A PRACTICAL APPROACH TO

ENVIRONMENTAL LAW

A PRACTICAL APPROACH TO

ENVIRONMENTAL LAW

Paul Stookes

OXFORD

UNIVERSITY PRESS

OXFORD
UNIVERSITY PRESS

Great Clarendon Street, Oxford OX2 6DP

Oxford University Press is a department of the University of Oxford.
It furthers the University's objective of excellence in research, scholarship,
and education by publishing worldwide in

Oxford New York

Auckland Cape Town Dar es Salaam Hong Kong Karachi
Kuala Lumpur Madrid Melbourne Mexico City Nairobi
New Delhi Shanghai Taipei Toronto

With offices in

Argentina Austria Brazil Chile Czech Republic France Greece
Guatemala Hungary Italy Japan Poland Portugal Singapore
South Korea Switzerland Thailand Turkey Ukraine Vietnam

Published in the United States
by Oxford University Press Inc., New York

British Library Cataloguing in Publication Data

Data available

Library of Congress Cataloging in Publication Data

Stookes, Paul.
A practical approach to environmental law / Paul Stookes.
p. cm.
Includes bibliographical references and index.
1. Environmental law—Great Britain. I. Title.
KD3372.S76 2005
344.4104'6—dc22

ISBN 0–19–927921–7   978–0–19–927921–0

1 3 5 7 9 10 8 6 4 2

Typeset by RefineCatch Limited, Bungay, Suffolk
Printed in Great Britain
on acid-free paper by
Ashford Colour Press Ltd, Gosport, Hampshire

To Helen, Jack, Billy, and Mum, all my love

FOREWORD

Concern within society for the environment and for how we live our lives has never been more widespread. We now hear political leaders talk quite seriously about the fundamental problems we face. Yet the environment is very complex. The interrelation between different species, ecosystems, and life cycles is often not properly understood and is often ignored as a result. Similarly, environmental law is complex; it does not operate in an essentially autonomous legal system such as probate, housing, or employment law. It cuts across a number of disciplines and it is rare for even specialist environmental practitioners to be familiar with all its various facets. Environmental protection relies on criminal, public, and civil law. It includes negligence, nuisance, and trespass. It influences corporate, property, and housing law. It is increasingly influencing the town and country planning system.

Given the state of the world, and the state of environmental law, it is very encouraging to find a book that seeks to cover all key aspects of the topic in a concise, practical way that will assist the reader. It is a bold attempt to bring the various strands of the environment and law together. The author has himself achieved distinction in the field as Chief Executive of the Environmental Law Foundation. I strongly commend his efforts.

Stephen Hockman QC
Head of Chambers, 6 Pump Court, Temple
Vice Chairman of the Bar Council

ACKNOWLEDGEMENTS

I have very many people to thank in being able to complete this book: Richard Buxton, Susan Ring, Sally Tozer, Sara Ball, Cairo Robb, and all my colleagues at Richard Buxton Environmental and Public Law; Stephen Hockman QC at 6 Pump Court for his continuing support; David Whiting, Julia Say, and all my former colleagues at the Environmental Law Foundation; Paul Reader, Andrew Johnson, and Yashin Masoliver from Berry & Berry Solicitors, where my continuing requests for thoughts were at one point regarded as borderline harassment; Martin Baxter and Karl Fuller at IEMA; and James Roy, Charles Wild, and Gail Merry and my colleagues at the Faculty of Law, University of Herts. I thank Phil Michaels at Friends of the Earth, Ann Flintham at the Magistrates' Association, Lal Kurukulasuriya, former Chief of the Law Division at UNEP, Nairobi, and my associates at the EU Judges Forum for the Environment including Lord Justice Carnwath and Justice Lavrysen for maintaining my belief in the environmental justice system.

I must also thank and acknowledge the large number of authors and publishers that have allowed me to refer to their work including: John Bates, HHJ William Birtles, Martin Edwards, Greg Jones, Robert McCracken QC, James Pereira, Charles Pugh, and Stephen Tromans. To Trevor Hellawell and the Law Society, the Local Government Ombudsman, Louisa Frears and David Hicks at the University of Bath, Howard Price at the Chartered Institute of Environmental Health, Christopher Penn and Shaw & Son, Paul Langridge at A&C Black (Publishing) Ltd, Amy Woods at Thomson, Sweet & Maxwell, HMSO, Rachel Caldin at LawText Publishing, Roger Butterfield and Jessica Holroyd and Monitor Press, the Environment Times and Butterworths LexisNexis.

Finally, I would like to thank everyone at Oxford University Press for the support and assistance granted to me in publishing this book. Above all, I must thank Helen and the boys for their divine tolerance and patience — it must be hard living with a zealot.

For clarity, reference to the masculine form includes reference to the feminine as appropriate. All mistakes are entirely my own; the law is up to date to May 2005.

Paul Stookes
June 2005

CONTENTS SUMMARY

CONTENTS

PART I INTRODUCTION

THE CLIENT

1   ENVIRONMENTAL LAW IN OUTLINE

2   ENVIRONMENTAL RIGHTS AND PRINCIPLES

PART II SUBSTANTIVE ENVIRONMENTAL LAW AREAS

3   AIR

PART III PRACTICE AND PROCEDURE

17 CIVIL LAW PRACTICE AND PROCEDURE

TABLE OF CASES

TABLE OF STATUTES

TABLE OF STATUTORY INSTRUMENTS

TABLE OF EU AND INTERNATIONAL LEGISLATION

International Legislation

PART I

INTRODUCTION

THE CLIENT

A   INTRODUCTION

The primary purpose of the book is to provide a comprehensive yet practical practitioner's **IN.01**
text on environmental law. While there are specialist texts on specific aspects of the environment there is a need for a quality, affordable text for environmental law practitioners and
for those who are coming into contact with environmental matters during their work, but
do not necessarily practice in the area full time.

Environmental law is based on a wide range of environmental areas such as noise, air, water, **IN.02**
land use etc. It operates across a range of legal sectors such as land use planning, integrated
pollution control, and statutory nuisance. It also impacts on many other sector-specific
areas of law such as employment, housing, licensing, and property law. Environmental law
can be found at an international, regional, national, and local level. It can include policy,
legislation, and jurisprudence. Finally, it comprises a complex mix of civil, criminal, and
public law.

This book provides a guide through the maze of environmental law and policy. It will help **IN.03** readers understand how the law interacts with the environment and society in general and then to advise appropriately when environmental aspects may arise. It is divided into three parts.

Part I highlights the significance of the adviser/client relationship including aspects of an initial interview, document review, and early advice. It also puts environmental law into context including the impact of international and European law. Finally it sets out key environmental principles that cut across environmental law.

Part II examines the substantive areas of environmental law. These have been listed in alphabetical order from Air to Wildlife. The reason for this is that when practitioners come across an environmental concern for the first time they will want to go directly to the problem area to gain a greater understanding of how the law relates to that concern.

Part III covers practice and procedure. Most environmental impacts will have at least a civil and criminal aspect to them. Successive governments have sought to protect the environment on behalf of society and they have legislated for this. Often the legislation relies on criminal sanctions enforced by public bodies or agencies. As a result, both criminal law and public law review of any decisions, acts, or omissions is likely to be relevant. There may also be a private right to claim compensation or some other remedy for any harm caused.

IN.04 There is significant cross-referencing throughout the book. This is partly due to the complexity of environmental concerns and that they do not fall neatly into one specific legal area. It will always be worthwhile to check the relevant environmental aspect and then to cross-refer to the general practice and procedure for further insight into the matter. Similarly, the practice and procedure sections are often further elaborated in relation to specific problems. For example, Chapter 18: Statutory Nuisance considers material interference with property and personal comfort arising out of private nuisance. This aspect of private nuisance is also considered in the subsection on private nuisance in Chapter 10: Noise.

IN.05 The difficulty for any practitioner is to know which approach to take to resolve the concern. This may not always be an easy decision. In *Marcic v Thames Water Utilities Ltd* [2003] UKHL 66, a claim in nuisance for continuing sewage flooding, found the House of Lords stating that, in fact, a nuisance claim was not the appropriate action. Instead the regulator should have been pursued and if that had not provided a satisfactory remedy then the claimant should have considered judicial review. This book is unable to provide all the answers; they will only become evident on the facts of each case. However, it helps set out the options and enables the reader to assess when a particular course of action may be the most appropriate.

B PRELIMINARY MATTERS

IN.06 The remaining sections of this chapter provide guidance on taking initial instructions and providing early advice. It sets out some basic principles and highlights common areas of concern in environmental matters; it is not intended to be a definitive guide. Each case will have particular aspects that will be unique.

Who does what in environmental law?

There are likely to be three types of client in environmental matters: the polluter, the   **IN.07**
polluted, and the environmental protector.

The polluter

The polluter or developer may well have an interest in protecting the environment,   **IN.08**
but is also likely to be liable for potentially polluting activities as a result of his or her
activities.

The polluted

This is most likely to be the individual or community immediately affected by the potential   **IN.09**
or actual polluting activity. Often, one or two clients providing instructions will be representing their local community. In a report published by the Environmental Law Foundation
(ELF) in 2003, *Civil law aspects of environmental justice*, each client referred by ELF to one of its
members represented, on average, 869 others.

The environmental protector

The main protector of the environment is likely to be a public body such as the Environment   **IN.10**
Agency or a local authority. It is important to bear in mind that, *prima facie*, protecting
the environment is a government role taken on behalf of society. This has to be right when
protecting the environment includes not only protecting it for individuals and a local
community directly affected by pollution or potential environmental harm, but also on
behalf of distant communities that may suffer as a result of transboundary polluting effects,
future generations and wildlife, all of which are unlikely to have a voice or right of action of
their own. And so while private law interests may be involved, environmental protection
and improvement is primarily the responsibility of public bodies that are best equipped and
funded to resolve the concern.

The client

It will usually be quite clear who your client is, but clarifying the identity of any opponent   **IN.11**
or other interested party is also important. For example, with land use planning matters, a
local community may be concerned about the likely noise and pollution from a proposed
development. While at first glance, the concern may be about the polluter/developer,
any challenge is most likely to be against the local planning authority (LPA) that granted
permission for the proposal. However, it is also possible that final approval for the proposal is
a decision by the Secretary of State. In this scenario, the client may be a local community
group, any potential opponent could be either the LPA or the Secretary of State, and an
interested third party will be the developer.

Often a number of different parties will have an interest in a particular decision or action   **IN.12**
and ensuring that there is no conflict of interest when advising any one of these clients is
vital. Further, many industry operators that have the potential to pollute may well be owned
by parent companies and it is important to establish from the proposed client its status
in terms of the activities being carried on and any relationship with other relevant
organizations.

The environmental concern

What is the environmental concern or potential problem?

IN.13   It is important to clarify what the client's concern is. This may be clear, if for example, an industrial operator wishes to apply for an installation permit or a local nightclub operator has been issued with a noise abatement notice. However, if it is perhaps a local resident concerned about increased traffic generation by a proposal to develop a new shopping centre, then exploring what aspects of the traffic generation are of concern will be critical. There will be a number of ways to control such a problem and simply preventing the development may not be realistic.

What is the likely cause of the concern?

IN.14   There will always be a cause of the environmental problem. Again, this may often be clear; such as noise and air pollution coming from a local factory. However, if water pollution is a concern, it may be more difficult to pinpoint the pollution source and further investigation may be necessary. For any decision that has been taken in controlling an activity or development the cause of the problem is likely to be the decision taken by the regulator in authorizing the activity.

How many people is the problem likely to affect?

IN.15   The number of people (or variety of wildlife) that the environmental problem may affect is important, not only to highlight the significance of the problem but also to see whether anyone else may be interested in pursuing any claim.

What does the client want to achieve?

IN.16   A company that has breached an enforcement notice under the Pollution, Prevention and Control regime (see Chapter 11: Pollution prevention and control) may simply be trying to mitigate their loss and get their installation operating again. If so, early negotiations with the regulator may be the best approach.

IN.17   A local resident or community action group may be trying to prevent a development going ahead and, while there has been no formal approval of the development, discussion and constructive representations to the LPA may be the best approach. However, discussion and debate will be of less value if, for example, a decision has been taken and there is as little as six weeks to apply for statutory review of an appeal decision.

Relevant documents

IN.18   All decisions taken that may result in environmental harm are likely to have a number of supporting documents. Many pollution incidents that arise will be regulated in some way and so have documents relating to the regulation. Important documents could include:

- a formal notice or decision letter;
- a court order;

- committee reports;
- diary notes of continuing or regular events; or
- expert reports.

The list may be large. Information from the regulator, the LPA or other public body should be sought at the earliest stage. For proposed activities or developments, relevant documents may be located on the public register. **IN.19**

However, it is important to note that with many formal decisions, the time for appealing or challenging any decision starts to run from the date of the decision, not the date of any notice given. It may be some weeks before a formal decision notice is issued and, if opponents of a decision were waiting for the formal notice, any time to prepare a challenge will have been lost: see para IN.25. **IN.20**

It is also important to check through the documents received to see what further documents may be required. For instance, an air pollution permit will have conditions attached that will set air emission levels. The levels and any local air quality management strategy will be contained in other documents. These will need to be obtained. **IN.21**

Which legal procedure?

With environmental law operating across the civil, criminal and public law fields, practitioners taking on environmental cases will have to have an appreciation of each main area of law. For example, action taken to stop noise nuisance will start as a civil matter and then following the laying of an information in the magistrates' court; is dealt with under criminal law principles from that point on. **IN.22**

C EARLY ADVICE

Confirming instructions

It may be difficult to provide any conclusive legal advice at or shortly after an initial inter- view, but the following will be useful: **IN.23**

- clarify, in writing, what you understand the client's concern to be and what initial advice has been given;
- provide advice on procedural matters that may be appropriate, e.g. that there are strict time limits for a claim for judicial review;
- suggest any appropriate practical steps, e.g. enlisting the help of a local wildlife expert to assess any woodland that may be threatened for rare or endangered species;
- suggest contacting neighbours to see whether they regard the matter to be a concern and whether they would be willing to assist in resolving the environmental concern;
- in appropriate circumstances, contact the relevant regulator about any incident and request that they investigate the matter.

Funding legal action

IN.24 One of the biggest concerns in resolving any issue is the cost of doing so. The expense incurred by corporate bodies in securing a permit or planning permission is likely to be included in any business plan. The cost to regulators of protecting the environment will be budgeted for in annual financial forecasts. By contrast, for communities and individuals looking to protect their environment, funding legal action can often be an insurmountable hurdle. Public funding may be available in limited circumstances. It is necessary to be able to give some estimate as to the likely cost and, importantly, any other costs liability, in funding action. Costs and funding are considered in the relevant chapters of Part III: Practice and procedure.

D   BEFORE ISSUING PROCEEDINGS

Time limits

IN.25 In many environmental cases time limits are a critical aspect of advice. The time limit to appeal a planning decision is six months. A claim for judicial review must be made within three months (and prompt in any event) under Part 54.5 of the Civil Procedure Rules 1998 (see Chapter 20: Public law), and a statutory review claim against a Planning Inspector's decision must be made within six weeks. For a continuing nuisance, it will be important to stop the nuisance as soon as possible.

IN.26 It is vital then to check the date of any decisions that have been taken and to ensure that if any proceedings are issued they fall within any relevant limitation periods.

Pre-action protocols

IN.27 Judicial review is subject to a pre-action protocol, which parties should follow before making a claim for judicial review. Similarly there is the personal injury pre-action protocol. It is acknowledged that in urgent judicial review cases, e.g. where it is important to compel a public body to act, compliance with protocol may not be appropriate.

Letter before action

IN.28 Pre-action protocols require a letter before action, and it should be regarded as good practice to send a letter to the opponent before issuing proceedings. This should set out:

- the client's details;
- details of the matter being challenged including the date of any decision, any act or failure to act, a brief summary of the facts and why these are being challenged;
- details of the action that the opponent is expected to take, any information sought, any documents that are relevant and necessary;
- the likely remedies to be sought from the court should the matter not be resolved;
- the details of any interested parties;
- the address for reply and service of documents;
- the date that the opponent should reply by.

E   ISSUING PROCEEDINGS

If proceedings are to be issued to resolve the problem then the best option to resolve the   **IN.29**
concern will have to be considered. For instance, there are up to six ways of responding to
the issue of an abatement notice:

- ignore the notice;
- comply with the notice;
- appeal to the magistrates' court;
- make a claim for judicial review;
- defend criminal proceedings; or
- complain to the Local Government Ombudsman.

Of these options, three relate to legal proceedings with two requiring positive legal action   **IN.30**
in different courts by the person served with the notice. Both of these, the appeal and
judicial review, have time limits and require that proceedings are issued using a specific
form, e.g. Form N461 for judicial review available from the court service website:
www.hmcourts-service.gov.uk.

F   SUMMARY CHECKLIST

Many environmental concerns raise complex issues that will require detailed analysis of the   **IN.31**
problem and careful consideration of the most appropriate solution. However, getting basic
information at an early stage can simplify this. This includes clarifying:

- All the parties involved, e.g. who is causing the pollution or harm, who is the regulator,
  if there is one, and who is suffering or could suffer any potential harm?
- What is the environmental concern or potential problem?
- What is the likely cause of the concern?
- How many people are likely to be affected?
- What does the client want to achieve?
- What further documents are required?
- What practical steps should be taken?
- What are the cost implications of taking certain steps and what funding options are
  available?
- What is the most appropriate legal procedure and in which court should proceedings
  commence?
- Any time limits.
- Does a pre-action protocol need to be followed if issuing proceedings?
- Is a letter before action appropriate?

1

ENVIRONMENTAL LAW IN OUTLINE

A   DEFINING THE ENVIRONMENT

In simple terms, the environment is the surroundings in which we live. However, there are a number of legal definitions. For some purposes, e.g. property transactions, the definition may be quite narrowly defined, for others it is more general. A common statutory definition, which is found in s 1(2) of the Environmental Protection Act 1990 (EPA 1990) provides that: **1.01**

> The 'environment' consists of all, or any, of the following media, namely the air, water, and land; and the medium of air includes the air within buildings and the air within other natural or man-made structures above or below ground.

This definition is then referred to in other legislation such as s 56(1) of the Environment Act 1995. It does not include the relationship between the environment and human beings or wildlife and should therefore be regarded as quite narrow and used only for its purpose in relation to the legislation.   **1.02**

1.03   A wide interpretation is contained in the Environmental Information Regulations 2004 (SI 2004/3391), which provides that:

> environmental information; has the same meaning as in Art 2(1) of the Directive [2003/4/EC on access to environmental information], namely any information in written, visual, aural, electronic or any other material form on the state of the elements of the environment.

1.04   This is set out more fully in Chapter 2: Environmental rights and principles. It should be contrasted with the very specific definition in Directive 2004/35/EC on environmental liability, which defines 'environmental damage' under Art 2(1) as: damage to protected species and natural habitats; water damage, and land damage.

1.05   In short, unless there is a statutory definition of the environment it should include wildlife, human health impacts such as noise, local environmental matters such as waste, dog fouling, and litter, which could equally be regarded as socio-environmental concerns, and wider environmental impacts such as energy use and climate change.

1.06   A pragmatic reason for a wide definition is to try and build a greater understanding in society, including the legal establishment, that almost all environmental activities are almost always going to have an impact much greater than the immediate impact that may be the symptom or cause of an initial complaint. Importantly, any definition of the environment should not be exclusive and should not, for example, exclude matters relating to neighbourhood regeneration even if there is the tendency by others, including government, to make such a distinction. The report *Environmental Quality and Social Deprivation* published by the Environment Agency in 2003 confirmed once again the link between poverty and poor environment, concluding that a greater burden of potential environmental impact is borne by deprived populations than by the more affluent.

Defining pollution

1.07   Many of the rules, regulations, and offences relating to environmental law refer to pollution. However, this is not defined in legislation. In *R v Dovermoss Ltd* [1995] Env LR 258 the Court of Appeal stated that 'pollute' and its derivatives should be given their ordinary meaning as in the Oxford English Dictionary definition 'to make physically impure, foul, or filthy; to dirty, stain, taint, or befoul.' In *Express Dairies Ltd v Environment Agency* [2004] EWHC 1710 (Admin), in which milk leaked from a tanker lorry into a watercourse, it was held that to pollute did not require any evidence of harmful effects. The definition of water pollution at common law was regarded in *John Young & Co v Bankier Distillery Co* [1893] AC 691 as doing something that changes the natural qualities or properties of water. This is considered further in Chapter 15: Water.

B   THE COMPLEXITY OF ENVIRONMENTAL LAW

1.08   It is accepted that the environment is complex. The interrelation between different species, ecosystems, and life cycles and the effect that activities have on both human health, flora, and fauna is not properly understood and is often ignored as a result. See, for example, *Malster v Ipswich Borough Council* [2001] EWCA Civ 1715 in which the court found that severe shadowing from a proposed stadium extension did not justify the need for an environmental statement to support the planning application for the proposal. Similarly, environmental law is complex; it does not operate in a broadly autonomous legal system such as probate, housing, or employment law. It cuts across a number of disciplines and it is rare for even environmental practitioners to be familiar with all its various facets. Environmental protection relies on criminal, public, and civil law. It includes negligence, nuisance, and trespass. It influences corporate, property, and housing law. It heavily influences the Town and Country Planning system. Further, the rules and regulations of environmental law are based on international, regional, European, national, and local legislation and decision-making.

The pervasive nature of environmental law is a key reason why it is becoming increasingly important in practice and policy. In 2003, the Department for Environmental, Food and Rural Affairs (Defra) commissioned four studies on access to environmental justice. Throughout 2004, there was a series of public inquiries by the Government's Environmental Audit Committee into environmental crime and the courts. Across Europe, leading members of the judiciary have formed the European Union Forum of Judges for the Environment (EUFJE), which aims to promote, in the perspective of sustainable development, the implementation of national, European, and international environmental law. At an international level the United Nations Environment Programme (UNEP) continues to pursue an extensive global programme of judicial training and awareness raising in environmental law. Meanwhile, the debate about whether there should be a discrete Environmental Court or Tribunal continues. **1.09**

It is then unsurprising that environmental law has been cited as a potentially huge growth area in the legal profession for some time, and despite not materializing into large environmental corporate departments, the interest and influence of environmental law does reflect society's notional awareness about the environment. Indeed, the number of environmental concerns being raised by community groups, individuals, corporate bodies, and government is rising fast. As Western society is placing increasing pressure on the environment through unsustainable patterns of consumption, travel, and living the law is being asked to define and clarify the scope and boundaries of modern life. **1.10**

C   HISTORY AND BACKGROUND

Environmental regulation and jurisprudence is not new. Britain's first recorded legislation dates from 1273 when King Edward I, better known for fighting the Scots and the Welsh, prohibited the burning of 'sea coal' in order to protect the health of his subjects. In the 1500s, it is understood that Elizabeth I banned the use of coal while Parliament was sitting with the penalty of death in default. **1.11**

By the 1840s Victorian England had to tackle the adverse consequences of the industrial revolution. During this period, the UK government began to legislate more generally for public health including the introduction of the Alkali Act 1863 to try and reduce the heavy build up of acid in the local atmosphere and the Public Health Act 1875; the **1.12** precursor to the current statutory nuisance regime. And, although there were cases in the courts such as *St Helen's Smelting Company v Tipping* (1865) 11 HLC 642 and *Rylands v Fletcher* [1861–73] All ER 1, which may now be regarded as environmental cases, the concept of environmental protection for the wider benefit of society and future generations was not evident.

1.13 It has really been in the latter part of the twentieth century that environmental law has evolved with perhaps the most significant changes brought about by the enactment of the Town and Country Planning Act 1947, which created local planning authorities and required all land to be subject to planning control recognizing that landowners could not simply build and use land at will and without planning permission. During the 1950s specific legislation was introduced to control smoke including the Clean Air Act 1956 as a response to the heavy London smog of the early 1950s, which was believed to have claimed thousands of lives.

1.14 In terms of private civil claims in courts, the 1960s seemed to mark a development in favour of claimants in the field of private nuisance, which until then had tended to support the polluter. In *Goldman v Hargreave* [1967] 1 AC 645 the court concluded that although a land-owner may not create a nuisance, he may adopt liability for it when he becomes the owner or occupier of the land. The Control of Pollution Act 1974 introduced a regime of pollution control covering different environmental sectors of waste disposal, water pollution, noise, atmospheric pollution, and public health and, although some parts of the Act such as Part III relating to noise remain in force, many were not implemented effectively and have since been repealed.

1.15 Despite some attempts to curb pollution and environmental harm, the 1980s saw some relaxation in environmental control, particularly in the land use planning system. The era also promoted car use and a shift from public transport to private vehicle use, with a massive road expansion scheme. This resulted in year-on-year increases in pollution from road vehicles and, again, loss of green, open land. By the end of the 1980s the UK had earned the title of the 'dirty man of Europe' due to its environmental performance. In response the EPA 1990 was introduced, which consolidated much of the existing environmental legislation such as the statutory nuisance regime contained in Part III of the Act. It also introduced a system known as Integrated Pollution Control (IPC), which acknowledged that various pol-luting activities were often interlinked and needed a holistic approach to their management and regulation. Ironically, IPC became the model for later European Union (EU) regulation of polluting activities introduced by the EU Directive concerning integrated pollution prevention and control 1996 (96/61/EC).

1.16 Environmental law in the twenty-first century is experiencing even more legislative control, while the courts are in some instances, such as *Marcic v Thames Water Utilities* [2003] UKHL 66 and *Transco plc v Stockport Metropolitan Borough Council* [2003] UKHL 61, continuing to adopt the conservative approach of the 1990s found in the House of Lords cases *Cambridge Water Company v Eastern Counties Leather* [1994] 1 AER 53 and *Hunter v Canary Wharf* [1997] 2 WLR 684.

D INTERNATIONAL LAW

Most people and practitioners will encounter environmental law at a national level. How- **1.17** ever, international and EU law will often be relevant for the interpretation or spirit of principles underpinning the legislation. There may be concern that an international obliga- tion has not been met and this may be subject to challenge; or a client may wish to prepare and plan for the proposed transposition of EU regulations. Much of the environmental law currently in force in the UK derives from international law and has been incorporated into national law via the European Union. National policy and legislation will often be enacted to ensure compliance with international obligations. Most international environmental legislation is sponsored and promoted by the United Nations (UN) and the United Nations Environment Programme (UNEP).

International environmental law operates through a range of governance mechanisms **1.18** such as treaties, policy statements, informal arrangements, recommendations, custom, arbitration, and litigation. It tends to be based upon relations and disputes between states and regional bodies such as the EU or the North American Free Trade Association (NAFTA). But the implementation or impact of international decisions can also be influential at vari- ous levels from the international level, through regional and national level, and with poten- tially local impact. For instance, the right of the public to participate in decision-making starts life as Principle 10 of the Rio Declaration 1992, which provides that, among other things:

> . . . environmental issues are best handled with the participation of all concerned citizens, at the relevant level.

In Europe, the principle is embodied in the United Nations Convention on Access to Infor- **1.19** mation, Public Participation in Decision Making and Access to Justice in Environmental Matters 1998 (the Aarhus Convention 1998), at least three EU Directives and a proposed Regulation. The participation rights and access to information are also contained in the new Environmental Information Regulations 2004 (SI 2004/3391) and at a local level local plan- ning authorities must now publish a Statement of Community Involvement setting out their policy for involving interested parties in preparing and revising local planning documents and for consulting on planning applications: see Planning Policy Statement (PPS) 1: *Delivering Sustainable Development* (2005).

Treaties

International legislation is often divided into hard and soft law. Hard law includes formal **1.20** written agreements such as treaties, conventions, and protocols finalized between countries and regions. Soft law includes all non-binding agreements, which may not be legally bind- ing but can be persuasive. The terms 'treaty', 'convention', and 'statute' are synonymous. Most of the major treaties are given common names that usually adopt the city of adoption or conclusion, e.g. the Montreal Protocol 1987 for the Protocol on Substances that Deplete the Ozone Layer. UNEP suggests that there are well over 500 international environmental treaties currently in force, although the number varies depending on who, what, and when the count takes place. They operate to tackle a range of environmental concerns including transboundary pollution, environmental impact assessment, hazardous chemicals in international trade, and persistent organic pollutants. A treaty is defined in the Vienna Convention on the Law of Treaties (1969) as:

> An international agreement concluded between states in written form and governed by international law, whether embodied in a single instrument or in two or more related instruments and whatever its particular designation.

1.21 An example of an international treaty is the Convention on Biological Diversity 1992, which came into force in December 1993 and aims to provide a comprehensive approach to the conservation of biological diversity, the sustainable use of natural resources and the fair and equitable sharing of benefits deriving from the use of genetic resources. By June 2004, 188 countries had ratified the Convention. It is considered to be the most widely ratified environmental treaty in force.

Non-binding agreements

1.22 Non-binding agreements will include recommendations, declarations, resolutions etc. and are often regarded as soft law. They are, however, something more than simple policy statements. They aim to secure some commitment from signatory states even though they cannot be enforced. An example of soft law is the Declaration of the UN Conference on Environment and Development 1992 (the Rio Declaration), which is a statement of 27 principles for sustainable development including the precautionary principle and the polluter pays principle (considered in Chapter 2: Environmental rights and principles). The reason for developing soft law is largely political in that some proposals may be so contentious that they would never secure the commitment of the majority of states and would not materialize into a formal agreement or treaty.

1.23 This proved to be the difficulty with the Kyoto Protocol 1997, which was adopted under the UN Convention on Climate Change 1992 in order to develop policies and measures to reduce anthropogenic emissions of greenhouse gases. The Protocol required ratification by at least 55 countries that were parties to the Climate Change Convention and who, collectively, accounted for 55% of the global carbon dioxide emissions at 1990 levels. The Protocol did not enter force until February 2005 following ratification of the Protocol by Russia, which accounted for 17.4% of all greenhouse gas emissions. Thus, the Protocol took eight years to enter into force. It is often considered better to get informal commitment to some measures rather than failing to get any formalized commitment at all.

Dispute settlement and international law

1.24 There are a number of dispute resolution mechanisms in international law although, compared with the development of legislation over the last few decades, litigation and court decisions play a relatively minor role in international environmental law. The International Court of Justice (ICJ) can hear cases between two or more states, but not private individuals or organizations. It can also be asked to provide an advisory opinion on a question of law. To refer a matter to the ICJ usually requires the consent of all parties to the dispute. A leading case heard by the ICJ included the *Gabcikovo-Nagymaros Project* [1997] ICJ Rep 7, which considered a dispute between Hungary and Czechoslovakia over the construction of a dam and the diversion of the River Danube. The UN Convention on the Law of the Sea 1982 (UNCLOS 1982) provides its own compulsory dispute procedure by establishing the International Tribunal for the Law of the Sea that hears disputes relating to marine activities such as fishing rights, exploration, and exploitation.

Many international environmental disputes arise from trade matters where one state has imposed trade restrictions to protect the environment. To hear disputes the World Trade Organization has established three bodies: the Dispute Settlement Body, *ad hoc* panels, and the Appellate Body. Important environment and trade cases are the *Beef Hormones* case (1998) WT/DS48/AB/R relating to the EU ban on imported meat and meat products from cattle that had been subjected to growth hormones and the *Shrimp/Turtle* case (1999) 38 ILM 118, which considered the US import ban on shrimps and shrimp products that were harvested in a way that endangered sea turtles. **1.25**

In a similar fashion to the Tribunal established by UNCLOS, many agreements may establish a clarification or dispute settlement mechanism. For instance, the Cartagena Protocol on Biosafety 2000 that aims to provide protection in the field of living modified organisms, sets up a Biosafety Clearing House (Art 10) and the ability to set up a process to secure liability and redress for damage resulting from transboundary movements of living modified organisms (Art 27). **1.26**

The relevance of international environmental legislation is that it often precedes and informs national law. It is referred to whenever appropriate throughout this book. **1.27**

E THE EUROPEAN UNION

Over 80% of all environmental legislation in the UK now emanates from the EU and, of the 500 plus EU Directives that have been adopted to date, over 250 relate to the environment. For this reason, EU institutions and laws have a significant influence on the environmental justice system. **1.28**

EU institutions

The EU institutions include: **1.29**

- the European Commission;
- the Council of the European Union;
- the European Parliament;
- the European Court of Justice (ECJ); and
- the Court of Auditors.

The role of each body is outlined below. **1.30**

The European Commission

The European Commission plays an executive role in the EU; it is primarily a civil service. There are currently 25 Commissioners that are chosen from among the Member States, **1.31** with at least one representative from each state. They hold office for five years. They are responsible for 30 Directorates including the Environment Directorate, which is responsible for environmental matters. Each Directorate will devise and propose EU legislation.

The Council of the European Union

1.32 The Council of the European Union comprises one political representative from each Member State. The Environment Council covers environmental matters. It meets twice a year. The UK's Minister for the Environment is the UK representative. Its role is to promote the political interests of the Member States and carry out a regulatory function in terms of EU law.

The European Parliament

1.33 The European Parliament comprises 785 directly elected members from the Member States. Parliament has democratic control over the EU institutions, legislative power in conjunction with the Council and is involved in approval of financial matters including consultation in appointment of the Court of Auditors. There are a number of standing committees specializing in aspects of EU policy and law. The Committee on Environment, Public Health and Consumer Policy covers environmental matters.

European Court of Justice

1.34 The European Court of Justice (ECJ) can determine actions against decisions from any EU specialized court. It can review the legality of any EU laws and framework laws and review the legality of any EU bodies or agencies. It can give preliminary rulings on the interpretation of the Constitution and legislation. The Court can hear disputes between Member States about EU matters providing the case is submitted by agreement between the states. It has wide jurisdiction to hear various types of action and to give preliminary rulings. In its direct jurisdiction, the proceedings are generally for judicial review of action or inaction by Member States or Community institutions. A key responsibility of the Commission is to ensure that EU law is applied properly by Member States. Since the Court of Justice was set up in 1952, more than 8,600 cases have been brought before the Court.

1.35 Judges are appointed from each Member State and enjoy the usual guarantees of independence and impartiality. At present, eight Advocate-Generals, who are required to consider a case impartially and come to a personal conclusion as to what in law should be done, assist the judges. Prior to judgment the Advocate-General publicly states what he or she considers the facts and the law to be and suggests what matters should be considered in the judgment. However, the Advocate-General does not participate in that judgment. Article 222 of the EU Treaty requires each Advocate-General to act:

> with complete impartiality and independence to make, in open court, reasoned submissions, on cases before the Court.

1.36 The ECJ has concluded that, among other things:

(i) EU law takes precedence over national law, any incompatible domestic legislation should not be applied (*R v Secretary of State for Transport ex p Factortame (No. 2)* C-1213/89 (1990)).

(ii) If a treaty is clear as to the rights and obligations created it can be used in national courts as if it were national legislation (*Van Gend en Loos* [1963] ECR 3).

(iii) Where national law is open to interpretation, national courts should interpret that law as far as possible in line with the wording and purpose of EU legislation (*Marleasing SA v La Comercial Internacional* C-106-90 (1990)).

(iv) Member States are liable to remedy any loss suffered by individuals arising from a failure to implement an EU obligation (*Francovich v Italy* C-497/93 (1995)).

The most common environmental cases before the ECJ relate to air, EIA, nature, water, and waste. Leading cases include *UK v EC Commission* [1998] ECR I-2265 relating to the precautionary principle that the EU may take precautionary measures without having to wait until the seriousness of risks become fully apparent, and *Palin Granit Oy* Case C-9/00 in which the ECJ held that leftover stone from quarrying should be classified as waste for the purpose of the Waste Directive 75/442/EEC and that the storage place for leftover stone is not relevant for determining whether or not the stone is waste. **1.37**

The Single European Act 1986 created the Court of First Instance, which began hearing matters in 1989. It has limited jurisdiction but hears matters that have been transferred to it from the ECJ by act of Council from time to time. The European Court of Human Rights, which considers breaches of human rights, has always operated entirely separate from the ECJ. Human rights and the environment are considered in Chapter 2: Environmental rights and principles. ECJ procedure is considered in Chapter 20: Public law. **1.38**

Court of Auditors

The Court of Auditors is responsible for examining the financial accounts of the community and all institutions that operate under it. It provides the European Parliament and the Council with a statement of assurance as to the veracity of the account and the legality of transactions. **1.39**

EU legislation

EU legislation comprises a mix of binding legislation (hard law) and non-binding plans and polices (soft law) including: **1.40**

- Treaties;
- Regulations;
- Directives;
- Decisions;
- Recommendations and Opinions;
- Plans and Policies.

Treaties

Treaties are the highest level of law. They are the constitutional basis for the EU, its organizations, and functions. Successive treaties since the inception of the EU have broadened the role, scope, and purpose of the EU itself. Prominent EU treaties have been: **1.41**

- the Treaty of Rome 1957, which first established the EU;

- the Treaty of Accession 1972, which brought the total number of EU countries to nine, including the UK;
- the Single European Act 1986, which introduced express provision for environmental protection;
- the Maastricht Treaty 1992, which implemented the concept of European Monetary and Political Union;
- the Treaty of the European Union 1997, which increased the number of EU member states to fifteen and entered into force in 1999.

Regulations

1.42 Regulations have general application, Article 249 of the EU Treaty states that they are binding in their entirety and are directly applicable in all Member States. Regulations enter into force 20 days after publication in the Official Journal of the EU. Regulations do not allow any discretion in their transposition or implementation, indeed the ECJ ruled in *Variola v Amministrazione Italiana delle Finanze* [1973] ECR 981 that Member States must not pass national legislation to implement a regulation. Regulation (EC) 761/2001 allowing voluntary participation by organizations in a Community eco-management and audit scheme (EMAS) is an example of an environmental regulation, and while the participation in EMAS is voluntary for organizations in Member States, the regulation itself places a number of obligations on Member States to ensure its effective implementation.

Directives

1.43 Directives are binding on the Member States to which they apply, and often they apply to all Member States. They are not directly applicable but leave the method of transposition up to each Member State. They are however, under Art 249 of the EU Treaty, binding as to the result to be achieved upon each Member State to which they are addressed. Directives are implemented in the UK by both primary and secondary legislation, e.g. Directive 85/337/EEC on the assessment of the effects of certain public and private projects on the environment (the EIA Directive) was originally transposed via the Town and Country Planning (Assessment of Environmental Effects) Regulations 1988 (SI 1988/1199). Later amendments by EU Directive 97/11/EC were transposed by similar regulations (see Chapter 24: Environmental assessment). Important environmental directives over the past 30 years have included the Waste Directive (75/442/EEC), the Wild Birds Directive (79/409/EEC), the EIA Directive, as amended, the Habitats Directive (92/43/EEC), and the IPPC Directive (96/61/EC).

Decisions

1.44 Decisions by the Council or the Commission are, under Art 249, binding in their entirety upon those they address. They may apply to Member States, corporate bodies, or individuals. Because decisions are binding in their entirety there is no discretion for the addressee as to how the decision should be implemented.

Recommendations and Opinions

1.45 Recommendations and Opinions are non-binding instruments. They are listed in Art 249, but it may be argued that they are not legislative provisions because they have no binding force. KPE Lazok in *The Law and Institutions of the European Union* (9/e, Butterworths, 2001) suggests that their role should be persuasive and constructive in the formulation and execution of the policies of the Community.

Plans and policies

The EU also prepares a range of non-binding plans and policy statements for environmental   **1.46** protection and improvement. It has adopted six Environmental Action Programmes (EAPs). The sixth EAP, covering a ten-year period from July 2002, aims to promote the integration of environmental concerns in all EU policies and contribute to the achievement of sustainable development. It promoted the European Spatial Development Perspective 1998 that set out how to incorporate all aspects of sustainable development into long-term planning, including land use planning. To demonstrate the significance of non-binding policy, spatial development has been incorporated into the land use planning system via s 334 of the Greater London Authority Act 1999, which provides that the Mayor shall prepare and publish a spatial development strategy, and s 1 of the Planning and Compulsory Purchase Act 2004, which states that for each region there shall be a regional spatial strategy.

The EU Official Journal

The EU Official Journal formally publishes all enacted legislation. It is the key publication by   **1.47** which dates are set when considering the interpretation and implementation of legislation. It is available from the EU website: www.europa.eu.int.

A new European Constitution?

The legislative structure of the EU may well be subject to another overhaul with the approval   **1.48** in June 2004 of a new EU Treaty establishing a Constitution for Europe. Article 3 of the Constitution sets out EU objectives that include, among other things:

(a) To promote peace, its values, and the well-being of its peoples.
(b) To offer its citizens an area of freedom, security, and justice with internal frontiers, and a single market where competition is free and undistorted.
(c) To work for the sustainable development of Europe based on economic growth, a social market economy aiming at full employment and social progress and with a high level of protection and improvement of the quality of the environment.
(d) To uphold and promote its values in relations with the wider world.

The Constitution has to be ratified, following referenda in Member States by October 2006.   **1.49** Articles III-129 to III-131 of the Constitution relate to the environment noting that EU policy on the environment shall aim at a high level of protection taking into account the diversity of situations throughout the Union. Environmental objectives include preserving, protecting, and improving environmental quality, protecting, human health, prudent use of natural resources, and tackling regional and worldwide environmental problems. The legislation of Treaties, Regulations, Directives, Decisions, Opinions, and Recommendations will be replaced by the legal instruments found in Arts 32 to 38 of the Constitution:

• *European law*; a legislative act of general application binding in its entirety and directly applicable in all Member States.

- *European framework law*; a legislative act binding, as to the result to be achieved, on the Member States to which it is addressed, but leaving the national authorities free to choose the form and means of achieving the result.
- *European regulation*; a non-legislative act of general application that may be binding in entirety and directly applicable or binding only with regard to the result to be achieved.
- *European decision*; a non-legislative act binding only on those it specifically refers to.
- *Recommendations and opinions*; having no binding force.

F NATIONAL LAW

Legislation and policy

1.50 National environmental law includes policy, legislation, and jurisprudence. To transpose EU legislation effectively the UK government enacts either primary legislation or secondary legislation such as statutory instruments, e.g. the Town and Country Planning (Environmental Impact Assessment) (England and Wales) Regulations 1999 (SI 1999/293) (see Chapter 24: Environmental assessment). Other environmental legislation derives from national policy such as the new public nuisance aspects of entertainment licensing and anti-social behaviour orders (s 4 of the Licensing Act 2003 and s 40 of the Anti-social Behaviour Act 2003).

1.51 A proportion of environmental legislation is to be found in the EPA 1990 (as amended) including integrated pollution control in Pt I (now being superseded by the IPPC regime), waste management in Pt II, contaminated land in Pt IIA, statutory nuisance in Pt III, and genetically modified organisms in Pt VI. Other key pieces of legislation include the Wildlife and Countryside Act 1981 (as amended), the Water Resources Act 1991, and the Environment Act 1995. Many of the environmental protection measures are based on regulation underpinned by criminal penalties.

Plans and policies

1.52 As with international law, policy is important at a national and local level. It influences the strict letter of the law. Also, with public bodies such as local authorities responsible for implementing the vast majority of environmental protection measures, failure to properly consider policy may give rise to an application for judicial review. Over the next few years, local authorities may be subject to challenge if they consistently fail to use their powers to promote the environmental and social wellbeing in their communities as required by s 2 of the Local Government Act 2000. The courts have taken care to avoid any limitation of the power. In *R (J) v London Borough of Enfield and the Secretary of State for Health* [2002] EWHC 432 (Admin) Elias J that it would be 'inapt' to describe a situation where no power had been conferred as a prohibition, restriction, or limitation. Further, if there was a human rights aspect to the use of the power then it is likely that those rights would be infringed if no assistance under the power was provided.

Environment and the national courts

The court's approach to the environment and specific environmental sectors is considered in **1.53** detail in Parts II and III, but it is important to set environmental law in context within the legal justice system and to emphasize how environmental concerns arise in private civil claims, criminal cases, and public law matters.

The private civil law system

Almost all environmental problems arising out of disputes between two or more parties **1.54** are based upon the common law torts of negligence, nuisance, and trespass. Of these, negligence actions will be based upon claiming compensation for personal injury and the impact on human health. There is no clear division between personal injury claims and the environment, and a distinction may not be necessary. It is suggested that the case of *Lubbe & ors v Cape Plc* [2000] UKHL 41 in which 3,000 miners and their families claimed compensation for exposure to asbestos fibres may equally be regarded as both a personal injury and an environmental claim. Nuisance claims have a long history; in *William Aldred's* case (1610) 9 Co Rep 57b the court found that light and clean air was necessary for wholesome habitation after the claimant objected about his neighbour's pigsty built near to his house. In nuisance claims the court's have tended to favour the pollutant, often regarding the courts as the wrong forum for securing environmental protection (*Cambridge Water Company v Eastern Counties Leather* [1994] 2 AC 264. Nuisance actions also extend beyond the civil courts as public nuisance and statutory nuisance bridge both civil and criminal law.

Environmental crime

The criminal justice system assists environmental protection by providing sanctions for the **1.55** regulation and control of polluting and environmentally harmful activities. Prosecutions are investigated and pursued by a number of different government agents and public bodies including the Environment Agency, local authorities, the Police, English Nature, and HM Customs & Excise. Individuals and organizations are also able to bring private prosecutions. In *R v Anglian Water Services Ltd* [2003] EWCA Crim 2243 a local resident successfully prosecuted Anglian Water who were fined £200,000 at the Crown Court, albeit reduced later on appeal to £60,000.

Public law

Environmental protection is primarily the responsibility of the government, its agents and **1.56** other public bodies who work on behalf of society and the public good. Each of these must ensure that their decisions, acts, and omissions are procedurally correct, if not they may be subject to an application for judicial review by people and organizations with an interest in the decision taken. In *R v Secretary of State ex p Greenpeace* [1994] 4 All ER 352 the judge noted that whether he would have directed a public inquiry was neither here nor there, the question was whether the Secretary of State acted lawfully in refusing to call a public inquiry. One of the most common environmental public law challenges in recent years has been in the way the EIA regulations have been implemented when local planning authorities have granted planning permission for major developments.

During 2003, research by the Environmental Law Foundation sought to establish the level **1.57** of private civil claims in environmental law and found any analysis to be inconclusive, a best guess from the research was that there could be anything from between 300 to 3,000 civil environmental claims each year. Contrast this with, for example, around 200,000 employment cases each year. A similar pattern emerges with environmental prosecutions where there could be anything from 3,000 to 8,000 environmental cases coming before the courts each year compared to around 33,000 for burglary offences according to the Criminal Statistics for 2002 published by the Home Office. However, the modest numbers of environmental cases reaching final judgment underplays the significance and impact that environmental concerns have on neighbourhoods, local communities, future generations, and often the wider world. It also highlights the fact that using the legal justice system often requires innovation, determination, and funds. With just one incident or concern often affecting many hundreds or thousands of people, environmental legal action is unique.

Role of the case law and precedent decisions

1.58   It is, as with most other areas of law, important to appreciate the precedent nature of case law in environmental matters. As a simple principle, the decisions of the highest appellate courts such as the House of Lords are binding on all courts below. Whereas the decisions of the lower courts do not bind other courts including themselves but may be persuasive or give an indication of how other courts are approaching a particular matter. This is particularly the case in magistrates' courts and appeal matters, where it is important to consider each case on its facts. Any reference to lower court or planning appeal decisions is by way of illustration of the nature of cases coming before these courts.

KEY DOCUMENTS AND MATERIALS

Environmental Protection Act 1990

Walker, D, and others (2003). *Environmental Quality and Social Deprivation*. Environment Agency: Bristol

The European Union: www.europa.eu.int
United Nations Environment Programme (UNEP): www.unep.org

2

ENVIRONMENTAL RIGHTS
AND PRINCIPLES

A SUSTAINABLE DEVELOPMENT

The concept of sustainable development is the most important principle of environmental **2.01** law. It is, in the author's view, unfamiliar to most people and properly understood by even fewer. This is no surprise. It has been given a multitude of meanings, often self-serving, and its definitions tend to be long and various.

Defining sustainable development

2.02 Put simply, sustainable development means leaving the planet as we found it. The World Commission on Environment and Development, in its report *Our Common Future* (1987) (the Brundtland Report — after the Commission's President; Gro Harlem Brundtland), emphasized the needs of the world's poor in the now popular definition of sustainable development as:

> . . . development that meets the needs of the present without compromising the ability of future generations to meet their needs. It contains within it two concepts: the concept of 'needs', in particular the essential needs of the world's poor, to which overriding priority should be given; and the idea of limitations imposed by the state of technology and social organisation on the environment's ability to meet present and future needs.

2.03 The Brundtland Report and definition provided the backdrop for the Rio Earth Summit in 1992 and subsequent Rio Declaration 1992. The present needs of the world's poor and how they interrelate with the environment was reiterated at the Johannesburg Summit in 2002, ten years after Rio.

2.04 The UK Government published a new sustainable development report: *Securing the Future* in March 2005. It provides that:

> The goal of sustainable development is to enable all people throughout the world to satisfy their basic needs and enjoy a better quality of life, without compromising the quality of life of future generations. For the UK Government and the Devolved Administrations, that goal will be pursued in an integrated way through a sustainable, innovative and productive economy that delivers high levels of employment; and a just society that promotes social inclusion, sustainable communities and personal wellbeing. This will be done in ways that protect and enhance the physical and natural environment, and use resources and energy as efficiently as possible. Government must promote a clear understanding of, and commitment to, sustainable development so that all people can contribute to the overall goal through their individual decisions. Similar objectives will inform all our international endeavours, with the UK actively promoting multilateral and sustainable solutions to today's most pressing environmental, economic and social problems. There is a clear obligation on more prosperous nations both to put their own house in order, and to support other countries in the transition towards a more equitable and sustainable world.

2.05 The strategy states that the UK Government and devolved administrations will pursue the primary goal using the following five guiding principles:

- *Living within environmental limits* Respecting the limits of the planet's environment, resources, and biodiversity — to improve our environment and ensure that the natural resources needed for life are unimpaired and remain so for future generations.
- *Ensuring a strong, healthy, and just society* Meeting the diverse needs of all people in existing and future communities, promoting personal wellbeing, social cohesion and inclusion, and creating equal opportunity for all.
- *Achieving a sustainable economy* Building a strong, stable, and sustainable economy, which provides prosperity and opportunities for all, and in which environmental and social costs fall on those who impose them (polluter pays), and efficient resource use is incentivized.

- *Using sound science responsibly* Ensuring policy is developed and implemented on the basis of strong scientific evidence, whilst taking into account scientific uncertainty (through the precautionary principle) as well as public attitudes and values.
- *Promoting good governance* Actively promoting effective, participative systems of governance in all levels of society — engaging people's creativity, energy, and diversity.

All environmental legal activity including property transactions, environmental auditing, and concerns about pollution, will always have at least one and often two or more aspects of sustainable development. Communicating the principles and justification of sustainable development to the client, court, or any other party should be central to advising on environmental law matters. **2.06**

Development within the earth's environmental capacity

Sustainable development is often regarded as pursuing the three goals of: **2.07**

(1) social development;
(2) economic development; and
(3) environmental protection and enhancement.

These broadly match the UK Government's five guiding principles of sustainable develop- **2.08** ment set out above. However, taking these in isolation can be misleading. First, consideration of the goals should not be restricted to a balancing exercise between these apparently competing aims. For example, if we want to achieve a particular social goal of providing homes for all, then this cannot be achieved in a sustainable way simply by subsidizing development and building a few parks close to housing development. These balancing factors may assist but they should not be regarded as successfully achieving sustainable development. Rather, when seeking to achieve a certain aim, say homes for all, then economic and environmental development should be integrated within the decision-making process taken.

Achieving effective sustainable development will be difficult; and is why legislation, which **2.09** itself begins life as politics and policy, always works towards it, rather than making a commitment to securing it. Perhaps most important of all is that the pursuit of economic, social, or environmental development must be undertaken within the environmental capacity of the earth. It requires rethinking how we all live our lives and not necessarily following current patterns of economic growth, consumption, and travel. It means taking economic, social, and environmental decisions within the carrying capacity (the environmental limits) of the planet. It means building homes that, when occupied and used, do not have an overall adverse impact on the environment, whether through energy use, construction, loss of open land, or waste arising. It means ensuring that travel patterns do not produce carbon emissions that cannot be wholly used up (sequestrated) by the earth itself. To put *sustainable* development into perspective, by pursuing conventional economic development policy the world is presently using *three* planet's worth of resources (and generating the subsequent pollution) in the pursuit of progress and development. This cannot continue in the long term; and is therefore unsustainable. It is vital that, sooner rather than later, decision-makers begin to tackle the issue.

2.10 There are some tough and politically unpopular decisions to be taken if society is to make any significant progress in tackling some of the biggest environmental problems we now face, such as climate change. And, whether it is a local community seeking to protect a village green or a large multinational company committing itself to an effective management system that ensures compliance with the latest regulatory regime, environmental law will be at the heart of this.

Sustainable development in legislation

2.11 Sustainable development was introduced into UK legislation in the Environment Act 1995, which, among other things, established the Environment Agency and the Scottish Environment Protection Agency. Section 4(1) of the Act provides that:

> It shall be the principal aim of the Agency (subject to and in accordance with the provisions of this Act or any other enactment and taking into account any likely costs) in discharging its functions so to protect or enhance the environment, taken as a whole, as to make the contribution towards attaining the objective of achieving sustainable development . . .

2.12 It is encouraging to see that sustainable development is the Agency's principal aim, but it is important to note that it is qualified by aspiration (. . . contributing towards attaining . . .) and the need to carry out cost-benefit analysis (. . . taking into account any likely costs . . .). The requirement to contribute towards achieving sustainable development is also contained in local government legislation. Section 4(1) of the Local Government Act 2000 provides that:

> Every local authority must prepare a strategy . . . for promoting and improving the economic, social and environmental well-being of their area and contributing to the achievement of sustainable development in the UK.

2.13 Further, s 39 of the Planning and Compulsory Purchase Act 2004 provides that local planning authorities in England and Wales must exercise the functions conferred by the Act with the objective of contributing to the achievement of sustainable development.

2.14 While the inclusion of sustainable development into national legislation should be seen as a positive step, the UK's efforts may best be regarded as 'modest' and falling somewhat short of its enactment in other jurisdictions. For instance, Art 24 of the South African Constitution 1994 states that everyone has the right to:

(a) have an environment that is not harmful to his or her health or well-being;
(b) an environment protected for the benefit of present and future generations, through reasonable legislative and other measures that—
   (i)   prevent pollution and ecological degradation;
   (ii) promote conservation; and
   (iii) secure ecologically sustainable development and use of natural resources,
while promoting justifiable economic and social development.

Sustainable development and the courts

2.15 In the Indian case of *Vellore Citizens Welfare Forum v Union of India* (1996) SC 2715 Kuldip Singh, J commented that the Supreme Court had:

no hesitation in holding that 'Sustainable Development' [defined by the Brundtland Report] as a balancing concept between ecology and development has been accepted as a part of the customary international law . . .

In the case of *Rajendra Parajuli and ors v Shree Distillery Ltd and ors* (1996) Nepal 2 UNEP **2.16** Compendia, the Supreme Court of Nepal held that having a licence for the operation of industry does not excuse its obligation to protect the environment. It added that in line with the principle of sustainable development 'every industry has an obligation to run its development activities without creating environmental deterioration' and that the environment should not be viewed narrowly. While in the case of *Contact Energy Ltd v Waikato Regional Council* (2000) ECD A04/2000 the New Zealand Environment Court held that a modified proposal to build a geo-thermal power station would overall serve the purpose of sustainable management of natural and physical resources, and that the resource consents needed should be granted subject to conditions imposed by the court.

English and Welsh courts have considered sustainable development on a number of **2.17** occasions. In *Fairlie v Secretary of State for the Environment and South Somerset DC* [1997] EWCA Civ 1677 the court considered an appeal against planning enforcement against Tinkers Bubble Trust; a group who had set up a permaculture farm with the aim of living off the land, i.e. growing organic produce, relying on renewable energy and causing little or no impact on the environment. The enforcement action was for siting and occupying seven tents without planning permission. Part of the appeal was because the Secretary of State misunderstood his own planning guidance when applying the concept of sustainable development as contained in para 4 of Planning Policy Guidance (PPG) 1. The appeal by the Trust was dismissed. However, it seems that the difficulty wasn't so much the understanding or application of PPG1 but the mistaken objective of sustainable development contained in the guidance with emphasis on economic goals. This has been rectified in the new Planning Policy Statement (PPS) 1: *Delivering Sustainable Development* (2005), which, at para 4, seeks to ensure that the four aims of sustainable development are tackled in an integrated way.

In the case of *Goldfinch (Projects) Ltd v National Assembly for Wales and Flintshire County* **2.18** *Council* [2002] EWHC 1275 (Admin) the claimant challenged a planning inspector's decision to dismiss an appeal against the refusal of planning permission for the development of 23 homes. There had been a previous grant of permission that had lapsed. The inspector found that the proposal was objectionable on the grounds that it would not be well integrated with the existing pattern of settlement and was in conflict with the objectives of sustainable development. In his judgment, Scott Baker J stated that 'sustainable development is defined as development that meets the needs of the present without compromising the ability of future generations to meet their needs.' He noted the Government's vision based upon the four aspects of: use of natural resources, social progress, economic growth, and full employment. However, he concluded that the inspector had elevated the seriousness of flooding to a serious issue, which it was not, and that he had failed to give adequate weight to why permission had originally been granted. On this basis the inspector had erred in law and the decision was quashed and remitted for a rehearing by a different inspector.

In *Sherburn Sand Company Ltd v First Secretary of State and Durham County Council* [2004] **2.19** EWCH 1314 (Admin), the High Court dismissed a challenge to a planning inspector's decision refusing permission to mine 56,320 tonnes of magnesium limestone and 288,800 tonnes of sand. In summary, the county's sand and gravel needs until 2016 could be met from existing permitted sources. See also *LB Bromley v Susanna and ors* [1998] EWCA Civ 1444 and *Fagg v Secretary of State for Transport and ors* [2002] EWHC 1327.

B　PREVENTION, PRECAUTION, AND THE POLLUTER PAYS PRINCIPLES

2.20　There are three key environmental principles that can be considered as a hierarchy of effective environmental protection. These principles have been incorporated into EU law. Article 174(2) of the Consolidated EU Treaty (OJ C325/107) affirms that EU policy on the environment shall be based on the precautionary principle, that preventative action should be taken, that environmental damage should as a priority be rectified at source, and that the polluter should pay.

Figure 2.1 The hierarchy of environmental principles

....

Prevention of environmental harm should be the ultimate goal when taking decisions, actions, or omissions with potentially adverse environmental impacts.

A *precautionary* approach should be taken whenever there is uncertainty as to whether environmental harm will arise.

The *polluter should pay* for any environmental harm that does arise from its decisions, acts, or omissions.

....

The preventative principle

2.21　The preventative principle is based on an obligation to avoid environmental harm. It is similar to the duty of care doctrine in negligence. It is also, to an extent, implied in private nuisance claims where a neighbour may be prevented by way of an injunction from the unlawful interference with a person's use or enjoyment of land or some right over, or in connection with it (*Read v Lyons* [1947] AC 156). Although there should be caution in relying on a nuisance action as a means of environmental protection, with the courts more willing to award compensation and allow the polluting activity to continue rather than grant injunctive relief to prevent it; see e.g. *Dennis v Ministry of Defence* [2003] EWHC 793 (QB). Injunctions are always at the discretion of the trial judge with an appeal court unable to consider the merits of the case (see also Chapter 17: Civil law practice and procedure). Further, if any claim relates to obligations imposed by statute then the administrative remedies under that statute should be exhausted and if necessary make an application for judicial review. In *Marcic v Thames Water Utilities Ltd* [2003] UKHL 66 Lord Nichols commented in para 33 that: 'The common law of nuisance should not impose on Thames Water obligations inconsistent with the statutory scheme', which, in this instance, was the Water Industry Act 1991.

2.22　The preventative principle has evolved in the international arena over many years. In the *Trail Smelter Arbitration (US v Canada)* 3 RIAA (1941) the tribunal held that no state had the right to permit the use of its territory in a way that would cause injury by fumes to the territory, people, or property of another; in this instance that Canada should prevent pollution entering the US. The principle has been recognized in both international and national legislation. Article 2 of the Framework Convention on Climate Change 1992 states that: 'the ultimate objective is to achieve the stabilization of greenhouse gas emissions in the atmosphere to a level that would prevent dangerous anthropogenic interference with the climate system'.

In the Pollution Prevention and Control Act 1999 (transposing Directive 96/61/EC concern- **2.23** ing integrated pollution prevention and control (IPPC Directive), s 1 states that regulations may make provision for regulating activities that are capable of causing any environmental pollution and otherwise preventing or controlling emissions capable of causing pollution.

The precautionary principle

The precautionary principle has a more recent history in environmental law, arising from **2.24** the West German environmental policy of *Vorsorgeprinzip* meaning 'prior worry or care' (see Royal Commission on Environmental Pollution 12th Report Cm310 1988). The courts were initially reluctant to recognize precaution. In *R v Secretary of State for Trade and Industry ex p Dudderidge* [1995] (The Times 26 October 1995), the Court of Appeal held that the precautionary principle had no distinct legal effect in the UK and, although there may be a need to take environmental risk into account as a material consideration in decision-making, Art 130r of the EC Treaty did not impose any obligation on the Secretary of State to issue regulations restricting electromagnetic fields from electric cables being laid as part of the national grid. However, in the case of *R (AMVAC Chemical UK Ltd) v The Secretary of State for Environment, Food & Rural Affairs and ors* [2001] EWHC Admin 1011 the court considered the precautionary principle in some detail. Crane J stated that the precautionary principle as defined in the Rio Declaration 1992, requires that where there are threats of serious or irreversible damage, lack of scientific certainty should not be posed as a reason for post-poning cost-effective measures to prevent environmental degradation (Principle 15 of the Declaration). He then referred to the UK Sustainable Development Strategy 1999 that states:

> The precautionary principle means that it is not acceptable just to say we can't be sure that serious damage will happen, so we'll do nothing to prevent it. Precaution is not just relevant to environmental damage — for example, chemicals which may affect wildlife may also affect human health.

Crane J then continued referring also to the EU Communication in February 2000 on the **2.25** precautionary principle, the Cartagena Protocol on Biosafety 2000, and then finally the Art 174(2) of the EU Treaty. In conclusion, the judge found that the claim failed on the issues relating to the precautionary principle but nevertheless found the Respondent's decision procedurally flawed and made a quashing order.

In *UK v Commission* [1998] Case C-180/96, the UK Government applied under Art 173 of the **2.26** EU Treaty to annul Commission Decision 96/239/EC on emergency measures to protect against BSE. The ECJ held that the EU institutions could take protective measures without having to wait until the reality and seriousness of those risks became fully apparent. More recently, in *Pfizer Animal Health SA v Council of the European Union* [2002] T13-99 the EU Court of First Instance affirmed that under the precautionary principle EU institutions are entitled in the interests of human health to adopt, on the basis of as yet incomplete scientific knowledge, protective measures that may seriously harm legally protected provisions, and that they enjoy a broad discretion in this respect.

2.27   The precautionary principle is now being incorporated into land use policy. PPG 25: *Development and flood risk* (2001) notes that the principle is particularly relevant to dealing with the hazard of flooding. Its application acknowledges the uncertainty inherent in flood estimation and, by proceeding from the known facts and taking a precautionary approach to uncertainties, enables more open and better-informed decisions to be made. This can reduce the environmental impact and improve the safety of people and property, despite the existence of risk that may change with time.

The polluter pays principle

2.28   The polluter pays principle may be regarded as a response to pollution and environmental harm rather than an effective mechanism for environmental protection. By implication, it accepts that pollution will arise, but that the polluter should pay for it. It is used as a financial incentive to operate more efficiently and as a sanction for carrying out polluting activities. It should also operate as a deterrent in helping to ensure that prevention of harm arises in similar situations in the future. Importantly, it is not a polluter's charter relying on the fact that those that can afford to pollute may do so with impunity. In international law, Principle 16 of the Rio Declaration 1992 provides that:

> National authorities should endeavour to promote the internalization of environmental costs and the use of economic instruments, taking into account the approach that the polluter should, in principle, bear the costs of pollution, with due regard to the public interest and without unduly distorting international trade and investment.

2.29   Countries adopt the principle, rather than individual or corporate polluters, placing the obligation on states to ensure that the polluters within their jurisdiction pay the price of polluting. The principle acknowledges the concept of internalizing the cost of pollution, i.e. that the full cost of many polluting activities such as emissions to air and water are often paid by society as a whole, e.g. by suffering poor air and water quality. Often, these costs are not incurred by the polluter and are therefore said to be external to their business. Internalizing the costs of pollution means that the polluter should pay the full cost of pollution. However, Principle 16 notes the potentially adverse financial consequences of paying the price for pollution control and so qualifies the principle to avoid distorting trade and investment. Internalizing costs may be achieved by introducing state of the art technology to reduce or eliminate emissions. It may be by paying additional taxes for using polluting energy processes, e.g. the climate change levy imposed by s 30 of the Finance Act 2000 and designed to encourage business and other organizations to reduce energy use or transfer energy supply to a more environmentally friendly means.

2.30   In the UK, the principle underpins much of the environmental regulatory regime and in particular the criminal sanctions used as a means of enforcement. Many sentences for environmental crimes greatly exceed Level 5 of the standard scale of maximum fines for summary offences contained in s 37(2) of the Criminal Justice Act 1982 by a factor of four. For example, maximum summary fines for most waste, water, and air offences are £20,000 compared to the current Level 5 maximum of £5,000.

C   PROCEDURAL RIGHTS: INFORMATION, PARTICIPATION, AND ACCESS TO JUSTICE

One of the most important pieces of environmental legislation in recent years has been the   **2.31** UNECE Convention on Access to Information, Public Participation in Decision-making and Access to Justice in Environmental Matters 1998 (the Aarhus Convention). This is reproduced in Appendix 1. Although regional in scope it sets out a comprehensive framework for procedural environmental rights and is a model that is being used in countries throughout the world.

The UK Government ratified the Aarhus Convention in February 2005 and considers that   **2.32** since the introduction of new Environmental Information Regulations 2004 (SI 2004/3391) (the Environmental Information Regs 2004), the UK is Aarhus compliant.

The EU also signed the Aarhus Convention to ensure that all Member States would meet the   **2.33** environmental obligations equally and to ensure that all EU citizens would have at least a minimum standard of environmental rights under the Convention. EU legislation is being implemented to secure certain rights being imposed on Member States. This includes Directive 2003/4/EC on public access to environmental information and repealing Directive 90/313/EEC to be transposed by February 2005; Directive 2003/35/EC providing for public participation in respect of the drawing up of certain plans and programmes relating to the environment and amending with regard to public participation and access to justice Directives 85/337/EEC and 96/61/EC to be transposed by June 2005; and the draft Directive on access to justice in environmental matters COM(2003) 614 final, which has yet to enter into force. The EU has also prepared legislation to ensure that the EU's own institutions comply with the Aarhus Convention with the proposed Regulation on the application of the Aarhus Convention COM (2003) 622 Final.

As its title suggests, there are three key parts to the Convention. These may be regarded as the   **2.34** environmental procedural rights of:

(1) access to information;
(2) public participation in decision-making; and
(3) access to justice.

The rights afforded by the Convention should be regarded as minimum requirements rather   **2.35** than an optimum level to be attained; a floor, not a ceiling. Articles 3(5) and (6) state that the Convention provisions:

> shall not affect the right of a Party to maintain or introduce measures providing for broader access to information, more extensive public participation and wider access to justice than required by [the Convention] . . . and shall not require any derogation from existing rights.

Access to information

Effective access to environmental information is vital if any representations or potential   **2.36** challenge is proposed relating to the environment. Without proper access to information, the other procedural rights of public participation and access to justice are likely to be far less effective.

2.37   Access to information usually comes in two forms: passive information provision covered by Art 4 of the Aarhus Convention and active information provision contained in Art 5.

Passive information provision

2.38   Passive information provision is where a public body, such as a local authority, provides information following the request by an individual or organization. If no request for information is made then that particular information may not necessarily be put into the public domain and the public body will simply hold the information and publish upon request. This should not be seen as withholding the information but rather that it requires a positive request to disclose it. A simple example is making available the public file in relation to an application for planning permission. Article 4 obligations under the Aarhus Convention include a requirement that public authorities make information available upon request and supply it, subject to exceptions, within set time limits.

Active information provision

2.39   Active information provision is where a public body, such as central government, publishes and promotes information generally. The information should be widely and easily available for all. An example of this type of published information is a 'state of the environment' report setting out how well a country or region is performing in terms of the environment, e.g. the UK Government report *Achieving a better quality of life 2004*. Other important information is the digest of environmental statistics published on Defra's website setting out general information on a range of environmental matters. Importantly, this information should be actively promoted to help ensure that all members of the public are made aware of the environmental information made available. Article 5 of the Convention requires public authorities to collect, possess, and disseminate environmental information including that on decision and policy making.

The Environmental Information Regulations 2004

2.40   The Environmental Information Regs 2004 are made pursuant to s 82(2) of the Freedom of Information Act 2000 (FoI Act 2000). Under reg 2(1) environmental information is given a wide meaning and includes information in written, visual, aural, electronic, or any other material form on:

(a)   the state of the elements of the environment such as air and atmosphere, water, soil, land, landscape, and natural sites including wetlands, coastlands, and marine areas, biological diversity and its components, including GMOs, and the interaction among these elements;

(b)   factors, such as substances, energy, noise, radiation, or waste, including radioactive waste, emissions, discharges, and other releases into the environment, affecting or likely to affect the elements of the environment referred to in (a);

(c)   measures (including administrative measures), such as policies, legislation, plans, programmes, environmental agreements, and activities affecting or likely to affect the elements and factors referred to in (a) and (b) as well as measures or activities designed to protect those elements;

(d) reports on the implementation of environmental legislation;

(e) cost-benefit and other economic analyses and assumptions used within the frameworks of the measures in (c); and

(f) the state of human health and safety, including the contamination of the food chain, where relevant, conditions of human life, cultural sites and built structures inasmuch as they are or may be affected by the state of the elements of the environment referred to in (a) or through those elements, by any of the matters referred to in (b) or (c).

In *R v British Coal Corporation ex p Ibstock Building Products Ltd* [1995] JPL 836, a case relating   **2.41** to the earlier Environmental Information Regulations 1992, the court held that the name of someone providing information about the state of land was 'environmental information' on the basis that the information was necessary to assess the credibility of other information on the state of the land. In *R v Secretary of State for the Environment and Midland Expressway Ltd ex p Alliance Against Birmingham Northern Relief Road and ors* [1998] EWHC Admin 797, the court held that the test as to whether or not information was 'environmental information' was objective.

Regulation 3 of the Environmental Information Regs 2004 sets out who is covered by the   **2.42** regulations and who can be required to provide information. Regulation 3(2) states that the regulations apply to public authorities. Regulation 2(1) defines public authority as:

(a) government departments;

(b) any other public body as defined in s 3(1) of the Freedom of Information Act 2000 (FoI Act 2000), subject to exceptions;

(c) any other body or other person, that carries out functions of public administration; or

(d) any other body or other person, that is under the control of a person under sub-para (a), (b), or (c) and:

    (i)   has public responsibilities relating to the environment;

    (ii)   exercises functions of a public nature relating to the environment; or

    (iii) provides public services relating to the environment.

Regulation 4 of the Environmental Information Regs 2004, requires that a public authority   **2.43** must make environmental information that it holds progressively more available to the public by electronic means and take reasonable steps to organize the information with a view to the active and systematic dissemination to the public of the information. This is the obligation for active information provision.

Regulation 5 provides that a public authority that holds environmental information shall   **2.44** make it available on request. This is passive information provision, where the information won't be made publicly available until a request has been received. Under reg 5(2), public authorities have 20 working days to provide information. An extension to this period may be secured under reg 7 if the authority believes that the complexity and volume of the information requested means that it is impracticable either to comply with the request within the earlier period or to make a decision to refuse the request. Regulation 8 provides that public authorities may charge for costs reasonably attributable to the supply of information, which is conditional on payment of any charge, although this is subject to exceptions such as when allowing access to public registers or lists of environmental information held by the public authority (reg 8(2)(a)).

2.45 Regulation 9 of the Environmental Information Regs 2004 provides that public authorities must provide advice and assistance in relation to environmental information so far as it would be reasonable to expect the authority to do so, to applicants and prospective applicants. For example, under reg 9(2), where an applicant has requested information in too general a manner the authority shall ask the applicant as soon as possible and within 20 working days, to provide more particulars in relation to the request.

2.46 Public bodies must disclose the environmental information requested unless one of the exceptions to the disclosure duty under Pt 3 of the Regulations applies. Regulation 12(1) provides that, subject to exceptions, a public body may refuse to disclose environmental information if requested if:

    (a)   an exception to disclosure applies under paras (4) or (5); and

    (b)   in all the circumstances of the case, the public interest in maintaining the exception outweighs the public interest in disclosing the information.

2.47 Regulation 12(2) adds that a public authority shall apply a presumption in favour of disclosure. Phil Michaels, in an article in Environmental Law and Management: 'Guide to the Environmental Information Regulations' (Lawtext, 2004), emphasizes the presumption in favour of disclosure by explaining that: 'in contrast to the FoI Act 2000, there are no absolute exceptions under the regulations and an authority wishing to refuse to release information must satisfy itself as to the balance of public interest.'

2.48 The reg 12 exceptions to disclosure of information arise in two ways, under subparas:

    (4)   where the disclosure relates to, among other things, procedural matters such as: that the authority does not hold the information when the applicant's request is made; and

    (5)   where the disclosure would adversely affect specified matters which include defence, national security, commercial confidentiality, or intellectual property rights.

2.49 Unless the exceptions apply, taking into account the public interest presumption in favour of disclosure, any failure by a public authority to provide information following a request may be subject to review and/or enforcement action. An internal review procedure is required by reg 11. Regulation 11(1) provides that an applicant may make representations to a public authority in relation to a request for environmental information if it appears to the applicant that the authority has failed to comply with the Regulations. Representations must be made within 40 working days after the date on which the applicant believes that the public authority has failed to comply with the requirement. The review process is free of charge. A public authority shall notify the applicant within 40 days of the date of representations.

2.50 Regulation 18 of the Environmental Information Regs 2004 applies the enforcement and appeal provisions of the FoI Act 2000. A person who has made a request for environmental information from a public authority may complain to the Information Commissioner if he believes that the public authority has not dealt with the request, or representations to the authority about the request, in accordance with the requirements of these Regulations. The Commissioner has equivalent powers to enforce the Regulations as under Pt IV of the FoI Act 2000. These include powers of entry and inspection and, in respect of the exercise of those powers, the offence of obstruction. There is also a right of appeal from a Commissioner's decision to the Information Tribunal.

Further, there is an offence under reg 19(1) whereby if a request for environmental informa-   **2.51**
tion has been made and the applicant would have been entitled to the information, a person
is guilty of an offence if he alters, defaces, blocks, erases, destroys, or conceals any record
held by the public authority, with the intention of preventing the disclosure by that
authority of all, or any part, of the information to which the applicant would have been
entitled. The offence does not cover a government department. The prosecuting authority is
the Commissioner or the Director of Public Prosecutions. The offence, which is a summary
offence, is liable to a maximum penalty of a £5,000 fine.

There are a number of cases relating to the former EU Directive 90/313/EEC on the Freedom   **2.52**
of Access to Information on the Environment and the related Environmental Information
Regulations 1992. In the *Salisbury Bypass* case [1996] (unreported but considered in the REC
Handbook on Access to Justice (2003) (REC Handbook)) Friends of the Earth asked the
Department of Transport (DoT) for a copy of an 'induced traffic assessment report', which
had been prepared on a proposed bypass and had predicted how much extra traffic would
be generated by building the new road. DoT refused the request arguing that, among other
things, the report was not 'environmental information' within the meaning of 1992
Regulations. Friends of the Earth made an application for judicial review and two weeks
before the hearing the DoT provided a copy of the report accepting that it was 'capable of
falling within the scope of "environmental information" '.

The *Birmingham Northern Relief Road* case concerned a concession agreement for the construc-   **2.53**
tion of a toll road scheme containing commercially confidential information. The court held
that as a matter of precedent fact the agreement was 'information relating to the environment'. Also, even though the agreement could contain genuine commercially confidential
information that argument could not be used to prevent disclosure of the main body of the
agreement. And finally, that the applicant's purpose in seeking the information was irrelevant.

Publication participation in decision-making

There are a number of levels of participation. There is the right to be informed, the right to   **2.54**
be consulted, to make representations, to be heard, the right of appeal (considered in more
detail below under access to justice), and, ultimately, being in a position of direct control of
the relevant decision, act, or omission. This is illustrated below.

Figure 2.2 Levels of participation in decision-making

Active member of the decision-making body

Right to appeal a decision

Right to be heard and make oral representations to decision-makers

Right to make (usually written) representations

Right to be consulted

Right to be informed of the decision-making process

Articles 6 to 8 of the Aarhus Convention require all signatory states to provide for early   **2.55**
public participation, adding that only when all options are open and effective can public

participation take place. Public participation is not defined, although the Preamble to the Convention suggests that the values central to participation are ensuring that there is a means for the public to assert the right to live in an environment adequate for his or her health and wellbeing. Article 6 seeks to guarantee participation in decision-making that may have potentially significant environmental impacts. Article 7 sets out the need to establish a transparent and fair framework for public involvement in plans and programmes and Art 8 promotes participation in the preparation of law and rules that may have an environmental impact.

2.56   The UK Government considers that its present provision for public participation in environmental decision-making complies with the Aarhus Convention. Public participation rights in environmental matters most frequently arise under the land use planning regime. Article 8 of the Town and Country Planning (General Development Procedure) Order 1995 (SI 1995/419) states that an application for planning permission shall be publicized in the manner set out within the Article and under Art 19 representations made to the local planning authority about planning applications shall be taken into account. This level of participation is at the lower end of the participation ladder but nevertheless complies with the basic requirements of the Aarhus Convention.

2.57   The level of participation conferred by local planning authorities often goes much further than the minimum legislative requirements with many allowing oral representations to be made to planning committees. Further, under Directive 85/337/EEC on the assessment of the effects of certain public and private projects on the environment (as amended by Directive 97/11/EC) (the EIA Directive) major development projects may be subject to environmental impact assessment (EIA) and requires that any information gathered under Art 5 of the Directive is made available to the public within a reasonable time in order to give the public concerned the opportunity to express an opinion before planning permission is granted. The judiciary have expressed their support for meaningful public involvement. In *Berkeley v Secretary of State for the Environment* [2000] 2 AC 603, the House of Lords emphasized that token participation was not enough and that the public should be properly involved in EIA-related decisions. This is discussed more fully in Chapter 8: Land use.

2.58   The infringement of the participation rights of NABU, a German nature conservation group, was found to be unlawful in the case of *NABU Landesverband Sachsen-Anhalt v Federal Republic of Germany* (12 November 1997) file no. 11 A 49/96. NABU were participating in the development stage of a rail track extension and were denied access to amended expert reports. The Federal Administrative Court held that the development permit issued following the planning proceedings was unenforceable and could not be rectified by holding supplementary planning proceedings.

2.59   The REC Handbook (p 27) suggests that there are three categories of procedural errors in public participation:

   • failure to disclose all information to the public relevant to its participation;
   • improper procedures for public participation, such as timely or adequate notice, opportunity to comment, timeframes, restrictions on 'administrative standing' or other conditions; and

- inadequate response to comments received (failure to take due account), or failure to reveal the reasons or considerations for the decision.

There are many examples of participation best practice. In 2002, IEMA published guidelines **2.60**
on participation in environmental decision-making, which aims to improve participation by demonstrating its importance, offering advice on how to achieve effective participation and providing practical examples of what has been achieved such as the local community participation in the Crick bypass scheme, which involved a continuous consultation process over three years.

In *R v North and East Devon Health Authority ex p Coughlan* [2001] 1 QB 213 the Court of **2.61**
Appeal at 258 held that:

> whether or not consultation of interested parties and the public is a legal requirement, if it is embarked upon it must be carried out properly. To be proper, consultation must be undertaken at a time when proposals are still at a formative stage; it must include sufficient reasons for particular proposals to allow those consulted to give intelligent consideration and an intelligent response; adequate time must be given for this purpose; and the product of consultation must be consciously taken into account when the ultimate decision is taken.

Access to justice

Environmental justice has at least two meanings. The first involves access to the law and **2.62**
the courts in order to resolve environmental problems and to ensure that communities and individuals have the same rights and remedies as corporate and state organizations. Environmental justice in its broader sense may be referred to as environmental equity, which means ensuring that everyone, regardless of means, where they live, or their background, enjoys a clean and healthy environment. Environmental equity includes equity between nations and between generations.

In terms of procedural rights, access to environmental justice takes the first, more direct, **2.63**
definition. It provides the checks and balances for the procedural rights of information and participation. It should also provide a right of review of other more substantive rights such as a right to healthy environment. It is important that if such a right exists then it must be supported by the rule of law and access to the courts, when the right is breached. Securing environmental equity will almost certainly rely on providing effective access to justice; environmental justice in its direct form.

Articles 9(1) and (2) of the Aarhus Convention provide review procedures for any breach **2.64**
of the access to information and participation provisions contained in Arts 4 and 6 respectively. Article 9(3) requires signatory states to ensure that there is public access to administrative or judicial procedures to challenge acts or omissions by private persons or public authorities contravening national environmental law. The principle of *actio popularis* whereby anyone can sue the government when it acts unlawfully, regardless of whether they have standing in a strict sense, is said to be consistent with Art 9.

One of the critical aspects of the Aarhus Convention, and an area that has been the subject **2.65**
of concern in the way the UK Government has approached compliance (see the Coalition for Access to Justice for the Environment Briefings 2004), is the need to provide a fair review process. Article 9(4) provides that:

the procedures referred to in [Art 9] shall provide adequate and effective remedies, including injunctive relief as appropriate, and be fair, equitable, timely and not prohibitively expensive. Decisions under this article shall be given or recorded in writing. Decisions of courts, and whenever possible of other bodies, shall be publicly accessible.

2.66   Judicial review under Pt 54 of the Civil Procedure Rules 1998 is the system of review largely relied upon by the UK to secure compliance. Using this form of administrative review has caused difficulty in securing injunctive relief and a system that is not prohibitively expensive as required by the Convention.

2.67   In *R v Secretary of State for the Environment ex p RSPB* [1997] Env LR 431 the House of Lords refused to grant interim relief to RSPB while the matter was referred to the ECJ without a cross-undertaking in damages in relation to the large economic loss that could have arisen from development delay. Ultimately, the ECJ ruled that the UK was not entitled to take economic requirements into account when designating a Special Protection Area under the Wild Birds Directive. However, 12 months had elapsed between the application for interim relief and the ECJ ruling during which the site, Lappel Bank mudflats in Kent, had been turned into a car park.

2.68   In terms of prohibitive expense, the case of *Shirley v Secretary of State for Transport Local Government and the Regions* [2002] CO/4505/2001 highlights the difficulties with costs, when lawyers representing the interested party, Canterbury College, informed the applicant that if the matter went to hearing and the applicant lost, she would face a costs bill from them of £126,000. Despite this, the applicant pursued the case, the High Court found in favour of the Applicant and quashed the Respondent's decision. A similar scenario arose in *Friends of the Earth v Environment Agency* [2003] EWHC 3193 Admin when, the day before the hearing, Friends of the Earth were served with a Schedule of Costs of just over £100,000 for a one-day judicial review hearing on a preliminary issue by the Interested Party, Able UK Ltd. Again, Friends of the Earth were successful and were not required to pay those costs. For further discussion on this see Chapter 20: Public law.

D   SUBSTANTIVE ENVIRONMENTAL RIGHTS

2.69   Substantive environmental rights are those rights that set clear objectives and may be secured without any reference to any other rights, e.g. the right to a clean and healthy environment, and the right to clean, fresh drinking water. These could also be regarded as human rights. The UNEP Judges Guide notes that almost every national constitution adopted or revised since 1970 either states that an environment or a certain standard is a human right, or imposes environmental duties upon the state. More than 100 state constitutions guarantee a right to a clean environment, impose a duty on the state to prevent environmental harm, or mention the protection of the environment or natural resources. For example, s 4 of the National Environment Statute 1995 of Uganda provides that:

(1)   Every person has a right to a healthy environment.

(2)   Every person has a duty to maintain and enhance the environment including the duty to inform the Authority or the local environment committees of all activities and phenomena that may affect the environment significantly.

Substantive rights can be found in a wide range of legislative texts from international treaties   **2.70**
to local laws with many incorporating the protection of wildlife as well as human rights,
e.g. the Convention on Illegal Trade in Endangered Species of Wild Fauna and Flora 1973
(CITES), which aims to regulate international trade in endangered species, and the Wildlife
and Countryside Act 1981 (as amended), which provides protection for specific species in
England and Wales. The UNEP guide even points to the regional German law of Thuringen,
which provides that: 'Animals are to be respected as living beings and fellow creatures.
They will be protected from treatment inappropriate to the species and from avoidable
suffering.'

The UK does not confer any substantive environmental rights although Art II-37 of the draft   **2.71**
EU Constitution provides that a 'high level of environmental protection and the improvement of the quality of the environment must be integrated into the policies of the Union
and ensured in accordance with the principle of sustainable development.' And so, whereas
national governments across the UK do not recognize or confer any substantive environmental rights for humans, EU policies may shortly be required to.

E   HUMAN RIGHTS AND THE ENVIRONMENT

The European Convention for the Protection of Human Rights and Fundamental Freedoms   **2.72**
1950 (ECHR) provides a number of basic human rights and freedoms. The Human Rights
Act 1998 (HRA 1998) brought the Convention closer to home by giving 'further effect to the
rights and freedoms' guaranteed under the ECHR, while not formally incorporating the
Convention into domestic law or restricting parliamentary sovereignty. However, the Convention has been persuasive, and the European Court of Human Rights (ECtHR) provided
redress for UK citizens for some time. The *Human Rights Act Study Guide* published by the
DCA explains that the HRA works in three main ways:

(1) It requires all legislation to be interpreted and given effect as far as possible compatibly
     with the Convention rights. Where this is not possible, a court may quash or disapply
     secondary legislation and make a declaration of incompatibility for primary legislation.
(2) It makes it unlawful for a public authority to act incompatibly with the Convention
     rights and allows for a case to be brought in a UK court or tribunal against the authority
     if it does so.
(3) UK courts and tribunals must take account of Convention rights in all cases that come
     before them. They must develop the common law compatibly with the Convention
     rights and they must take account of Strasbourg (ECtHR) case law.

The HRA 1998 emphasizes that the Convention governs relationships between the state and   **2.73**
individuals, yet the Convention does cover certain matters between private persons. Section
6(3) of the Act states that a public authority includes a court and tribunal and that it will act
unlawfully if it fails to develop the law in line with the Convention. However, the HRA 1998
does not create any new, free-standing, rights. *Blackstone's Guide to the Human Rights Act 1998*
explains that if a claimant wishes to use a Convention argument in a case against a private
defendant, then the claimant must find an existing private law argument on which to hang

the Convention argument or, alternatively, focus the action on a public body that has failed to protect the claimant's rights from being violated by the defendant.

2.74 Human rights legislation draws on a number of procedural and administrative law concepts including restriction of rights available, the margin of appreciation, and proportionality. An outline of ECtHR Procedure is provided in Chapter 20: Public law.

General principles

Environmental human rights are qualified

2.75 The Convention is a mix of absolute and qualified rights. Absolute rights include the protection from torture (Art 3) and the near-absolute right to life (Art 2). Qualified rights such as the right to respect for private life (Art 8) are restricted in application or provide certain exceptions when the right or freedom does not apply. Many of the rights and freedoms relied upon in environmental matters (Arts 8, 10, 11, and Art 1, Protocol 1) are qualified and allow exceptions to those rights. The qualifications are usually found in the text of the Convention after the right itself has been established, e.g. Art 8(1) provides the right to respect for private life; Art 8(2) allows interference 'as is necessary in a democratic society'.

Margin of appreciation in balancing competing interests of society

2.76 For the Convention rights that provide for some qualification or limitation, which are generally requiring a balance to be struck between competing interests in society, public authorities enjoy a 'margin of appreciation' when exercising their functions. The ECtHR is said to recognize that national authorities should be better placed to make decisions about the merits of a case. The margin of appreciation was considered in *Hatton & ors v UK* [2003] 36022/97 (discussed in para 2.86 and Chapter 10: Noise).

Proportionality

2.77 When considering a restriction or qualification of a right, public authorities must act in a way that is proportionate to the legitimate aim pursued. In *R (Daly) v Secretary of State for the Home Department* [2001] UKHL 26 (a prisoner's rights case) Lord Steyn noted that the principle of proportionality was familiar, suggesting that the approach taken by the Privy Council in *de Freitas v Permanent Secretary of Ministry of Agriculture, Fisheries, Lands and Housing* [1999] 1 AC 69 should be applied in determining whether a limitation (by an act, rule, or decision) is arbitrary or excessive and that the court should ask itself whether:

(a) the legislative objective is sufficiently important to justify limiting a fundamental right;
(b) the measures designed to meet the legislative objective are rationally connected to it; and
(c) the means used to impair the right or freedom are no more than is necessary to accomplish the objective.

2.78 Neither the Act nor the Convention provides a specific right to a clean and healthy environment, although national and international case law is defining the extent to which the Convention and its related Protocols can be relied upon to confer rights that provide some form of environmental protection and means of redress. The following rights and freedoms have been found to have some relevance in environmental matters:

Article 2: right to life
Article 6: right to a fair trial
Article 8: right to respect for private and family life
Article 10: freedom of expression
Article 1 of Protocol 1: protection of property

Article 2: right to life

Article 2 of the Convention provides that everyone's right to life shall be protected by law.   **2.79**
This is qualified slightly in the event of a court sentence and if death results from the use of
necessary force. For the most serious environmental concerns, the right to life may be at
issue. In *Oneryildiz v Turkey* [2004] 48939/99, the applicant claimed a breach of human rights
under Articles 2, 6, 8, 13 (the right to an effective remedy) and Art 1 of Protocol 1 when a
council-run rubbish tip experienced a methane explosion causing a landslide and then the
death of 39 people, including nine members of the applicant's family. The ECtHR held that
there had been a violation of Art 2 on account of the deaths and the ineffectiveness of the
Turkish judicial machinery. The Grand Chamber, which heard the final appeal noted that:

> the Court reiterates that Article 2 does not solely concern deaths resulting from the use of force
> by agents of the State but also . . . lays down a positive obligation on States to take appropriate
> steps to safeguard the lives within their jurisdiction.

Article 6: right to a fair trial

The right to a fair trial under Art 6(1) is a procedural and qualified right, providing that: **2.80**

> In the determination of his civil rights and obligations or of any criminal charge against him,
> everyone is entitled to a fair and public hearing within a reasonable time by an independent
> and impartial tribunal established by law.

In *Zander v Sweden* (1993) 18 EHRR 175 the claimant's land was adjacent to a waste tip,   **2.81**
which had polluted the local water supply. When an application to dump more waste on the
tip was granted, the claimant's only means of appeal was to the government who dismissed
an appeal that any permit to dump waste must be subject to the waste company taking
precautionary measures to avoid further pollution. The ECtHR held that there was a breach
of Art 6(1) and awarded damages of Kr30,000 (around £5,000). However, in *Balmer-Schafroth
v Switzerland* [1997] ECHR 46 the ECtHR found that the claimants had failed to show that the
operation of the power station exposed them to a danger that was serious, specific, and
imminent. The connection between the government decision and the Art 6(1) right was
regarded as too remote to qualify as a civil right.

In *Alconbury v Secretary of State for the Environment* [2001] UKHL 23 the House of Lords   **2.82**
reviewed Art 6(1) in terms of land use planning. The Lords found that administrative matters
such as planning decisions could involve the determination of civil rights and obligations
and that there could be protection under Art 6. However, in the present case the Secretary of
State had not claimed that he was acting as an independent or impartial tribunal and the
availability of judicial review of the Secretary of State's decision satisfied the rights under the
Convention.

2.83   The court in *R (Kathro) v Rhondda Cynon Taff CBC* [2002] PLCR 304 suggested that where a public body had to determine a disputed issue of fact the decision-making process may not comply with Art 6(1) and in those circumstances there would be no review of the substantive merits of the case, thus leaving a potential gap in human rights provision. However in *R (Vetterlein) v Hampshire CC* [2001] EWHC Admin 560 the court held that the claimants' opportunity to make detailed representations during a public consultation process and then to address the planning committee had satisfied the Art 6(1) obligations.

2.84   In *Steel & Morris v UK* (2005) (No. 68416/01), a claim arising out of breaches relating to the 'McLibel' case *Steel & Morris v McDonald's Corporation* [1999] (CA) QBENF 97/1281/1, the applicants' principal complaint under Art 6(1) was that they were denied a fair trial because of the lack of legal aid. The ECtHR held that:

> the question before the court was whether the provision of legal aid was necessary for a fair hearing to be determined on the basis of the particular facts and circumstances of each case and depended *inter alia* upon the importance of what was at stake for the applicant in the proceedings, the complexity of the relevant law and procedure, and the applicant's capacity to represent him or herself effectively.

2.85   The Court held unanimously that there had been a violation of Art 6.1 and of Art 10 (freedom of expression) of the Convention. Under Art 41 of the ECHR (just satisfaction), the Court also awarded €20,000 to the first applicant and €15,000 to the second applicant for non-pecuniary damage, and €47,311.17 for costs and expenses.

Article 8: right to respect for private and family life

2.86   Article 8 provides that:

> (1)   Everyone has the right to respect for his private and family life, his home and his correspondence.
>
> (2)   There shall be no interference by a public authority with the exercise of this right except such as is necessary in a democratic society in the interests of national security, public safety or the economic well-being of the country, for the prevention of disorder or crime, for the protection of health or morals, or for the protection of rights and freedoms of others.

2.87   The main purpose of Art 8 is to protect against public interference or action in private matters. The provisions in Art 8(2) restrict the right conferred under Art 8(1). It imposes positive and negative obligations on public bodies; positive obligations include taking measures to secure the rights conferred, negative obligations involve refraining from interfering action. The approach to whether there may be a breach of Art 8 is:

(a)   To decide whether there is, in principle, a right protected under Art 8(1). The definitions of private life, family life, and home are broad and the indirect intrusion from pollution and environmental harm is covered, see e.g. *Hatton & ors v UK* where although, ultimately, the ECtHR found against the applicants this has been based upon the qualifications or the Art 8 right, not on its initial scope.

(b)   If a right exists under Art 8, there should be consideration of whether there has been any state interference with that right.

(c)   Finally, if there has been interference, is that interference within the law? Does it pursue a legitimate aim? And, is it necessary in a democratic society?

The right is regularly relied upon in environmental matters and a common concern has been   **2.88**
noise. In *Powell and Rayner v UK* (1986) 12 EHRR 335, the court found that interference of private life from aircraft noise was justified. The problem of aircraft noise was revisited in the case of *Hatton & ors v UK*. In *Hatton* the ECtHR Grand Chamber considered a referral from its own Third Chamber following a request (as an appeal) from the UK Government. The Court held that the Government policy on night flights at Heathrow airport did not violate the applicants' Art 8 right to respect for private life. Both courts considered that there was a balance between competing interests of society. The first court found in favour of the applicants, the Grand Chamber tended towards more general economic interests adding that authorities, when balancing interests, were afforded a 'margin of appreciation'. It stated that:

> The Court must consider whether the Government can be said to have struck a fair balance between [the interests of the economic well-being of the country and for the protection of the rights and freedoms of others] and the conflicting interests of the persons affected by noise disturbances, including the applicants. Environmental protection should be taken into consideration by Governments acting within the margin of appreciation and by the Court in its review of that margin, but it would not be appropriate for the Court to adopt a special approach in this respect by reference to a special status of environmental human rights.

Relying on the Art 8(2) qualification the ECtHR held that it was legitimate for the Govern-   **2.89**
ment to have taken the economic interests of the airline operators, other businesses and their clients, and those of the country as a whole when developing policy. Although the substantive right in Art 8 was found not to be violated the Court held the scope of the review by the domestic courts was not sufficient to comply with Art 13 (the right to an effective remedy before a national authority).

One of the leading cases on environmental protection under the Art 8 is *Lopez Ostra v Spain*   **2.90**
(1994) 20 EHRR 277 in which the applicant complained that a neighbouring waste treatment plant emitting fumes, noise, and strong smells made her family's living conditions unbearable and was causing serious health problems. Prior to the ECtHR hearing, Mrs Lopez Ostra, had tried numerous civil and criminal actions in domestic law, each of which failed to adequately resolve the problem. The court found that there had been a breach of Art 8 and awarded the applicant 4 million pesetas (around £20,000) in damages. It held that, despite the margin of appreciation left to the state, it had not succeeded in striking a fair balance between the interests of the town's economic wellbeing, that of having a waste treatment plant, and the applicant's effective enjoyment of her right to respect for her home and her private and family life.

Guerra & ors v Italy (1998) 26 EHRR 3577 concerned the failure to provide a local community   **2.91**
with information about risk and how to proceed in the event of an accident at a nearby chemical factory. The Court held that the potential direct effect of toxic emissions on the applicants' right to respect for their private and family life meant that Art 8 was applicable. The applicants had complained of an omission by state authority in its failure to act, rather than positive interference.

2.92   In *Chapman v UK* (2001) 33 EHRR 18 the ECtHR found that the interference of rights to private life by a local planning authority's enforcement of planning controls were expressed primarily in terms of environmental policy and, in those circumstances, the local authority were pursuing the legitimate aim of protecting the 'rights of others' through the preservation of the environment.

Article 10: freedom of expression

2.93   Article 10 provides that:

> everyone has the right to freedom of expression, which includes holding opinions, receiving and imparting information. The right may be restricted by a licensing regime or any restrictions or penalties necessary in a democratic society.

2.94   The right to freedom of expression may be relevant in instances where environmental activists are prosecuted for carrying out protesting activities. In *Percy v DPP* [2001] EWHC Admin 1125, a protestor who defaced a US flag in front of servicemen was convicted of causing harassment, alarm, or distress under s 5 of the Public Order Act 1986. The claimant challenged the conviction relying on Art 10 (holding an opinion). The Divisional Court held that the conviction was excessive and that peaceful protest may cause affront, which is not criminal. The conviction was quashed having failed to give sufficient weight to the defendant's Art 10 right.

2.95   However, in *Persey v SSEFR* [2002] EWHC 371 (Admin) the decision to hold private rather than public inquiries into the Foot & Mouth outbreak was held not to breach Art 10 and the right to receive information. The court noted that Art 10 imposes no positive obligation on government to provide, in addition to existing means of communication, an open forum to achieve yet wider dissemination of views.

2.96   In *Steel & Morris v UK* the ECtHR held that, in relation to the Art 10 point, the central issue that fell to be determined was whether the interference with the applicants' freedom of expression had been 'necessary in a democratic society'. It noted that:

> The Government had contended that, as the applicants were not journalists, they should not attract the high level of protection afforded to the press under Article 10. However, in a democratic society even small and informal campaign groups, such as London Greenpeace, had to be able to carry on their activities effectively. There existed a strong public interest in enabling such groups and individuals outside the mainstream to contribute to the public debate by disseminating information and ideas on matters of general public interest such as health and the environment.

Article 1 of Protocol 1: protection of property

2.97   Article 1, Protocol 1 provides that:

> Every natural person is entitled to the peaceful enjoyment of his possessions. No one shall be deprived of his possessions except in the public interest and subject to conditions provided by law and by the general principles of international law.
>
> The preceding provisions shall not, however, impair the right of a State to enforce such laws as it deems necessary to control the use of property in accordance with the general interest or to secure the payment of taxes or other contributions or penalties.

The term 'possessions' referred to in Art 1, Protocol 1 is broad and, importantly for environmental matters, includes land and other property. It may also include the maintenance of a licence: *Tre Traktorer v Sweden* (1989) 13 EHRR 309, and a permit to exploit a gravel pit: *Fredin v Sweden* (1991) 13 EHRR 784. However, a possession does not extend to a regulatory approval for the production of chemical pesticides: *R (Amvac) v SSEFR and ors* [2001] EWHC Admin 1011. **2.98**

In *Aston Cantlow & ors v Wallbank* [2003] UKHL 37 Lord Hope stated at para 67 that there were three rules within Art 1, Protocol 1: **2.99**

(1) the right to peaceful enjoyment of possessions as set out in the first sentence is of a general nature;
(2) there are then two forms of interference; the deprivation of possessions that it subjects to conditions, and the control of the use of property in accordance with the general interest.

He added that: **2.100**

(3) In each case a balance must be struck between the rights of the individual and the public interest to determine whether the interference was justified. These rules are not unconnected, as before considering whether the first rule has been complied with, the court must first determine whether the last two rules are applicable.

In *Sporrong & Lonnroth v Sweden* (1982) 5 EHRR 35, the ECtHR found that Stockholm City Council had interfered with the applicants' right to enjoyment of their possessions due to development and construction restrictions in an area where they owned property. In the case of *Chassagnou & ors v France* [1999] ECHR 22 the Grand Chamber considered the objections by small landowners to a municipal hunting association requiring rights of hunting across all land in the region. The court found that: **2.101**

> compelling landowners to transfer hunting rights over their land so that others can make use of them in a way which is totally incompatible with their beliefs imposes a disproportionate burden which is not justified under the second paragraph of Article 1 of Protocol 1.

It also held that there had been a violation of Art 1, Protocol 1 in conjunction with Art 14 of the Convention (the enjoyment of rights and freedoms without discrimination) and Art 11 (the right to freedom of peaceful assembly and association). The Grand Chamber considered an alleged violation of Art 9 (the right to freedom of thought, conscience, and religion), but found that it was unnecessary to conduct a separate examination from that standpoint. However, Judge Fischbach, in a separate opinion stated that he took the view that: **2.102**

> 'environmentalist' or 'ecological' beliefs come within the scope of Article 9 in so far as they are informed by what is a truly societal stance. They are closely bound up with the personality of each individual and determine the decisions he takes about the type of life he wishes to lead. Moreover, it is undeniable that the question of preservation of our environment, and of wild animals in particular, is now a much-debated one in our societies.

In *R (Langton & Allen) v Defra and Derbyshire CC* [2002] Env LR 20 the issue and enforcement of a notice under the Animal By-Products Order 1999 by the local authority after a failure to dispose of maggot waste adequately was proportionate to the interference rights under Art 1, Protocol 1 because matters of public and animal health required prompt action. **2.103**

KEY DOCUMENTS AND MATERIALS

The Human Rights Act 1998.
Freedom of Information Act 2000
Environmental Information Regulations 2004 (SI 2004/3391)

UNECE Convention on Access to Information, Public Participation in Decision-making and
    Access to Justice in Environmental Matters 1998 (the Aarhus Convention).
    www.unece.org (reproduced in Appendix 1)

Department of Constitutional Affairs (2002). *Human Rights Act 1998 Study Guide*. 2nd ed.
    DCA: London
IEMA (2002): *Perspectives: Guidelines on Participation in Environmental Decision-making*. IEMA:
    Lincoln. www.iema.net
Regional Environment Center (2003). *Handbook on Access to Justice under the Aarhus
    Convention*. REC: Hungary. www.rec.org
Wadham and others (2003). *Blackstone's Guide to the Human Rights Act 1998*. 3rd ed. Oxford
    University Press: Oxford

PART II
SUBSTANTIVE ENVIRONMENTAL LAW AREAS

3

AIR

A INTRODUCTION

Air pollution illustrates the wide range of impacts that can arise from quite discrete **3.01** activities. It can cause localized problems of increased smoke and dust emissions resulting in immediate injury to health, e.g. by aggravating asthma and contributing to premature death. It also creates global concerns like the destruction of the ozone layer through the increased use of chloroflourocarbons (CFCs) and other stratospheric ozone-depleting compounds. A perhaps simplistic, but nevertheless useful, distinction between the adverse impacts on air is to refer to the two categories of (local) air pollution and (global) atmospheric pollution.

3.02 Early legislation such as the Alkali Act 1863, sought to tackle localized air pollution and in particular to regulate hydrochloric gas emissions from caustic soda works. Successive amending legislation through the Victorian period revised the legislation. By the introduction of the consolidating Alkali, etc, Works Regulation Act 1906, the legislation sought to confine 95% of acid gas within the alkali works and had introduced the concept of 'best practical means' to, for example, prevent the escape of noxious or offensive gases. The Government, in its Air Quality Strategy 2000, has set objectives to reduce the eight key pollutants, outlined in section B below, by 2008.

3.03 The main sources of pollution are from burning fossil fuel for energy and emissions from vehicles. Sulphur dioxide from power stations and nitrogen oxides from road traffic contribute to acidification and local air pollution. They can affect human health and vegetation. Particulate matter comes from a range of sources but significantly from diesel engines.

3.04 Ozone occurs naturally but levels are aggravated by reactions with volatile organic compounds and nitrogen oxide. It can cause damage to the airway lining, as well as eye and nose irritation. It can also harm vegetation.

3.05 It can be said that air pollution in the UK is in decline. This is partly due to the reduction in heavy industry and the switch to power stations that pollute less (i.e. from coal to gas). Nevertheless, air pollution remains responsible for up to 24,000 premature deaths every year. Climate change is causing ever more frequent extreme weather patterns throughout the world. For example, in 2004, Bangladesh experienced its worst floods for decades with over 600,000 people affected. The monsoon season always brings flooding to Bangladesh with severity operating on a ten-year cycle. However, in 2004 the most severe floods arrived three years early, with deforestation, irrigation, and global warming being blamed for, among other things, speeding up the melting of the Himalayan snows.

3.06 Air quality management is based upon strategic policy and decision-making, regulation, and more recently, the use of economic instruments. Liability for air pollution arises through civil and criminal sanctions that may ultimately be put before the courts. Research also plays a role. For instance Defra recently commissioned research on how much people were prepared to pay for reductions in health risks relating to air pollution: *Valuation of Health Benefits Associated with Reductions in Air Pollution* (Defra, 2004).

B   DEFINING AIR POLLUTION

3.07 Air pollution in its simplest form is unwelcome particles and substances in the air. Particles, often too small to see, range in size from grit to fine vapours. Odour may also be described as air pollution. There are two general forms of air pollution: dust and gas. These are defined by various standards, largely according to the diameter of the particle and are often based on monitoring devices designed to mimic the characteristics of the human respiratory system or on the equivalent physical characteristics of spherical particles, i.e. aerodynamic diameter. Useful definitions of particulate matter are contained in the former Department of Environment *Quality of Urban Air Review Group 3rd Report: Airborne Particulate Matter in the UK 1996*. Some simple definitions are set out below.

Grit

Grit, the largest particulate, is defined by the Clean Air (Emission of Grit and Dust from Furnaces) Regulations 1971 (SI 1971/162) as particulate matter exceeding 76 μm in diameter. **3.08**

Dust

Dust is defined in BS 3405 1983: *Method for Measurement of Particulate Emission Including Grit and Dust (Simplified Method)* as 'particulates between 1 and 75 μm in diameter'. The particle size and shape govern its physical transport characteristics with small, irregularly shaped particles being more likely to remain airborne than large, dense, spherical particles. Airborne particulate matter can cover a wide range of sizes from a few nanometres (nm) (1 nm = 10^{-9} metre = one billionth of a metre) to tens of micrometers μm (1 μm = 10^{-6} metre = one millionth of a metre). Despite the BS definition, the word 'dust' is often used to cover substances between 1 and 300 μm in diameter (0.001 to 0.3 mm). Particulates have a number of subcategories: **3.09**

- *Coarse particle mode* is greater than 2 μm in diameter within the spectrum of airborne particles, in which particles have arisen mostly from disintegration of bulk solid and liquid materials.
- PM_{15} is particulate matter less than 15 μm in aerodynamic diameter or, more strictly, particles that pass through a size-selective inlet with a 50% efficiency cut off at 15 μm in aerodynamic diameter.
- PM_{10} is particulate matter less than 10 μm in aerodynamic diameter (or more strictly, particles that pass through a size-selective inlet with a 50% efficiency cut off at 10 μm in aerodynamic diameter). Within the PM_{10} range, particles less than 2.5 μm in diameter (known as $PM_{2.5}$) are described as fine, while particles between 2.5 and 10 μm are described as coarse.
- $PM_{2.5}$ (fine particles) is particulate matter less than 2.5 μm in aerodynamic diameter (or more strictly, particles that pass through a size-selective inlet with a 50% efficiency cut off at 2.5 μm in aerodynamic diameter). These arise mainly from the condensation of hot vapours and chemically driven gas to particle conversion processes.

Particulates can be carried into the lungs and are a known carcinogen. The airborne particulate matter that enters the nose and mouth during breathing is defined as total inhalable dust and is often referred to as PM_{10}. The smaller particle mass, which penetrates to the gas exchange region of the lung, is defined as respirable dust and is often referred to as PM_4. **3.10**

Fume

Fume is defined by s 63 of the Clean Air Act 1993 as airborne solid matter smaller than dust. **3.11**

Aerosol

3.12 Aerosol is an atmosphere or system containing particles, between 10^{-5} and 10^{-7} cm in diameter, dispersed in a gas, smoke, or fog.

Smoke

3.13 Smoke is a particulate matter of less than 15 μm, derived from the incomplete combustion of fuels. Dark smoke is a non-reflective (dark) particulate matter, measured according to the Ringelmann Chart: see para 3.28.

Volatile organic compound

3.14 Volatile organic compounds (VOCs) are defined in Art 1(9) of the VOCs Protocol 1991 as 'all organic compounds of anthropogenic nature, other than methane, that are capable of producing photochemical oxidants by reactions with NOx in the presence of sunlight.' They evaporate easily at ambient temperatures and contribute to air pollution largely though the formation of secondary pollutants such as hydrocarbons. They contribute to ground level ozone and depletion of the ozone layer. They also include greenhouse gases. VOCs arise from the incomplete combustion of fuel from vehicle engines and from the use of solvents in paint and glue.

Carbon combustion

3.15 Carbon dioxide (CO_2) is a colourless, odourless, non-reactive gas from the combustion of carbon and the respiration of fauna. It is the most significant greenhouse gas and contributor to global warming, not so much of its potency but from the vast emissions that arise. Carbon monoxide (CO) is an odourless gas from the incomplete combustion of carbon including that from road vehicles.

Clarifying the source of air pollution

3.16 Any claim relating to air pollution will require evidence that the deposits, particulates, or gases travel from a specific source to the point of harm. This distance will depend on wind speed and direction and other weather conditions. It will also be determined by the nature of the emission source, e.g. the height of a factory chimney will influence the distance airborne pollutants will travel. The location of the polluting source will be another determining factor. This was key during the 1960s and 1970s when Scotland, Northern England, and Scandinavia suffered the most from acid rain caused by coal-fired power stations operating across the UK and emitting large quantities of sulphur dioxide.

C   AIR QUALITY MANAGEMENT

3.17 Part IV of the Environment Act 1995 (EA 1995) required a strategic approach to tackling air pollution and the Government published the UK Air Quality Strategy in 2000. Part IV also requires local authorities to review the air quality in their area. The reviews must consider the present and likely future air quality. Such reviews must be accompanied by an assessment of whether any air quality objectives are being achieved or are likely to be achieved.

Where any objectives are not likely to be achieved, the local authority must, by order, designate that area an air quality management area (AQMA) (s 83 of the EA 1995). On designation of an AQMA, local authorities must prepare an action plan that relates to the use of all the authority's powers (see below) in achieving the air quality objectives and a timetable for completion of any proposed action.

The Air Quality (England) Regulations 2000 (SI 2000/928) and Air Quality (Wales) **3.18** Regulations 2000 (SI 2000/1940) set targets for the reduction of seven of the eight key pollutants listed in the Schedule to the Regulations. These are set out below.

Table 3.1 The Government's eight key pollutants

Pollutant	Main cause	Objective	Measured as	Target date
benzene	petrol vehicles	16.25 µg/m^3 (5 ppb)	running annual mean	31.12.03
1,3-butadiene	road transport	2.25 µg/m^3 (1 ppb)	running annual mean	31.12.03
carbon mono.	petrol vehicles & ind.	11.6 µg/m^3 (10 ppb)	running 8-hour mean	31.12.03
lead	petrol vehicles & ind.	0.5 µg/m^3 (1 ppb)	annual mean	31.12.04
		0.25 µg/m^3 (1 ppb)	annual mean	31.12.08
nitrogen dioxide	road transport power gen.	200 µg/m^3 (105 ppb) not exceeded > 18 × yr (provisional targets)	1-hour mean	31.12.05
particles (PM$_{10}$)	road transport power gen. & ind.	50 µg/m^3 (1 ppb) not exceeded < 35 × yr	24-hour mean	31.12.04
sulphur dioxide	power gen. & ind.	350 µg/m^3 (132 ppb) not exceeded < 24 × yr	1-hour mean	31.12.04
		125 µg/m^3 (47 ppb) not exceeded < 3 × yr	24-hour mean	31.12.04
		266 µg/m^3 (100 ppb) not exceeded < 35 × yr	24-hour mean	31.12.05
ozone	mix of oxygen atoms, inc NOx from car exhaust		no target	

The Air Quality Strategy calls upon a range of stakeholders to help manage local air quality **3.19** including public bodies such as local authorities, private organizations, and the public. For example, the Highways Agency, the public body responsible for the network of trunk roads including motorways published: *The Role of the Highways Agency in Local Air Quality Management* in 2003. Section 3 of the report explains that for all major pollutants from road vehicles the highest emission rates occur at the lowest speeds although there is an optimum speed of around 100 km/h. It suggests that one option to reduce emissions would be to reduce the maximum speed limit to 100 km/h.

By July 2004, 125 local authorities had identified pollution hotspots and designated these as **3.20** AQMAs, mainly in respect of the objectives for nitrogen dioxide and PM$_{10}$s. Road traffic emissions were the main source of pollution in 95% of AQMAs.

D   AIR QUALITY CONTROL

3.21   The local authority powers available to implement an action plan under Pt IV of the EA 1995 include:

- the integrated pollution control (IPC) and pollution prevention and control (PPC) regimes;
- local air pollution control (APC) and air pollution prevention and control regimes;
- the prohibition or control of dark smoke, grit dust, and fumes from activities not covered by IPPC, IPC, or APC and the creation of smoke control areas under the Clean Air Act 1993; and
- the regulation of highways, transport, and vehicle emissions.

There are also local authority controls under the land use planning system, and residual powers under the statutory nuisance regime and the civil law, principally in nuisance.

IPC and PPC

3.22   IPC and PPC are considered in detail in Chapter 11: Pollution, prevention and control. IPC was introduced under Pt I of the EPA 1990; PPC by the Pollution Prevention and Control Act 1999. They operate in tandem until IPC is phased out and PPC fully replaces it by the end of 2007. IPC and PPC both make a distinction between Pt A, the more polluting activities and Pt B, the less polluting ones. Part B covers polluting processes emitting to air alone and controls the APC or APPC regimes. Some of the most polluting emissions to air are from waste incineration discussed in Chapter 14: Waste.

APC and APPC

3.23   In terms of the procedure, authorizations/permits, appeals enforcement, and sanctions, APC and APPC operate under the same regulations as IPC and PPC respectively and are considered in Chapter 11. In 2004, the Chartered Institute of Environmental Health (CIEH) produced a second edition of its publication: *Industrial Pollution Control by Local Authorities — a Management Guide*. This provides guidance on local authority functions, procedures, and enforcement together with model agreements and enforcement policies. It is available from the CIEH website: www.cieh.org.

3.24   In summary, the regulation of pollution is by the grant of authorizations or permits to pollute with conditions limiting the polluting processes. The Pt B processes referred to are those releasing emissions to air regulated by local authorities such as: Sch 1 para 1.3 Pt B of the PPS Regs 1991 'burning fuel in a boiler or furnace with a net rated thermal input of not less than 20 megawatts (but less than 50 megawatts)' or, one of the more common processes, found in Sch 1 para 5.1 Pt B of the PPS Regs 1991: the process of cremation of human remains; an activity generally undertaken by local authorities themselves.

3.25   Over 80 guidance notes covering different industry sectors are produced by the Secretary of State and available from the Department of Environment, Food and Rural Affairs (Defra) such as:

- PG1/9(91): Poultry litter combustion processes between 0.4 and 3 MW net rated thermal input;
- PG2/9(91): Metal decontamination processes; and
- PG6/39(92): Animal by-product dealers.

Enforcement of APC/APPC

The enforcement of the APC and APPC regime includes non-compliance action by the regulator including prosecution for breach of the regulations and breach of any notice served on an operator. There are very few reported decisions relating to air pollution control and any that do arise tend to fall under the IPPC regime and are therefore considered in Chapter 11: Pollution prevention and control. **3.26**

The Clean Air Act 1993

The Clean Air Act 1993 (CAA 1993) provides further control of air pollution that falls outside IPC/PPC and APC/APPC regimes (Pt VI of the CAA 1993 specifically excludes special cases including processes controlled under the EPA 1990 and activities under the PPCA 1999). The Act enables local authorities to: **3.27**

- prohibit dark smoke from chimneys of any building or an industrial or trade premises (Pt I);
- control smoke, dust, and grit emissions from industrial furnaces and regulate the height of chimneys (Pt II);
- designate smoke control areas (Pt III); and
- publish information about air pollution (Pt V).

Part IV of the Act also enables the Secretary of State to make regulations to control certain forms of air pollution such as motor fuel.

Part I: dark smoke

Dark smoke is defined according to the Ringelmann Chart (s 3(1) of the CAA 1993) as being 'as dark or darker than shade 2 on the chart'. The Ringelmann Chart is a simple card with five squares with 0 being clear and the shades of grey becoming progressively darker as the numbers rise to the darkest at 4. **3.28**

Section 1 of the CAA 1993 states that it is an offence to emit dark smoke from a chimney of any building or a furnace. Certain emissions may be permitted by regulation, e.g. the Dark Smoke (Permitted Periods) Regulations 1958 (SI 1958/498) allow blowing soot from boilers for ten minutes in an eight-hour period. Section 1(4) also provides a defence that an emission was solely due to (a) lighting up a furnace, (b) the failure of a furnace, (c) the use of unsuitable fuel, or a combination of these causes. A person guilty of an offence under s 1 shall be liable on summary conviction to a maximum fine of £5,000 (or £1,000 if a private dwelling). **3.29**

Section 2 of the CAA 1993 prohibits dark smoke from any industrial or trade premises other than considered in s 1. Again, certain emissions may be permitted, e.g. under the Clean Air (Emission of Dark Smoke) (Exemption) Regulations 1969 (SI 1969/1263). In terms of evidence, s 2(3) provides that there shall be taken to have been an emission of dark smoke **3.30** in any case where material is burned on the premises and the circumstances are such that their burning would be likely to cause dark smoke, unless the contrary can be shown. It is a defence, under s 2(4) to prove that the emission was inadvertent or that all practicable steps had been taken to prevent or minimize the emission. Someone guilty of an offence under s 2 shall be liable on summary conviction to a maximum fine of £20,000.

Part II: smoke, grit, dust, and fumes

3.31 The aim of Pt II of the CAA 1993 is to prevent or limit emissions of smoke, grit, dust, and fumes by requiring that:

- new furnaces shall be, so far as practicable, smokeless (s 4);
- emissions of grit and dust from non-domestic furnaces are limited according to prescribed limits contained in regulations (s 5);
- certain furnaces burning pulverized fuel must not be used unless fitted with arrestment plants (ss 6 and 8); and
- the height of furnace chimneys has been approved before an occupier uses certain furnaces burning certain fuels (s 14).

3.32 It is an offence to breach any of the requirements of Pt II. There is the defence of 'best practical means' for the s 5 grit and dust emissions under s 5(4). There are exemptions to the use of arrestment plant under s 7 and an appeal against non-approval of any plans for arrestment plant (s 9). There are further requirements to provide information to local authorities about furnaces and fuel consumed if requested and with non-compliance being an offence.

3.33 Chimney height approval under s 14 will not be granted unless a local authority is satisfied that the height proposed will be sufficient to prevent, so far as practicable, the emissions from becoming prejudicial to health or a nuisance having regard to the chimney's purpose, the type and position of nearby buildings, the levels of neighbouring ground, and any other relevant matter. Guidance on chimney heights is provided in the Government's *Third Memorandum on Chimney Heights* (1981).

3.34 A person guilty of one of the offences in Pt II shall be liable on summary conviction to a maximum fine of £5,000 (or £1,000 for failing to give notice of installation under s 4(1)).

Part III: smoke control areas

3.35 Part III of the CAA 1993 includes provisions on the adaptation of fireplaces and declaring smoke control areas. Section 18(1) provides that a local authority may by order, declare the whole or any part of the district to be a smoke control area. The Secretary of State may also direct that a local authority make a smoke control order. Under s 20 it is an offence to emit smoke from a chimney within a smoke control area, although s 20(4) provides a defence, if proven, that the emission was not caused by the use of any fuel other than authorized fuel. A person guilty of an offence under s 20 shall be liable on summary conviction to a maximum fine of £1,000.

3.36 In 2004 a new website was launched containing information on smoke control areas in the UK to allow people to see if a local authority has smoke controls: www.uksmokecontrolareas.co.uk. The aim is to provide the public, local authorities, and manufacturers of fuels and fireplaces access to information on the location of smoke control areas.

Part IV: control of certain forms of pollution

Part IV of the CAA 1993 enables the Secretary of State to make regulations regarding motor **3.37** fuels and the content of fuel for furnaces and engines. It also creates an offence of cable burning, which is subject to a maximum fine on summary conviction of £5,000.

The regulations relating to motor vehicle emissions are numerous, almost all of which derive **3.38** from the EU, e.g. Directive 91/441/EEC amending Directive 70/220/EEC on the approximation of the laws of the Member States relating to measures to be taken against air pollution by emissions from motor vehicles. However, prior to enacting regulations relating to fuels in Pt IV, the Secretary of State must, under ss 30(2) and 31(2) of the CAA 1993, consult representatives of vehicle manufacturers and users, representatives of fuel producers and users, and air pollution experts. The control of vehicle emissions is considered in more detail in para 3.65.

Part V: information about air pollution

A local authority may undertake investigation and research on air pollution and then **3.39** publicize and promote the problem (s 34 of the CAA 1993). Under s 35 it can obtain information from an occupier by issuing a notice requesting specific details on pollutants and emissions. Section 37 provides a right of appeal against a s 36 notice. Failure, without reasonable excuse, to comply with the requirements of a notice or to provide any information is an offence and subject on summary conviction to a maximum fine of £5,000.

Part VI: special cases

Part VI of the CAA 1993 applies regulations and exceptions in particular circumstances such **3.40** as the use of certain railway engines and vessels, e.g. s 1 of the CAA 1993 prohibiting dark smoke does not apply to merchant shipping being used by the Navy within territorial waters. Related regulations include the Dark Smoke (Permitted Periods) (Vessels) Regulations 1958 (SI 1958/878).

Part VII: miscellaneous and general

The miscellaneous provisions in Pt VII of the CAA 1993 include the rights and obligations **3.41** of local authority officers responsible for regulating and enforcing controls under the Act. These include, under s 51 of the CAA 1993, the duty to notify the occupier as soon as possible of an offence being committed under ss 1, 2, or 20. There are also rights of entry, inspection, and power to serve a notice to obtain information requested under Pt V of the Act.

E OTHER LEGAL CONTROLS OF AIR POLLUTION

Land use planning

Planning decisions have a significant impact on air and other sources of pollution, e.g. by **3.42** allocating an area in a local development framework as high density housing, which, unless managed sustainably, will give rise to a significant increase in transport emissions; or by granting planning permission for a new fossil fuel-based power station in an area where levels of nitrogen dioxide or other pollutants are already high. Government guidance PPS 23: *Planning and Pollution Control* (2005) provides at para 1.12, Annex 2 that planning, transport, and air quality control functions should work closely together in:

- carrying out the reviews and assessments of air quality, especially where new development is likely;
- considering the possible impact of new development in drawing up any air quality action plans and local air quality strategies;
- considering the results of air quality reviews and assessments in the preparation of development plans; and
- taking any development control decisions that may have a direct or indirect bearing on existing air quality or creating exposure to poor air quality.

3.43   In terms of development control PPS 23 states at para 8 that:

> Any consideration of the quality of land, air or water and the potential impacts arising from development, possibly leading to an impact on health, is capable of being a material planning consideration, in so far as it arises or may arise from any land use.

3.44   Appendix A to PPS 23 notes that the following matters, among other things, should be considered in the preparation of development plans and may also be material in the consideration of individual planning applications:

- the existing, and likely future, air quality in an area;
- compliance with any statutory environmental quality standards or objectives prescribed by the Air Quality Regulations 2000;
- the need to limit and where possible reduce greenhouse gas emissions and take account of potential effects of climate change;
- relevant action and management plans, e.g. AQMA action plans; and
- the possibility that emissions of smoke, fumes, gases, dust, steam, smell, or noise from the development constitute a statutory nuisance: see paras 3.50–3.55.

3.45   Other aspects of the relationship between land use planning and pollution control are considered in Chapter 11: Pollution prevention and control.

Building regulations

3.46   The design, construction, and use of buildings play a key role in reducing emissions from buildings, particularly CO_2. Part L, of the Building Regulations 2000 (SI 2000/2351), as amended, covers the conservation of fuel and power. L1 provides that reasonable provision shall be made for the conservation of fuel and power by controlling space and hot water heating, and limiting heat loss in dwellings and buildings whose floor area exceeds 30 m². L2 requires energy efficient artificial lighting to be installed in buildings, other than dwellings, of more than 100 m² floor area. Part L relates to building work and where there is a material change of use. The Building Regulations in general are considered in Chapter 8: Land use planning.

Waste management

Certain forms of waste management, such as incineration, are likely to be covered by the PPC/APPC regime. However, the Waste Management Licensing System under Pt II of the EPA 1990 may also control air pollution. For instance, s 33(1) of the EPA 1990 includes, among other things, that no person shall '(b) dispose of controlled waste in or on any land except in accordance with a waste management licence, and (c) dispose of controlled waste in a manner likely to cause pollution of the environment or harm to human health'. **3.47**

In *R v Biffa Waste Services* (2002) Env Times, Vol 8.3 p 37, the defendant was fined £7,000 and ordered to pay costs of £5,881 after concerns were raised about severe odour problems from one of its waste sites. The Environment Agency had received earlier reports of offensive smells from the same site. In *R v Reading Skips Hire Ltd* (2004) Environment Times website 27 July 2004, the defendant was found guilty of breaching four conditions of its Waste Management Licence after it was found unlawfully burning large quantities of waste over a four day period. Waste management is considered further in Chapter 14: Waste. **3.48**

Agricultural pollution

Certain agricultural practices can cause significant air pollution such as stubble and crop burning, the spreading of sewage sludge on farmland causing offensive smells and the release of GMOs. The control of agricultural pollution including GMOs is covered in Chapter 6: Fishing, farming, and animal health. **3.49**

Statutory nuisance

Part III of the EPA 1990 covers statutory nuisance, and although activities and pollution that fall within the PPC regime are excluded from statutory nuisance through the various statutory nuisance exceptions, there are three nuisance categories that specifically relate to air pollution: **3.50**

- certain smoke emissions from premises;
- fumes or gases emitted from premises; and
- any dust, steam, smell, or other effluvia arising on industrial, trade, or business premises.

Chapter 19: Criminal law practice and procedure covers the practice and procedure of statutory nuisance, this section covers the topic with special interest to air pollution. **3.51**

Certain smoke emitted from premises

Section 79(1)(b) of the EPA 1990 states that smoke emitted from premises so as to be prejudicial to health or a nuisance is a statutory nuisance. Section 79(7) states that smoke includes soot, ash, grit, and gritty particles emitted in smoke. Subsection (1)(b) includes garden bonfires and barbecues (providing they comply with the regularity and frequency principles). Most smoke emissions from business premises or land are covered by the PPC legislation or the Clean Air Act 1993 and are excluded from the statutory nuisance provisions. **3.52**

There are many exceptions to this category contained in s 79(2) and (3) including smoke from private dwellings within a smoke control area and dark smoke from industrial or trade **3.53** premises. In *Griffiths v Pembrokeshire County Council* [2000] EWHC Admin 319, the defendant continued to burn animal carcasses in contravention of an abatement notice, he argued that although there may have been a smell of smoke that would not amount to smoke as a statutory nuisance. The High Court dismissed an appeal by way of case stated and held that the term smoke could apply to the smell of smoke.

Fumes or gases emitted from premises

3.54 Section 79(1)(c) of the EPA 1990 provides that fumes or gases emitted from premises so as to be prejudicial to health or a nuisance constitutes a statutory nuisance. Section 79(4) of the EPA provides that s 79(1)(c) only applies to private dwellings.

Dust, steam, smell, or other effluvia arising on industrial, trade, or business premises

3.55 Section 79(1)(d) of the EPA 1990 states that a statutory nuisance includes any dust, steam, smell, or other effluvia arising on industrial, trade, or business premises and being prejudicial to health or a nuisance. The subsection does not cover residential property. Section 79(7) provides that dust under s 79(1)(d) does not include dust emitted from a chimney as an ingredient of smoke. Steam, smell, or effluvia are not specifically defined. A common definition of effluvia is unpleasant smells or exhalation from gas or decaying matter.

Private nuisance

3.56 Private nuisance is considered in detail in Chapter 17: Civil law practice and procedure. It was defined in *Read v Lyons (J.) & Co.* [1947] AC 156 as the 'unlawful interference with a person's use or enjoyment of land or some right over, or in connection with it.' In terms of nuisance caused by air pollution, interference may be physical damage to land, property, and chattels, e.g. from dust and smuts landing on property and having a corrosive effect, or from the restricted use, e.g. where someone is unable to sit outside due to dust, smoke, or smells.

3.57 *St Helens Smelting Co v Tipping* (1865) 11 HL Cas 642 continues to be an important case in nuisance, in which Mr Tipping successfully claimed compensation for damage caused to trees, crops, and cattle and illness to himself and servants by noxious gases and vapours being emitted from nearby smelting works. In *Wheeler v JJ Saunders Ltd* [1996] Ch 19 CA, nuisance was caused by smells arising from two pig rearing houses for which the claimant's neighbour had been granted planning permission to erect and use. The Court of Appeal upheld the judge's award of damages and an injunction. In *Southwork LBC v Long* [2002] EWCA Civ 403, the Court of Appeal upheld an award of £13,500 in damages for nuisance caused by smell and infestation following the landlord's failure to keep the common parts clean. Similarly, in *Wilson v Southwick Contractors* [1996] CLY 2157, a District Judge awarded general damages to the claimant for suffering smell, smoke, and loud noise arising from the defendant's garage workshop.

Public nuisance

3.58 The practice and procedure of public nuisance is considered in Chapter 19: Criminal law practice and procedure. In *A-G v PYA Quarries Ltd* [1957] 2 QB 169, public nuisance was said to include an act or omission that obstructs or causes inconvenience or damage to the public. In *Shoreham-by-Sea UDC v Dolphin Canadian Proteins Ltd* (1972) 71 LGR 261, unpleasant smells from the production of animal feed, manure, and tallow was held to be a public nuisance.

Judicial review

Because of the mainly regulatory nature of air pollution control and the role of public bodies   **3.59**
such as the Environment Agency and local authorities, judicial review may be appropriate in challenging any decision taken. This may arise in the way that a permit or notice has been served on an operator or from a local community group concerned that any permit or condition attached to it is unlawful.

In *R (Westminster City Council & ors) v The Mayor of London* [2002] EWHC 2440 (Admin), the   **3.60**
claimants challenged the Mayor's decision to introduce a Congestion Charging Scheme (CCS) in central London. The grounds of challenge regarded deficiencies in the consultation process and provision of information, the decision not to carry out an EIA on the scheme, the decision not to hold a public inquiry into the implementation and operation of the scheme, and alleged breaches of human rights. The claim failed. In his judgment Justice Kay referred to various reports carried out before implementing the CCS; these concluded that estimated changes in vehicle emissions would be limited by the introduction of the scheme, although there would be some variation between localities with increases outside the CCS zone and some modest decreases within the zone.

F   TRANSPORT AND AIR POLLUTION

One of the main sources of air pollution in the UK is from road transport. According to the   **3.61**
Government's *Air Quality Strategy 2000* it contributed to 56% of benzene and 18% of PM_{10} emissions in 1997. It is responsible for 26% of all UK CO_2 emissions and almost half of certain smog-forming pollutants. According to government statistics, road traffic has more than doubled since 1970 and is now estimated to be nearly 500 billion vehicle kilometres a year. Between 1970 and 2002, some emissions such as NO_X and $PM10_s$ have decreased slightly, mainly due to better engine design and increased fuel efficiency, although CO_2 emissions have increased by 130%. There are a number of legislative controls on air pollution from transport regulating emissions from and the use of road vehicles.

Air transport is rising rapidly in the UK and is estimated to contribute around 3.5% to   **3.62**
human induced global warming. In the UK air passenger traffic has grown nearly six fold in just over 30 years from 32 million passengers per year in 1970 to 189 million in 2002. It is continuing to grow at around 6% per annum, fuelled by a growth in low cost air flights and the promotion of air travel as an alternative to land-based transport. In December 2003, the UK Government published its Aviation White Paper: *The Future of Air Transport* setting out its strategic framework for the development of airport capacity for the next 30 years. In terms of environmental impact, the Intergovernmental Panel on Climate Change (IPCC), a body of over 700 scientists from around the world, published a detailed study of the impact of air

pollution on the atmosphere: *Aviation and the Global Atmosphere* (1999) reporting that aircraft release more than 600 million tonnes of CO_2, the world's major greenhouse gas, every year.

Regulating pollution from road vehicles

3.63   The EU Auto-Oil II Programme takes a strategic approach to reducing air pollution from road transport incorporating the role of public transport, traffic management, and new technology. It sets the policy for the range of EU Directives on vehicle emissions, which in turn, require transposition into UK law, usually by enacting regulations. The Communication from the Commission *A Review of the Auto-Oil II Programme* COM (2000) 626 noted that:

> The Auto-Oil II results have confirmed that road transport is responsible for a declining relative share of total emissions of the most common atmospheric pollutants. Although road transport will on current trends remain a major contributor to poor air quality until 2010 and beyond, not least because of the location of the emissions, it is equally clear that further improvements in air quality will require an approach that addresses other sources more systematically.

3.64   Regulations made by the Secretary of State under Pt IV of the CAA 1993 include the Motor Fuel (Composition and Content) Regulations 1999 (SI 1999/3107), which transposes the EU Directive 98/70/EC relating to the quality of petrol and diesel fuels. The regulations control the distribution and sale of fuel from filling stations and included a general ban on marketing leaded petrol, although it may be used in some limited circumstances. The Motor Fuel (Composition and Content) (Amendment) Regulations 2003 (SI 2003/3078) transposes EU Directive 2003/17/EC (which amends Directive 98/70/EC) and requires sulphur-free fuel to be made widely available in the UK and prohibits the distribution or sale of petrol or diesel fuel with a sulphur content exceeding 10 mg/kg from 1 January 2009.

3.65   Regulations 61 and 61A of the Road Vehicles (Construction and Use) Regulations 1986 (SI 1986/1078) as amended, control the emission of smoke, vapour, gases, oily substances, etc. from vehicles. The regulations specify in tables what emissions are controlled, and any exemptions that may apply, to various categories of vehicles. An example of a direct prohibition is in reg 61(5), which provides that:

> No person shall use, or cause or permit to be used, on a road any motor vehicle . . . from which any smoke, visible vapour, grit, sparks, ashes, cinders or oil substance is emitted if that emission causes, or is likely to cause, damage to any property or injury or danger to any person who is, or who may reasonably be expected to be, on the road

3.66   Schedule 2 of the Road Traffic Offenders Act 1988 (RTOA 1988) provides that someone in breach of the construction and use requirements of s 42 of the Road Traffic Act 1988 (which covers reg 61(5)) is liable on summary conviction to a maximum fine of £2,500 for goods vehicles and passenger vehicles of more than eight passengers and £1,000 in any other case.

3.67   Other emission controls relate to engineering, construction, and development. The Road Vehicles (Construction and Use) (Amendment) Regulations 2004 (SI 2004/1706) updates the Department for Transport (DfT) document: *In Service Exhaust Emission Standards for Road Vehicles Booklet 2004*, which contains emission limits that all petrol engine cars and light vans are required to meet at MoT tests and roadside checks. The 200-page booklet is revised on a regular basis to include new models that have recently come onto the market.

The progressive nature of EU legislation and its transposition in the UK highlights how air **3.68** quality in urban areas has, to an extent, been stabilized, despite a large increase in vehicle use.

Controlling road and vehicle use

Regulation 98 of the Road Vehicles (Construction and Use) Regulations 1986 (SI 1986/1078) **3.69** enables an authorized person from a local authority to ask the driver of a vehicle with its engine running while stationary to turn the engine off. Failure to do so is an offence. Further Regulation 107 creates an offence for a person to leave or cause to permit to be left a motor vehicle unattended by a person unless its engine has been turned off and its parking brake set. In *Butterworth v Shorthouse* (1956) Crim LR 341 the High Court upheld a conviction of a motorist charged with not stopping his engine and using his brake even though the magistrates had found that he had, in fact, turned his engine off.

Section 42 of the RTA 1988 provides that breach of any construction or use requirement, **3.70** which includes regs 98 and 107 is an offence. Schedule 2 of the RTOA 1988 provides that a person who breaches regs 98 and 107 is liable on summary conviction to a maximum fine of £2,500 for goods vehicles and vehicles with more than eight passengers and £1,000 in any other case.

In an effort to try and prevent air pollution rather than prosecute for an offence, it is possible **3.71** to report trucks and public service vehicles such as buses and coaches with smoky exhausts to the Vehicle Inspectorate (0870 6060440 or e-mail www.vosa.gov.uk). The Inspectorate will contact the operator and ask that the problem be resolved. The reporting service does not cover privately owned vehicles.

Fixed penalty notices

The Road Traffic (Vehicle Emissions) (Fixed Penalty) (England) Regulations 2002 (SI 2002/ **3.72** 1808) (the VEFP Regs 2002) aim to help improve local air quality by reducing unnecessary exhaust emissions from vehicles by targeting more serious offenders (e.g. coaches that park in busy town centres, buses standing idle, and vehicles parked outside schools) and when appropriate issuing fixed penalty notices to those who leave their engines running while parked. The purpose is to encourage all drivers to have due regard to the local environment. The DfT has issued guidance entitled: *Local Authority Powers to Require Drivers to Switch Off Engines when Parked* (2002).

In line with other fixed penalty schemes, payment of the penalty discharges liability. Under **3.73** reg 17 of the VEFP Regs 2002, proceedings are not issued until the payment period has expired, unless the alleged offender has requested a hearing. If the penalty is not paid and the offender has not requested a hearing the sums due are increased to £90 for unlawful emissions and £40 for leaving an engine running. Under reg 21 of VEFP Regs 2002 These sums become enforceable in the county court.

Traffic management

The Road Traffic Reduction Act 1997 requires local authorities to prepare a report assessing **3.74** local traffic levels and to forecast growth. The Road Traffic Reduction (National Targets) Act 1998 requires the Secretary of State to publish reports that include targets for traffic reduction across the country and reduce the adverse environmental, social, and economic impacts of road traffic.

3.75 The land use planning system also provides for transport management. PPG 13: *Transport* (2002) considers a sustainable travel pattern to make optimum use of the transport system and so reduce the need to use the car.

Aviation and air pollution

3.76 The main pollutants generated from aviation are CO_2 and nitrogen oxide. Emission levels from aircraft are comparatively high. Their impact on local air quality gives rise to local concentrations of air pollutants, although the more significant impact is in the atmosphere and in terms of the contribution to global warming and ozone depletion.

3.77 The Air Navigation (Environmental Standards Order 2002 (SI 2002/798) bans aircraft from taking off or landing in the UK unless they comply with fuel venting requirements and emission obligations relating to smoke, unburned hydrocarbons, carbon monoxide, and nitrogen.

3.78 Any civil claim against air pollution from aircraft will be limited to non-civil aircraft, as in *Dennis v Ministry of Defence* EWHC 793 (QB) (a claim against military aircraft: see Chapter 10: Noise). Section 76(1) of the Civil Aviation Act 1982 provides that no action shall lie in respect of trespass or nuisance, against aircraft flying over any property, which, having regard to wind, weather, and all the circumstances of the case, is reasonable so long as there has been compliance with any navigation order, no dangerous flying, or that it is not an emergency or time of war.

3.79 As a signatory to the Kyoto Protocol 1997, the UK must include emissions from domestic flights as greenhouse gas emissions that fall within agreed reduction targets. However, international flights fall outside the Protocol. Instead, parties to the Climate Change Convention 1992 are required to limit or reduce emissions from international services through the International Civil Aviation Organisation (ICAO). Annex 16 to the Convention on International Civil Aviation 1944 provides for rules on environmental protection for noise and aircraft engine emissions. To assess the impact of aviation on the atmosphere the ICAO asked the IPCC to consider this and the IPCC subsequently published the *Special Report on Aviation and the Global Atmosphere* (1999). See also para 3.82 on climate change.

G   MANAGING ATMOSPHERIC POLLUTION

3.80 The management and control of air pollution at a local and national level will also influence atmospheric or global pollution. A good example of this is the efforts to reduce CO_2 emissions. However, there are many concerns that require international action and co-operation; it cannot be solved by individual countries. Global atmospheric pollution problems include climate change, the depletion of the ozone layer, and transboundary air pollution, which recognises that airborne pollutants often travel thousands of miles. In the *Trail Smelter* case (16 April 1938) the United States claimed compensation from a Canadian company for damage to crops, trees, and agriculture caused by sulphur dioxide emissions. The arbitral tribunal commented that, under international law:

> no state has the right to use or permit the use of territory in such a manner as to cause injury by fumes in or to the territory of another or the properties or person therein, when the case is of serious consequence and the injury is established by clear and convincing evidence.

Climate change

What is climate change?

Probably the most serious global environmental problem today is climate change. The UN   **3.81** Framework Convention on Climate Change defines it in Art 1(2) as:

> a change of climate which is attributed directly or indirectly to human activity that alters the composition of the global atmosphere and which is in addition to natural climate variability observed over comparable periods.

The IPCC Third Assessment Report in 2001 concluded that an increasing body of observa-   **3.82** tions give a collective picture of a warming world and other changes in the climate system. They reported that emissions of greenhouse gases and aerosols due to human activities continue to alter the atmosphere in ways that are expected to effect the climate. They added that there was new and stronger evidence that most of the global warming observed over the last 50 years was attributable to human activities.

The average surface temperature of the earth increased by 0.6° Celsius last century while UK   **3.83** sea levels are rising at an average of 1 cm every 10 years. Climate change is producing more unstable and extreme weather conditions that are devastating large areas of the world. In November 1999 a cyclone devastated parts of eastern India killing up to 10,000 people and in the following month over 30,000 people died in violent storms in Venezuela. In the UK, a very wet winter in 2000 resulted in widespread flooding followed by an unusually mild autumn the following year. Central Europe witnessed violent storms in summer 2002 resulting in up to 100 deaths and the following year a heat wave caused over 20,000 premature deaths across the same region.

The financial impact of climate change is also of concern. A report published in 2004 by   **3.84** the Association of British Insurers: *A Changing Climate for Insurance* concluded that if present weather trends continue, subsidence claims were likely to double and claims for storm damage were likely to treble. While the Royal Liver Assurance considers that around 10% of land area in the UK is at risk of flooding affecting two million homes and 185,000 businesses.

The most important greenhouse gases controlled by international legislation, such as the   **3.85** Kyoto Protocol 1997, and national policy, e.g. the UK Climate Change Programme, are:

- carbon dioxide;
- methane;
- nitrous oxide;
- hydrofluorocarbons;
- perfluorocarbons; and
- sulphur hexafluoride.

3.86 Other important greenhouse gas emissions include chlorofluorocarbons (CFCs), and hydro-chlorofluorocarbons (HCFCs), which are being phased out under the Vienna Convention 1985 and Montreal Protocol 1987 in efforts to protect the ozone layer. Also, VOCs are significant greenhouse gases but are controlled under the Convention on Transboundary Air Pollution 1979.

Climate Change Convention 1992

3.87 The IPCC conclusion affirms the need for enactment of the Climate Change Convention 1992, which to March 2005 had secured 191 state and region parties including the UK and the EU. The convention's objective contained in Art 2 is to stabilize greenhouse gas concentrations in the atmosphere at a level that prevents dangerous anthropogenic interference with the climate system. Under Art 4(1) of the Convention all signatory states shall, among other things:

  (a) publish national inventories of anthropogenic emissions;
  (b) publish national and regional programmes to mitigate climate change by addressing anthropogenic emissions;
  (c) promote and cooperate in the development, application, and diffusion practices and processes that control, reduce, or prevent emissions; and
  (d) and (i) promote sustainable management and education.

3.88 Under Art 4(2) of the Convention developed countries are required to:

  (a) adopt national policies and measures to mitigate climate change;
  (b) communicate detailed information on policies;
  (c) calculate emissions by sources and removals by sinks of greenhouse gases, taking into account best available scientific information.

3.89 Further, under Art 4 developed countries must:

  (3) provide financial resources to developing countries in helping them to meet their obligations;
  (4) provide financial assistance to those developing countries that are particularly vulnerable to the adverse impacts of climate change in meeting adaptation costs; and
  (5) promote, facilitate, and finance, as appropriate, the transfer of technology and know-how to developing countries.

3.90 While the Climate Change Convention provides quite specific obligations it nevertheless remains a framework convention leaving the implementation of action and specific requirements to the Kyoto Protocol 1997 adopted under the Convention.

Kyoto Protocol 1997

3.91 The Kyoto Protocol to the United Nations Framework Convention on Climate Change 1997 (the Kyoto Protocol) ties developed countries to specific policies to achieve quantified targets for reducing greenhouse gas emissions and provide a number of ways they can assist developing countries in mitigating and adapting to climate change. Article 25 of the Protocol required ratification by at least 55 countries including those listed in Annex 1 that accounted for in total at least 55% of the total CO_2 emissions for 1990. In 2004, Russia ratified the Protocol and it entered into force in February 2005. The status and detail of countries can be found on the UNFCCC website: www.unfccc.org.

The Protocol provides that the developed countries listed in Annex 1 should ensure that **3.92** their anthropogenic emissions do not exceed their assigned amounts and that they should have made demonstrable progress towards achieving their individual commitments and with a view to reducing their overall emissions of greenhouse gases by at least 5% below 1990 levels by 2012.

Under the Protocol the UK is committed to greenhouse gas emissions of 12.5% of 1990 levels **3.93** by 2012 and has also set a national target of reducing CO_2 emissions by 20% of 1990 levels by 2010. The government strategy *Climate Change — the UK Programme* published in 2000 aims to reduce greenhouse gas emissions by 23% of 1990 levels by 2010. The UK's *Third National Communication under the UN Framework Convention on Climate Change 2001* reported that in 1999 the UK's total greenhouse gas emissions were about 14.5% below 1990 levels. More recently, however, the UK's CO_2 emissions have risen to show only a 7% reduction since 1990, this is attributed to a greater use of coal in electricity generation. The Climate Change Programme is under review. The consultation paper published in December 2004 noted that:

> The UK's greenhouse gas emissions are already below the level required to achieve our target under the Kyoto Protocol, . . . It is estimated that in 2003, total greenhouse gas emissions were 14 per cent below base year levels.

The UK is meeting its Convention obligations to developing countries through assistance in **3.94** emissions reduction, adaptation, technology transfer, and science. For example between 1997 and 2000 the UK spent over £244 million on bilateral aid projects either wholly or partly concerned with energy efficiency and climate change. UK activity is carried out by a number of government departments including the Climate Change Project Office at Defra, the Foreign and Commonwealth Office, and the Department for International Development, which supports the UN Global Environment Fund.

Action to reduce UK emissions relates to energy use, transport, and trading in emission **3.95** quotas. Strategic aims set out in the White Paper *Our Energy Future — Creating a Low Carbon Economy* (2003) are to:

- cut CO_2 emissions by 60% by 2050;
- maintain reliable energy supplies;
- promote competitive markets in the UK and abroad; and
- ensure that every home is adequately and affordably heated.

The Home Energy Conservation Act 1995 requires local authorities to regularly report **3.96** on how energy savings from residential properties could be achieved while the Building Regulations (see para 3.46) has minimum energy requirements for buildings. Further, the Sustainable Energy Act 2003 requires targets for combined heat and power (CHP) use and energy conservation and the publication of progress reports towards sustainable energy aims. Efforts to reduce emissions from transport are discussed in Section F.

Emissions trading

In 2002, the UK Government, as part of its Kyoto Protocol commitments, introduced the UK **3.97** Emissions Trading Scheme and in January 2005, the EU Emissions Trading Scheme began operation. These are considered further in Chapter 12: Property and land rights.

Liability for climate change

3.98   While it is never likely to be possible to link any particular decision, act, or omission to any
given weather condition, climate change litigation is beginning to emerge. In 2002, US
export credit agencies were sued by a number of city authorities, NGOs, and concerned
citizens for deciding to back fossil fuel projects overseas. Similarly, in 2004 NGOs claimed
against the German government for failing to disclose details of foreign fossil fuel projects
supported by the German export credit agency. In *State of Connecticut & ors v American Electric
Power Co. Inc* (writ issued 21 July 2004) 04 CV 05669 & 05670 the claimants are seeking an
order requiring the defendants, who represent the five large energy producers in the US, to
reduce their emissions of CO_2, and thereby abating their contribution to a public nuisance,
i.e. global warming. More details of climate change litigation are available from the Climate
Justice Programme at www.climatelaw.org.

Long-range transboundary air pollution

3.99   The Long-Range Transboundary Air Pollution Convention 1979 recognized that air pollution is not just a problem at a local level but that emissions can travel long distances and
remain harmful to health and the environment. Article 2 of the Convention requires signatory states: 'shall endeavour to limit and, as far as possible, gradually reduce and prevent air
pollution including long-range transboundary pollution.'

3.100   The definition of air pollution in Art 1 of the Convention is wide and can include greenhouse gases and ozone-depleting chemicals and while the commitment required under
the Convention is quite vague, a number of specific air pollution protocols have since been
agreed and ratified.

Monitoring and Evaluation Protocol 1984

3.101   Article 2 of the Monitoring and Evaluation Protocol 1984 (signed in Geneva, 28 September
1984) aims to provide long-term financing of the cooperative programme for monitoring
and evaluation of the long-range transmission of air pollutants in Europe. There are 35
signatory countries, including the UK, that are required under Art 4 to provide financial
contributions to programmes set up under the Protocol, e.g. the European programme for
monitoring and evaluating air pollution (the EMEP programme).

Sulphur Protocol 1985

3.102   The Sulphur Protocol 1985 (signed in Helsinki, 8 July 1995) required the reduction of
sulphur emissions or their transboundary fluxes (flows or discharges) by at least 30% of the
1980 levels by 1993. Ratified by 22 countries, all signatories met the target set. The UK did
not ratify the convention but did secure a reduction of 45% sulphur emissions by 1994.

Further Reduction on Sulphur Emissions Protocol 1994

3.103   The second sulphur emissions protocol the Further Reduction on Sulphur Emissions
Protocol 1994 (signed in Oslo, 14 June 1994) provided for tougher targets, i.e. to secure a
60% reduction of sulphur emissions across the UN Economic Commission for Europe
(UNECE) by 2000, but allowed a more flexible approach to securing these. The UK ratified

the second Protocol and published a national strategy in compliance. By 2000, UK emissions of sulphur dioxide had fallen by 77% compared to 1980 levels.

Nitrogen Oxides Protocol 1988

The Nitrogen Oxides Protocol 1988 (signed in Sofia, 31 October 1988) requires the control **3.104** and reduction of annual emissions of nitrogen oxides (NOx). Article 2(1) provides that by 1994, all parties must have reduced their national annual emissions of NOx to at least 1987 levels. By 2001, UK NOx levels had fallen by 39%.

Volatile Organic Compounds Protocol 1991

The Volatile Organic Compounds Protocol 1991 (signed in Geneva, 18 November 1991) **3.105** seeks to control the emissions of VOCs and their transboundary fluxes. Parties to the Protocol were required to make a 30% reduction of 1988 VOC emission levels by 1999.

Heavy Metals Protocol 1998

The Heavy Metals Protocol 1998 (signed at Aarhus, 24 June 1998) requires parties to reduce **3.106** emissions of lead, cadmium, and mercury below 1990 levels (or any predetermined year between 1985–1995). The UK ratified the Protocol and, by 1999, had reduced emissions of each heavy metal significantly: see the Defra digest of environmental statistics available at www.defra.gov.uk/environment/statistics.

Persistent Organic Pollutants Protocol 1998

The Persistent Organic Pollutants Protocol 1998 (signed at Aarhus, 24 June 1998) aims to **3.107** prevent discharges, emissions, and losses of persistent organic pollutants (POPs) to the atmosphere. The Protocol lists 16 substances including pesticides such as aldrin, dieldrin, and DDT; industrial chemicals such as PCBs; and by-products and contaminants such as dioxins and furans, which should be phased out. The Protocol entered into force in 2003.

Acidification, Eutrophication, and Ground Level Ozone Protocol 1999

Article 2 of the Acidification, Eutrophication and Ground Level Ozone Protocol 1999 (signed **3.108** at Gothenburg, 30 November 1999) provides that the parties should control and reduce anthropogenic emissions of sulphur, NOx, ammonia, and VOCs that are likely to cause adverse effects on human health, natural ecosystems, materials, and crops. The Protocol requires ratification by 16 states to enter into force. The UK has signed but not yet ratified the Protocol. It entered into force in May 2005.

Ozone depletion

In 1974 scientists warned that certain chemicals including CFCs, halons, solvents, and **3.109** aerosol product propellants were destroying the stratospheric ozone layer that protects the earth from the harmful effects of ultraviolet radiation. A few countries banned cosmetic aerosol products but the CFC industry protected its markets. In 1977 the United Nations Environment Programme (UNEP) began to organize action to protect the ozone layer and following five years of negotiation the Vienna Convention for the Protection of the Ozone Layer 1985 (signed in Vienna, 22 March 1985) entered into force. Around the same time, scientists discovered that the ozone layer above the Antarctic was severely depleted.

The Montreal Protocol on Substances that Deplete the Ozone Layer 1987

3.110 The Vienna Convention required commitment to the concern but did not include the necessary obligations to secure the necessary reductions in ozone-depleting chemicals. The Montreal Protocol on Substances that Deplete the Ozone Layer 1987 (signed in Montreal, 25 September 1987) provided specific legal obligations to reduce ozone-depleting chemicals. The Protocol has been amended four times since its introduction. Articles 2 to 2H provide control measures for CFCs, halons, carbon tetrachloride, 1,1,1-trichloroethane, HCFCs, hydrobromofluorocarbon, and methyl bromide, including significant reductions in use and the prohibition of certain chemicals. While cuts in ozone-depleting chemicals have occurred, the World Meteorological Organisation is still recording large ozone holes over the Antarctic, and the need for still greater action is necessary. The British Antarctic Survey Ozone Bulletin (http://www.antarctica.ac.uk/met/jds/ozone) monitors the size of the ozone hole. In March 2005 it reported that:

> The circulation over the Antarctic continent is in its autumn state. This is the time of year when ozone levels were at the lowest prior to the mid 1970s. The ozone layer over much of the Southern Hemisphere south of 50° remains around 10–15% below the long term normal. . . . The ozone hole (where ozone values are below 220 DU) grew rapidly from mid August to early September [2004] to reach around 19 million square kilometres.

KEY DOCUMENTS AND MATERIALS

Clean Air Act 1993
Environmental Protection Act 1990
Environment Act 1995
Air Quality (England) Regulations 2000 (SI 2000/928)
Air Quality (Wales) Regulations 2000 (SI 2000/1940)
Building Regulations 2000 (SI 2000/2351)

UN Framework Convention on Climate Change 1992
Kyoto Protocol to the United Nations Framework Convention on Climate Change 1997

APC Part B process guidance notes
CIEH (2004) *Industrial Pollution Control by Local Authorities — a Management Guide*. CIEH: London
Communication from the Commission *A Review of the Auto-Oil II Programme* COM (2000) 626
Defra (2000) *Air Quality Strategy*. Defra: London
Defra (2002) *Emissions Trading Scheme User Manual*. Defra: London
Defra (June 2004) *Valuation of Health Benefits Associated with Reductions in Air Pollution*. Defra: London
Department for Transport. *Local Authority Powers to Require Drivers to Switch Off Engines when Parked*. DfT: 2002
DETR (2000) *Climate Change — the UK Programme*. Defra: London
IPCC (1999) *Aviation and the Global Atmosphere*. IPCC: Geneva

IPCC (2001) *Third Assessment Report*. IPCC: Geneva
Office of Deputy Prime Minister: PPS 23: *Planning and Pollution Control*

British Antarctic Survey Ozone Bulletin at www.antarctica.ac.uk/met/jds/ozone
Climate Justice Programme at www.climatelaw.org
www.defra.gov.uk.etr

4

ANTI-SOCIAL BEHAVIOUR, HOUSING, AND LOCAL CONCERNS

A   INTRODUCTION TO ANTI-SOCIAL BEHAVIOUR

4.01   Many of the environmental impacts in the local community are not from what may be regarded as conventional polluters such as factories or road transport, but come from the way people behave in the local community. Some behaviour in a neighbourhood may be so excessive and persistent that it can be very distressing and amount to harassment, e.g. excessive noise and graffiti. Of course, some of the anti-social behaviour cannot itself be regarded as an environmental concern such as drug dealing, drunken behaviour, and abusive language, although the indirect effects of these actions may be, e.g., discarding litter such as bottles, cans, and used syringes. In summary, many forms of anti-social behaviour can have a serious adverse effect on the quality of the local environment and, in turn the quality of life of local people.

4.02   In 2003, the Anti-Social Behaviour Unit at the Home Office held a one-day count of anti-social behaviour and recorded over 72,000 incidents. One of the concerns with local environmental harm is of its cumulative effect. The 'broken windows' theory is that one apparently insignificant incident, such as a broken window left in a state of disrepair, can send out the message to people that it is acceptable to degrade the environment and this leads on to other acts of damage. A study by Philip Zimbardo (1969) in the Bronx, New York highlighted this when a car that was deliberately abandoned on the street, was a shell within three days following 23 'incidents of destructive contact'.

4.03   Many anti-social behaviour acts are offences and are subject to criminal sanctions. However, since the introduction of the Crime and Disorder Act 1998 (CDA 1998), as amended by the Police Reform Act 2002 and Pt 9 of the Anti-social Behaviour Act 2003, relevant authorities can seek an anti-social behaviour order (ASBO) from the court or enter into an acceptable behaviour contract (ABC) with anyone involved in anti-social activities. The anti-social behaviour provisions aim to be preventative, not punitive, and rely on relevant authorities and other local organizations working together in order to resolve local problems. They should create local crime and disorder partnerships, which then take a strategic approach to improving their areas by collaboration.

Defining anti-social behaviour

4.04   The term 'anti-social behaviour' is not expressly defined although s 1 of the CDA 1998 provides that a relevant authority may apply for an anti-social behaviour order with respect to any person aged ten years or over if the following conditions are fulfilled:

(a)   that the person has acted . . . in an anti-social manner, that is to say, in a manner that caused or was likely to cause harassment, alarm or distress to one or more persons not of the same household as himself; and

(b)   that such an order is necessary to protect persons from further anti-social acts by him.

Under s 1A of the CDA 1998, a relevant authority means: **4.05**

- the police (including the transport police);
- local district authorities, London boroughs, county boroughs in Wales (and other equivalent authorities), and county councils;
- registered social landlords under the Housing Act 1996 (RSLs); and
- housing action trusts established under the Housing Act 1988 (HATs).

The ASBO powers available are being construed widely. In *R v Murphy* (2005) (unreported, **4.06** 28 January 2005) Dartford Magistrates' Court fined the defendant £2,000 and made an ASBO following fly-tipping incidents. In January 2005 it was reported that a Norfolk farmer pleaded not guilty to failing to comply with an ASBO without reasonable excuse. It was alleged that he failed to constrain his pigs from straying on to a neighbour's land, in breach of an interim order. (Law Gazette, p 5, 6 January 2005).

The Home Office *Guide to Anti-Social Behaviour Orders and Acceptable Behaviour Contracts* **4.07** (rev 2002) (*Guide to ASBOs and ABCs*) states that:

ASBOs are civil orders that exist to protect the public from behaviour that causes or is likely to cause harassment, alarm or distress. An order contains conditions prohibiting the offender from specific anti-social acts or entering defined areas and is effective for a minimum of two years. The orders are not criminal penalties and are not intended to punish the offender. An order should not be viewed as an option of last resort.

It adds that ASBOs are community-based orders that involve local people in the collection of **4.08** evidence and in helping to enforce breaches. They encourage local communities to become actively involved in reporting crime and disorder, and protecting the community. An ASBO can be obtained in one of three ways:

(1) on application to a magistrates' court;
(2) following conviction of a relevant offence in criminal proceedings; or
(3) on application in any county court proceedings where a relevant authority is a party to those proceedings.

Each of these is considered below, although the emphasis is on the stand-alone application **4.09** made to the magistrates' court.

B   APPLICATION FOR AN ANTI-SOCIAL BEHAVIOUR ORDER

Pre-action procedure and considerations

The *Guide to ASBOs and ABCs* suggests that fully coordinated partnership working is essential **4.10** in successfully tackling anti-social behaviour. This includes ensuring that there is a lead agency, which is most likely to be one of the relevant authorities, capable of commencing legal proceedings. It also suggests that any potential applicants seeking an ASBO consider the Model Protocol on information exchange protocol available from the Crime Reduction website www.crimereduction.gov.uk.

Section 1E of the CDA 1998 sets out the consultation requirements for an applicant when **4.11** applying for an ASBO including that:

- the police and local authorities must consult each other; and
- RSL and British Transport Police must consult both the local authority and police in their area.

4.12   The court requires a signed document of consultation, although this should not necessarily indicate whether the party consulted was in agreement or not. Supporting statements or reports from partner agencies should be provided separately.

Commencing proceedings

4.13   Under s 1(3) of the CDA 1998 an application for a stand-alone ASBO is made by way of complaint to a magistrates' court. The proceedings are civil, not criminal, and are not designed to punish the defendant but to prevent him acting in an anti-social manner. The prescribed form of complaint is contained in Sch 1 of the Magistrates' Courts (Anti-Social Behaviour Orders) Rules 2002 (SI 2002/2784) (ASBO Rules 2002) and should be filed at court together with completed documentary evidence, any notice of hearsay evidence, and details of other evidence in support.

4.14   Following receipt of the complaint the court will issue a summons to the defendant requiring that he appear before the magistrates' court to answer an application for an ASBO. The defendant should also be served with a copy of the ASBO application (the complaint), documentary evidence, notice of hearsay evidence, other evidence in support, guidance on how the defendant may obtain legal advice and representation, and a warning letter to the defendant that it is an offence to pervert the course of justice and that witness intimidation is liable to lead to prosecution. Where a child or juvenile is involved, someone with parental responsibility must also receive a copy of the summons.

Public funding for the defendant

4.15   Public funding for defendant representation by solicitors is available for any ASBO proceedings. Advocacy assistance is available in defending an ASBO, an interim order under s 1D of the CDA 1998 (para 4.29), for an application to vary or discharge an ASBO or to appeal, under s 4 of CDA 1998, against an order (para 4.36). Solicitors can grant advocacy assistance. There are no defendant financial criteria. Assistance may not be provided where it appears unreasonable that approval should be granted or where the interests of justice test is not met, although there is an additional factor where there is a real risk of imprisonment on breach of an ASBO.

4.16   In exceptional circumstances a defendant may apply for a representation order to the Criminal Defence Service. Although the availability of advocacy assistance will be a relevant factor in whether or not representation is granted, normally the Legal Services Commission will refuse an application for a representation order where advocacy assistance is available. Funding is considered further in Chapter 21: Funding civil and public law litigation.

Time limits

4.17   Under s 127 of the Magistrates' Court Act 1980 a court shall not hear a complaint unless it was made within six months from the time the matter relevant to the complaint arose. One incident of severe anti-social behaviour may be sufficient for an order, although other incidents will assist to show a pattern of behaviour.

Evidence

Because ASBO proceedings are civil in nature they are based upon civil rules of evidence 4.18
with the exception of proving the acts of anti-social behaviour that have already occurred.
The *Guide to ASBOs and ABCs* suggests that the evidence in support of an application should
prove:

- that the defendant acted in a specific way on specific dates and at specific places; and
- that these acts caused or were likely to cause harassment, alarm, or distress to one or more persons not in the same household as the defendant.

It adds that it is the effect or likely effect of the behaviour on other people that determines 4.19
whether the behaviour is anti-social. The authority applying for the order does not have to
prove an intention on the part of the defendant to cause harassment, alarm, or distress and
evidence may include:

- breach of an ABC;
- witness statements of officers who attended incidents or from people affected by the behaviour;
- evidence of complaints reported by the police, housing providers, or other agencies;
- statements from expert and professional witnesses, e.g. local authority officers, health visitors, police officers, and doctors — all of whom can be called to give opinion on matters within their expertise;
- video or CCTV evidence;
- supporting statements from other agencies;
- previous successful relevant civil proceedings, e.g. an eviction order for similar behaviour;
- previous relevant convictions;
- copies of custody records of previous arrests relevant to the application; and
- information from witness diaries.

Disclosure of information to a relevant authority

Section 115(1) of the CDA 1998 provides that any person who, apart from this subsection, 4.20
would not have power to disclose information to a relevant authority or someone acting
on behalf of them shall have power to do so in any case where the disclosure is necessary or
expedient for the purpose of any provision of this Act.

Standard of proof for past anti-social acts

Magistrates must apply the criminal standard of proof, i.e. beyond reasonable doubt, when 4.21
considering s 1(1)(a) of the CDA 1998. In *R (McCann) v Crown Court at Manchester, Clingham v
Kensington & Chelsea RLBC* [2002] UKHL 39, Lord Steyn stated at para 39 that:

> [magistrates] must in all cases under s 1 apply the criminal standard . . . it will be sufficient for
> magistrates, when applying s 1(1)(a) to be sure that the defendant has acted in an anti-social
> manner, that is to say in a manner which caused or was likely to cause harassment, alarm, or
> distress to one or more person not of the same household as himself.

Evaluation of future behaviour

4.22   However, consideration of future behaviour of the defendant required under s 1(1)(b) is not a determination of proof of future incidents but an evaluation. In *R (McCann) v Crown Court at Manchester* [2002], Lord Steyn noted, 'The inquiry under s 1(1)(b), namely that such an order is necessary to protect persons from further anti-social acts by him, does not involve a standard of proof: it is an exercise of judgment or evaluation.'

Hearsay evidence

4.23   In *R v Marylebone Magistrates' Court ex p C* [2001] EWHC Admin 1 the High Court affirmed that the admissibility of hearsay evidence under s 1 of the Civil Evidence Act 1995 applied to ASBO proceedings. In the particular case, the applicants sought to rely on evidence of a police officer of complaints made to him about the defendant's behaviour. *Stone's Justices' Manual 2004* notes at para 1–3804 that the fact that some evidence is hearsay, without the possibility of cross-examination, does not have the automatic result that the trial is not fair trial under Art 6(1) of the European Convention of Human Rights (ECHR). The court will have to consider what weight to give to the evidence in the light of criticisms that can be made of hearsay evidence. In *R (McCann) v Crown Court at Manchester* [2002], Lord Steyn affirmed at paras 35 to 37 that:

> Having concluded that the proceedings in question are civil under domestic law and Art 6, it follows that the machinery of the Civil Evidence Act 1995 and the Magistrates' Court (Hearsay Evidence in Civil Proceedings) Rules 1999 allow the introduction of such evidence under the first part of s 1.
>
> . . . use of the Civil Evidence Act 1995 and the Rules in cases under the first part of s 1 are not in any way incompatible with the Human Rights Act 1998.
>
> . . . hearsay evidence will often be of crucial importance. For my part, hearsay evidence depending on its logical probativeness is quite capable of satisfying the requirements of s 1(1).

Applicant's case

4.24   Section 1(6) of the CDA 1998 provides that local authorities and the police may apply for an ASBO where they consider it necessary to protect persons in their area regardless of where the original anti-social behaviour arose. An ASBO can be sought against anyone aged ten years or more who has behaved in an anti-social way and it is necessary to protect persons in the locality.

4.25   Under s 1(1B) of the CDA 1998, applications from the British Transport Police or registered social landlords must relate to anti-social behaviour related to the premises for which they are responsible by persons who are on or in the vicinity of such premises or likely to be either on or in the vicinity of such premises. Applications by HATs are limited to applications for an order, which would protect persons who reside in or who are in the vicinity of premises provided or managed by HATs. Applications by county councils are limited to orders that would protect persons within the county.

4.26   An ASBO will relate to a specific defendant. Where there is more than one person acting in an anti-social manner, an order should be sought against each person or, if possible, against potential ringleaders of a group. Page 13 of the *Guide to ASBOs and ABCs* provides a case study from West Mercia Police where a group of youths hanging around a village that engaged in drink and drug abuse, conducted racially motivated incidents and caused damage. Four ASBOs were obtained on the gang ringleaders that resulted in reports of disorder dropping from 24 in the month before the ASBOs were made to five in the month after.

Defence

There are no statutory defences under the CDA 1998, however under s 1(5) of the CDA 1998, **4.27** the court must disregard any act of the defendant that he shows was reasonable in the circumstances.

Disclosure

Before disclosure of evidence, including that filed at court and served on the defendant, the **4.28** applicant should consult the police to ensure that all reasonable steps have been taken to support witnesses. Any evidence should not be disclosed without the express permission of the witness. However, if it is not disclosed, it cannot be relied upon in proceedings. The applicant should seek to maintain witness anonymity and ensure that it does not identify them by accident.

The hearing

The hearing will follow a conventional trial with applicant evidence given first, followed **4.29** by any defence evidence. There is likely to be a brief opening speech by the applicant and a summary closing speech by the defendant. It is for the applicant to prepare the court bundles. At least eight bundles must be prepared containing all relevant documents for the hearing. These should be indexed and paginated.

Interim orders

Under s 1D of the CDA 1998 the court may grant an interim order. Section 1D(2) provides **4.30** that, 'If, before determining an application . . . the court considers that it is just to make an ASBO pending the determination of that application ("the main application"), it may make such an order.'

An interim order may be made, subject to leave being given by the justices' clerk, at an initial **4.31** hearing without the defendant having notice of the proceedings. However, if the order is made without notice, it will not take effect until it has been served on the defendant together with the application for a full order and a summons giving a date for the defendant to attend court.

A without notice interim order will be made without all the evidence in the case being heard **4.32** and will only be made on the basis that there is sufficient evidence of an urgent need to protect the community. Rule 5 of the ASBO Rules 2002 covers the procedures and forms to be used for an interim order. It will be limited in scope by s 1D(4), which states that the interim order must be for a fixed period; that it may be varied, renewed, or discharged; and shall, if it has not previously ceased to have effect, cease to have effect on the determination of the main application.

Final order

4.33 The *Guide to ASBOs and ABCs* notes that although it is for the court to decide what prohibitions are to be imposed by the order, the relevant authority should propose conditions (including for a duration of a minimum two years) to the court. A full order should be drawn up according to r 4 and Sch 3 of the ASBO Rules 2002. The order cannot impose any positive requirements on the defendant and can only prohibit certain acts. It should, among other things:

- cover the range of anti-social acts committed by the defendant;
- be necessary to protect people within the defined areas;
- be reasonable, proportionate, realistic, and practical; and
- be clear, concise, and easy to understand.

4.34 Examples of prohibitions are available at www.crimereduction.gov.uk. An ASBO can extend across any defined area, which may extend to cover the whole of England and Wales if appropriate.

Orders against children and juveniles

4.35 An application for an ASBO against a child or juvenile will be heard in the magistrates' court as opposed to the youth court, however there are no automatic reporting restrictions under s 39 of the Children and Young Persons Act 1933. The court does have the power to impose reporting restrictions although this may limit the effectiveness of an ASBO, which relies on the community being aware of the order. In *R (T) v Crown Court at St Albans* [2002] EWHC 1129 (Admin) the High Court held that an anonymity order under s 39 was not appropriate for ASBO applications because publicity is essential to the operation of ASBOs even where the defendant is a minor.

Parenting order

4.36 For ASBOs that involve a child the court may, under s 8 of the CDA 1998, make a parenting order in the interests of preventing a repetition of the kind of behaviour that led to the order.

Appeals

4.37 Section 4(1) of the CDA 1998 provides that an appeal shall lie to the Crown Court against the making by a magistrates' court of an ASBO and an interim order under s 1D. Any order of the Crown Court, other than one directing that an application be re-heard by a magistrates' court, shall be treated, for the purpose of s 1(8) (i.e. applications to vary, renew, or discharge), as if it were an order of the magistrates' court from which the appeal was brought. There is no provision for automatic suspension or stay of the order pending appeal and breach of the order before appeal is an offence.

4.38 Rules 74 and 75 of the Magistrates' Courts Rules 1981 (SI 1981/552), as variously amended, and the Crown Court Rules 1982 (SI 1982/1109) apply to the s 4 appeal. Notice of appeal must be given in writing to the court clerk within 21 days.

4.39 Alternatively, it is open for the parties to make a claim for judicial review. An applicant authority may also, under s 111 of the Magistrates' Courts Act 1980, seek to challenge the magistrates' refusal to grant an ASBO by way of case stated to the Divisional Court.

Variation and discharge of an ASBO

Under s 1(8) of the CDA 1998, the applicant or defendant may apply by complaint to the court, which made an ASBO for it to be varied or discharged by a further order. The procedure for variation or discharge is contained in r 6 of the ASBO Rules 2002. An ASBO cannot be discharged before the end of two years of entering into force, unless (except for order on conviction) it is with agreement of the parties. **4.40**

Enforcement

Breach of an ASBO is an offence under the CDA 1998. Section 1(10) of the Act provides that if, without reasonable excuse, a person does anything that he is prohibited from doing by an ASBO, he is guilty of an offence liable on summary conviction to a maximum penalty of a £5,000 fine and/or six months' imprisonment; or an unlimited fine and/or five years' imprisonment following conviction on indictment. **4.41**

Sections 10A and 10B of the CDA 1998 allows a local authority to prosecute for breach of an ASBO where it obtained the order or if the defendant resides or appears to reside in its area. **4.42**

The maximum sentence for breach of an ASBO by a juvenile is a detention and training order, which has a maximum term of 24 months: 12 months in custody and 12 months in the community. The maximum sentence for breach of an ASBO by a child aged between 10 and 11 years old is a community order. **4.43**

C ANTI-SOCIAL BEHAVIOUR ORDERS ON CONVICTION

The Government encourages authorities to use publicity to enforce ASBOs. It has published *Guidance on Publicising Anti-Social Behaviour Orders* (2005) (available from www.together.gov.uk), emphasizing that an ASBO is not a punishment in itself but a preventative order and, similarly, publicity should not intend to punish an individual. **4.44**

Under s 1C of the CDA 1998 a magistrates' court, youth court, or the Crown Court may make an ASBO following conviction of a relevant offence in criminal proceedings. The *Guide to ASBOs and ABCs* provides that the order on conviction is not part of the criminal sentence and it can only be made in addition to a sentence or a conditional discharge. The order will be granted on the basis of the evidence presented to the court during the criminal proceedings and any additional evidence provided to the court after the verdict in any related civil proceedings. **4.45**

The court can make an ASBO on conviction on its own initiative or at the request of the prosecutor, who may make representations to the court in support. Any evidence that is submitted for the purpose of considering the ASBO will be under the civil evidence rules. The prosecution may propose prohibitions for the ASBO or the court may prepare these on its own volition in similar fashion to an application for an ASBO: see paras 4.10–4.30. If **4.46** an offender is imprisoned on sentence for the main offence, the court may direct that the ASBO becomes effective on release from prison.

4.47   Appeal against an ASBO made in the Crown Court is to the Divisional Court.

D   ANTI-SOCIAL BEHAVIOUR ORDERS IN CIVIL PROCEEDINGS

4.48   Section 1B of the CDA 1998, which enables a relevant authority to obtain an ASBO in related county court proceedings, was designed to remove the need for a separate legal process in the magistrates' court and so provide public protection against anti-social behaviour sooner and more effectively. Most proceedings will be possession proceedings by registered social landlords but it could also be by a private landlord seeking a possession order: see Section F.

4.49   The relevant authority must be a party in the principal proceedings to be able to apply for an ASBO. If not, the authority may apply under s 1B(3) of the CDA 1998 to be joined in the proceedings so that it may apply for an ASBO. The *Guide to ASBOs and ABCs* notes that where a relevant authority is not a party, an application should be made as soon as possible after the authority becomes aware of the proceedings. The county court will be able to grant orders where the principal proceedings include evidence of anti-social behaviour.

4.50   Sections 1B(3A) to (3C) of the CDA 1998 enable relevant authorities to apply to join a person who is not a party to the principal county court proceedings, but is material to those proceedings, so that an order can be applied for against that person.

4.51   An application for an ASBO in the county court must be made in accordance with the procedure set out in rr 65.21 to 65.26 of the Civil Procedure Rules 1998 (CPR 1998) and Practice Direction 65. Where the relevant authority is a defendant in the principal proceedings the application should accompany the defence. Any proposed order with draft prohibitions should accompany the application along similar lines to an application for an ASBO: see paras 4.10–4.36.

E   ACCEPTABLE BEHAVIOUR CONTRACTS

4.52   The *Guide to ASBOs and ABCs* defines an ABC as a written agreement between a person involved in anti-social behaviour and one or more local agencies whose role it is to prevent such behaviour. The contract is agreed and signed by the defendant and relevant agencies. ABCs are more commonly used for children and juveniles but may also be used for adults.

The relationship between ASBOs and ABCs

4.53   If an ABC is identified as the most appropriate step to take in tackling anti-social behaviour, it should contain a statement that continuation of unacceptable behaviour may lead to an application for an ASBO. Where an ABC is broken, that should be used as evidence in the application for an ASBO as well as any evidence originally collated to prepare the ABC.

Importantly, it is not suggested that an ASBO must follow on from an ABC as a means of last resort. It may often be more effective simply to apply for an ASBO from the outset.

Entering into a contract

Preparatory meeting

Where anti-social behaviour is causing a problem, an early stage to resolve the problem will be consulting the relevant agencies and inviting them to take part in a meeting with other relevant parties, the individual and, if appropriate, his or her family. The purpose of the meeting is to discuss the actions, the meaning of anti-social behaviour, and the impact it has on others. **4.54**

Drafting the contract

The terms of the ABC should include a list of anti-social acts in which the person has been involved and should cease. Where possible, the individual should help draw up the contract list, something that may help them recognize the impact of their behaviour. The number of anti-social activities to be avoided should be limited to ensure that the individual is not overwhelmed. They should be written in plain English and set out clearly. Examples of terms to agree may include: **4.55**

- I will not write graffiti.
- I will not climb on public or private property.
- I will not damage property.
- I will not throw stones or other objects.
- I will not harm the environment.

The contract will normally last for six months, although this is flexible. Support to address the underlying causes of the behaviour should be offered by the relevant agencies and in parallel to the contract. This may include attendance at a youth project or support for the family. Legal action in the form of an ASBO or possession order (if the person is in social housing) should be stated in the contract where this is a potential consequence of the breach. **4.56**

Managing the contract

Monitoring

Monitoring compliance of the ABC is critical. Information on breaches can be collected from the same sources that the original anti-social behaviour was identified. If the contract is breached there must always be a response and it will therefore be essential that there are adequate resources available to ensure monitoring is effective. **4.57**

Responding to breaches of contract terms

The type of breach will influence any response to a breach of an ABC. A structured approach is suggested by the *Guide to ASBOs and ABCs*, which may involve: **4.58**

- verbal warnings;
- written warnings, if appropriate;

- an interview to discuss and reiterate the contract terms;
- proceedings for an ASBO; and/or
- proceedings for a possession order.

F   ANTI-SOCIAL BEHAVIOUR, ENVIRONMENTAL HARM, AND HOUSING

Possession proceedings

4.59   There are a number of grounds for possession of rented accommodation by the landlord that relate to environmental harm, and most often noise nuisance. Outlined below are the main grounds for possession. For further analysis of the procedure on possession consider: Garner and Frith's: *A Practical Approach to Landlord and Tenant* (4/e, OUP, 2004) or Woodfall's *Landlord and Tenant* (Sweet & Maxwell, regular updates).

4.60   Many tenancy agreements will provide an express covenant prohibiting the tenant from causing or allowing any acts that may be a nuisance or annoyance to other tenants, occupiers of neighbouring properties, or the landlord, or which may cause damage to the property or others. However, in *O'Leary v LB of Islington* (1983) 9 HLR 81 the court would not imply a duty on the landlord to enforce a clause contained in another tenant's lease to prevent that noisy tenant from causing a nuisance.

4.61   Rented accommodation is provided by both the public and private sectors although much of the housing provision provided by RSLs (formerly housing associations) may often be regarded as public sector provision but now comes within the private sector under the Housing Act 1988.

Rent Act 1977

4.62   The Rent Act 1977 covers private sector tenancies entered into before 1 January 1989. Schedule 15, Pt 1 of the Act lists a series of cases in which the court may order possession under s 98(1) of the Act. Case 2: nuisance, annoyance, used for immoral or illegal purposes, includes:

> Where the tenant or any person residing or lodging with him or any sub-tenant of his has been guilty of conduct which is a nuisance or annoyance to adjoining occupiers, or has been convicted of using the dwelling-house or allowing the dwelling-house to be used for immoral or illegal purposes.

4.63   Under Case 2 of the Rent Act 1977 nuisance or annoyance are given their common meaning, rather than the more defined legal definition for private and statutory nuisance; see Chapters 18 and 19 respectively. In *Cobstone Investments Ltd v Maxim* [1985] QB 140 the court held that this ground could include drunkenness, abusive and obstructive behaviour towards other occupiers, and noise. It also noted that 'adjoining occupiers' should be used in the wider sense of neighbouring occupiers.

Housing Act 1988

4.64   The Housing Act 1988 covers private sector tenancies entered on or after 1 January 1989. Schedule 2 of the Housing Act 1988 provides a number of grounds upon which the court may, or in some circumstances must, grant possession, if the ground is found to exist.

Ground 14: nuisance, annoyance, or conviction for illegal or immoral use is a discretionary ground where the court will only grant a possession order if, under s 7(4) of the Housing Act 1988, it considers it reasonable to do so. Ground 14 (as amended by the Housing Act 1996) provides that the tenant or a person residing or visiting the dwellinghouse:

(a) has been guilty of conduct causing or likely to cause a nuisance or annoyance to a person residing, visiting or otherwise engaging in lawful activity in the locality, or

(b) has been convicted of:

    (i) using the dwelling-house or allowing it to be used for immoral or illegal purpose, or

    (ii) an arrestable offence committed in, or in the locality of the dwelling-house.

Ground 14 enables the landlord to take action against anti-social behaviour. The behaviour only needs to be likely to cause a nuisance, rather than actual nuisance. The nuisance or annoyance can extend to neighbours and anyone visiting or carrying out a lawful activity, which enables local authority or housing officers to witness activities and provide evidence at a subsequent hearing and so avoid the need for local residents to give evidence. Also, following the Court of Appeal decision in *Frederick Platts Co v Grigor* [1950] 1 All ER 941 the court may be able to infer that nuisance or annoyance has been caused without hearing evidence from anyone affected.   **4.65**

Any possession order granted by the court may be suspended, but may be brought back to court if further nuisance arises. In *New Charter Housing (North) Ltd v Ruth Ashcroft* [2004] EWCA Civ 310 the Court of Appeal allowed an appeal by the claimant housing authority against a suspended possession order granted following proceedings under Ground 14 against the defendant arising out of the behaviour and activities of her 17-year-old son. The Court of Appeal set aside the county court order substituting for it an order that possession be given to the claimant in six weeks from the date of the decision. The son had some months earlier been convicted of offences under s 4 of the Public Order Act 1986 and breach of an interim ASBO order and had been sentenced to six months' detention and training order. He was also made subject to a full ASBO under s 1C of the CDA 1998.   **4.66**

Arrestable offences are those defined by s 24 of the Police and Criminal Evidence Act 1984. Any proceedings and consideration of behaviour must take account of the tenant's mental state and any illness that the tenant may be suffering. In *North Devon Homes v Brazier* [2003] EWHC 574 medical evidence suggested that her nuisance behaviour was likely to arise from her mental illness and her eviction on grounds of nuisance would be discriminatory under the Disability Discrimination Act 1995.   **4.67**

Proceedings under ground 14 are those envisaged by s 1B of the CDA 1998 (see paras 4.47–4.50), whereby a relevant authority, including an RSL, can apply for an ASBO in relation to county court proceedings.   **4.68**

Housing Act 1985

The Housing Act 1985 covers public sector tenancies. Schedule 2 of the Act contains grounds for possession. Ground 2 covers nuisance and annoyance by the tenant. The wording of Ground 2 is identical to Ground 14 under the Housing Act 1988.   **4.69**

4.70 Under s 82 of the HA 1985, as amended by the Anti-social Behaviour Act 2003 (ASBA 2003), the court can, following an application by the landlord, make an order for possession, or that the secure tenancy is transferred to a periodic tenancy, or for a demotion order. Under s 82A(4) the court must not make a demotion order unless it is satisfied that:

(a) the tenant or a person residing in or visiting the dwelling-house has engaged or has threatened to engage in conduct to which ss 153A or 153B of the HA 1996 (anti-social behaviour or use of premises for unlawful purposes) applies, and

(b) that it is reasonable to make the order.

4.71 In *Kensington v Chelsea RLBC v Simmonds* (1997) 29 HLR 507 the nuisance and annoyance had persisted for several months from the tenant's son. The Court of Appeal found it unnecessary to show fault on the part of the tenant and that they must consider the interests of the neighbours as well as the tenant. Although in *Portsmouth CC v Bryant* (2000) 32 HLR 906, the extent of personal fault is relevant when considering reasonableness (in this case the court granted a suspended possession order).

Introductory tenancies under the Housing Act 1996

4.72 Section 124 of the Housing Act 1996 (HA 1996) creates a new probationary form of tenancy for local housing authorities and housing action trusts called an introductory tenancy. The tenancy is on a trial period for one year and does not provide security of tenure for that period. During the trial period, the landlord can take proceedings for possession under s 127 of the HA 1996 and the court shall make such an order unless the provisions of s 128 apply, which include, among other things, that a notice of proceedings has not been served. The tenant has a right to review the decision to take possession. However, if the council has complied with the requirements contained in s 128 the court must make an order for possession. However, following the case of *Manchester CC v Cochrane* [1999] 1 WLR 809 the court may allow judicial review proceedings to begin, e.g. to review the local authority's possession proceedings review procedure. However, in *Merton LBC v Williams* [2002] EWCA Civ 980 the court held that a possession action should not be adjourned if the claim for judicial review has no realistic prospect of success. The trial period enables landlords to consider whether anti-social behaviour may arise from a tenant and it has much greater flexibility in tackling this.

4.73 Each of the possession proceedings outlined above should come within Pt 55 of the CPR 1998. Claims should commence using the claim form for possession of property, Form N5.

Injunctions under the Housing Act 1996

4.74 Chapter III of Pt V of the HA 1996, as amended by s 13 of ASBA 2003, enables local authorities and other social landlords to obtain injunctions against anti-social behaviour. Section 153A(2) of the Act provides that the court may, on the application of a relevant landlord, grant an anti-social behaviour injunction if each of the following conditions is satisfied:

• that the person against whom the injunction is sought is engaging, has engaged, or threatens to engage in conduct to which the section applies; and

- that the conduct is capable of causing nuisance or annoyance to either a person with a right to reside in or occupy accommodation owned or managed by the landlord, a person engaged in lawful activity in the neighbourhood, or a person employed in connection with the exercise of the landlord's management functions.

The relevant conduct is described in s 153A(1) of the HA 1996 as conduct: **4.75**

   (a)   which is capable of causing nuisance or annoyance to any person, and
   (b)   which directly or indirectly relates to or affects the housing management functions of a relevant landlord.

If the application for an injunction is successful the order granted may prohibit the person **4.76** served from engaging in the conduct referred to in the injunction. In *R v P* [2004] EWCA Crim 287 the Court of Appeal recently affirmed, in relation to an ASBO, that the conduct prohibited in the order should be clearly specified on the face of that order. The court added that if an order is to protect someone who is not party to the proceedings, the judge should make a finding of fact that there is a significant risk of harm to such persons.

Rules 65.2 to 65.10 of the CPR 1998 cover an application for an injunction under the **4.77** HA 1996. Rule 65.3(1) provides that such an application shall be subject to the Pt 8 procedure as modified by this rule and the relevant practice direction.

Policies and procedures on anti-social behaviour

Section 218A of the Housing Act 1996 provides that local housing authorities, housing **4.78** action trusts, and RSLs must prepare a policy in relation to anti-social behaviour and also a procedure for dealing with anti-social behaviour. The landlords must have published a statement of the policy and procedures by the end of 2004.

G HOUSING: ENVIRONMENTAL HARM AND DISREPAIR

Residents who experience environmental harm or pollution may be able to abate the **4.79** nuisance or claim compensation for the damage caused under the statutory nuisance regime, see paras 4.108–4.114, or in a claim in common law nuisance, see Chapter 17: Civil law practice and procedure. If the harm is being caused to rented accommodation and the reason for the harm or pollution arises from the actions of the landlord or someone acting on his behalf then the tenant may also be able to claim damages and/or an injunction to prevent the harm under the tenancy agreement. Also, if damage is caused through the tenant's action, then the landlord may be able to take certain steps. Two important areas of relevance to environmental protection are:

(1)   breach of covenant for quiet enjoyment; and
(2)   breach of repair covenants or implied obligations.

These are discussed below based upon summary and extracts from Garner and Frith's *A* **4.80** *Practical Approach to Landlord and Tenant* (4/e, OUP, 2004).

Covenant for quiet enjoyment

4.81   A covenant for quiet enjoyment protects a tenant from interference from the right to exclusive possession of the property. The covenant is often expressly provided for in the tenancy agreement, but if not, it will be implied into the contract in any event and so all tenancy agreements will contain a covenant for quiet enjoyment.

4.82   An important aspect of the covenant for quiet enjoyment is that it does not effectively provide what may be understood from a common reading of the term, i.e. protection from noise. Instead, quiet enjoyment means exclusive possession without substantial interruption or interference in the land. In *Kenny v Preen* [1963] 1 QB 499 Pearson LJ explains the distinction at p 511 by stating that:

> I think the word 'enjoy' used in this connection is a translation of the Latin word '*fruor*' and refers to the exercise and use of the right and having the full benefit of it, rather than deriving pleasure from it.

4.83   That said, a breach of exclusive possession might arise from noise created by the landlord. In *Southwark LBC v Mills* [1999] 3 WLR 939, a council tenant complained of regular excessive noise from an upstairs flat due to lack of adequate sound insulation and successfully sued the council landlord for breach of covenant for quiet enjoyment and nuisance. However, it could equally arise from other sources of interference. The importance in terms of protecting the environment is that the covenant provides a remedy that may stop the problem and/or give rise to compensation for any harm or damage that has arisen.

Landlord's acts that cause a breach of quiet enjoyment

4.84   Whether or not a landlord's acts interfere with a tenant's quiet enjoyment depends upon whether they disturb the tenant's enjoyment of possession rather than whether there has been physical damage. This is a question of fact arising out of the particular circumstances of each case. In *Kenny v Preen* there had been a deliberate, persistent, and prolonged course of intimidation and persecution, which, in so far as physical interference was necessary, was present in the form of knocking on the door and shouting threats at the tenant. In *Booth v Thomas* [1926] Ch 397 CA a lack of repair to a culvert on neighbouring land resulted in water escaping from the culvert and damaging the tenant's property. While in *Lavender v Betts* [1942] 2 All ER 72 the landlord entered the tenant's premises and removed the windows and doors.

4.85   In contrast, in *Kelly v Battershall* [1949] 2 All ER 830 CA noise from the landlord, which caused mere inconvenience to the tenant, was not held to be a breach of quiet enjoyment. Also, a temporary disturbance is unlikely to cause a breach, see *Phelps v City of London Corporation* [1916] 2 Ch 255.

Remedies for interfering with quiet enjoyment

4.86   Garner and Frith state that an action for breach of covenant for quiet enjoyment is an action for breach of contract. Damages will be available that will normally be calculated on contractual principles. However, the act that gives rise to the breach may also involve the tort of nuisance and trespass, which could give rise to damages based on the diminution in the loss of land. Any personal injury suffered as a result of the breach, e.g. for mental distress, will need to be based upon a personal injury (negligence) claim.

An injunction may be granted by the court restraining the landlord for any further breaches   **4.87**
of the covenant for quiet enjoyment, although this is a discretionary remedy where the
court will take into account a number of factors unique to the case, see Chapter 17: Civil law
practice and procedure.

Breach of obligations to repair

Much of the harm caused to buildings and the immediate environment is from a failure to   **4.88**
keep buildings in good repair. Disrepair can also have an adverse impact on the wider built
environment and on human health, in extreme circumstances reaching the point of being
unfit for human habitation. Repair obligations can be entered into as express, contractual
obligations by each party or may be implied obligations on both the landlord and tenant.

Express obligations to repair will arise under the tenancy agreement under which the parties   **4.89**
may apportion obligations. Usually, a landlord will be liable for external and structural
repairs while the tenant will be responsible for internal repairs and decoration.

Repair obligations of the landlord

Implied repairing obligations on the landlord include: **4.90**

- providing a dwelling fit for human habitation;
- keeping the common parts in good condition;
- tortious liability at common law and under statute;
- covenants implied by statute.

In *Smith v Marrable* (1843) 11 M&W 5, Parke B stated that premises were unfit for human   **4.91**
habitation 'if the demised premises are incumbered with a nuisance of so serious a nature
that no person can reasonably be expected to live in them.'

Unfitness for human habitation included defective drains in *Wilson v Finch Hatton* (1877)   **4.92**
2 Ex D 3356 and inadequate water supply in *Chester v Powell* (1885) 53 LT 722.

The landlord's obligation to keep the common parts in good condition was found to exist by   **4.93**
the House of Lords in *Liverpool CC v Irwin* [1977] AC 239 in which the claimants rented a flat
in a 15-storey block from the defendant local authority. The lifts in the block regularly failed
and the upper staircases were said to be dangerous and often unlit, all largely as a result of
vandalism. However, in *Duke of Westminster v Guild* [1985] QB 688 the court did not imply a
duty to repair a drain where there was said to be a lease that appeared to be complete.

If the landlord retains part of the building and its disrepair interferes with the tenant's   **4.94**
enjoyment, the landlord may be liable in nuisance. In *Tennant Radiant Heat Ltd v Warrington
Development Corporation* (1988) 11 EG 71 water entered into the tenant's property from the
landlord's failure to maintain the roof and guttering. However, the courts have been
reluctant to extend a landlord's liability in negligence to his tenant or any other person
for disrepair. In *Cavalier v Pope* [1906] AC 428 the House of Lords held that the owner of a
dilapidated house contracted with his tenant to repair a floor but failed to do so. The tenant's
wife, who lived in the house and was well aware of the danger, fell through the floor and was
injured. The court held that the wife, being a stranger to the contract, had no claim for
damages against the owner. Lord Atkinson stated on page 432 that:

> it is well established that no duty is, at law, cast upon a landlord not to let a house in a dangerous or dilapidated condition, and further, that if he does let it while in such a condition, he is not thereby rendered liable in damages for injuries which may be sustained by the tenant, his (the tenant's) servants, guests, customers, or others invited by him to enter the premises by reason on this defective condition.

4.95 However, in *Green v Chelsea BC* [1954] 2 QB 127 the claimant, a licensee of the defendant, successfully claimed in negligence after a ceiling fell on her head, Denning LJ stated at 138 that the principle as set out in *Cavalier v Pope* was a relic of an out-of-date doctrine that must be kept in close confinement.

4.96 The Occupiers Liability Act 1957 and the Defective Premises Act 1972 (DPA 1972) may in certain circumstances give rise to statutory liability for failure to repair, e.g. s 4(1) of the DPA 1972 provides that:

> Where premises are let under a tenancy which puts on the landlord an obligation to the tenant for the maintenance or repair of the premises, the landlord owes to all persons who might reasonably be expected to be affected by defects in the state of the premises a duty to take such care as is reasonable in all the circumstances to see that they are reasonably safe from personal injury or from damage to their property caused by a relevant defect.

4.97 Section 8(1) of the Landlord and Tenant Act 1985 (LTA 1985) provides that where a house is let on a very low rent there is implied on the landlord a condition that the house is fit for human habitation at the start of the tenancy and that during the course of the tenancy the house will be kept in all respects reasonably fit for human habitation. Section 11(1) of the LTA 1985 provides that for short or period tenancies there is implied a covenant by the landlord to keep in repair, among other things, the structure and exterior of the dwelling-house including drains, gutters, and external pipes.

Repair obligations of the tenant

4.98 Implied repairing obligations on the tenant will be to use the premises in a tenant-like manner such as not intentionally or negligently damaging the property, and not to commit waste, i.e. causing the property to deteriorate either by actively doing something that should not be done or by passively letting a property fall into disrepair and taking no preventative action.

Liability to repair

4.99 Liability to repair will only arise when there has been some disrepair. Condensation and dampness is a common concern for repair with the real potential to adversely impact on the indoor environment in the home, yet often it does not give rise to a state of disrepair but is caused by the design of the building, or by remedial work to homes such as installing replacement windows. In *Quick v Taff Ely BC* [1985] 3 WLR 981 severe condensation caused by the installation of metal framed windows caused the claimant's furniture to be damaged through damp to the point where some rooms were uninhabitable. However, the Court of Appeal held that the local authority landlord was only liable under s 11 of the LTA 1985 to keep the structure and exterior in repair. While the dwelling was unfit for human habitation, the structure and exterior were not in a state of disrepair. However, in *Staves & Staves v Leeds CC* (1992) 29 EG 119 CA the claimant successfully sued for disrepair after damp had caused parts of the plaster on internal walls to deteriorate. In *Lee v Leeds CC* [2003] 34 HLR 367 the Court of Appeal affirmed the decision of *Quick v Taff Ely BC* [1985] but suggested that severe levels of condensation may give rise to a breach of a tenant's rights to family and private life under Art 8 of the ECHR. See Garner and Frith for further analysis of what constitutes repair and the standards of repair required.

Remedies for failing to repair

A landlord's remedy against a tenant who fails to repair may include: **4.100**

- a right of re-entry, if this is provided for in the tenancy agreement;
- forfeiture, although the landlord will need to serve notice on the tenant under s 125 of the Law of Property Act 1925; or
- damages, based on the diminution in value of the property caused by the lack of repair, assessed at the time the property reverts back to the landlord at the end of the lease.

The tenant's remedies against the landlord for failing to repair may include: **4.101**

- damages, based on the cost of repair to the standard that the property would have been in had there been no repair;
- special damages for ruined furniture;
- general damages for personal injury and discomfort, e.g. suffering ill health due to damp conditions, see *Alienus v Tower Hamlets LBC* [1998] CLY 2987;
- carrying out the repairs and deducting the cost from future rent (self-help), see *Lee-Parker v Izzet* [1971] 3 All ER 1099. In *British Anzani (Felixstowe) Ltd v International Marine* [1980] QB 137, the landlord sued for unpaid rent and the tenant counter-claimed for the cost of repairs;
- specific performance under s 17 of the LTA 1985;
- appointment of a manager under Pt II of the Landlord and Tenant Act 1987;
- appointment of a receiver by the court under s 37 of the Supreme Court Act 1981, where the landlord cannot be traced; or
- requesting that the local housing authority issue a repair notice under the Housing Act 1985 (HA 1985), see para 4.67.

In *Toff v McDowell* (1995) 69 P&CR 535 the High Court granted damages for breach of   **4.102**
covenant to repair after the landlord had removed the floor covering from the flat above the claimant and then rented it out to noisy tenants. See also *Bird v Hackney LBC* (2001) July 2001 LAB 25. Legal proceedings for disrepair and breach of quiet enjoyment should normally commence in the county court and must comply with CPR 1998, using the Pt 7 rules, see Chapter 17.

Housing repair notice

Sections 189 and 190 of the HA 1985 enable local authorities to serve a housing repair notice   **4.103**
on any dwelling house or house in multiple occupation that is unfit for human habitation or in a state of disrepair. Section 604 of the HA 1985 provides that a dwellinghouse is fit for human habitation unless, in the opinion of the local housing authority, it fails to meet one or more of the following requirements:

(a)   it is structurally stable;

(b)   it is free from serious disrepair;

(c)   it is free from dampness prejudicial to the health of the occupants (if any);

(d)   it has adequate provision for lighting, heating, and ventilation;

(e)   it has an adequate piped supply of wholesome water;

(f)   there are satisfactory facilities for the preparation and cooking of food including a sink with a satisfactory supply of hot and cold water;

(g)   it has a suitably located water-closet for the exclusive use of the occupants;

(h)   it has, for the exclusive use of the occupants, a suitably located fixed bath or shower and wash-hand basin, each of which is provided with a satisfactory supply of hot and cold water; and

(i)   it has an effective system for the draining of foul, waste, and surface water.

4.104   In *Dover DC v Sherred* (1997) 29 HLR 864 the Court of Appeal held that unfit for human habitation should be based upon standards of ordinary user on issues of fact without applying any special rules as to expert evidence. Section 207 of the HA 1985 provides that a dwelling-house or house in multiple occupation includes any yard, garden, outhouses, and appurtenances belonging to it or usually enjoyed with it.

4.105   Once the local authority have determined that a house is unfit for human habitation under s 189 of the HA 1985 they must, following the Court of Appeal judgment in *R v Kerrier DC ex p Guppy's (Bridgport) Ltd* (1976) 32 P&CR 411, serve a repair notice. There is no similar mandatory requirement for a repair notice under s 190 of the Act.

4.106   Under s 191 of the HA 1985 a person aggrieved by a repair notice can, within 21 days of the date of service, appeal against it in the county court. Appeals under this section are regarded as statutory appeals and are governed by Pt 52 of the CPR 1998. Statutory appeals are not subject to a need to seek permission to appeal. The 21-day limitation period overrides the general 28-day period provided for in Pt 52.

4.107   Section 189(4) of the HA 1985 provides that if no appeal is brought, after 21 days of service the notice is final and conclusive and becomes operative. Under s 189(5) an operative repair notice is a local land charge.

Slum clearance

4.108   Part IX of the HA 1985 provides for slum clearance and the demolition or closing of unfit premises beyond repair at reasonable cost. Powers of a local housing authority include making a demolition order. A person aggrieved by a demolition order may, within 21 days of service of the order, appeal to the county court.

Statutory nuisance

4.109   There have been a number of cases heard by the courts where a tenant has claimed that the landlord's act or default has given rise to a statutory nuisance. Under Pt III of the Environmental Protection Act 1990 (EPA 1990) a statutory nuisance includes premises in such a state as to be prejudicial to health or a nuisance. This is considered in detail in Chapter 18: Statutory nuisance, although housing-related cases are considered below.

In *Pollway Nominees Ltd v LB of Havering* (1989) 21 HLR 462, the landlord company was held **4.110** liable for the statutory nuisance of damp conditions in a flat even though the damp arose from a wall that was not considered to be part of the demised premises. The court held that the 'premises' that were prejudicial to health was the flat itself.

Where the harm or injury has been to a third party, the phrase 'person responsible' has **4.111** caused difficulties between the landlord and tenant. In *Gwinnel v Eamer* (1875) LR 10 CP 658, a landlord knew that the nuisance existed but had, by covenant, agreed that the tenant would keep it in repair, and so the tenant was liable. Also in *Nelson v Liverpool Brewery Co* (1877) 2 CPD 311 the landlord was not held liable for damage caused by a falling chimney pot on the basis that he had let the premises in good repair, while in *Todd v Flight* (1860) LR 8 CP 401, the reverse was true and the landlord was liable for a falling chimney pot.

A landlord may be liable for the nuisance regardless of whether he is aware of the nuisance **4.112** act or state of affairs, as in the case of *Gandy v Jubber* (1865) 9 B&S 15 in relation to a defective grating. Butterfield R and Holroyd J in *Statutory Nuisance: a Guide for Professionals* (Monitor Press, 2000) summarize the general principles of liability in the landlord and tenant relationship as:

- unless there is a statutory or contractual provision to the contrary it is the tenant as occupier who is liable for statutory nuisance;
- if the tenant has covenanted to do repairs he is liable to the exclusion of all others, and this is so even though the nuisance existed when the tenancy began, see *Gwinnel v Eamer*;
- if there is no contractual obligation to repair the landlord may be liable if he has reserved the right to enter to carry out necessary repairs, see *Heape v Ind Coope & Allsop Ltd* [1940] 2 KB 476;
- if there is no contractual obligation to repair the landlord will be liable if the nuisance existed at the time of the letting, see *Todd v Flight*;
- the landlord will be liable where he lets premises for a specific purpose that gives rise to a nuisance *Harris v James* (1876) 45 LJ QB 545; and
- if the nuisance arises from a structural defect the responsibility, under s 80(2)(b) of the EPA 1990, will in every case fall to the landlord.

H LOCAL ENVIRONMENTAL CONCERNS

Local environmental concerns often fall outside the scope of environmental practice and **4.113** procedure but for most people it is as important an issue as any other. Local concerns include graffiti, fly-posting, dog fouling, litter and refuse, abandoned vehicles, waste and fly-tipping (see Chapter 14: Waste), and noise (see Chapter 10: Noise).

The Government has sought to strengthen many of the laws relating to local environmental **4.114** crime with the enactment of the Clean Neighbourhoods and Environment Act 2005 (CNEA 2005). The Act contains points that affect all the concerns discussed below as well as others relating to noise, statutory nuisance, waste, advertising etc. It also introduces new sanctions for illegal and nuisance parking of vehicles and abandoned shopping and luggage trolleys. The various provisions are to come into force by order of the Secretary of State and National

Assembly for Wales. Therefore the introduction of commencement provisions should be followed carefully.

Graffiti and fly-posting

4.115 ASBA 2003 has increased certain powers, sanctions, and options in relation to graffiti and fly-posting. Section 48(12) of ASBA 2003 provides certain definitions including graffiti, which is defined as 'painting, writing, soiling, marking, or other defacing by whatever means.'

4.116 Graffiti and fly-posting can cause the built environment to deteriorate and adversely impacts on visual amenity. In doing so it reduces the quality of the local environment generally. Graffiti and fly-posting incidents are more common in urban areas although this is not exclusively so. Causing graffiti or carrying out fly-posting gives rise to a range of offences under various pieces of legislation including those set out in s 44 of ASBA 2003:

- s 54(10) of the Metropolitan Police Act 1839 (fixing posters);
- s 20(1) of the London County Council (General Powers) Act 1954 (defacement of streets with slogans);
- s 1(1) of the Criminal Damage Act 1971 (damaging property etc.), which involves only the painting or writing on, or the soiling, marking, or other defacing of, any property by whatever means;
- ss 131(2) and 132(1) of the Highways Act 1980 (damaging, painting, or affixing things onto the highway including signs and structures); and
- s 224(3) of the Town and Country Planning Act 1990 (TCPA 1990) (displaying an advertisement in contravention of obligations).

Fixed penalty notice

4.117 Sections 43 to 47 of ASBA 2003 enable local authorities to issue fixed penalty notices to those found causing graffiti or fly-posting. Section 43(1) provides that:

> Where an authorised officer of a local authority has reason to believe that a person has committed a relevant offence in the area of that authority, he may give that person a notice offering him the opportunity of discharging any liability to conviction for that offence by payment of a penalty in accordance with the notice.

4.118 The fixed penalty notice, currently set at £50, must be in the prescribed form and must include the details of the offence, the period within which proceedings will not begin and the penalty amount and who to pay it to. Payment can be made by post. In line with most other fixed penalty notices, where a person has been given a notice no proceedings may be instituted for that offence until 14 days after the date of the notice and, if he pays the penalty within 14 days he may not be convicted of the relevant offence. If the penalty notice is unpaid the matter can then be prosecuted under the relevant offences.

4.119 For fly-posting offences under s 224 of the TCPA 1990, the fixed penalty scheme only operates in relation to the person who has personally fixed the advertisement and so the person whose goods or services are being promoted will not be liable to receive a fixed penalty. Also, under s 43(2) of ASBA 2003 a fixed penalty notice cannot be served if the offence is motivated by racial or religious hatred. Section 31 of CNEA 2005 extends the principle of graffiti removal notices (see below) to fly-posting offences.

Graffiti removal notice

Under s 48 of ASBA 2003 a local authority may serve a graffiti removal notice upon any **4.120** person responsible for the surface if it is satisfied:

(a) that a relevant surface in an area has been defaced by graffiti, and
(b) that the defacement is detrimental to the amenity of the area or is offensive.

The graffiti removal notice imposes a requirement that the defacement be removed, cleared, **4.121** or otherwise remedied within a period specified in the notice being not less than 28 days from service of the notice. If the person responsible is unknown after reasonable inquiry then the authority may fix the notice to the surface, entering any land that may be necessary. Under s 48(4) of ASBA 2003, if the notice is not complied with the authority may remove the graffiti and recover expenditure reasonably incurred in doing so. Guidance on the use of graffiti removal notices has been published by Defra entitled: *Guidance for Local Authorities on the Operation of Sections 48 to 52 of the Anti-Social Behaviour Act 2003: Graffiti Removal Notices.*

Miscellaneous amendments and provisions

ASBA 2003 has increased the maximum fine for the unlawful display of advertisements from **4.122** £1,000 to £2,500 per offence. While s 54 of the Act creates a new offence of selling an aerosol spray paint to a person under the age of 16. It is a defence under s 54(4) to provide that the seller took all reasonable steps to determine the purchaser's age and that he reasonably believed that the person was not under 16 years. Also, under s 55(5) if the sale is effected by another person, that the defendant took all reasonable steps to avoid the offence. The maximum penalty on summary conviction is a £2,500 fine. Section 32 of the CNEA 2005 creates enforcement provisions relating to the sale of aerosol paint to children.

Litter and refuse

Litter, refuse, and waste generally is becoming an acute problem throughout the UK. There **4.123** has been an increase in litter particularly near fast-food and late night take-away outlets, and this has, in turn, resulted in an increase in the rat population in the UK to the point where it is greater than the human population. Weil's disease, affecting the liver, kidneys, and sometimes causing meningitis, is spread by the urine of rats and is a recurrent threat.

Part IV of the EPA 1990 makes provisions relating to litter to be implemented by principal **4.124** litter authorities, who include under s 86(2) of the Act county councils, county borough councils, district councils, and London borough councils. Part IV provides for a number of options to control litter including an offence of dropping litter and keeping land defaced by litter, a duty to keep land and highways clear, and designating litter control areas. Section 18 of the CNEA 2005 extends the areas covered by the offence to all open places.

Under s 87(1) of the EPA 1990 it is an offence for any person to throw down, drop, or **4.125** otherwise deposit litter in, into, or from any place to which the section applies. Applicable places include under s 87(2), among others any public open space or relevant land. In *Felix v*

DPP [1998] Crim LR 675 the High Court allowed an appeal by way of case stated for a defendant convicted of depositing litter under s 87(1) after affixing three cards advertising prostitution services inside a telephone kiosk. The court held that a public open space did not include a telephone kiosk, which was enclosed on three sides and had a roof, and that 'otherwise deposit' may be construed very widely and means no more than placing or putting.

4.126   In *Westminster CC v Riding* [1996] Env LR 95, the court held that commercial rubbish including plastic refuse sacks, empty beer and crisp cartons, and bread bags can amount to litter contributing to the defacement of a highway. The supporting commentary to *Felix v DPP* at 658 suggests that litter can be 'anything whatsoever' but a thing does not become litter unless something is done with it; and the mere deposit is apparently not enough: the deposit must at least 'tend' to the defacement by litter of any place. Under the Litter (Animal Droppings) Order 1991 (SI 1991/961), Pt IV of the EPA 1990 applies to dog faeces.

4.127   A person guilty of an offence under s 87(1) shall be liable on summary conviction to a fine not exceeding £2,500. Where an authorized officer of a litter authority finds a person he has reason to believe has committed a litter offence he may, under s 88 of the EPA 1990, serve a fixed penalty notice on that person. If the person served pays the penalty within 14 days of the date of service no proceedings under the offence shall be instituted. The Litter (Fixed Penalty Notices) Order 1991 (SI 1991/111) prescribes the form of fixed penalty notice.

4.128   Under s 89 of the EPA 1990 each local authority is under a duty to ensure that its land is, so far as is practicable, kept clear of litter and refuse. Section 91 provides that summary proceedings may be brought by any persons aggrieved by the defacement, by litter or refuse, of any highway or land specified in the Act. The proceedings are brought against the person who has a duty to keep the land clear under s 89(1). Under s 91(3) a principal litter authority shall not be treated as a person aggrieved. Where the standards of cleanliness are not met, the aggrieved person must give the authority five days' notice of its intention to make a complaint to the magistrates' court. If the magistrates find that the duty has not been met it may issue a litter abatement order. Under s 91(9) of the EPA 1990 a person who, without reasonable excuse, fails to comply with a litter abatement order shall be guilty of an offence and liable on summary conviction to a fine not exceeding £2,500 together with a further fine of an amount equal to 1/20 of that level for each day on which the offence continues after conviction.

4.129   Section 92 of the EPA 1990 provides that where a principal litter authority is satisfied that any land set out in that section is defaced by litter or refuse or that such defacement is likely to recur, the authority shall serve a litter abatement notice imposing the requirement to clear the litter and/or a prohibition on permitting the land to become defaced. Under s 92(4) a person served with a litter abatement order may appeal against the notice to a magistrates' court by way of summary application within 21 days of service of the notice.

4.130   Under s 92(6) of the EPA 1990, if someone served with a litter abatement notice fails, without reasonable excuse, to comply with or contravenes the requirement or prohibition imposed by the notice, he shall be guilty of an offence. It is a defence under s 92(7) to prove that he has complied, as respects the land in question with the duty under s 89(1) above. Someone convicted of an offence under s 92 is liable on summary conviction to a maximum fine of

£2,500 together with a further fine of 1/20 of £2,500 for each day on which the offence
continues after the conviction.

Codes of Practice

In compliance with the obligation under s 89(7) of the EPA 1990 Defra has published *Code*   **4.131**
of Practice (1999) on the Standards of Cleanliness. This provides for certain standards of
cleanliness from Grades A to D in various localities referred to by the guidance as zones. The
standards of cleanliness include:

Grade A   no litter or refuse;
Grade B   predominantly free of litter, apart from small items such as cigarette ends;
Grade C   widespread distribution of small items and larger items and animal faeces; and
Grade D   heavily littered.

The zones are referred to by numbers and include: **4.132**

(1)   Town centres, shopping areas, railway and bus stations etc.;
(2)   High density residential areas, recreational areas etc.;
(3)   Low density residential areas, public parks, and industrial estates;
(4)   All other areas;
(5)   Local authority beaches;
(6)   Motorways and other main routes;
(7)   Other roads;
(8)   Educational establishments; and
(9)   Railway embankments (within 100 m of platform).

Dog fouling

Under s 2 of the Dogs (Fouling of Land) Act 1996 (DFLA 1996) a local authority can designate   **4.133**
land in its area where it is a crime not to clear up after your dog.

Section 3(1) of the DFLA 1996 provides that if a dog defecates at any time on designated land   **4.134**
and a person in charge of the dog at that time fails to clear it up that person is guilty of an
offence, which, on summary conviction has a maximum penalty of a £1,000 fine. Under s 4
of the DFLA 1996, a local authority officer may give a person contravening s 3 of the Act an
opportunity of discharging liability by the payment of a fixed penalty. This Act is subject to
repeal under Pt 6 of the CNEA 2005. Controls on dogs to be replaced with more effective
powers for local authorities to control this problem.

Abandoned vehicles

Abandoned vehicles are becoming a particularly acute problem for most local authorities as   **4.135**
the cost of vehicle disposal increases. In 2000/01, over 238,000 vehicles were abandoned in
England and Wales, to be dealt with at the expense of local authorities. Section 2(1)(a) of the
Refuse Disposal (Amenity) Act 1978 (RDAA 1978) provides that any person who, without
lawful authority:

abandons on any land in the open air, or on any other land forming part of a highway, a motor vehicle or anything which formed part of a motor vehicle and was removed from it in the course of dismantling the vehicle on the land . . . shall be guilty of an offence and liable to summary conviction to a maximum fine of £2,500 and/or three months' imprisonment.

4.136 Section 2(2) of the Act provides that for the purpose of s 2(1), a person may leave any thing on any land in such circumstances or for such a period that he may reasonably be assumed to have abandoned it unless the contrary is shown. Following *Vaughan v Biggs* [1960] 2 All ER 473 the time limit for proceedings runs from the date of leaving the vehicle and the offence is not a continuing one. As a summary offence, the matter will commence by laying an information see Chapter 19: Criminal law practice and procedure.

4.137 Part 2 of the CNEA 2005 creates various offences relating to vehicles including creating certain nuisance parking offences such as exposing vehicles for sale on a road and repairing vehicles on a road. Sections 10 to 14 of the Act amend the abandoned vehicle provisions of RDAA 1978 by creating a fixed penalty notice scheme by creating new ss 2A to 2C. It also revises the removal and disposal provisions contained in ss 3 and 4 of the RDAA 1978.

KEY DOCUMENTS AND MATERIALS

Rent Act 1977
Refuse Disposal (Amenity) Act 1978
Housing Act 1985
Housing Act 1988
Environmental Protection Act 1990
Dogs (Fouling of Land) Act 1996
Housing Act 1996
Crime and Disorder Act 1998
Magistrates' Courts (Anti-Social Behaviour Orders) Rules 2002 (SI 2002/2784)
Anti-Social Behaviour Act 2003

Clean Neighbourhoods and Environment Bill

Part 8 Civil Procedure Rules 1998 and Practice Direction 8
Part 55 Civil Procedure Rules 1998 and Practice Direction 55
Part 65 Civil Procedure Rules 1998 and Practice Direction 65

Butterfield, R and Holroyd, J (2000). *Statutory Nuisance: A Guide for Professionals*. Monitor Press: Suffolk
Defra, *Code of Practice (1999) on the Standards of Cleanliness*, available at www.defra.gov.uk
Garner, S and Frith, A (2004). *A Practical Approach to Landlord and Tenant*. 4/e. OUP: Oxford
Home Office (2002) *Guide to Anti-Social Behaviour Orders and Acceptable Behaviour Contracts*. Home Office: London
Home Office (2005). *Guidance on Publicising Anti-Social Behaviour Orders*, available at www.together.gov.uk

Woodfall, W and Lewison, K *Woodfall's Landlord and Tenant.* (Regular updates). Sweet & Maxwell: London

Zimbardo, PG (1969). 'The Human Choice: Individuation, Reason and Order Norms vs. Deindividuation, Impulse and Chaos.' *Nebraska Symposium on Motivation,* 17, pp 237–307

www.crimereduction.gov.uk

5

CONTAMINATED LAND

A   INTRODUCTION

5.01   Land contaminated by pollution and other human activities has presented problems for the environment for many years. Until recently, communities have either lived with the contamination or moved elsewhere. Some contamination is ancient and could have arisen from the spoil heaps of Roman lead mines, other contamination could be naturally occurring. However, most of the current contamination arose from a lack of care from industry and waste management, particular from the early 1800s and through the industrial revolution when harmful substances were released onto the land and into watercourses. Historic sources of contamination may arise from oil refineries, gas works, heavy industry, and illegal landfill.

5.02   As the pressure to use land has become more acute and polluting activities more common, there has been a need to either prevent contamination or begin to decontaminate the affected areas. With an increasing demand for more homes and a spiralling waste disposal problem, land contamination in the UK has become critical. Land contamination may arise by accident or from intentional acts or omissions. Intentional actions can result from the unlawful disposal of waste or from the lawful use of land such as depositing waste in landfill sites.

B   THE CONTAMINATED LAND REGIME

5.03   The government White Paper: *Paying for our Past* set out proposals for tackling the problem of contaminated land by introducing a nationwide scheme to identify areas of contamination, register them, and then proceed to improve the areas. The proposal was implemented under s 57 of the Environment Act 1995, which inserted Pt IIA into the Environmental Protection Act 1990 (EPA 1990). Part IIA ranges from s 78A to s 78YC. The contaminated land regime came into force in April 2000, following the enactment of the Contaminated Land (England) Regulations 2000 (SI 2000/227) and the Contaminated Land (Wales) Regulations 2001 (WSI 2001/2197).

Objectives of the contaminated land regime

5.04   The primary objectives of the Pt IIA contaminated land regime are set out in para 7 of the DETR Circular 2/2000 *Contaminated Land: Implementation of Part IIA of the Environmental Protection Act 1990* (Circular 02/2000), i.e.

(a)   to identify and remove unacceptable risks to human health and the environment;
(b)   to seek to bring damaged land back into beneficial use; and
(c)   to seek to ensure that the cost burdens faced by individuals, companies, and society as a whole are proportionate, manageable, and economically sustainable.

5.05   The legislative framework is discussed below. Up to June 2004, there were 74 contaminated land sites in England and Wales. Fifty-nine of these had an area of less than five hectares. The most common pollutants at the sites were organic compounds, such as pesticides, dyes, solvents, and metals.

Enforcing authorities

The contaminated land regime is managed in England and Wales by local authorities, **5.06**
i.e. district and unitary authorities and the Environment Agency working together. Section
78A(9) of the EPA 1990 states that the enforcing authority means:

(a)　in relation to a special site, the [Environment Agency];
(b)　in relation to contaminated land other than a special site, the local authority in whose area
　　　the land is situated;

Defining contaminated land

The Environment Agency, on its website, defines contaminated land as land that has been **5.07**
polluted with harmful substances and so is a serious risk to human health and or the
environment (habitats and wildlife). Contamination can be on the surface or below it. Even
small amounts of heavy organic compounds like pesticides, dyes, solvents or paints, oils,
and metals can pollute land. It is often confused with the term 'brownfield land'. Brownfield
sites are land or premises that have previously been used or developed. They may also be
vacant or derelict, but are not necessarily contaminated. There is increased pressure to
redevelop brownfield sites and greater awareness of environmental issues means there is a
general need to know whether a site is contaminated. The Government has a target that
60% of new homes should be built on brownfield land. Greenfield land is land that has never
been built on.

Section 78A(2) of the EPA 1990 defines contaminated land as land that appears to the local **5.08**
authority in whose areas it is situated to be in such a condition, by reason of substances in,
on, or under the land, that:

(a)　significant harm is being caused or there is a significant possibility of such harm being
　　　caused; or
(b)　pollution of controlled waters is being, or is likely to be, caused;

Section 78A(4) of the EPA 1990 defines harm as harm to the health of living organisms or **5.09**
other interference with the ecological systems of which they form a part and, in the case of
man, includes harm to his property. Section 78A(5) of the EPA 1990 further provides that
significant harm shall be determined in accordance with guidance. Circular 2/2000 provides at para A.23 that the local authority should regard as significant only harm that is
both:

(a)　to a receptor of a type listed in Table 5.1 (see below), and
(b)　within the description of harm specified for that type of receptor in Table 5.1.

Table 5.1 Categories of significant harm

Type of receptor	Description of harm to that type of receptor that is to be regarded as significant harm
1. Human beings	Death, disease, serious injury, genetic mutation, birth defects or the impairment of reproductive functions. For these purposes, disease is to be taken to mean an unhealthy condition of the body or a part of it and can include, for example, cancer, liver dysfunction

Table 5.1—*continued*

Type of receptor	Description of harm to that type of receptor that is to be regarded as significant harm
	or extensive skin ailments. Mental dysfunction is included only insofar as it is attributable to the effects of a pollutant on the body of the person concerned. In this chapter, this description of significant harm is referred to as a 'human health effect'.
2. Any ecological system, or living organism forming part of such a system, within a location which is: • an area notified as an area of special scientific interest under s 28 of the Wildlife and Countryside Act 1981; • any land declared a national nature reserve under s 35 of that Act; • any area designated as a marine nature reserve under s 36 of that Act; • an area of special protection for birds, established under s 3 of that Act; • any European Site within the meaning of reg 10 of the Conservation (Natural Habitats etc) Regulations 1994 (ie Special Areas of Conservation and Special Protection Areas); • any candidate Special Areas of Conservation or potential Special Protection Areas given equivalent protection; • any habitat or site afforded policy protection under paragraph 13 of Planning Policy Guidance Note 9 (PPG9) on nature conservation (ie candidate Special Areas of Conservation, potential Special Protection Areas and listed Ramsar sites); or • any nature reserve established under s 21 of the National Parks and Access to the Countryside Act 1949.	For any protected location: • harm which results in an irreversible adverse change, or in some other substantial adverse change, in the functioning of the ecological system within any substantial part of that location; or • harm which affects any species of special interest within that location and which endangers the long-term maintenance of the population of that species at that location. In addition, in the case of a protected location which is a European Site (or a candidate Special Area of Conservation or a potential Special Protection Area), harm which is incompatible with the favourable conservation status of natural habitats at that location or species typically found there. In determining what constitutes such harm, the local authority should have regard to the advice of English Nature and to the requirements of the Conservation (Natural Habitats etc) Regulations 1994. In this Chapter, this description of significant harm is referred to as an 'ecological system effect'.
3. Property in the form of: • crops, including timber; • produce grown domestically, or on allotments, for consumption; • livestock; • other owned or domesticated animals; • wild animals which are the subject of shooting or fishing rights.	For crops, a substantial diminution in yield or other substantial loss in their value resulting from death, disease or other physical damage. For domestic pets, death, serious disease or serious physical damage. For other property in this category, a substantial loss in its value resulting from death, disease or other serious physical damage. The local authority should regard a substantial loss in value as occurring only when a substantial proportion of the animals or crops are dead or otherwise no longer fit for their intended purpose. Food should be regarded as being no longer fit for purpose when it fails to comply with the provisions of the Food Safety Act 1990. Where a diminution in yield or loss in value is caused by a pollutant linkage, a 20% diminution or loss should be regarded as a benchmark for what constitutes a substantial diminution or loss. In this Chapter, this description of significant harm is referred to as an 'animal or crop effect'.

Type of receptor	Description of harm to that type of receptor that is to be regarded as significant harm
4. Property in the form of buildings. For this purpose, 'building' means any structure or erection, and any part of a building including any part below ground level, but does not include plant or machinery comprised in a building.	Structural failure, substantial damage or substantial interference with any right of occupation. For this purpose, the local authority should regard substantial damage or substantial interference as occurring when any part of the building ceases to be capable of being used for the purpose for which it is or was intended. Additionally, in the case of a scheduled Ancient Monument, substantial damage should be regarded as occurring when the damage significantly impairs the historic, architectural, traditional, artistic, or archaeological interest by reason of which the monument was scheduled. In this Chapter, this description of significant harm is referred to as a 'building effect'.

The following excerpt from the Circular 02/2000 further defines significant harm: **5.10**

A.24 The local authority should not regard harm to receptors of any type other than those mentioned in [Table 5.1] as being significant harm for the purposes of Part IIA. For example, harm to ecological systems outside the descriptions in the second entry in the table should be disregarded. Similarly, the authority should not regard any other description of harm to receptors of the types mentioned in Table A as being significant harm.

A.25 The authority should disregard any receptors which are not likely to be present, given the 'current use' of the land or other land which might be affected.

A.26 For the purposes of this guidance, the 'current use' means any use which is currently being made, or is likely to be made, of the land and which is consistent with any existing planning permission (or is otherwise lawful under town and country planning legislation). This definition is subject to the following qualifications:

(a) the current use should be taken to include any temporary use, permitted under town and country planning legislation, to which the land is, or is likely to be, put from time to time;

(b) the current use includes future uses or developments which do not require a new, or amended, grant of planning permission (but see also paragraph A.34 below);

(c) the current use should, nevertheless, be taken to include any likely informal recreational use of the land, whether authorised by the owners or occupiers or not, (for example, children playing on the land); however, in assessing the likelihood of any such informal use, the local authority should give due attention to measures taken to prevent or restrict access to the land; and

(d) in the case of agricultural land, however, the current agricultural use should not be taken to extend beyond the growing or rearing of the crops or animals which are habitually grown or reared on the land.

The definition of contaminated land is limited to the boundaries set in Circular 02/2000, i.e. **5.11** that the contamination must affect one of the four receptors taking into account the current use of the land. There is no definition of 'land' under the EPA 1990. Schedule 1 of the Interpretation Act 1978 provides that land includes buildings and other structures, land covered with water, and any estate, interest, easement, servitude, or right in or over land.

Risk assessment

5.12   Paragraph A.9 of Circular 02/2000 explains that the definition of contaminated land is based upon the principles of risk assessment, which is defined as the combination of:

(a)   the probability, or frequency, of occurrence of a defined hazard (for example, exposure to a property of a substance with the potential to cause harm); and

(b)   the magnitude (including the seriousness) of the consequences.

5.13   Circular 02/2000 further explains, at paras A.10 to A.14, that a conventional approach to risk assessment is taken, which incorporates the concept of the 'contaminant-pathway-receptor'. It advises that there are two steps the local authority must take when applying the definition of contaminated land:

(1)   it must satisfy itself that a contaminant, a pathway (or pathways), and a receptor have been identified with respect to that land; and

(2)   it must satisfy itself that both a pollutant linkage exists in respect of a piece of land; and that pollutant linkage:

(i)   is resulting in significant harm being caused to the receptor in the pollutant linkage,

(ii)   presents a significant possibility of significant harm being caused to that receptor,

(iii) is resulting in the pollution of the controlled waters which constitute the receptor,

(iv)   or is likely to result in such pollution.

5.14   The Environment Agency and Defra have produced the *Contaminated Land Exposure Assessment Model* that aims to help assess the risk to human health from land contamination and is available from www.defra.gov.uk. To support the Regulations and Circular 02/2000, the Environment Agency, in collaboration with the Local Government Association (LGA) and the Chartered Institute of Environmental Health (CIEH), has published the *Local Authority Guide to the Application of Part IIA of the EPA 1990* available from www.lga.gov.uk. Defra has produced a number of industry profiles that may give rise to certain forms of contamination. These are available at www.defra.gov.uk.

C   INVESTIGATING CONTAMINATED LAND UNDER PART IIA

Contaminated land strategies

5.15   Circular 02/2000 requires each local authority to prepare a contaminated land strategy for its area, helping them to take a strategic approach to identifying land that merits detailed individual inspection. Many local authorities have published their strategies on their local authority websites, see e.g., the North Lincolnshire Council Contaminated Land Strategy, which contains seven chapters and six appendices and discusses the characteristics of the area, the aims, procedures, and communication of the strategy, as well as mechanisms for review and training provision. It is available at: www.northlincs.gov.uk.

Inspection and identification

5.16   Under s 78B of the EPA 1990, local authorities are under a duty to inspect their land to identify whether there are any areas of contamination and whether any such land should be designated a special site. The inspection must be in accordance with the requirements of Circular 02/2000. Under s 78X(1) of the EPA 1990, where there are two or more sites that, individually would not be regarded as contaminated, but together would, then each site should be treated as being contaminated.

If a local authority identifies land as contaminated land it must, under s 78B(3) of the EPA 1990, notify: **5.17**

(a) the Environment Agency;
(b) the owner of the land;
(c) any person occupying all or any part of the land; and
(d) any other appropriate person.

Appropriate person and apportionment

Section 78F of the EPA 1990 provides that an appropriate person is any person(s) who caused   **5.18** or knowingly permitted the land to become contaminated land. The appropriate person may then be liable for cleaning up the contaminated land. It is likely, and has been envisaged by the legislation, regulations, and guidance, that there will often be more than one appropriate person and that there must be some way of allocating or apportioning responsibility for cleaning the land among those identified. It is therefore necessary to consider who is an appropriate person and apportionment.

Appropriate person

Section 78F of the EPA 1990 determines who is the appropriate person to bear responsibility   **5.19** for anything the enforcing authority determines is needed to remediate contaminated land. To begin with s 78F(2) provides that:

> any person, or any of the persons, who caused or knowingly permitted the substances, or any of the substances, by reason of which the contaminated land in question is such land to be in, on or under land is an appropriate person.

Paragraph 9.5, Annex 2 of Circular 02/2000 advises that an appropriate person (referred to in   **5.20** the Circular as a Class A person) will be the appropriate person only in respect of any remediation that is referable to the particular substances that he caused or knowingly permitted to be in, on, or under the land. This means that the question of liability has to be considered separately for each significant pollutant linkage identified on the land.

A second category of appropriate person arises where it is not possible to find a Class A   **5.21** person, either for all of the significant pollutant linkages or for a particular one. These circumstances are addressed in s 78F, which provides that:

> (4) If no person has, after reasonable inquiry, been found who is by virtue of subs (2) an appropriate person to bear responsibility for the things which are to be done by way of remediation, the owner or occupier for the time being of the land in question is an appropriate person.
>
> (5) If, in consequence of subs (3), there are things which are to be done by way of remediation in relation to which no person has, after reasonable inquiry, been found who is an appropriate person by virtue of subs (2), the owner or occupier for the time being of the contaminated land in question is an appropriate person in relation to those things.

5.22 Under para 9.7, Annex 2 of Circular 02/2000, a person who is an appropriate person under s 78F(4) or (5) is referred to as a Class B person.

5.23 Paragraph 9.8, Annex 2 of Circular 02/2000 states that the test of 'causing or knowingly permitting' has been used as a basis for establishing liability in environmental legislation for more than 100 years. In the context of Pt IIA, what is 'caused or knowingly permitted' is the presence of a pollutant in, on, or under the land. In the Government's view, the test of 'causing' will require that the person concerned was involved in some active operation, or series of operations, to which the presence of the pollutant is attributable. Such involvement may also take the form of a failure to act in certain circumstances.

5.24 The meaning of the term 'knowingly permit' was considered during a House of Lords debate prior to enactment of the legislation (see *Hansard*, 11 July 1995, col 1497). The then Minister for the Environment, the Earl Ferrers, stated that:

> The test of 'knowingly permitting' would require both knowledge that the substances in question were in, on or under the land and the possession of the power to prevent such a substance being there.

5.25 In *Environment Agency v Empress Car Co (Abertillery) Ltd* [1999] AC 22 the House of Lords held that the defendant's act may be a 'cause' of the pollution without being the most immediate cause; but the court must also consider whether an intervening event was a normal fact of life or something extraordinary. This is considered further in Chapter 19: Criminal law practice and procedure.

5.26 Reference to an appropriate person may be any person including a company. Section 157 of the EPA 1990 applies to Pt IIA and a company director or managing person may be liable for an offence committed by a corporate body.

Liability of owners and occupiers of land

5.27 Only where no Class A person can be found who is responsible for any particular remediation action will the owner or occupier be liable for remediation by virtue solely of that ownership or occupation. Although owners and occupiers may be Class A persons because of their own past actions or omissions. Circular 02/2000 states at para 9.17, Annex 2 that:

> It is ultimately for the courts to decide whether, in any case, it can be said that no Class A person has been found. In the Government's view, the context in which the word is used in Part IIA implies that a person must be in existence in order to be found. Section 78F(4) provides that the owner or occupier shall bear responsibility only 'if no person has, after reasonable inquiry, been found who is an appropriate person to bear responsibility for the things which are to be done by way of remediation.'

5.28 The term 'occupier' is not defined in Pt IIA and it will therefore carry its ordinary meaning.

Apportioning liability

5.29 Annex 3 of Circular 02/2000 provides a comprehensive and complex procedure for determining and apportioning liability for contaminated land remediation, which includes:

(a)   Identifying potential appropriate persons and liability groups;
(b)   Characterizing remediation actions;
(c)   Attributing responsibility to liability groups;
(d)   Excluding members of a liability group; and
(e)   Apportioning liability between members of a liability group.

Special sites

For the more serious incidents of contaminated land the local authority may designate   **5.30**
the land as a special site. Less than one-third of the registered contaminated land sites in
England and Wales are currently designated as special sites. Section 78C of the EPA 1990
provides that if the local authority considers the land that it has identified as being
contaminated warrants being designated a special site then it should seek the Environment Agency's advice on designation. Under s 78C(2) the local authority must also notify
the relevant persons (i.e. the same categories as in s 78B(2)) that it considers a site should
be designated a special site. Section 78C(4) provides that the Environment Agency may
also advise the local authority that it considers certain land to be designated as a special
site.

Regulation 2 of the Contaminated Land Regs 2000 requires the following types of   **5.31**
contaminated land to be designated as a special site:

(a)   land to which reg 3 applies, i.e. where controlled waters are being affected by con-
      tamination and where that water is used for the supply of drinking water fit for human
      consumption, where the water does not meet the requirement of s 82 of the Water
      Resources Act 1991 and where the water is being affected by substances listed in Sch 1 of
      the Contaminated Land Regs 2000 or where it is contained in substrata comprising the
      formation of rocks listed in Sch 1;
(b)   where there is the presence of waste acid tars in, on or under the land (these include tars
      which contain sulphuric acid, were produced from refining benzole, used lubricants or
      petroleum, and are or were stored on land used as a retention basin for the disposal of such
      tars (reg 2(2));
(c)   land which has been used for purification, including refining of crude petroleum or oil
      extraction from petroleum, shale or other bituminous substance, except coal, or for manu-
      facture or processing of explosives;
(d)   land on which an Integrated Pollution Control (IPC) process operates and is controlled by
      the Environment Agency and is unconnected with a remediation process;
(da) land on which a Pollution Prevention Control (PPC) permit has been granted and does not
      comprise solely of things being done under a remediation notice;
(e)   land within a nuclear site;
(f)   land owned or occupied by or on behalf of the Secretary of State for Defence or other
      defence organisation which is being used for naval, military or air force purposes;
(g)   land on which chemical weapons or biological weapons have been or are being, manu-
      factured, produced or disposed of;
(h)   land which has been designated under the Atomic Weapons Establishment Act 1991;
(i)   land for the use of Greenwich Hospital;
(j)   any land adjoining or adjacent to the land above, if it appears to have been contaminated
      as a result of an escape from the actual site.

5.32   Other subsections in reg 2 expand on the categories of land to be designated as a special site.

Designation as a special site

5.33   Section 78D of the EPA 1990 provides that if, on being notified that contaminated land is to be designated a special site, the Environment Agency disagrees with the proposed designation, it must notify the local authority within 21 days of the notice to designate. The local authority will then refer the matter to the Secretary of State for determination under s 78D(1). The Secretary of State will then either confirm or reverse the decision with respect to the whole or any part of the land and will give notice of his decision to the relevant persons and to the local authority (s 78D(4)). The land is not designated as a special site until a determination has been made. If the Agency either approves or provides no objection to the designation, then, under s 78C(6), the designation becomes effective 21 days after the notice to designate. The local authority must then inform everyone that was notified of the proposal to designate that this has taken effect. On designation as a special site the Environment Agency usually becomes the enforcing authority in place of the local authority under s 78Q of the EPA 1990.

5.34   If the Environment Agency decides that a special site should no longer be designated as a special site then it may, under s 78Q(4) of the EPA 1990, give notice to the Secretary of State and the local authority terminating its special site designation.

Duty to maintain a public register of contaminated land

5.35   Section 78R of the EPA 1990 provides that each local authority must maintain a public register containing particulars relating to contaminated land and special sites in its area. The registers must be available for public inspection at all reasonable times, although a reasonable charge may be made for copy documents from the register. Schedule 3 of the Contaminated Land Regs 2000 sets out what details should be held on the register. These include:

- remediation notices, appeals against remediation notices, and any appeal decisions, remediation declarations, and statements;
- appeals against charging notices under s 78P of the EPA 1990 and any appeal decision;
- designation of special sites;
- notification of claimed remediation;
- convictions for offences under s 78M (non-compliance with a remediation notice);
- any guidance; and
- any other environmental controls.

Excluding information from the register

5.36   Certain information may be excluded from the contaminated land register on the ground of national security under s 78S of the EPA 1990 and commercial confidentiality under s 78T. A request to treat information as commercially confidential should be made to the local authority. If the request is approved the information remains commercially confidential for four years, although the person concerned can apply to the local authority for the exclusion of the information to be extended beyond four years.

The refusal of a request may be appealed within 21 days of the date of the refusal. An **5.37** appeal is made to the Secretary of State, whose functions are carried out by the Planning Inspectorate. The appeal may be by way of written representations or a hearing. Where either party, i.e. the appellant or the local authority, requests a hearing or if the Secretary of State decides on a hearing, this must be held in private. If the appeal fails then the information will be placed on the public register seven days after the date of the appeal.

Duty to report on the state of contaminated land

In addition to the local authority obligations of maintaining a public register, under s 78U **5.38** of the EPA 1990 the Environment Agency must prepare and publish from time to time reports on the state of contaminated land. These can be found at: www.environment-agency.gov.uk.

D REMEDIATION

Remediation notice

Where land has been designated land as a special site or land has been identified as con- **5.39** taminated land, under s 78E of the EPA 1990, the enforcing authority (i.e. either the local authority or the Environment Agency) must take steps to ensure that the land is cleaned up. This requires serving a remediation notice on every appropriate person (for appropriate person see paras 5.18 to 5.22).

Consultation prior to service of notice

Section 78H(1) of the EPA 1990 provides that before serving a remediation notice the **5.40** enforcing authority shall reasonably endeavour to consult on what is to be done by way of remediation with:

(a) the person on whom the notice is served;

(b) the owner of any land to which the notice relates;

(c) any person who appears to that authority to be in occupation of the whole or any part of the land; and

(d) any person as may be prescribed by regulations.

Section 78G of the EPA 1990 recognizes that a remediation notice may require an appro- **5.41** priate person to do things by way of remediation that he is not entitled to do. Section 78G(2) enables the enforcing authority to secure any necessary consents while s 78G(5) provides that any person granting consent may be entitled to compensation for doing so. Regulation 6 and Sch 2 of the Contaminated Land Regs 2000 prescribes the procedure for granting compensation.

Contents of the notice

5.42 Under reg 4(1) of the Contaminated Land Regs 2000 a remediation notice must state, among other things:

(a) the name and address of the person on whom the notice is served;

(b) the location and extent of the contaminated land;

(c) the date of any notice under s 78B (identification of contaminated land);

(d) whether the enforcing authority considers the person on whom the notice is served is an appropriate person;

(e) particulars of the significant harm or pollution of controlled waters;

(f) the substances by reason of which the contaminated land in question is contaminated land and if any substances have escaped;

(g) the enforcing authority's reasons for its decisions as to remediation steps;

(k) the name and address of the owner of the contaminated land;

(l) the name and address of any person from whom consent to carry out remediation works is required;
and

(n) that it is an offence, without reasonable excuse, not to comply with the terms of the notice noting the penalties for non-compliance.

5.43 Under reg 4(2) the remediation notice must also state:

(a) that there is a right of appeal against the notice under s 78L;

(b) how, within what period, and on what grounds an appeal may be made;
and

(c) that a notice is suspended, where an appeal is duly made, until the final determination and abandonment of the appeal.

5.44 Under s 78E(3) of the EPA 1990, where two or more persons are appropriate persons in relation to any particular thing that is to be done by way of remediation, the remediation notice must be served on each of them and it must state the proportion of the cost of doing that thing that each person should bear.

Restrictions on serving the notice

5.45 There are certain restrictions and limitations on serving a remediation notice, some of which are considered below.

Time period

5.46 Section 78H(3) of the EPA 1990 sets out time periods for serving a remediation notice this includes that it should not be served within three months of service of the initial notice identifying the contaminated land. Although s 78H(4) provides an exception where:

> it appears to the enforcing authority that the land in question is in such a condition, by reason of substances, in, on or under the land, that there is imminent danger of serious harm, or serious pollution of controlled waters being caused.

Unreasonable cost of remediation

Section 78E(4) of the EPA 1990 provides that the only things that the enforcing authority **5.47** can require to be done by way of remediation are things that it considers reasonable having regard to:

(a)   the likely cost of the work; and

(b)   the seriousness of the harm or pollution of controlled waters.

When deciding what remediation work is to be done, the standard to which any land is, **5.48** or waters are, to be remediated, and to what is, or is not, to be regarded as reasonable, the enforcing authority must, under s 78E(5) have regard to any guidance, e.g. Circular 02/2000, issued for this purpose by the Secretary of State.

Express prohibition on serving a remediation notice

Section 78H(5) provides that the enforcing authority must not serve a remediation notice on **5.49** a person if one or more of the following conditions apply:

(a)   that, taking into account the cost and reasonableness under s 78E, there is nothing by way of remediation that could be specified in a remediation notice;

(b)   that the authority is satisfied that appropriate steps are being, or will be, done by way of remediation without the service of a remediation notice;

(c)   that the person being served with the notice is the authority itself; or

(d)   that the authority is satisfied that using its own powers of remediation under s 78N, it should do what is appropriate by way of remediation.

Remediation declaration

If the enforcing authority does not issue a remediation notice for contaminated land then **5.50** it must issue a remediation declaration, under s 78H(6), setting out what would have been required in a remediation notice and stating why it was precluded from issuing such a notice.

Remediation statement

Section 78H(7) of the EPA 1990 provides that if the enforcing authority cannot issue a **5.51** remediation notice because conditions under subs (5)(b), (c), or (d) apply then the responsible person under those conditions must publish a remediation statement. If they refuse to do so, the enforcing authority may publish the statement and recover the cost of doing so from the responsible person. The remediation statement should state:

(a)   the things that are being, have been, or are expected to be, done by way of remediation in the particular case;

(b)   the name and address of the person who is doing those things; and

(c)   the periods within which each of those things is being, or is expected to be, done.

Section 78H(10) enables the enforcing authority to serve a remediation notice if any of the **5.52** prohibitions contained in subs (5) no longer apply and no other restrictions prevent this.

Other regulatory controls

Section 78YB of the EPA 1990 restricts the use of a remediation notice in cases where other **5.53** regulatory controls apply including:

- IPC;
- waste management under Pt II of the EPA 1990;
- PPC; and
- water regulation under the Water Resources Act 1991.

These controls are discussed further in Section E.

Appeal against remediation notice

5.54   There is a right of appeal against a remediation notice. Section 78L of the EPA 1990 provides that where a remediation notice has been served by a local authority the person served may appeal to the magistrates' court within 21 days of the date of service. If the remediation notice relates to contaminated land designated as a special site then the appeal against the remediation notice is to the Secretary of State. The appeal body (i.e. the magistrates' court or the Secretary of State) is referred to in the legislation as the appellate authority.

Grounds of appeal

5.55   There are 19 separate ground of appeal against a remediation notice contained in the Contaminated Land Regs 2000 and Contaminated Land (Wales) Regs 2001. These include, among other things, that:

(a)   the local authority failed to act in accordance with any guide (e.g. Circular 02/2000) or unreasonably identified all or any of the land to which the notice relates as contaminated land; . . .

(c)   the enforcing authority unreasonably determined the appellant to be the appropriate person who is to bear responsibility for any thing required by the notice to be done by way of remediation; . . .

(g)   service of the notice contravened a provision of s 78H (restrictions and prohibitions on serving remediation notices) . . . ; . . .

(p)   a period specified in the notice within which the appellant is required to do anything is not reasonably sufficient for the purpose; . . .

(s)   there has been some informality, defect or error in, or in connection with, the notice, in respect of which there is no right of appeal under the grounds set out in sub-paras (a) to (r) . . . Although this is subject to reg 7(3) which provides that an appeal based on information, defect or error in the notice will be dismissed if the information, defect or error was not a material one.

5.56   Where an appeal against a remediation notice is duly made, the notice is suspended until determination of the appeal or abandonment of the appeal procedure.

Procedure for appeal to the magistrates' court

5.57   The appeal procedure to the magistrates' court is contained in reg 8 of the Contaminated Land Regs 2000. Regulation 1 provides that an appeal should be made by way of complaint for an order and that subject to s 78L(2) and (3) and regs 7(3), 12, and 13 the Magistrates' Courts Act 1980 shall apply to the proceedings. Because the appeal is made by way of a complaint, the proceedings are regarded as civil proceedings and civil rules of evidence and proof will apply. These are discussed more fully with regard to an appeal against an abatement notice in Chapter 18: Statutory nuisance.

Regulation 8(2) of the Contaminated Land Regs 2000 provides that at the same time as the **5.58** appellant makes a complaint, he should:

(a) file a notice of appeal and serve a copy of it on:
  (i) the enforcing authority;
  (ii) any person named in the remediation notice as an appropriate person;
  (iii) any person named in the notice of appeal as an appropriate person; and
  (iv) any person named in the remediation notice as the owner or occupier of the whole or any part of the land to which the notice relates;
(b) file a copy of the remediation notice to which the appeal relates and serve a copy of it on any person named in the notice of appeal as an appropriate person who was not so named in the remediation notice; and
(c) file a statement of the names and address of any person falling within either (ii), (iii) or (iv) of sub-para (a) above.

Under reg 8(3) of the Contaminated Land Regs 2000 the notice of appeal should state the **5.59** appellant's name, address, and the grounds on which the appeal is made.

Regulation 8(4) provides that in appeal proceedings the justices' clerk or the court may give, **5.60** vary, or revoke directions for the conduct of proceedings, including the timetable, service of documents, submission of evidence, and the order of speeches. Any person that is served with a copy of the notice of appeal under reg 8(2) shall be given notice of and an opportunity to be heard at the hearing of the complaint and any hearing for directions, in addition to the appellant and the enforcing authority.

Procedure for appeal to the Secretary of State

Under s 114(1) of the Environment Act 1995, the Secretary of State may appoint any **5.61** person to exercise any function relating to an appeal under ss 78L or 78T of the EPA 1990. Accordingly, an Inspector from the Planning Inspectorate carries out the appeal functions of the Secretary of State.

Regulation 9(1) of the Contaminated Land Regs 2000 provides that an appeal to the **5.62** Secretary of State against a remediation notice shall be made by notice of appeal that must state:

(a) the name and address of the appellant;
(b) the grounds on which the appeal is made; and
(c) whether the appellant wishes the appeal to be in the form of a hearing or to be disposed of on the basis of written representations.

Regulation 9(2) covers service of the notice of appeal on other specified persons, including **5.63** the Environment Agency, and that the Secretary of State should be served with a statement of names and addresses of any persons on whom the notice of appeal has been served. A copy of the remediation notice should be also be served on all those receiving the notice of appeal. The appellant or the Environment Agency can request, under reg 10 of the Contaminated Land Regs 2000, that the appeal be heard by either a hearing or local inquiry as opposed to being dealt with by written representations. It is the Secretary of State who decides which of the two fora is most appropriate, if at all. If the appeal proceeds as a hearing, the Secretary of State must decide whether it will be held in private or in public at a local inquiry.

5.64 Regulation 11 of the Contaminated Land Regs 2000 provides that on the conclusion of the appeal the Inspector will (unless the power of determining the appeal has also been delegated to the Inspector) write to the Secretary of State with his conclusions and recommendations. The Secretary of State will then make a decision and either accept the recommendations or reject them and make his own determination. The Secretary of State shall then notify the appellant in writing and send copy documents to the Environment Agency and any other person on whom the appellant was required to serve a copy of the notice of appeal.

Determining an appeal against a remediation notice

5.65 Section 78L(2) of the EPA 1990 provides that on any appeal under subs (1) the appellate authority:

(a)   shall quash the notice, if it satisfied that there is a material defect in the notice; but

(b)   subject to that, may confirm the remediation notice, with or without modification, or quash it.

5.66 Under s 78(L)(3), where the appellate authority confirms a remediation notice, with or without modification, it may extend the period specified in the notice for doing what the notice requires to be done. If the remediation notice is modified in a way that is less favourable to the appellant or any other person on whom the notice was served, the appellate authority shall, under reg 12(1) of the Contaminated Land Regs 2000:

(a)   notify the appellant and any person on whom the appellant was required to serve a copy of the notice of appeal of the proposed modification;

(b)   permit any person so notified to make representations in relation to the proposed modification; and

(c)   permit the appellant or any other person on whom the remediation notice was served to be heard if any such person so requests.

5.67 One of the first cases to be heard under Pt IIA of the EPA 1990 has been *Circular Facilities (London) Ltd v Sevenoaks DC* [2004] Env L Rev 283, and brings together a number of the elements of the contaminated land regime. Land in the local authority's area had at one time been clay pits. These had become ponds and then, over time, had been filled with organic matter. The appellant, Circular Facilities, eventually bought the site and in collaboration with the former owner, began to construct houses on the land. A geotechnical survey found that there was organic matter trapped in the clay pits and that this was producing significant quantities of carbon dioxide and methane. The local authority (as the enforcing authority) classified the site as contaminated land under Pt IIA and served a remediation notice. They identified Circular Facilities as the only appropriate Class A person, on the basis that they had constructed the housing and that this had created a significant pollutant linkage by introducing receptors to the land, i.e. the houses and the residents. The appellant appealed against the notice on the grounds that the local authority had unreasonably determined that it was the appropriate Class A person and that the former site owner was the appropriate person. Before the appeal was heard the enforcing authority carried out remedial works on the basis that there was imminent danger of serious harm. At the hearing the appellant argued that the proceedings would be sterile because the remedial works set out in the remediation notice had been carried out. The court held that the proceedings would not be sterile and confirmed the remediation notice adding that the regime and accompanying statutory guidance contemplated this and that determining the appeal would establish who was the appropriate person to bear responsibility for the remediation. District Judge Kelly decided that:

(a) the appellant was an appropriate Class A person, that must have been aware of the content of the geotechnical report and the presence of the organic matter under the land; and

(b) the enforcing authority had not unreasonably excluded the former site owner from being the appropriate person; the appellant had introduced the pathways and/or the receptors in the significant pollutant linkage, and it did not matter that it had not introduced the contaminants to the land, it was enough that it knew of their presence and did nothing to remove them or break the pollutant linkage. The appellant appealled the magistrates' court decision: see below.

Challenging the appeal decision

The appellant may challenge an appeal decision of the magistrates' court or the Secretary **5.68** of State on a point of law by way of a claim for judicial review. In *Circular Facilities v Sevenoaks DC* [2005] EWHC 865 (Admin) the High Court allowed the claim for judicial review of the earlier decision on the basis that the District Judge had given inadequate reasons for his determination and not addressed the relevant facts. The case was remitted for retrial to a different District Judge.

Non-compliance of a remediation notice

Part IIA provides a criminal sanction for non-compliance of a remediation notice. Criminal **5.69** law practice and procedure is covered in Chapter 19: Criminal law practice and procedure. The contaminated land offence is under s 78M(1) of the EPA 1990, which provides that:

If a person on whom an enforcing authority serves a remediation notice fails, without reasonable excuse, to comply with any of the requirements of the notice, he shall be guilty of an offence.

Defence to prosecution for non-compliance of a remediation notice

There is a defence of reasonable excuse contained within the wording of the offence itself. **5.70** Reasonable excuse is considered in Chapter 19: Criminal law practice and procedure. A further statutory defence is provided in s 78M(2) of the EPA 1990, which provides that where the remediation notice is required, under s 78E(3), two or more persons to state the proportion of cost involved in remediation to that person, it shall be a defence to prove that the only reason why it has not been complied with is that one or more of the other persons who are liable to bear the proportion of the cost refused or was unable to comply with the requirement.

Section 78M(3) provides that a defendant guilty of an offence under subs (1) is liable on **5.71** summary conviction to a fine not exceeding £5,000 and to a further fine of £500 for each day on which the offence continues after the conviction. If the offence relates to industrial, trade, or business premises the maximum fine is, under subs (4), £20,000 plus up to £2,000 for each day the offence continues after conviction. See a brief discussion of daily fines in Chapter 19: Criminal law practice and procedure.

Remediation by the enforcing authority

5.72   Section 78N of the EPA 1990 empowers an enforcing authority to do what is appropriate by way of remediation to the relevant land or waters including, under s 78N(3):

(a)   where it is necessary to prevent the occurrence of serious harm or serious pollution of controlled waters, of which there is imminent danger;

(b)   where an appropriate person has agreed in writing for the authority to carry out the work, at the cost of that person;

(c)   where there is non-compliance with a remediation notice;

(d)   where the enforcing authority is precluded by ss 78J or 78K from including something in a remediation notice;

(e)   where the enforcing authority considers that, it would not seek to recover costs or a portion of costs of remediation; or

(f)   where no person has, after reasonable inquiry, been found who is an appropriate person.

Recovering the cost of remediation

5.73   Where the enforcing authority does anything by way of remediation it is, under s 78P of the EPA 1990, entitled in certain circumstances to recover the reasonable cost of all or part of that remediation. Although in deciding how much of its cost to recover, if anything, it must, under s 78P(2) have regard to any hardship that the recovery may cause and to any guidance published for that purpose. Following a decision to recover costs the local authority must serve a charging notice on the person concerned setting out the amount to be charged and the rate of interest to be paid on that amount.

5.74   Section 78P(8) provides that a person served with a charging notice may appeal against the notice to the county court within 21 days of the date of service of the notice. On commencement of the appeal proceedings the charging notice will be suspended. Regulations cover the procedure of appeal against a charging notice.

5.75   On hearing an appeal the court can, under s 78P(9):

(a)   confirm the charging notice without modification;

(b)   order that the notice is to have effect with the substitution of a different amount of the amount originally specified in it; or

(c)   order that the notice is to be of no effect.

5.76   If, following an appeal or after 21 days from service of the charging notice, the charging notice remains, s 78P(11) empowers the enforcing authority to secure the charge as a local land charge on the property and this can be registered against its title. Where a land charge is placed on the property the enforcing authority may, by order, recover the costs to be paid over a specified period until the whole amount is paid.

Civil proceedings

Section 78M(5) of the EPA 1990 provides that if the enforcing authority is of the opinion that   **5.77**
criminal proceedings would afford an ineffectual remedy against someone who has failed
to comply with a remediation notice, the authority may take civil proceedings in the High
Court, for the purpose of securing compliance with the remediation notice. The civil claim
envisaged under this section would be an injunction ordering compliance. Civil law practice
and procedure is discussed in Chapter 17.

E   ALTERNATIVE CONTAMINATED LAND CONTROLS

Breach of other regulatory controls

Section 78YB of the EPA 1990 expressly prohibits the use of Pt IIA where the contaminated   **5.78**
land is regulated under other legislation. It is considered that those operating regimes will
provide a more effective mechanism for control and introducing further regulation of Pt IIA
will simply complicate the situation.

Pollution prevention and control

If contamination of land has occurred in relation to an activity controlled under the PPC or   **5.79**
IPC regimes, enforcement or prohibition proceedings should be taken under the PPC Regs
2000 or Pt I of the EPA 1990 respectively instead of action by the enforcing authority under
Part IIA of the EPA 1990. The PPC/IPC regimes have power to remove the contamination,
i.e. the regulator's power to prevent or remedy harm, under reg 26 of the PPC Regs 2000 and
the power of the chief inspector to remedy harm under s 27 of the EPA 1990, see Chapter 11:
Pollution prevention and control.

Waste management

If a breach of a waste management licence granted under Pt II of the EPA 1990 caused land   **5.80**
to be contaminated, then remediation and sanctions should be pursuant to Pt II. While
land contamination from unlawful waste deposits should be dealt with under s 59 of the EPA
1990, see Chapter 14: Waste.

Water pollution

Under s 161 of the Water Resources Act 1991, the Environment Agency may serve an anti-   **5.81**
pollution works notice on any person who has caused or knowingly permitted a pollutant
to enter controlled waters, including from contaminated land, requiring them to deal with
the problem. If urgent action is necessary the Agency may, under s 161D of the Act, take
remedial action to deal with the pollution and recover the costs from the person responsible
for the pollution. The Environment Agency has published *Policy and Guidance on the Use
of Anti-Pollution Works Notices*, setting out how the Agency intends to use the works notice
powers, particularly when there is an overlap with the contaminated land regime. See also
Chapter 15: Water.

Radioactive substances legislation

5.82   Section 78YC of the EPA 1990 excludes the use of Pt IIA remediation in relation to harm or
pollution of controlled waters from radioactivity, although it enables the Secretary of
State to make further regulations on this if required. Any land contaminated by radioactive
substances will come under the Radioactive Substances Act 1993, which is considered in
Chapter 13: Radiation.

Statutory nuisance

5.83   The statutory nuisance controls under Pt III of the EPA 1990 are not available in resolving
contaminated land problems. Section 79(1A) of the EPA 1990 provides that no matter shall
constitute a statutory nuisance to the extent that it consists of, or is caused by, any land
being in a contaminated state. Under s 79(1B), land is in a contaminated state if, and only if,
it is in such condition, by reasons of substances in, on or under the land that:

> (a)   harm is being caused or there is a possibility of harm being caused; or
> (b)   pollution of controlled waters is being, or is likely to be, caused; . . .

5.84   The section adds that 'harm', 'pollution of controlled waters', and 'substances' have the
same meaning as in Pt IIA of the EPA 1990. However, the exclusion only relates to harm
from contaminated land. This is explained in paras 60–63 of Annex A to Circular 02/2000:

> 60   Parliament has considered that the Part IIA regime, as explained in the statutory guidance,
> sets out the right level of protection for human health and the environment from the
> effects of land contamination. It has therefore judged it inappropriate to leave in place
> the possibility of using another, less precisely defined, system which could lead to the
> imposition of regulatory requirements on a different basis.
>
> 61   From the entry into force of the new contaminated land regime, most land contamination
> issues are therefore removed from the scope of the Statutory Nuisance regime. . . . Any
> matter which would otherwise have been a statutory nuisance will no longer be treated
> as such, to the extent that it consists of, or is caused by, land 'being in a contaminated
> state'. The definition of land which is 'in a contaminated state', and where the statutory
> nuisance regime is therefore excluded, covers all land where there are substances in, on
> or under the land which are causing harm or where there is a possibility of harm being
> caused.
>
> 63   . . . the statutory nuisance regime will continue to apply to the effects of deposits of
> substances on land which give rise to such offence to human senses (such as stenches) as to
> constitute a nuisance, since the exclusion of the statutory nuisance regime applies only
> to harm (as defined in section 78A(4)) and the pollution of controlled waters.

Other regimes

5.85   Annex A to Circular 02/2000 notes that there may be potential overlap between the
regulation of contaminated land under Pt IIA and other regimes including

> (a)   *Food Safety* under Pt I of the Food and Environment Protection Act 1985 which gives
> ministers emergency powers to issue orders for the purpose of prohibiting specified
> agricultural activities in a designated area, in order to protect consumers from exposure
> to contaminated food. The 1985 Act provides for ministers to designate authorities for
> the enforcement of emergency control orders. . . . This includes, for example, the power
> to issue consents in relation to certain activities and the power to give directions on

compliance with the provisions of an order. Enforcing authorities under Part IIA should liaise with the Food Standards Agency about any possible use of the powers in Part I of the 1985 Act. (See Chapter 6: Fishing, farming, and animal health.)

(b) *Health and Safety* — The Health and Safety at Work etc Act 1974, the Construction (Design and Management) Regulations 1994 (SI 1994/3140) and their associated controls are concerned with risks to the public or employees at business and other premises; risks of these kinds could arise as a result of land contamination. Liaison between Part IIA enforcing authorities and the Health and Safety Executive will help to ensure that unnecessary duplication of controls is avoided, and that the most appropriate regime is used to deal with any problems. (See Chapter 7: Human health.)

(c) *Landfill Tax* — The Finance Act 1996 introduced a tax on the disposal of wastes, including those arising from the remediation and reclamation of land. However, an exemption from this tax can be obtained where material is being removed from contaminated land in order to prevent harm, or to facilitate the development of the land for particular purposes. An exemption certificate has to be specifically applied for, through HM Customs and Excise, in each case where it might apply. No exemption certificate will be granted where the material is being removed in order to comply with the requirements of a remediation notice served under section 78E of the 1990 Act. This provides a fiscal incentive for those responsible for carrying out remediation under Part IIA to do so by agreement, rather than waiting for the service of a remediation notice.

(d) *Major Accident Hazards* — The Control of Major Accident Hazards Regulations 1999 (SI 1999/743) (COMAH Regs 1999) require operators of establishments handling prescribed dangerous substances to prepare on-site emergency plans, and the local authorities to prepare off-site emergency plans. The objectives of these emergency plans include providing for the restoration and clean up of the environment following a major accident. The Health and Safety Executive are responsible for overseeing the COMAH Regs 1999. (See Chapter 24: Environmental assessment.)

Civil liability for contaminated land

In certain circumstances, it may be possible for a person with an interest in land to commence civil proceedings in nuisance for land contaminated by the acts or omissions of a neighbour. Although there needs to be some escape from the neighbour's land that causes the contamination. The procedural aspects of nuisance and civil law are considered in Chapter 17: Civil law practice and procedure.   **5.86**

Blue Circle Industries plc v Ministry of Defence, [1999] Env LR 22 the Court of Appeal awarded £5 million for the radioactive contamination of land. See also *Cambridge Water Co v Eastern Counties Leather* [1994] 2 AC 264, although the claim was based upon contamination of an aquifer some distance below ground.   **5.87**

F   PREVENTING LAND CONTAMINATION

Land use planning

5.88   One of the most effective ways of preventing land contamination, and any form of pollution, is to prepare and plan land use to ensure that contamination will not occur or that the risk of contamination is very low. Land use planning is discussed in Chapter 8. One of the fundamental principles is that, under s 57(1) of the Town and Country Planning Act 1990, planning permission is required for the carrying out of any development of land. A potential developer must obtain consent before developing any project and a local planning authority (LPA) must take into account any potential land contamination as a material consideration when determining a planning application.

5.89   As well as preventing land contamination, land use planning influences the way land is used if it is already contaminated. The LPA may attach conditions to the planning permission to ensure that the proposed development will be safe and any contamination is either removed or is rendered harmless. PPS 23: *Planning and Pollution Control* (2005) explains the relationship of the contaminated land regime under Pt IIA of the EPA 1990 to the planning system. It advises that the broad approach, concepts, and principles of that regime with respect to identifying risks for land contamination and dealing with them should be applied to plan-making and the determination of planning applications. The aim is to ensure that planners, developers, and their advisers address contamination at the appropriate stage and consistently with the arrangements under Pt IIA.

5.90   In *Angele Dowmunt-Iwaszkiewicz v First Secretary of State* [2004] EWHC 2537 (QB), the High Court quashed a Planning Inspector's decision to not grant planning permission for residential homes where the development would have meant removing asbestos from the site and justified planning permission for only very special circumstances. It was held that the inspector had not made a quantitative judgement about the level of contamination and any risk relating to it and so the claimant had been genuinely prejudiced by the failure of the Inspector to provide reasons.

Waste management under Part II of the EPA 1990

5.91   Under s 34 of the EPA 1990, those responsible for lawfully depositing waste on land, e.g. landfill operators, are under a duty, among other things, to take all reasonable measures to prevent the escape of waste from his control or that of any other person. The duty of care for managing landfill sites covers sites no longer used and continues until a certificate of completion has been issued for the site. There is, therefore, if the duty of care is met, the opportunity to prevent contamination of land.

KEY DOCUMENTS AND MATERIALS

Environmental Protection Act 1990
Water Resources Act 1991

Environment Act 1995

Contaminated Land (England) Regulations 2000 (SI 2000/227)

Contaminated Land (Wales) Regulations 2001 (WSI 2001/2197)

DETR Circular 2/2000 *Contaminated Land: Implementation of Part IIA of the Environmental Protection Act 1990*

Environment Agency: *Policy and Guidance on the Use of Anti-Pollution Works Notices.* Environment Agency: Bristol

PPS 23: Planning and Pollution Control (2005)

Contaminated Land Exposure Assessment Model www.defra.gov.uk.

LGA and CIEH, *Local Authority Guide to the Application of Part IIA of the EPA 1990* www.lga.gov.uk

www.environment-agency.gov.uk

6

FISHING, FARMING, AND ANIMAL HEALTH

A INTRODUCTION

6.01 Sustainable development, discussed in Chapter 2: Environmental rights and principles, relies on the principle that the pursuit of social, economic, and environmental goals must be integrated instead of trying to balance these, often competing, aims. Further, pursuing the three goals has to be within the environmental capacity of the earth, if meaningful and effective sustainable development is to be achieved. The social function of providing food has one of the greatest adverse impacts on the environment, often unnecessarily so. However, food production is often calculated in terms of financial gain to the producer rather than the number of people that are fed or the loss of life by starvation. At present, the production of food is unsustainable, this is evidenced by the fact that one-fifth of the world's population is malnourished and hungry; over 1 billion people.

6.02 The legal control of food production and consumption is highly regulated and covers a number of apparently discrete areas. As with all environmental areas, the distinction between each area is far less clear than it appears. Outlined below are some of the key areas of food production and consumption that have related environmental concerns including fisheries, farming, animal health, and genetically modified organism (GMOs).

B MARINE FISHERIES

The problem of over-fishing

6.03 Over-fishing in coastal waters is leading to a level of fish stocks where the fish are unable to replenish themselves. This is an international problem. In its 25th report: *Turning the Tide: Addressing the Impact of Fisheries on the Marine Environment* (TSO, 2004) the Royal Commission on Environmental Pollution (RCEP) explained that cod were caught off Newfoundland since the early 1500s and that until the early 1900s, they were mainly caught with hook and line but in later years, much more effective fishing techniques began to be used such as bottom trawling, traps, and gill nets. By 1992 the six Canadian populations of Atlantic Cod had collapsed. The size of the spawning stock had fallen from around 1.6 million tonnes in 1962 to 22,000 tonnes in 1992. The region had been fished to commercial extinction and was the direct result of setting excessive quota levels and over-fishing.

6.04 In 2004, the European Commission predicted that a total ban on fishing for cod, haddock, and whiting in UK coastal waters was now necessary. According to Defra figures to 2002, cited in the RCEP report, of the main commercial fish populations of UK importance just 29% were regarded as within safe biological levels according to population size and fishing rates, and only 47% were above precautionary biomass levels (below which management action should be taken). The tonnage of fish landed in England and Wales decreased by 23% between 1996 and 2003, reflecting declines in population levels. Over-fishing threatens fish as a renewable resource and a vital source of food. It risks fishing and way of life to many.

Legislative control of marine fishing

Marine fishing is subject to strict legislative control that derives from EU Regulations and the **6.05** Common Fisheries Policy. Council Regulation (EC) No. 2371/2002 on the conservation and sustainable exploitation of fisheries resources under the Common Fisheries Policy is the main regulatory control. This has direct effect in the UK. Supporting domestic legislation includes the Fisheries Act 1981. Section 30(2) of this Act provides that:

> Ministers may by order make such provision as appears to them to be requisite for the enforce-
> ment of any enforceable Community restriction or other obligation relating to sea fishing; and
> any such order may in particular contain provisions which (with any necessary modification)
> apply or correspond to any relevant provisions of the [Sea Fish (Conservation) Act 1967] or the
> [Sea Fisheries Act 1968].

There are a number of enforcement regulations made under this provision including, for **6.06** example, the Sea Fishing (Enforcement of Community Control Measures) Order 2000, SI 2000/51 (Sea Fishing Enforcement Order).

For commercial sea fishing, fish quotas are set annually on a national basis and run for the **6.07** calendar year from 1 January. The quotas are set on the basis of scientific samples of fish populations and from the data provided from fishing boats. It is essential that the data as to species, amounts, and area of capture are correct so that scientists have an accurate picture of fish stocks and can advise on action to protect species of fish in areas under pressure from over-fishing. If not, then fish stocks are likely to fall below viable levels before unsustainable fish stocks become detected and corrective action can be taken.

UK regulatory bodies

The UK Fisheries Departments include, among others, Defra and the National Assembly **6.08** for Wales Agriculture Department. The Centre for Environment Fisheries and Aquaculture Science (CEFAS) is a government department that operates in this area. Licensing and quota management are devolved to national governments. There are also 12 Sea Fisheries Committees (SFCs) that regulate 72 local sea fisheries around England and Wales covering waters up to six nautical miles out to sea. Defra's Sea Fisheries Inspectorate carries out the compliance and enforcement of fishing regulation although the national quota management system is based upon informal agreement between government and fishing groups known as Producer Organisations, which were set up under the Common Fisheries Policy.

Licensing fishing vessels

Under EC Regulation 2371/2002, Member States are required to operate a fishing vessel **6.09** licensing system for fishing operations and national fishing fleets. The UK operates a restrictive licensing system for commercial fishing whereby owners of new fishing vessels must secure a licence from an existing licensed vessel and transfer the licence to the new vessel. A transfer is only approved if the capacity, tonnage, and engine power of the new vessel is no greater than that of the existing vessel. Further, there may be a surcharge on the new vessel to account for its increased catching efficiency.

6.10 The vessel licence defines the type and, in some circumstances, the volume of fish that can be caught and landed. Licence restrictions may be adjusted throughout the year as quotas are exhausted or increased. All fishing vessel masters and owners must keep an accurate record of fish species caught and landed, which are sent to Defra. Sales notes produced by sales agents must also be forwarded to Defra and these are checked against the figures submitted by fishing operators. The information provided is used to ensure that those limits are not exceeded. When the UK's fish quota for a species is reached, fishing for that species should stop to help fish stocks recover. Licences may contain procedural restrictions such as the requirement to land at specified ports or to give prior notification of landing and the need for vessels to maintain a genuine economic link with the UK.

Offences under the Fisheries Act 1981

6.11 Section 30(1) of the Fisheries Act 1981 provides that enforceable Community restrictions relating to sea fishing are applicable and that if any fishing boat fishes within British fishery limits in contravention of such restriction the master, the owner, and the charterer (if any) are each guilty of an offence. Article 4(3) of the Sea Fishing Enforcement Order provides that owners and masters of fishing vessels found fishing without a licence or breaching the conditions are liable on summary conviction to a maximum fine of £50,000 plus an additional sum up to the value of the fish. Courts also have the power to disqualify a person from holding a licence.

Other relevant marine environment legislation

6.12 SFCs must also have regard to the Sea Fisheries (Wildlife Conservation) Act 1992 and the Environment Act 1995 (EA 1995), which requires that they have regard for the wider implications of their actions in relation to fisheries as far as other flora and fauna are concerned. The EA 1995 gives SFCs the power to promote bye-laws to control fishing if there is a wider environmental need for such action. Further, Pt II of the Food and Environmental Protection Act 1985 (FEPA 1985) seeks to protect the marine ecosystem by requiring a licence to be obtained from the licensing authority to deposit any articles or substances in the sea or under the seabed.

Proposals for reform

6.13 The European Commission in its Green Paper: *The Future of the Common Fisheries Policy* (2001) suggested that overall the European fishing fleet should be reduced by up to 40% to help sustain the marine environment. The RCEP concluded that a new framework was required to provide the proper legal and institutional context for measures to secure environmental improvements. It recommended that the UK Government should develop a comprehensive system of marine spatial planning that sets out the principles and long-term goals for protecting the marine environment and promoting the sustainable use of the sea. It added that, among other things, the devolved administrations should introduce Marine Acts in their areas that set out the principles for managing human impacts on the marine environment.

In 2004, Defra published the *Review of the Marine Fisheries and Environmental Enforcement*, **6.14** which recommended that the idea of a single marine enforcement agency be pursued.

C INLAND FISHING

For inland waterways, environmental concerns relating to fishing arise from water **6.15** pollution, illegal fishing, and unlawful movement of fish. The impact of illegal fishing and movement is that fish stocks in rivers are well below what may be regarded as a level to sustain a particular population. The Environment Agency reported in evidence to the Government's Environmental Audit Committee in 2004 that two-thirds of the 63 principal salmon rivers were not achieving conservation limits and that fish moved into a new environment can have a harmful effect on indigenous species with the transfer of diseases and parasites. The regulatory control of inland fishing is outlined below; water pollution is considered in Chapter 15: Water.

Unlicensed fishing, illegal fish removals, transfer and introduction

The key legislative control of unlicensed fishing and poaching is the Salmon and Freshwater **6.16** Fisheries Act 1975 (SFFA 1975). The Environment Agency is the regulatory authority. This operates through a series of prohibitions that are supported by criminal penalties if convicted of a related offence. For example, s 1(1)(a) of the SFFA 1975 provides that no person shall:

(a) use . . . a firearm; an otter lath or jack, wire or snare; a crossline or setline; a spear, gaff, stroke-haul, snatch or other like instrument; a light; . . . for taking or killing salmon, trout or freshwater fish for the purpose of taking or killing salmon, trout or freshwater fish;

(b) have in his possession any instrument mentioned in para (a) above intending to use it to take or kill salmon, trout or freshwater fish; or

(c) throw or discharge any stone or other missile for the purpose of taking or killing, or facilitating the taking or killing of any salmon, trout or freshwater fish.

Section 1(2) of the SFFA 1975 provides that anyone contravening s 1 shall be guilty of an **6.17** offence. It is a defence to prove that the act done was for the purpose of the preservation or development of a private fishery and with the prior written permission of the Environment Agency. A person guilty of an offence against any provision of the Act will be subject on summary conviction to the sentence specified in Sch 4, Pt 1 of the SFFA 1975, which includes for example, a s 1 offence on summary conviction, a maximum penalty of a £5,000 fine and/or three months' imprisonment and an unlimited fine and/or two years' imprisonment for conviction on indictment.

Other offences under the SFFA 1975 include, among other things: **6.18**

s 2(4) wilfully disturbing spawning fish (maximum penalty £2,500 fine on summary conviction);

s 19   fishing during the closed season (maximum penalty £2,500 fine on summary
        conviction);

s 27   unlicensed fishing (with a net) (maximum penalty £5,000 fine and/or three months'
        imprisonment on summary conviction, and an unlimited fine and/or two years'
        imprisonment for conviction on indictment).

s 31   the offence of obstruction of a water bailiff (maximum penalty £2,500 fine on
        summary conviction).

General nature conservation protection

6.19   As well as regulating fishing activities, fish species are also covered by more general nature
        conservation laws, e.g. those contained in the Wildlife and Countryside Act 1981 (WCA
        1981). This is more fully considered in Chapter 16: Wildlife and nature conservation. There
        are a number of fish species protected under Sch 5 of the WCA 1981 and the Conservation
        (Natural Habitats, etc) Regulations 1994 (SI 1994/2716) such as the Atlantic Salmon (which
        is protected only in fresh water).

6.20   There is very active support for clean rivers in the UK by fishermen and fishing groups. For
        example, the Anglers' Conservation Association, formed in 1948 to tackle water pollution,
        has pursued a number of civil claims and criminal prosecutions on behalf of members to
        ensure that loss and harm to watercourses are compensated and protected.

D   ANIMAL HEALTH

6.21   There was a stark reminder of the link between environment and animal health during the
        foot and mouth crisis of 2001. The topic is large and includes the following:

- animal by-products;
- animal health and welfare;
- diseases such as BSE, foot and mouth, rabies, scrapie, and tuberculosis;
- illegal imports;
- international trade; and
- livestock movements.

6.22   Defra is the government department with overall responsibility for animal health and
        welfare and further reference for any of the above should be made to the Defra website. For
        the purpose of illustrating aspects of animal health and its interaction with environmental
        law and the environment there is further consideration of the interlinked topics of animal
        health and welfare and illegal import. International trade is considered in Chapter 16:
        Wildlife and nature conservation.

Animal health and welfare

6.23   In 2003, Defra published an animal health and welfare strategy that aimed to achieve a
        continuing improvement in the health and welfare of kept animals and to protect the public

from animal diseases. The current law on protecting animals from cruelty and suffering is found in a number of specific pieces of legislation. These are outlined below.

Protection of animals

There are a number of related pieces of legislation arising from and amending the Protection **6.24** of Animals Act 1911 (PAA 1911). These include, for example, the Cock Fighting Act 1952, under which it is illegal to organize or advertise cockfights, the Abandonment of Animals Act 1960 and the Protection of Animals (Amendment) Act 2000 which make provision for the care, disposal, and slaughter of animals. Collectively, the Acts cover domestic and captive animals with a view to preventing cruelty and suffering. Under s 1(1) of the PAA 1911 it is an offence to, among other things:

(a) cruelly beat, kick, ill-treat, over-ride, over-drive, over-load, torture, infuriate, or terrify any animal, . . .;
(b) cause unnecessary suffering through transportation;
(c) take part in the fighting or baiting of an animal;
(d) administer poisonous or injurious substances without reasonable excuse;
(e) permit operations to be carried out without due care and humanity; or
(f) tether any horse, ass or mule in such a manner as to cause unnecessary suffering.

There are defences within the elements of some of the offences, e.g. without reasonable **6.25** excuse and without due care and humanity. Further, s 1(3) of the PAA 1911 also provides that nothing in s 1 renders illegal any act carried out lawfully under the Animal (Scientific Procedures) Act 1986, or shall apply:

(a) to the commission or omission of any act in the course of the destruction, or the preparation for destruction, of any animal as food for mankind, unless such destruction or such preparation was accompanied by the infliction of unnecessary suffering; or
(b) to the coursing or hunting of any captive animal, unless such animal is liberated in an injured, mutilated, or exhausted condition; but a captive animal shall not, for the purposes of being coursed or hunted, or after it has been recaptured, or if it is under control and a captive animal shall not be deemed to be coursed or hunted within the meaning of this subsection if it is coursed or hunted in an enclosed space from which it has no reasonable chance of escape.

Under s 1(2) of the Act, an owner is deemed to have permitted cruelty if he fails to **6.26** exercise reasonable care and supervision in respect of the protection of the animal from cruelty. Unnecessary suffering can be caused by either acts or omission. In *Whiting v Jones* (1910) 74 JP 324 this included where an owner knew the condition of a horse was poor when he bought it and then failed to take steps to prevent it being worked in that condition.

There have been a number of cases defining s 1 of the PAA 1911 and the related legislation **6.27** enacted both before and after this Act. *Johnson v Needham* [1909] 1 KB 626 held that each of the words contained in s 1(1) of the Act (e.g. beat, kick, ill-treat etc.) create separate offences. In *Ford v Wiley* (1889) 23 QBD 203 the court held the mere infliction of pain for a necessary purpose was not cruelty but that unnecessary and unreasonable use was. In *RSPCA v Isaacs* [1994] Crim LR 517 the suffering becomes unnecessary when it is not inevitable, in that it can be terminated or alleviated by some reasonably practicable measure. In *Bandeira &*

Brannigan v RSPCA (2000) 164 JP the court affirmed that whether any countryside activity amounted to ill treatment was a question of fact for the magistrates.

Prosecution for cruelty and breach of animal welfare

6.28 Anyone can prosecute an offence under the animal welfare Acts although prosecutions are usually brought by the police, local authority, or certain animal welfare organizations such as the RSPCA. Under s 1 of the PAA 1911, a person convicted of an offence is liable on summary conviction to a maximum penalty of a £5,000 fine and/or six months' imprisonment. There is a right of appeal to the Crown Court against an order under s 14 of the Act.

Transfer of ownership and destruction of animal

6.29 Sections 2 and 3 of the PAA 1911 provides that if the owner of an animal is convicted of an offence under the Act, the court may, if it thinks fit, deprive the owner of ownership of the animal. Where the court is satisfied that it would be cruel to keep the animal alive, it may direct that the animal be destroyed and that the owner pays any reasonable cost of destruction. Section 14 states that there is no right of appeal against an order for destruction of the animal.

Training animals

6.30 The Performing Animals (Regulation) Act 1925 requires trainers and exhibitors of such animals to be registered with the local authority. It also empowers the police and local authority officers, who may include a vet, to enter premises where animals are being trained and exhibited, and if cruelty and neglect is detected, a magistrates' court can prohibit or restrict the training or exhibition of the animals and suspend or cancel registration.

Pet animals

6.31 The Pet Animal Acts 1951, as amended by the PAA (Amendment) 1983, protects the welfare of animals sold as pets. Section 1 of the Act requires any person keeping a pet shop to be licensed by the local authority. Before granting a licence the authority must be satisfied that the animals are kept in clean and suitable accommodation, that they are supplied with appropriate food and drink, and that they are adequately protected from disease and fire. The local authority may attach conditions to a licence, they may inspect licensed premises, and may refuse a licence if conditions at the premises are unsatisfactory or if the terms of the licence are not being complied with.

6.32 A person aggrieved by a local authority decision not to grant a licence or against conditions attached may, under s 1(4) of the PAA 1951, appeal to the magistrates' court. Any person contravening the provisions of s 1 shall be guilty of an offence and is liable on summary conviction of a maximum penalty of £500 and/or three months' imprisonment.

6.33 The Abandonment of Animals Act 1960 provides that it is an offence to abandon any animal without reasonable excuse in circumstances likely to cause it unnecessary suffering. In *Hunt v Duckering* [1993] Crim LR 678 the court held that abandonment meant leaving an animal unattended in circumstances where suffering was likely and where there was sufficient evidence to prove that the defendant had relinquished, wholly disregarded, or given up his duty of care for the animal. Other legislation aimed to protect animals includes:

- Slaughter of Poultry Act 1967;
- Agriculture (Miscellaneous Provisions) Act 1968, which covers the welfare of livestock;
- Conservation of Seals Act 1970;
- Slaughterhouses Act 1974;
- Dangerous Wild Animals Act 1976;
- Bees Act 1980, controlling the pests and diseases affecting bees;
- Animal Health Act 1981, as amended, which provides general powers to Ministers to make orders and to authorize regulations relating to the prevention and spreading of disease;
- Animal Health and Welfare Act 1984;
- Protection of Badgers Act 1992;
- Wild Mammals (Protection) Act 1996; and
- Fur Farming (Prohibition) Act 2000.

Defra guidance

The Defra Circular 1/2002: *The Keeping of Wild Animals* outlines government policy on the   **6.34**
keeping of wild animals in captivity and provides general guidance to local authorities on their duties and powers under the Protection of Animals Act 1911 and other related legislative provisions. This is available from www.defra.gov.uk. There are a number of organizations that aim to help animals suffering from cruelty and abuse including Animal Aid, RSPCA, RSPB, and WWF-UK. See further on the protection of animals and wildlife in Chapter 16: Wildlife and nature conservation.

Illegal imports

Securing animal health includes regulating the trade and international movement of meat   **6.35**
and animal products. For example, it is now commonly accepted that the foot and mouth disease epidemic of 2001 began by cattle being fed inadequately boiled swill that contained infected meat. The swill was believed to have been smuggled into the UK from countries with foot and mouth disease.

HM Customs and Excise (HMCE) have been given the legal powers and responsibility for   **6.36**
enforcing controls on illegal smuggling of products of animal origin from countries outside the EU. Import controls help to ensure that they meet the same standards as food produced within the EU. The Products of Animal Origin (Third Country Imports) (England) Regulations 2004 (SI 2004/1214) are the main regulations relating to imports of products of animal origin and give effect to Directive 97/78/EC laying down principles governing the organization of veterinary checks on products entering the Community from third countries. The Regulations also confer responsibility to HMCE to enforce controls on prohibited goods at points of entry who can use its powers under the Customs and Excise Management Act 1979 (CEMA 1979) under which it has wide-ranging powers, including powers of search, seizure, and arrest. Section 170 of CEMA 1979 smuggling prohibited or restricted items is an offence with unlimited fines and/or a maximum of seven years' imprisonment. HMCE would use the CEMA 1979 provisions for repeat offenders and who have knowingly imported illegal products.

6.37 Other regulatory control comes under the Products of Animal Origin (Import and Export) Regulations 1996 (SI 1996/3124), as variously amended (PAO Regs 1996). Regulation 20(1) provides that no person shall import any product of animal origin except at a border inspection post. Under reg 21(1) of the PAO Regs 1996 no person shall import any product of animal origin unless he has given to either the official veterinary surgeon at the border inspection post or the Minister the required advance notice. Under regulation 37(1) of the PAO Regs 1996, a person contravening any provision of the Regulations or any notice served under them shall be guilty of an offence. Under reg 37(3) of the PAO Regs 1996, a person found guilty of an offence is liable, on summary conviction, to a maximum penalty of a £5,000 fine and/or three months' imprisonment, or an unlimited fine and/or two years' imprisonment for conviction on indictment.

E FARMING

Introduction

6.38 Agriculture is the science, art, and occupation of cultivating land and rearing livestock. Farming is the business of agriculture. It has a profound effect on the environment and, in providing the main source of the world's food, it has a critical role to play in the pursuit of sustainable development. However, intensive farming can have highly adverse impacts. For example, in many countries, the demand for meat production to meet western consumption patterns has resulted in the clearance of ancient forests. On deforestation, these regions soon deteriorate to unmanageable desert areas. Similar patterns of intensive and unsustainable agricultural practices are found in the UK, with large areas of intensive farming having an adverse effect on a locality by, for example, the compacting of soil causing significant water run off and consequent flooding, and the pollution of watercourses by pesticides and slurry contamination. Yet UK farming contributes over £6 billion a year to the economy, it employs over half a million people and uses around three-quarters of the national land area.

Defra's action on agriculture

6.39 Defra is the government department responsible for farming and agriculture. It recognizes that there are a number of contemporary concerns with farming and highlights the following areas of environmental activity:

- tackling air quality and, in particular, ammonia produced in farming;
- the impact of climate change and the need to adapt to the changing weather patterns and more extreme weather conditions;
- farmland conservation; and
- water pollution, including publishing the *Code of Good Agricultural Practice for the Protection of Water* (1998), *Guidelines for Farmers in NVZs* (2002), and a review of obligations relating to nitrate vulnerable zones to meet the requirements of the EU Directive 2003/35/EC providing for public participation in respect of the drawing up of certain plans and programmes relating to the environment (the Public Participation Directive). The Nitrates Directive Action Programme is one of the plans and programmes identified.

Common Agricultural Policy

Farming practice in the UK is dominated by the Common Agricultural Policy (CAP), which was introduced in 1962 to meet a strategic need for food security in Europe. CAP created a deliberate increase in domestic food production and reduced dependence on imports. Its main mechanisms were market management to remove surpluses and protection for the domestic market through import taxes and export subsidies. EU agreement on reform of the CAP was reached in 2003 with a simplified scheme that aims to encourage more environmentally friendly farming practices, such as organic production.   **6.40**

Legal framework for the CAP

The 2003 CAP agreement was formalized by the adoption of seven EU Regulations. These include regulations dealing with rural development and market reforms (covering cereals, rice, dried fodder, and milk). Arguably the most important is Council Regulation (EC) No. 1782/2003 of 29 September 2003 establishing common rules for direct support schemes under the common agricultural policy and establishing certain support schemes for farmers (the CAP Reform Regulation 2003). It amended the following EU Regulations: **6.41**

- 2019/93 relating to small Aegean islands;
- 1452/2001 on measures for agriculture in French overseas departments;
- 1453/2001 for products of the Azores and Madeira;
- 1454/2001 for certain products of the Canary Islands;
- 1868/94 on potato starch;
- 1251/1999 on arable crops;
- 1254/1999 on beef and veal;
- 1673/2000 on flax and hemp grown for fibre;
- 2358/71 on the common organization of the market in seeds; and
- 2529/2001 on the common organization of the market in sheep meat and goat meat.

The CAP Reform Regulation 2003 sets out a legal framework for the new decoupled scheme of agricultural subsidy; the Single Payment Scheme. It has been subject to further amendment relating to specific farming areas such as cereals (Reg 1784/2003), rice (Reg 1785/2003), dried fodder (Reg 1786/2003), and milk (Reg 1787/2003).   **6.42**

In addition to the CAP Reform Regulation 2003, as amended, there are a number of detailed rules set out in Commission Regulations such as Commission Regulation 795/2004 relating to the Single Payment Scheme and Commission Regulation 1973/2004, which includes the rules for all the coupled schemes that apply from 1 January 2005 of which Protein Premium, Nuts, and Energy crops are relevant for the UK context.   **6.43**

Communications to the European Commission

Under the terms of Commission Regulation 795/2004, Member States were obliged to communicate to the European Commission, by August 2004, the basis on which they would implement the Single Payment Scheme and associated issues, including any proposed recoupling of support. The communication by the UK to the Commission may be found on the Defra website.   **6.44**

Environmental protection and farming

6.45   The legal controls on agricultural activities relating to the environment are outlined below. These include a number of different legal sectors such as land use planning and waste as well as specific agricultural regulation with environmental aspects.

Pollution, prevention and control

6.46   The larger farming operations are controlled under the pollution, prevention and control regime. Section 6.9, Pt 1, Sch 1 of the Pollution Prevention and Control (England and Wales) Regulations 2000 (SI 2000/1973) covers intensive farming including rearing poultry or pigs intensively in an installation with more than 40,000 places for poultry; 2,000 places for production of pigs (over 30 kg) or 750 places for sows. Such agricultural activities require a PPC permit to operate. Similarly, certain operations will be regulated under the integrated pollution control (IPC) regime. It is an offence to carry on activities without a permit, see Chapter 11: Pollution prevention and control.

Control of air pollution

6.47   The legislative control of farming in terms of air pollution includes:

- The Heather and Grass Burning (England and Wales) Regulations 1986 (SI 1986/428) as amended by SI 1987/1208 and made under s 20 of the Hill Farming Act 1946. Section 20(2) of the Act provides that any person contravening regulations made under this section shall be liable on summary conviction to a maximum fine of £1,000.
- Under s 161A of the Highways Act 1980 if a person lights a fire on land next to a highway or either directs or permits this and as a result a highway user is injured, interrupted, or endangered by the fire, or by smoke from the fire, that person is guilty of an offence and on summary conviction is liable to a maximum penalty of a £5,000 fine.
- Section 79 of the Environmental Protection Act 1990 (EPA 1990) that covers air emissions from farms causing a statutory nuisance, see Chapter 18: Statutory nuisance.
- Parts I and III of the Clean Air Act 1993 that prohibits the emission of dark smoke and smoke from a chimney apply to farming. Although the Clean Air (Emission of Dark Smoke) Exemption Regulations 1969 (SI 1969/1263) allow the limited burning of farm wastes including animal carcasses and pesticide containers.
- The Crop Residue (Burning) Regulations 1993 (SI 1993/1366) prohibits the burning of cereal straw and stubble and the residue of field beans and peas. Exceptions to the prohibition are to eradicate pests, provided a notice has been served under the Plant Health (GB) Order 1993 (SI 1993/1320), for education and research, and to dispose of broken bales and the remains of straw stacks. A person contravening the Regulations is subject to, on summary conviction, a maximum fine of £5,000.
- Air emissions from farms regulated under PPC and IPC will be subject to restrictions through conditions in permits or authorizations: see Chapter 11: Pollution prevention and control.

6.48   Defra has published guidance on air pollution: *The Code of Good Agricultural Practice for the Protection of Air* (1998), which outlines relevant legislation for farmers including advice on the reduction of odour and reducing the need to burn waste and other matter such as straw.

Waste

Illegal disposal of waste on farmland is a continuing problem, and although, on occasions, **6.49** the owner/occupier may be responsible, quite often the farmer is quite innocent and is as much a victim of the waste disposal as the environment itself. Waste, including fly-tipping and unlawful disposal is considered in Chapter 14: Waste.

Water pollution

Many water pollution incidents arise from agricultural operations. Pollutants include pesti- **6.50** cides and nitrates; solid wastes and sewage cause deoxygenation (arising from farm waste and sewage), nutrient enrichment such as fertilisers encourages algae and plant growth. For example, in *R v Lomas & ors* (2003) Env Times Vol. 9.2 p 35, three farmers were convicted of allowing silage effluent to enter a watercourse and resulting in the death of around 100 trout. The clean up and restocking operation costs of over £11,500 were recharged and paid by the defendants. They were also fined £1,000 each and ordered to pay costs of £556. In *R v Coles* (2004) Env Times Vol. 10.1 p 31 the defendant was found guilty of polluting a tributary with agricultural effluent. The pollution incident was traced to vegetable washings water that had been spread on a field and then entered the farm's drainage system and discharged into the watercourse. On summary conviction, the defendant was fined £11,255 including costs. The water pollution regime under the Water Resources Act 1991 is covered further in Chapter 15: Water.

Nuisance and other controls

Nuisance claims, whether private, public, or statutory can be used either to prevent or abate **6.51** a nuisance arising from agricultural operations. These are considered in Chapters 17 to 19. The use of Anti-social Behaviour Orders has recently extended to farming operations. In *R v Hagan* (2005) (unreported, but see Law Gazette 6.1.05, p 5), a farmer pleaded not guilty to failing to comply with an ASBO without reasonable excuse after it is alleged that he failed to constrain his pigs from straying on to a neighbour's land.

Land use planning

While some development on agricultural land falls outside the Town and Country Planning **6.52** regime, there is still the need for certain activities to be subject to control. In particular, environmental impact assessment (EIA) has a useful role to play in informing major agricultural development proposals. In *R (Lebus & ors) v South Cambridgeshire DC* [2002] EWHC 2009 (Admin) the court held that an EIA was required for an egg production unit for 12,000 'free range' chickens. See also Chapters 8: Land use planning and 24: Environmental assessment.

Landscape, recreation, and public access

The Countryside and Rights of Way Act 2000 (CRoW Act 2000) repealed a number of areas **6.53** of law in relation to access to the countryside and public rights of way. To clarify the rights and responsibilities of users, owners, and occupiers of land Defra published the guide: *Landscape Protection, Recreation and Public Access* (2003).

Removal of surface soil on agricultural land

6.54   Under s 1(1) of the Agricultural Land (Removal of Surface Soil) Act 1953 a person is guilty of an offence if he:

(a)   removes surface soil from agricultural land with a view to the sale of that soil, and

(b)   the removal of that soil constitutes development within the meaning of the Town and Country Planning Act 1990 (TCPA 1990), and

(c)   the quantity of soil so removed in any period of three months amounts to more than five cubic yards.

6.55   Prosecution under the Act requires the consent of the Attorney General or the DPP. Further, s 1(2) of the Act provides that s 1(1) does not apply to the cutting of peat or to the removal of so much surface soil as it is reasonably necessary to remove in the course of cutting turf. Also, s 2(3) of the Act provides that it shall be a defence to show that, before carrying out the removal of soil, it was determined under s 64 of the TCPA 1990, that the operations would not constitute development. A person guilty of an offence under s 1(1) shall be liable on summary conviction to a maximum penalty of a £1,000.

Collection of kitchen waste for animal feedstuffs

6.56   A local authority may collect kitchen and other waste in their area for use as animal feeding stuffs. Section 9 of the Agriculture (Miscellaneous Provisions) Act 1954, provides for the collection of kitchen waste etc. for animal feeding stuffs under which a local authority may make bye-laws regulating such kitchen or other waste.

Prevention of the spread of weeds

6.57   If certain specified weeds are growing on land the Secretary of State may, under s 1 of the Weeds Act 1959, serve on the occupier of the land written notice requiring him, with a specified time, to take necessary action to prevent the weeds from spreading. Examples of such weeds include spear thistle, creeping or field thistle, curled dock, broad-leaved dock, and ragwort. It is an offence to unreasonably fail to comply with the notice. A person guilty of such an offence is liable, on summary conviction, to a maximum penalty of £1,000. A Minister may only commence proceedings, although under s 5, this power may be delegated to a county council or metropolitan district council.

Risk of poisoning

6.58   Poisoning on farms may arise through the use of a number of chemicals used in controlling pests and diseases. Pesticides are a common form of control and are considered in Section F below.

F   PESTICIDES

6.59   Pesticides is a general term for a number of poisons including herbicides, rodenticides, and insecticides. Some of the most highly toxic insecticides are organophosphate and organochlorine. While pesticide use is used in a number of industries, e.g. in spraying timbers used in buildings, they are predominantly used in agriculture.

Regulation and control of pesticides is undertaken by the Pesticide Safety Directorate (PSD), **6.60** an executive agency of Defra responsible for the issue of consents including licences for sale, supply, storage, and use. Approval depends on the provision of safety and efficacy data showing that the product works and is safe to operators, consumers, and the environment in general.

Legislation

There are various EU Directives controlling pesticides and similar chemicals. EU Directive **6.61** 79/117/EEC prohibiting the placing on the market and use of plant protection products containing certain active substances, as variously amended, bans the use and marketing of plant protection products. While EU Directive 98/8/EC on the placing of biocidal products on the market regulates many of the chemicals not already covered by earlier legislation.

The Directives are transposed in the UK by both primary and secondary legislation. Part III of **6.62** FEPA 1985 as variously amended by e.g. the Pesticides Act 1998, provides under s 16(1) that Pt III shall have effect with a view to:

(a) the continuous development of means:
    (i) to protect the health of human beings, creatures and plants;
    (ii) to safeguard the environment; and
    (iii) to secure safe, efficient and humane methods of controlling pests; and
(b) making information about pesticides available to the public;

Section 16(2) and (3) of FEPA 1985 confers wide powers on Ministers to make regulations **6.63** relating to pesticides such as prohibiting and controlling their use, reviewing, revoking, amending or suspending any approvals granted, controlling the import, sale, supply, use, or storage and advertisement. Examples of regulations include the Plant Protection Products Regulations 2003, as amended (SI 2003/3241) and the Pesticides (Maximum Residue Levels in Crops, Food and Feeding Stuffs) (England and Wales) Regulations 1999 (SI 1999/3483) to identify certain pesticide residues that may be left in a crop, food, or feeding stuff, and to specify maximum levels of pesticide that crops, food, and feeding stuffs may contain, implementing to a limited extent EU Directives 86/362/EEC, 86/363/EEC, and 90/642/EEC on maximum levels of pesticides in crops, food, and feeding stuffs.

The Control of Pesticides Regulations 1986 (1986/1510), as amended, provide for the control **6.64** of pesticides and apply to certain substances, preparations, or organisms prepared or used for specified purposes (including protecting plants or wood or other plant products from harmful organisms, regulating the growth of plants, giving protection against harmful creatures and rendering such creatures harmless) as if they were pesticides. The safe use of a pesticide product is set out in Conditions of Approval under the Control of Pesticides Regulations 1986 and should be repeated on every product label. The conditions are based on the safe use of the pesticide and to prevent exposure to wildlife species and humans. Control of pesticides is largely implemented by the use of consents granted to applicants by the PSD to enable them to carry out an activity that is otherwise prohibited.

Regulatory control

6.65 Section 19 of FEPA 1985 sets out the enforcement powers that may be exercised by the PSD. These include the power to enter land if there are reasonable grounds to believe that any pesticide is being or had been applied to or stored on it. If an authorized person considers that an offence is being committed under s 16(12) of the Act then he may serve a notice to that effect stating that the physical circumstances of the situation must remain undisturbed for as long as is reasonably necessary and that any reasonable remedial or preventive measures shall be taken.

6.66 Under s 16(12) of FEPA 1985, a person who, without reasonable excuse, contravenes any regulations made under the Act shall be guilty of an offence. Under s 16(13) 'contravenes' includes 'fails to comply with'. Section 22 of FEPA 1985 provides a general defence of due diligence whereby it is a defence for the person charged to prove that he took all reasonable precautions and exercised all due diligence to avoid the commission of the offence. Section 21(3) of the Act provides that a person, on summary conviction, shall be liable to a £5,000 fine, or an unlimited fine for conviction on indictment.

Aerial crop spraying

6.67 Schedule 4 of the Control of Pesticides Regulations 1986 sets out conditions relating to consent to the use of pesticides by aerial application. Paragraph 1 or Sch 4 provides that:

> No person shall undertake an aerial application of a pesticide unless (a) an aerial application certificate granted under article 42(2) of the Ari Navigation Order 1985 is held by that person, that person's employer or the main contractor undertaking the aerial application, and (b) the pesticide to be used has been approved for the intended aerial application.

6.68 Schedule 4 provides further restrictions including a requirement to contact the relevant authority of any Local Nature Reserve, SSSI etc. that lies within 1,500 metres of the land to be sprayed.

Related pesticides regulation and other materials

6.69 Other pesticides regulation includes sections of the Control of Substances Hazardous to Health Regulations 2002 (SI 2002/2677), which aims to protect employees and others in the workplace from hazardous substances; it is regulated by the Health and Safety Executive. The Government has published Codes of Practice for the use of pesticides. The Yellow Code related to the storage, transportation, and disposal of pesticides. The Green Code covers, among other things, crop spraying and disposal. Failure to comply with the codes may be regarded as evidence of an offence under s 16(12) of FEPA 1985. The PSD provides details of all banned and non-authorized pesticides in the UK at www.pesticides.gov.uk.

G GENETICALLY MODIFIED ORGANISMS

6.70 There has been widespread concern across Europe about genetic modification (GM) and, in particular, genetically modified food. GM is a technology that allows scientists to take genes from one organism and put them into another. This changes the way the organism develops, making new types of plants and animals. It is often claimed that genetic modification is just an extension of the plant and animal breeding that has been going on for hundreds of years, although traditional breeders are restricted by natural barriers that stop unrelated organisms (such as a rat and a cotton plant) from breeding with each other. Genetic modification allows genes to be crossed between organisms that could never breed naturally. A gene from a fish, for example, has been put into a tomato.

There is uncertainty surrounding GM research and food production and, at present, they **6.71** are only being grown in the UK in trials that aim to clarify some of the uncertainty. All the trials being undertaken must be carefully monitored and the seeds being trialled placed on the National Seed Lists. The National Seed Lists contain the varieties of agricultural and vegetable species eligible for certification and marketing in the UK. All seeds to be released commercially must be placed on the National Seed List.

Defra is the main government body responsible for the development and control of **6.72** genetically modified organisms (GMOs). There are two main areas of legislative control transposing EU Directive 98/81/EC amending Directive 90/219/EEC on the contained use of genetically modified micro-organisms:

- Part VI of the EPA 1990, as amended, which aims to ensure that all appropriate measures are taken to avoid damage to the environment that may arise from the escape or deliberate release from human control of GMOs; and
- the Genetically Modified Organisms (Contained Use) Regulations 2000 (SI 2000/2831), which seeks to ensure that any work with GMOs takes place in conditions that will prevent any escape of the organisms into the environment.

Part VI of the EPA 1990

The operative elements of Pt VI of the EPA 1990 are based upon general controls, consents, **6.73** enforcement powers, and offences. Many of the sections within this Part were revised by the Genetically Modified Organisms (Deliberate Release) Regulations 2002 (SI 2002/2443). Part VI, as amended, transposes EU Directive 2001/18/EC on the deliberate release into the environment of GMOs and repealing Council Directive 90/220/EEC. Sections 106 and 107 of the EPA 1990 provide definitions for this Part of the Act:

- *organism* means any acellular, unicellular, or multicellular entity (in any form) other than humans, or human embryos, and, unless the context otherwise requires, the term also includes any article or substance consisting of or including biological matter;
- *environment* includes land, air, and water and living organisms supported by any of those media;
- *damage to the environment* is caused by the presence in the environment of GMOs that have (or a single such organism that has) escaped or been related from a person's control and are (or is) capable of causing harm to the living organisms supported by the environment;
- *GMOs are capable of causing harm* if they are individually capable, or are present in numbers such that together they are capable, of causing harm; or they are able to produce descendants that will be capable, or that will be present in numbers such that together

they will be capable, of causing harm; and a single organism is capable of causing harm either if it is itself capable of causing harm or if it is able to produce descendants that will be so capable;

- *harm* means adverse effects as regards the health of humans or the environment;
- *organisms are under the control* of a person where he keeps them contained in measures that are designed to limit their contact with humans and the environment and to protect or minimize the risk of harm;
- *an organism is released* if the person controlling it, deliberately causes or permits it to cease to be under his control or the control of any other person and to enter the environment;
- *an organism escapes* if, otherwise than by being released, it ceases to be under his control or that of any other person and enters the environment; and
- *GMOs are marketed* by a person when products consisting of or including such organisms are placed on the market by being made available to another person, whether or not for consideration.

Risk assessment and notification requirements

6.74   Under s 108 of the EPA 1990 no person shall import or acquire, release, market, or keep any GMOs unless, before doing so, he has carried out a risk assessment of damage to the environment being caused as a result of doing that act, and in such cases, he has given the Secretary of State notice of his intention of doing that act and such information that may be prescribed.

6.75   Section 108 does not apply to anyone who is required to have consent from the Secretary of State for carrying out the activity or keeping the organism or who may be exempt from the requirements by Regulations enacted by the Secretary of State or by specific exemptions by the Secretary of State and Food Standards Agency. Regulations may be prescribed under s 108 for exemptions and for the way in which assessments may be carried out, e.g. the GMO (Risk Assessment) (Records and Exemptions) Regulations 1996 (SI 1996/1106).

General duties regarding handling, releasing, or marketing of organisms

6.76   Under s 109(2) of the EPA 1990, a person who proposes to import or acquire GMOs shall take all reasonable steps to identify what risks there are of damage to the environment arising from their importation or acquisition and shall not import or acquire the organisms if it appears that there is a risk to the environment from their importation or acquisition.

6.77   Section 109(3) provides that a person who is keeping GMOs shall take all reasonable steps to keep himself informed of any damage to the environment that may have arisen; shall cease keeping if, despite any additional precautions, there is a risk of environmental damage from continuing to keep them; and shall use the best available techniques not entailing excessive cost (BATNEEC) for keeping the organisms under his control and for preventing any damage being caused as a result of his continuing to keep the organisms.

6.78   Under s 109(4) a person who proposes to release GMOs:

(a)   shall take all reasonable steps to keep himself informed of what risks there are of damage to the environment arising from the release;

(b)   shall not release the organisms if it appears that, despite the precautions that can be taken, there is a risk of damage to the environment; and

(c) subject to para (b), shall use BATNEEC for preventing any damage to the environment being caused as a result of their being released;

There requirements under s 109 do not apply to persons proposing to import, acquire, release, market, or keep GMOs in cases where they are not required to carry out a risk assessment under s 108 or to holders of consents, in the case of acts authorized by those consents. **6.79**

Prohibition notice

The Secretary of State may, under s 110(1) of the EPA 1990, serve a prohibition notice on any person whom he has reason to believe is proposing to import, acquire, release, market, or keep GMOs if he is of the opinion that doing such an act would risk causing damage to the environment. The prohibition notice must state the opinion of the Secretary of State as described in s 110(1), specify what is to be prohibited, and if the prohibition does not take effect on service, the date on which it should take effect. **6.80**

Conditions and limitations

Section 111(1) of the EPA 1990 provides that no person shall import, acquire, release, or market GMOs except in pursuance of a consent granted by the Secretary of State and in accordance with any limitations and conditions. Section 112 provides that the Secretary of State may include in a consent such limitations and conditions as he thinks fit for the purpose of ensuring that all appropriate measures are taken to avoid damage to the environment. There is also an implied condition in a consent for importation, acquisition, keeping, marketing, or releasing GMOs under s 112(3), (4), and (5) that the holder of a consent shall, among other things: **6.81**

- take all reasonable steps to keep himself informed of any risks there are of damage to the environment from the activity being carried out;
- (for import, acquisition, and keeping GMOs) if at any time it appears that any such risks are more serious than were apparent when the consent was granted, notify the Secretary of State forthwith;
- use BATNEEC for keeping the GMOs under his control and for preventing any damage to the environment being caused as a result of his continuing to keep them;
- (for marketing and release) notify the Secretary of State of any new information that becomes available with regard to risks, the effects of any release and any unforeseen event, occurring in connection with a release by him, which might affect the risks there are of damage to the environment, take such measures as are necessary to prevent damage to the environment, notify the Secretary of State of such measures; and
- (for marketing, release, and keeping) take all reasonable steps to keep himself informed of developments in the techniques that may be available in preventing damage to the environment and if it appears at any time that any better techniques are available to him than is required by any condition, shall notify the Secretary of State of that fact forthwith.

Powers of Inspectors and the Secretary of State

Section 114 of the EPA 1990 provides for the appointment of GMO inspectors. Under s 115, an inspector has a right of entry and inspection of premise where there is reason to believe a **6.82** person is keeping or had kept any GMOs on his land or for which he has reason to believe any such organisms have been released or have escaped and where the inspector has reason to believe they may be harmful GMOs or that there is evidence of damage to the environment by the GMOs. The inspector also has power, under s 117, to deal with the cause of imminent danger of damage to the environment.

Offences and conviction

6.83 There are various offences contained in s 118(1) including, among others:

(a), (b)   failing to comply with any requirements relating to risk assessment contained in s 108;

(c)   doing anything in contravention of s 111 in relation to consents;

(d)   to fail to comply with any requirement of s 109 and the general duties imposed on importation, acquisition, keeping, marketing, or release of GMOs;

(e)   to fail, without reasonable excuse, to comply with s 108(5) of keeping records of risk assessments;

(f)   to contravene a prohibition notice;

(g)   failing, without reasonable excuse, to comply with any requirement imposed under s 115 relating to the rights of entry and inspection or GMO inspectors; and

(h)   to intentionally obstruct an inspector in the exercise of his powers or duties under s 117 above.

6.84 Section 119(1) of the EPA 1990 provides that for offences under s 118(1)(c) and (d) it shall be for the accused to prove that no measure, other than the measures taken by him, were necessary to prevent damage being caused to the environment from the release, or where he took no measures that no measures were necessary. Further, where an entry is required by a condition in a consent to be made in any record as to the observance of any other condition and the entry has not been made, that fact shall be admissible as evidence that that other condition has not been observed.

6.85 A number of the offences provide a defence of reasonable excuse, e.g. s 118(1)(e) of the EPA 1990. Others require intention to be proved and so should not be regarded as strict liability offences, e.g. s 118(1)(h). The maximum penalties for offences under s 118(1) range from, on summary conviction, a £5,000 fine for an offence under s 118(1)(g) to £20,000 fine and/or six months' imprisonment. Maximum penalties following conviction on indictment include an unlimited fine and/or two years' imprisonment.

6.86 Under s 120 of the EPA 1990 where a person is convicted of an offence under s 118(1)(a) to (f) in respect of any matters that appear to the court to be matters that are in his power to remedy, the court may, in addition to or instead of imposing any punishment, order him, within such time as may be fixed in the order, to take such steps as may be specified in the order for remedying those matters. Alternatively, the Secretary of State has the power, under s 121 to remedy any harm caused from an offence and to recover the cost of taking those steps from any person convicted of the offence.

Public register

6.87 Section 122 of the EPA 1990, the Secretary of State must maintain a GMO register containing any notices, directions, prohibition notices, applications for consents, consents granted and any information in support, and any convictions for an offence. Certain information can be excluded from the public GMO register including matters that would be contrary to the national interest and any information deemed to be commercially confidential.

GMO (Contained Use) Regulations 2000

The Genetically Modified Organisms (Contained Use) Regulations 2000 (SI 2000/2831) **6.88** (GMO Contained Use Regs 2000) are enacted under the Health and Safety at Work Act etc 1974. It has been amended by GMO (Contained Use) (Amendment) Regulations 2002 (SI 2002/63). The Regulations provide for human health and safety and environmental protection from genetically modified micro-organisms in contained use, and additionally the human health and safety from genetically modified plants and animals (GMOs). The key requirement of the Regulations is to assess the risks of all activities and to make sure that any necessary controls are put in place. They provide a framework for making these judgments, and place clear legal obligations on people who work with GMOs. The main features of the GMO Contained Use Regs 2000 are

regs 6–8	the prohibition on activity involving GMOs unless a suitable and sufficient risk assessment for human health and the environment has been carried out, including the need to review risk assessment where an assessment may no longer be valid;
reg 9	no person shall use premises for the first time involving GMO activities unless the competent authority (i.e. the Defra) has been notified of the intention;
regs 12, 13	requiring notification of individual activities of Class 2 (low risk) to Class 4 (high risk) to be notified to the Competent Authority (which HSE administers). (Consents are issued for all Class 3 (medium risk) and Class 4 activities. Sch 1 sets out the four classes of risk: Class 1 (no or negligible risk) activities are not notifiable, although they are open to scrutiny by HSE's specialist inspectors who enforce the Regulations);
reg 17	setting out principles of occupational and environmental safety such as a person who undertakes an activity involving genetic modification shall ensure that the exposure of humans and the environment to genetically modified micro-organisms is reduced to the lowest level that is reasonably practicable; and harm to humans arising from an activity involving genetic modification of organisms other than micro-organisms is reduced to the lowest level that is reasonably practicable; and
reg 20	where an assessment carried out pursuant to reg 6(1) shows that, as a result of any reasonably foreseeable accident the health or safety of persons outside the premises in which an activity involving genetic modification is carried on is liable to be seriously affected; or there is a risk of serious damage to the environment, the person undertaking that activity shall ensure that, before the activity to which the assessment relates begins, a suitable plan is prepared with a view to securing the health and safety of those persons and the protection of the environment;
reg 24	requiring the competent body to maintain a public register of GM premises and certain activities; and

reg 26   ss 16–26 (approved codes of practice and enforcement), ss 33–42 (provisions as
              to offences), and s 47 (civil liability) of the HSWA 1974 Act shall apply to these
              Regulations as if they were health and safety regulations for the purposes of
              that Act, and any function of the Health and Safety Commission under any
              other provision of the 1974 Act, which is exercisable in relation to any function
              of the Executive under or in respect of health and safety regulations (including
              their enforcement) shall be exercisable as if these Regulations were, to the
              extent they would not otherwise be so, health and safety regulations for the
              purposes of that Act.

6.89 The Contained Use Regs 2000 were amended by the GMO (Contained Use) (Amendment)
          Regulations 2002 (SI 2002/63), which inserted a new reg 23A, providing for keeping
          information confidential in the interests of national security; and a new reg 24A, which
          makes provision for the exclusion from the register of information where, in the opinion of
          the Secretary of State, the inclusion of such information on the register would be contrary to
          the interests of national security.

6.90 Other pieces of health and safety legislation are relevant to work with GMOs. These
          include the general requirements of the Health and Safety at Work etc Act 1974, the
          Management of Health and Safety at Work Regulations 1999, and the Carriage of Dangerous
          Goods legislation. There are also some biological agents aspects of the Control of Substances
          Hazardous to Health Regulations 2002 (SI 2002/2677).

KEY DOCUMENTS AND MATERIALS

Protection of Animals Act 1911
Salmon and Freshwater Fisheries Act 1975
Customs and Excise Management Act 1979
Fisheries Act 1981
Food and Environmental Protection Act 1985
The Control of Pesticides Regulations 1986 as amended (SI 1986/1510)
Environmental Protection Act 1990
Genetically Modified Organisms (Contained Use) Regulations 2000 (SI 2000/2831)
Plant Protection Products Regulations 2003, as amended (SI 2003/3241)
Products of Animal Origin (Third Country Imports) (England) Regulations 2004 (SI 2004/
    1214)

Council Regulation (EC) No. 1782/2003 of 29 September 2003 establishing common rules
    for direct support schemes under the common agricultural policy and establishing certain
    support schemes for farmers
Council Regulation (EC) No. 2371/2002 on the conservation and sustainable exploitation of
    fisheries resources under the Common Fisheries Policy
EU Directive 79/117/EEC prohibiting the placing on the market and use of plant protections
    products containing certain active substances
EU Directive 2001/18/EC on the deliberate release into the environment of genetically
    modified organisms and repealing Council Directive 90/220/EEC

EU Directive 98/81/EC amending Directive 90/219/EEC on the contained use of genetically modified micro-organisms

Defra (2004). *Review of the Marine Fisheries and Environmental Enforcement*. Defra: London

Defra Circular 1/2002: *The Keeping of Wild Animals*. Defra: London

Defra (2005). *Nitrates, Reducing Water Pollution from Agriculture*. Defra: London

Defra (1998). *The Code of Good Agricultural Practice for the Protection of Air*. Defra: London

Defra (2001). *Groundwater Protection Code — Use and Disposal of Sheep Dip*. Defra: London

Royal Commission on Environmental Pollution (RCEP) (2004) 25th report: *Turning the Tide: Addressing the Impact of Fisheries on the Marine Environment*. The Stationery Office: London

Pesticide Safety Directorate at www.pesticides.gov.uk

7

HUMAN HEALTH

A INTRODUCTION

There is a danger, when considering environmental protection, in attempting to cover too **7.01**
much. The boundaries of what constitutes environmental law are vague and the law relating
to human health is a good example. Clearly, many environmental impacts will affect human
health but it is uncertain at what point a line should be drawn and it becomes a topic that
should really be considered elsewhere. For instance, a road crash that causes injury is
unlikely to be regarded as having direct environmental concern focusing mainly on the
injury to victims and damage to property. However, the indirect impacts from any consequent fuel spill, traffic congestion, and the damage to any vehicles will have significant
adverse environmental effects. Should carbon monoxide poisoning from a faulty gas boiler
fall outside of the boundaries of environmental law simply because it may only affect one or

two individuals in their home? On balance, health impacts are too closely associated to what may be regarded as a clean and healthy environment and are therefore too important to ignore.

7.02 Health and safety at work is well regulated, while the common law of personal injury and negligence is highly developed and is now regarded by some as encouraging a compensation culture, even though there is a significant decline in the number of claims being issued in the courts. It is important to clarify the relationship between human health and the environment and to ensure that any practitioner recognizes the potentially wide consequences of a case that may, at first sight, appear to be a straightforward matter of compensation for personal injury. This chapter considers the protection and regulation in place aimed at trying to prevent injury in the workplace and beyond. It then outlines what may be relevant in a claim for personal injury arising out of adverse environmental effects.

7.03 There is increasing concern about the effects on health and the environment by operating what may be regarded as public services and utilities in that they provide some form of public benefit, albeit that many will be operating primarily for financial gain. The operation, regulation, and liability of these services is considered in the chapters dealing with the specific environmental concern, e.g. radiation from telecommunication masts are covered in Chapter 13: Radiation, incinerators are discussed in Chapter 14: Waste, and the control of sewerage and water quality in Chapter 15: Water.

B   ENVIRONMENTAL EFFECTS ON HEALTH

7.04 The impact on human health from environmental effects will often be injuries to internal organs such as the lungs, or to the senses and, in particular, deafness.

Injuries to internal organs

7.05 Injuries to internal organs can be complex, often with long periods of latency and the development of disease. Most claims will be based on harm arising from industrial disease rather than a traumatic injury such as a car crash. Adverse environmental impacts may cause harm to the following:

The lungs

7.06 Lung disease is a common form of environmental harm with many cases arising from asbestos inhalation, such as: Mesothelioma, which can be fatal within months of diagnosis, is often regarded as the most serious; and asbestosis, which restricts the use of the lungs and so limits normal activities. Lung cancer can also be asbestos-related but can arise in other circumstances as well. Other lung diseases include emphysema, bronchitis, and asthma, which in the worst instances can cause severe and permanent disability.

The digestive system

7.07 Harm to the digestive system, e.g. from poisoning, can cause vomiting, diarrhoea, and fever. It may also lead on to cause associated damage in the kidney and reproductive system.

Bowels and bladder

Harm to the bowels could include a loss of natural function and dependence on colostomy, **7.08**
while harm to the bladder can be a complete loss of function. Disease to the bladder may
arise from carcinogenic exposure.

Reproductive system

Damage to a male victim may include impotency, sterility, and loss of sexual function. **7.09**
Damage to a female victim may include infertility. The seriousness of the harm will be
influenced by age and whether the victim has children before the disease or injury caused
the infertility or sterility.

Injury to the senses

Injury and harm to health from adverse environmental impacts are most likely to impact on **7.10**
sight and hearing, although the loss of smell and taste may also arise, particularly with the
close relationship between the ear, nose, and throat.

Sight

Blindness may result from some exposure to environmental hazards. The seriousness and **7.11**
level of damages will depend upon the loss of sight experienced by the victim together with
the permanence to the loss of vision.

Deafness

Deafness will usually result from exposure to noise. It can range from slight loss of hearing to **7.12**
total deafness. Loss of hearing may be temporary or permanent. Tinnitus, a noise heard in
the ear without any external cause, regularly accompanies deafness. Any claim for loss of
hearing should consider whether there is further disability from tinnitus. Noise is considered
in Chapter 10.

Occupational diseases

Occupational disease is a human illness or injury arising from work or the workplace. *Black's* **7.13**
Medical Dictionary (41/e, A&C Black, 2005) outlines the main types of occupational disease:

- *Pneumoconiosis* covers a group of diseases that cause lung disease following the inhalation
  of dust. Around 300 new claimants receive benefit each year. Most are coal miners
  suffering from the inhalation of coal dust, but also arising from stone-masons, steel-
  grinders, millers, and workers in cotton, flax, or wool mills.
- *Occupational asthma* develops after a short symptonless period of exposure and is relieved
  by absences from work.
- *Dermatitis* is the most common occupational disease. About three-quarters of cases
  are irritant-contact dermatitis due to acids, alkalis, soap, and water. Allergic contact
  dermatitis is a more specific response by those susceptible to certain allergens.
- *Musculo-skeletal disorders*, the most common of which are injured backs and two groups
  of repeat injury disorder such as 'beat' conditions to the knee and elbow from repeated
  kneeling or crawling and work-related upper limb disorders, which include carpal

tunnel syndrome, tendonitis, and less common disorders such as repetitive posture disorders.

- *Physical agents* can cause ill health and the most significant is occupational deafness. Workplace noise exposures in excess of 85 decibels for a working day are likely to cause damage to hearing.
- *Radiation.* Non-ionizing radiation from lasers or microwaves can cause severe localized heating leading to tissue damage of which cataracts are a particular variety. Ionizing radiation can cause acute tissue damage as well as cell damage where longer term effects include genetic damage and various malignant disorders such as leukaemia.
- *Occupational cancers.* Work is directly responsible for around 5% of all cancers and contributes to a further 5%.
- *Infections.* Two broad categories of job carry occupation risk: work with animals and those in contact with human sources of infection, e.g. health care staff and sewage workers.
- *Poisonings,* The most common poison agents are solvents, gases, acids, alkalis, and irritant vapours.

Poisons and toxins

7.14 A poison is any substance that, when ingested, introduced into, or absorbed by a human or living organism, injures health or causes death. To poison is to kill or injure by means of poison or poisonous gases. Toxicology is the science of poisons. However, a toxin is one form of poison produced by bacteria. The phrase 'toxic torts' refers to environmental tort claims based on poisoning of some form. An ancient statement by Paracelsus early in the fifteenth century remains relevant today, which is, 'All substances are poisons: there is none that is not a poison. The right dose differentiates a poison and a remedy.'

Thus, the concept of dose-response is critical when assessing the risk of exposure to any substance.

C HEALTH AND SAFETY AT WORK etc.

The Health and Safety at Work etc. Act 1974

7.15 The protection of health and prevention of injury from adverse environmental impacts is regulated by:

- the Health and Safety Executive (HSE);
- environmental health officers (EHOs) from local authorities; and
- the Environment Agency.

7.16 These public bodies regulate those more directly responsible for safety in the workplace and in the local community. For instance, the HSE inspectors and EHOs enforce many of the regulations enacted under the Health and Safety at Work etc. Act 1974 (HSWA 1974), which places obligations on employers to protect employees and other persons exposed to danger and harm in the workplace and beyond. EHOs are also responsible for ensuring that shops and local services operate within the law, covering areas such as waste disposal and food hygiene requirements.

Part 1 of the HSWA 1974 covers health, safety, and welfare in connection with work and **7.17** control of dangerous substances and certain emissions into the atmosphere. It was introduced because of the need to ensure high standards of health and safety in the workplace, but covers activities and impacts outside of work. Section 1 provides that Pt 1 shall have effect with a view to:

(a) securing the health, safety, and welfare of persons at work;

(b) protecting persons other than persons at work against risks to health or safety arising out of or in connection with the activities of persons at work;

(c) controlling the keeping and use of explosive or highly flammable or otherwise dangerous substances, and generally preventing the unlawful acquisition, possession, and use of such substances.

Under the Health and Safety at Work etc. Act 1974 (Application to Environmentally **7.18** Hazardous Substances) Regulations 2002 (SI 2002/282) reference to dangerous substances is extended to include environmentally hazardous substances. Under reg 2, environmentally hazardous substances means substances that are dangerous to the environment (whether or not they are already within s 1(1)(c) of the Health and Safety at Work etc. Act 1974 as dangerous substances).

General duties under the HSWA 1974

Section 2 of the HSWA 1974 creates general duties for employers to their employees, e.g. **7.19** s 2(1) provides that: 'it shall be the duty of every employer to ensure, so far as is reasonably practicable, the health, safety and welfare at work of his employees.'

The duty in s 2(1) is not limited to employees in work but, for instance, if the workers are **7.20** on a lunch break or not operating machinery for some reason, see *Bolton MBC v Malrod Insulation Ltd* [1993] ICR 358. Liability under s 2(1) is strict but subject to the employer taking all reasonable precautions in trying to protect health, safety, and welfare. There are further obligations imposed on employers and others under:

s 3 general duties of employers and self-employed to persons other than employees;

s 4 general duties of persons concerned with premises to persons other than their employees;

s 6 general duties of manufacturers etc. as regards articles and substances for use at work; and

s 7 general duties of employees at work.

Powers of inspectors

Sections 20 to 25 of the HSWA 1974 set out the powers of HSE inspectors, including: **7.21**

s 20 to enter premises, and to make such examination and investigation as is necessary to effect any relevant statutory provisions;

s 21 serving an improvement notice if a person has contravened, is continuing, or is likely to continue to contravene one or more relevant statutory provisions;

s 22 serving a prohibition notice if any activity under the relevant statutory provisions will involve a risk of serious personal injury; and

s 25 the power to deal with the cause of imminent danger.

7.22 The HSWA 1974 also plays a critical role in creating a large volume of secondary legislation to improve workplace and environmental conditions. For instance, in 1992 a 'six-pack' of regulations was introduced, which includes (as amended):

- Health & Safety (Display Screen Equipment) Regulations 1992 (SI 1992/2792);
- Management of Health and Safety at Work Regulations 1999 (SI 1999/3242) (Management of HSW Regs 1999);
- Manual Handling Operations Regulations 1992 (SI 1992/2793);
- Personal Protective Equipment at Work Regulations 1992 (SI 1992/2966) (PPE Regs);
- Provision and Use of Work Equipment Regulations 1998 (SI 1998/2306) (PUWER Regs); and
- Workplace (Health, Safety and Welfare) Regulations 1992 (SI 1992/3004) (the Workplace Regs 1992).

Offences under the HSWA 1974

7.23 The HSWA 1974 and supporting regulations are supported by criminal sanctions contained in s 33(1). This provides, among other things, that is an offence for a person to:

(a)   fail to discharge a duty under ss 2 to 7;

(c)   to contravene any health and safety regulations or any requirement or prohibition imposed under any regulations; and

(d)   to contravene any requirement imposed by an inspector under s 20 or s 25.

7.24 Section 33(1A), (2A), and (3) sets out the maximum penalties for conviction of offences under the HSWA 1974. For example, a person guilty of an offence under s 33(1)(a) shall be liable on summary conviction to a maximum fine of £20,000 and an unlimited fine on indictment. For s 33(1)(c) offences there is (subject to exceptions) a maximum fine of £5,000 on summary conviction and an unlimited fine and/or imprisonment for two years on indictment. For s 33(1)(d) offences there is a maximum penalty of £5,000 on summary conviction.

7.25 Offences attract strict liability and if someone causes an offence they will be liable regardless of any intention. However, many of the duties imposed on employers are qualified by requiring actions that are reasonably practicable. For example, s 3(1) of the HSWA 1974 provides that:

> It shall be the duty of every employer to conduct his undertaking in such a way as to ensure, so far as is reasonably practicable, that persons not in his employment who may be affected thereby are not exposed to risk to their health and safety.

7.26 In *R v British Steel plc* [1995] Crim LR 654 the Court of Appeal held that s 3(1) of the HSWA 1974 is an absolute liability offence that is only subject to a defence of reasonable practicability. Further, the defence is a narrow one, which incorporates the idea of measures necessary to avert the risk to health and safety. However, under *R v Nelson Group Services (Maintenance) Ltd* [1998] 4 All ER 331 where an employee has carried out work carelessly or has omitted to take a precaution it does not preclude the employer from establishing that everything that was reasonably practicable in the conduct of the employers' undertaking to ensure that third persons were not exposed to risks had been done. In *Edwards v National Coal Board* [1949] 1 All ER 743 the court noted that the term 'reasonably practicable' was:

a narrower term than 'physically possible' and implies that a computation must be made in which the quantum of risk is placed in one scale and the sacrifice, whether in time, money or trouble, involved in the measures necessary to avert the risk is placed in the other; and that, if it be shown there is a gross disproportion between them, the risk being insignificant in relation to the sacrifice, the person upon whom the duty is laid discharges the burden of proving that compliance was not reasonably practicable. This computation falls to be made at a point in time anterior to the happening of the incident complained of.

What is reasonably practicable will be a question of fact in each case. However, it is important to note that some sections in the Act and certain regs are not qualified by reasonable practicability, e.g. reg 19 of the Workplace Regs 1992 provides that 'escalators and moving walkways shall . . . function safely'. Further, s 40 of the HSW 1974 provides that in any proceedings for an offence of failing to comply with a duty or requirement to do something so far as is practicable, or so far as is reasonably practicable, or to use the best practicable means to do something, it shall be for the accused to prove that it was not practicable or reasonably practicable or that there was no better practicable means than was in fact used to satisfy the duty or requirement. **7.27**

For criminal liability under the various regulations consider: *R v Nelson Group Services (Maintenance) Ltd* [1998] 4 All ER 331. In *R v Sanyo Electrical Manufacturing (UK) Ltd* (1992) 156 JP 863 minimal risk to employees was not considered to be a mitigating factor in sentencing. Criminal procedure is considered in more detail in Chapter 19: Criminal law practice and procedure along with the health and safety cases of *R v F Howe and Son (Engineers) Ltd* [1999] 2 All ER 249 and *R v Friskies Petcare (UK) Ltd* [2000] 2 Cr App Rep (S) 401 for their relevance to environmental sentencing. **7.28**

Much of the detailed protection relating to specific activities or concerns, e.g. management, work equipment, and construction are contained in secondary legislation. The health and safety regulations that have a clear environmental and human health (as opposed to personal injury) impact are hazardous substances, radiation, and noise. Each of these is considered below. **7.29**

Hazardous substances

Many of the chemicals used or dispersed by society are harmless. However, many others have the potential to cause significant environmental harm and personal injury. These are often referred to as hazardous substances and include: **7.30**

- asbestos, a collection of impure mineral fibres, which, if they enter the body, can trigger a number of diseases;
- benzene, used in the manufacture of chemicals, as a solvent and as a fuel;
- lead, which is added to petrol to increase combustion; and
- trichloroethylene, used for degreasing metals, as a solvent and cleaning agent in dry cleaning.

There is particular concern in relation to the use, handling, and movement of hazardous substances with separate legislation being enacted to control each activity. **7.31**

Safe use of hazardous substances

7.32 The Control of Substances Hazardous to Health Regulations 2002 (SI 2002/2677) (COSHH Regs 2002) define a substance hazardous to health as any substance listed in Pt 1 of the approved supply list contained in the Chemicals (Hazard Information and Packaging for Supply) Regulations 2002 (SI 2002/1689) (CHIP Regs 2002) including those that are: very toxic, toxic, harmful, corrosive, an irritant, sensitizing, carcinogenic, mutagenic, and toxic for reproduction.

7.33 The COSHH Regs 2002 transpose the health requirements of EU Directive 98/24/EC on the protection of the health and safety of workers from the risks related to chemical agents at work. Further, under reg 3 employers have a duty to ensure that chemicals are used and handled in such a way that no one is put a risk, while under reg 6, they must carry out a sufficient risk assessment wherever employees may be subject to a health risk. Where any risk assessment shows that employee protection is necessary, reg 10 provides that the atmosphere should be monitored and readings recorded. General area monitoring records must be kept for five years, while exposure records of identified employees must be kept for 40 years.

Handling of hazardous substances

7.34 The CHIP Regs 2002 aim to protect human health and the environment from harmful chemicals by ensuring that they are packaged and labelled correctly. They provide detailed rules on advertising, packaging, labelling, and, where appropriate, secure fastenings, e.g. reg 8 states that labels for dangerous substances must include:

- the name, address, and telephone number of the supplier
- the name of the substance or trade name of preparation;
- an indication of the danger and appropriate hazard symbol;
- the risk and safety phrases set out in full;
- any EU number;
- for any substance classified as carcinogenic, mutagenic, or toxic for reproduction, a label restricting it to professional users; and
- labels for dangerous preparations must additionally state 'if for sale to the general public, the nominal quantity'.

Movement of hazardous substances

7.35 The Carriage of Dangerous Goods (Classification, Packaging and Labelling) and Use of Transportable Pressure Receptacles Regulations 1996 (SI 1996/2092) impose requirements and prohibitions in relation to the classification, packaging, and labelling of dangerous goods for carriage by road or on a railway. They implement two Directives as well as making other provision: Directive 94/55/EC on the approximation of the laws of the Member States with regard to the transport of dangerous goods by road, and Directive 96/49/EC on the approximation of the laws of the Member States with regard to the transport of dangerous goods by rail.

Asbestos

7.36 The regulation of asbestos is not covered by the general legislative control of hazardous substances but is covered by specific legislation. Asbestos has been responsible for thousands of deaths and many more cases of chronic ill-health from diseases such as asbestosis, which is widespread scarring of the lungs and leads to severe breathing difficulties, and mesothelioma, which is cancer of the lung, pleura, or sometimes the ovary.

The Control of Asbestos in the Air Regulations (SI 1990/566) implements the air pollution **7.37** aspects of EU Directive 87/217/ECC on the prevention and reduction of environmental pollution by asbestos and where all scheduled asbestos works must meet an emission limit of 0.1 mg m^{-3}. Further, the Asbestos (Prohibitions) Regulations 1992 (SI 1992/3067 as amended by SI 1999/2373), require asbestos emissions to be monitored at intervals of not less than six months to prevent significant emission from the working of products containing asbestos.

Under the Control of Asbestos at Work Regulations 2002 (SI 2002/2675 as amended by **7.38** SI 2004/568) (CAW Regs 2002) employers have a duty to protect employees who may be exposed to asbestos at work requiring employers to, among other things:

reg 6   review asbestos assessments at regular intervals;
reg 7   prepare a work plan where the activity involves the removal of asbestos from plant, buildings, or other sources; and
reg 10   preventing or reducing exposure by using alternatives, including ensuring only essential workers enter an affected area if there is an unforeseen escape or concentrations are likely to exceed limits.

To assist employers HSE recently published an Approved Code of Practice and Guidance **7.39** booklet: *The Management of Asbestos in Non-domestic Premises* (2004).

Lead

Chronic lead poisoning is relatively common. Symptoms include nausea, anaemia, and **7.40** peripheral nerve damage. The Control of Lead at Work Regulations 2002 (SI 2002/2676 as amended by SI 2004/568) require employers to assess the risk of lead exposure in the workplace and to take steps to control or prevent the exposure. Under reg 6 if lead exposure is unavoidable then specific controls are required including designating appropriate work processes and providing suitable protective clothing, Also where the risk assessment indicates that any employees are liable to receive significant exposure to lead then under reg 9 air monitoring should be carried out and medical surveillance provided under reg 10.

Major accident hazards

The Control of Major Accident Hazards Regulations 1999 (SI 1999/743) (COMAH Regs 1999) **7.41** applies to the most hazardous operations, e.g. those operating in the chemical and oil industry. The emphasis of the regs is on planning, assessment, and approval of actions plans. It is considered further in Chapter 24: Environmental assessment.

Radiation

Exposure to radiation can have a number of health implications from skin inflammation, **7.42** cataracts, and loss of fertility for minimal local exposure to nausea, and cancer for exposure to the whole body. There are two types of radiation: ionizing and non-ionizing. Working

with ionizing radiation is covered by the Ionising Radiations Regulations 1999 (SI 1999/
3232). Non-ionizing radiation includes ultraviolet, infra-red, radio frequencies, and
electromagnetic radiation and is considered in Chapter 13: Radiation.

Noise

7.43   The Noise at Work Regulations 1989 (SI 1999/1790) provide the main workplace legislative
protection for noise and are considered in Chapter 10: Noise. The Workplace Regs 1992 may
also be relevant in ensuring that welfare facilities are available for workers such as adequate
rest rooms.

7.44   The Workplace Regulations 1992 set out the requirements for safety in the workplace.
Detailed guidance for compliance with the Regulations is contained in the Approved Code
of Practice L 24. The Regulations cover a wide range of safety considerations from maintaining correct room temperatures (reg 7) to ensuring that rest room facilities have adequate
tables and chairs and are kept clean and tidy (reg 25). The Regulations that are relevant to
environmental protection (albeit predominantly the indoor and working environment)
include:

reg 5   that the workplace, its fixtures, fittings, and equipment are well maintained,
         kept clean, in an efficient state, in efficient working order, and in good
         repair;
reg 6   that the workplace atmosphere is kept wholesome and well ventilated;
reg 8   that lighting is suitable and sufficient; and
reg 25   that rest rooms are available.

Risk assessment under the Management of HSW Regulations 1999

7.45   The Management of HSW Regulations 1999 play an important role in managing and trying
to avoid the risk of harm. Under the Regulations employers are required to:

reg 3   carry out suitable and sufficient risk assessments of any work activities that may
         put anyone at risk;
reg 4   employ a systematic approach to implementing preventative and protective
         measures;
reg 5   implement effective planning, organization, control, monitoring, and review of the
         preventative and protective measures taken;
reg 6   provide health surveillance for employees where an occupational disease or health
         risk is identified;
reg 7   provide access to competent health and safety advice;
reg 8   inform employees where danger exists in the workplace;
reg 9   establish contact with the emergency services and inform employees of the
         procedures in contacting them;
reg 10   provide all employees with comprehensible and relevant information on risks at
         work, precautions and preventative measures, and emergency procedures;
reg 13   take account of employees' abilities to do the work required, ensuring that they are
         adequately trained;

reg 15   provide temporary workers with information on special qualifications or skills required and health surveillance associated with the work;

reg 16   for women of child-bearing age, who are pregnant, or nursing mothers, the employer must assess the additional risk they face; and

reg 19   where young persons are employed, ensure that the young person is not put at risk because of inexperience, lack of awareness of dangers, or physical immaturity and not employ them where the work is likely to affect their health.

Under reg 14 employees are also under an obligation to follow any training they have been given, follow their employer's instructions to ensure legal requirements are met, and report any serious risks to health and shortcomings in safety arrangements.   **7.46**

Risk assessment

The reg 3 obligation for employers to carry out a risk assessment of work activities that may put anyone at risk reflects a modern approach to management. Banks and insurers aiming to assess the potential liability for environmentally-related lending and insurance regularly undertake a risk assessment. In terms of human health and safety, risk assessment and management involves: **7.47**

(a)   identifying hazards, i.e. something that has the potential to cause harm;

(b)   removing or reducing those hazards wherever possible;

(c)   assessing the severity of harm of each unavoidable hazard;

(d)   evaluating probability, i.e. the likelihood that the hazard will cause harm;

(e)   assessing risk, i.e. the hazard x probability x severity;

(f)   developing a plan to avoid or reduce risk;

(g)   implementing a risk management plan including training employees;

(h)   monitoring and reviewing when necessary, the performance of the risk management plan.

By way of example, the framework of risk assessment and management would be as follows: **7.48**

• Identifying the hazard that is, say, keeping of large quantities of petrol and chemicals on site. This is found to be unavoidable due to the nature of the activity carried out on site.

• The severity of harm for that risk is considerable and includes fatal accidents, acute poisoning, and, if there is an explosion, air pollution and contamination of the surrounding area.

• The probability of such an event is, according to analysis of similar accidents across the UK over the past 30 years, quite high at one event every 20 years per site.

• Assessing the risk involves multiplying the hazard (storage of chemicals) by high severity of harm (fatalities, explosions etc.) and the likelihood of such an event occurring (once every 20 years). This analysis provides that the storage of chemical is a high-risk activity.

• In order to prevent loss of life, injury, and property damage a robust risk management regime must be put in place with a formal action plan that includes training, emergency provisions, and other actions that will minimize risk.

• The risk management plan, as with an environmental management system, must be effectively implemented and monitoring of the plan will assist this. If there are gaps in the implementation of the risk management plan, then these should be identified, reviewed, and resolved.

7.49 The principles of management systems are considered further in Chapter 23: Environmental management.

The health and safety provisions beyond the working environment

7.50 An employer's liability under the health and safety provisions extends to people other than employees, including members of the public. For instance, s 3(1) of the HSWA 1974 provides:

> It shall be the duty of every employer to conduct his undertaking in such a way as to ensure, so far as is reasonably practicable, that persons not in his employment who may be affected thereby are not thereby exposed to risk to their health or safety.

7.51 Also, s 4(1) of the HSWA 1974 imposes duties in relation to those other than employees who use non-domestic premises made available to them as a place of work or as a place where they may use a plant or substance provided for their use. In *R v Board of Trustees of the Science Museum* [1993] 1 WLR 1171 the court held that it was sufficient for the prosecution to prove that the public were exposed to a possibility of danger and that constituted risk for the purpose of s 3(1).

7.52 Regulation 20 of the Genetically Modified Organisms (Contained Use) Regulations 2000 (SI 2000/2831) provides that where a risk assessment shows that, following a reasonably foreseeable accident, the health or safety of persons outside premises in which GMO activity is carried on is liable to be seriously affected, or that there is a risk of serious damage to the environment, the person responsible must ensure that, before the activity begins, an emergency plan is prepared to secure the health and safety of those persons and the protection of the environment: see also Chapter 6: Fishing, farming, and animal health.

D PERSONAL INJURY

7.53 Personal injury claims are a distinct area of the tort of negligence. They make up a significant minority of environmental claims. An action for personal injury will aim to compensate the claimant for the harm caused; injunctive relief is not available. It may be that any incident, act, or omission that prompts a personal injury claim may also cause property damage. However, environmental damage to property is likely to relate to land or buildings and a claim in nuisance will be a more appropriate course of action. In *Transco plc v Stockport MBC* [2003] UKHL 61 the House of Lords affirmed that a personal injury claim should not be based upon a nuisance action. Other claims may arise through negligence, statutory nuisance, and other criminal cases. The general principles of negligence are covered in Chapter 17: Civil law practice and procedure. Particular areas of negligence relating to personal injury are considered below and include causation and compensation. Distinct areas of environmental/personal injury concerns are found in specific chapters e.g. Chapter 10: Noise.

Causation

Once it has been established that a duty of care was owed by the defendant to the claimant   **7.54**
(see *Caparo Industries plc v Dickman* [1990] 2 AC 605), and that the defendant breached that
duty of care by doing something a reasonable person would not do (*Blyth v Birmingham
Waterworks Co* (1856) 11 Exch 781), then the claimant must establish that the defendant
caused the harm and that his original act or omission was not too remote. Remoteness
and proving causation can be particularly difficult in environmental personal injury
claims, because the majority of claims are where claimants have contracted certain diseases
through living and working in a particular environment that, it is alleged, has caused the
disease.

How the injury arises

Charles Pugh in *Liability for Environmental Harm* (LexisNexis, 2004) explains that under-   **7.55**
standing who caused the injury requires analysis of the mechanism in which the injury
arose. He suggests that there are three mechanisms:

- *traumatic injuries*, which occur following a single or instantaneous event, e.g. a car crash,
  a fall, or malfunction of machinery;
- *cumulative injuries*, which are caused by stress, strain damage, or exposure over a long time,
  where the injury accumulates over a long period of time and where all exposure contributes to take the claimant to the point where he will develop the disease and once that
  threshold has been reached, all exposure contributes equally to worsening the disease;
  and
- *'one off' cases*, where the injury is caused by a single event that takes place within the
  context of multiple events. An example of this is cancer, where medical opinion believes
  that mesothelioma can be caused by a single asbestos fibre triggering a cancer. The risk
  of the disease arising is increased by exposure to a much greater number of asbestos
  fibres. However, this is distinct from cumulative injury where each exposure is probably
  increasing the severity of the injury rather than increasing the risk of injury.

Cases of environmental personal injury tend to arise from either cumulative or one-off   **7.56**
injury, as opposed to traumatic injuries.

With disease cases it will be almost impossible to meet the conventional 'but for' test of   **7.57**
causation, i.e. if the harm would not have happened *but for* a particular fault then that fault
is the cause of the damage. This was recognized by the House of Lords in *Bonnington Castings
Ltd v Wardlaw* [1956] AC 618 in which the respondent claimed damages for contracting
pneumoconiosis during his eight years employment at the defendant's steelworks by inhal-
ing air that contained particles of silica. Lord Keith at 626 stated that:

> It was . . . maintained for the defenders that the pursuer must show that the dust released by
> their negligence from the swing grinders had contributed materially to the dangerous dust
> inhaled by the pursuer. As there was no evidence to show the proportions of the dust emanating
> from the various sources in the dressing shop inhaled by the pursuer, his case, it was said, must
> fail. The pursuer has, however, in my opinion, proved enough to support the inference that
> the fault of the defenders has materially contributed to his illness. During the whole period of
> his employment he has been exposed to a polluted atmosphere for which the defenders are in
> part to blame. The disease is a disease of gradual incidence. Small though the contribution of

pollution may be for which the defenders are to blame, it was continuous over a long period. In *cumulo* it must have been substantial, though it might remain small in proportion. It was the atmosphere inhaled by the pursuer that caused his illness and it is impossible, in my opinion, to resolve the components of that atmosphere into particles caused by the fault of the defenders and particles not caused by the fault of the defenders, as if they were separate and independent factors in his illness. Prima facie, the particles inhaled are acting cumulatively, and I think the natural inference is that had it not been for the cumulative effect the pursuer would not have developed pneumoconiosis when he did and might not have developed it at all.

7.58 In *McGhee v National Coal Board* [1973] 1 WLR 1 medical evidence could not prove that the claimant's dermatitis was caused while he was exposed to dust during his working day. However, the House of Lords held that because the defendant had not provided showers at its brick kilns, it was the claimant's continued exposure to dust after leaving the works and travelling home that exacerbated the injury. The medical evidence could show that if there had been showers available at the works, using them would have reduced the risk of the skin disease. In essence, the defendant was negligent in not providing showers for the claimant and other workers to minimize the exposure to dust. It was a material increase in exposure and therefore risk of dermatitis that was sufficient, in law, to prove a material contribution to the injury. The principle from *McGhee* is that, following expert evidence that a causal link exists, it is possible to establish causation by showing that a 'guilty' cause of harm, albeit not the sole cause, makes it more likely that the victim would suffer the harm that he did.

7.59 The approach in *McGhee v National Coal Board* was considered in detail by the House of Lords in *Fairchild v Glenhaven Funeral Services Ltd* [2002] UKHL 22. In *Fairchild* the widow of an asbestos worker claimed compensation for her late husband's death from mesothelioma from two defendants. The Court of Appeal, applying the conventional *but for* test, held that it was not possible to prove, on a balance of probabilities, that either or both defendants were liable. The House of Lords reversed the Court of Appeal decision and found for the claimant. Lord Roger in his speech set out at para 169 certain conditions for the application of the *McGhee* principle to apply:

(1) Where the claimant has proved all that he possibly can, but the causal link could only ever be established by scientific investigation and the current state of the relevant science leaves it uncertain exactly how the injury was caused and, so, who caused it e.g. *McGhee* and the present case.

(2) That part of the underlying rationale of the principle is that the defendant's wrongdoing has materially increased the risk that the claimant will suffer injury. It is therefore essential not just that the defendant's conduct created a material risk of injury to a class of persons but that it actually created a material risk of injury to the claimant himself.

(3) That the defendant's conduct must have been capable of causing the claimant's injury.

(4) The claimant must prove that his injury was caused by the eventuation of the kind of risk created by the defendant's wrongdoing. In *McGhee*, for instance, the risk created by the defendant's failure was that the pursuer would develop dermatitis due to brick dust on his skin and he proved that he had developed dermatitis due to brick dust on his skin. By contrast, the principle does not apply where the claimant has merely proved that his injury could have been caused by a number of different events, only one of which is the eventuation of the risk created by the defendant's wrongful act or omission. *Wilsher v Essex AHA* [1988] AC 1074 is an example.

(5) This will usually mean that the claimant must prove that his injury was caused, if not by exactly the same agency as was involved in the defendant's wrongdoing, at least by an

agency that operated in substantially the same way. A possible example would be where a workman suffered injury from exposure to dusts coming from two sources, the dusts being particles of different substances each of which, however, could have caused his injury in the same way. Without having heard detailed argument on the point, I incline to the view that the principle was properly applied by the Court of Appeal in *Fitzgerald v Lane* [1987] 1 QB 781.

(6) The principle applies where the other possible source of the claimant's injury is a similar wrongful act or omission of another person, but it can also apply where, as in *McGhee*, the other possible source of the injury is a similar, but lawful, act or omission of the same defendant. I reserve my opinion as to whether the principle applies where the other possible source of injury is a similar but lawful act or omission of someone else or a natural occurrence.

Pugh concludes that following *Fairchild* there seem to be different tests for different cases: **7.60**

(a) in traumatic injury cases, the 'but for' test applies;
(b) in cumulative injury cases, the claimant need only show that the defendant's breach of duty made a material contribution to the injury, i.e. caused part of the injury; and
(c) in 'one off' cases, the claimant need only show that the defendant's breach of duty increased the risk that the claimant might suffer the relevant injury.

It is recognized by practitioners that environmentally based personal injury claims tend to **7.61** be expensive to investigate and progress. Sean Humber (APIL, 2004) has noted that during the last decade, there have been a succession of unsuccessful chronic exposure/PI claims including:

- *AB v South West Water Service Ltd* [1993] QB 507 in which residents in Camelford claimed compensation for health problems relating to exposure to aluminium sulphate in drinking water;
- *Reay v British Nuclear Fuels Plc* [1994] Env LR 320 in which children living close to Sellafield nuclear plant claimed personal injury on the basis of paternal irradiation from Sellafield, with the case involving 35 experts and the trial lasting almost a year; and
- *Studholme v Norweb* (1997) unreported involving a claim where an electromagnetic field was alleged to result in cancer cases of children.

More recently, the Court of Appeal in *Sutradhar v National Environment Research Council* **7.62** [2004] EWCA Civ 175 allowed the defendant's appeal against a preliminary High Court decision to proceed with the case on the basis that it raised a novel point of law. In 1992, a National Environment Research Council (NERC) subsidiary reported to the Bangladeshi Government that certain water resources were safe to drink. The claimant suffered arsenic poisoning after drinking some of the water and claimed against NERC. The majority of the Court held that if the defendants were held liable they would be explicitly developing the law and that this was not appropriate for the judiciary. Further, they held that allowing the case to proceed to such an extent would render the notion of foresight meaningless.

Liability for breach of statutory duty

Section 47(1) of the HSWA 1974 provides that none of the offences arising under the Act **7.63** confer a right of action in any civil proceedings, although s 47(2) states that a breach of a duty imposed by health and safety regulations shall, so far as it causes damage, be actionable except in so far as the regulations provide otherwise. For example, reg 22 of the Management of HSW Regs 1999 expressly prevents a civil liability claim arising from any action, although this is subject to exceptions relating to pregnant mothers and young persons. However, the remaining health and safety regulations are silent in this regard and, because there is no contrary indication to s 47(2) of the HSWA 1974 within the remaining acts, a conviction under those regulations, may assist any civil claim.

Practice and procedure

7.64 Personal injury claims come within the Civil Procedure Rules 1998, which are considered in Chapter 17: Civil law practice and procedure. However, of particular note for personal injury claims are:

Pre-action Protocol

7.65 The Pre-Action Protocol for Personal Injury Claims. The protocol provides guidance and encourages early notification of claim, that a letter of claim be sent before proceedings are issued and standard procedures for disclosure.

Limitation period

7.66 That the limitation period for personal injury claims is three years. Section 11 of the Limitation Act 1980 applies to where claims include damages in respect of personal injuries to the claimant or any other person. Section 11(4) of the Act states that the period applicable under the section is three years from:

(a) the date on which the cause of action accrued; or

(b) the date of knowledge (if later) of the person injured.

7.67 Section 11(5) of the Limitation Act 1980 provides that if the person dies before the expiration of the period in s 11(4) the period applicable as respects the cause of action surviving for the benefit of his estate shall be three years from the date of death or the date of the personal representative's knowledge, whichever is the later. Under s 38(1) of the Act, 'personal injuries' includes any disease or impairment of a person's physical or mental condition, and 'injury' and cognate expressions shall be construed accordingly.

Assessing compensation

7.68 The only remedy generally available in negligence is compensation, or damages. The reasoning behind paying damages is that the claimant should be fully compensated for any suffering and loss and be restored, in the best way money can assist this, to the position he or she would have been in if the negligent act, default, or omission had not occurred. In *Livingstone v Rawyards Coal Co.* (1880) 5 App Cas 25 Lord Blackburn at 41 stated that the measure of damages was:

> that sum of money which will put the party who has been injured, or who has suffered, in the same position as he would have been in if he had not sustained the wrong for which he is now getting his compensation or reparation.

The calculation of the level of compensation due is complex and involves considering a **7.69** number of elements. There are a number of practitioners' works available to assess compensation. Kemp and Kemp: *The Quantum of Damages* (Sweet & Maxwell, regular updates) is comprehensive. In outline, compensation for personal injury claims can include the following:

Damages for non-pecuniary loss

Damages for non-pecuniary loss (general damages) includes pain, suffering, and loss of **7.70** amenity. The assessment of general damages is based on court decisions. The Judicial Studies Board's *Guidelines for the Assessment of General Damages in Personal Injury* (7/e, OUP, 2004) is a concise reference guide. Excerpts from the JSB guidelines include:

- *Total deafness* (p 17, (B)(b)) The lower end of the bracket is appropriate for cases where there is no speech deficit or tinnitus. The higher end is appropriate for cases involving both of these — £50,000 to £60,000.
- *Lung cancer* (p 21, (B)(c)) (typically in an older person) causing severe pain and impairment of breathing, prolonged and frequent coughing, sleep disturbance and restriction of physical activity and employment — £30,000 to £43,750.
- *Mesothelioma* (p 22, (C)(a)) causing severe pain and impairment of both function and quality of life. This may be of pleura (the lung lining) or of the peritoneum (the lining of the abdominal cavity); the latter being typically more painful. The duration of pain and suffering accounts for the variations within this bracket. For periods of up to 18 months, awards in the bottom half of the bracket may be appropriate; for longer periods of four years or more, an award at the top end — £45,000 to £70,000.

A claim in general damages must take into account a wide range of factors that will influence **7.71** a decision and award such as the level of pain, suffering, and loss of amenity, pre-existing conditions, multiple injuries, sex, age, means of the claimant, lifestyle prior to the incident, circumstances of the incident, and loss of leisure. Any cases or damages referred to and used as part of an assessment must be updated to take account of inflation. In *Wright v British Railways Board* [1983] 2 AC 773 the House of Lords affirmed that the judge should assess general damages at the date of trial not in terms of value at the date of injury.

Special damages

A compensation award in personal injury will not only look at the injury, it will also **7.72** look forward at a number of other areas of loss collectively regarded as special damages. The original intention of special damages was to compensate the claimant for financial loss between the date of injury and the date of the trial. However, modern reference to special damages also includes a number of other losses including future loss and expenditure, e.g.:

- loss of earnings, earning capacity, and pension;
- medical expenses;
- care and housing costs; and
- transport costs.

The principle is, as with general damages although perhaps more realistically so, that the **7.73** claim of special damages should put the claimant in the position that he or she would have been in had the injury or harm not occurred. The claim for loss of earnings and earning capacity may include profit as well as income. Damages are awarded without consideration for how they are spent although the award under this head should be reduced by any cost of earning that may have been incurred had the harm not arisen.

7.74   Multipliers are used to calculate any sum required to cover future loss and expenditure. This is based on the assumption that any award given will be invested and generates interest. The sum awarded by the court should include interest on any sum awarded. The date of accrual of interest differs between general and special damages.

7.75   In certain cases, it may be appropriate to apply for provisional damages and in larger claims interim payments and structured settlements may be appropriate. Importantly, to ensure that all areas of a potential claim are covered it is advisable to consider specialist works on personal injury and, where appropriate, seek opinion from a specialist practitioner in this area.

7.76   Organizations that can assist in personal injury work include the Association of Personal Injury Lawyers (APIL) and the Law Society Personal Injury Panel.

Reduction in award by apportionment

7.77   When considering the level of damages the court may be asked by the defendant to apportion some of the responsibility for the harm caused to some other, possibly unknown, factor. The Court of Appeal in *Allen v British Rail Engineering* [2001] EWCA Civ 242 considered apportionment concluding that the extent of an employer's liability can be limited to the extent that its conduct contributed to the claimant's injury. Apportionment among employers was considered in *Thompson & ors v Smiths Shiprepairers (North Shields) Ltd* [1984] QB 405: the case is discussed in Chapter 10: Noise.

KEY DOCUMENTS AND MATERIALS

The Health and Safety at Work etc. Act 1974

The Asbestos (Prohibitions) Regulations 1992 (SI 1992/3067, as amended)

Workplace (Health, Safety and Welfare) Regulations 1992 (SI 1992/3004) (the Workplace Regs 1992)

HSW (Application to Environmentally Hazardous Substances) Regulations 2002 (SI 2002/282)

The Control of Major Accident Hazards Regulations 1999 (SI 1999/743) (COMAH Regs 1999)

Management of Health and Safety at Work Regulations 1999 (SI 1999/3242) (Management of HSW Regs 1999)

Chemicals (Hazard Information and Packaging for Supply) Regulations 2002 (SI 2002/1689) (CHIP Regs 2002)

Control of Asbestos at Work Regulations 2002 (SI 2002/2675) (CAW Regs 2002)

The Control of Substances Hazardous to Health Regulations 2002 (SI 2002/2677) (COSHH Regs 2002)

Bates J, Birtles, W, and Pugh C (2004). *Liability for Environmental Harm*. LexisNexis: London

Black's Medical Dictionary. 41/e (2005). A&C Black: London

HSE: Approved Code of Practice and Guidance booklet (2004). *The Management of Asbestos in Non-domestic Premises*

Judicial Studies Board's *Guidelines for the Assessment of General Damages in Personal Injury.* 7/e. (2004). OUP: Oxford

Kemp and Kemp: *The Quantum of Damages* Sweet & Maxwell: London

8

LAND USE PLANNING

A   OVERVIEW AND PRINCIPLES OF LAND USE PLANNING

8.01 Possibly the most influential area of law on the environment relates to land use. The UK has developed a complex system of statutory control over its development and use, commonly referred to as the Town and Country Planning system, although its scope is far wider. Its significance in influencing environmental law is that whatever change or use land is put to it is likely to have an environmental impact. For instance, building homes on a floodplain will not only put those homes at risk of flooding, it will take much of the undeveloped land used as a natural soakaway for rain water and concentrate the water that does fall through run-off from the homes and associated hard surface infrastructure.

8.02 The land use planning system is considered fully in Victor Moore's book, *A Practical Approach to Planning Law* (9/e, OUP, 2005). It is, nevertheless, important to cover the key parts of the regime in a book dealing with environmental law.

8.03 Local authorities are primarily responsible for land use planning. There has been a long history in the UK of local self-government. The Housing, Town Planning etc. Act 1909 authorized the council of any borough or urban district to prepare a town planning scheme to assist slum clearance and develop new homes and neighbourhoods. The Town and Country Planning Act 1947 (TCPA 1947) consolidated and repealed a number of land use Acts. There was by this time a pressing need to control the use of land in both town and country and left unrestricted, it was envisaged that the UK would soon be overwhelmed by inappropriate development. Moore explains that the TCPA 1947 set up a comprehensive system of land use for the country by:

- creating local planning authorities (LPAs) and requiring each authority to prepare a development plan for their area, which would state how land in the area should be used.
- developing a system whereby all land was subject to control and that anyone seeking to develop land had to obtain permission from the LPA. In reaching a decision, the LPA were to refer to their development plans. LPAs were given powers to deal with development carried out without planning permission.
- LPAs were given powers to preserve trees, protect buildings of architectural interest and historic buildings, and to control advertising displays.
- a compensation fund was set up to compensate landowners who suffered a drop in the value of their land as a result of the introduction of the new planning system.

Further planning schemes have been introduced since and much is now contained in one **8.04** of the principle pieces of planning legislation, the Town and Country Planning Act 1990 (TCPA 1990). Other important Acts are the Planning (Listed Buildings and Conservation Areas) Act 1990, the Planning and Compensation Act 1991, and the latest Planning and Compulsory Purchase Act 2004 (PCPA 2004); the last two both amending the TCPA 1990 to some degree.

Purpose of the land use planning system

The purpose of the land use planning system is to control land use and physical develop- **8.05** ment often with the general intention of improving the environment and surroundings. Importantly, the planning regime enables local authorities to have a high degree of control over the way land is used in their area. While much of the land use planning legislation is to protect, preserve, and enhance the environment, the Government in *Planning; Delivering a Fundamental Change* (2001), believes that a successful planning system will:

- promote economic prosperity by delivering land for development in the right place at the right time;
- encourage urban regeneration by ensuring that new development is channelled towards existing town centres rather than adding to urban sprawl;
- help to conserve greenfield land and re-use urban brownfield land;
- value our countryside and our heritage while recognizing that times move on;
- play a critical part in achieving the Government's commitment to sustainable development.

Principles of land use planning

Sustainable development

The concept of sustainable development is discussed in Chapter 2: Environmental rights and **8.06** principles. It has been given statutory status in land use planning. Section 39 of the PCPA 2004 states that:

(1) This section applies to any person who or body which exercises any function:
    (a) under Part 1 in relation to a regional spatial strategy;
    (b) under Part 2 in relation to local development documents; and
    (c) under Part 6 in relation to the Wales Spatial Plan or a local development plan.
(2) The person or body must exercise the function with the objective of contributing to the achievement of sustainable development.
(3) For the purpose of subs 2 the person or body must have regard to national policies and advice contained in guidance issued by:
    (a) the Secretary of State,
    (b) the National Assembly for Wales.

8.07 Sustainable development is not defined in the Act. However, Planning Policy Statement 1 (PPS 1): *Delivering Sustainable Development* (2005) provides at para 3 that:

> Sustainable development is the core principle underpinning planning. At the heart of sustainable development is the simple idea of ensuring a better quality of life for everyone, now and for future generations. A widely used definition was drawn up by the World Commission on Environment and Development 1987: 'development that meets the needs of the present without compromising the ability of future generations to meet their needs.'

8.08 Development in terms of *sustainable development* does not mean the development of land although it does impact on land development and construction. It does not mean that construction and development should continue in the long term. Sustainable development refers to the development of society as a whole; it includes future generations and the wider world. The Government has, in the planning reforms, recognized the wide impact that land use planning has on society noting, again in para 1 of PPS 1 that, 'Planning shapes the places where people live and work and the country we live in.'

Public participation in planning

8.09 The Government has placed emphasis on public participation and consultation in planning but the right to participate remains notional. There is a right, in certain circumstances, to be informed about a planning application and a right to make written representations on that application. Certain statutory consultees, e.g. the Environment Agency and Parish Councils have a right to be consulted. Also, certain major projects require the planning application to be supported by an environmental statement (ES). In these cases the public has a right of access to the ES and to make representations on this.

8.10 Section 18 of the PCPA 2004 provides that the LPA must prepare a statement of community involvement (SCI), which is a statement of the authority's policy as to the involvement in preparing local development documents, The SCI is not regarded by the Act as a document itself, although it is subject to independent examination in common with every development plan document.

The need for planning permission

8.11 The planning system is based on the key principle that, to be lawful, all development requires planning permission granted by the LPA to be lawful. Section 57 of the TCPA 1990 provides that subject to certain exceptions and exemptions, 'planning permission is required for the carrying out of any development of land.'

The term 'development' has a legal definition contained in s 55 of the TCPA 1990 providing **8.12** for two broad areas of development; operational development and material change of use. It also excludes certain types of land use activity from the definition.

The administration of land use

Land use planning is primarily an administrative rather than legal system. It is run by LPAs **8.13** on behalf of society. In *R v Secretary of State for the Environment, Transport and the Regions ex p Alconbury* [2001] UKHL 23 Lord Hoffman stated that, 'In a democratic country, decisions as to what the general interest requires are made by democratically elected bodies or persons accountable to them.'

In determining whether Art 6(1) of the European Convention on Human Rights (the right to **8.14** the determination of civil rights by an independent and impartial tribunal) was applicable he added that:

> I would have said that a decision as to what the public interest requires is not a 'determination' of civil rights and obligations. It may affect civil rights and obligations but it is not, and ought not to be, a judicial act such as article 6 has in contemplation. . . . But a decision as to the public interest (what I shall call for short a 'policy decision') is quite different from a determination of right. The administrator may have a duty, in accordance with the rule of law, to behave fairly ('quasi-judicially') in the decision-making procedure. But the decision itself is not a judicial or quasi-judicial act. It does not involve deciding between the rights or interests of particular persons. It is the exercise of a power delegated by the people as a whole to decide what the public interest requires.

The role of policy and decision-makers in planning

Planning law derives from statute. There are planning-related rules, decisions, and actions at **8.15** a number of levels of government including some (albeit a few) at EU level, national, and local levels. The relevant organizations include the Office of the Deputy Prime Minister, Regional Planning Bodies (introduced in the PCPA 2004), County Councils, District Councils (or Metropolitan Borough Councils, Unitary Councils, and, in Wales, County Borough Councils) and Parish Councils. Central government also publishes a range of Planning Policy Guidance Notes (PPGs) and Planning Policy Statements (PPSs) that set out government policy on different aspects of land use planning. LPAs must take their content into account in preparing their local development schemes. They may also be material to decisions on individual planning applications and appeals.

An important PPS in terms of environmental protection is PPS 23: *Pollution and Planning* **8.16** *Control* (2004). As well as affirming the role of pollution prevention and control and sustainable development in relation to planning matters it also notes that the Government is committed to using the precautionary principle highlighting that the Government's Interdepartmental Liaison Group on Risk Assessment considered that the precautionary principle should be invoked when:

• there is good reason to believe that harmful effects may occur to human, animal, or plant health, or to the environment; and

- the level of scientific uncertainty about the consequences or likelihood of the risk is such that the best available scientific advice cannot assess the risk with sufficient confidence to inform decision-making.

8.17 LPAs may also prepare policy documents in addition to the local development plans. These are referred to as supplementary planning documents and where prepared should be included in the local development framework. They are not subject to independent examination although the Government advises in para 2.42 of PPS 12: *Local Development Frameworks* (2004) they should be subjected to rigorous procedures on community involvement.

Strategic planning

8.18 Strategic planning is the system of devising and implementing a long-term plan for an area, e.g. the local development plan or a regional spatial strategy. It includes specific documents with maps and descriptions of projected land use. It includes planning guidance and policy at a regional and sub-regional level. It also includes the concept of spatial planning, which incorporates into regional plans matters that will influence the way land is used and required. An example of this is the recently published London Plan. The strategic planning process has recently been overhauled with the coming into force of the PCPA 2004. Section 120 and Sch 9 of the PCPA 2004 repeal Pt 2 of the TCPA 1990, which is replaced by Pts 1 and 2 of the new Act for England and Pt 6 for Wales.

Part 1 of the PCPA 2004: regional functions

8.19 Part 1 of the PCPA 2004 introduces Regional Spatial Strategies (RSSs) to replace Regional Planning Guidance and County Structure Plans. RSSs have legal status as opposed to guidance and should provide a broad development strategy for the region for a 15- to 20-year period. Paragraph 1.3 of PPS 11: *Regional Spatial Strategies* (2004) states that the following matters should be taken into account in an RSS:

- identification of the scale and distribution of provisions for new housing;
- priorities for the environment, such as countryside and biodiversity protection; and
- transport, infrastructure, economic development, agriculture, minerals extraction, and waste treatment and disposal.

8.20 The RSS, incorporating a Regional Transport Strategy, provides a spatial framework to inform the preparation of Local Development Documents (LDDs), Local Transport Plans, and regional and sub-regional strategies and programmes that have a bearing on land use activities. It is the responsibility of Regional Planning Bodies to prepare the RSS for their region. They must seek advice from each LPA in their region and can arrange to discharge their function through a relevant authority.

8.21 In similar fashion to the former development plans, a draft (or draft revision) RSS will be prepared upon which anyone is entitled to make representations. If the Secretary of State feels that it is appropriate he may order an examination in public of the draft revision RSS inviting certain relevant bodies to attend any hearing. While RSSs are being introduced, county structure plans will remain in force, some of which may have only recently been adopted. For instance, Kent County Council introduced a new structure plan as late as 2004.

In *JS Bloor (Northampton) Ltd & anor v Warwickshire CC* [2002] EWHC 334 the claimants   **8.22** sought to challenge the adoption of the Warwickshire Structure Plan under s 287 of the TCPA 1990 (see paras 8.207 to 8.215) in relation to a particular policy, GD5. The claimants alleged that the change in the policy on allocations of land was perverse, that the Council had acted unlawfully in not deciding to hold a new examination in public, that the Council should have had regard to material considerations in terms of Policy GD5, and that it failed to comply with its obligation to provide an explanatory memorandum. All four grounds of challenge were dismissed by the High Court. In *Watson v Essex CC* [2002] EWHC 669 Admin, the High Court dismissed an application under s 287 to quash a policy relating to the incineration of waste.

Part 2 of the PCPA 2004: local development

Part 2 of the PCPA 2004 provides for the preparation of LDDs that will collectively make   **8.23** up the local development framework for an area. The framework will replace local plans, unitary development plans, and structure plans. Every LPA must prepare and maintain a local development framework. County councils must prepare and maintain a minerals and waste development framework. PPS 12 provides at para 1.4 and figure 1.1 that each frame- work will set out what LDDs the authority must prepare and a timetable for operation. They must include:

- the local development scheme;
- core strategy;
- site specific allocations;
- adopted proposals map;
- statement of community involvement;
- annual monitoring report.

They may also include: **8.24**

- area action plans;
- supplementary planning documents;
- local development orders;
- simplified planning zones; and
- other development plan documents.

PPS 12 is supported by *Creating Local Development Frameworks: A Companion Guide to PPS 12*   **8.25** (2004).

Section 54A of the TCPA 1990 required that, when granting permission, there had to be   **8.26** regard to the development plan etc., but this has been replaced by s 38(6) of the PCPA 2004 which provides that:

> If regard is to be had to the development plan for the purpose of any determination to be made
> under the Planning Acts, the determination must be made in accordance with the plan unless
> material considerations indicate otherwise.

8.27 LDDs should integrate with other local authority strategies such as the community strategy and the local transport plan. Parts 1 to 3 of the PCPA 2004 came into force in September 2004.

Development control

8.28 The system by which planning applications are determined and other regulation such as enforcement is carried out is usually referred to as development control. A developer submitting a planning application may be an individual homeowner building a loft extension or a multinational company wishing to build a housing estate with over 1,000 homes. The application is, in general, decided by the LPA either through the elected members or by LPA officers who have delegated powers to determine the application. Development control is discussed further below.

Human rights and planning

8.29 The European Convention on Human Rights is discussed in Chapter 2: Environmental rights and principles. In relation to land use planning, there are three important Convention rights that have been claimed in the UK courts:

Art 6	the right to a fair hearing.
Art 8	the right to respect for private and family life.
Art 1 of Protocol 1	the right to peaceful enjoyment of possessions.

8.30 While some Convention rights are absolute, such as the right to life under Art 2, the planning-related rights are qualified and the public body is entitled to take account of other factors when considering whether to restrict the rights of individuals.

8.31 In *R v Secretary of State for the Environment, Transport and the Regions ex p Alconbury* the House of Lords held that administrative matters such as planning decisions did involve the determination of civil rights and obligations and that there could be protection under Art 6. However, the Secretary of State had not claimed that he was acting as an independent or impartial tribunal and the option to judicially review the Secretary of State's decision satisfied the Convention rights.

8.32 In *Lough v First Secretary of State* [2004] the Court of Appeal considered that the Art 8(1) right to respect for private life, family, and home, and Art 1 of Protocol 1 right to peaceful enjoyment of possessions were central to the planning decision-making process and it was to expressly reference the need to carry out a balancing exercise.

Matters related to land use planning

Building Regulations

8.33 The Building Regulations 2000 (SI 2000/2531), as amended, aim to ensure the health and safety of people in and around all types of buildings. They also provide for energy conservation, and access to and use of buildings. The Regulations may apply regardless of whether planning permission is required or permitted under the GPDO 1995.

The Regulations are made under powers contained in the Building Act 1984 and comprise **8.34** a range of definitions and procedures contained in 13 Parts to Sch 1 of the Regulations. These are:

Part	A	Structure
	B	Fire safety
	C	Site preparation and resistance to moisture
	D	Toxic substances
	E	Resistance to the passage of sound
	F	Ventilation
	G	Hygiene
	H	Drainage and waste disposal
	J	Combustion appliances and fuel storage systems
	K	Protection from falling, collision, and impact
	L	Conservation of fuel and power
	M	Access to and use of buildings
	N	Glazing — safety in relation to impact, opening, and cleaning

The Building Regulations 2000 apply if you are carrying out 'building work'. The definition **8.35** of 'building work' in reg 3 means that it includes:

• the erection of extension of a building;
• the installation or extension of a service or fitting, which is controlled under the Regulations;
• an alteration project involving work that will temporarily or permanently affect the ongoing compliance of the building, service, or fitting with the requirements relating to structure, fire, or access to and use of the buildings;
• the insertion of insulation into a cavity wall; and
• the underpinning of the foundations of the building.

The local authority enforces the Regulations. Under s 35 of the Building Act 1984, it can issue **8.36** an enforcement notice requiring specific work to be undertaken. The notice must be issued within one year of completion of the building works. Failure to comply with a notice may result in prosecution in the magistrates' court of the person carrying out the building works. The maximum penalty is a £5,000 fine and £50 for each day that the contravention continues.

Alternatively, the authority may issue an injunction under s 36(6) of the Building Act **8.37** 1984 for which there is no time limit; see *Cottingham v Attey Bower & Jones* [2000] Lloyd's Rep PN 591.

Party Wall etc. Act 1996

The Party Wall etc. Act 1996 (PWA 1996) aims to prevent and resolve disputes in relation to **8.38** party walls, boundary walls, and excavations near neighbouring buildings. The Act covers:

various works carried out directly to an existing party wall or structure; new building either at or astride the boundary line between properties; excavation within 3 or 6 metres of a neighbouring building(s) or structure(s) depending upon the depth of the hole or the proposed foundations.

A wall is a 'party wall' if it stands astride the boundary of land belonging to two (or more) **8.39** owners or if it stands on one owner's land, but is used by two (or more) owners to separate their buildings.

8.40 Under s 3 of the PWA 1996, all adjoining owners must be informed of proposed works at least two months before they commence by receiving formal notice. This should be in writing and include the developer's name and address, the building's address (this may be the same), a full description of what building works are proposed, and when they are expected to start. Someone receiving the s 3 notice may either give written consent or give a counter-notice proposing conditions or modifications to the works: s 4 of the Act.

8.41 Under s 5 of PWA 1996, if an owner on whom a party structure notice or a counter-notice has been served does not serve a notice indicating his consent to it within 14 days, he shall be deemed to have dissented from the notice and a dispute shall be deemed to have arisen between the parties.

Hierarchy of legislation

8.42 There is a complex legislative hierarchy in land use planning system from EU Directives down to local policies. A simplified hierarchy of planning legislation with examples is set out below.

Figure 8.1 Simplified hierarchy of planning legislation and regulation

···

EU Directives

Directive 85/337/EC on the assessment of the effect of certain public and private projects on the environment (as amended) (the Environmental Impact Assessment Directive 2001/42/EC on the assessment of the effects of certain plans and programmes on the environment (the Strategic Environmental Assessment)

National legislation

The Town and Country Planning Act 1990 (TCPA 1990)
The Planning and Compulsory Purchase Act 2004 (PCPA 1990)

Secondary legislation

The TCP (Use Classes) Order 1987 (SI 1987/764) (Use Classes Order 1987)
The TCP (General Permitted Development) Order 1995 (SI 1995/418) (GPDO 1995)
The TCP (General Development Procedure) Order 1995 (SI 1995/419) (GDPO 1995)

National policy guidance

Planning policy guidance notes (PPGs), e.g. PPG 24: Noise
Planning policy statements (PPSs), e.g. PPS 23: Planning and pollution control
Circulars, e.g. Circular 1/97: Planning Obligations

Regional policy

Regional Spatial Strategies and the London Plan 2003

Local policy

Local development documents, e.g. Statement of Community Involvement
Local Development Orders for permitted development

···

B   MANAGING SPECIFIC LAND USE ACTIVITIES

The planning system must balance competing interests and pressures on land placed upon   **8.43**
it by modern living. There are many sites that need specific protection from potentially
harmful use such as ancient monuments, buildings of special character, wildlife habitats,
coastal areas, trees and woodland. It is worth noting the scale of the demands on land.

The ODPM statistics provide that in 2002/03 district planning authorities in England alone   **8.44**
received 634,000 planning applications and made decisions on 586,000. Over half of all
decisions were for minor 'householder' development within the curtilage (area about a
building) of a residential property, e.g. home extensions, garages, and swimming pools and
11% were for new residential development. There were also decisions by county councils on
minerals and waste developments. The range of development is set out in the table below;
the ODPM adopts the definitions of development contained in the Use Classes Order 1987.
The main types of development are considered in the following sections.

Table 8.1 Development decisions in 2002/03

Type of development	Total
Minor dwellings, commercial and industrial	146,500
Householder	304,500
Change of use	35,000
Listed buildings/conservation areas	35,000
Advertisements	29,500
Major dwellings, commercial and industrial	11,500
Other, e.g. lawful certificate.	23,500
Waste developments	1,000
Minerals	500

Residential development

Housing and newbuild is the most common form of land use development. The Use Classes   **8.45**
Order 1987 defines a residential property or dwelling as a property in:

Use as a dwellinghouse (whether or not as a sole or main residence) —
  by a single person or by people living together as a family, or
  by not more than 6 residents living together as a single household (including a household
where care is provided by residents).

The ODPM considers major residential development to include where 10 or more dwellings   **8.46**
are to be constructed or, if this is not known, where the site is 0.5 hectares or more.

The Government considers that there is a chronic housing shortfall in certain parts of the   **8.47**
UK fuelled by increases in house prices, changing lifestyles, and developers reluctant to
release land from their land reserves to build homes. The Government set out its vision for
home building in the policy document; *Sustainable Communities* (2003). This provided
that the housing shortage would be addressed by tackling the mismatch of housing provisions between the South East and the North and Midlands. The growth of housing is to be
accelerated in four areas (Thames Gateway, London–Stansted–Cambridge corridor, Ashford,
and Milton Keynes–South Midlands).

8.48 The problems of abandonment and low demand for housing in the North and the Midlands is to be turned around through the use of nine pathfinder schemes. These schemes include plans to replace the obsolete housing with modern sustainable accommodation.

8.49 Social housing is to be brought up to decent standards by 2010. Efforts to improve the local environment of communities are proposed by making streets clearer and improving public spaces and parks. The countryside is to be protected with new developments being built on previously developed land. Greenbelt land is to be increased and maintained. It is difficult to see how this approach will, in fact, be sustainable. Securing a significant number of homes in an already overcrowded area such as the south-east of England is likely to place even greater stress on land and the other environmental media such as air quality and water resources, and add to the level of waste being produced and noise being generated.

8.50 Residential development is covered by the general legislation controlling development contained in Pt III of the TCPA 1990. The detail of how residential development should proceed is currently contained in PPG 3: *Housing* (2000). The Government intention is for everyone to have the opportunity of a decent home. Key aims contained in PPG 3 include:

- Widening housing opportunity and choice by, among other things, providing sufficient housing, creating mixed communities, assessing local housing needs, and delivering affordable housing.
- Maintaining a supply of housing by re-using urban land and buildings and assessing urban housing capacity.
- Creating sustainable residential environments through better links to public transport, the promotion of mixed use developments, greening the residential environment, and making best use of land

Commercial and industrial development

8.51 Commercial and industrial development is a broad category that includes shops, offices, general industrial buildings, storage and warehousing. The ODPM regards major development of this nature to include anything where the floorspace to be built is over 1,000 sq. metres or more, or the site area is one hectare or more. This adopts the definition of major development from Art 8(7) of the GDPO 1995. There is also a high level of development that will be a material change of use but that will not require formal building development. Further, there will be considerable change of use of properties within the same use class.

Business planning zones

8.52 Sections 82 to 87 of the TCPA 1990 enable, and in some instances now require, LPAs to make a simplified planning zone scheme for all or part of their area, if desirable. The main benefit of a simplified planning zone scheme is that it is unnecessary to secure planning consent for development allowed by the scheme, although this does not extend to development proposals requiring an environmental statement in support. Under Sch 7, para 1(2) of the TCPA 1990 any designated scheme shall specify:

(a) the development or classes of development permitted by the scheme,
(b) the land in relation to which permission is granted, and
(c) any conditions, limitations or exceptions subject to which it is granted; and shall contain such other matters as may be prescribed.

There are around ten simplified planning zones throughout England and Wales. The PCPA **8.53** 2004 has removed some discretion in adopting a simplified planning zone from LPAs and placed this with either the Regional Planning Bodies, Secretary of State, or Welsh Assembly. Section 83(1A) provides that if a Regional Spatial Strategy or the Welsh Assembly identifies the need for a simplified planning zone in an area, then the relevant LPA must consider which part(s) of their area are desirable for such a scheme (inserted by s 45 of the PCPA 2004). If that LPA then concludes an area to be desirable as a simplified planning zone, or if it is directed to do so by the Secretary of State or Welsh Assembly, then it must make a simplified planning zone scheme for all or part of its area.

Schedule 7 of the TCPA 1990 sets out the adoption process including that a proposed scheme **8.54** or the alteration of an existing scheme is subject to statutory consultation and publicity. For instance, where objections to a proposed scheme are received, the LPA may cause a local inquiry or other hearing to be held or require the objections to be considered by someone appointed by the Secretary of State. Under para 1(1) of Sch 7, once adopted, the scheme should include a map, a written statement, and other documents that the LPA thinks appropriate.

Advertising

Advertising consents accounted for 5% of all district planning authority development **8.55** decisions in 2002–3. The display of any advertisement outdoors generally requires the consent of the LPA. Sections 220 to 225 of the TCPA 1990 provides for control, enforcement, and the power to make regulations.

The Town & Country Planning (Control of Advertisements) Regulations 1992 (SI 1992/666) **8.56** (Control of Advertisement Regulations) provide the detailed planning control measures such as the type of advertising covered, e.g. Class (a) posters and notices, (c) fascia signs and projecting signs, and (k) traffic signs. Advertisements outside the Regulation are contained in Sch 2, e.g. Class (b) advertisements on enclosed land (sports grounds and forecourts). Schedule 3 sets out when deemed consent for advertisements may be given and includes (a) various official signs, (b) estate agents' boards, and (j) neighbourhood watch signs. The advertisements covered by Sch 3 are subject to limitations in terms of size, height, location, and the size of letters and symbols. If the limits are exceeded, express consent for the advertisement will be required.

Deemed planning consent is granted for advertisements displayed on a site as of 1 April 1974 **8.57** and for those granted express consent for the statutory period of five years, but where the express consent has expired.

Under the Control of Advertisement Regulations the power to control advertising is exercised **8.58** in the interests of amenity or public safety. One of the biggest problems with advertisement control is fly-posting, where posters are unlawfully stuck to buildings and street furniture. Although the maximum penalty for unlawful advertising, including fly-posting, has recently been increased to £2,500, the enforcement measures in s 224 of the TCPA 1990 are considered inadequate. New reforms include changing the statutory defence of lack of knowledge and consent to align with the defence in s 25 of the London Local Authorities Act 2004 where the beneficiary of any advertisement must demonstrate either a lack of knowledge of the display or that he took all reasonable steps and exercised all due diligence to prevent or discontinue their display (see s 33 of the Clean Neighbourhoods and Environment Act 2005).

8.59   Under s 43 of the Anti-social Behaviour Act 2003 new powers have been granted to local authorities and the police to issue a fixed penalty notice of £50 in relation to minor fly-posting offences. If issued by the local authority they may keep the fine.

Ancient monuments and areas of archaeological and historic importance

Ancient monuments and archaeological areas

8.60   Ancient monuments are protected under the land use planning system and the Ancient Monuments and Archaeological Areas Act 1979 (AMAA 1979). The Act requires the Secretary of State for Culture, Media and Sport to compile a schedule of monuments of national importance and any monument listed is then referred to as a 'scheduled monument'. There is also protection for any monument that has 'historic, architectural, traditional, artistic or archaeological interest attached to it'. Under s 61(7) of AMAA 1979 a monument can include buildings, structures, caves, excavations, vehicles, vessels, aircraft, and any machinery attached to a monument that cannot be detached without being dismantled. There are around 17,500 scheduled monuments including sites such as Stonehenge and Hadrian's Wall.

8.61   Under the AMAA 1979, the Secretary of State also has power to designate areas of archaeological importance, which helps ensure that any development proposal at sites within an area will allow time for the sites to be excavated and recorded.

8.62   Protection under the planning system is contained in PPG16: *Archaeology and Planning* (1990), which provides that detailed development plans, e.g. the new Local Development Frameworks, should include policies for the protection, enhancement, and preservation of sites of archaeological interest and their settings

Historic parks, gardens, and battlefields

8.63   English Heritage maintains a register of parks and gardens with special historic interest. There are no formal protective measures for the sites, although under Art 10(1) of the GDPO, English Heritage must be consulted before an LPA grants planning permission for development that may affect a Grade I or II* park or garden (not so for standard Grade II listed parks and gardens). English Heritage also maintains a register of historic battlefields. These historic sites will be a material consideration when deciding relevant planning applications.

Listed buildings

8.64   Listed buildings are buildings with an architectural or historic interest. Under s 1 of the Planning (Listed Buildings and Conservation Areas) Act 1990 (LBCA 1990) the Secretary of State for Culture, Media and Sport must either compile lists of such buildings or approve lists compiled by English Heritage. In Wales, the National Assembly takes similar responsibilities.

8.65   Under s 91 of the LBCA 1990, building has the same meaning as that given under s 336(1) of the TCPA 1990 (s 336(1) is a long interpretation section for the Act). Paragraph 6.10 of PPG 15: *Planning and the Historic Environment* (1994) sets out the criteria for deciding which buildings should be listed; para 6.11 suggests that those buildings will include:

(a)   all buildings built before 1700;

(b)   most buildings built between 1700 and 1840;

(c)   buildings of quality and character between 1841 and 1914;

(d)   selected buildings after 1914; and

(e)   buildings of outstanding quality and under threat that are 10 to 30 years old.

Listed buildings are classified in the following grades: **8.66**

Grade I   of outstanding architectural interest or historic buildings.

Grade II* important buildings of more than special interest that are not Grade I.

Grade II   buildings of special interest.

According to English Heritage, there are around 9,000 Grade I listings, 19,000 Grade II*   **8.67**
listings, and around 472,000 Grade II listings in England alone.

Protecting listed buildings

Unlawful demolition, alteration, or extension

Listed buildings are protected in a number of ways. Under ss 7 and 9 of the LBCA 1990 if any   **8.68**
person executes or causes to be executed any works for the demolition of a listed building
or the alteration or extension of a building in a way that would affect its character as a
listed building he shall be guilty of an offence. The maximum penalty is a £20,000 fine on
summary conviction, or an unlimited fine and/or two years' imprisonment on indictment.
Section 9(3) of the LBCA 1990 provides a statutory defence where:

(a)   the works were urgently necessary for health and safety or building preservation;

(b)   it was not practicable to preserve the building by repair;

(c)   the works were limited to those minimum measures immediately necessary; and

(d)   notice in writing detailing the works was given to the LPA as soon as reasonably
       practicable.

It is for the defendant to show that the defence applies (s 101 of the Magistrates' Courts Act   **8.69**
1980 and *R v Edwards* [1975] QB 27).

Requirement for listed building consent

Section 8 of the LBCA 1990 allows alterations to listed buildings if written consent is granted   **8.70**
by the LPA or the Secretary of State. The procedure for securing consent is under s 10 of the
Act and in the Planning (Listed Buildings and Conservation Areas) Regulations 1990 (SI
1990/1519). Conditions to any consent may be attached by the LPA (or the Secretary of
State, if he is determining it). There is a right of appeal against a refusal to grant consent or
against conditions attached to a grant under s 20 of the LBCA 1990. An appeal must be made
within six months of the decision. In *Costas Georgiou v LB Enfield & ors* [2005] JPL 62, the
High Court quashed a grant of listed building consent and planning permission for the
conversion of a Grade II listed building to offices, a consulting room, and the development
of a mental health nursing home for up to 60 persons within the curtilage of the house. The
court quashed the consent and permission on the basis of an appearance of bias in that a
fair-minded and informed observer would conclude that was the case. This arose because

members of the local authority's conservation advisory group were also members of the planning committee who granted the listed building consent.

Enforcement notice

8.71   An LPA may, under s 38 of LBCA 1990, issue an enforcement notice to require any works carried out without building consent to be remedied by either restoration, requiring further works to be done or bring the building to the state it would have been had any building consent conditions been complied with.

LPA power to carry out repair works

8.72   Local planning authorities have the power under s 54 of LBCA 1990 to execute any works that appear to be urgently necessary for the preservation of listing buildings. Under s 55, the LPA may recover the costs in carrying out urgent works: see *R v Secretary of State for Wales ex p City & County of Swansea* [1999] JPL 524.

Compulsory purchase of buildings needing repair

8.73   Under s 47 of the LBCA 1990, the Secretary of State may, after consulting with English Heritage, make a compulsory purchase of any listed building where he believes that reasonable steps are not being taken for the building's proper preservation. He may also authorize an LPA to make a compulsory purchase, following the normal compulsory purchase procedures (see s 8) including that prior to the acquisition, the LPA must serve on the owner a repair notice specifying the works that the authority believes are reasonably necessary to preserve the building and that if those works are not carried out then the LPA may issue compulsory purchase proceedings. Compensation paid on compulsory purchase is based upon market value.

Building preservation notice

8.74   Buildings that are not listed but nevertheless have special architectural or historic interest may be protected by the relevant LPA issuing a building preservation notice (s 3 of the LBCA 1990). The notice should confirm a building's special interest and that the LPA is requesting that the Secretary of State should list the building. The notice lasts for six months. However, under s 29 of the Act, compensation must be paid for any loss arising from the notice if the building is not listed.

Options for owners of listed buildings

Certificate of immunity

8.75   Section 6 of the LBCA 1990 enables any person to apply to the Secretary of State for a certificate of immunity from listed building status. If issued, a certificate of immunity will last for five years or be the subject of a building preservation notice. This will assist anyone who has applied for planning permission that involves the demolition, alteration, or extension of a building.

Listed building purchase notice

8.76   Owners of properties that have been refused listed building consent, or granted consent subject to conditions, and wish to sell the land may serve a listed building purchase notice on the LPA requiring the authority to purchase it (ss 32 to 37 of the LBCA 1990). The owner must show that the land has become 'incapable of reasonably beneficial use'.

Conservation areas

Local planning authorities must, from time to time, determine areas of special architectural **8.77** or historic interest in their district and then designate any such areas as conservation areas. The LPA must publish policies (usually in their local development plan) on the preservation and enhancement of conservation areas. Any development within a conservation area will be subject to stricter planning controls, e.g. permitted development rights under the GPDO 1995 tend to be restricted and any relevant conservation policies of an LPA must be taken into account as a material planning consideration.

Mining and minerals

Mining, quarrying, and minerals excavation have significant environmental effects. There **8.78** is the removal of finite resources, e.g. the sand, rock, or slate being extracted. There is the noise, dust, and vibration generated during extraction. There is also the impact of transporting the materials to their destination. The works can continue for long periods. Mines and quarries can be worked for decades. For these reasons, among others, mining and minerals development are considered, at times, separately from conventional development. For instance, the relevant authorities, i.e. mineral planning authorities (MPAs), are, under s 1(4) of the TCPA 1990, county planning matters. There are also 15 national policy statements; Minerals Planning Guidance Notes (MPGs) numbered 1 to 15, such as MPG 1: *General Considerations and the Development Plan System* (1996), which sets out the main principles and objectives for minerals planning and MPG 5: *Stability in Surface Mineral Workings and Tips* (2000), which gives advice on design, assessment, and inspection of surface mining workings.

Section 55(4) of the TCPA 1990 provides that mining operations include: **8.79**

   (a) the removal of material of any description—
      (i)   from a mineral-working deposit;
      (ii) from a deposit of pulverised fuel ash or other furnace ash or clinker; or
      (iii) from a deposit of iron, steel or other metallic slags; and
   (b) the extraction of minerals from a disused railway embankment.

Section 336(1) adds that: **8.80**

'mineral-working deposit' means any deposit of material remaining after minerals have been extracted from land or otherwise deriving from the carrying out of operations for the winning and working of minerals in, on or under land;

'minerals' includes all substances of a kind ordinarily worked for removal by underground or surface working, except that it does not include peat cut for the purposes other than sale;

When granting permission to mine, the MPA can grant conditions of restoration requiring **8.81** the return of any subsoil or topsoil to the site and to contour the site appropriately. The MPA can also grant aftercare conditions that are implemented after the restoration works are complete (para 2, Sch 5 of the TCPA 1990). The MPA should place a time limit on the permission. If they fail to do so there is a statutory time limit of 60 years under paras 1 to 6 of Sch 5.

8.82   Under s 96 of the Environment Act 1995, MPAs must review the minerals sites in their area and decide whether to revoke or modify the permission granted. They have other regulatory powers such as the power to prohibit or suspend mineral works.

8.83   Due to the long-term nature of mining activities there have evolved different laws relating to mining permissions before 1948, known as old mining permissions; mining permissions granted between 1948 and 1982; and mining permissions since 1982. Due to the size and environmental impact, many planning applications will require an environmental state- ment (ES) in support: see Chapter 24: Environmental assessment. It will also be required when considering an existing mine or site that is being reconsidered or new conditions being set. In *R v North Yorkshire CC ex p Brown* [1999] JPL 616 the Court of Appeal quashed the determination of conditions attached to an old mining permission, because an ES had not been prepared and the determination of the conditions equated to the grant of permission to proceed with mining. In *R (Wells) v Secretary of State for Transport, Local Government and the Regions* [2004] Case C-201/02 the ECJ held that a purposive approach is required to be taken when considering development consent with LPAs under a continuing duty to make good past breaches of EIA where possible.

Nature conservation

General protection for wildlife

8.84   Nature conservation is considered in Chapter 16: Wildlife and nature conservation. It is relevant to land use planning at both the strategic and development control stage in land use planning. Sections 12(3A), 31(3), and 36(3) of the TCPA 1990 provide that plans shall include policies on the conservation of the natural beauty, amenity of land, and the physical environment. PPG 9: *Nature Conservation* (1994) sets out Government objectives, the role of LPAs, English Nature and the Countryside Commission for Wales (the main nature conservation bodies), and advises on the various aspects of nature conservation such as designated sites and the treatment of nature conservation in development plans. Paragraph 19 of PPG 9 provides that nature conservation objectives should be taken into account in all planning activities that affect rural and coastal land use, and in urban areas where there is wildlife of local importance.

Designated sites

8.85   One of the more effective ways to protect wildlife is to designate special conservation sites. PPG 9, Annex A describes the range of designations and includes:

- Sites of Special Scientific Interest (SSSIs).
- Limestone Pavement Orders (LPOs). The removal of stone from land subject to an LPO requires an application under Pt III of the TCPA 1990.
- National Nature Reserves (NNRs).
- Special Protection Areas (SPAs) and Special Areas of Conservation (SACs).
- Ramsar sites are listed by the Secretary of State in accordance with the Convention on Wetlands of International Importance Especially of Waterfowl Habitat 1971 (the Ramsar Convention).
- Biogenetic Reserves tend to be sites already designated as SSSIs or NNRs.
- Marine Nature Reserves (MNRs) are designated under the WCA.

- The Secretary of State may designate Areas of Special Protection for Birds.
- Local authorities may establish Local Nature Reserves (LNRs) under the National Parks and Access to the Countryside Act 1949.

Trees and hedgerows

The protection of trees and hedgerows arises in a number of ways in land use planning. This is also considered in Chapter 16: Wildlife and nature conservation   8.86

The Government's *Tree Preservation Orders: A Guide to the Law and Good Practice* (2000) states at para 5.5 that the presence of trees and woodlands has always been recognized as an important material consideration in determining planning applications. Section 197 of the TCPA 1990 places a duty on LPAs to ensure that, whenever appropriate, adequate provision is made for trees when granting planning permission. This may be achieved by conditions for preservation or planting.   8.87

Sections 198 to 214D of the TCPA 1990 provides powers for local authorities to make provision for the preservation of trees or woodlands through tree preservation orders (TPOs) and for trees in conservation areas. In defining a tree, Phillips J suggested in *Bullock v Secretary of State* (1980) 40 P&CR 246 that for the purposes of the Act : 'anything that ordinarily one would call a tree is a "tree" . . .'   8.88

The main protection for hedgerows, other than their consideration as a matter of general planning principles, is under the Hedgerows Regulations 1997 (SI 1997/1160). Government guidance, *The Hedgerows Regulations: A Guide to the Law and Good Practice* (1997), suggests that a hedgerow is a row of bushes forming a hedge, with the trees, etc., growing in it.   8.89

Types of developers

There are as many types of developers as there are types of land use. Most are subject to the general planning rules and regulations; some are subject to special control, e.g. local authorities seeking to develop land themselves.   8.90

Private land and home owners

As indicated above, the majority of planning applications relate to private land owners such as householders wishing to make small extensions to their homes. These proposals will often be non-contentious although they could develop into neighbour disputes.   8.91

Corporate bodies including building/construction companies

Most new construction work will be by companies carrying out their main business as developers. This accounted for over 30% of the planning decisions in 2002–3. Collectively, developers own large areas of land across the country and develop this by building homes, industrial units, offices, or shops.   8.92

General corporate activities

Many other companies will be making planning applications to carry on the business activity although the development itself will not be the primary purpose of their business,   8.93

e.g. applications for displaying advertisements and change of use. A typical example will be a chain of pubs applying for a change of use for a high street office building into a public house.

Local authorities

8.94　The local authority itself may wish to develop its own land. This will often be to further a policy that it regards will benefit its local community such as building a library or a school. It may also buy land from other landowners to do this under the Compulsory Purchase regime (see Chapter 12: Property and land rights). LPAs must apply for planning permission in the same way as any other developer; although, if it is the planning committee itself that is developing the land then the rules of delegation do not apply and the application would have to be heard either by full council or another committee with the same delegated powers to consider the application.

Central government and the Crown

8.95　Part 7 of the PCPA 2004 abolished the Crown immunity to require planning permission. Central government and the Crown must now make an application for planning permission whenever necessary, although provisions have been introduced to cover development relating to national security and emergencies.

Statutory undertakers

8.96　Statutory undertakers include gas, electric, and water companies as well as organizations operating railways, road and water transport services, and airport operators (s 262 of the TCPA 1990). Any statutory undertaker wishing to carry out development should apply to the LPA, although much of the proposed development will be covered under the GDPO 1995. If any matter is referred to the Secretary of State either on appeal or 'call in', the relevant government department should also be informed, e.g. for a road proposal it would be the Department for Transport.

C　APPLYING FOR PLANNING PERMISSION

Is planning permission necessary?

8.97　Before applying for planning permission and incurring the direct and indirect costs involved it is important to check whether permission to develop is actually necessary. As a starting point s 57(1) of the TCPA 1990 provides that:

> planning permission is required for the carrying out of any development of land.

8.98　However, s 57 contains specific exceptions relating to the reversion of land to its original purpose after the change of use for a limited period. Some land use development will not fall within the legal definition of development under the planning regime. Further, some works that are within the legislative definition of development may be classed as permitted development or exempt from development due to the nature of the development, e.g. a change in the use of building from one purpose to another within the same class. The exceptions to s 57 are considered below.

What is development for the purpose of land use planning?

Development is defined in s 55(1) of the TCPA 1990 as: **8.99**

> the carrying out of building, engineering, mining or other operations in, on, over or under land, [often referred to as *operational development*] or the making or any *material change in the use* of any buildings or other land.

The two parts of the definition are distinct to the extent that a material change of use **8.100** cannot authorize any operational development (s 336(1) of the TCPA 1990). In contrast, it is accepted under s 75 of the TCPA 1990 that operational development will almost always result in a change of use. It is often convenient for practical purposes to consider development to be in two parts: operational development and change of use.

Operational development

Section 55(1A) provides that building operations includes: **8.101**

(a) the demolition of buildings;
(b) rebuilding;
(c) structural alterations of or additions to buildings; and
other operations normally undertaken by a . . . builder.

Section 55(2) of the TCPA 1990 provides that the following shall *not* be regarded as **8.102** development:

(a) the carrying out for the maintenance, improvement or other alteration of any building of works which:
  (i) affect only the interior of the building, or
  (ii) do not materially affect the external appearance of the building . . . and are not works for making good war damage or . . . for alterations providing additional underground space;
(b) necessary maintenance and improvement works on roads;
(c) inspection, repairs and other works on utility services (e.g. sewers, pipes cables);
(d) use within the curtilage of a dwelling house that is incidental to the enjoyment of the dwelling house;
(e) use of land and buildings for agriculture and forestry;
(f) buildings or land used for a purpose in the same class [under the Use Classes Order];
(g) the demolition of any building specified in a Direction by the Secretary of State e.g. the Town & Country Planning (Demolition — Description of Buildings) Direction 1995.

'Building' is defined by s 336 of the TCPA 1990 as: 'any structure or erection and any part of a **8.103** building so defined, but does not include plant or machinery comprised in a building'. This is wider than the ordinary meaning and may include cranes, masts, and fences. The court in *Cardiff Rating Authority v Guest Keen Baldwin's Iron and Steel Co Ltd* [1949] 1 KB 385 identified three relevant factors to determine what a building was:

• size, such that a building would normally be constructed on site as opposed to being brought already made to the site;
• permanence, some degree of permanence was required; and
• physical attachment, some degree of attachment should be evident, although this is not conclusive.

8.104   In *Parkes v Secretary of State for the Environment* [1979] 1 All ER 211 Lord Denning MR stated that:

> [building operations are] . . . activities which result in some physical alteration to the land which have some degree of permanence to the land itself, whereas 'use' comprises activities which were done in, alongside, or on the land but did not interfere with the actual physical characteristics of the land.

8.105   The court in *Sunbury on Thames UDC v Mann* [1958] 9 P&CR 309 stated that the planning legislation distinguished between use and operation. Permission for change of use did not authorize a building erected without planning permission and the occupier had to comply with the enforcement notice served and demolish the building.

8.106   Demolition requiring planning permission mainly applies to dwellinghouses or buildings adjoining dwellinghouses. The Town and Country Planning (Demolition — Description of Buildings) Direction 1995 states that planning permission is not required for the demolition of:

- listed buildings, buildings in conservation areas, and scheduled monuments, although listed building consent may be required;
- buildings not exceeding 50 cubic metres; and
- buildings other than dwellinghouses or buildings adjoining dwellinghouses.

8.107   Section 336(1) of the TCPA 1990 provides that 'engineering operations' includes the formation or laying out of means of access to highways, but note the highways exceptions to development in s 55(2)(b). In *Fayrewood Fish Farms Ltd v Secretary of State for the Environment* [1984] JPL 267 the judge noted that engineering operations must mean 'operations of the kind usually undertaken by engineers' and in *RFW Copper v K J Bruce Smith* [1998] JPL 1077 the Court of Appeal found that the removal of tennis courts was engineering as opposed to building (demolition) operations. In *Field v First Secretary of State and Crawley BC* [2004] EWHC 147 Sullivan J allowed an appeal against an Inspector's decision concluding, among other things, that the demolition of cottages did amount to development and so a permission granted in 1967 to demolish four cottages and build two bungalows remained valid because the demolition had taken place before 1 April 1969, the date that the TCPA 1968 required development work to commence if outline permission granted before that date was to remain valid and not expire.

8.108   Mining is discussed in Section B.

8.109   There is no statutory definition of 'other operations' and very little case law for clarification. In *Cambridge CC v Secretary of State for the Environment* (1991) 89 LGR 1015, the Court of Appeal held that the term did not mean all other operations and that they had to be of a constructive character that were similar to building or engineering operations.

8.110   In the Inspector's decision *North Norfolk DC, M Crane* [2004] JPL 1723, the Planning Inspector refused to grant a certificate of lawful use or development in respect of the temporary use of two growing tunnels on agricultural land. The tunnels were regarded as operational development and did not have the appropriate planning permission.

Material change of use

'Material change of use' is not defined in the TCPA 1990 although s 55(2)(d) to (f) set out **8.111** what is not development, i.e. incidental enjoyment of a house, agriculture or forestry use, and change of use within the same use class. Outside this, there is a wide discretion for an LPA to decide what activities are considered development and the courts have been reluctant to interfere with this discretion, subject to irrationality. It is a question of fact and degree. For instance, in *Bendles Motors v Bristol Corporation* [1963] 1 WLR 247, the court found that the erection of an egg-vending machine on the forecourt of a garage was held to be a material change of use of the site from, one assumes, a garage to a garage and egg shop. The critical test is whether a change is material or whether it will have an impact in planning terms. Schiemann LJ in *Thames Heliport plc v Tower Hamlets LBC* [1997] JPL 448 stated that one should ask: 'has someone made a material change in the use of land from the point of view of human beings likely to be affected by the change which had occurred.'

Forty years on from *Bendles*, the Inspector in the planning appeal decision *Pendle Borough* **8.112** *Council App/E2340* [2002] JPL 1303 had to consider whether hot food sales were ancillary to a petrol filling station shop after the LPA had served an enforcement notice that the petrol station was using the shop unlawfully, i.e. selling hot food when it did not have planning permission to do so. The Inspector held that whether there had been a material change of use of the land was a matter of fact and degree. The Inspector allowed the appeal concluding that permission should be granted.

In terms of agriculture, the change from non-agricultural to agricultural use does not require **8.113** planning permission: see *McKellen v Minister of Housing & Local Government* (1966) EG 683. Further, placing an existing building on agricultural land may not be building operations. In *Wealden DC v SSE* (1987) 56 P&CR 286 CA a residential caravan that provided a weatherproof store and place for mixing cattle feed was not development.

For 'change of use within the same use class' The Use Classes Order 1987 (as amended) **8.114** removes the need for planning permission where there is a change of use within certain specified uses of land or buildings. The aim is to reduce the number of unnecessary planning applications. There are 14 different classes of development:

A1   Shops, e.g. retail, post office, hairdressing, funeral directors.
A2   Financial and professional services.
A3   Food and drink, i.e. for consumption on the premises.
A4   Pubs and bars.
A5   Takeaways.

B1   Business, e.g. for offices other than in A2, research and development.
B2   General industrial.
(B3 to B7 repealed and the activities incorporated into B2.)
B8   Storage or distribution.

C1   Hotels and hostels.
C2   Residential institutions, e.g. hospital or nursing home.
C3   Dwellinghouses.

D1 Non-residential institutions, e.g. museum, public library.

D2 Assembly and leisure.

D3 Late night leisure.

8.115 The operation of the Use Classes Order 1987 would enable, for example, a hairdressing salon (Class A1) to convert to a post office (also in Class A1) without requiring planning permission. However, the change of use from a hairdresser's to a pub (Class A4) would require an application for planning permission.

8.116 Some changes of use are regarded as permitted development within Pt 3 of the GPDO 1995 even though they are across classes, e.g. the change between the use of building in Class A3 to Class A1. The rationale is that the new use is less problematic, in planning terms, than the existing use. However, in *Corporation of City of London v Secretary of State for the Environment & anor* [1972] 23/24 P&CR 169 the court held that, provided an LPA had regard to the development plan and to other material considerations and that any conditions imposed were reasonable and reasonably related to the permitted development, it might impose restrictions beyond those laid down specifically in the legislation even if that meant a restriction on a use that would not amount to development.

8.117 Section 55(2A) of the TCPA 1990 (inserted by s 49 of the PCPA 2004) amends the definition of development in s 55(2) to include the creation of additional floorspace within buildings under planning control. Secondary legislation will enable the Secretary of State, by development order, to bring specified proposals for the provision of additional floorspace in existing buildings within the definition of 'development'.

8.118 Section 55(3) of the TCPA 1990 states that, 'for the avoidance of doubt' (a) the division of a single dwellinghouse into two or more separate dwellinghouses (a building of multiple occupation) is a material change of use. However, there is no statutory provision that states that the conversion of a multiple occupation building into a single dwelling constitutes a material change of use. The court in *Richmond LBC v Secretary of State for the Environment & ors* [2001] JPL 84 held that whether such a conversion was a planning matter was a question of fact and degree. Further, the conversion would have to comply with s 55(2) of the TCPA 1990 and not materially affect the external appearance of the building.

8.119 Section 55(3)(b) then provides that:

the deposit of refuse or waste materials on land involves a material change in its use, notwithstanding that the land is comprised in a site already used for that purpose if:

(i)   the superficial areas of the deposit is extended, or

(ii) the height of the disposal is extended and exceeds the level of the land adjoining the site.

8.120 If a use falls outside of the scope of the Use Classes Order 1987 the general principle is that planning permission will be required for any material change of use, however it may well be appropriate to consider the GPDO 1995. Such uses include petrol stations, launderettes, and scrap yards.

8.121 Section 55(5) of the TCPA 1990 provides an additional means of control emphasizing that the use of any external part of a building for advertising, when it is not normally used as such, is a material change of use and requires planning permission.

Where current use is intensified, this may amount to a material change of use if the increase **8.122** in activity has significant planning impacts. *Guildford RDC v Perry* [1959] 2 QB 112 considered that increasing intensity of use may involve a substantial increase in the burden of services that a local authority would have to supply. This may be a material factor in some cases as to whether the use of the land has materially changed.

In the Inspector's Appeal Decision of *Bradford MDC, C Cockayne and J Sampson* [2002] JPL **8.123** 1413, two enforcement notices were upheld alleging a breach of planning control from a dwellinghouse to a mixed use of residential and the keeping of an excessive number of cats. The Inspector, in dismissing the appeal noted:

> It appears from the evidence that activities on the appeal site in connection with the cat refuge and keeping of pet cats has resulted in a significant change in the residential character of the property.

The appeal decision noted that a statutory nuisance abatement notice had also been served **8.124** by the local authority arising from complaints from residents that cats were regularly defecating in their gardens.

Permitted development

Article 3 of the GPDO 1995 provides that, subject to exceptions, planning permission is **8.125** automatically granted for the classes of development described as permitted development contained in Sch 2 of the Order. The permitted development classes are set out in Figure 8.2 below.

It is important to note that each class is often divided into categories. For example, Class 2: **8.126** Minor operations, has within it Classes A to C, with A being the erection, construction, maintenance, improvement, or alteration of a gate, fence, wall, or other means of enclosure. Further, each class (or sub-class) will often be divided into permitted development, permitted development with conditions, or development not permitted. For example, Pt 32: Schools, colleges etc., permits the erection of any building for a purpose incidental to the use of a school, college, university, or hospital. Paragraph A.2 provides that:

> Development is permitted by Class A subject to the condition that, in the case of any article 1(5) land, any materials used shall be of a similar appearance to those used for the original school, college, university or hospital buildings.

Article 1(5) land includes land within a National Park, area of outstanding natural beauty, **8.127** a conservation area, an area for the enhancement and protection of the natural beauty and amenity of the countryside and the Broads).

Directions restricting permitted development rights

Article 4(1) of the GPDO 1995 provides that if the Secretary of State or the appropriate LPA is **8.128** satisfied that it is expedient that development described in any Part, Class, or paragraph in Sch 2, except Class B of Pts 22 and 23, should not be carried out unless permission is granted for it on an application, he or they may give a direction that the permitted development rights under Art 3 should not apply. The Government discourages the blanket use of Art 4 directions and for the majority of occasions, the LPA must seek the Secretary of State's approval before making such a direction. If, following an Art 4 direction, planning permission is refused or granted subject to more stringent conditions than those provided

Figure 8.2 Schedule 2 of the GPDO 1995: Permitted development

Part

1	Development within the curtilage of a dwellinghouse
2	Minor operations, e.g. erection or alteration of gates, fences, and walls
3	Changes of use
4	Temporary buildings and uses
5	Caravan sites
6	Agricultural buildings and operations
7	Forestry buildings and operations
8	Industrial and warehouse development
9	Repairs to unadopted streets and private ways
10	Repairs to services
11	Development under local or private Acts or orders
12	Development by local authorities
13	Development by local highway authorities
14	Development by drainage bodies
15	Development by the Environment Agency
16	Development by or on behalf of sewerage undertakers
17	Development by statutory undertakers
18	Aviation development
19	Development ancillary to mining operations
20	Coal mining development by the Coal Authority and licensed operators
21	Waste tipping at a mine
22	Mineral exploration
23	Removal of material from mineral-working deposits
24	Development by telecommunications code system operators
25	Other telecommunication developments
26	Development by the Historic Buildings and Monuments Commission for England
27	Use by members of certain recreational organizations
28	Development at amusement parks
29	Driver information systems
30	Toll road facilities
31	Demolition of buildings
32	Schools, colleges, universities, and hospitals
33	Closed circuit television cameras

under the GPDO 1995, then the landowner may claim compensation under ss 107 and 108 of the TCPA 1990.

8.129   To gain a full understanding of the GPDO 1995 and the development classed as permitted development the legislation should be considered in full. This can be downloaded from www.odpm.gov.uk, although the original legislation has been amended on several occasions. To put the Order into context, there is a brief consideration of two aspects of the GPDO 1995: Pt 1 — development within the curtilage of a dwellinghouse and Pt 24 —

development by telecommunications code system operators, which was revised by the TCP (GPD) (Amendment) (England) Order 2001 (SI 2001/2718).

Development within the curtilage of a dwellinghouse

There has been some difficulty in assessing what is meant by incidental use within the curtilage of a dwellinghouse. First, certain activities within the curtilage of a dwellinghouse will not be regarded as development at all by virtue of s 55(2)(d) of the TCPA 1990. Also, what is regarded as a curtilage is vague. It is simple to assess in terms of a house with a small front or back garden because the curtilage could be regarded as the boundary of the title to the land. However, if there is any larger area of land attached then it will be hard to justify all the area forming part of the title as the curtilage. **8.130**

Certain classes within Pt 1 provide that the use should be incidental to the use and enjoyment of the dwellinghouse. In *Wallington v Secretary of State for Wales* [1990] P&CR 150 the Court of Appeal, considering 44 dogs in a dwellinghouse, concluded that incidental use could not be determined by the subjective views of the owner; the LPA should apply an objective standard. In *Holding v First Secretary of State* [2003] EWHC 3148 Admin, a hanger in which three aircraft were kept was held not to be for a purpose incidental to the enjoyment of the dwellinghouse. **8.131**

The size and nature of any development will also be significant. In general, most small garden structures are likely to be regarded as permitted development, e.g. a tool shed or garden ornaments, providing they are within the curtilage and they are a reasonable size. In the planning appeal decision *Sevenoaks DC, App/G 2245* [2002] JPL 1305 an enforcement notice ordered the demolition of a large garage and replacement with a smaller one. The Inspector held that the extent of the permitted development rights had been exaggerated although a garage up to 174 cu m in size would fall within the permitted development rights under Pt 1, Classes A and E. **8.132**

Part 24: development by telecommunications code system operators

The development of mobile phone masts has given rise to great concern and litigation over the last decade. The Mobile Operators Association estimates that there will be up to 50,000 masts by the end of 2007. There is concern about the impact on visual amenity particularly in the countryside. There is also fear about the health impacts from the emission of radioactive waves. One of the important provisions under Pt 24 is that the development of masts under 15 metres in height are, subject to exceptions, granted permitted development rights. The development of mobile phone masts is considered further in Chapter 13: Radiation. **8.133**

Local development orders: ss 61A to 61C of the PCPA 2004

Section 40 of the PCPA 2004 inserts three new sections into the TCPA 1990. Section 61A provides that an LPA may by order (a local development order (LDO)) implement policies that provide for permitted development rights in addition to those contained in the GPDO 1995. Government guidance on the types of development that could be included within an LDO is expected. **8.134**

Pre-application consultation and other action

Informal consultation with the LPA

8.135   Circular 28/83 suggests that, before applying for planning permission, it is useful to discuss the proposal with an LPA officer. If there is any doubt whether a matter is not regarded as development or is permitted development then this can be confirmed before an application is made. Paragraph 5.9 of *Delivering a Fundamental Change* (DTLR, 2001) affirmed that it wanted to encourage pre-application discussions between applicants and local authorities to help guide applicants through the process, clarify what is required, and help them formulate acceptable proposals. However, an LPA is under no duty of care to an applicant: *Tidman v Reading BC* [1994] 3 PLR 72, although a complaint may be made to the Local Government Ombudsman (Section E).

Notice of the proposed application to the owner

8.136   Section 65 of the TCPA 1990 requires, via Art 7 of the GDPO 1995, for an applicant to certify his/her interest in the land relating to the application and that he has notified the owner(s) of the land at the prescribed date, i.e. 21 days before the planning application. Any know- ingly or recklessly misleading statement is an offence subject to a maximum penalty of a £5,000 fine on summary conviction. Article 6 of the GDPO 1995 provides detail as to service of the notice, local advertising when necessary, and specific requirements for certain appli- cations. Parts 1 and 2 of Sch 2 of the TCPA 1990 set out the forms of the Art 6 Notice and the Art 7 Certificate(s) A to D.

Certificate of lawfulness of proposed use or development (CLOPUD)

8.137   Formal clarification is possible by making an application under s 192 of TCPA 1990 for a CLOPUD. Under s 192(2), if the LPA is satisfied that the use or operations proposed would be lawful they must issue a certificate to that effect. In the Inspector's appeal decision *Canter- bury CC, South East Parks Ltd* [2005] JPL 136, the Planning Inspector allowed an appeal against the refusal of the LPA to grant a CLOPUD in relation to the seasonal use of land as a caravan site. In this case, there was a planning permission to use the land from 1960 for the continuation of use as a seasonal caravan camp but no conditions attached to the per- mission. The Inspector held that following the decision of *I'm Your Man Ltd v Secretary of State* [1998] 4 PLR 107 that a condition implying seasonal restrictions is not possible.

Development without making an application

8.138   Many developers may decide not to make any application for planning either because they are confident the development does not require a formal application (because it does not constitute development or because it is permitted development under the GPDO 1995) or because they do not realize that permission is required. It may also be that they are prepared to take the risk of developing without planning permission and either not be found out or that no enforcement action is taken. This may be an attractive option for unscrupulous developers who are aware that their LPA does not have the resources to properly administer the enforcement side of their planning responsibilities, but is, of course, unlawful.

Certificate of lawfulness of existing use or development (CLEUD)

Similar to CLOPUD, any person can apply under s 191 of the TCPA 1990 for a CLEUD that **8.139**
will confirm that the existing use or development of land is lawful. Once satisfied of the
lawfulness of the use, operations, or other matter described in the CLEUD application, the
LPA must issue a certificate to that effect (s 191(4) of the TCPA 1990).

It is, however, an offence under s 194 for someone, for the purpose of procuring either a **8.140**
CLOPUD or CLEUD, to knowingly or recklessly make a false statement, to use a false or
misleading document, or to withhold information with intent to deceive. The maximum
penalty is £5,000 on summary conviction or an unlimited fine and/or two years' imprisonment on indictment.

Time limits for enforcement action

Any LPA wishing to take enforcement action against unlawful development must do so **8.141**
within a certain time period. For operational development, enforcement action must be
commenced within four years of completion of the unlawful works; for a material change of
use, the action must begin within 10 years.

Preparing an EIA in support of the planning application

Planning applications for the largest projects must have an environmental statement (ES) in **8.142**
support. This will need to be prepared following an environmental impact assessment (EIA)
that must take place prior to the application for permission. Often, it is a matter for the LPA
whether a proposal requires an ES. Any discussions and consideration by the LPA must be
prior to the application: see Chapter 24: Environmental assessment.

Applying for planning permission

Application fees

TCP (Fees for Application and Deemed Applications) Regulations 1989 (SI 1989/193) as **8.143**
amended by SI 2002/768 set out the costs of submitting a planning application. These vary
according to the type and size of proposal, e.g. para 1.1 on the scale of fees provides that for
the erection of dwellinghouses the cost is currently £220 per 0.1 hectare of the site area for
outline permission and, in other cases, £220 for each dwellinghouse to be created by the
development, subject to a maximum of £11,000.

Form and content of planning application

Under reg 3(1) of the TCP (Applications) Regs 1988 (SI 1988/1812) (The Applications Regs **8.144**
1998), a planning application shall:

(a) be made on a form provided by the LPA;
(b) include the particulars specified in the form and be accompanied by a plan, which
     identifies the land and any other plans, drawings, and information necessary to describe
     the development; and
(c) be accompanied by three copies of the plans and drawing submitted with it.

The style of the application form can be left for the LPA, although certain basic information **8.145** will always be required. Under reg 4 the LPA may direct that further necessary information and plans are provided or evidence is provided to verify matters in order to determine the application.

8.146 A new s 62 of the TCPA 1990 has been introduced by s 42 of the PCPA 2004. The new section should simplify the current requirement that planning applications and other consents must be prescribed by regulations. The new process will prescribe forms through the use of a development order. The section also requires planning applications to be accompanied by a design statement, access statement, or both.

Outline permission

8.147 The grant of planning permission required under s 57 of the TCPA 1990 may be for outline permission. Section 92 of the TCPA 1990 defines 'outline planning permission' as:

> permission granted, in accordance with the provisions of a development order, with the reservation for subsequent approval by the LPA or Secretary of State of matters not particularised in the application ('reserved matters').

8.148 Regulation 2 of the Applications Regs 1988 defines outline planning permission and the reserved matters as permission for the erection of a building, subject to a condition requiring the subsequent approval of one or more reserved matters, i.e. siting, design, external appearance, means of access, and landscaping. In *Kebbel Development Ltd v the First Secretary of State and Harrogate BC* [2003] EWCA Civ 1855, the Court of Appeal affirmed the Inspector's decision to refuse the grant of reserved matters following a failure to apply for these within the time specified in the outline planning permission.

The General Development Procedure Order 1995

8.149 Once the LPA has received a planning application there are a number of procedural requirements such as placing the matter on the planning register and publicizing the application locally, which are contained within the GDPO 1995. This is considered further in Section D.

Duty on statutory consultees to respond to consultation

8.150 Section 54 of the PCPA 2004 introduced a requirement that bodies required to be consulted by the Secretary of State, the National Assembly for Wales, or an LPA before the grant of any permission, approval, or consent under the planning Acts must respond to consultation requests within a prescribed period. It also applies to pre-application consultation. Statutory consultees must respond within 21 days and provide a substantive response of either: no comment, content with the development, reference to existing standing advice (already enacted by Art 4 of the TCP (GDP) (England) (Amendment) Order 2003 (SI 2003/2047)), together with the provision of helpful advice.

D   DETERMINING APPLICATIONS, CONDITIONS, AND OBLIGATIONS

Determining planning applications

What is planning permission?

In essence planning permission is the right to carry out the process of developing land. It   **8.151**
can be limited in its scope and can have obligations attached to it.

Section 75 of the TCPA 1990 provides that, subject to other provisions, any grant of   **8.152**
planning permission shall enure for the benefit of the land and of all persons for the
time being interested in it. Section 75(2) and (3) provides that where permission is granted
for the erection of a building, the grant may specify a purpose. If no purpose is specified that
permission shall include the use of the building for which the building is designed. Under ss
97 to 100 of the TCPA 1990 an LPA or Secretary of State can revoke or modify a planning
permission where it is expedient to do so.

Nature of permission

In *R v Ashford BC ex p Shepway DC* [1999] PLCR 12 the court held that, generally, the permis-   **8.153**
sion granted should be defined by looking at the permission document itself, with any
conditions. The application is not part of the formal permission unless expressly referred
to in the permission document. If there is uncertainty, ambiguity, or the permission is
challenged then it is appropriate to look at any documents supporting the application,
including the application itself.

It is not conclusive that the grant of permission for a site completely extinguishes the   **8.154**
existing use right. In some cases this may be obvious. In *Petticoat Lane Rentals v Secretary of
State for the Environment* [1971] 1 WLR 1112, the court suggested that in cases where open
space was fully built upon following grant of permission that grant does extinguish the
former use. However, it was less certain where the grant of permission covers an area of open
space and only part of that space is built upon. Moore's *A Practical Approach to Planning Law*
(p 324, 2005) suggests that until the problem is resolved, a developer applying for permission
to develop part of its land should consider restricting the application to the relevant part
only, leaving the authority to restrict, if necessary, the existing use rights of the remaining
land by express condition.

Who determines the planning application?

The LPA is, for the majority of applications, the district council, metropolitan/city council,   **8.155**
or unitary authority. It may also be the county council, particularly for mining permissions,
or the Secretary of State, usually acting through his regional Government offices such as the
Government Office of the South West (GOSW).

If it is the LPA that is determining applications then, as a starting point, it should be acting   **8.156**
on a council-wide basis. However, LPAs will delegate authority to decide the majority of
applications to committees, sub-committees, or planning officers under s 101 of the Local
Government Act 1972. The Government aims to ensure that over 90% of all planning applications are determined by planning officers under delegated authority. There are a number
of principles relevant to delegated authority in this context:

- The decision of the delegate becomes the decision of the public body itself.
- Delegation to a committee must involve delegation to more than one member of the local authority.
- The delegate cannot usually itself further delegate the decision-making power.
- Where authority to take decisions is lawfully delegated, the decision-maker must act within the scope of his delegated authority.

Called-in applications

8.157 The Secretary of State has the power, under s 77 of the TCPA 1990, to call-in planning applications and decide these in place of the LPA. A Government statement in 2000 on call-in applications noted that the powers would only be used very rarely and that it would be considered on a case-by-case basis. Section 55 and Sch 2 of the PCPA 2004 requires the Secretary of State to set a timetable for his decisions on called-in applications and recovered appeals, together with any other decisions for which he is responsible and which are connected to those decisions.

Major infrastructure projects

8.158 The Government determines the largest development proposals such as the construction of motorways, nuclear power stations, and ports. Under the Town and Country Planning (Major Infrastructure Project Inquiries Procedure) (England) Rules 2002 (SI 2002/1223) such projects are defined with reference to Sch 1 of the EIA Regulations. Also, new ss 76A and 76B of the TCPA 1990 by s 44 of the PCPA 2004 enable the Secretary of State to call in applications 'of national or regional importance' and for a public inquiry to be held.

Powers and procedure for determining a planning application

Determining planning applications with regard to the development plan

8.159 Section 70(1) of the TCPA 1990 provides that where an application is made to an LPA for planning permission they may grant permission unconditionally, subject to conditions or refuse permission. Section 70(2) of the TCPA 1990 provides that in dealing with a planning application, the LPA shall have regard to the provisions of the development plan, so far as material to the application, and to any other material considerations. Section 38(6) of the PCPA 2004 provides that:

> If regard is to be had to the development plan for the purpose of any determination to be made under the Planning Acts, the determination must be made in accordance with the plan unless material considerations indicate otherwise.

8.160 If the development plan contains relevant policies and there are no other material considerations then the application must be determined in accordance with the plan. Recent guidance published by the ODPM, *The Planning System: General Principles* (2005), notes that where there are other material considerations, the development plan should be the starting point and other material considerations should be taken into account in reaching the decision.

Material considerations

A material consideration will be, for example, if the plan is up to date. It cites *Stringer v*   **8.161**
Minister for Housing and Local Government [1970] 1 WLR 1281 in that:

> In principle . . . any consideration which relates to the use and development of land is capable
> of being a planning consideration. Whether a particular consideration falling within that broad
> class is material in any given case will depend on the circumstances.

An LPA (or the Secretary of State) must take into account 'relevant' or 'material' considera-   **8.162**
tions in reaching its decision and must not take into account irrelevant considerations.
Whether or not a particular matter is a *material* consideration depends upon the facts and
legislative context of the particular decision. However, *taking into account* a relevant consideration does not necessarily mean giving effect to it, e.g. the noise impact of a proposal
may be a relevant consideration in deciding whether to permit it, but the mere fact that a
proposal will have a noise impact on neighbours does not mean that it cannot be permitted.

It is for the LPA to decide what weight, or significance, to give that noise impact when   **8.163**
assessing all the competing interests. Also, a judicial review challenge based on the contention that an LPA failed to take into account a particular consideration does not need to show
that taking it into account would necessarily have changed the outcome; it need only show
that it might have made a difference. Any consideration that relates to the use and development of land is capable of being a material planning consideration. Material considerations
that may be relevant in land use planning decision-making could include:

- The development plan for the area either adopted or in the course of preparation.
- Protection of certain wildlife habitats.
- Environmental impact assessments.
- Representations received from consultees and members of the public.
- Government guidance in PPSs, PPGs, and other policy guidance. If it contains relevant
  policies, the planning authority must take them into account.
- Public fears of the proposed development.
- The impact of the proposal on residential amenity.
- The planning history of the site.
- The availability of alternative sites.
- The precedent effect of granting planning permission.

In practice, the list is almost endless and much will depend upon the facts of the particular   **8.164**
case. In *R v Westminster CC ex p Monahan* [1988] JPL 107 the court held that material considerations must be genuine planning considerations that relate to the development and use
of land in the public interest and to the application concerned.

Procedure in determining planning applications

The procedure that an LPA should follow in determining a planning application is found in   **8.165**
the GDPO 1995. The main articles are:

Art 2 *Application.* GDPO 1995 applies to all land in England and Wales.
Art 3 *Applications for outline planning permission.* Where an application is made for outline
       permission, the LPA may grant permission subject to a condition specifying reserved
       matters for the authority's subsequent approval.

Art 4   *Applications for approval of reserved matters.* This shall be made in writing, with sufficient information, and such plans and documents required to deal with the matters reserved in the outline permission.

Art 5   *General provisions relating to applications.* Any application for permission or reserved matters shall be made to the relevant planning authority together with an Art 7 certificate if necessary. If any application is invalid then the LPA shall notify the applicant as soon as reasonably practicable.

Art 6   *Notice of applications for planning permission.* The applicant shall give notice of the application to the owner or tenant of the land to which the application relates by serving notice and (if required) by local advertisement. Also procedures for removal of obscured or defaced notices.

Art 7   *Certificates in relation to notice of applications for planning permissions.* The applicant shall certify that the requirements of Art 6 have been satisfied.

Art 8   *Publicity for applications for planning permission.* An application for planning permission shall be publicized by the LPA in the manner described in this article, e.g. for EIA development, Art 8(3) an application shall be publicized by site notice for not less than 21 days and by local advertisement.

Art 9   *Applications for planning permission referred to the Secretary of State and appeals to the Secretary of State.* Articles 6 and 7 apply to any appeal to the Secretary of State.

Art 10   *Consultations before grant of permission.* Before granting permission for development that, in their opinion, falls within a category in the table set out in Art 10, an LPA shall consult the authority or person mentioned in relation to the particular category.

Art 11   *Consultation with county planning authority.* Where required, the LPA must consult and give 14 days for a county planning authority to respond, before granting permission.

Art 12   *Applications relating to county matters.* Where applicable, a county planning authority shall give an LPA 14 days within which to make recommendations before determining a planning application.

Art 13   *Notice to parish and community councils.* Where a parish or community council are given information in relation to applications, they shall notify the LPA whether they are going to make representations and make any representations within 14 days of notification to them.

Art 14   *Directions by the Secretary of State.* The Secretary of State may give directions restricting the grant of planning permission by an LPA.

Art 15   *Special provisions as to permission for development affecting certain existing and proposed highways.* Where a planning application relates to the formation, layout, or alteration to a main road, or any development within 67 metres of a specified highway the LPA shall notify the Secretary of State.

Art 16   *Notification of mineral applications.* Notice of an application to win and work any mineral must be given to the relevant mineral authority, e.g. the Coal Authority, before determining any application.

Art 17   *Development not in accordance with the development plan.* The LPA may, subject to consideration by the Secretary of State, grant permission for development that is not in accordance with the development plan.

Art 18   *Notice of reference of applications to the Secretary of State.* When referring a matter under s 77 of the TCPA 1990, the LPA shall serve a notice on the applicant.

Art 19   *Representations to be taken into account.* An LPA shall, in determining a planning application, take into account any representations made. An LPA shall give notice of their decision to every person who has made representations that they were required to take into account.

Art 20   *Time periods for decision.* Provisions for time periods relating to determinations and any extended periods in particular that an LPA shall give the applicant notice of their decision within eight weeks of the date the application was received.

Art 21   *Applications made under planning condition.* Subject to exceptions, an LPA will give notice of a decision relating to any consent, agreement, or approval required by a condition within eight weeks from the date the application was received by the LPA.

Art 22   *Written notice of decision relating to a planning application.* Where the LPA gives notice of a decision or determination of a planning application or reserved matters the notice shall state clearly and precisely the reasons for the decision — as amended by para 5 of the TCP (GDP) (England) (Amendment) Order 2003 (SI 2003/2047) (GDP Amendment Order (2003)).

Art 23   *Appeals.* An applicant who wishes to appeal an LPA decision under s 78 of the TCPA 1990 shall serve on the Secretary of State and the LPA a notice of appeal within six months (reduced to three months by para 6 of the GDP Amendment Order (2003) then reverting to six following a Ministerial Statement of December 2004)

Art 24   *Certificate of lawful use or development.* An application for a CLEUD or CLOPUD, shall among other things, be in writing and shall specify the land, the relevant section from the TCPA 1990 under which the application is made. The article contains other procedural requirements for applications.

Art 25   *Register of applications.* Each LPA shall keep, in two parts, a register of every application for planning permission relating to their area. The article prescribes what should be contained in each Part. See also s 69(1) of the TCPA 1990 the register must be available for public inspection at all reasonable hours.

Art 26   *Register of enforcement and stop notices.* The article prescribes what information should be held on the register of enforcement and stop notices under s 188 of the TCPA 1990.

Notice and publicity

Article 7 of GDPO

In *Main v Swansea CC* [1985] JPL 558 the Art 7 Certificate, which had been submitted with   **8.166** the planning application, stated that all owners of the land to be developed had been notified of the proposal, whereas in fact an unidentified owner had not been notified, in which case a local advertisement should have been prepared by the developer. On the facts, the Court declined to quash the grant of planning permission but noted that in certain circumstances such a failure to properly inform all owners may be sufficient to quash a planning decision. In *R (Pridmore) v Salisbury DC* [2004] EWHC 2511 (Admin) the court did quash the permission where the facts provided that it would be just to do so.

Article 8 of the GDPO

8.167 Under Art 8 the LPA is required to publicize a planning application according to the size of the proposed development:

Art 8(3)   for development that requires an EIA, does not accord with the development plan or affects a right of way under Pt III of the WCA 1981, (para(2)) the LPA must give requisite notice by:
   (a) site display in at least one place on or near the land to be developed for not less than 21 days, and
   (b) local advertisement;

Art 8(4)   for development that is not within para (2) but is major development the application shall be publicized by:
   (a) either (i) site notice for 21 days or (ii) serving the notice on any adjoining owner or occupier, and
   (b) by local advertisement;

Art 8(5)   For cases outside of paras (2) or (4) notice shall be by either
   (a) site display for 21 days, or
   (b) serving the notice on any adjoining owner or occupier.

8.168 In *R (Gavin) v Haringey LBC* [2003] EWHC 2591 (Admin), the LPA failed to notify the claimant about a new warehouse development across the road from his home. There had not been a site notice. Planning permission was granted and around two and half years later construction work began. The claimant challenged the permission. The High Court declined to quash the planning decision but granted a declaration that the LPA had failed to comply with the Art 8 publicity requirements for EIA development. The case is considered in Chapter 20: Public law, raising a number of interesting points of public law.

Power to decline to determine applications

8.169 Under new ss 70A and 70B of the TCPA 1990 (inserted by s 43 of the PCPA 2004) an LPA may refuse to determine one or more planning applications for substantially the same form of development, where the decision was issued during the last two years, and there has been no significant change in the relevant considerations. This extends the power that was only previously available if the matter had gone to appeal.

Conditions

Circular 11/95: The Use of Conditions in Planning Permission

8.170 The power in s 70(1) of the TCPA 1990 to grant planning permission subject to conditions is very wide. According to Government Circular 11/95: *The Use of Conditions in Planning Permission*, if used properly, conditions can enhance the quality of development and enable many development proposals to proceed where it would otherwise have been necessary to refuse planning permission. The Circular states that the objectives of planning are best served when the power to impose conditions is exercised in such a way that conditions are clearly seen to be fair, reasonable, and practicable and provides a six-part test for conditions that they should be:

(1) *Necessary*. Authorities should ask themselves whether permission would have to be refused if the condition were not imposed. If not, then the condition needs special and precise justification.

(2) *Relevant to planning*. A condition, which has no relevance to planning, is *ultra vires*. For instance, a condition that the first occupants of dwellings must be drawn from a local authority's housing waiting list would be improper because it would intend to meet housing objectives and not a planning need.

(3) *Relevant to development*. A condition should fairly and reasonably relate to the development permitted. If not, it will be *ultra vires*, e.g. permission for factory alterations cannot impose conditions for improving the appearance of an adjoining site simply because that site is untidy, despite the desirability in planning objectives terms.

(4) *Enforceable*. A condition should not be imposed if it cannot be enforced under either ss 172 or 187A of the TCPA 1990. Sometimes a condition will be unenforceable because it will, in practice, be impossible to detect a contravention.

(5) *Precise*. A condition that is too vague for the applicant to ascertain what must be done for compliance will be *ultra vires*. Conditions should not only be precise but also clear.

(6) *Reasonable*. A condition may be *ultra vires* because it is unreasonable. An unreasonable condition does not become reasonable on consent of the applicant.

Part 2 of Circular 11/95 provides for the specific use of conditions for matters such as trees, time limits, highway conditions, and noise. Appendices A and B set out suggested models of acceptable and unacceptable conditions respectively. **8.171**

Conditions on duration of permission

Section 91(1) of the TCPA 1990 (as amended by s 51 of the PCPA 2004) provides that every grant of planning permission shall be subject to the condition that the development shall begin within five years from the date of the grant; or such other date as the LPA may direct. Thus, an LPA may direct longer or shorter periods where appropriate. However, an extension to an agreed period is not possible without the submission of a new application (s 73(5) of the TCPA 1990). **8.172**

For outline permission, the approval of reserved matters shall be within three years from the date of the grant of outline permission (s 92 of the TCPA 1990). A condition may be imposed on the grant of permission for a limited period under s 72 of the TCPA 1990, e.g. s 72(1)(b) requiring the removal of any buildings or works authorized by the permission or the discontinuance of any use of land so authorized at the end of a specified period. **8.173**

Under s 94(2) of the TCPA 1990, if an LPA is of the opinion that development will not be completed within a reasonable period, it may serve a completion notice stating that the permission will cease to have effect at the expiration of a further period specified in the notice. **8.174**

Grampian conditions

An LPA can impose negative conditions on a planning permission that relates to the actions of others, e.g. activity on land not under control of the applicant. These types of conditions are often referred to as *Grampian* conditions after the House of Lords decision in *Grampian Regional Council v City of Aberdeen DC* [1984] 47 P&CR 633. One way **8.175** of achieving this is by prohibiting development (a restrictive or negative condition) until a specified action has been taken. Paragraph 40 of *Circular 11/95* states, in relation to these conditions that:

> It is the policy of the Secretaries of State that such a condition should only be imposed on a planning permission if there are at least reasonable prospects of the action in question being performed within the time-limit imposed by the permission

Obligations

8.176 Landowners and LPAs have for some years been able to enter into agreements in regulating land use. The latest provisions are contained in ss 106, 106A, and 106B of the TCPA 1990. Planning obligations, also referred to as s 106 agreements, are usually negotiated between local authorities and developers while considering and determining planning permission. They can also be unilateral undertakings made by the developer. They can help ensure that a proposed development has an element of socio-environmental benefit, e.g. by securing contributions towards the infrastructure required in a locality.

Section 106 of the TCPA 1990: planning obligations

8.177 Section 106(1) of the TCPA 1990 provides that any person interested in land in the area of an LPA may enter into a planning obligation:

(a) restricting the development or use of land in any specified way;

(b) requiring specified operations or activities to be carried out in, on, under, or over the land;

(c) requiring the land to be used in any specified way; or

(d) requiring a sum or sums to be paid to the authority on a specified date or dates or periodically.

8.178 Under s 106(2) a planning obligation may be unconditional, conditional, or impose restrictions or requirements contained in (1)(a) to (d) for specified periods or indefinitely. Section 106(9) of the TCPA 1990 provides that a planning obligation must be executed as a deed that states that (a) it is a planning obligation, and identifies (b) the land of interest, (c) the person entering into the obligation, and (d) the LPA. Subsection (11) provides that a planning obligation shall be a local land charge and therefore runs with the land.

8.179 Under s 106(3) to (8) a planning obligation may be enforced by the LPA through injunctive relief and by entering the land, carrying out operations relating to the obligations and recovering any costs reasonably incurred. Any person who wilfully obstructs a person entering land and carrying out such operations shall be guilty of an offence subject to a maximum fine of £1,000.

Modification and discharge of planning obligations

8.180 Section 106A(1) of the TCPA 1990 provides that a planning obligation may not be modified or discharged except by agreement between the LPA and those against whom the obligation is enforceable (providing such agreement is executed as a deed) or under ss 106A and 106B. Section 106A(3) enables a planning obligation to be discharged in certain circumstances by application to the LPA. If an LPA fails to determine an application or determine that the obligation shall continue without modification, the applicant may appeal to the Secretary of State (s 106B). In the Planning Appeal decision *West Wiltshire DC, Mr & Mrs Austin* [2002] JPL 1417, the Inspector considered appeals against the LPA's refusal to discharge planning obligations, this included an assessment as to whether the obligation contained in a s 106 agreement 'no longer served a useful purpose'. The Inspector noted that this should be considered in land use planning terms and concluded that on this basis the obligation did continue to do so.

Circular 1/97

Circular 1/97: *Planning Obligations* sets out the Government's current policy on the use of planning obligations. It advises that negotiation between the LPA and developer should allow development to go ahead, which may otherwise be refused. It sets out how LPAs should approach obligations and, in particular, that they should only be sought where they meet the tests of being: **8.181**

(a) necessary;
(b) relevant to planning;
(c) directly related to the proposed development;
(d) fairly and reasonably related in scale and kind to the proposed development;
(e) reasonable in all other respects.

Annexes A, B, and C to the Circular expand on these tests. Two points of interest are: para B19 provides, under the heading public involvement, that planning obligations should be conducted as openly, fairly, and reasonably as possible; and under B20 that if there is a choice between imposing conditions and entering into planning obligations, the imposition of a condition that satisfies Circular 11/95 is preferable because it provides the developer with a right of appeal.   **8.182**

The courts have refined the scope of the planning obligations. In *Tesco Stores Ltd v Secretary of State for the Environment* [1995] 1 WLR 759 the House of Lords held that an LPA would not be acting unlawfully by taking into account a planning obligation that did not comply with the policy test, provided that the relevant matters regarding the obligation were capable of being material planning considerations; to be a material consideration, the relevant matters should have a more than nominal connection with the development.   **8.183**

An example of when a planning obligation may be used is where a development may create a need for something related to planning that cannot be secured through imposing planning conditions, e.g. the provision of a bus service where the development will create a demand for this. In *Patel v Brent LBC* [2004] EWHC 763 (Ch) the court held that a planning obligation could not be discharged by breach. Hart J held, on the facts, that it was necessary to imply a term into the agreement, in order to give it business efficacy, that the local authority would continue to use its reasonable endeavours to complete the works specified in the agreement after the contractual completion date.   **8.184**

Revising planning obligations and introducing planning contributions

As part of the planning reforms the Government is proposing to revise planning obligation policy and also to introduce a new system of planning contributions under ss 46 and 47 of the PCPA 2004. The revised policy, which will replace Circular 1/97, aims to simplify   **8.185** the policy tests, place a stronger emphasis on national, regional, and local plans and to encourage the use of standard charges. The draft revised Circular on planning obligations was published in November 2004 and can be obtained from www.odpm.gov.uk.

8.186   The new planning contribution provisions are expected in 2006. They will enable the Secretary of State to make regulations for planning contributions to be made to an LPA for certain development projects or use of land. The LPA could be required by the regulations to set out in a document:

- which developments and uses they will seek contributions for;
- where they will not seek a contribution;
- the purposes to which receipts from contributions may be made, either in whole or in part; and
- the criteria for determining the value of the contribution.

8.187   The contributor may make a contribution by the optional planning charge or by a means agreed by negotiation, or a combination of both.

Duty to give reasons for planning decision

8.188   Under Art 22 of the GDPO the LPA must give summary reasons for both refusing and granting planning permission. In *R (Wall) v Brighton & Hove City Council* [2004] EWHC 2582, the LPA failed to give reasons for the grant of permission and the High Court quashed the decision. Mr Justice Sullivan held at para 69 that:

> Parliament intended that the defendant should set out its summary reasons for granting planning permission in the decision notice. This is not a case of summary reasons being inadequate because, for example, the planning authority has failed to mention a particular reason or reasons. No reasons were given at all. While it is true that the claimant cannot point to any specific prejudice having been caused by the defendant's omission, neither can the defendant nor any interested party point to any particular prejudice if the decision notice is quashed and the Committee has to reconsider the matter.

8.189   In *R (Chisnell) v Richmond upon Thames LBC* [2005] EWHC 134 the court quashed a planning decision where there had been a failure to give adequate reasons for the decision and that simply referring to the public or interested parties in the officer's report was insufficient. In *Angele Dowmunt-Iwaszkiewicz v First Secretary of State* [2004] EWHC 2537 (QB), the High Court quashed a Planning Inspector's decision where the claimant had been genuinely prejudiced by the failure to give reasons for the refusal of permission.

E   CHALLENGING PLANNING DECISIONS

8.190   The developer has a right of appeal against an adverse planning decision and, in some instances, the right of statutory review. Further, all interested parties (including the developer) may challenge a determination by way of an application for judicial review. They may also make a complaint to the Local Government Ombudsman.

Appeals relating to planning decisions

Section 78(1) of the TCPA 1990 provides that where an LPA has: **8.191**

(a) refused an application for planning permission or that the grant is subject to conditions;
(b) refused an application for any consent, agreement or approval required by a condition; or
(c) refused any approval required under a development order;

the applicant, i.e. the developer, may appeal to the Secretary of State.

Under s 78(2) the developer may also appeal where the LPA has not given notice of either: **8.192**

(a) its decision;
(aa) its decision to use its s 70A power (to decline to determine applications); or
(b) a referral to the Secretary of State under s 77 (call in).

Generally, it is the Planning Inspectorate that handles the appeal process on behalf of the **8.193** Secretary of State, although he has the power to 'recover' cases relating to certain development. In 2002–3, the Planning Inspectorate decided 15,021 appeals of which 36% were successful.

Section 78A of the TCPA 1990 inserted by s 50 of the PCPA 2004 allows a short period of **8.194** dual jurisdiction between the Secretary of State and the LPA where an appeal has been made against non-determination of an application. The additional period of time will be determined by a development order.

Grounds of appeal

Blackstone's Planning Law Practice (Blackstone Press, 1999) suggests that grounds of appeal **8.195** can take four basic forms:

(1) They may challenge the relevance of a reason for refusal, e.g. a reason for refusal may be that the development is contrary to certain policies within the local development scheme. An appeal ground may be that the policy has been misapplied, or that its terms are outweighed by another development document.
(2) The appeal might challenge the facts on which reasons for refusal are based, e.g. if a reason for refusal was the impact of a proposal on the amenity of nearby residents, then the ground for appeal might deny that the development would have that effect, or that the LPA has failed to take into account mitigating proposals.
(3) Grounds of appeal may comment on facts and assertions made by the LPA within the refusal notice. For example if an application for a change of use of premises is refused on grounds of a development policy that encourages mixed use, then the appellant may comment that the LPA's view of the mixed use character is out of date.
(4) An appeal may raise matters to which the refusal decision makes no reference. For example if permission is refused for development that is broadly in line with previous planning permission granted for the same or a similar site, then the appeal grounds may point out the inconsistency of the LPA's approach.

Power of the Secretary of State and Inspectorate

8.196 Under s 79(1) of the TCPA 1990 the Secretary of State may allow or dismiss the appeal; reverse or vary any part of the LPA (whether the appeal related to that part or not); and may deal with the application as if it had been made to him in the first instance. Section 79(5) provides that the appeal decision shall be final, although see below paras 8.208 to 8.215 on statutory review. Under s 79(6A) the Secretary of State may dismiss the appeal on the grounds of unreasonable delay by the appellant.

Appeal procedure

8.197 There are a number of different procedures of appeal depending on the form it takes, i.e. whether by written representations, hearing, or by public inquiry. As a rule, the simpler appeals may be made by written representations, and as an alternative to written appeals, s 79(2) provides that these, more simple appeals, may be by way of a hearing. The more complex appeals are heard as a local inquiry. There are separate regulations for each procedure:

- *Written representations:* Town and Country Planning (Appeals) (Written Representations Procedure) (England) Regulations 2000 (SI 2000/1628).
- *Hearings:* Town and Country Planning (Hearing Procedures) (England) Regulations 2000 (SI 2000/1626).
- *Local inquiries:* Town and Country Planning (Determination by Inspectors) (Inquiries Procedures) (England) Regulations 2000 (SI 2000/1625), where the matter is 'transferred' to the Inspector to hear the inquiry.

8.198 Town and Country Planning (Inquiries Procedures) (England) Regulations 2000 (SI 2000/1624) relate to where the Secretary of State 'recovers' the matter following a recommendation by the Inspector.

8.199 Article 23(2) of the GDPO 1995 provides that a notice of appeal against a refusal or any conditions must be made within six months from the date of determination.

8.200 The general rule as to costs on appeal is that each party pays their own costs. However, s 320 of the TCPA 1990 provides that the evidence and costs rules from s 250(2) to (5) of the Local Government Act 1972 apply to local planning inquiries. Further, s 322 of the TCPA 1990 provides that the Secretary of State has similar powers for appeal hearings and appeals on written representations. Circular 8/93 provides guidance as to when costs awards may be made by the Inspector including those for unreasonable behaviour both through the appeal process and prior to submission of the appeal. Applications for costs are normally heard at the end of proceedings, but before the close of proceedings and will only be allowed if the party claiming them can show that the other party behaved unreasonably and put them to unnecessary expense.

8.201 Following an application for costs the Inspector or Secretary of State should take into account Circular 8/93: *Award of Costs in Planning and Other Proceedings*, which provides general principles for awards of costs for unreasonable behaviour and applications of costs policy to third parties. According to Circular 8/93 unreasonable behaviour on behalf of an appellant may include failure to comply with normal procedural requirements, failing to pursue an appeal, and the introduction of new grounds of appeal late in the proceedings. Regulators may be at risk of a costs award against them if they fail to provide evidence to substantiate reasons for refusal or fail to take into account relevant policy statements. Section 250(5) of the Local Government Act 1972 applies to PPC appeals and enables the Secretary of State to make an order as to the costs of the parties at an inquiry and that an order for costs if unpaid becomes a civil debt. An appellant may be awarded an adverse costs order if it pursues an appeal that had no reasonable prospect of success. An LPA may be at risk of a costs order if it failed to substantiate reasons for refusing planning permission.

In cases where the Secretary of State, rather than an Inspector, is actually determining the appeal, the Inspector will carry out a site visit, hearing, or inquiry and then prepare a report for the Secretary of State.   **8.202**

Circular 05/2000 guidance and the Planning Inspectorate website

Circular 05/2000 provides guidance on each type of appeal. The tables below are extracts from the Planning Inspectorate website and provide an outline guide for each appeal procedure, i.e. the written procedure, the hearing procedure, and the inquiry procedure.   **8.203**

Recent appeal decisions

Certain planning appeal decisions are considered throughout this book where relevant to the matter being considered. Summarized below are three further recent examples of decisions.   **8.204**

Wokingham DC: McCarthy & Stone (Developments) Ltd [2004] JPL 1439. An appeal against refusal to grant planning permission to build a new country house. The issue was whether a proposed house was within para 3.21 of PPG 7L: *The Countryside* (1997), which provides that 'an isolated new house in the countryside may also exceptionally be justified if it is clearly of the highest quality, is truly outstanding in terms of its architecture and landscape design, and would significantly enhance its immediate setting and wider surroundings. The Inspector allowed the appeal. Granting permission he concluded that the building was neither a slavish reproduction nor overly modern.   **8.205**

Epsom & Ewell BC [2004] JPL 1451 (App/P3610/x/03/1129273). A lawful development certificate (LDC) was sought for the erection of dormers to each side of a roof of a dwellinghouse. The LPA considered that the proposal did not fall within Class B of the GPDO 1995 but that it amounted to an extension of the house. The Inspector allowed the appeal. There was nothing in Class B that did not include an alteration to the roof. This view was consistent with the judgment in *Richmond LBC v SSE* [1991] JPL 948 in which it was held that vertical parapet walls erected on a flat roof of an existing extension involved an alteration to the roof. An LDC was granted.   **8.206**

Waveney DC [2004] JPL 1453 (App/P3535/c/03/1136819). This involved an appeal against an enforcement notice requiring the removal of two stables and a tack room. The ground (c) appeal was that the horses were no longer ridden and simply grazed the land, this amounted to an agricultural use and so no material change had occurred. The enforcement notice was upheld. The horses permanently occupied the site. This went beyond the grazing of the land by the animals. Grazing was incidental to the primary use of the land for the keeping of the horses and so a breach of planning control had occurred.   **8.207**

Figure 8.3 Making your planning appeal

Extract from the Planning Inspectorate website: www.planning-inspectorate.gov.uk.

Appendix — 3.1 The Written Procedure

Timetable	You	LPA	Interested people
Appeal made (within the 6-month time limit) **We set a starting date**	You send your appeal form and all supporting documents to us and the LPA. Your grounds of appeal should make up your full case.	If they don't want the written procedure, we will tell you and arrange a hearing or inquiry.	
Within 2 weeks from the starting date	You receive from the LPA a filled-in questionnaire and any supporting documents.	The LPA send you and us a filled-in questionnaire and supporting documents. They also write to interested people about the appeal.	Interested people receive the LPA's letter about the appeal.
Within 6 weeks from the starting date (see the note below) (We will not normally accept late statements. Instead, we will return them to you.)	You send us 2 copies of any further statement. This should relate only to issues raised by the questionnaire and any supporting documents.	The LPA send us 2 copies of any further statement.	Interested people send us any comments.
Within 9 weeks from the starting date (see the note below) (We will not normally accept late statements. Instead, we will return them to you.)	You send us 2 copies of your final comments on the LPA's statement and on any comments from interested people. **No new evidence is allowed.**	The LPA send us 2 copies of their final comments on your statement and on any comments from interested people.	**No new evidence is allowed.**

Note: We send copies of statements and comments to you and the LPA by first-class post. We aim to do this within a week of the deadlines.

Decision:
After the site visit, the Inspector writes the decision or sends a report to the Secretary of State. We will send a copy of the decision notice to you, the LPA and anyone else who asks us for a copy.

Appendix — 3.2 The Hearing Procedure

Timetable	You	LPA	Interested people
Appeal made (within the 6-month time limit) **We set a starting date**	You send your appeal form and all supporting documents to us and the LPA.	They let us know if they don't think a hearing is suitable.	
Within 2 weeks from the starting date	You receive from the LPA a filled-in questionnaire and any supporting documents.	The LPA send you and us a filled-in questionnaire and supporting documents. They also write to interested people about the appeal.	Interested people receive the LPA's letter about the appeal.

Timetable	You	LPA	Interested people
Within 6 weeks from the starting date (see the note below) (We will not normally accept late statements. Instead, we will return them to you.)	You send us 2 copies of your hearing statement.	The LPA send us 2 copies of their hearing statement.	Interested people send us any comments.
Within 9 weeks from the starting date (see the note below) (We will not normally accept late comments. Instead, we will return them to you.)	You send us 2 copies of your final comments on the LPA's statement and on any comments from interested people. **No new evidence is allowed.**	The LPA send us 2 copies of their final comments on your statement and on any comments from interested people. **No new evidence is allowed.** They tell interested people about the arrangements. They may put a notice in a local paper about the hearing two weeks before the date.	Interested people are told about the hearing by the LPA. They may go to the hearing and, if the Inspector agrees, give their views.

Note: We send copies of statements and comments to you and the LPA by first-class post. We aim to do this within a week of the deadlines.

Decision:
After the hearing, the Inspector writes the decision or sends a report to the Secretary of State. We will send a copy of the decision notice to you, the LPA and anyone else who asks us for a copy.

Appendix — 3.3 The Inquiry Procedure

Timetable	You	LPA	Interested people
Appeal made (within the 6-month time limit) **We set a starting date**	You send your appeal form and all supporting documents to us and the LPA.	The LPA receive the appeal documents.	
Within 2 weeks from the starting date	You receive from the LPA a filled-in questionnaire and any supporting documents.	The LPA send you and us a filled-in questionnaire and supporting documents. They write to interested people about the appeal. The LPA send us 2 copies of their inquiry statement.	Interested people receive the LPA's letter about the appeal.
Within 6 weeks from the starting date (see the note below) (We will not normally accept late statements. Instead, we will return them to you.)	You send us 2 copies of your inquiry statement.	The LPA send us 2 copies of their inquiry statement.	Interested people send us any comments.

Figure 8.3—*continued*

Timetable	You	LPA	Interested people
Within 9 weeks from the starting date (see the note below) (We will not normally accept late comments. Instead, we will return them to you.)	You send us 2 copies of your final comments on the LPA's statement and on any comments from interested people. **No new evidence is allowed.**	The LPA send us 2 copies of their final comments on your statement and on any comments from interested people. **No new evidence is allowed.**	
4 weeks before the inquiry (see the note below) (We will not normally accept late proofs of evidence. Instead, we will return them to you.)	You send us 2 copies of your proof of evidence and 1 copy of the statement of common ground. You put up a notice on the site about the inquiry two weeks before.	The LPA send us 2 copies of their proof of evidence. The LPA put a notice in a local paper about the inquiry and tell interested people.	Interested people are told about the inquiry by the LPA. They may attend the inquiry and, if the Inspector agrees, give their views.

Note: We send copies of statements, comments and proofs of evidence to you and the LPA by first-class post. We aim to do this within a week of the deadlines

Decision:
After the inquiry, the Inspector writes the decision or sends a report to the Secretary of State. We will send a copy of the decision notice to you, the LPA and anyone else who asks us for a copy.

Statutory review

8.208   Section 284(1) of the TCPA 1990 provides that the validity of many LPA activities such as an appeal decision under s 78, development plans, and orders relating to TPOs may not be questioned in any legal proceedings, except in so far as may be provided by Pt XII of the Act. Thus, despite the finality of s 78, there is an opportunity to challenge an appeal decision of the Secretary of State or Inspectorate. It is often called statutory review as distinct from the more general judicial review process, although the two review procedures are similar; in particular in the limited scope of order that can be made.

Grounds for statutory review

8.209   Section 287 of the TCPA 1990 provides the opportunity to question development plans and certain schemes and orders. Section 288 states that the validity of other orders, decisions, and directions may be questioned by an application to the High Court on the grounds that:

(i)   the order is not within the powers of the Act, or

(ii) that any of the relevant requirements have not been complied with in relation to that order.

Power of the High Court on review

8.210   Under ss 287(2) and 288(5) of the TCPA 1990, if the High Court is satisfied that the order or actions in question are not within powers of the Act, or that the interests of the applicant have been substantially prejudiced by a failure to comply with any of the relevant requirements, it may quash the order or action. The court may also make an interim order to suspend operation of the order or action until determination of the proceedings.

In *Kingswood DC v Secretary of State for the Environment* [1988] JPL 248, it was held that, **8.211** following the court's decision to quash the order, the Secretary of State was obliged to hear the matter anew. It is important to note that the court cannot substitute the LPA's decision with its own judgment on the merits of the case.

Procedural aspects of statutory review

Important procedural requirements in statutory review include standing, time limits, and **8.212** costs.

Sections 287(1) and 288(1) provide that any 'person aggrieved' may apply for review. This **8.213** includes the developer (the appellant) and the LPA in planning decisions. It also includes any interested party that may have made representations at the appeal.

Under ss 287(4) and 288(3) of the TCPA 1990 an application must be made within six weeks **8.214** from the date on which the order is confirmed or as the case may be, the date on which action is taken.

In *Bolton MDC v Secretary of State for the Environment* [1995] 3 PLR 37 the House of Lords **8.215** affirmed that there were no rules as to costs in relation to a s 288 review and that costs were always at the discretion of the court. If successful, the SSE would normally be entitled to his costs. The developer would not normally be entitled to costs unless he could show that there was likely to be a separate issue, not covered by lawyers for the SSE. In *Dacorum BC v Secretary of State for the Environment* [1997] EWHC Admin 562 (17 June 1997) the court awarded two sets of costs for the SSE and the developer (Tesco) where the SSE was successful in defending an application by the LPA, the judge also awarded costs against a third party who had withdrawn from the proceedings at a late stage.

Judicial review

A claim for judicial review is the control exercised by the High Court over the decisions of **8.216** public bodies. It may be available in land use planning to challenge the decision of an LPA or the Secretary of State. It is discussed in Chapter 20: Public law.

Nuisance

The possibility of a cause of action in nuisance relates to land use planning in two ways: **8.217**

• a nuisance being caused by a new development and affecting long-standing neighbours, and
• a nuisance by long-term residents that affects new neighbours in the locality.

In both instances the claimants must establish that a nuisance does exist and that the use is **8:218** unreasonable. However, the character of the locality has been a significant aspect of reasonableness of use since the case of *Sturges v Bridgman* (1879) LR 11 Ch D 852. In terms of planning law, while the grant of planning permission is no defence to a nuisance claim it can result in a change of the character of an area, e.g. from employment/business use to residential and so the reasonableness of use is taken into account after planning permission is granted.

8.219   In *Gillingham BC v Medway (Chatham Docks) Co Ltd* [1993] QB 343, permission was granted to reuse the former docks and resulted in heavy lorry use in a quiet neighbourhood. In dismissing the nuisance claim the judge noted that the LPA, in determining the application, had to balance the interests of the local community with the new industrial neighbour.

8.220   However, even where planning permission changes the character of an area, any potential nuisance maker must still act reasonably otherwise a nuisance claim may succeed. In *Wheeler & anor v JJ Saunders Ltd* [1995] 2 AER 61 where permission had been granted for pig rearing houses, the Court of Appeal accepted that planning permission may change the local environment but did not find that it authorized a nuisance.

8.221   In *Nichols & ors v Powergen Renewables Ltd & anor* (2004) unreported (discussed by Stephen Tromans in [2004] JPL 1023) a group of residents brought statutory nuisance proceedings for noise caused by a wind farm operated by the defendants. Noise limits had been set as conditions as part of the original planning permission. The proceedings were dismissed. Nuisance is discussed further in Chapters 17 and 18.

Negligence

8.222   There is a reluctance to hold an LPA liable in negligence. In *R v ex p Chung Tak Lam Borough of Torbay* [1998] EWHC Admin 671 the Court of Appeal upheld the High Court decision to dismiss a claim in negligence, nuisance, and breach of statutory duty. Collins J in the High Court stated:

> It seems to me that it would be wholly detrimental to the proper process of considering planning applications if the local authority, in addition, had to have regard to the private law interests of any persons who might be affected by the grant of permission. . . . If it were potentially liable to actions in negligence in those circumstances, it seems to me that the carrying out of its important functions in the public interest would be likely to be adversely affected.

8.223   Generally, if loss, damage, or injury occurs in relation to a development, the developer will have caused it and they will be the primary defendants. However, if the developer becomes insolvent or has inadequate funds, then the claimant may turn to the LPA. The case of *Kane v New Forest DC* [2001] 3 All ER 914 provides that, in certain circumstances, an LPA may be liable for problems arising out of a development; in *Kane* there was a failure by the LPA to require safe sight lines.

Misrepresentation

8.224   The House of Lords in *R v East Sussex CC ex p Reprotech* [2002] JPL 821 clarified that the administration of the land use planning regime is a public not private law matter and that, in that instance, the notion of estoppel by representation of an LPA officer could not be relied upon. However, an LPA and its officers must act honestly. In *Slough Estates plc v Welwyn Hatfield DC* [1996] EGCS 132 the claimants were awarded damages of nearly £30 million following deceit by the LPA.

Reporting to the Chief Monitoring Officer

Under s 5 of the Local Government and Housing Act 1989 every local authority must appoint a Chief Monitoring Officer who must report to the council at any time if it appears to him that any proposal, decision, or omission by the authority has given rise or is likely to give rise to a contravention of any enactment or any maladministration or injustice. The report is to the full council within 21 days of being prepared. **8.225**

Local Government Ombudsman

If reporting to the Chief Monitoring Officer does not resolve the concern, it is also possible to challenge local authority actions by way of complaint to the Local Government Ombudsman. The Ombudsman is discussed further in Chapter 22: Extra-legal options, however some recent Ombudsman decisions relevant to planning are summarized below. For full details see the Local Government Ombudsman website at www.lgo.org.uk. **8.226**

In *West Dorset DC (02/B/13675)* the LPA had failed to properly consider objections to a neighbour's house extension. They had also wrongly informed the objectors about their legal rights and that they could contact the Ombudsman. The Ombudsman found maladministration and injustice and recommended that the LPA pay the complainants £1,000 to assist them in taking mitigation measures for overlooking that they now suffer and in recognition of the trouble in pursuing the complaint. **8.227**

In *Warrington BC (02/C/6932)* the complainant bought his home following an assurance by the LPA that the land immediately in front of it, a woodland with several mature trees, was protected 'in perpetuity' from development. The LPA failed to take action when one of the trees that were subject to a tree preservation order was felled and the LPA later granted permission to develop the site. The Ombudsman found maladministration leading to injustice and recommended that the LPA pay the complainant a sum equivalent to the difference between the value of his home before and after development and a further £500 for the time and trouble of making the complaint. **8.228**

In *City of York Council (02/B/10098)* the complainant alleged that the LPA gave inadequate consideration to the way surface water would drain from land adjacent to her property when granting planning permission for the development of the land for new housing. After the development was complete, her garden was sodden and repeatedly flooded. She added that the LPA had acted unreasonably in responding to her concerns. The Ombudsman found maladministration causing injustice and recommended that the LPA pay £2,000 in compensation, arrange for a land drainage investigation and remedial works at its own expense to stop the flooding, and review its procedures for the discharge of planning conditions and approval of drainage plans. **8.229**

F ENFORCEMENT

Unlawful development is underpinned by enforcement measures that aim to assist LPAs in carrying out their development control functions. Part VII of the TCPA 1990 contains a **8.230** number of provisions including the issuing of notices and powers of investigation. Many of these are underpinned by criminal sanctions.

8.231   Under s 171A(1) of the TCPA 1990:

    (a)   carrying out development without the required planning permission; or

    (b)   failing to comply with any condition or limitation subject to which planning permission has been granted,

constitutes a breach of planning control.

8.232   Section 171A(2) provides that:

    (a)   the issue of an enforcement notice (defined in s 172); or

    (b)   the service of a breach of condition notice (defined in s 187A),

constitutes taking enforcement action.

Gathering information

8.233   Section 324(1) of the TCPA 1990 enables an LPA and the Secretary of State to enter, at any reasonable time, any land for the purpose of surveying it in connection with, among other things:

    (b)   any application under Pt III (control over development)

    (c)   any proposal . . . to make, issue or serve any order [subject to exceptions].

8.234   Under s 330 of the TCPA 1990, an LPA and the Secretary of State has the power to require information as to interests in land by the service of a notice. Failure to comply with such a notice, without reasonable excuse, is an offence with a maximum sentence on summary conviction of £1,000. Anyone knowingly giving false information shall be guilty of an offence liable to a maximum penalty of a £5,000 fine and/or six months' imprisonment on summary conviction; or an unlimited fine and/or two years' imprisonment on indictment.

8.235   Further, s 196A of the TCPA 1990 provides a right of entry at any reasonable hour to an officer of an LPA to enter any land without the need of a warrant to, among other things, ascertain whether there has been a breach of planning control. If the admission to land under s 196A has been refused or the case is one of urgency s 196B enables an LPA officer to apply to the magistrates' court for a warrant to enter the premises.

Contravention notice

8.236   LPAs can gather information about activities on land that they believe may be in breach of planning control. The power contained in s 171C of the TCPA 1990 is designed to resolve potential concerns without the need to take more stringent enforcement action.

8.237   Section 171C(2) provides that a planning contravention notice may require the person on whom it is served to give such information as to:

    (a)   any operations being carried out on the land, any use of the land and any other activities being carried out on the land; and

(b) any matter relating to the conditions or limitations subject to which any planning permission in respect of the land has been granted,

as may be specified in the notice.

Section 171D provides a sanction for non-compliance with the contravention notice in that **8.238** if, after 21 days of service of a notice, any person served has not complied with any requirement of the notice, he shall be guilty of an offence with a maximum penalty of £1,000 on summary conviction (s 171D(4)).

Temporary stop notice

Section 52 of the PCPA 2004 inserts new ss 171E to 171H into the TCPA 1990, providing LPAs **8.239** with a discretionary power to serve temporary stop notices to halt breaches of planning control for a period of up to 28 days. It enables them to prevent unauthorized development at an early stage without the need to issue an enforcement notice.

Enforcement notice

Issuing an enforcement notice

Under s 172 of the TCPA an LPA may issue an enforcement notice where it appears: **8.240**

(a) that there has been a breach of planning control; and

(b) that it is expedient to issue the notice, having regard to the provisions of the development plan and to any other material consideration.

Section 173(1) provides that an enforcement notice shall state the matters that appear to **8.241** the LPA to constitute the breach of planning control and s 171A(1) within which the breach falls, i.e. carrying out development without permission or failing to comply with any condition or limitation.

Once issued, an enforcement notice must be served not more than 28 days after the date **8.242** of issue; and not less than 28 days before the date specified as the date on which it is to take effect (s 172 of the TCPA 1990).

Limitation period

The legislation provides for two limitation periods in taking enforcement action. Sections **8.243** 171B(1) and (2) of the TCPA 1990 provide that where there has been a breach of planning control relating to building, engineering, mining, or other operations in, on, over, or under land, or where there has been a change of use to a use as a single dwellinghouse, no enforcement action may be taken after four years from the date the operations were substantially completed. For all other breaches, no action may be taken after ten years from the date of the breach.

Appeal against an enforcement notice

There is a right of appeal against an enforcement notice. Section 174(1) of the TCPA 1990 **8.244** provides that a person having an interest in land to which an enforcement notice relates or a relevant occupier may appeal to the Secretary of State against the notice, whether or not a copy has been served on him.

8.245 Section 174(2) sets out the grounds for appeal including:

    (a)   that planning permission should have been granted or a condition or limitation should be discharged;

    (b)   that those matters [in the notice] have not occurred;

    (c)   that those matters (if they occurred) do not constitute a breach of planning control;

    (d)   that, at the date when the notice was issued, no enforcement action could be taken;

    (e)   that copies of the enforcement notice were not served as required by s 172;

    (f)   that the steps required, or activities that are required to cease, exceed what was necessary to remedy any breach of planning control or remedy any injury to amenity;

    (g)   that any period specified in the notice falls short of what should be reasonably allowed.

8.246 In *R (Sevenoaks DC) v First Secretary of State and Pedham Place Golf Course* [2005] JPL 116, the High Court dismissed the LPA's claim to quash an Inspector's decision allowing an appeal against an enforcement notice.

Stop notice

8.247 A stop notice allows an LPA (and the Secretary of State) to take urgent and necessary action in support of an enforcement notice. It can serve a stop notice with the enforcement notice or at any time after its service but before it comes into effect. The intention is to avoid any delay that may arise during the compliance period required by an enforcement notice. The statutory provisions are contained in ss 183 to 187 of the TCPA 1990. Section 183(1) provides:

> Where the LPA consider it expedient that any relevant activity should cease before the expiry of the period for compliance with an enforcement notice they may, when they serve the copy of the enforcement notice or afterwards, serve a [stop] notice prohibiting the carrying out of that activity on the land to which the enforcement notice relates, on any part of that land specified in the stop notice.

8.248 Sections 183 and 184 define the scope and procedures of the stop notice, e.g. that it cannot prohibit the use of a building as a dwellinghouse and that it must not take effect within three days and after 28 days from the date it is served.

8.249 Section 186 of the TCPA 1990 provides that compensation may be payable if either the relating enforcement notice is quashed in some circumstances, varied, or withdrawn or if the stop notice itself is withdrawn. Although under s 186(5) no compensation is payable if the activity to which the notice was in force constitutes or contributes to a breach of planning control.

8.250 Under s 187 of the TCPA 1990 if any person contravenes a stop notice after a site notice has been displayed or the notice has been served on him he shall be guilty of an offence. The maximum penalty is a £20,000 fine on summary conviction and an unlimited fine on indictment.

LPA carrying out works to remedy breach

8.251 If any steps required by an enforcement notice are not taken an LPA may carry out the works and then recover the reasonable costs of doing so from the owner (s 178 of the TCPA 1990). Any person wilfully obstructing the LPA shall be guilty of an offence with a maximum penalty of £1,000 fine on summary conviction (s 178(6)).

Breach of an enforcement notice

The TCPA 1990 creates an offence of breach of enforcement notice. Section 179 provides: **8.252**

(a) Where, at any time after the end of the period for compliance with an enforcement notice, any step required by the notice to be taken has not been taken or any activity required by the notice to cease is being carried on, the person who is then the owner of the land is in breach of the notice.

(b) Where the owner . . . is in breach of an enforcement notice he shall be guilty of an offence.

This applies to the owner or any person who has control of the land. A statutory defence is   **8.253** provided by s 179(3) in that any person charged did everything he could be expected to do to secure compliance with the notice.

The maximum penalty for breach of an enforcement notice is a £20,000 fine on summary   **8.254** conviction and an unlimited fine on indictment (s 179(8)). Significantly, when sentencing the court should have regard for any financial benefit that has accrued or appears likely to do so (s 179(9)).

Long-term operation of an enforcement notice

Section 180 of the TCPA 1990 provides that if planning permission is granted for any develop-   **8.255** ment after the service of an enforcement (or breach of condition) notice, then the notice shall no longer have effect so far as it is inconsistent with the permission.

However, under s 181 of the TCPA 1990 compliance with either an enforcement or breach of   **8.256** condition notice does not, by itself discharge the notice and, if the breach resumes, it is an offence with a maximum penalty of a £5,000 fine on summary conviction.

Breach of conditions or limitations of planning permission

Section 171A(1) of the TCPA 1990 provides for the failure to comply with any condition or   **8.257** limitation placed on the grant of planning permission by the service of a breach of condition notice.

The main provisions are contained in s 187A of the TCPA 1990. A breach of condition notice   **8.258** is served upon anyone who is carrying out (or carried out) the development or any person having control of the land. It should specify the steps to be taken or which activities should cease providing a minimum 28-day compliance period. It is an offence not to comply with any of the conditions in the notice. The maximum penalty is a £1,000 fine on summary conviction.

Injunctions

If an LPA needs to act urgently to stop any particular development or other breach of   **8.259** planning control they may apply for an injunction. Section 187B provides:

(1) Where [an LPA] consider it necessary or expedient for any actual or apprehended breach of planning control to be restrained by injunction, they may apply to the court for an

injunction, whether or not they have exercised or are proposing to exercise any of their other powers under this Part [i.e. powers to issue contravention, enforcement, stop, and breach of condition notices].

(2)   On an application under (1) the court may grant such an injunction as the court thinks appropriate for the purpose of restraining the breach

8.260   However, recent House of Lords decisions in *South Bucks DC v Porter* [2003] UKHL 26 and the associated cases have affirmed that s 187B should be used sparingly and other options of control should be considered and properly exhausted before issuing proceedings.

8.261   In *South Bucks DC v Porter* the county court granted injunctions to the LPA ordering gypsies living in mobile homes to move from land that they owned because they did not have planning permission. It was accepted that this was an interference with the Art 8 ECHR right of respect of private life, family, and home. It was accepted by the gypsies that the interference was lawful. The issue was whether the injunction was a proportionate interference to protect the environment. The Court of Appeal held that a judge should not injunct unless he would be prepared to commit the defendant to prison for breach and overturned the injunction. The House of Lords dismissed the LPA's appeal.

8.262   In *Slough BC v Prashare & ors* [2004] JPL 1718 an injunction was granted to restrain continued breaches of planning control. The defendant challenged the order on the basis that it should be restricted to the areas imposed on enforcement notices issued by the LPA. The Court of Appeal dismissed the appeal holding that there was no requirement under s 187B of the TCPA 1990 to confine the area in such a way. Injunctions are considered further in Chapter 17: Civil law practice and procedure.

G   HAZARDOUS SUBSTANCES

Overview of the hazardous substances regime

8.263   Some of the worst environmental disasters and human tragedies have arisen through incidents relating to the use or misuse of hazardous substances. In 1974, a large explosion at an oxidizing plant in Flixborough, North Lincolnshire, killed 28 workers and led to the formation of the Advisory Committee on Major Hazards. In 1976 a chemical plant operating in Seveso, Italy caused a large dioxin emission to enter the air and settle on an area of around 1,800 hectares around the plant. Local people were evacuated but widespread damage and pollution was caused. As a result EU Directive 82/501/EEC on the major accident of certain industrial activities (the Seveso Directive) was enacted. Similar chemical incidents have arisen in Bhopal, India where thousands of people died and the effects are still being felt 20 years on.

8.264   Partly in response to the Seveso Directive, the UK introduced legislation to control hazardous substances; the Housing and Planning Act 1986. This and other legislation was consolidated in the Planning (Hazardous Substances) Act 1990 (PHSA 1990), which remains in force. Secondary legislation made under s 5 of the PHSA 1990 includes the Planning

(Hazardous Substances) Regulations 1992 (SI 1992/656), as amended (PHS Regs 1992) and the Planning (Control of Major Accident Hazards) Regulations 1999 (SI 1999/981), which were introduced to implement EU Directive 96/82/EC on the control of major accident hazards involving dangerous substances (the Seveso II Directive), which aims under Art 1:

> at the prevention of major accidents which involve dangerous substances, and the limitation of their consequences for man and the environment, with a view to ensuring high levels of protection throughout the Community in a consistent and effective manner.

Hazardous substances are controlled through a consent procedure to operate with such substances. Hazardous substances consent is granted by the relevant hazardous substances authority (HSA), which, under s 1 of the PHSA 1990, is the council of the district, Welsh county, county borough, or London borough in which the land is situated. Section 4 of the PHSA 1990 provides that, 'the presence of a hazardous substance on, over or under land requires the consent of a hazardous substances authority'   **8.265**

Section 4(2) of the PHSA 1990 adds that hazardous substances consent is not required if the aggregate quantity of the substance on, over, or under the land is less than the quantity prescribed as the controlled quantity for that substance. Various definitions are provided in s 39(2) of the PHSA 1990 although many cross-refer to 'the principal Act', which is the TCPA 1990. Guidance on how the consent procedure for hazardous substances operates is provided by DETR Circular 04/00: *Planning Controls for Hazardous Substances* (Circular 04/00).   **8.266**

Hazardous substances consent procedure

Circular 04/00 advises that the requirement for hazardous substances consent does not override the need for planning permission to be obtained where the development of land is necessary. Where planning permission is required, two distinct applications will be necessary and the respective statutory requirements must be followed for each. It adds that developers and local authorities will wish to ensure that related applications are dealt with together, avoiding unnecessary duplication and providing a speedier resolution of the applications.   **8.267**

Pre-application requirements

Under reg 6(1) of the PSH Regs 1992, the applicant must, during the 21-day period immediately preceding the application is made, publicize the application by way of site notice, notice in a local newspaper, and under reg 7 give notice to any persons other than the applicant who is an owner of the land relevant to the application, providing an opportunity for representations to be made to the HSA. The applicant is required, during the periods afforded for representations, to make a copy of the application available for inspection in the locality.   **8.268**

Applying for consent

An application for hazardous substances consent must be made in the form prescribed in Form 1 of Sch 2 of the PSH Regs 1992. The application must include any named substances appearing in Pts A to C of Sch 1. Regulations 24 and 25 provide that a fee shall be payable   **8.269** when seeking consent starting from £200 and varying according to the application being made. Regulation 10 of the PSH Regs 1992 lists the organizations that the HSA must consult before determining the application including, among others, the Health and Safety Executive, the district (etc.) council, where that council is not also the hazardous substances authority and the Environment Agency.

Determination of consent

8.270 Under reg 11 of the PSH Regs 1992, the HSA must not determine an application for consent before the expiry of the periods allowed for making representations, and not within 28 days of contacting one of the statutory consultees. The HSA must give the applicant written notice of their decision within eight weeks, except where the applicant has already given notice to the Secretary of State, or an extension has been agreed by consent, or where the fee paid by the applicant has not been honoured.

Variation, modification, and revocation of consent

8.271 Section 13 of the PHSA 1990 provides that a consent holder may apply to remove or vary one or more conditions attached to a consent. Other options include, under s 17, applying to continue a consent after a control of land. This is required because if there is change of control of part of the land relating to a consent the whole consent will be revoked.

8.272 Under s 14(1) of the PHSA 1990 the HSA may by order revoke a hazardous substances consent if it appears to them, having regard to any material consideration, that it is expedient to revoke or modify it. Under s 14(2) they may also revoke it, if it appears to them:

    (a)   that there has been a material change of use of land to which the hazardous substances consent relates; or

    (b)   that planning permission has been granted for development, the carrying out of which would involve a material change of use of such land and the development to which the permission relates has been commenced; or

    (c)   in the case of a hazardous substances consent that relates only to one substance, that that substance has not for at least five years been present on, over, or under the land to which the consent relates in a quantity equal to or exceeding the controlled quantity; or

    (d)   in the case of a hazardous substances consent that relates to a number of substances, that none of those substances has for at least five years been so present.

8.273 Section 14(3) provides that an order under s 14(2)(a) or (b) may revoke the consent entirely or in part relating to only a specified substance. Under s 16 compensation may be payable in respect of a s 14 order.

Appeals

8.274 Section 21 of the PHSA 1990 provides that an applicant may appeal to the Secretary of State against a decision or a failure to determine an application by the HSA. An appeal must be made within six months of the date that gave rise to the appeal or from the expiry period provided in reg 11.

Enforcement

Section 23(1) of the PHSA 1990 provides that if there is a contravention of hazardous sub- **8.275** stances control, the appropriate person shall be guilty of an offence. Section 23(2) sets out the various circumstances for a contravention. Section 23(5) provides a defence for the accused to prove that he took all reasonable precautions and exercised due diligence, or that the commission of the offence could only have been avoided by the taking of action amounting to a breach of a statutory duty. Under s 23(4) a person guilty of an offence under s 23 shall be liable on summary conviction to a maximum penalty of a £20,000 fine and an unlimited fine for conviction on indictment.

Hazardous substances consent register

Under s 28 of the PHSA 1990 every HSA must keep a register containing information about **8.276** applications for hazardous substances consent and all other decisions and determinations relating to any consents.

KEY DOCUMENTS AND MATERIALS

The Town and Country Planning (Use Classes) Order 1987 (SI 1987/764)
Planning (Hazardous Substances) Act 1990
The Town and Country Planning Act 1990
Planning (Hazardous Substances) Regulations 1992 (SI 1992/656)
The Town and Country Planning (General Permitted Development) Order 1995
    (SI 1995/418)
The Town and Country Planning (General Development Procedure) Order 1995
    (SI 1995/419)
Building Regulations 2000 (SI 2000/2531)
Planning and Compulsory Purchase Act 2004

EU Directive 96/82/EC on the control of major-accident hazards involving dangerous
    substances (the Seveso II Directive)

Circular 05/2000
Circular 1/97: *Planning Obligations*
Circular 11/95: *The Use of Conditions in Planning Permission*
Department of Transport Local Government and the Regions (2001). *Delivering a
    Fundamental Change*. DTLR: London. See: www.odpm.gov.uk
DETR Circular 04/00: *Planning Controls for Hazardous Substances* (Circular 04/00)
Moore, V (2005). *A Practical Approach to Planning Law*. 9/e. OUP: Oxford
ODPM (2004). *Creating Local Development Frameworks: A Companion Guide to PPS 12*
ODPM (1997). *The Hedgerows Regulations: A Guide to the Law and Good Practice*. ODPM:
    London
ODPM (2000). *Tree Preservation Orders: A Guide to the Law and Good Practice* ODPM: London
ODPM (2001). *Planning; Delivering a Fundamental Change*. ODPM: London
Planning Policy Statement 1 (PPS 1): *Delivering Sustainable Development* (2005)
PPG 8: *Telecommunications* (2001)

PPS 11: *Regional Spatial Strategies* (2004)
PPS 12: *Local Development Frameworks* (2004)
PPS 23: *Planning and Pollution Control* (2004)

Local Government Ombudsman: www.lgo.org.uk.
The Planning Inspectorate website: www.planning-inspectorate.gov.uk

9

LIGHT

A INTRODUCTION

Daylight and artificial light at night raise two distinct concerns. The environmental concern **9.01** relating to natural daylight is when such light is restricted, whereas nighttime light becomes a problem when there is too much. In law, both areas are inadequately controlled leaving those experiencing problems without any effective means of resolution. Yet both aspects of light can have significant influence on human health and the wider environment. A lack of daylight can give rise to Seasonal Affective Disorder Syndrome (SADS) whereby a sufferer is commonly depressed in winter and picks up again in spring. *Blacks Medical Dictionary* (41/e, A&C Black, 2005) suggests that the mood change is probably related to light, with melatonin playing a key role. Artificial night light causes wild animals and birds to be disorientated and to remain awake at times when they would rest, although it is unknown how this impacts on their health. The duration and intensity of exposure to light can modify sleep profoundly. Light promotes wakefulness and is the main factor that adjusts the internal human body rhythm to the 24-hour day. Excessive artificial light at night can disturb sleep patterns and cause stress and anxiety.

The consideration of light in law has tended to avoid an overly technical assessment of light, **9.02** particularly in relation to interference with the right to light. In *Carr-Saunders v Dick McNeil Associates Ltd & ors* [1986] 2 All ER 888 the court concluded that it was unnecessary to enter into a technical assessment of what could be regarded as a sufficient level of light. Nevertheless, it is useful to have an outline of the principles of light production and measurement. Some simplified definitions are:

- *Radiant flux* is the physical energy radiated by an energy source in a certain time. The watt is the measurement of radiant flux.
- *Luminous flux* is the total amount of light energy from a single source. It is measured in Lumens. A conventional 100 watt light bulb is 1,740 lumens.
- *Illuminance* is the luminous flux from an object that hits a surface and is defined as Lux. By way of example, a full moon has an illuminance of 1 Lux, street lighting has an illuminance of 10 Lux and sunlight has an illuminance of 100,000 Lux.

B   RIGHT TO LIGHT

9.03 There are a number of ways that natural light may be interrupted or interfered with. This is particularly so in urban areas where between 5% to 10% of land is being redeveloped in some way or another at any one time. With the lifespan of buildings steadily decreasing, this turnover of buildings and redevelopment will continue.

Right acquired by prescription

9.04 There is no statutory right to light, although a right to light may be acquired by an express grant or by prescription. The right is only in relation to light in buildings. In *Tapling v Jones* (1865) 11 HLC 290, the court held that if a right to light is acquired by prescription then it must be for windows or other openings that admit light. The right to light, if acquired, is referred to as 'ancient lights'. An interference of ancient lights will give rise to a claim in private nuisance; see also Chapter 17: Civil law practice and procedure. The discussion below considers the court's approach to ancient lights, determining its scope and limitations.

9.05 The House of Lords in *Colls v Home & Colonial Stores* [1904] AC 179 considered the right to ancient lights in some detail. It overruled a decision of the Court of Appeal granting a mandatory injunction to demolish a partly-built building. It held that to constitute an actionable obstruction of ancient lights it is not enough that the light is less than before. The court stated that there must be a substantial deprivation of light, enough to render the occupation of the house uncomfortable according to the ordinary notions of mankind and (in the case of business premises) to prevent the claimant from carrying on his business as beneficially as before. Lord Robertson explained at para 205 that s 3 of the Prescription Act 1832 shows that in order to acquire a right to light there must be:

(1)   Access and use of light, not access alone. Access here is understood to refer to free passage of light over the servient tenement [the premises obstructing the light].

(2)   Such access and use must be to and for some dwelling-house, workshop, or other building.

(3)   Such access and use must be actually enjoyed therewith.

(4)   Such enjoyment must be without interruption for 20 years.

(5)   If all these are proved, the right to the access and use of light so enjoyed becomes absolute and indefeasible, unless it can be explained by some deed or writing.

. . . It will be observed that the statute does not in terms confer a right to light, but rather it assumes its acquisition by use and enjoyment, and declares it to be 'absolute and indefeasible'.

The courts have, since *Colls v Home & Colonial Stores*, refined the opportunity to claim against **9.06** an interference with ancient lights. In *Horton's Estate Ltd v James Beattie Ltd* [1927] 1 Ch 75 Russell J, at para 78, considered the doctrine of locality commenting that location may be irrelevant when considering interference with right to light he added that: 'the human eye requires as much light of comfortable reading or sewing in Darlington Street, Wolverhampton as in Mayfair'.

However, the Court of Appeal in *Ough v King* [1967] 1 WLR 1547 has since ruled that the **9.07** general nature of the locality may be relevant and that higher standards of comfort demanded in modern times may also be taken into account. Further, in *Carr-Saunders v Dick McNeil Associates Ltd & ors* the court concluded that there should be light that will leave premises adequately lit for the ordinary purposes for which they may reasonably be expected to be used. Light from other sources must be taken into account: in *Smith v Evangelization Society* [1933] 1 Ch 515 the claimant had obstructed light from skylights and then claimed a right to ancient lights through other windows. The court held that the burden on a servient tenement could not be increased by any merely voluntary action of the owner of the dominant tenement (the premises enjoying the right to light). The court must also take into consideration light enjoyed by the dominant tenement at the time the prescriptive right began and at the time the claim was issued. In *Sheffield Masonic Hall Co v Sheffield Corporation* [1932] 2 Ch 17 the court held that when a room in a building receives light through windows on different sides, which are ancient lights, the owner of land on either side as a general rule can build only to such a height as, if a building of like height were erected on the other side, would not deprive the room of so much light as to cause a nuisance. It noted that reflected or diffused light should not be ignored.

In *Carr-Saunders v Dick McNeil Associates Ltd & ors* the court held that the rights acquired **9.08** under s 3 of the Prescription Act 1832 was an easement for the access of light to a building and not to a particular room within it and it was unnecessary to measure the internal arrangements of the building.

In *Allen v Greenwood* [1980] Ch 119 the claimant sued for interference with his right to **9.09** light for his greenhouse, which was regarded as more light than was required simply for illumination. The Court of Appeal held that claimant had acquired by prescription a right to the level of light necessary for the proper use of a greenhouse as a place for growing plants. Goff LJ at 133 noted that interference with a use of abnormal sensitiveness would not be a nuisance in the first place. If the owner of the dominant tenement carries out building works to his property he does not lose his right to light, although he cannot increase the burden on the servient tenement beyond a reasonable amount of light. The court in *News of the World v Allen Fairhead & Sons Ltd* [1931] 2 Ch 402 held that an owner of ancient lights cannot reduce his ancient light area in a way that increases the burden on the servient tenement. While Farwell J held that the mere lack of evidence of any intention to preserve the ancient lights was not by itself sufficient to prove an intention to abandon them, the claimant cannot, after reducing the size of windows in its buildings, say:

> . . . 'owing to your own fault we have got very dark rooms and you are not entitled to make them darker, though if we had not ourselves darkened them your obstruction would have caused no nuisance at all.'

9.10   Further, in *W H Bailey & Son Ltd v Holborn and Frascati Ltd* [1914] 1 Ch 598 the acquiescence to a restriction of light by one neighbouring building does not entirely negative the dominant tenement's right to light relating to other neighbouring properties, although such an acquiescence does not give the dominant tenement any greater rights than it was previously entitled to.

Remedies

9.11   As with all nuisance claims, the court may grant an injunction to prevent the interference with the claimant's right, although this is a discretionary remedy and there is often reluctance to do so, particularly if the right found to exist is unsubstantial and can be adequately compensated by the payment of damages. In *Leeds Industrial Co-operative Society v Slack* [1924] AC 851 the claimant sought an injunction to restrain the obstruction of ancient lights and, in particular, to prevent the further erection of certain buildings and an order to pull down so much of the building as caused an obstruction and damages. The Chancery Division found that the Co-operative Society's buildings, when completed, would cause an actionable obstruction to the claimant's lights, but that no such obstruction had yet taken place, expressing the view that the interference with the respondent's legal rights when the building was completed would be small, and could be adequately compensated by damages, even though the law constrained the court from doing so and they reluctantly granted an injunction. The Court of Appeal agreed. The House of Lords on an appeal limited to whether damages would be appropriate in lieu of an injunction reversed the decision of the Court of Appeal and held that the court under s 2 of Lord Cairns's Act 1858 had jurisdiction to award damages in lieu of an injunction.

9.12   In *Midtown Ltd v City of London Real Property Co Ltd* [2005] EWHC 33 (Ch) the claimants claimed a right to light acquired by prescription for their property and sought an injunction to prevent the defendants from developing a neighbouring building, which the claimant's alleged would interfere with the building's light to a substantial degree. The High Court found an infringement of the right to light but rejected the claim for an injunction determining that there was entitlement to damages instead. Similarly, in *Deakins v Hookings* [1994] 1 EGLR 190, the county court awarded damages in lieu of a mandatory injunction for obstruction of the claimant's right to light.

9.13   When damages are awarded the level of such an award is based upon the diminution in the value of the whole of the site, rather than just the building or windows affected by the interference with the light. In *Griffith v Richard Clay & Sons Ltd* [1912] AC 291 the Court of Appeal affirmed that damages recoverable by the claimant were not limited to the depreciation in the value of the houses, but extended to the diminution in value of the whole of the claimant's premises considered as one building site. Buckley LJ explained that:

> No room enjoys the same light exactly as another room; the action is not in respect of that, but in respect of the injury to the house as a whole. The thing to be ascertained is the injury to the house as a whole by reason of the infringement of the right to light to certain of its windows. . . . The house as a whole does not mean merely those rooms which look to the front. It includes rooms which look to the back. These do not get any light from the front, of course, but . . . the whole property is to be taken into consideration in determining what is the amount of the damage sustained.

Rights of Light Act 1959

The Rights of Light Act 1959 aims to assist persons with a reversionary interest in land, **9.14** e.g. a landlord, who cannot gain access to their land to protect neighbours from securing a prescriptive right to light. For example, if a landlord owned a piece of land and his neighbour built a house next door and the landlord was unable to gain access to his land to erect a physical obstruction to interfere with the neighbours right to light, after 20 years, the neighbour could prevent the landlord from developing the land further by claiming a right to light for windows in the house. Under the Act, a servient owner can register a statutory notice against a prospective dominant building that effectively breaks the period of prescription to protect the landlord's interest and preserve his ability to develop the land without interfering with any right to light that may have been acquired by a neighbour.

C LIGHT POLLUTION

Light, as a pollutant, is difficult to counter. Much of the light now produced at night is from **9.15** road lighting, which aims to increase safety on the roads. Owners and occupiers of property are also free to install outside lighting, which is either sensitive to movement or turned on permanently, often without any control in the nature or extent of the light being produced. Outlined below are the options open to prevent light pollution and any remedial action that may be taken to counter light pollution that has occurred.

Land use planning

It should not be assumed that street lighting is universally desired. Practical steps may be **9.16** taken to ensure that assumptions taken at a strategic level are not implemented on the ground through uncertainty or apathy. For instance, there is an increasing trend for many parish councils to oppose the installation of street lamps in villages after considering the matter with local residents.

Strategic planning

Development plans prepared by local planning authorities (LPAs) should include policies **9.17** on light pollution. Planning policy statement PPS 23: *Planning and pollution control* (2005) notes that the need to limit and, where possible, reduce the adverse impact of light pollution, e.g. on local amenity, rural tranquility, and nature conservation, should be considered in the preparation of development plan documents and may also be material in the consideration of individual planning. An annex to PPS 23 on planning and light pollution is to be prepared. However, not all LPAs have a strategic policy on light pollution. A survey by CPRE and reported in *Night blight!* (2003) found that over one-third of district and unitary councils surveyed had no light pollution policies of any kind and no plans to introduce them.

Development control

9.18 On granting planning permission, conditions may be attached to control the level of external lighting. Light pollution may well be a material consideration in the decision-making process, see Chapter 8: Land use planning.

9.19 For major project proposals, the Town and Country Planning (Environmental Impact Assessment) Regulations 1999 (SI 1999/293) may apply. Environmental statements that must be in support of certain major project proposals must have a description of the development including an estimate, by type and quantity, of expected residues and emissions of, among other things, light, heat, etc. resulting from the operation of the proposed development see further Chapter 24: Environmental assessment.

Pollution, prevention and control

9.20 Regulation of major polluting activities under the pollution, prevention and control regime provides an opportunity for the regulator, i.e. either the Environment Agency or local authority, to prevent or control light pollution from all activities that fall within the regime. The Pollution Prevention and Control Act 1999 (PPCA 1999) aims to regulate activities that are capable of causing environmental pollution. Environmental pollution is defined under s 1(2) of the PPCA 1999 as pollution of the air, water, or land that may give rise to any harm, while: 'pollution includes pollution caused by noise, heat or vibrations, or any other kind of release of energy'

9.21 As indicated in para 9.02, light pollution is a release of energy and therefore falls within the definition of pollution for the purposes of the PPC regime.

Nuisance

Statutory nuisance

9.22 Light pollution did not come within the defined areas of statutory nuisance under s 79(1) of the Environmental Protection Act 1990 (EPA 1990) or any other enactment declared as a statutory nuisance. However, in its consultation, *Clean Neighbourhoods* (2004), Defra proposed extending the list of statutory nuisance to one covering artificial light from residential, commercial, and industrial premises, although premises used for activities where artificial light is essential or required by legislation for operational, security, or health and safety reasons would be exempt, as would street lighting. Section 102 of the Clean Neighbourhoods and Environment Act 2005 provides that s 79(1) of the EPA 1990 be amended to provide that the following constituted a statutory nuisance:

> (fb) artificial light emitted from premises so as to be prejudicial to health or a nuisance.

9.23 The amendment to s 79, once brought into force by a commencement order (due Spring 2006), will include various exceptions including light emitted from, among other things: an airport; harbour, railway and tramway premises; a lighthouse; and a prison. The defence of best practicable means will be available in proceedings commenced under s 80 but not for proceedings under s 82 by any person aggrieved.

Private and public nuisance

There are few cases where claimants have pursued a claim for light pollution and, as a result, **9.24** there is little reference to the subject in case law or texts or guidance. Birtles *et al* in *Liability for Environmental Harm* (LexisNexis, 2004) usefully consider the problems of light pollution explaining that a claimant must satisfy the court of the following:

(a) The existence of the light source by evidence from the claimant, e.g. when and from where the pollution arises, its frequency, and duration. Photographs would assist.

(b) The effect the light has on the claimant's use and enjoyment of his property taking into account that the use must be reasonable and consider locality and utility of the defendant's conduct; the level of brightness in relation to surroundings may be of significance.

(c) Evidence of intensity will be relevant and it may be necessary to obtain an expert lighting engineer's report to explain the problem to the court. The Institution of Lighting Engineers at www.ile.org.uk. should assist in offering guidance notes for reducing light pollution.

When the courts have considered light as a pollutant they have tended to take a pragmatic **9.25** approach. In *Racti v Hughes* (1995) NSW Supreme Court (considered by Birtles *et al*) the claimants complained of floodlights and camera equipment installed in their neighbour's garden, which were activated each time the claimant went into his own garden. The court held that the lighting was a nuisance. In *Hunter v Canary Wharf* [1997] AC 655 Lord Goff considered the New Zealand case of *Bank of New Zealand v Greenwood* [1984] 1 NZLR 525 in which a dazzling glare caused by sunlight deflecting from the glass roof of a verandah was held to create a nuisance. The court in *Greenwood* declined to grant an injunction ordering that the verandah be demolished and awarded damages to the claimant to install blinds.

KEY DOCUMENTS AND MATERIALS

Prescription Act 1832

Clean Neighbourhoods and Environment Act 2005

Birtles *et al* in *Liability for Environmental Harm* (LexisNexis, 2004)
PPS 23: *Planning and Pollution Control* (2005)
CPRE (2003). *Night blight!* CPRE: London

Institution of Lighting Engineers at www.ile.org.uk

10

NOISE

A INTRODUCTION

The number of noise complaints received by environmental health officers has risen sharply **10.01** over the last 15 years with around 300,000 per annum now being made. This suggests that noise is of only recent concern to people, yet, in its 1963 report, the Government Committee on the Problem of Noise (the Wilson Report 1963) in one survey asked people living in London: 'If you could change just one thing that you don't like about living round here, what would you choose?' In reply the highest number of people most wanted to change either the amount of traffic or the noise. This was followed by public facilities, transport, and the council.

10.02   Noise is a pollutant because it can seriously impact on quality of life and have physical, psychological, and social effects on those exposed to it. One of the difficulties with noise is that it is subjective. Something that is acceptable to person X may not be so to person Y. For instance, noise complaints from buildings will generally arise when unreasonable use is made of the building, e.g. general office noise generated during the working day is unlikely to be intrusive or a nuisance, but the same noise may be unacceptable at 8.00 am on a Sunday morning or at midnight on a Tuesday night. Noise from homes can cause particular anxiety and contribute to a breakdown of neighbour relations.

10.03   There are two ways to approach noise or potential noise:

(1)   to prevent it occurring in the first place or to ensure that any noise does not reach an unacceptable level; and
(2)   to respond to a continuing or recurring noise and to take steps to reduce it or stop it completely.

These are considered below. It is important first to define noise and to clarify some of the terms and phrases used in noise measurement.

Defining noise

10.04   The Wilson Report 1963 accepted the definition of noise as 'sound which is undesired by the recipient'. This simple description emphasises the cardinal fact that noise is subjective; a noise problem must involve people and their feelings, and its assessment is a matter rather of human values and environments than of precise physical measurements.

10.05   In a technical sense, sound is the variation of (usually) air pressure that can be detected by the ear. The variation of pressure itself shifts and is referred to as a frequency and this is measured in Hertz (Hz). The human ear can usually hear pressure variations in the range of 20 to 20,000 Hz. Very low frequency sound such as a bass drum will resonate at around 120 Hz whereas a piccolo flute is more likely to register between 2,000 to 5,000 Hz. However, it is not just the frequency that changes sound and, importantly, will determine when sound becomes noise. It is the level of sound, or how loud something is, which will cause any sound to be undesirable.

Sound levels

10.06   Sound level is measured in decibels (dB). Average audible levels start at around 5 dB and may continue to increase until they reach what most people will consider intolerable at around 120 dB, e.g. if someone was standing next to a pneumatic drill breaking up concrete. To create results that are similar to the human ear, dB measurements are weighted, with the most common, A weighting, written as dBA. Sound pressure measurements (dBAs) are measured according to a logarithmic scale in which an increase of 6 dB will be heard as a doubling of sound level.

Variation in impact

Sound impacts are cumulative whereby additional sources of noise will add to noise levels. **10.07** Also, some noise is of concern because it is continuing or repetitive whereas another because it is relatively loud, albeit intermittent. The analysis of sound can be further complicated by the fact that levels will vary even though they are continuous. For instance, if a prevailing wind is causing a particular sound to increase and decrease, at some points it may be loud while at others almost inaudible. This may occur at outdoor public events such as pop concerts. A distinction is made between the following two measurements:

(1) LAeq: the single value equivalent continuous sound level (A weighted). This is the average steady sound level taken over a certain period that accounts for any fluctuation in level. A common sound source will be a building site.
(2) LA Max: the maximum sound level reached over a period, e.g. a single firework being set off.

There is a range of guidance for assessing noise including: **10.08**

- World Health Organization (1999) *Guidelines for Community Noise*. The guidance states that in order to avoid moderate community annoyance a noise level of 50 $LAeq_T$ or below should be achieved. Serious community annoyance will arise at anything over 55 $LAeq_T$;
- British Standard Institute: BSI 7445; and
- Environment Agency: IPPC Technical Guidance Notes.

There is no formally agreed definition, nor a single principle of when sound levels becomes **10.09** noise or when noise becomes a nuisance. Each case should be considered on its facts.

Low frequency noise

Low frequency noise is often a cause for concern. One of the difficulties is that it can be **10.10** difficult to detect and it can travel through walls and ceilings more effectively than higher frequency sound. Also, quite low levels of low frequency noise can become a nuisance, particularly if it is persistent. Research on low frequency noise published in 2002 entitled: *Low Frequency Noise Technical Research Report for Defra Noise Programme* is available at www.defra.gov.uk.

Vibration

Sound is effectively the variation of pressure that is audible. However, there are other **10.11** pressure variations that cannot be heard but may be felt, in particular very low frequency pressure variations (between 3 Hz to 100 Hz) are often experienced as vibration. The similarity in the generation of noise and vibration means that they are often considered together in preventative measures and regulations designed to limit their impact. The statutory nuisance provisions in Pt III of the Environmental Protection Act 1990 (EPA 1990) (see Section E and Chapter 18) include vibration (s 79(7)).

Measuring sound and vibration

10.12 Specialist equipment is used to measure sound and vibration including a microphone, decibel meter, and other recording and analysis tools. The operator should be experienced in taking and reporting on the findings. There are numerous influences on sound levels including the shape, size, design, and contents of a room; humidity, wind, and background interference. Further, noise travels through objects such as walls and water as well as through air, and on occasions, natural conditions may amplify noise. It is important, when relying on sound or vibration measurements, that reliable and objective evidence is obtained. However, the High Court in *Lewisham LBC v Hall* [2003] Env LR 4 held that magistrates should not refuse to convict a person charged with an alleged breach of a noise abatement notice on the basis that no evidence of acoustic measurements had been produced.

The impact of noise and vibration on human health

10.13 The human ear first receives sound in the outer ear and on the eardrum. Vibration on the ear drum sends signals into the middle ear and then on to the inner ear, which, in turn, sends signals via tiny hairs connected to nerve cells to the brain. The brain then recognizes the sound and responds accordingly. The complexity of sound and the way it is interpreted by individuals through the aural system lends it to being a subjective sensation. It can also lead to a number of responses that impact on human health including causing deafness, tinnitus (a ringing, hissing, or booming sensation in the inner ear), sleep interference and deprivation, fatigue, headaches, stress, and anxiety.

Summary of definitions

10.14 The various definitions and concepts considered above are outlined below:

noise	sound that is unwanted by the recipient
sound	variation in air pressure detectable by the human ear
frequency	pressure variations
hertz (Hz)	measurement of frequency
decibel (dB)	measurement of sound level
dBA	A-weighted decibels (to resemble the human ear)
LA$_{eq}$	the single value equivalent (A-weighted) continuous sound
LA Max	the maximum sound level reached over a period
vibration	very low frequency pressure variation

B   NOISE PREVENTION AND REDUCTION

10.15 The law has developed quite erratically in trying to prevent noise or to limit it to acceptable levels. It has tended to respond to societal trends with, for example, the introduction of the measures to tackle nuisance car alarms under the Noise and Statutory Nuisance Act 1993 following their widespread introduction during the 1980s. Preventative measures include the opportunity to develop noise abatement zones, to minimize construction site noise, land use planning controls over development, measures under the integrated pollution, prevention and control regime, and limits to reduce transport noise.

Ambient noise strategy

Directive 2002/49/EC relating to the assessment and management of environmental noise aims to limit exposure to environmental noise in built-up areas, public parks, quiet areas, and in noise-sensitive buildings, e.g. schools and hospitals. It requires Member States to prepare noise maps for large urban areas, major roads, railways, and airports. Action plans to reduce noise should be developed following publication of the noise maps. **10.16**

Directive 2002/49/EC is being implemented by Defra and under the project: Noise Mapping England, the first map prepared under the strategy is the *London Road Traffic Noise Map* (2004). This is available at www.noisemapping.org. The Mayor also published the London Ambient Noise Strategy in 2002 as required by the Greater London Authority Act 1999. **10.17**

Noise abatement zones

Under s 63 of the Control of Pollution Act 1974 (CoPA 1974) a local authority may by order designate all or any part of its area a noise abatement zone (NAZ). The purpose of a zone is to minimize the effects of noise in urban areas and to try to avoid deterioration in the overall noise of a neighbourhood. This is said to be achieved by a local authority through a process of review, noise abatement orders, maintaining a noise level register, issuing noise reduction notices, and the opportunity to determine the acceptable noise levels for proposed development **10.18**

NAZ procedure

The procedure for operating a noise abatement zone is provided in ss 64 to 67 and Sch 1 of CoPA 1974. Section 63(2) provides that a noise abatement order shall specify the classes of premises to which it applies while Sch 1 provides that before a noise abatement order is made the local authority shall serve on every owner, lessee, and occupier of any premises within the area, and of a class to which the order will relate, a notice about the proposal, details on its scope, and other publicity requirements. A notice should also be placed in the London Gazette for two successive weeks. Before an order is made all owners, occupiers, and lessees are to be notified and given at least six weeks to lodge an objection with the local authority. **10.19**

Section 64 of CoPA 1974 requires every local authority that has designated an NAZ to measure and record in a register the level of noise emanating from premises within the zone that are of the specified classes. On recording any measurement the local authority shall serve a copy of the record on the owner and occupier of the premises. There is a right of appeal to the Secretary of State against the record in the register. **10.20**

Section 65 of CoPA 1974 provides that the recorded noise level shall not be exceeded except with the written consent of the local authority, which may be given subject to conditions. If, following a request for consent, this is refused or the local authority does not respond to the **10.21** request within two months, then under s 65(3) the applicant may appeal to the Secretary of State against the local authority's decision or failure to determine.

Noise reduction notice

10.22   Under s 66 of CoPA 1974, if it appears to the local authority that the level of noise from any premises to which a noise abatement order applies is not acceptable, that an acceptable level is practicable at reasonable cost and would afford a public benefit, the local authority may serve a noise reduction notice on the person responsible. The notice shall require that noise levels are reduced and that any subsequent increase in levels should be prevented unless consent from the authority is obtained. A person served with a noise reduction notice may appeal against the notice to a magistrates' court.

New buildings

10.23   Where a building is to be constructed within a NAZ and that on completion will become premises, to which the noise abatement order applies then, under s 67 of CoPA 1974, the local authority may determine the acceptable level of noise from the premises and record this in the noise level register. The local authority shall give notice of its intention to record the noise level in the register to the owner or occupier and the recipient may appeal to the Secretary of State within three months of the date of notification.

10.24   While the idea of implementing noise abatement zones has the potential to tackle unacceptable noise levels in practice, local authorities have been slow to implement the measures, mainly due to the resources needed for the scheme. In *Noise Control: The Law and its Enforcement* (3/e, Shaw & Sons, 2002), Christopher Penn notes that between 1976 and 1993 only 58 zones had been designated throughout the UK and that 40 of those were no longer in operation, with only very limited enforcement action being taken in any event.

Land use planning

10.25   The implementation of the land use planning system will have a considerable influence on the generation of noise, its prevention, and reduction. Strategic planning and development control decisions are likely to need consideration of noise on the local community. The general operation of the planning system is considered in Chapter 8: Land use planning; its impact on noise is considered below.

Planning policy

10.26   Planning policy guidance and statements set out government policy on aspects of land use planning. Local planning authorities (LPAs) must take their content into account in preparing their local development schemes. They may also be material to decisions on individual planning applications and appeals. All current guidance and statements are available from the ODPM at www.odpm.gov.uk.

10.27   PPG 24: *Planning and Noise* (1994) provides advice to LPAs on the use of their planning powers to minimize the adverse impacts of noise. It outlines the considerations to be taken into account in determining planning applications both for noise-sensitive developments and for those activities that will generate noise; It introduces the concept of noise exposure categories for residential developments, encourages their use, and recommends appropriate levels for exposure to different sources for noise. It also advises on the use of conditions to minimize the impact of noise. The annexes to PPG 24 include:

1   Noise exposure categories (NECs) for dwellings (set out below).
2   An explanation of noises levels for the NECs during day and night.
3   Detailed guidance on the assessment of noise from different sources.
4   Examples of planning conditions.
5   Specifying noise limits.
6   Insulation of buildings against external noise.
7   More information on other noise control regimes.
8   Relevant Statutory Instruments and British Standards.

Table 10.1 PPG 24: Noise exposure categories

A	Noise need not be considered as a determining factor in granting planning permission, although the noise level at the high end of the category should not be regarded as a desirable level.
B	Noise should be taken into account when determining planning applications and, where appropriate, conditions imposed to ensure an adequate level of protection against noise.
C	Planning permission should not normally be granted. Where it is considered that permission should be given, e.g. because there are no alternative quieter sites available, conditions should be imposed to ensure a commensurate level of protection against noise.
D	Planning permission should normally be refused.

Spatial and strategic planning

Part I of the Planning and Compulsory Purchase Act 2004 requires Regional Planning Bodies   **10.28**
to prepare Regional Spatial Strategies for their region. Because these strategic planning documents and plans set out how land in an area is to be used in the medium term (say, 5 to 15 years) they will strongly influence the levels of noise and other environmental impacts in the locality. When LPAs determine planning applications they are likely to have regard to the development plan and, under s 38(6) of the PCPA 2004, any determination must be made in accordance with the plan unless material considerations indicate otherwise.

Development control

Under s 55 of the TCPA 1990 planning permission is required for either operational develop-   **10.29**
ment or a material change in use of land and buildings. In terms of operational development, any grant of building, engineering, mining, or other operations, is likely to generate some form of noise. Noise is likely to be a material consideration that must be taken into account when granting planning permission. Importantly, the grant of planning permission may well change the nature of the locality and noise that would at one time be unacceptable could, following the grant of permission, be acceptable. Similarly, the grant of permission and subsequent development may result in noise that was at one time tolerable, being no longer the case and an action in noise nuisance could arise.

In *Gillingham BC v Medway (Chatham Docks) Co Ltd* [1993] QB 343 the court suggested that   **10.30**
the grant of planning permission to reopen the docks for commerce effectively changed the character of the neighbourhood to the extent that a nuisance action had to be considered

in the light of the existing environment, not one in the past. However, the Court of Appeal accepted in *Wheeler & anor v JJ Saunders Ltd* [1995] 2 All ER 61 that planning permission may change the local environment but did not agree that such permission authorized any nuisance that arose from it. Further, and although not a point for the House of Lords on appeal, Lord Hoffman and Lord Cooke in *Hunter v Canary Wharf* [1997] AC 655 confirmed that compliance with planning control was not in itself a defence to a nuisance action while both Lordships agreed with the proposition that planning permission may be relevant indirectly.

10.31   In terms of a material change of use, the Use Classes Order 1987 (as amended) largely governs what types of change of use require planning permission and those that do not. However, some uses, while remaining in a particular class, will nevertheless require planning permission, e.g. under s 55(3)(a) of the TCPA 1990 the division of a single dwellinghouse into two or more separate dwellinghouses (a building of multiple occupation) is a material change of use. In *LB of Newham v SSE* [1986] JPL 607 the court held that the need for sound insulation and increased noise arising from the conversion of a dwellinghouse into flats were material considerations in determining a planning application based upon a material change of use. Noise problems were attributable to the character of the use of the land.

Building regulations

10.32   Neighbour noise is the most common form of noise complaint to environmental health departments. Concerns can arise from the use of domestic appliances and playing loud music and much of the noise will travel through a building such as walls and ceilings. Other sound may be external to the building but penetrate through the building via windows, doors, and external walls. Schedule 1, Pt E of the Building Regulations 2000 (SI 2000/2531), as amended by SI 2002/2871, (the Building Regulations) sets sound insulation targets for floors and walls in newly built and converted residential accommodation. Local authority building inspectors regulate development and are responsible for securing compliance with the regulations. Part E1 of the Building Regulations covers airborne sound through walls, Pt E2 airborne sound through floors and stairs and Pt E3 impact sound through floors and stairs. Approved Document E: *Resistance to the Passage of Sound* (2004) explains how to meet the requirements in the regulations.

Pollution, prevention and control

10.33   The integrated pollution, prevention and control (IPPC) regime is considered in Chapter 11. It takes an integrated approach to the regulation of industrial activities and their emissions to air, water, and land. Section 2 of the Pollution Prevention and Control Act 1999 (PPCA 1999) provides that:

> 'environmental pollution' means pollution of the air, water and land which may give rise to any harm; and for the purposes of this definition . . . a) 'pollution' includes pollution caused by noise, heat or vibrations or any other kind of release of energy . . .

Best available techniques

10.34   The general principle of best available techniques (BAT) is to be taken into account when determining permit conditions (reg 11(2) of the PPC Regs 2000): see Chapter 11: Pollution prevention and control for full definition. The Environment Agency internal document H3: *IPPC: Horizontal Guidance for Noise, Part 1 — Regulation and Permitting* (2001) provides that:

> in determining BAT across an installation, noise will have to be considered and balanced within the wider context of other releases to different media (air, land and water) and taking issues such as usage of energy and raw materials into account. Noise cannot, therefore, be considered in isolation from other impacts on the environment.

Guidance adds that the purpose of BAT should be to underpin good practice, e.g. plant **10.35** maintenance; achieve noise levels that do not give reasonable cause for annoyance to persons in the vicinity; and to prevent creeping ambient noise. It suggests that when considering an application for a PPC permit the Environment Agency will take account of other, related statutory controls that may already be in place to control noise, e.g. noise abatement zones, and any conditions on the grant of planning permission already granted. The Agency will also look to any agreements with associated regulated bodies and their representative organizations, e.g. the *Local Government Association — Environment Agency Protocol on Implementing the IPPC Directive* (2003).

C   SPECIFIC NOISE CONCERNS

Construction sites

Development and construction on land gives rise to significant levels of noise, vibration, **10.36** and dust. In *Hunter v Canary Wharf* the joined claims included two related actions for interference with television signals by the development itself and damage and annoyance from dust caused by the construction of a 1,800 metre link road to the development site. The House of Lords dismissed the claims and so affirming the decision in *Andreae v Selfridge* [1938] 3 All ER 255, which held that noise and dust from demolition and construction was not actionable providing all reasonable steps are taken to avoid inconvenience to neighbours and that any compensation that may be payable will be over and above what is permissible. Nevertheless, there is some statutory control of noise from construction sites under Pt III of CoPA 1974.

Section 60 of CoPA 1974 (which applies to, among other things, construction, repair, and **10.37** demolition) provides that where it appears to a local authority that construction works are to be carried out, the authority may serve a notice on the person due to carry out the works imposing requirements as to the way the works are to be carried out, and it may publish notice of those requirements. The notice may specify the plant or machinery to be used, the hours during which work may be carried out and the level of noise that may be emitted (s 60(3)). It may also specify the time within which the notice is to be complied with and require the execution of specific action. In serving a notice the local authority, under s 60(4), shall have regard to:

(a)   any code of practice issued under the Act;
(b)   the need for ensuring that the best practical means are employed to minimize noise;
(c)   the desirability, according to the person being served the notice, of specifying

alternative methods, plant, or machinery, which may be substantially as effective in minimizing noise and more acceptable to them; and

(d)   the need to protect persons in the locality from the effects of noise.

Codes of Practice

10.38   The Control of Noise (Codes of Practice for Construction and Open Sites) (England) Order 2002 (SI 2002/461) and the Control of Noise (Codes of Practice for Construction and Open Sites) (Wales) Order 2002 (SI 2002/1795) approved the current Code of Practice BS 5228: *Noise Control on Construction and Open Sites* (1997), which helps secure compliance with s 60 of CoPA 1976. The Code is in five parts covering:

(1)   basic information and procedures for noise and vibration control;

(2)   guidance to noise and vibration control legislation for construction and demolition including road construction and maintenance;

(3)   surface coal extraction by open cast methods;

(4)   noise and vibration relating to piling operations; and

(5)   surface mineral extraction (except coal) sites.

Challenging the s 60 notice

10.39   Section 60(7) provides a right of appeal to a magistrates' court within 21 days from service of the notice. The Control of Noise (Appeals) Regulations 1975 (SI 1975/2116) provide, under reg 5(2), the following grounds of appeal:

(a)   that the s 60 notice is not justified;

(b)   that there has been some [material] informality, defect, or error in, or in connection with, the notice;

(c)   that the local authority have unreasonably refused to accept compliance with alternative requirements, or that the requirements, are unreasonable in character or extent, or are unnecessary;

(d)   that the time, or times, in which requirements of the notice are to be complied with is not reasonably sufficient;

(e)   that the notice should have been served on someone else;

(f)   that the notice could lawfully be served on some person in addition to the appellant and that this would have been equitable; and

(g)   that the authority have not had regard to some or all of the provisions of s 60(4).

On hearing the appeal, the court may quash or vary the notice, or dismiss the appeal.

Failing to comply with a s 60 notice

10.40   Under s 60(8) of CoPA 1974, if a person served with a notice, without reasonable excuse contravenes any requirement of the notice, he shall be guilty of an offence. A person guilty of an offence shall, under s 74, be liable on summary conviction to a £5,000 fine, with a further fine not exceeding £50 for each day that the offence continues following conviction.

10.41   The High Court in *Wiltshier Construction (London) Ltd v Westminster CC* [1997] Env LR 321 dismissed an appeal by the developer against a conviction under s 60(8). It was held that the local authority was entitled to serve a s 60 notice whenever matters appeared to exist.

The magistrate was entitled to adopt the approach that there had been a misdescription in the notice that put the authority at a serious disadvantage, save as against proceedings against a person who was well aware of the misdescription and clear as to the site that it was intended to describe.

In *Amec Building Ltd & Squibb & Davies Ltd v LB Camden* [1997] Env LR 330, a building **10.42** company and demolition company had been convicted in the magistrates' court of 16 out of 18 summonses and 19 out of 21 summonses respectively brought under s 60(8) of CoPA 1974 and s 80(4) of the EPA 1990. The first appellant successfully appealed the convictions because service of the s 60 notice was on a related company Amec Construction Ltd. However, the other appeal was dismissed with the court concluding that it was only necessary for the magistrate to consider whether the notice had been complied with where it related to the abatement of an existing nuisance, it was irrelevant whether the statutory nuisance had occurred: see also Section E on noise and statutory nuisance.

In *City of London Corporation v Bovis Construction Ltd* [1992] 3 All ER 697 the local authority **10.43** obtained an interlocutory injunction to restrain the breach of a s 60 notice. The Court of Appeal dismissed the defendant's appeal stating that it was appropriate to issue an injunction in exceptional circumstances and when criminal proceedings were likely to be ineffective.

Section 74(2) provides that in determining whether an offence is a second or subsequent **10.44** offence, under Pt III of CoPA 1974, account shall be taken of any offence under s 95 of the Public Health Act 1936 by way of contravening a nuisance order relating to noise or under s 80 of the EPA 1990 as if it were an offence against this Part. Also see the requirements to protect employees on construction sites under the Noise at Work Regulations 1989 (SI 1989/1790): see paras 10.70 to 10.73 and also Chapter 7: Human health.

It is unlikely that a private claim for noise nuisance will arise out of work being carried on **10.45** at construction sites. The principles that the development will bring benefit to the local economy and community and that the development will be temporary in nature are likely to outweigh any inconvenience to local residents.

Transport

Despite the concerns about road transport and traffic noise highlighted over 40 years ago **10.46** in the Wilson Report 1963. The Government White Paper: *A New Deal for Transport: Better for Everyone* (1998) acknowledged that traffic noise continued to have an adverse impact on health. Everyone would agree that the problem has clearly not gone away and, if anything, has deteriorated. Concern regarding transport noise arises in three main areas: road, air, and rail.

Road

Noise from road vehicles is from three main sources: **10.47**

(1) engines;
(2) vehicle movement; and
(3) intermittent noise from horns and alarms.

The Road Vehicles (Construction & Use) Regulations 1986 (SI 1986/1078), as amended, **10.48** (RV (Construction & Use) Regs 1986) enacted under the Road Traffic Act 1988 set maximum noise limits from engines and exhausts. Regulation 55(3) provides that every vehicle to which the regulation applies shall be constructed so that it complies with the requirements under the regulations and if:

(a) its sound level does not exceed the relevant limit specified in the Regulations; and

(b) for certain vehicles, the device designed to reduce the exhaust noise meets the requirements specified.

10.49 Regulations 56 to 60 of the RV (Construction & Use) Regs 1986 provide for exceptions, motorcycles, and radio interference suppression. The Motor Cycle Noise Act 1997 provides further regulation including making it an offence to sell certain exhaust and silencer systems. The current maximum noise limits are found in EU legislation. These limits are periodically increased. The first EU legislation was Council Directive 70/157/EEC on the approximation of the laws of the Member States relating to the permissible sound level and the exhaust system of motor vehicles. This has been variously amended; the most recent of which was Directive 99/101/EC. The Directives apply to any vehicle used on the road having at least four wheels and a maximum excess speed of 25 km/h, with the exception of agricultural and forestry vehicles and mobile machinery. They set limits for the noise level of the mechanical parts and exhaust systems of the vehicles concerned. Limits range from 74 dB(A) for cars to 80 dB(A) for high-powered goods vehicles.

10.50 Regulation 98 of the RV (Construction & Use) Regs 1986 provides that when a vehicle is stationary a driver must stop the engine for the prevention of noise (or exhaust emissions) except when in the necessities of traffic, to examine the machinery or when it is a vehicle propelled by gas. The regulations may be enforced by a local authority officer who may issue a fixed penalty notice under the Road Traffic (Vehicle Emissions) (Fixed Penalty) Regulations 1997 (SI 1997/3058).

10.51 Noise from vehicle movement is caused by friction between vehicle tyres and the road, the movement of vehicles through the air and the noise arising from the vehicle itself such as engine and brake use. Vehicle movement noise levels are influenced by:

- *The type of vehicle.* Heavy goods vehicles and large cars generate more noise than conventional cars.
- *The speed and nature of the driving.* Smooth driving style at speeds within the relevant speed limit will generate less noise than erratic driving involving acceleration and braking.
- *The type of road surface.* For example, thin surface dressing on roads is known to significantly reduce noise levels, whereas some traffic calming measures can increase noise, but this may be dependent on driving style, i.e. if a driver speeds up and brakes hard between road humps this will generate more noise than a driver driving slowly but consistently along a humped road. The Highways Agency supports the use of quieter road surfaces with work being carried out on a number of primary routes including the M1, M2, and M5 see further: www.highways.gov.uk.
- *The nature of the local environment.* Noise in an urban setting will reverberate among tall buildings. It will also have a greater number of people potentially affected by the noise.

10.52 Under reg 97 of the RV (Construction & Use) Regs 1986 no motor vehicle shall be used on a road in such manner as to cause any excessive noise that could have been avoided by the exercise of reasonable care on the part of the driver. This covers the case where a driver revs up a vehicle engine repeatedly and unnecessarily.

Regulation 99 of the RV (Construction & Use) Regs 1986 provides that, subject to exceptions, **10.53** no person shall sound, or cause or permit to be sounded, any horn, gong, bell, siren fitted to or carried on a vehicle, which is:

(a) stationary on a road, at any time, other than at times of danger due to another moving vehicle on or near the road;

(b) in motion on a restricted road, between 23.30 hours and 07.00 hours in the following morning.

In *Andrews v Reading BC* [2005] JPL 129, the claimant issued a small claim in the county **10.54** court seeking £4,207 in compensation for the cost of noise insulation carried out in order to mitigate excessive traffic noise created by a traffic regulation order made by the defendant. The Noise Insulation Regulations 1975 (SI 1975/1763) did not apply. The claimant stated that to impose an increased level of road traffic noise and disturbance on his house, his family, and himself without any assistance or attempt at mitigation was breach of his Art 8 right to family life under the ECHR. The defendant made an application to strike out the matter, which was dismissed. The defendant then sought summary judgment on the ground that the claim had no real prospect of success together with an application for security of costs. The matter was transferred to the High Court to clarify the statement in *Anufrijeva v LB of Southwark* [2004] 2 WLR 605 (considered in Chapter 20: Public law). The High Court referred the matter back to the county court with the following directions: that the application for summary judgment failed, that there should be no security for costs, and that the claimant was not barred from claiming damages under Art 8 for the loss suffered.

See also the controls under s 62 of the Control of Pollution Act 1974 and the statutory **10.55** nuisance provision: see Section E. See generally Chapter 3: Air, for breach of the construction and use requirements under the RV (Construction & Use) Regs 1986 in accordance with s 42 of the Road Traffic Act 1988.

Air

UK airports handled over 180 million passengers during 2002–3 and Government forecasts **10.56** are that this will rise to 500 million passengers in the next 30 years. The most common environmental concern from air transport is noise, caused by engines and rapid movement of aircraft through air. Aircraft are built to comply with international standards prepared by the International Civil Aviation Organisation (ICAO) and implemented in the UK via EU Directives. The first noise standard was Chapter 1, and was followed by Chapter 2. Chapter 3 is the current standard and includes aircraft such as Boeing 747 and airbus. Chapters 1 and 2 aircraft are now banned in the EU. The relevant UK legislation is the Aeroplane Noise Regulations 1999 (SI 1999/1452). The ICAO has adopted a Chapter 4 standard and new aircraft must meet this by the end of 2005. Directive 2002/30/EC on the establishment of rules and procedures with regard to the introduction of noise-related operating restrictions at Community airports has been transposed in the UK by the Aerodromes (Noise Restrictions) (Rules and Procedures) Regulations 2003 (SI 2003/1742) (the Aerodrome Noise Restrictions Regs 2003). It applies to all public airports with over 50,000 aircraft movements per year and to certain city airports. This includes Birmingham, Gatwick, Heathrow, London City, Luton, Manchester, and Stansted.

10.57   The Civil Aviation Act 1982 (CAA 1982) controls the operation of aircraft and airports, principally in terms of safety, although under ss 5 and 6 of the Act the Secretary of State can direct the Civil Aviation Authority (CAA) to consider environmental concerns including noise, vibration, and other forms of pollution. Recent guidance issued to the CAA covers s 78 of the CAA 1982 which enables the Secretary of State to enforce noise control on aircraft and airports. Section 79 of the Act empowers him to make noise insulation grant schemes for designated airports. Heathrow, Gatwick, and Stansted airports are currently designated, under s 80, to confer direct responsibility to the Secretary of State to enforce ss 78 and 79.

10.58   The Rules of the Air Regulations 1996 (SI 1996/1393) restrict the way aircraft are flown. For example para 5(1)(a) of Sch 1 provides that, subject to exceptions, an aircraft other than a helicopter shall not fly over any congested area of a city, town, or settlement below:

> (i)   such height as would enable the aircraft to alight clear of the area and without danger to persons or property on the surface, in the event of failure of a power unit and if such an aircraft is towing a banner such height shall be calculated on the basis that the banner shall not be dropped within the congested area;
>
> (ii)   a height of 1500 feet above the highest fixed object within 600 metres of the aircraft: whichever is the higher;

10.59   The Aerodromes (Noise Restrictions) (Rules and Procedures) Regulations 2003 (SI 2003/1742) set out the procedures that major airports, i.e. those with over 50,000 movements of civil subsonic jet aeroplanes a year, should follow when considering noise amelioration measures. Rules under the Regulations include that airports:

- shall set environmental objectives for the airport before considering any measures under the Regulations;
- shall not impose measures that are more restrictive than necessary to achieve the airport's environmental objectives;
- shall not discriminate on grounds of the nationality or the identity of the air carrier or the aircraft manufacturer;
- should take into account the likely costs and benefits of noise measures available as well as airport-specific characteristics; and
- may consider economic incentives as a noise measure;

10.60   Further, the Air Navigation (Environmental Standards) Order 2002 (SI 2002/798) provides that certain supersonic aeroplanes, helicopters, and microlight aircraft are banned from using UK airports unless they have a noise certificate from the Civil Aviation Authority.

10.61   Daytime noise limits at Heathrow, Gatwick, and Stansted airports require noise from aircraft not to exceed 94 db(A) between 7.00 am and 11.00 pm. The airport operators monitor compliance. Breach of limits by anything up to 3 db(A) will result in a maximum £500 fine. Anything above 3db(A) is subject to a maximum penalty of £1,000. Night-time noise limits and flight restrictions are also in place at Heathrow, Gatwick, and Stansted airport. A maximum noise limit between 11.00 pm and 11.30 pm is 89 db(A) and 87 db(A) from 11.30 pm to 7.00 am. The Government paper *Night Restrictions at Heathrow, Gatwick and Stansted:*

Revised Restrictions with Effect from 31 October 1999 were subject to review and consultation during 2004.

Night flight restrictions for Heathrow, Gatwick, and Stansted operate by limiting the number **10.62** of flights in and out of each airport during the night quota period of 11.30 pm to 6.00 am. The number of flights varies according to the time of year and the airport, e.g. there are currently around 16 flights at Heathrow and over 30 at Stansted. The night flight quota system operates by each aircraft being awarded a quota certificate (QC) with points ranging from QC 0.5 (the quietest) to QC 16 (the noisiest). At present, aircraft in class QC 4 and above are banned from taking off during 11.30 pm and 6.00 am. Each airport is allocated a maximum number of quota points for night flights; so, if, for example, Gatwick was allocated 90 points per night it could control anything from a minimum of 30 flights from QC 3 type aircraft to 180 flights of QC 0.5 aircraft. The case of *Hatton & ors v UK* [2003] 36022/97 (discussed in relation to human rights in Chapter 2) unsuccessfully challenged the implementation of the quota system at Heathrow. The court held that there was nothing to suggest that the authorities' decision to introduce a scheme based on the quota-count system was as such incompatible with Art 8.

The development of airports is subject to planning control. Applications for planning per- **10.63** mission will almost certainly require an environmental statement in support; the larger proposals will be regarded as major infrastructure projects and will be referred to the Secretary of State for determination. Any grant of planning permission will be subject to conditions on limiting noise and emissions. Temporary helicopter landing sites (up to 28 days) are permitted under the T&CP (General Permitted Development) Order 1995 (SI 1995/419).

In 2002, the Government produced a White Paper: *The Future Development of Air Transport in* **10.64** *the UK* comprising regional policies on significant airport expansion in the UK. In *LB Wandsworth and ors v Secretary of State and ors* [2005] EWHC 20 (Admin) the High Court found that elements of the consultation process in relation to expansion at Stansted and Luton airports were unlawful and required further consultation.

Section 79(6) of the EPA 1990 states that the statutory nuisance provisions under Pt III of **10.65** the EPA 1990 does not apply to noise by aircraft other than model aircraft. While s 76 of the CAA 1982 provides that:

> no action shall lie in respect of trespass or nuisance, by reason only of the flight of an aircraft over any property at a height above the ground which, having regard to wind, weather and all the circumstances of the case is reasonable, or the ordinary incidents of such flight, so long as the provisions of any Air Navigation Order and of any orders under s 62 [aviation control during times of war or emergency] have been duly complied with and there has been no breach of s 81 [dangerous flying].

In *Bernstein of Leigh v Skyviews & General Ltd* [1978] QB 479 the defendants flew over the **10.66** claimant's home, took a photograph, and then tried to sell it to him. The claimant sued in trespass and lost; the court finding no authority for the view that a landowner's rights in the air space above his property extended to an unlimited height. However, see *Roedean School Ltd v Cornwall Aviation Co Ltd* (1926) The Times, 3 July 1926 where the claim was based on regular low flights near the school grounds. In relation to a claim for depreciation in the value of land caused by public works, noise can be taken into account under s 4 of the Land Compensation Act 1973.

Rail

10.67   Noise from railways is significant: generated by the movement of air particularly with speed trains, vibration of rolling stock and from friction of wheels on track, and, of more recent concern, the use of rail horns used to alert people of an oncoming train. The Noise Insulation (Railways and Other Guided Transport Systems) Regulations 1996 (SI 1996/428) as amended by SI 1998/1701, requires rail authorities to provide insulation to homes within 300 metres of new or improved railway lines.

Health and safety at work

10.68   Noise is a common cause of workplace harm and injury to health. Health and safety at work provisions are generally considered in Chapter 7: Human health.

10.69   The latest EU legislation, Directive 2003/10/EC on the minimum health and safety requirements regarding exposure of workers to the risks arising from physical agents (noise) will replace Directive 86/188/EEC and must be transposed by Member States by February 2006.

10.70   Current statutory protection in the UK is via the Health & Safety at Work etc. Act 1974 (HSWA 1974) and the Noise at Work Regulations 1989 (SI 1989/1790) (the Noise at Work Regs 1989). These set out the steps required to reduce noise levels at work and places responsibility on employers and employees in protecting health and promoting safety.

10.71   Regulation 2 of the Noise at Work Regulations 1989 defines the measurement of noise as the daily personal noise exposure ($L_{EP,d}$), which is the integrated noise exposure over the working day that can be calculated from sound readings and also from a dosimeter, which is a measuring device worn by an employee that measures and records sound levels throughout an employee's shift. It also defines three action levels that are introduced by the Regulations, i.e.:

(1)   the first action level, which is a continuous $L_{EP,d}$ of 85 db(A);
(2)   the second action level, which is a continuous $L_{EP,d}$ of 90 db(A); and
(3)   the peak action level, which covers impact noise, such as hammering or drilling, and is measured at a sound pressure level of 200 pascals (equivalent to about 140 db(A)).

10.72   Under reg 4, employers are required to carry out a noise assessment where employees are exposed to excessive noise. The noise assessment must identify employees exposed to noise at or above the specified action levels and provide an employer with information that allows him to comply with his obligations under:

reg 7   by reducing the exposure of noise at the second action level;
reg 8   by providing suitable and efficient ear protection;
reg 9   identify ear protection zones within the workplace; and
reg 11   provide adequate information and training to all employees likely to be exposed to noise at or above the first or peak action levels

10.73   As with many of the obligations under the health and safety provisions, some are absolute duties and many others are qualified to the extent that they are practicable or reasonably practicable. The Health and Safety Executive has published a series of guidance notes on noise for employers including Noise Guide 1: *Legal Duties of Employers to Prevent Damage to Hearing* (1989) and Noise Guide 8: *Exemption from Certain Requirements of the Noise at Work Regulations 1989* (1989).

Industrial injuries benefit and statutory right to benefit

If hearing loss has been caused due to working conditions then a compensation claim for noise-induced harm may be made to the Department of Social Security. Between 1,200 to 1,500 cases of noise exposure industrial disease are recorded every year. Deafness and hearing loss is a prescribed disease under the Social Security (Industrial Injuries) (Prescribed Diseases) Regulations 1985 (SI 1985/967) as variously amended including by the Social Security (Industrial Injuries) (Prescribed Diseases) Amendment Regulations 2005 (SI 2005/324) (the IIPD Regs 1985). Occupational deafness is defined in Sch 1 of the IIPD Regs 1985 as: **10.74**

> Sensorineural hearing loss amounting to at least 50dB in each ear, being the average of hearing losses at 1, 2 and 3 kHz frequencies, and being due in the case of at least one ear to occupational noise.

It requires that the injured person must have worked in: **10.75**

• one or more specified jobs for at least 10 years; and
• one or more of those jobs at the same time during the five years prior to the claim.

The jobs specified in the Regulations include using, or working very near, powered grinding tools on metal (other than sheet metal or plate metal), using, or working very near, pneumatic percussive tools on metal and using chainsaws in forestry. Certain vibration is also included. If an injured person submits a claim, the DSS will arrange a medical examination. If this reveals a degree of permanent hearing loss sufficient to meet the regulations, an independent medical board will assess the disability and decide the level to be paid. **10.76**

Music, entertainment, and street noise

Noise from music and entertainment is controlled by an assortment of legislation with restrictions placed on bars, nightclubs, and other entertainment venues; prohibitions on using loudspeakers in the street; and powers of local authorities to tackle night-time noise from dwellings including to seize equipment. Each is considered below. **10.77**

Noise in the street

Section 62(1) of CoPA 1974 provides that a loudspeaker shall not be operated: **10.78**

(a) between 9.00 pm and 8.00 am for any purpose; and
(b) at any time, for the purpose of advertising any entertainment, trade or business.

Any person who operates or permits the operation of a loudspeaker in contravention of the subsection is guilty of an offence subject to a maximum penalty of £5,000 on summary conviction, with a further fine of £50/day for each day the offence continues after the conviction. Section 62(2) of CoPA 1974 provides certain exceptions for, among other things, an emergency and for use by the emergency services, utility operators, public bodies, and **10.79** public transport operators. Section 62(3) also provides a limited exception between 12.00 noon and 7.00 pm for vehicles selling food providing they do not give reasonable cause for annoyance. Further, s 62(3A) of CoPA 1974 provides that a s 62(1) prohibition does not apply if consent to use the loudspeaker has been granted by the local authority in accordance with s 8 and Sch 2 of the Noise and Statutory Nuisance Act 1993.

10.80   Section 79(1)(ga) of the EPA 1990 states that a noise that is prejudicial to health or is a nuisance and is emitted from or caused by a vehicle, machinery, or equipment in a street shall constitute a statutory nuisance. Noise from traffic, military forces, or from a political demonstration are excluded under s 79(6A).

10.81   Proceedings to abate a statutory nuisance are considered in Chapter 18: Statutory nuisance. However, for street noise arising from a vehicle, machinery, or equipment s 80A(2) of the EPA 1990 provides that an abatement notice shall be served:

(a)   on the person responsible for the vehicle, machinery, or equipment where that person can be found; or

(b)   otherwise by fixing the notice to the vehicle, machinery, or equipment.

10.82   If the notice is served under s 80A(2)(b) of the EPA 1990 and the person responsible for the vehicle can be found within an hour of fixing the abatement notice on the vehicle, machinery, or equipment, then the notice should also be served on that person. A local authority may, under s 81(3), abate a nuisance by taking whatever action may be necessary in the execution of the notice. However, it must comply with the provisions of para 2A, Sch 3 of the EPA 1990. Paragraph 2A(1) of Sch 3 provides that any person authorized by a local authority may:

(a)   enter or open a vehicle, machinery, or equipment, if necessary by force, or

(b)   remove a vehicle, machinery, or equipment from a street to a secure place.

10.83   Importantly, para 2A(5) provides that: 'Before a vehicle, machinery or equipment is entered opened or removed under subpara (1), the local authority shall notify the police of the intention to take action under sub-paragraph.' In *Westminster CC v French Connection Retail Ltd* [2005] BLD 020505/861, the Divisional Court allowed an appeal by way of case stated after the defendant was prosecuted for broadcasting pop music and advertisements for its shop into the street contrary to s 62(1)(b) of CoPA 1974. The matter was remitted to the magistrates with a direction to convict.

Nightclubs and music venues

10.84   All nightclubs and music venues whether for public and private events require a licence to be issued by the local authority, either under the Local Government (Miscellaneous Provisions) Act 1982 or the Private Places of Entertainment (Licensing) Act 1967. For each licence, the local authority can impose certain licence conditions relating to noise; a breach of such conditions is subject to a maximum fine of £20,000 on summary conviction. The Licensing Act 2003, which transferred the liquor licensing regime from magistrates to local authorities, sets four key objectives for local authorities in carrying out its functions. These include, under s 4(2):

(a)   the prevention of crime and disorder;

(b)   public safety;

(c)   the prevention of public nuisance; and

(d)   the protection of children from harm.

Public nuisance is not defined in the Act, although in the Parliamentary debates of both the   **10.85**
Licensing Bill and the Anti-Social Behaviour Bill it was concluded that public nuisance
should retain its common law meaning. Public nuisance can include noise nuisance. For
instance, s 161(1) of the Licensing Act 2003 provides that a senior police officer may make a
closure order in relation to any relevant premises if he reasonably believes that a public
nuisance is being caused by noise coming from the premises and the closure of the premises
is necessary to prevent that nuisance.

Section 40 of ASBA 2003 also provides a local authority with the power to make a 24-hour   **10.86**
closure order in relation to premises if it reasonably believes that, under s 40(1):

(a)   public nuisance is being caused by noise coming from the premises, and

(b)   the closure of the premises is necessary to prevent that nuisance.

Under s 40(4) and (5) of ASBA 2003, a person who, without reasonable excuse, permits   **10.87**
premises to be open in contravention of a closure order shall be liable on summary conviction to a maximum fine of £20,000 and/or three months' imprisonment. Finally, the police
have powers under the Criminal Justice and Public Order Act 1994 to tackle illegal raves
including asking people to leave land and to confiscate equipment.

In *Gomez v Spain* [2004] ECHR (No. 4143/02) the claimant lived in a residential area in   **10.88**
Valencia that had suffered a continuing increase in noise levels from clubs, bars, and discos
in her neighbourhood. After the locality had been designated an 'acoustically saturated
zone' by the local authority a further licence was granted to a disco. Mrs Gomez sought relief
from the European Court of Human Rights after domestic litigation failed. The court held
that the local authority had breached Mrs Gomez' Art 8 right to respect for private and
family life by failing to prevent the continuing and chronic noise being generated over
many years.

Audible intruder alarms

Part 7 of the Clean Neighbourhoods and Environment Act 2005 (CNEA 2005) provides that   **10.89**
a local authority may designate its area as an alarm notification area within which any
person responsible for premises with an alarm must notify the authority of the name,
address and telephone number of the key holder for the premises. Failure to do so is an
offence under s 73(4) with a maximum fine of £1,000 on summary conviction. A fixed
penalty notice procedure is available. In addition local authority officers have powers of
entry under ss 77–79 of the CNEA 2005.

Fireworks

Fireworks are subject to new control under the Fireworks Act 2003, although there has   **10.90**
been regulation under the Explosives Act 1875, the Protection of Animals Act 1911, the
HSWA 1974, the Consumer Protection Act 1987, and the Noise Act 1996. The Fireworks
Regulations 2004 (SI 2004/1836) made under s 2 of the Fireworks Act 2003, aim to minimize
the risk of firework use and to avoid the harmful consequences for people, animals,
or property. Regulation 8 prohibits the supply, purchase, or possession of any Category 3

fireworks (categorized under BS 7114) whose noise levels exceed 120 decibels and includes provision for measuring these noise levels. Section 11 of the Act provides that it is an offence to contravene a prohibition imposed by fireworks regulations. A person guilty of a s 11 offence is liable on summary conviction to a maximum fine of £5,000 and/or six months' imprisonment.

Residential night-time noise

10.91 The Noise Act 1996 confers additional legislative powers on local authorities to deal with noise at night. Section 42 of the Anti-social Behaviour Act 2003 (ASBA 2003) amends the provisions in that all local authorities will have these powers (whereas before they were only available to those authorities who had adopted the night-time noise regime) and that the duty of investigation formerly required under the Noise Act 1996 becomes a discretionary power of investigation.

10.92 Under s 2(1) of the Noise Act 1996 a local authority may, if they receive a complaint of excessive noise from a dwelling, arrange for an officer of the authority to take reasonable steps to investigate the complaint. Under s 2(4), if the officer is satisfied that:

(a) noise is being emitted from the offending dwelling during night hours (between 11.00 pm and 7 am), and

(b) the noise, if it were measured from within the complainant's dwelling, would or might exceed the permitted level,

he may serve a warning notice stating that an officer considers that noise being emitted from the offending dwelling exceeds, or may exceed, the permitted level, and which gives warning that any person who is responsible may be guilty of an offence.

10.93 Defra Circular NN/31/03/2004 and National Assembly for Wales Circular NAFWC 22/2004 provides that in any case where the underlying level of noise does not exceed 25 db, the permitted level of noise should be 35 db and in any case where the underlying level of noise exceeds 25 db, the permitted level shall be 10 db in excess of that underlying level of noise.

10.94 Section 4 of the Noise Act 1996 states that if a warning notice has been served any person responsible for noise emitted exceeding the permitted level and in the period specified in the notice is guilty of an offence with a maximum penalty of a £1,000 fine on summary conviction. A defence of reasonable excuse is available. Under s 8 of the Act, an officer who believes a s 4 offence has been committed may serve a fixed penalty notice of £100 on the person responsible.

10.95 Under s 10 of the Noise Act 1996 an officer, or authorized person, may enter the offending dwelling to seize and remove any equipment that it appears is being used or has been used in emitting the noise. The Schedule to the Noise Act 1996 sets out the powers in relation to seized equipment including that the equipment may be retained for a period of 28 days or until any person who has been charged with an offence under the Act is sentenced or when proceedings are discontinued, although para 2(2) of the Schedule provides that equipment seized when a fixed penalty notice was served may not be retained if the penalty is paid before the end of the period allowed for payment, which is, under s 8(3)(b), 14 days.

Section 42(5) of the ASBA 2003 specifies what local authorities may do with penalty receipts including for the purpose of carrying out its functions under the Act.

The Chartered Institute for Environmental Health published the *Noise Liaison Guide — Good* **10.96** *Practice for Police and Local Authority Cooperation* (1997) to help ensure that police and local authorities work together effectively when attending to noise complaints under the Noise Act 1996.

Section 84 of the CNEA 2005 extends the provisions of the Noise Act 1996 to cover licensed **10.97** premises.

Power equipment and domestic appliances

There is regulatory control of domestic and business equipment. Outdoor equipment is **10.98** covered by the Noise Emission in the Environment by Equipment for Use Outdoors Regulations 2001 (SI 2001/1701), which implements EU Directive 2000/14/EC relating to noise from outdoor equipment. The Regulations cover lawn mowers, lawn trimmers, leaf blowers, etc. and require manufacturers of the equipment to fix labels to each product confirming its sound level. Further, on certain equipment, labels should show that the equipment meets certain noise levels.

The Household Appliances (Noise Emission) Regulations 1990 (SI 1990/161) transposes **10.99** EU Directive 86/594/EEC on airborne noise emitted by household appliances and sets out requirements if manufacturers choose to provide information about the noise levels of their products.

D   NOISE AND THE COMMON LAW

Private nuisance

Many of the common law claims in private nuisance arise from noise complaints and **10.100** concerns. Private nuisance is defined in *Read v Lyons & Co.* [1947] AC 156 as the unlawful interference with a person's use or enjoyment of land or some right over, or in connection with it. It is explained in some detail in Chapter 18: Statutory nuisance, but in summary, a finding of nuisance requires that:

- there has been material interference or harm suffered by the claimant;
- the claimant has an interest in the land affected;
- there is an appropriate defendant;
- there has been unreasonable use of neighbouring land by the defendant; and
- the defendant could reasonably foresee the harm caused.

Some of these components with a particular reference to noise are considered below. **10.101**

Material interference or harm

The act or default of the defendant that constitutes material interference with the claimant's **10.102** property or personal comfort does not have to be the only cause of the problem. In *Polsue & Alfieri Ltd v Rushmer* [1907] AC 121 the House of Lords dismissed an appeal by a printing firm who had been restrained from working machinery throughout the night even though similar activities operated at that time and that, by itself, the noise from the operation was not great but did cause such additional disturbance significant enough to give rise to a finding of nuisance.

10.103   In *Murdoch & Murdoch v Glacier Metal Co Ltd* [1998] Env LR 732 the Court of Appeal dismissed an appeal by the claimants who lived near to the defendant's factory. The claim was that fluctuating noise and glare arising from night-time operations at the factory caused sleep disturbance and was, in the circumstances, a nuisance. The court held that noise exceeding the maximum level recommended by the World Health Organization did not constitute an actionable nuisance *per se*. It was not necessarily the case that there was a common law nuisance if sleep in a house in an area of mixed uses was disturbed by noise. While the question of sleep disturbance was an important matter to take into account, it was necessary to consider the overall situation. The Court of Appeal believed that the judge in the lower court had applied the right test by taking into account the standards of the average person and the character of the neighbourhood when deciding whether the noise was sufficiently serious to amount to a nuisance. The lack of complaints by other local residents, the presence of a bypass in close proximity to the claimants' home, and evidence from the local environmental health officer that there was no statutory nuisance were relevant considerations.

10.104   The harm suffered by the claimant does not have to be physical injury. In *Hampstead Suburban Properties Ltd v Diomedous* [1968] 3 All ER 545 the court considered that the noise causing the nuisance need not be injurious to health. In considering the balance of competing interests, i.e. the claimant's wish for peace and quiet and the defendant's desire to play loud music, the court found for the claimant. Megarry J commented at 551 that: 'A home in which sleep is possible is a necessity, whereas loud music as an accompaniment is, for those who enjoy it, relatively a luxury.'

10.105   Temporary interference such as noise from a construction site is unlikely to give rise to a finding of nuisance. It will either not be a material interference, or if it is, the benefit or utility from the interference may well be regarded as justified. In *Andreae v Selfridge* the court held that providing building works are carried out reasonably and proper steps are taken to avoid undue inconvenience to neighbours, then the activities will not be a nuisance in legal terms. However, exceptional activity such as pile driving at night, as in *De Kuysers Royal Hotel Ltd v Spicer Bros & Minter* (1914) 30 TLR 257, may constitute a nuisance.

Unreasonable use of neighbouring land by the defendant

10.106   The use of the defendant's land must be unreasonable. In assessing reasonableness, it is no defence to state that activities are carried on in a reasonable manner, see Veale J in *Halsey v Esso Petroleum Co Ltd* [1961] 2 All ER 145 considered in Chapter 17: Civil law practice and procedure. In *Sturges v Bridgman* (1879) 11 Ch D 852 the defendant caused noise and vibration by operating two large pestle and mortars and had been doing so for more than 20 years without actual interference in the claimant's use of his land. When the claimant built a consulting room at the end of his garden the noise and vibration materially interfered with his consulting practice. The defendant argued that he had acquired a prescriptive right to carry out his work in this way by more than 20 years of continuing activity. The court found for the claimant, despite the fact that (a) the claimant had effectively 'moved' to the nuisance, and (b) that there had been continuing nuisance activity for over 20 years. The judge also emphasized that the nature of the locality will influence whether or not noise or any other nuisance is reasonable or not.

Other relevant factors to a finding of nuisance

There are a number of other factors to consider when determining whether a noise nuisance **10.107** has arisen. Whether any one or more of these factors are relevant will depend on the facts of the case. In *Noise Control*, Penn considers further noise-related factors in nuisance which derive from general principles of private nuisance such as malice (see *Christie v Davey* [1893] 1 Ch 316) and the normal use of residence (see *LB Southwark v Mills* [1999] HL).

Statutory prohibition to a legal claim

A number of statutory provisions prevent a common law claim arising. Section 76 of the **10.108** CAA 1982 provides that no action shall lie in respect of trespass or nuisance, by reason only of the flight of an aircraft, see para 10.65. However, s 7 of the Road Traffic (Consequential Provisions) Act 1988 states that:

> Nothing in the Road Traffic Acts authorises a person to use on a road a vehicle so constructed or used as to cause a public or private nuisance . . . or affects the liability, whether under statute or common law, of the driver or owner so using such a vehicle.

Remedy

Successful claims in nuisance can result in either an award of damages or an injunction that **10.109** either orders the nuisance to stop and/or prohibits further nuisance activity from occurring. However, the courts have a wide discretion as to whether they award an injunction. In *Kennaway v Thompson* [1981] QB 88 there was a finding of nuisance caused by powerboat racing: an injunction to prevent the noise was not granted although damages in lieu were awarded. Similarly, in *Dennis v Ministry of Defence* [2003] EWHC 793 (QB) noise interference with the claimants' land by jet fighters flying overhead was found to be unreasonable. Damages were awarded in lieu of an injunction.

Personal injury

If someone is seeking to claim compensation for personal injury or harm arising out of **10.110** exposure to noise then a private civil law claim for personal injury may be possible. However, there are a number of important qualifications to this including the nature of noise and the option for alternative types of claim.

General or ambient noise

It is unlikely that general or ambient noise is likely to cause direct personal injury such as **10.111** deafness and tinnitus, even though these levels may be quite high. It is likely that if levels were such that they could cause direct personal injury after prolonged exposure, most people would be forced to move from the noise source or take measures to reduce the levels, before physical personal injury arose. There are instances where stress following prolonged exposure to noise may cause psychiatric illness, but it is unlikely that any claim may arise from this because of the difficulty in proving causation and that it is the prolonged exposure that is responsible for the illness. In summary, any common law personal injury claims based upon harm from noise are likely to arise from work-related conditions.

Statutory right to benefit for harm

10.112   Most compensation claims for noise-induced harm should be made to the Department
of Social Security which manages the benefit claims for occupational deafness: see paras
6.68–6.76.

Civil law claim for personal injury

10.113   If a statutory right to benefit is unavailable (if, for example, the noise did not fall into one of
the statutory lists of noisy occupations) a private law civil claim for personal injury may be
necessary if compensation is sought. Certain aspects of personal injury law such as causation
are considered in Chapter 7: Human health. Civil law procedural matters are covered in
Chapter 17: Civil law practice and procedure.

10.114   In *Berry v Stone Manganese Marine Ltd* (1971) 12 KIR 12 the claimant worked for the defendant
using pneumatic hammers. This included generating noise levels of up to 120 dBA. The
claimant became aware of hearing loss and eventually took proceedings against his
employer claiming compensation for loss of hearing. The court awarded compensation and
held that the ear plugs available to employees were of limited sizes and there was no supervision as to the correct and most effective ear plugs to be used. Penn notes that the case raises
the following points of interest for employers including:

- in cases where harm to hearing is obvious, protection must be provided and employees
  made aware of this;
- in some instances, the risk to hearing may be less obvious but serious hearing impairment
  may still arise. A reasonable employer should take steps to establish the possible risks of
  exposure to a noisy environment;
- the correct type of hearing protection must be provided under supervision and not left
  solely to the individual and any protection must be adequate; and
- it is no defence to say that the employee would not have worn hearing protection
  if supplied. The employer is under a duty to educate the employee to ensure that ear
  protection is used.

10.115   The court in *Thompson & ors v Smiths Shiprepairers (North Shields) Ltd* [1984] QB 405 held that
following the publication of *Noise and the Worker* in 1963 it would be assumed that employers were aware that excessive exposure to noise could lead to hearing loss and, thereafter,
they would be liable for personal injury, loss of amenity, and social handicap to employees
experiencing such exposure. The court added that where harm occurs through successive
jobs, liability may be apportioned between employers: see further Chapter 7: Human health.
See also *Kill v Sussex Coastline Buses Ltd* (2000) Current Law Year Book, p 1115, and *Sykes v
Chief Constable of West Yorkshire Police* (1997) Current Law Year Book p 226.

E   NOISE AND STATUTORY NUISANCE

10.116   Noise complaints account for a significant proportion of the claims and investigations for
statutory nuisance under Pt III of the EPA 1990. The principles and procedure of statutory
nuisance are covered in Chapter 18; some aspects of statutory nuisance in terms of noise are

considered below. Section 86 of the CNEA 2005 enables the local authority to defer its duty to issue an abatement notice for a period of up to seven days.

Noise abatement under Part III of the EPA 1990

Noise abatement under Pt III of the EPA 1990 falls into two categories. Section 79(1) of the **10.117** EPA 1990 provides that a statutory nuisance includes:

(g) noise emitted from premises so as to be prejudicial to health or a nuisance;
(ga) noise that is prejudicial to health and is emitted from or caused by a vehicle, machinery or equipment in a street; . . .

Section 79(1)(ga) was inserted into the EPA 1990 by the Noise and Statutory Nuisance Act **10.118** 1993. It applies to individual vehicles including those with refrigerated lorries, car alarms, and reversing signals. Section 79(6A) of the EPA 1990 provides that subsection (ga) does not apply to noise made by:

(a) traffic;
(b) any naval, military, or air force; or
(c) a political demonstration or those supporting or opposing a cause or campaign.

Section s 79(7) of the EPA 1990 provides that noise includes vibration but provides no **10.119** further definition. It adds that equipment includes a musical instrument.

In *Gillingham BC v Medway (Chatham Docks) Co Ltd* and *Wheeler & anor v JJ Saunders Ltd* the **10.120** courts considered the relevance of planning permission in changing the local environment but did not agree that such permission authorized any nuisance that arose from it. In *Hunter v Canary Wharf* the House of Lords approved this approach: see paras 10.30 and 10.36.

Traffic exemption

In *Haringey LBC v Jowett* (1999) The Times, 20 May 1999, a council tenant complained under **10.121** s 82(1) that his home, by virtue of the lack of sound insulation and the consequent intrusion of traffic noise from outside, was in such a state under s 79(1)(a) of the EPA 1990 as to constitute a statutory nuisance. The court regarded this approach as an attempt to circum-vent the traffic exemption under s 79(6A) that applied to the street noise under category (ga). Accordingly, the court extended the s 79(6A) exemption to s 79(1)(a) and dismissed the complaint. It also noted that s 79(1)(ga) could apply to railway noise.

Noise and the abatement notice

Specification of works or steps in an abatement notice

In *Lambie v Thanet DC* [2001] Env LR 397 the local authority had required in an abatement **10.122** notice that the defendant install noise limiters to reduce noise levels from their public house. This was considered acceptable by the High Court, subject to a slight variation of the abatement notice. The court also affirmed that it was unnecessary to specify the steps required to abate a nuisance in an abatement notice. If, however, the local authority thought that this was necessary then, following *R v Falmouth & Truro Port Health Authority ex p South West Water Ltd* [2000] Env LR 658, they should be stated with clarity.

10.123 In *Budd v Colchester BC* [1999] Env LR 739 the local authority had served an abatement notice on the appellant requiring him to abate the nuisance of dog barking. The appeal was on the ground that the notice had not specified the works to be undertaken in abating the noise. The Court of Appeal held that in a case of barking dogs causing a nuisance the steps to be taken were straightforward and it was unnecessary to specify any steps.

Appealing against the abatement notice

10.124 The recipient of an abatement notice can appeal to the magistrates' court against the notice on a number of grounds set out in reg 2(2) of the Statutory Nuisance (Appeals) Regulations 1995 (SI 1995/2644) (the Appeal Regs 1995). The following points have arisen in instances of noise.

10.125 A ground of appeal under reg 2(2)(b) of the Appeal Regs 1995 is that there has been some informality, defect, or error in connection with the abatement notice. In *Lowe & Watson v South Somerset DC* [1998] Env LR 143 the court considered noise nuisance caused by cockerels and waterfowl and held that it was unnecessary to state whether the noise complained of was either prejudicial to health or a nuisance and declined to conclude that such noise was no more than should be expected in the country, see also Chapter 18: Statutory nuisance.

10.126 Regulation 2(2)(c) of the Appeal Regs 1995 provides a ground of appeal against the requirements of the notice that are unreasonable in character or extent, or are unnecessary. In *Brighton and Hove Council v Ocean Coachworks (Brighton) Ltd* [2001] Env LR 77 QBD the court held that the request by the local authority to keep garage doors closed was reasonable in the circumstances. See also *St Helen's Smelting Co v Tipping* (1865) 11 HLC 642 and *Baxter v London Borough of Camden* [2000] Env LR 112 HL.

Noise levels in support of statutory nuisance

10.127 In *Godfrey v Conwy CBC* [2001] Env LR 674 the court held that noise can constitute a statutory nuisance even if it does not exceed background noise levels and is not injurious to health, but it has qualities that are nevertheless irritating. However, in *Lewisham LBC v Fenner* (1995) ENDS Report 248 p 44, a case brought under s 82 proceedings, the Crown Court found on appeal by the defendant local authority that the noise generated by a humidifier at a public swimming pool was way below the threshold recommended for intrusive noise in BS 8233 and, although irritating, the noise did not constitute a nuisance.

Expert evidence and measurement of noise levels

10.128 In *Godfrey v Conwy CBC* the court held that the test for a statutory nuisance was the common law test for nuisance, which did not require that a particular noise level or level above background noise be identified. The test to determine whether a nuisance existed was whether it caused an unreasonable interference with the claimant. Further, in *Lewisham LBC v Hall* [2003] Env LR 4 the High Court held that magistrates should not refuse to convict a person charged with an alleged breach of a noise abatement notice merely on the basis that no evidence of acoustic measurements had been produced.

KEY DOCUMENTS AND MATERIALS

Control of Pollution Act 1974

Health & Safety at Work etc. Act 1974

The Control of Noise (Appeals) Regulations 1975 (SI 1975/2116)

Social Security (Industrial Injuries) (Prescribed Diseases) Regulations 1985, as amended (SI 1985/967)

Road Vehicles (Construction & Use) Regulations 1986 (SI 1986/1078), as amended

Noise at Work Regulations 1989 (SI 1989/1790)

Environmental Protection Act 1990

Noise and Statutory Nuisance Act 1993

Statutory Nuisance (Appeals) Regulations 1995 (SI 1995/2644)

Noise Act 1996

Pollution Prevention and Control Act 1999

PPG 24: *Planning and noise* (1994)

Control of Noise (Codes of Practice for Construction and Open Sites) (England) Order 2002 (SI 2002/461)

Air Navigation (Environmental Standards) Order 2002 (SI 2002/798)

Control of Noise (Codes of Practice for Construction and Open Sites) (Wales) Order 2002 (SI 2002/1795)

Aerodromes (Noise Restrictions) (Rules and Procedures) Regulations 2003 (SI 2003/1742)

Licensing Act 2003

Clean Neighbourhoods and Environment Act 2005

Directive 2002/30/EC on the establishment of rules and procedures with regard to the introduction of noise-related operating restrictions at Community airports

Directive 2002/49/EC relating to the assessment and management of environmental noise

Directive 2003/10/EC on the minimum health and safety requirements regarding exposure of workers to the risks arising from physical agents (noise)

British Standard Institute. *BSI 7445*

Building Regulations 2000: Approved Document E: *Resistance to the Passage of Sound*

CIEH *Noise Liaison guide — Good Practice for Police and Local Authority Cooperation* 1997

Environment Agency: IPPC Technical Guidance Notes

The Government Committee on the Problem of Noise (1963). *Noise, Final Report*. HMSO: London (the Wilson Report)

Noise Guide 1: *Legal Duties of Employers to Prevent Damage to Hearing* (1989)

Noise Guide 8: *Exemption from Certain Requirements of the Noise at Work Regulations 1989*. (1989)

Penn, C (2002). *Noise Control: The Law and its Enforcement*. 3rd ed. Shaw & Sons: Crayford, Kent

Schedule 1, Part E of the Building Regulations 2000 (SI 2000/2531), as amended by SI 2002/2871

World Health Organization (1993). *Task Force on Community Noise Recommendations*. EUR/ICP/RUD. WHO: Geneva

Low Frequency Noise Technical Research Report for Defra Noise Programme from
www.defra.gov.uk

*Night Restrictions at Heathrow, Gatwick and Stansted: Revised restrictions with effect from
31 October 1999*

11

POLLUTION PREVENTION AND CONTROL

A   INTRODUCTION

11.01   The system of Pollution Prevention and Control (PPC) aims to control and, where possible, prevent pollution from polluting activities. It takes an integrated approach to protecting the environment, which means that emissions to air, land, and water must be considered together. Integrated pollution control (IPC) was introduced by Pt I of the Environmental Protection Act 1990 (EPA 1990). The EU Directive 96/61/EC concerning integrated pollution prevention and control (IPPC Directive) required more stringent standards than those contained in the EPA 1990; the Pollution Prevention and Control Act 1999 (PPCA 1999) was enacted to transpose the IPPC Directive.

11.02   There are many similarities and areas of overlap between IPC and PPC. They have operated in tandem since 1999 although PPC will replace IPC by 2007. Installations being controlled by IPC before 31 October 1999 continued to be regulated under IPC unless there was a substantial change in the process, whereas activities requiring a new permit to pollute after that date were managed under the new regime. All activities must have fully transferred to PPC by 2007. The operation of the two regimes are contained in:

(1)   For IPC: Pt I of the EPA 1990, the Environmental Protection (Prescribed Processes and Substances) Regulations 1991 (SI 1991/472) as amended (PPS Regs 1991) and the Environmental Protection (Applications, Appeals and Registers) Regulations 1991 (SI 1991/507) as amended (EPAAR Regs 1991).

(2)   For PPC: the Pollution Prevention and Control (England and Wales) Regulations 2000 (SI 2000/1973) as amended (PPC Regs 2000). These are to be further amended by the

forthcoming PPC (Public Participation) (England and Wales) Regulations 2005 amending Schs 4 and 7 in relation to public participation.

The list below highlights the types of activities controlled under each regime. The transfer **11.03** from IPC to PPC has been simplified by drafting the regulations in similar fashion with each Chapter covering similar themes.

Table 11.1 Activities under the IPC and PPC regulations

	Sch 1 of the PPS Regs 1991	Sch 1 of the PPC Regs 2000
Chapter 1	fuel production processes, combustion processes (including power generation and associated processes)	energy industries
Chapter 2	metal production and processing	production and processing of metals
Chapter 3	mineral industries	mineral industries
Chapter 4	the chemical industry	the chemical Industry
Chapter 5	waste disposal and recycling	waste management
Chapter 6	other industries	other activities

IPC and PPC both make a distinction between Part A, the more polluting activities, and **11.04** Part B, the less polluting ones. Part B processes cover polluting processes emitting to air alone and controlled under the Air Pollution Control (APC) or Air Pollution Prevention and Control (APPC) systems. PPC and the majority of the Part A activities are managed by the Environment Agency, whereas APPC is controlled by local authorities, who also manage the activities under Part A(2) (the less polluting processes that nevertheless emit into more than one media), e.g. Sch 1, s 5.1 of the PPC Regs, Part A(1) includes, among other things:

(a) the incineration of any waste chemical or waste plastic arising from the manufacture of a chemical or the manufacture of a plastic.

Whereas Sch 1, s 5.1, Part B includes:

(b) The incineration of specified hazardous waste in an incineration plant with a capacity of 10 tonnes or less per day and less than 1 tonne per hour, unless the plant is an exempt incineration plant.

Differences between IPC and PPC

While IPC and PPC are similar in many ways such as taking an integrated approach to **11.05** regulation. There are some key differences:

- PPC covers a wider range of environmental impacts, in addition to air, land, and water it covers energy use, resources, noise, vibration, and heat outputs;
- PPC covers a larger number of polluting activities than IPC with up to 7,000 expecting to be under its control by 2007; and
- the Environment Agency or local authority grants an IPC or APC authorization under IPC. Under PPC the polluter applies for a permit to pollute.

In this chapter IPC and PPC are considered separately. APC and APPC simply relate to the **11.06** less polluting activities that emit solely to air. They are managed under the IPC and PPC regimes respectively and it is unnecessary to consider them separately. However, other aspects of air pollution and operation are considered in Chapter 3: Air.

11.07   A summary of the pollution control regimes is provided below adapted from the Defra guidance: *Industrial Pollution Control Regimes*. Defra is the main government department responsible for PPC.

Table 11.2 Summary of pollution control regimes

Legislation	Regime	Regulator	Classification of industrial processes/activities	Scope of regulatory control
EPA 1990 and PPS Regs 1991	IPC	Environment Agency	Part A processes/installations	air, water, land
	APC	local authorities	Part B processes/installations	air
PPCA 1999 and PPC Regs 2000	IPPC	Environment Agency	Part A (1) activities/ installations (about 5,000 in England/Wales	air, water, land, odour, waste, energy, accident prevention, noise, and vibration
	LA IPPC	local authorities	Part A(2) activities/installations (about 1,000 in England/ Wales — gen. smaller and less polluting than Part A(1)	air, water, land, odour, waste, energy, accident prevention, noise, and vibration
	LA PPC	local authorities	Part B activities/installations	air

11.08   Each of the regulatory systems is considered in detail. PPC as the now, more dominant system is considered first and in more detail. However, both regimes remain relevant until IPC is repealed in 2007. Both systems are also relevant in considering air emissions alone.

B   OVERVIEW OF PPC

11.09   The PPC Regs 2000 provide three related systems of pollution control:

- Integrated Pollution Prevention and Control (PPC), which covers Part A(1) Installations regulated by the Environment Agency;
- Local Authority Integrated Pollution Prevention and Control (LA-PPC), which covers Part A(2) Installations regulated by local authorities; and
- Local Authority Pollution Prevention and Control (APPC), which covers Part B installations emitting to air regulated by local authorities.

11.10   The PPC Regs 2000 have been amended by SI 2001/503, SI 2002/275, SI 2002/1702, SI 2003/ 1699, and SI 2003/3296. The Landfill (England & Wales) Regs 2002 (SI 2002/1559), the Waste Incineration (England & Wales) Regs 2002 (SI 2002/2980), and the Solvent Emissions (England & Wales) Regs 2004 (SI 2004/107) also make amendments.

11.11   The preamble to the IPPC Directive states that:

the objective of an integrated approach to pollution control is to prevent emissions into air, water or soil wherever this is practicable, taking into account waste management, and, where it is not, to minimise them in order to achieve a high level of protection for the environment as a whole.

Section 1(1) of the PPCA 1999 states that the purpose of the Act is to provide for: **11.12**

(a)   the implementation of the IPPC Directive;
(b)   regulating, otherwise than in pursuance with the Directive, activities which are capable of causing environmental pollution; and
(c)   otherwise preventing or controlling emissions capable of causing any such pollution.

Under s 2(2) of the PPCA 1999 'environmental pollution' means pollution of the air, water,   **11.13**
and land, which may give rise to any harm; and for the purposes of this definition

(a)   'pollution' includes pollution caused by noise, heat, vibrations, or any other kind of release of energy, and
(b)   'air' includes air within buildings and air within other natural or man-made structures above or below ground.

Under each system of pollution control (PPC, LA-PPC, and APPC) the operators of industrial   **11.14**
and other installations covered in the regime must obtain a permit to pollute. Regulation 9(1) of the PPC Regs 2000 provides that:

> No person shall operate an installation or mobile plant after the prescribed date for the installa-tion or mobile plant except under and to the extent authorised by a permit granted by the regulator.

An installation is defined in reg 2(1) of the PPC Regs 2000 as a stationary technical unit   **11.15**
where one or more activities listed in Pt 1, Sch 1 of the Regs are carried out, and any other location on the same site where any other directly associated activities are carried out, which have a technical connection with the activities in the stationary unit that could have an effect on pollution. Mobile plant is defined as plant that is designed to move or to be moved whether on roads or otherwise and that is used to carry out one or more activities listed in Pt 1, Sch 1. Regulation 32 of the PPC Regs 2000 provides that to operate an installation or mobile plant without a permit is an offence.

The Defra publication: *Integrated Pollution Prevention and Control: A Practical Guide* (3/e, 2004)   **11.16**
provides a clear explanation of how the PPC regulations work in practice and is available from the Defra website. The PPC regime is not straightforward and further reference to the relevant legislation and to the Defra, Environment Agency, and local authority guidance is recommended. The key parts of the PPC regime are considered below.

C   THE PPC PERMIT SYSTEM

The prohibition in reg 9(1) of the PPC Regs 2000 means that operators must apply for a   **11.17**
permit for a new or substantially changed installation before the activity operates.

Pre-application considerations

11.18   The permit application procedure is set out in both the PPC Regs 2000 and the Defra *Guide*, which suggests that where installations are not particularly complex a permit application could be submitted at the design stage of the proposal and that this would be best before any construction work begins.

11.19   An installation may also need planning permission and it is recommended that the operator make the permit application and an application for planning permission in parallel wherever possible. The regulator must take account of information contained in any environmental impact assessment that has been prepared, see Chapter 8: Land use planning and Chapter 24: Environmental assessment.

11.20   For particularly complex installations, the *Guide* suggests that the operator should negotiate and agree a 'staged application' process, whereby a plan for achieving the permit is prepared. The regulator will assess the proposed installation at intervals with the final stage resulting in a determination of whether to grant or refuse a permit.

Form of application

11.21   Regulation 10(1) provides that a permit application shall be made to the regulator in accordance with paras 1 to 3 of Pt 1, Sch 4 and shall be accompanied by a fee. Part 1 requires the permit application to be in writing and then lists from (a) to (p) the information required in submitting the application. Important features of the list are the request for:

(a)   contact details;

(e)   a description of the installation and activities to be carried out;

(f)   details of raw materials, other substances, and energy use;

(g)   the nature, quantities, and sources of foreseeable emissions;

(h)   details of technologies and other techniques that the operator proposes to use; and

(p)   a non-technical summary of all the information listed from (a) to (o).

11.22   The Environment Agency provides comprehensive guidance for applicants including *IPPC: Part A(1) Installations: Guide for Applicants* (2000) and a range of technical guidance notes such as:

• IPPC S6.01: *Sector Guidance: Pulp and Paper* (2000);
• IPPC Regulatory Guidance Series No. 3: *Understanding the Meaning of 'Operator' under IPPC* (2001); and
• IPPC Regulatory Guidance Series No. 1: *Change in Operation and Substantial Change under IPPC* (2004).

Fees and charges

11.23   Sections 41 to 43 of the Environment Act 1995 empower the Environment Agency to prepare a charging scheme for the recovery of costs incurred in performing its operator functions and in relation to Part A(1) installations. Charges are reviewed each year and will depend upon the installation proposed. The current fees are published by the Environment Agency on their website at www.environment-agency.gov.uk. For Part A(2) and Part B installations, the Secretary of State sets the fees and charges to be paid for a permit application under reg 22 of the PPC Regs 2000. The current fees payable are available from Defra at www.defra.gov.uk.

Pre-application discussions

The Defra *Guide* suggests that operators, regulators, and possibly some statutory consultees **11.24** may hold pre-application discussions before a formal application is made. The regulator may clarify whether a permit is likely to be required, offer general advice on preparing applications and more specific guidance on the relationship with land use planning and whether a staged application is appropriate. However, the parties cannot imply any advance agreement or outcome.

Operators may use other information or documents they hold in support of the application, **11.25** e.g. documents relating to certified environmental management systems, or the responsibilities under the Control of Major Accident Hazards Regulations 1999 (SI 1999/743). If they wish to rely on associated documents then there should be some explanation as to how and why they relate their PPC permit application.

Regulator's action on receipt of a permit application

On receipt of a permit application, the regulator will check to see whether the application **11.26** has been 'duly made'. Instances where the application has not been 'duly made' include:

- that the standard application form issued by the regulator has not been used;
- that the installation falls outside the PPC regime;
- that it has been sent to the wrong regulator; or
- that the necessary fee has not been paid.

The regulator should be reasonable when assessing applications. If certain information is **11.27** missing then the regulator may simply request that information. Alternatively, the regulator may return the application and fee informing the operator why the application has not been duly made. Either way, the determination of the application will be delayed.

Statutory consultation

If the application has been duly made then the regulator must begin the consultation **11.28** process. It should consult with the specified statutory consultees listed in Sch 4, Pt 2 of the PPC Regs 2000 and the public. Part 2, para 9 provides that the regulator should give notice to statutory consultees within 14 days of receiving the application. There are ten specific statutory consultees such as the Health Authority (now the Primary Care Trust) and the Food Standards Agency. The regulations specify when and for which type of installation i.e., Part A or Part B, the consultee should be contacted. There is also a catch-all section of 'such other persons as the Secretary of State may direct'. Under Pt 2, para 12(2)(a) statutory consultees have 28 days to make representations from the date on which notice is given.

Public consultation

The level of public consultation required by the PPC Regs 2000 relates to information **11.29** provision and the opportunity to make representations on a permit application. The Defra

Guide suggests that the purpose of the consultation is to provide the regulator with facts and views that it might not otherwise have to help with its determination. It also allows people to bring local or wider issues or concerns to the regulator's attention.

11.30   It is the duty of each regulator to maintain a public register of information under reg 29(1) of the PPC Regs 2000. Schedule 9 lists what the register should contain including under para 1(a) all particulars of any application made to the regulator for a permit. The application should be placed on the public register as soon as possible. The introduction of the Freedom of Information Act 2000 and the Environmental Information Regulations 2004 (SI 2004/ 3391) provide a right of access to environmental information subject to any non-disclosure on the grounds of commercial confidentiality or national security. However, there is a presumption in favour of disclosure, placing the burden on those wishing not to disclose to prove their case, see Chapter 2: Environmental rights and principles.

11.31   Schedule 4, para 5 of the PPC Regs 2000 requires the operator to advertise the application by advertising it in one or more local newspapers and in the London Gazette, within a period of 28 days beginning 14 days after the date on which the application is made. This gives the regulator time to check the application and place it on the public register for inspection. Under para 6 of the PPC Regs 2000 the advertisement must state the operator's name, the address of the installation, and describe the activities proposed. It should also provide details of the public register and that this may be inspected free of charge. It must explain that any person may make representations in writing to the regulator within 28 days from the date the application is advertised.

Determining the application

Time period for determination

11.32   Paragraph 15, Sch 4 of the PPC Regs 2000 provides that the regulator should give notice of its determination of a permit application within four months from the date the application was received or after such longer period as agreed. This may be extended if the regulator had to request further information from the operator. Under para 16, if the regulator fails to make a determination within the time period the operator may regard this as a refusal and can appeal against the decision.

The role of conditions

11.33   Regulation 10(2) of the PPC Regs 2000 provides that a regulator shall either grant the permit subject to conditions or refuse it. The regulation and control of the installation or mobile plant is based upon the conditions attached to a permit. Regulation 11 sets out general principles for permit conditions such as under 11(2) that:

    (a)   all the appropriate preventative measures are taken against pollution, in particular through application of the best available techniques; and

    (b)   no significant pollution is caused.

11.34   There are specific condition requirements contained in reg 12, which include, among other things, emission limit values for pollutants, in particular those pollutants listed in Sch 5 to the PPC Regs 2000. The regulator must either grant a permit with conditions or refuse it.

Compensation for off-site conditions

On some occasions, a permit may include a condition requiring an operator to carry **11.35** out works or do other things in relation to land not forming part of the installation site. This requires the provision of an off-site condition under reg 12(12) of the PPC Regs 2000. Regulation 12(13) and Sch 6 of the PPC Regs 2000 provide for a scheme of compensation to be paid to any person who has granted the operator any rights to use the land.

Determination by the Secretary of State

Under para 14, Sch 4 of the PPC Regs 2000, the Secretary of State can direct that a permit **11.36** application be referred to him for determination. This will be exceptional, for example, if the application were of national significance. If a referral is made, the regulator will continue to carry out the application procedure but will forward documents and representations to the Secretary of State. The Secretary of State may direct that there is a hearing on the matter and will do so if requested by both the operator and regulator. After considering the application the Secretary of State will direct the regulator either to grant a permit with any conditions or to refuse the application.

Refusing the permit

The Defra *Guide* states that the regulator must refuse a permit in certain circumstances and **11.37** that there are three main criteria:

(1) That the regulator is unable to reasonably grant the permit subject to conditions e.g. where the environmental impact would be unacceptable, the information provided does not provide a reasonable basis to determine conditions or the additional requirements of landfill, waste incineration or solvent emissions regulations cannot be complied with.

(2) That the operator will not comply with its conditions. For instance, Regulation 10(3) of the PPC Regs 2000 provides that a permit shall not be granted if the regulator considers that the applicant will not be the person in control of the installation or mobile plant or will not ensure that it is operated so as to comply with its conditions.

(3) Because the permit may authorize a specified waste management activity without the pre-requisites for these installations being met.

The operator may wish to appeal against a regulator's determination to refuse a permit, **11.38** against certain conditions imposed on a permit, or the action for closure of an existing landfill to the Secretary of State. However, there is no right of appeal against the decision of the regulator to treat an application as withdrawn following the operator's inaction in not providing further information in the time given. In this instance, the operator would need to make a fresh permit application. Appeals are considered below.

D PPC PRINCIPLES

Best available techniques

The principle of best available techniques (BAT) is central to the PPC regime. It is a general **11.39** principle to be taken into account when determining permit conditions (reg 11(2) of the PPC Regs 2000). There is also an implied, default condition provided by reg 12(10) that states:

there is implied in every permit a condition that, in operating the installation or mobile plant, the operator shall use the best available techniques for preventing or, where that is not practicable, reducing emissions from the installation or mobile plant.

Defining BAT

11.40   Regulation 3 of the PPC Regs 2000 defines BAT as:

the most effective and advanced stage in the development of activities and their methods of operation which indicates the practical suitability of particular techniques for providing in principle the basis for emission limit values designed to prevent and where this is not practicable, generally to reduce emissions and the impact on the environment as a whole; and for the purpose of this definition—

(a)   'available techniques; means those techniques which have been developed on a scale which allows implementation in the relevant industrial sector, under economically and technically viable conditions, taking into consideration the cost and advantages, whether or not the techniques are used or produced inside the UK, as long as they are reasonably accessible to the operator;

(b)   'best' means, in relation to techniques, the most effective in achieving a high general level of protection of the environment as a whole;

(c)   'techniques' includes both the technology used and the way in which the installation is designed, built, maintained, operated and decommissioned.

Identifying BAT options

11.41   The Defra *Guide* suggests that where there is a choice, the technique that is best overall will be BAT unless it is not an 'available technique' and that there are two aspects to availability:

(1)   a cost-benefit analysis, which means that a technique may be rejected if its costs far outweigh its environmental benefits, and

(2)   can the operator obtain the technique? This does not mean that the technique must be in general use. It could have been the subject of a successful pilot that the industry is confident about introducing. Also, the technique may come from outside the EU.

11.42   Determining BAT involves comparing the techniques that prevent and reduce emissions and identifying the best in terms of the lowest environmental impact. The environmental assessment should consider both direct and indirect effects and look at the techniques proposed to tackle these. Schedule 2, para 1 of the PPC Regs 2000 provides that in determining BAT special consideration, bearing in mind the likely costs and benefits, shall be given to a list of 12 specific matters including:

(5) technological advances and changes in scientific knowledge and understanding;

(8) the length of time needed to introduce the BAT;

(11) the need to prevent accidents and to minimise the consequences for the environment; and

(12) the information published by the Commission pursuant to Art 16(2) of the Directive or by international organisations.

11.43   The Defra *Guide* concludes that in some cases a judgement will need to be made about the relative significance of different environmental effects, sometimes in different media. In comparing these, certain parameters may assist, e.g. long-term irreversible effects are worse than short-term reversible ones, if all other factors such as immediate severity are equal although comparisons will often be an inexact science.

After the environmental assessment an economic assessment of BAT options may be made. **11.44** The cost assessment should include operating as well as capital costs and any savings that may arise. The lack of profitability of any business should not affect a regulator's determination in assessing what is BAT for a particular industry.

BREF notes

Article 16(2) of the IPPC Directive provides that Member States should exchange informa- **11.45** tion on BAT. The European Commission publishes BAT Reference documents (BREF notes) for 30 industry sectors. These are not binding requirements but should be taken into account when Member States determine BAT. The BREF notes are available from the European IPPC Bureau website: http://eippcb.jrc.es/pages.Fevents.htm.

Emission limit values

Regulation 2 of the PPC Regs 2000 provides that 'emission limit value' (ELV) means the **11.46** mass, expressed in terms of specific parameters, concentration, or level of an emission, which may not be exceeded during one or more periods of time. For all activities, except landfills, applying BAT will usually set ELVs. However, ELVs must also satisfy reg 12(7), which provides that where an EU environmental quality standard (EQS) requires stricter ELVs than those achievable under BAT the regulator must impose the stricter limits.

Environmental Quality Standards

EU Environmental Quality Standards

The Defra *Guide* states that an EQS includes several numerical standards that specify **11.47** maximum concentrations of named pollutants for air and water. There are also qualitative EU EQSs, which, again, may require ELVs stricter than those by working to BAT. Further, if an EU EQS changes or a new one is introduced the regulator may need to vary an operator's permit conditions. If an EU EQS is already being breached in a particular locality, then a permit should not be issued to any new installation that would cause anything beyond a negligible increase in the exceedence. If a combination of controls on the proposed installation and measures to reduce emissions from other sources will achieve compliance with an EQS, then the installation may be permitted. If an existing installation makes only a minor contribution to a breach of an EU EQS caused mainly by other, non-PPC sources, ELVs for the installation should reflect that.

National Environmental Quality Standards

The regulators should ensure that national EQSs should be observed to adequately protect **11.48** the environment. For instance, in terms of water quality these include:

(a)   Government river quality objectives;
(b)   Environment Agency national standards to protect the quality of water and aquatic life; and
(c)   Environment Agency local standards to control specific sources of substances.

Regulation proportionate to risk

11.49   The Defra *Guide* states that the PPC regime should be applied proportionately to the environmental risk presented by the operation. The Environment Agency has developed the Environment Protection Operator Performance and Risk Appraisal (OPRA) methodology to help evaluate risk and operator performance when carrying out its regulatory functions. Details of OPRA can be obtained from the Agency.

Site-specific permitting and general binding rules

11.50   Any permits granted to an operator are generally site-specific and they will take account of the particular installation, its location, and the local environmental conditions. However, under reg 14 of the PPC Regs 2000, the Secretary of State may make 'general binding rules', which, at the request of the operator, may be included in permits for certain installations. The 'general binding rules' may be appropriate for certain industries where similar installations share similar characteristics. No general binding rules have been made to date, although the Environment Agency has published *Standard Farming Installation Rules and Guidance* (2005) for intensive agricultural practices that fall within PPC (available on the Agency's website: www.environment-agency.gov.uk).

Management systems and operator competence

11.51   Effective management systems are regarded as an integral part of BAT. Some operators may be implementing one of the recognized environmental management systems such as ISO 14001 or the Eco-Management and Audit System (EMAS). Regulators are encouraged to take account of the systems. They are discussed in Chapter 23: Environmental management. At a minimum the Defra *Guide* provides that management systems need to cover:

(a)   staff numbers;
(b)   training;
(c)   personnel competencies;
(d)   working methods;
(e)   maintenance;
(f)   records; and
(g)   monitoring of releases.

11.52   A regulator must not issue a permit if it will not comply with its conditions. This may be doubtful if an operator's management system is inadequate.

Public register

11.53   Regulation 29 of the PPC Regs 2000 requires all regulators to maintain a public register on all the installations they regulate and that the register maintained by the local authority must also contain particulars on installations in their area managed by the Environment Agency. The register must be available at all reasonable times for free public inspection and to be copied on payment of a reasonable charge (reg 29(6)). The Defra *Guide* states that the register can be of any form that allows proper public access, e.g. a computerized register. If a computer-based register is maintained, assistance to enable anyone to effectively inspect the register must be available.

Paragraph 1 of Sch 9 to the PPC Regs 2000 lists the information that must be contained on a register. This includes, for example: **11.54**

(a) details of any application permit;
(f) details of any permit granted by the regulator;
(q) details of any conviction or caution under reg 32(1) of any person relating to the operation; and
(v) all particulars of any report published by a regulator relating to an environmental assessment of the operation.

National security and commercial confidentiality

Regulation 30 excludes from registers information affecting national security. The Secretary of State determines whether or not the information that should be placed on the register would be against the national interest following an application by the operator. **11.55**

Regulation 31 of the PPC Regs 2000 enables regulators to exclude information from the register on the ground that it is commercially confidential, something that is determined by the regulator. If a regulator decides that the information is commercially confidential then it may be excluded from the register for a period of up to four years. After this period a person may reapply for confidential status. The register must note that commercially confidential information is protected. **11.56**

Under reg 31(4), if a regulator fails to determine an application within 28 days the applicant can treat the failure as a determination that the information is not commercially confidential and may appeal to the Secretary of State against this decision. **11.57**

E OPERATIONS AND PERMIT REQUIREMENTS

Once the installation or mobile plant has been granted a permit, its operation should be in compliance of the conditions of the permit. It should also operate in accordance with the general principles contained in reg 11 of the PPC Regs 2000 including taking appropriate preventative measures, without significant pollution, and in a way that waste production is avoided, energy is used efficiently, and accidents are prevented. **11.58**

Effective management is required as outlined in para 11.51 and Chapter 23: Environmental management. There will also be conditions requiring site protection and monitoring programmes. The Defra *Guide* suggests that the following techniques may be relevant to the programme: **11.59**

• integrity testing of containment measures such as pipes, bunds, hard standing etc.;
• monitoring of preventative measures through sampling and checking of soil and/or water; and
• maintenance of operating records through the life of the permit.

11.60   Regulations 15 to 21 of the PPC Regs 2000 cover the situation when there is a permit in place but there is a change in circumstances that may need to be reflected in either the conditions of an existing permit being varied, the permit being transferred, or the surrender of the permit. These are considered below.

Permit review

11.61   Regulation 15(1) of the PPC Regs 2000 provides that regulators shall periodically review the conditions of permits and may do so at any time. Also, reg 15(2) requires a permit review when:

(a)   pollution from the installation or mobile plant is of such significance that the existing emission limit values need to be revised;

(b)   substantial changes in BAT make it possible to reduce emissions significantly without imposing excessive costs; or

(c)   the operational safety of activities requires other techniques to be used.

Proposed changes in operation and variation of conditions

11.62   Under reg 16 of the PPC Regs 2000 an operator proposing any change in operations shall notify the regulator in writing at least 14 days before making the change providing the proposed change does not require permit conditions to vary. The regulator should then acknowledge receipt of any notification. An example of such a change falling under reg 16 would be a change in the company name providing this did not, in fact, mean a change in operator.

11.63   Regulation 17(2) of the PPC Regs 2000 allows an operator to apply to the regulator to apply for the variation of the conditions of his permit that will authorize a 'substantial change' in the operation of an installation or mobile plant. The application to vary conditions should be made in accordance with the procedure contained in Sch 7, Pt 1 and be sent with the relevant fee. The variation procedure is similar to the initial permit application process with the requirement to publicize and offer the opportunity of representations on the application. The regulator may also decide to vary permit conditions at any time, e.g. following a review of the permit under reg 15.

Substantial change

11.64   Regulation 2(1) of the PPC Regs 2000 provides that:

'change in operation' means, in relation to an installation or mobile plant, a change in the nature or functioning or an extension of the installation or mobile plant which may have consequences for the environment; and
'substantial change in operation' means, . . . a change in operation, which, in the opinion of the regulator may have significant negative effects on human beings or the environment.

11.65   The Defra *Guide* suggests that whether any particular change proposed by an operator would constitute a substantial change is something that can only be determined on the facts of each case and requires consideration of all impacts of any proposed change rather than just the net environmental effect.

Receipt of variation application

On receipt of a variation application, the regulator will confirm that the application has **11.66** been duly made and, if not, the regulator may request further information. If this is not provided in time the regulator may treat the application as withdrawn.

The public consultation requirements for a substantial change in operations are the same as **11.67** a new permit application. For variations not involving a substantial change, the regulator may decide that a similar approach to public consultation is still required for some other reason.

Determination of permit variation

When considering the application to vary conditions, the regulator may accept the con- **11.68** ditions proposed, provide alternative conditions, or refuse the application. The operator may appeal the decision of the regulator.

If the regulator decides to vary the conditions either in response to an application or on **11.69** its own motion under reg 17(1) of the PPC Regs 2000, it will issue a variation notice. The regulator must determine a variation application within four months from the date the regulator received the application (para 7, Sch 7 of the PPC Regs 2000).

Permit transfer

Regulation 18(1) of the PPC Regs 2000 provides that where the operator of an installation **11.70** or mobile plant wishes to transfer, in whole or in part, his permit to another person the operator and the proposed transferee shall jointly make an application to the regulator to effect the transfer.

Surrendering a permit

Under reg 19 of the PPC Regs 2000 an operator of a Part A installation may apply to surrender **11.71** a permit where he ceases or intends to cease operating an installation (in whole or in part) or a mobile plant and, in accordance with reg 11(3), upon definitive cessation of activities, take necessary measures to avoid any pollution risk and to return the site of the installation or mobile plant to a satisfactory state.

The operator must make an application in the form prescribed in reg 19(3) and submit the **11.72** form with an application fee. The regulator must determine the surrender application and either accept or refuse the surrender application within three months. If the regulator fails to make a determination in the time period, the operator may write to the regulator stating that he treats the non-determination as a refusal.

F   APPEAL AGAINST DETERMINATIONS

Right of appeal

Regulation 27(1) of the PPC Regs 2000 provides that an operator may appeal to the Secretary **11.73** of State against a regulator's:

(a)   refusal to grant a permit under reg 10;

(b)   refusal to vary conditions under reg 17(2);

(c)   conditions attached to a permit under reg 10 or 17(2);

(d)   refusal to transfer a permit under reg 18 or any conditions attached to a transfer;

(e)   refusal to surrender a permit under reg 19(2) or any conditions attached to a surrender.

11.74   An operator also has under reg 27(2) a right of appeal to the Secretary of State against the service of a variation notice, other than under reg 17(2), and against service of a revocation, enforcement, or suspension notice.

11.75   Although an appeal is formally to the Secretary of State, it is generally an Inspector appointed from the Planning Inspectorate that decides most appeals with the Secretary of State taking over a case if it is particularly important or controversial. The appeal procedure is not available for permit decisions taken by the Secretary of State when considering the most complex installations. The only form of challenge in these cases will be to unlawful procedure by judicial review, see Chapter 20: Public law.

11.76   There is no right of appeal for any other interested party such as a statutory consultee or a local resident that had made written representations in any particular application process.

Appeal procedure

11.77   Schedule 8 of the PPC Regs 2000 sets out the appeal procedure. This includes, under para 1, the documents required in support of the notice of appeal including:

(a)   a statement of grounds of appeal;

(b)   a copy of any relevant application;

(c)   a copy of any relevant permit;

(d)   a copy of any relevant correspondence between the appellant and the regulator;

(e)   a copy of any decision or notice, which is the subject matter of the appeal; and

(f)   a statement indicating whether the appellant wishes the appeal to be in the form of a hearing or to be disposed of on the basis of written representations.

Time limits

11.78   The time limit for appealing is provided in para 2 of the PPC Regs 2000, and varies according to the subject of appeal. For an appeal under reg 27(1) it is six months, whereas an appeal under reg 27(2) is two months from the date of the notice which is the subject matter of the appeal. Paragraph 2(2) provides that the Secretary of State may, in a particular case, allow notice of appeal after the limitation periods. This should be regarded as exceptional.

Notice of appeal

11.79   Within 14 days of receiving the operator's notice of appeal, the regulator must, under para 3(1), give notice to:

(a)   any person who was required to be given notice of the subject matter of the appeal under para 9, Sch 4 of the PPC Regs 2000, i.e. the relevant statutory consultees;

(b)   any person who made representations to the regulator with respect to the subject matter of the appeal; and (c)　any person who appears to the regulator to have a particular interest in the subject matter of the appeal.

Written representations

Paragraph 5, Sch 8 of the PPC Regs 2000 sets out the procedure where an appeal is to be dealt with by written representations. This requires the regulator to submit any written representations within 28 days after receiving a copy of the notice of appeal documents. The appellant and the regulator are also given an opportunity to make written representations on any other representations received by people given notice under para 3. There is discretion to vary the written representation procedures by setting later time limits and also require exchanges of representations in addition to those mentioned in the regulations (para 6, Sch 8). **11.80**

Requesting a hearing or public inquiry

An appeal may be conducted either by written representations, a hearing, or, in more complex and exceptional cases, by public inquiry. A hearing may be in part or wholly in private. If a hearing is requested, the Secretary of State must give the appellant and the regulator at least 28 days' notice of the date, time, and place of the hearing. Hearings should be conducted in the spirit of the Town and Country Planning Act (Hearing Procedure) Rules 2000 (SI 2000/1626); public inquiries should follow the Town and Country Planning (Inquiries Procedure) Rules 2000 (SI 2000/1624 and 1625), see Chapter 8: Land use planning. Section 250(2) of the Local Government Act 1972 applies to PPC appeals including provision for requiring persons to attend a hearing, if necessary by summons. **11.81**

A right to be heard

Paragraph 4(7) provides that the following have a right to be heard at a hearing: **11.82**

(a)　the appellant;
(b)　the regulator; and
(c)　any person required by para 3(1) to be notified of the appeal.

Determination of an appeal by an Inspector

Following the receipt of all written representations, or at the conclusion of a hearing or public inquiry, the Inspector will prepare a written decision and send it to the regulator and operator. The decision will also be placed on the public register. The Inspector may affirm or quash the regulator's decision, conditions, and notices. They can also direct the regulator to grant or vary permit conditions. The Inspector shall also make a report in writing to the Secretary of State, which shall include conclusions and recommendations or any reasons for not making recommendations. **11.83**

Determination by the Secretary of State

If the Secretary of State is determining the appeal, following the conclusion of the case the Inspector will report to the Secretary of State making a recommendation as to whether or not the appeal should be allowed. The Secretary of State will consider the matter and the decision will be sent to the regulator and operator with a copy of the Inspector's report. **11.84**

Costs of an appeal

11.85   The general rule to as to costs at an appeal is that each party pays their own costs. However, if there is a hearing or inquiry then costs may be awarded against any side for unreasonable behaviour in the conduct of proceedings that leads to unnecessary or wasted costs. Appeal costs are considered in Chapter 8: Land use planning.

11.86   If the operator or an interested party considers that the appeal decision is unlawful, then this may be challenged by a claim for judicial review: see Chapter 20: Public law. Practical guidance on the PPC appeal procedure is available from the Planning Inspectorate website: www.planning-inspectorate.gov.uk.

G   PPC ENFORCEMENT

11.87   Operators are largely responsible for monitoring and reporting on operations under the PPC regime, although the regulator does have monitoring and inspection obligations. Under reg 23 of the PPC Regs 2000, the regulator is under a duty to take such action as required to ensure that permit conditions are complied with. This will include permit review (see para 11.61) and, if necessary, enforcement action.

Non-compliance action by the regulator

Enforcement notice

11.88   Regulation 24 of the PPC Regs 2000 provides that if a regulator considers that an operator has contravened, is contravening, or is likely to contravene any permit condition, the regulator may serve an enforcement notice. This will specify the contravention (or likely contravention) and the steps that must be taken to remedy this, together with a period of compliance. An operator may appeal against an enforcement notice.

Suspension notice

11.89   Under reg 25 of the PPC Regs 2000, the regulator may serve a suspension notice on an operator if it considers that the operation of the installation of mobile plant involves an imminent risk of serious pollution. Regulation 25(4) states that a suspension notice shall:

(a)   state the regulator's opinion;
(b)   specify the imminent risk involved and the steps to be taken to remove it;
(c)   state that the permit shall, until the suspension notice is withdrawn, cease to authorize the operation of the installation; and
(d)   state any steps, in addition to those required under the permit that the operator must comply with.

11.90   A suspension notice applies regardless of whether the operator has breached a permit condition. Further, while the suspension notice ceases to authorize the operation, it does not suspend the permit *per se* or any other obligations attached to it.

Variation notice

The regulator has the power under reg 17(1) to vary permit conditions at any time by serving **11.91** a variation notice on the operator.

Power of regulator to prevent or remedy pollution

Under reg 26 of the PPC Regs 2000, if the regulator is of the opinion that the operation of **11.92** an installation or mobile plant involves imminent risk of serious pollution, it may arrange for steps to be taken to remove that risk. If intending to do so, then under reg 26(3) it must notify the operator of such steps giving at least seven days' notice.

Revocation notice

Regulation 21 of the PPC Regs 2000 provides that the regulator may revoke a permit, in **11.93** whole or in part, at any time by serving a revocation notice on the operator. A revocation notice that revokes in part must specify the extent to which the permit is being revoked. For all revocations the notice must state the date that the revocation will take effect, which has to be at least 28 days after the date of service. From the date the revocation takes effect, the permit is no longer in force although any restoration requirements may remain in force. The Defra *Guide* suggests that revocation may be appropriate where other enforcement tools have failed to protect the environment properly.

Criminal sanctions

Offences

Regulation 32 of the PPC Regs 2000 provides a number of offences covering the operation of **11.94** the PPC regime. These include under reg 32(1):

(a) contravening reg 9(1) by operating an installation without a permit;
(b) contravening a permit condition;
(c) failing to comply with reg 16(1) by notifying the regulator of a proposed change in operation;
(d) failing to comply with an enforcement or suspension notice;
(e) failing, without reasonable excuse, to comply with any information obligations under reg 28;
(f) making a false or misleading statement;
(g) intentionally making a false entry in any records required under permit condition;
(h) intending to deceive or forging a document relating to a permit condition;
(i) failing to comply with a court order made under reg 35 ordering a convicted person to take remedial steps in relation to an offence under reg 32(1)(a), (b), or (d).

Many of the offences are of strict liability although entering a false record under reg 32(1)(g) **11.95** requires intention.

Defences

There are no statutory defences to the offences under reg 32(1) except under reg 32(1)(e), **11.96** which provides a defence of reasonable excuse.

Penalties

11.97   Regulation 32(2) of the PPC Regs 2000 provides that a person guilty of an offence under reg 32(1)(a), (b), (d), or (i) shall by liable to a maximum fine of £20,000 and/or six months' imprisonment on summary conviction; and an unlimited fine and/or five years' imprisonment on indictment.

11.98   A person guilty of an offence under reg 32 (1)(c), (e), (f), (g), or (h) shall by liable to a maximum fine of £5,000 on summary conviction; and an unlimited fine and/or two years' imprisonment on indictment.

Liability of the managing officers of a company

11.99   Regulation 32(4) of the PPC Regs 2000 provides that where an offence has been committed by a company and has been proved to have been committed with the consent or connivance of, or attributable to any neglect of, a director, manager, secretary, or other similar officer of that company then he shall be guilty of the offence and shall be liable to be proceeded against and punished accordingly. Regulation 32(5) provides that where shareholders manage a company's affairs then they are regarded as directors for the purposes of reg 32(1) and may be personally liable: see Chapter 19: Criminal law practice and procedure.

Remediation order

11.100   Under reg 35 of the PPC Regs 2000 the court may make an order, in addition to any other order or sentence, requiring the defendant to remedy the environmental harm resulting from the offence.

11.101   An example of a conviction under the PPC regime is summarized in *R v Kvaerner Engineering & Construction UK Ltd* (2003) Env Times, Vol 9.3 p 37, in which the defendants held a contract to run a combined heat and power plant at the AstraZeneca site in Macclesfield. The plant was regulated under a PPC permit issued by the Environment Agency. During development the defendant allowed 22 tonnes of sodium hydroxide to be released into the site's trade effluent system. The defendant was, on summary conviction, fined £6,000 plus costs of £2,946.

Civil proceedings

11.102   If the regulator considers that prosecuting an operator will be ineffective, e.g. due to the lack of response to enforcement or suspension action, the regulator may, under reg 33 of the PPC Regs 2000 take civil proceedings in the High Court to secure compliance, in particular, by applying for an injunction.

H   OVERVIEW OF IPC

11.103   Part I of the EPA 1990, the PPS Regs 1991, and the EPAAR Regs 1991 create two related systems of pollution control:

- Integrated Pollution Control (IPC), which covers Part A processes regulated by the Environment Agency; and

• Local Authority Pollution Control (APC), which covers Part B processes emitting to air regulated by local authorities.

Part I of the EPA 1990 has had a number of amendments and is to be repealed by s 6(2) and Sch 3 of the PPCA 1999 on a date to be appointed, expected in 2007. The PPS Regs 1991 have been amended by SI 1992/614, SI 1993/1749, SI 1993/2405, SI 1994/1271, SI 1994/1329, and SI 1995/3247 as well as the Environmental Protection (PPS) (Petrol Vapour Recovery) Regulations 1996 (SI 1996/2678) and the Environmental Protection (PPS) (Hazardous Waste Incineration) Regulations 1998 (SI 1998/767) (Hazardous Waste Incineration Regs).   **11.104**

The amending regulations generally make minor revisions to what falls within the IPC regime, although the Hazardous Waste Incineration Regs make provision for the implementation of EU Directive 94/67/EC on the incineration of hazardous waste. SI 1996/667 and SI 1996/979 have amended the EPAAR Regs 1991. This legislation does not apply to Part A1 and A2 installations that have come into operation since 31 October 1999, which fall within the PPC regime discussed above.   **11.105**

The main purpose of the IPC regime was set out in Britain's Environmental Strategy 1990: *This Common Inheritance*, which stated that preventative action was at the heart of IPC and that it would 'control releases to air, water and land from the most polluting industrial processes'.   **11.106**

For both pollution control regimes (IPC and APC), it is an offence to operate a prescribed process in any way without being authorized to do so. Section 6(1) of the EPA 1990 provides that: **11.107**

> No person shall carry on a prescribed process . . . except under an authorisation granted by the enforcing authority and in accordance with the conditions to which it is subject.

Contravention of s 6(1) is an offence under s 23 of the EPA 1990.   **11.108**

I THE IPC AUTHORIZATION SYSTEM

The prohibition in s 6(1) of the EPA 1990 meant that operators of polluting processes had to apply for an authorization for a new or substantially changed process before it began operating. With the introduction of the PPC regime, this requirement is no longer relevant, IPC should now only be regarded in the limited terms of varying an existing authorization or to taking enforcement action. If a new potentially polluting process is proposed then a PPC permit must be sought.   **11.109**

Prescribed processes

Section 2(1) of the EPA 1990 enables the Secretary of State to make regulations as to what may be referred to as a prescribed process and therefore require an authorization to operate; Sch 1 of the PPS Regs 1991 describes these processes. Section 2(5) of the EPA 1990 allows for the description of what substances may be regarded as prescribed substances, the release of which may be controlled: Schs 4 to 6 of the PPS Regs 1991.   **11.110**

Authorizations

11.111   The authorizations were granted by the regulator, i.e. the Environment Agency for Part A processes and local authorities for Part B air pollution processes, following an application process that required details under reg 2 of the EPAAR Regs 1991 of, among other things:

(a)   the proposed operator;

(b)   the relevant local authority;

(d)   a description of the prescribed process;

(e)   a list of prescribed substances and other substances that may cause harm, if released;

(f)   a description of the techniques to be used for preventing or minimizing the release into any environmental medium of such substances;

(g)   details of any proposed release;

(h)   proposals for monitoring any release; and

(i)   the matters on which the applicant relies to establish that the principle of BATNEEC (see below) will be used to prevent releases.

11.112   These details should have been placed and remain on the public register maintained by the regulator. They are also relevant to any application to vary the authorization conditions or enforcement action that may arise.

J   IPC PRINCIPLES

Best available techniques not entailing excessive costs

11.113   Section 7 of the EPA 1990 provides that in any authorization there should be specific conditions, as the regulator considers appropriate, for ensuring that the best available techniques not entailing excessive costs (BATNEEC) will be used in carrying on a prescribed process. Section 7(4) also creates an implied authorization condition that an operator, in carrying on a process, must use BATNEEC for preventing the release of substances and for rendering harmless any substances that may cause harm. In *R v Proctor & Gamble Product Supply (UK) Ltd* (2003) Env Times Vol 9.2 p 35 the defendant pleaded guilty to failing to comply with its implied BATNEEC conditions and failing in its duty towards employees under the Health & Safety at Work etc. Act 1974. The failure to use BATNEEC resulted in the unauthorized release of acid including traces of sulphur dioxide and dilute sulphur trioxide lasting between two to three minutes. Four employees suffered from eye and throat irritation and tightness to the chest. The company, on summary conviction, was fined £28,000 plus costs of £8,914.

11.114   The Department of Environment and Welsh Office publication: *Integrated Pollution Control: A Practical Guide* (3/e, 1996) (DoE Guide) defined BATNEEC by stating that:

• '*Best*' means most effective in preventing, minimizing, or rendering harmless polluting releases. There may be more than one set of techniques that achieves comparable effectiveness, i.e. there may be more than one set of 'best' techniques.

• '*Available*' should be taken to mean procurable by the operator of the process in question. It does not imply that the technique has to be in general use, but it does require general accessibility. It includes a technique that has been developed (or proven at a scale that allows its implementation in the relevant industrial context with the necessary business confidence). It does not imply that sources outside the UK are 'unavailable' nor does it imply a competitive supply market. If there is a monopoly supplier the technique counts as being available providing the operator can procure it.

- *'Techniques'* The term embraces both the plant in which the process is carried on and how the process is operated. It should be taken to mean the components of which it is made up and the manner in which they are connected together to make the whole. It also includes matters such as numbers and qualifications of staff, working methods, training and supervisions and also the design, construction, layout, and maintenance of buildings and will affect the concept and design of the process.

The DoE *Guide* added that: **11.115**

- the cost of the best available techniques must be weighed against the environmental damage from the process; the greater the environmental damage, the greater the costs of BAT that can be required before costs are considered excessive;
- the objective is to prevent damaging releases or to reduce such releases so far as this can be done without imposing excessive costs; if after applying BATNEEC serious harm would still result, the application can be refused;
- as objective an approach as possible to the consideration of BATNEEC is required. The concern is with what costs in general are excessive; the lack of profitability of a particular business should not affect the determination.

Defra publishes over 80 IPC and APC Process Guidance Notes that provide what the   **11.116**
BATNEEC for specific processes will be. They can be obtained by viewing the Defra website: www.defra.gov.uk. In *UK Renderers Association Ltd & anor v Secretary of State for the Environment, Transport and the Regions* [2002] JPL 1524, the Court of Appeal dismissed an appeal by the claimant that had challenged the lawfulness of Process Guidance Note (6/100) and Additional Guidance Note (AQ3(00)) in respect of conditions appropriate for the control of air pollution in relation to animal by-product rendering processes. Richard Harwood in his JPL commentary notes that:

> Attacking the adoption of policy is inherently difficult. This was doubly so in the present case as the Court of Appeal held that the qualified odour boundary condition proposed in the guidance could be lawfully imposed. A complexity in s 7 of the EPA 1990 is the relationship between the power to impose specific conditions under s 7(1)(a) relating to BATNEEC (subs (2)(a)) or the other objectives in subs (2), and the general power to impose conditions under s 7(1)(c). Parallel to this issue is the reference to statutory guidance relating to subs (2) objectives and the general ability to the Secretary of State to publish guidance.

In *Levy v Environment Agency* [2003] Env LR 11 the claimant challenged an Environment   **11.117**
Agency decision to permit the use of scrap tyres as a substitute fuel at a cement works in Wiltshire. The claim alleged that the Agency had failed to:

- ensure that BATNEEC was used for the emissions of prescribed substances, e.g. that sulphur scrubbers had not been used;
- consider whether in the light of the economic benefit of using waste tyres the use of tyres was now the BATNEEC; and

- make its decision without the objective of implementing material parts of the UK Waste Strategy 2000.

11.118 The High Court dismissed the claim and held, among other things, that the court would not interfere with a decision that called upon the Agency to exercise sophisticated, specialized, scientific knowledge and expertise and which accordingly had a wider margin of appreciation than that in the average case, and that a requirement to install sulphur scrubbers would have 'entailed excessive cost'.

Best practical environmental option

11.119 Section 7(7) of the EPA 1990 provides that where the process is for central control, i.e. by the Environment Agency and is likely to involve the release of substances into more than one environmental medium; then the BATNEEC objective will be used having regard to the best practical environmental option (BPEO) available as respects the substances that may be released.

11.120 BPEO is described in the 12th report of the Royal Commission of Environmental Pollution as:

> the outcome of a systematic consultative and decision-making procedure, which emphasises the protection and conservation of the environment across land, air and water. The BPEO procedure establishes, for a given set of objectives, the option that provides the most benefit of least damage to the environment as a whole, at acceptable costs, in the long term as well as in the short term.

11.121 However, s 7(7) of the EPA 1990 only relates to the BPEO of releases and not to all environmental impacts such as use of raw materials, energy, and other resources. This should be compared with the approach to minimizing a much wider range of environmental impacts through the PPC regime.

Public register

11.122 The regulator must maintain a public register of all IPC permits (ss 20 to 22 of the EPA 1990). Regulation 15 of the EPAAR Regs 1991 lists the information to be contained on the register. This includes, among other things, details of any application, advertisement, notice, representations, and grant of authorization.

Commercial confidentiality

11.123 Section 22 of the EPA 1990 enables operators to apply for certain documents and materials to be treated as commercially confidential and so not be placed on the public register. An application for commercial confidentiality is made when the information is sent to the regulator in support of an application for authorization or variation. The regulator must determine it within 14 days. If the application is successful then the information is excluded from the register for a period of four years. If the operator wishes, after this time, for the information to remain excluded then a further application must be made.

11.124 If the application for commercial confidentiality is refused then the regulator may appeal to the Secretary of State within 21 days (after which time the information is placed on the register), although if an appeal is made, the information is not placed on the public register until after the appeal has been determined.

K OPERATION AND AUTHORIZATION REQUIREMENTS

Installations and mobile plants still operating under IPC authorizations may continue to do so until the time required to transfer to the PPC regime is met. Operators must continue to comply with the conditions set out in the IPC authorization. There also remains the option to vary authorization conditions.

11.125

Transfer of authorizations

Section 9 of the EPA 1990 enables an operator to transfer an authorization to another person. Where an authorization is transferred the new operator must notify the regulator in writing of the transfer within 21 days of the transfer. The authorization transfer is otherwise a contractual arrangement between the parties; contrast this with the permit transfer under IPPC which requires both parties to make a joint application to the regulator under reg 18 of the PPC Regs 2000.

11.126

Variations to conditions

Under s 11 of the EPA 1990 an operator who wishes to make a relevant change in the prescribed process may either ask the regulator to determine whether the proposed change will require that the authorization conditions be varied to account for the proposed change or make a formal application to vary the conditions. Part II of Sch 1 of the EPA 1990 and reg 3 of the EPAAR Regs 1991 set out the procedure and the content of an application to vary authorization conditions. This provides for public and statutory consultation and the requirements on the regulator for determining the application. Paragraph 8 of Sch 1 enables the Secretary of State to call in variation applications and the option for holding a local inquiry to be held.

11.127

The regulator may, on its own motion, vary authorization conditions under s 10 of the EPA 1990 by serving a variation notice on the operator, for instance, to tighten emission limits on an activity. Section 15 of the EPA 1990 provides a right of appeal against a variation determination or a variation notice.

11.128

Information and consultation on variation applications

There is a right for statutory consultees (listed in reg 4 of the PAAR Regs 1991) to be consulted and the public to be informed by way of advertisement about a proposed variation: Pt 2 of the EPA 1990 and regs 4 and 5 of the EPAAR Regs 1991. The public are entitled to make written representations on any application. There are time limits for consultation.

11.129

L APPEAL AGAINST DETERMINATIONS

Right of appeal

Section 15(1) of the EPA 1990 provides that an operator who:

11.130

(a)   has been refused the grant of an authorization;

(b)   is aggrieved by conditions attached to an authorization;

(c)   has been refused a variation of an authorization; or

(d)   has had an authorization revoked

may appeal to the Secretary of State against the regulator's decision, unless the Secretary of State took the decision.

11.131   Under s 15(2) an operator may also appeal against either a variation, enforcement, or prohibition notice unless this was a decision by the Secretary of State. An Inspector appointed from the Planning Inspectorate decides most appeals, although the Secretary of State may determine cases of major significance.

Appeal procedure

Time limit for bringing an appeal

11.132   Regulation 10 of the EPAAR Regs 1991 states that appeals against the refusal of authorization or conditions must be made within six months of the decision date; appeals against revocation must be made before the revocation takes effect, which is generally 28 days after service of the notice. An appeal against a variation, enforcement, or prohibition notice must be made within two months of the date of notice. Finally an appeal against the refusal of commercial confidentiality is 21 days from the date of determination.

11.133   There is no appeal form or fee, although appellants must provide under reg 9 of EPAAR Reg 1991:

(1)   a written notice of appeal together with:

(2)   (a)   a statement of grounds of appeal;

    (b)   a copy of any relevant application;

    (c)   a copy of any relevant authorization;

    (d)   a copy of relevant correspondence between the appellant and the enforcing authority;

    (e)   a copy of any decision or notice that is the subject of the appeal; and

    (f)   a statement indicating whether the appellant wishes the appeal to be by written representations or by hearing.

11.134   For an appeal against a variation, revocation, enforcement, or prohibition notice the notice of appeal is sent to any person who appears to the regulator likely to have an interest in the appeal. In any other case, the regulator gives notice to any person who made representations to the authority with respect to the grant or variation: reg 11, EPAAR Regs 1991. An appeal does not suspend the relevant determination decision (except for revocation notices).

11.135   The Planning Inspectorate has published a brief guide to appeals: *EPA Part 1: LAPC/IPC Appeal Procedure Guidance* (2002) setting out in clear terms the appeal procedure. In summary the appeal may be heard in one of three ways:

Written representations

11.136   Appeal by way of written representations includes an exchange of statements. A statement should be submitted within 28 days of the start date of the appeal with an opportunity to submit further representations on exchange of statements. Following this, an Inspector will make a site visit and then in due course reach a decision.

Hearings

Either party may request a hearing or the Inspector may decide that this is necessary if **11.137** complex issues are involved. Hearings are conducted in the spirit of the Town and Country Planning Act (Hearings Procedure) Rules 2000 (SI 2000/1626): see Chapter 8: Land use planning.

Public inquiries

Either party may request a public inquiry or the Inspector may decide that one is necessary **11.138** in exceptional cases. An inquiry is more formal than a hearing and public inquiries are conducted in the spirit of the Town and Country Planning (Inquiries Procedure) Rules 2000 (SI 2000/1624 and 1625): see Chapter 8: Land use planning.

Appeal decisions

Following the appeal the Inspector's decision will be sent to the parties and to other inter- **11.139** ested parties who have requested it. In cases where the Secretary of State has recovered the appeal from the Inspector (in particularly complex cases or matters of significant impor- tance), the Inspector will send a report to the Secretary of State making a recommendation. The Secretary of State will then consider all the issues involved and a decision will be sent to all parties with a copy of the Inspector's report.

Costs of an appeal

As a general rule each party pays their own costs of the appeal. However, if there is a hearing **11.140** or inquiry then costs may be awarded against any side for unreasonable behaviour in the conduct of proceedings that leads to unnecessary or wasted costs. Appeal costs are considered in Chapter 8: Land use planning.

M   IPC ENFORCEMENT

Non-compliance action by the regulator

Revocation of authorization

Section 12 of the EPA 1990 provides that the regulator may at any time revoke an authoriza- **11.141** tion by written notice to the operator. The revocation notice shall have an effect from the date specified in the notice, which should not be less than 28 days from the date the notice is served. The operator may appeal against the revocation notice prior to it taking effect.

Enforcement notice

Under s 13(1) of the EPA 1990, if the regulator is of the opinion that the person carrying on a **11.142** prescribed process under an authorization is contravening any condition of the authoriza- tion or is likely to contravene any such condition, the authority may serve an enforcement notice. The enforcement notice should set out the reasons for the contravention, the remedial steps necessary, and the time within which those steps must be taken. The operator may appeal against the enforcement notice.

Prohibition notice

11.143 If the regulator is of the opinion that carrying on a prescribed process in a particular manner involves an imminent risk of serious pollution of the environment the regulator shall, under s 14 of the EPA 1990, serve a prohibition notice. A prohibition notice may be served whether or not the action in question contravenes an authorization condition. The notice must, under s 14(3):

(a) state the regulator's opinion;
(b) specify the risks involved;
(c) specify the steps necessary to remove the risk and the time within which the steps must be taken; and
(d) direct that the authorization shall cease to have effect until the prohibition notice is withdrawn.

Criminal sanctions

Offences

11.144 Section 23(1) of the EPA 1990 creates a number of offences including:

(a) operating a prescribed process without an authorization
(b) failing to give notice of transfer of an authorization;
(c) failing to comply with or contravene any requirement or prohibition imposed by an enforcement notice or a prohibition notice;
(g) failing, without reasonable excuse, to comply with any request for information;
(h) making a statement that is knowingly or recklessly false or misleading in a material particular, where the statement is made relating to information provision or for the purpose of obtaining a grant or variation of an authorization;
(i) intentionally to make a false entry in any record required to be kept under s 7;
(j) forging or using a document relating to conditions with intent to deceive; and
(l) failing to comply with a court order relating to remedial matters following conviction under s 23(1)(a) or (c).

11.145 All the offences under s 23(1) are of strict liability with the exception of subs (1) (h), which requires proof of intention or recklessness and subs (1)(i), which requires proof of intention.

Defences

11.146 There are no statutory defences to the s 23(1) offences except for the offence under s 23(1)(g), which provides the defence of reasonable excuse.

Penalties

11.147 Section 23(2) of the EPA 1990 provides that a person guilty of an offence under subs (1)(a), (c), or (l) shall be liable to a maximum fine of £20,000 and/or three months' imprisonment on summary conviction; and an unlimited fine and/or two years' imprisonment on indictment.

A person guilty of an offence under s 23 (1)(b), (g), (h), (i), or (j) shall be liable to a maximum **11.148** fine of £5,000 on summary conviction; and an unlimited fine and/or two years' imprisonment on indictment.

Examples of convictions under the IPC are summarized below. In *R v TXU Europe Merchant* **11.149** *Generation Ltd* (2002) Env Times, Vol 10.1 p 48 the defendant was found guilty of not having appropriate written operation instructions for staff in the control rooms at its Ironbridge Power Station, Shropshire, in accordance with the IPC regime. This followed an incident at the power station that involved excessive dust releases from the main stack. The defendant was fined £5,000 plus £2,000 costs.

In *R v UOP Ltd* (2004) Env Times, Vol 10.1 p 33 the defendant company was convicted of **11.150** exceeding emission limits set under an IPC authorization by allowing high concentrations of a corrosive acid to escape into the atmosphere. It was fined, on summary conviction, £12,000 plus £1,620 costs.

In *R v Landowner Liquid Fertiliser Ltd* (2003) Env Times Vol 9.3 p 35 the company was con- **11.151** victed of two incidents of failing to meet IPC conditions. The first was causing strong waste acid to enter a culvert. The second was the emission of nitrogen dioxide significant enough for a neighbour to call the fire brigade. The company was fined on summary conviction a total of £18,250 with £15,000 costs. The company's managing director, Mr Boon, was also convicted under s 157 of the EPA 1990 and fined £1,425.

Remediation order

Under s 26(1) of the EPA 1990 the court may make an order, in addition to any other order **11.152** or sentence, requiring the defendant to remedy the environmental harm resulting from the offence.

Liability of the managing officers of a company

Section 157(1) of the EPA 1990 provides that where an offence has been committed by a **11.153** company and has been proved to have been committed with the consent or connivance of, or attributable to any neglect of, a director, manager, secretary, or other similar officer of that company then he shall be guilty of the offence and shall be liable to be proceeded against and punished accordingly. Section 157(2) provides that where shareholders manage a company's affairs then they are regarded as directors for the purposes of subs (1) and may be personally liable: see Chapter 19: Criminal law practice and procedure.

Civil proceedings

If the regulator considers that prosecuting an operator will be ineffective, perhaps due to **11.154** the attitude taken to an enforcement or prohibition notice, under s 24 of the EPA 1990, the regulator may take civil proceedings in the High Court to secure compliance, in particular by applying for an injunction.

N   PPC, IPC, AND OTHER ENVIRONMENTAL CONTROL REGIMES

11.155   As will have been noted, in controlling environmental impacts in an integrated way PPC and IPC considers and reduces impacts on each of the environmental media collectively. The interaction with PPC/IPC in these areas is covered in Chapters 3: Air, 5: Contaminated Land, 14: Waste and 15: Water. There is also a close association with land use planning, which is outlined below.

Land use planning and PPC

11.156   The land use planning system is a separate but complementary system of environmental regulation. Its role influences the way PPC operates and is particularly relevant following the introduction of s 39 of the Planning and Compulsory Purchase Act 2004, which provides that any person involved in spatial strategies and local development documents must exercise their function with the objective of contributing to the achievement of sustainable development. The relationship between PPC and land use planning is comprehensively covered in Planning Policy Statement (PPS) 23: *Planning and Pollution Control* (2004), which advises local planning authorities (LPAs) at para 3 that, among other things:

- any consideration of the quality of land, air, or water and potential impacts arising from development, possibly leading to impacts on health, is capable of being a material planning consideration, in so far as it arises or may arise from or may affect any land use;
- the planning system plays a key role in determining the location of development that may give rise to pollution, either directly or indirectly, and in ensuring that other uses and developments are not, as far as possible, affected by major existing or potential sources of pollution;
- the controls under the planning and pollution control regimes should complement rather than duplicate each other;
- where pollution issues are likely to arise, intending developers should hold informal pre-application discussions with the LPA, the relevant pollution control authority, and/or environmental health departments of local authorities, and other authorities and stakeholders with a legitimate interest; and
- where it will save money, consideration should be given to submitting applications for planning permission and pollution control permits in parallel and coordinating their consideration by the relevant authorities.

11.157   PPS 23 further advises at para 8 that any consideration of the quality of land, air, or water and potential impacts arising from development, possibly leading to an impact on health, is capable of being a material planning consideration, in so far as it arises or may arise from any land use.

11.158   It adds at para 10 that the planning system should focus on whether the development itself is an acceptable use of the land, and the impacts of those uses, rather than the control of processes or emissions themselves. Planning authorities should work on the assumption that the relevant pollution control regime will be properly applied and enforced. They should act to complement but not seek to duplicate it.

In *Gateshead MBC v SSE and Northumbrian Water Group* [1995] JPL 432 the Court of Appeal **11.159**
held that, while IPC and the land use planning system may overlap, this should not prevent
an IPC regulator from refusing authorization if they concluded that this was the proper
decision to make. However, a local planning authority should take into account any relevant
IPC regime, which should be expected to be the primary form of pollution control. There is
no reason why this approach should not be applied to the PPC regime and permits.

KEY DOCUMENTS AND MATERIALS

Environmental Protection Act 1990

The Environmental Protection (Applications, Appeals and Registers) Regulations 1991
(SI 1991/507), as amended

The Environmental Protection (Prescribed Processes and Substances) Regulations 1991
(SI 1991/472), as amended

Pollution Prevention and Control Act 1999

The Town and Country Planning Act (Inquiries Procedure) Rules 2000 (SI 2000/1624 & 1625)

The Town and Country Planning Act (Hearing Procedure) Rules 2000 (SI 2000/1626)

The Pollution Prevention and Control (England and Wales) Regulations 2000 (SI 2000/1973)
as amended (PPC Regs 2000)

EU Directive 96/61/EC concerning integrated pollution prevention and control.
www.europa.eu.int

Defra (2004). *Integrated Pollution Prevention and Control: A Practical Guide*. 3/e. Defra: London.
www.defra.gov.uk/environment/ppc

Defra. *Industrial Pollution Control Regimes*. Defra: London www.defra.gov.uk/environment/
ppc

Department of Environment and Welsh Office (1996). *Integrated Pollution Control: A Practical
Guide*. 3/e. TSO: London

Environment Agency, Technical Guidance Notes

Environment Agency (2000). *IPPC: Part A(1) Installations: Guide for Applicants*. Environment
Agency: Bristol

Environment Agency. *Environment Protection Operator Performance and Risk Appraisal*.
Environment Agency: Bristol. www.environment-agency.gov.uk.

Planning Inspectorate (2002). *EPA Part 1: LAPC/IPC Appeal Procedure Guidance*. Planning
Inspectorate: Bristol

PPS 23: *Planning and Pollution Control*

BREF notes from the European IPPC Bureau at http://eippcb.jrc.es/pages.Fevents.htm

Netregs. www.environment-agency.gov.uk

Planning Inspectorate website: www.planning-inspectorate.gov.uk

Most Defra publications are available from:
Defra Publications, Admail 6000, London SW1A 2XX. tel. 08459 556000

12

PROPERTY AND LAND RIGHTS

A INTRODUCTION

12.01 Land ownership, occupation, and use has a significant impact on the environment and access to the environment. The law of property governs land ownership and rights and this is primarily based on private law principles of contract, although in many landlord and tenant matters there is statutory intervention for the benefit of each party and, more recently, the introduction of anti-social behaviour rules for the benefit of third parties: see Chapter 4: Anti-social behaviour, housing and local concerns. Of particular interest in relation to environmental matters is the use of freehold covenants to protect the environment, access to public open spaces and the countryside, and the acquisition of land for the public benefit and the environment.

12.02 Environmental rights in relation to land and property also cover non-land property or 'personalty'. For instance, there may be a remedy for harm to personalty under consumer protection laws. There is also a need to consider the new quasi-economic role being played by corporate bodies operating in pollution markets under the emissions trading schemes.

B CORPORATE AND PROPERTY TRANSACTIONS

Corporate transactions

12.03 In carrying out many of the larger transactions, businesses must now be aware of the environmental impact of the transaction itself or of the product or services that are being secured. It is hoped that business operators are highly conscious of their adverse effect of carrying on business and seek to minimize any impact for the sake of the environment and others that may be affected by the business operation. Regardless of this, the regulatory responsibilities may be quite onerous and the financial cost alone of carrying out business in accordance with the environmental regulations is likely to be significant. Thus, there are two areas where a business or other organization may wish to consider environmental regulation and law:

(1) in order to take a positive approach to reducing environmental impacts and to put effective and efficient procedures in place to ensure this, e.g. by implementing an environmental management system (EMS); or

(2) to avoid liability for breaches of those regulatory controls.

12.04 Environmental management is considered in Chapter 23; this section outlines steps to take to avoid liability, taking into account the aims of the corporate activity.

Assessing liability

12.05 Unless some or all of the objectives of a transaction are to secure some environmental benefit, then any environmental/legal liability is likely to be regarded as, at best, an inconvenience. Importantly, the liability arising must be identified at an early stage and will be determined by the nature of the corporate activity. Likely areas of corporate liability are:

- contaminated land;
- land use planning;
- noise;
- PPC requirements;
- statutory nuisance;
- waste management; and
- water pollution.

Often, a company will instruct a consultant to carry out an audit of the proposal to **12.06** identify where any environmental liability may arise. Auditing is considered further in Chapter 23: Environmental management. Trevor Hellawell in *Environmental Law Handbook* (5/e, The Law Society, 2002) suggests that the following issues should be considered at an early stage:

- *The product.* Check the product or service itself to see whether it is polluting or causes environmental harm, or has the potential to do either, but checking the product itself is not determinative and following further steps should be considered.
- *Raw materials.* Consider the components used in the production process. If toxic materials are used during manufacturing check how these are being dealt with. Under the pollution prevention and control (PPC) regime, operators are required to monitor raw material use and other inputs such as energy and water use. PPC is considered in Chapter 11.
- *Preparing for the production process.* All documents relating to the application for any licence or permit sought and obtained must be checked. This is important because at the end of a PPC process, the operator will be responsible for cleaning up any contamination to land not discovered in any contaminated land search done at the start of the production process and therefore a copy of any original land search should be sought and suitable indemnities secured.
- *Licences, permits, and consents.* It is necessary to check that all appropriate licences, permits, and consents have been obtained and that the conditions imposed are fully understood. It is important to check when any licences may be up for renewal or review.
- *The production process.* It is the responsibility of the proposed purchaser in a transaction as part of its due diligence assessment to find out whether any part of the production or development process will result in emissions to the environment and, if so, what steps are being taken to prevent or minimize any adverse impacts.
- *Historical use of any relevant site.* If the transaction includes the purchase or management of sites, then it is important to check the historical use of these sites. For example, an area that may currently be used for storage could have been a former gasworks with a mix of toxic substances percolating into the ground.
- *Waste disposal.* The obligations relating to waste disposal are increasing year on year. All waste management responsibilities including storage, transportation, disposal, and the duty of care must be complied with.
- *Site inspection.* An important aspect of the assessment of liability will be a site and local inspection carried out by specialist consultants. This may highlight matters that may not appear on any documents, licences, or conditions. For example, evidence of cracked flooring and hard surfaces or the positioning and routes of sewerage and surface water drainage systems may suggest potential contamination of groundwater.

12.07   With environmental regulation being introduced at an increasing rate, it will be vital to ensure that emerging as well as existing liability is considered. For example, the EU Directive 2004/35/EC on environmental liability with regard to the prevention and remedying of environmental damage entered into force during 2004. Its primary purpose is to ensure that a person causing certain environmental damage is held financially liable. It is not yet in force in the UK, but must be transposed by April 2007. Also, the extent of liability for many environmental offences extends beyond the corporate veil to the company officers for example, under s 157 of the Environmental Protection Act 1990, see Chapter 19: Criminal law practice and procedure.

Minimizing liability

12.08   The level of environmental liability of a purchaser may be minimized by securing either a warranty or indemnity from the vendor. A warranty is an undertaking that the person giving the warranty will be held answerable for the truth of some statement incidental to the contract. A breach of warranty will only give rise to a claim for damages. However, if the warranty is a condition of the contract then a breach of warranty may give rise to the right to terminate the contract.

12.09   An indemnity is a form of security or protection from any contingent damage or loss. It is common for purchasers to secure a general environmental indemnity for liability arising from all environmental incidents that arise out of the vendor's operation or any predecessor in title. The extent of indemnity may be limited by agreement to the extent of the nature of environmental incident, temporally or financially.

12.10   Insurance to cover environmental liabilities can be obtained. The scope and nature of any insurance will depend on the premium paid and on what is being covered. For larger operations, insurance companies will require an environmental investigation and will seek to limit the cover provided generally up to around £10 million. Insurance cannot cover the cost of any fines or other penalties arising from criminal proceedings. The person convicted must pay any fines imposed personally.

Buying property

12.11   The Government has set a target of ensuring that at least 60% of new development is to be on brownfield sites and so the pressure to ensure that any property bought is free from environmental problems has never been so intense. Many of the concerns or areas of environmental impact arising out of commercial transactions will be relevant when purchasing property although there will also be other considerations such as proposed new development in an area, the impact of living near or in nature reserves and conservation areas, and the risk of flooding from nearby water sources. Of particular concern is contaminated land.

12.12   In 2001, the Law Society issued the *Contaminated Land Warning Card* to all solicitors explaining that they should be aware that environmental liabilities may arise and consider what further enquiries and specialist assistance a client should be advised to obtain. The warning card suggests what particular action should be taken for particular property transactions. For example, it states that:

In purchases, mortgages and leases, solicitors should:

1. Advise the client of potential liabilities associated with contaminated land. Generally clients should be advised of the possibility and consequences of acquiring interests in contaminated land and the steps that can be taken to assess the risks.
2. Make specific enquiries of the seller.

It adds that for unresolved problems, lawyers should consider advising withdrawal, and noting advice or advising insurance (increasingly obtainable for costs of remediation of undetected contamination and any shortfall in value because of undisclosed problems). Most conveyancing practitioners will now carry out an environmental search on behalf of their clients. This should cover: **12.13**

- past land use;
- landfill and waste sites;
- industrial sites and processes;
- natural hazards such as flooding, subsidence, and radon;
- mining; and
- the environmental setting, which may include groundwater vulnerability and soil leaching potential, abstraction licences, river quality, and air quality.

There are a number of environmental search companies including *Envirosearch* (see www.landmark-information.co.uk) and *groundsure* at www.groundsure.com. **12.14**

C THE ACQUISITION OF LAND FOR PUBLIC BENEFIT

Power to acquire land

Compulsory acquisition may be regarded as one of the most powerful means of social intervention in property rights for the purpose of the community or public as a whole. Local authorities have been able to acquire land either by agreement, appropriation, or accepting as a gift in order to carry out their functions for over 150 years. There are a number of powers such as s 120 of the Local Government Act 1972, which enables a local authority to acquire any land inside or outside its area: **12.15**

(a) for the purposes of its functions under any enactment, or
(b) for the benefit, improvement, or development of its area,
whether it is immediately required for any such purpose or not.

Compulsory purchase for planning purposes has been revised under the PCPA 2004. Sections 226 and 227 of the Town and Country Planning Act 1990 (TCPA 1990), as revised, empower certain authorities including county councils, county boroughs, districts, London boroughs, and the Secretary of State (authorizing a local authority) to acquire compulsorily any land in their area. They can acquire land under s 226(1), **12.16**

(a) if they think the acquisition will facilitate the carrying out of development, redevelopment, or improvement of the land, or
(b) for a purpose that it is necessary to achieve in the interests of the proper planning of an area in which the land is situated.

12.17 However, under s 226(1A) a local planning authority (LPA) must not exercise the power under para (a) unless they think that the proposal is likely to contribute to the promotion or improvement of the economic, social, or environmental well-being of their area.

12.18 Importantly, the planning considerations formerly contained in s 226(2) have been removed although there remains the quite stringent requirement to demonstrate a compelling case in the public interest to justify compulsion.

12.19 More specific powers are contained in other enabling legislation such as ss 47 to 50 of the Planning (Listed Buildings and Conservation Areas) Act 1950 (often referred to as the Listed Buildings Act 1950), which relates to the compulsory acquisition of a listed building in need of repair, the service of a repairs notice, and the preparation of a direction for minimum compensation.

Procedure for compulsory acquisition

12.20 In most cases land is acquired by agreement and any compensation paid will be negotiated by agreement. Although, whichever way a local authority acquires land, it must almost always comply with the procedural requirements set out in the Acquisition of Land Act 1981 (ALA 1981) and the Compulsory Purchase Act 1965 (CPA 1965). An exception to this is the power to implement clearance areas under the Housing Act 1985, which provides for similar procedures.

12.21 Broadly, the ALA 1981 covers procedures relating to obtaining a Compulsory Purchase Order (CPO) in the early stages of acquisition, while the CPA 1965 covers the post-order matters such as serving a notice to treat on interested landowners and completion of the acquisition.

Confirmation of the CPO

12.22 The acquiring authority must apply to the appropriate Minister for confirmation of the CPO. For planning matters this will be the Deputy Prime Minister. Before making such an application the authority must advertise the proposed confirmation as a notice and send the notice to all people with an interest in the land, except tenants with a lease period of a month or less.

12.23 The authority may seek a technical examination from the confirming government department prior to submitting the Order to resolve any drafting defects, although each authority is expected to seek its own legal advice on whether the Order be confirmed.

12.24 If no objections are made or sustained, the Minister can confirm the Order. If objections persist that relate to the substance of the proposed Order, rather than compensation alone, then the objectors have the right to be heard at a public inquiry, although acquiring authorities are encouraged to continue negotiating with objectors with a view to securing the withdrawal of objections. For a CPO under s 226 of the TCPA 1990, the Minister may disregard objections that, in practice, relate to the development plan defining any proposed use. It is for the acquiring authority to justify its proposals for the compulsory acquisition. It must be ready to defend such proposals at an inquiry or through written representations and, if necessary, in the courts.

12.25 The Compulsory Purchase of Land (Written Representations Procedure) (Ministers) Regulations 2004 (SI 2004/2595) prescribe a procedure for considering objections in writing as an alternative to an inquiry, providing all objectors agree to this, and the confirming Minister deems it appropriate: see para 40 of Circular 06/2004: *Compulsory Purchase and the Crichel Down Rules*. There are two sets of rules governing the inquiry procedure:

(1) The Compulsory Purchase by Non-Ministerial Acquiring Authorities (Inquiries Procedure) Rules 1990 (SI 1990/512) with detailed guidance in Circular 1/90, and
(2) The Compulsory Purchase by Ministers (Inquiries Procedure) Rules 1994 (SI 1994/3264).

Publishing confirmation of the CPO

Following the inquiry or written representations, the confirming Minister either confirms or refuses the Order. He may confirm it with or without modification although he has no scope to add to or substitute the statutory purpose for which it was made see *Proctor & Gamble Ltd v Secretary of State for the Environment* [1991] EGCS 123.   **12.26**

Following confirmation by the Minister the CPO comes into effect on the first day it is published in the press by the acquiring authority. Section 23 of the ALA 1981 provides that a CPO may be challenged in the High Court on two specific grounds: that it is *ultra vires* or that there has been a failure to comply with some statutory requirement. There is a six-week time limit to make a challenge beginning from the date the notice of confirmation of the CPO was published. There is no discretion to extend the six-week period. Section 25 provides that, subject to s 23, a CPO or certificate under Pt III of the Act shall not, either before or after it has been confirmed, made, or given, be questioned in any legal proceedings whatsoever, although following the House of Lords decision in *Smith v East Elloe RDC* [1956] AC 736 an action for damages may lie against someone who in bad faith or by fraud secures a CPO.   **12.27**

Conveying the land to the acquiring authority

There are two ways to transfer the land to the acquiring authority on publication of the confirmed CPO: **12.28**

- by notice to treat, or
- by general vesting declaration.

In terms of the notice to treat. Under s 5 of the CPA 1965 the acquiring authority must serve notice on all parties interested in the land that it has been authorized to acquire the land and is willing to treat for its purchase and that they are required to convey their interest. Schedule 4 of the CPA 1965 sets out the procedure for the purchase of common land.   **12.29**

Once a notice to treat has been served, an acquiring authority may enter the land 14 days after it has been served and take possession. On possession, someone claiming compensation may request an advance payment of up to 90% of the estimated or agreed sum due. A notice to treat ceases to have effect after three years (s 5(2A) to (2E) of the CPA 1965).   **12.30**

The notice to treat requires interested parties to submit details of their claim for compensation. These are often settled by agreement. If not, claims are referred to the Lands Tribunal. The assessment of compensation is complex. It is considered in outline below. Following service of the notice to treat, and when agreement has been reached on compensation payments, the land can be conveyed to the acquiring authority under general conveyancing procedures. The acquiring authority generally covers the cost of acquisition.   **12.31**

12.32   General vesting declarations are made under the Compulsory Purchase (Vesting Declarations) Act 1981 and provide an alternative to the notice to treat procedure. It allows the acquiring authority to obtain title to the land without having first to be satisfied as to the 'vendor's' title or to finalize the level of compensation. It is often used where time is of the essence or where some of the landowners are unknown.

Compensation

12.33   Compensation payments are based on the principle that the owner should be paid neither less nor more than his loss. In *Horn v Sunderland Corporation* [1941] 2 KB 26 Scott LJ stated that the owner:

> has the right to be put, so far as money can do it, in the same position as if his land had not been taken from him. In other words, he gains the right to receive a money payment not less than the loss imposed on him in the public interest, but on the other hand, no greater.

12.34   The value of the owner's interest in land comprises:

- the amount that the interest in land might be expected to realize if sold on the open market by a willing seller — open market value;
- compensation for severance and/or injurious affection; and
- compensation for disturbance and other losses not directly based on the value of the land.

12.35   Alternatively, where the land or property is used for a purpose for which there is no general demand or market (e.g. a church) and the owner intends to reinstate elsewhere, he may be awarded compensation on the basis of the reasonable cost of equivalent reinstatement. See para 61 Circular 06/2004, s 5 of the Land Compensation Act 1961, and s 7 of the CPA 1965.

Rules of compensation

12.36   The Land Compensation Act 1961 (LCA 1961) sets out rules for assessing compensation. These are:

- General rules under ss 5 and 5A of the LCA 1961 such as that there should be no allowance for the compulsory nature of the acquisition, that land values shall be taken as the amount realized on an open market and that no adjustment should be made to the valuation in respect of anything that happens after the relevant valuation date.
- Special rules under ss 6 to 9 of the LCA 1961 such as no account being taken of any increase or decrease in the value of land attributable to development or the prospect of development
- Assumptions as to the grant or proposed grant of planning permission derived from the development plan or otherwise.

12.37   The assessment of compensation is a complex, specialized area, is governed by extensive case law and is outside the scope of this book. Acquiring authorities and those claiming compensation should seek specialist legal advice.

D COVENANTS ON LAND

The land use planning system discussed in Chapter 8: Land use planning has removed much **12.38**
of the need for restrictive freehold covenants on land to the point whereby Gray and Gray in
Elements of Land Law (Butterworths, 2001) suggest that:

> 'Property' in land has become in effect, a form of stewardship in which land resources are held
> on some kind of civic or environmental trust . . . far removed from the classic liberal perception
> of 'property' as a self-interested claim of absolute or arbitrary power.

This may be the case, but there nevertheless remains a need to consider certain freehold **12.39**
covenants that remain on land or the potential to introduce new covenants to protect the
socio-environmental rights or private interests in land.

A covenant is an obligation or agreement by way of deed, i.e. a written document that is **12.40**
signed in the presence of a witness and delivered (a commitment by the person signing the
deed that he or she adopts it irrevocably). The covenantor (the person making the promise)
promises the covenantee (the person receiving the benefit of the promise) that he or she
will undertake some positive act (referred to as a positive covenant) or refrain from certain
activities (a restrictive covenant). An example of a positive covenant is an obligation to
maintain a hedgerow. A restrictive covenant would be to prohibit the use of the land as a
tannery.

Elements of covenants in law

The application of covenants under property law is complex, incorporating a mix of ancient **12.41**
common law supplemented by the statutory provision, mainly from the Law of Property
Act 1925 (LPA 1925). However, a number of important elements relating to the utility of
covenants arise; these include that the covenant must 'touch and concern' the land, that the
benefit of positive covenants are largely unenforceable against successors in title, and the
rights of third parties under certain covenants.

Covenants that 'touch and concern' the land

A covenant will be ineffective unless it touches and concerns the land owned by the **12.42**
covenantee. In *P&A Swift Investments v Combined English Stores Group plc* [1989] AC 632 Lord
Oliver held, at 642, that a covenant touched and concerned the land providing:

(1) it benefited the covenantee for the time being, and if separated from the land, it ceased
    to be of benefit to him or her;
(2) the covenant must affect the nature, quality, mode of user, or value of the covenantee's
    land; and
(3) the covenant must not be personal to the covenantee.

Positive covenants largely unenforceable on assignment

While it will be quite straightforward to enforce a positive requirement to do something on **12.43**
someone who actually covenanted to do this, it is unlikely that the positive requirement can
be enforced against a successor in title. In *Austerberry v Corporation of Oldham* (1885) 29 Ch D

750 the Court of Appeal held that a positive covenant requiring the covenantor to pay expenses towards making up a road was unenforceable against the respondent local authority, who had bought the road from the original covenantor. Liability for making up the road was imposed on the frontagers by the Public Health Act 1875.

Third party rights and covenants

12.44   Under s 1 of the Contracts (Third Party Rights) Act 1999, a person who is not a party to a contract (including one entered into by covenant) may enforce a term of the contract in his or her own right if either the contract expressly provides for this or the contract purports to confer a benefit upon him. While the contract should provide an explicit reference to the third party, it need only do so by class or if that person answers a particular description. If these circumstances prevail it is likely that covenants can be enforced.

Covenants in equity

12.45   Because of the difficulties of enforcing covenants in law, the courts have, at times, invoked certain equitable principles to ensure that where it is fair to do so, a covenant could be enforced. However, the equitable right to enforce a covenant only relates to restrictive covenants.

Remedies for breach of covenant

12.46   The common law remedy for breach of covenant is damages for retrospective loss. Compensation for future loss may be recoverable under s 2 of the Chancery Amendment Act 1858 (Lord Cairns's Act). Injunctive relief may be available but unlikely. In *Wrotham Park Estate Co Ltd v Parkside Homes Ltd* [1974] 1 WLR 798 the Court declined to grant an injunction to demolish homes despite concluding that the defendant had built them in breach of covenant. Brightman J commented at 811 that it would be a waste of much needed houses to direct that they now be pulled down but added that developers who act in breach of covenant may be in for a rude awakening and granted damages in lieu of an injunction. In contrast, the Court of Appeal in *Wakeham v Wood* (1982) 43 P&CR 40 granted a mandatory injunction requiring the demolition of a building that obstructed the claimant's sea view.

Modification or discharge of the restriction

12.47   It is possible to modify or discharge a covenant relating to land by an application to the Lands Tribunal. Section 84(1) of the LPA 1925, as amended, provides that the Lands Tribunal shall have power, on an application of any person interested in freehold land affected by a restriction under covenant, wholly or partially to discharge or modify any such restriction on being satisfied:

    (a)   that by reason of changes in the character of the property or the neighbourhood or other circumstances of the case . . . the restrictions ought to be deemed obsolete;

    (aa)   that the continued existence would impede some reasonable user of the land for public or private purpose;

    (b)   those entitled to the benefit of the restriction have agreed to the restriction being discharged or modified; or

(c)   that the proposed discharge or modification will not injure the person entitled to the benefit of the restriction.

Section 84(1A) of the LPA 1925 provides that subs (aa) authorizes discharge or modification **12.48** of a restriction in any case that the Lands Tribunal is satisfied that the restriction, in impeding that user, either does not secure for the person entitled to the benefit any practical benefits of substantial value or advantage to them; or is contrary to public interest and that money will be adequate compensation for the loss of disadvantage (if any) arising from the discharge or modification. Section 84(1B) further provides that in determining an application, the Lands Tribunal must take into account the development plan and any declared or ascertainable pattern for the grant or refusal of planning permission in the relevant areas, as well as the period at which and the context in which the restriction was created or imposed and any other material circumstances. Under s 84(1C), the Lands Tribunal may, when considering a modification to a restriction, add further reasonable restrictions or may refuse to modify without such addition. The Lands Tribunal Rules 1996 (SI 1996/1022) govern the procedure for applications under s 84 of the LPA 1925.

Perhaps unsurprisingly, there have been numerous cases arising out of applications to **12.49** discharge or modify restrictive covenants. Often, applications have been strongly resisted by neighbouring landowners purporting to have a benefit from the restrictions. In *Re Bass Ltd's application* (1973) 26 P&CR 156 the Tribunal granted the modification of a covenant to enable the applicant to load and unload over 200 articulated lorries every day. The applicants had been granted planning permission. The Tribunal regarded the planning permission to be very persuasive but added that the issue of reasonable user: 'could not always be concluded in the affirmative by the production of a planning permission'.

In *Re Patten Ltd's application* (1975) 31 P&CR 180 an application to modify a covenant to **12.50** enable the development of ten homes behind homes that had the benefit of covenants prohibiting the development was refused. In *Re New Ideal Homes Ltd's Application* [1978] JPL 632 the applicant sought to modify a covenant restricting the number of homes to be built on land from 79 to 150. The Tribunal modified the application, requiring compensation to be paid. It noted the restriction was not against public interest simply because there was a housing need but felt that it did not secure practical benefits of substantial value to the objecting local authority.

For further analysis of freehold covenants and more generally on the role of property law **12.51** and the environment see Chapter 10 of Gray and Gray *Elements of Land Law* (Butterworths, 2001). For further case law see *Crest Nicholson v McAllister* [2004] 1 WLR 2409 CA (identifying the land that benefits from the covenant) and *Martin v David Wilson Homes Ltd.* [2004] EWCA Civ 1027 (what is a private dwelling house?).

E   ACCESS TO OPEN SPACES AND PUBLIC PLACES

Access to open spaces such as urban and country parks, woodland, beaches, and rivers, is **12.52** an essential element to a good quality of life. Indeed, many of the organizations responsible for providing and encouraging access to open spaces, such as local authorities and the forestry commission, aim to ensure that these areas are maintained in a way that encourages use. It is recognized that the majority of outdoor activities are generally beneficial to health providing exercise and clear air.

Amenity land

12.53 There is increasing opportunity to gain access to open spaces and countryside. Indeed for many, the countryside and its wild inhabitants are what many people regard as the environment. In terms of quality of life, it is vital that everyone has the chance to enjoy access to open spaces and country. This was and remains the rationale behind the access to the countryside legislation. Section 59 of the National Parks and Countryside Act 1949 provides that the Act shall have effect for enabling the public to have access for open-air recreation to open country. The Countryside and Rights of Way Act 2000 (CRoW Act 2000) developed these principles by improving public rights of access and rights of way.

Rights of access to specified land

12.54 Section 2(1) of the CRoW Act 2000 provides a new right of access on foot to specific types of land referred to as access land. This includes, under s 1, mountain (which is land over 600 metres), moorland, heath, downland, and registered common land. Access to certain types of land is excluded or restricted. Schedule 1 of the Act sets out the excepted land categories such as cultivated land, land covered by buildings or the curtilage of such land, land within 20 metres of a dwelling, and land used as a park or a garden. Schedule 2 of the Act restricts the use of access land for example by prohibiting the lighting of fires; or of taking, killing, or disturbing any animal, bird, or fish. A person may enter and remain on any land providing they do so without breaking or damaging any wall, fence, hedge, stile, or gate and comply with the Sch 2 restrictions.

12.55 Access land does not arise until it is designated and recorded as access land on official maps. This follows a process of designation, which includes preparing draft maps, consulting on these, and then producing conclusive maps that define where the rights of access arise. Section 6(1) of the CRoW Act 2000 provides that any person with an interest in the land to be designated may appeal to the Secretary of State or the National Assembly for Wales against the land showing on a map in provisional form as registered common land or as open country.

Public rights of way

12.56 A public right of way is a way over land to which everyone has a right of passage. The different types of public right of way include:

- footpaths;
- bridleways;
- permissive paths;
- tow paths; and
- the sea-shore.

12.57 A public right of way may be granted by statute, by the general grant of private landowners, and by agreement between landowners and certain users. Also, rights may be acquired under prescription or by registration of use, most particularly for use as a village or town green.

Under s 16 of the CRoW Act 2000, a public right of access may be dedicated by a person holding land in fee simple or for a legal term of which not less than 90 years remain unexpired. This provision builds upon s 193 of the LPA 1925, which has been repealed.

A person requiring vehicular access over land may apply, under s 68 of the CRoW Act 2000, **12.58** to secure a right of way that the owner or occupier (from time to time) of any premises has used as a means of access for vehicles to the premises, if that use of the way:

    (a)   was an offence under an enactment applying to the land crossed by the way, but

    (b)   would otherwise have been sufficient to create on or after [5 May 1993], and to keep in existence, an easement giving a right of way of vehicles.

The purpose of the provision was to overcome, or at least mitigate, the situation whereby an **12.59** owner of land would request payment for the privilege of vehicular access over land that had previously been used without charge, albeit that the use was unlawful. The Vehicular Access Across Common and Other Land (England) Regulations 2002 (SI 2002/1711) prescribe the procedure for making an application. Regulation 3(1) provides that: 'an owner of any premises may, as respects a way to which s 68 of the CRoW Act 2000 applies, apply for the creation of an easement in accordance with these Regulations.'

In *Bakewell Management v Brandwood* [2004] UKHL 14 Lord Hope noted the consequence of **12.60** the decision in *Hanning v Top Deck Travel Ltd* (1993) 68 P&CR 14 (the case that prompted the introduction of s 68 of the CRoW Act 2000):

> It is well known that opportunist companies have been buying up the freehold of common land in England and Wales for the sole purpose of extracting money from local residents, who had assumed that they had an established right of vehicular access across the common to their homes as they had been obtaining access in this way without interruption since time immemorial. Public authorities too had been exacting these charges, under pressure from the Treasury.

In *Bakewell*, the Lords found for the defendant users. At para 39, Lord Scott noted that: **12.61**

> A statutory prohibition forbidding some particular use of land that is expressed in terms that allows the landowner to authorise the prohibited use and exempts from criminality use of the land with that authority is an unusual type of prohibition. It allows a clear distinction to be drawn between cases where a grant by the landowner of the right to use the land in the pro-hibited way would be a lawful grant that would remove the criminality of the user and cases where a grant by the landowner of the right to use the land in the prohibited way would be an unlawful grant and incapable of vesting any right in the grantee. It is easy to see why, in the latter class of case, long and uninterrupted use of the land contrary to a statutory prohibition cannot give rise to the presumed grant of an easement that it would have been unlawful for the landowner to grant. It is difficult to see why, in the former class of case, the long and uninterrupted user should not be capable of supporting the presumed grant by the land owner of an easement that if granted would have been lawful and effective notwithstanding that the user was contrary to a statutory prohibition. I can see no requirement of public policy that would prevent the presumption of a grant that it would have been lawful to grant. On the contrary, the remarks of Lord Denning MR and Stamp LJ in *Davis v Whitby* [[1974] 1 Ch 186] and of Lord Hoffmann in *R v Oxfordshire CC ex p Sunningwell Parish Council* [2000] 1 AC 335 to which I have referred provide sound public policy reasons why, if a grant of the right could have been lawfully made, the grant should be presumed so that long de facto enjoyment should not be disturbed.

Private rights of way

12.62   A right of way over land benefiting an individual or group of individuals but not the public at large is referred to as a private right of way. Often the right will be granted as an easement, which is a right benefiting land rather than a particular person. For an easement to exist there must be:

(a)   land that is affected by it (a servient tenement);

(b)   land annexed to the servient land that takes the benefit (the dominant tenement); and

(c)   a right granted by the easement that is capable of forming the subject matter of an easement.

12.63   For further analysis see *Re Ellenborough Park* [1956] Ch 131. In terms of liability of the owner and occupier of the land an easement is not subject to the Occupiers Liability Act 1957 (OLA 1957), but may well be liable under the Occupiers Liability Act 1984 (OLA 1984). Further, anyone wishing to assert a private right of way may well have contractual or other rights under the law on easements.

Liability of owners and occupiers of land

12.64   In providing access to the countryside and open spaces there is a duty of care owed to people coming on to the land, which may give rise to liability if those persons are injured. The responsibility of owners and occupiers of land to visitors and other persons is largely governed by the OLA 1957 and OLA 1984. The legislation makes a distinction between visitors and other persons, e.g. trespassers and those exercising a statutory right. Each is considered below.

Visitors

12.65   Section 2(1) of the Occupiers Liability Act 1957 provides that:

> An occupier of premises owes the same duty, the 'common duty of care', to all his visitors, except in so far as he is free to and does extend, restrict, modify or exclude his duty to any visitors by agreement or otherwise.

12.66   To understand the extent of liability, key elements of the section should be considered further including: what are premises, who is an occupier, who is a visitor, and what is the scope of the duty of care and the exclusion of liability.

12.67   There is no definition of premises. *Clerk & Lindsell on Torts* (Sweet & Maxwell, 2002) suggests that premises is used in its legal, rather than popular, sense to include land whether or not there are buildings on it; and it therefore covers liability of, for example, the owner of a field with poisonous berries growing on it that caused injury to a child visitor who ate them.

12.68   An occupier is not defined under the OLA 1957. In *Wheat v E Lacon & Co Ltd* [1966] 1 AC 522 the House of Lords held that an occupier may be anyone who has a sufficient degree of control over premises to be able to ensure safety and to appreciate that a failure to use care may result in injury to a person coming on to the premises. Further, there may be more than one occupier of the same premises, each with a duty to use care based upon his or her degree of control, although occupation for the purpose of determining liability is dependent on some level of physical control. However, a highway authority is not an occupier of a public footpath or road for the purpose of the OLA 1957 although, under s 58 of the Highways Act 1980, it does owe a duty to keep the surface of the highway in good repair.

Section 1(2) of the OLA 1957 provides that visitors are defined as the persons who would at **12.69** common law be treated as invitees or licensees. A licence or an invitation to enter or use the premises may be express or implied. In *Lowery v Walker* [1911] AC 10 the House of Lords held that where the public had used a short-cut across the defendant's field over a period of 35 years, the claimant had an implied licence and so was not regarded as a trespasser. However, in *Edwards v Railway Executive* [1952] AC 737 the House of Lords held that where a claimant child had regularly used the defendant's land as a short-cut a licence to enter was not implied and the claimant was regarded as a trespasser. The distinction between *Edwards* and *Lowery* was that in *Edwards* the defendant had repeatedly taken efforts to keep the claimant and others off the land whereas in *Lowery* this was not proved to be the case.

Under s 2(2) of the OLA 1957 the common duty of care requires: **12.70**

> such care as in all the circumstances of the case is reasonable to see that the visitor will be reasonably safe in using the premises for the purpose for which he is invited or permitted by the occupier to be there.

In *Wheat v Lacon* [1966] the House of Lords equated the common duty of care to that **12.71** required under the law in negligence and considered that whether the occupier has fulfilled his duty to the visitor will depend upon the facts of the case. Under s 2(3) of OLA 1957 an occupier must be prepared for children to be less careful than adults. In *Glasgow Corporation v Taylor* [1922] 1 AC 44 a young boy died after eating poisonous berries from a plant in a public park. The court held that the local authority was liable for not fencing off the plant or providing a warning sign. However, *Winfield and Jolowicz on Tort* (Sweet & Maxwell, 2002) submit that the law remains as stated in *Phipps v Rochester Corporation* [1955] 1 QB 450 and that one of the circumstances that should be taken into account in measuring the occupier's obligation is the degree of care the occupier may assume will be exercised by a child's parents. In *Phipps* a five-year-old boy was blackberry picking with his seven-year-old sister in the defendant's field when he fell in a trench; the danger of which would have been clear to an adult. On the facts it was held that a prudent parent would not have allowed two small children to be alone in the field. The court considered that the defendant may assume that parents would behave in this way and so the claim failed. The Law Reform (Contributory Negligence) Act 1945 applies to an action for a breach of the common duty of care under OLA 1957.

Section 2(4)(a) of OLA 1957 provides that: **12.72**

> Where damage is caused to a visitor by a danger of which he had been warned by the occupier, the warning is not to be treated without more as absolving the occupier from liability, unless in all the circumstances it was enough to enable the visitor to be reasonably safe.

Whether the warning is sufficient will depend upon the facts of the case. In *Roles v Nathan* **12.73** [1963] 1 WLR 1117 the warning was sufficient. In *Rae v Mars (UK) Ltd* [1990] EG 90 the court noted that the more serious the danger the more specific the warning should be. Section 2(4)(b) of OLA 1957 states that an occupier will not be liable for faulty execution of work by an independent contractor provided that this was reasonable to entrust the work to a contractor, the occupier had taken reasonable care to see that the contractor was competent, and he had taken reasonable care to see that the work was properly done. Further, under s 2(5) of the Act, the common duty of care does not impose on an occupier any obligation in respect of risks willingly accepted by the visitor.

12.74 The ability to restrict, modify, or exclude an occupier's duty to any visitors by agreement or otherwise, e.g. by placing a warning sign and/or exclusion sign is limited by s 2 of the Unfair Contract Terms Act 1977 (UCTA 1977), which provides that:

(1) A person cannot by reference to any contract term or to a notice exclude or restrict his liability for death or personal injury resulting from negligence;

(2) in the case of other loss or damage, a person cannot so exclude or restrict his liability for negligence except in so far as the term or notice satisfies the requirement of reasonableness.

12.75 Section 1(1)(c) of UCTA 1977 provides that for the purpose of the Act 'negligence' includes the common duty of care under imposed by OLA 1957. Although, under s 1(3) of UCTA 1977, limitation of s 2 only relates to things done in the course of a business or from the occupation of premises used for business purposes.

Liability to users of open country

12.76 Section 1(4) of the OLA 1957 provides that:

> A person entering any premises in exercise of rights conferred by virtue of an access agreement or order under the National Parks and Access to the Countryside Act 1949 is not, for the purposes of this Act, a visitor of the occupier of those premises.

12.77 However, an occupier may still be liable for any harm or injury under the OLA 1984 or the common law.

Non-visitors

12.78 The OLA 1984 imposes a duty on an occupier to persons other than visitors who enter or use land. The term 'persons other than visitors' is not defined but will include:

- those entering land under rights conferred by the National Parks and Access to the Countryside Act 1949;
- those using a private right of way; and
- trespassers.

12.79 Section 1(3) of OLA 1984 provides that an occupier of premises owes a duty to another (not being a visitor) in respect of any risk of their suffering injury on the premises by reason of any danger due to the state of the premises or to things done or omitted to be done on them. The duty is set out in s 1(4) of the Act as:

> the duty to take such care as is reasonable in all the circumstances of the case to see that he does not suffer injury on the premises by reason of the danger concerned.

12.80 Subsections 1(5) to (8) of OLA 1984 limit the duty owed by:

(5) giving a warning to entrants and users of risk, although this will be subject to UCTA 1977, see para 12.75;

(6) any person willingly accepting the risk;

(7) excluding liability to persons using the highway; and

(8) excluding liability for loss or damage to property.

In *British Railways Board v Herrington* [1972] AC 877 a six-year-old claimant was badly burned **12.81** when trespassing on the defendant's land after gaining access through a fence. The House of Lords held that even though the claimant was a trespasser he was still owed a duty of care, albeit a lower duty of care, than a visitor or invitee on the land. A number of similar cases have held that a duty is owed to trespassers including *Southern Portland Cement v Cooper* [1974] AC 623 (13-year-old boy electrocuted after playing on the defendant's land) and *Harris v Birkenhead Corporation* [1976] 1 WLR 279 (where a local authority failed to block up doors and windows of a property it had acquired for demolition and a four-year-old child fell out of an upstairs window). However, in *Penny v Northampton BC* (1974) 72 LGR the court declined to hold the local authority liable after a child was injured while playing on a rubbish tip. The court considered that, on the facts, the local authority had taken all reasonable steps to prevent trespassers entering the site.

F   TOWN AND VILLAGE GREENS

Town and village greens provide a valuable area of public open space. Under the Commons **12.82** Registration Act 1965 (CRA 1965), local inhabitants of an area may acquire a right to use village greens for 'lawful sport and pastimes' where there has been a history of such use. The CRoW 2000 expanded the scope of the Act. Section 22(1) of the CRA 1965 provides that a town or village green is:

> Land which has been allotted by or under any Act for the exercise or recreation of the inhabitants of any locality or on which the inhabitants of any locality have a customary right to indulge in lawful sports and pastimes or on which the inhabitants of any locality have indulged in such sports and pastimes or which falls within subs. 1A of this section.

Section 1A of the CRA 1965 provides that land under s 22(1) will include land that for **12.83** not less than 20 years a significant number of the inhabitants of any locality, or of any neighbourhood within a locality, have indulged in lawful sports and pastimes as of right and either continue to do so, or have ceased to do so for not more than such period as may be prescribed.

In the *Sunningwell Parish Council* case the House of Lords held that the phrase 'sport and **12.84** pastime' could include informal activities such as blackberry picking.

Applying to register a town or village green

An application for registration of a town or village green is made under s 13 of the CRA 1965. **12.85** Under reg 3(4) of the Commons Registration (New Land) Regulations 1969 (SI 1969/1843) an application for the registration of any land as common land or as a town or village green may be made by any person, and a registration authority shall so register any land in any case where it registers rights over it under these Regulations. A registration authority for land is either the county council; the county borough council; the Greater London Council; or the metropolitan district council. If the land in question is partly in the area of one registration authority and partly in that of another, the authorities may by agreement have provided for one of them to be the registration authority for the whole of the land.

12.86   An application is made on Form 13 and must be supported by a land description and evidence that the land in question has become a town or village green. It requires a statutory declaration of the person making the application confirming the validity of the facts stated on the form. The registration authority will, on receipt of the application, carry out a preliminary assessment of the application. Unless the application has to be rejected after preliminary consideration, the registration authority will give publicity to it and will consider it further in the light of any objections that may be received. The applicant will be supplied with copies of all objections that fall to be considered and will have an opportunity of answering them. After determination by the authority, the applicant will be informed whether the application has been accepted or rejected. If it is accepted, the land will be registered as a town or village green, and the applicant will be supplied with particulars of the registration. If it is rejected, the applicant will be notified of the reasons for the rejection.

12.87   In *R v City of Sunderland ex p Beresford* [2003] UKHL 60 the court had to consider whether a use that is tolerated or encouraged by a landowner could constitute a customary right under s 22(1) of the CRA 1965. Earlier decisions had found that if there was implied permission to use land then this permission could be revoked and there was no use 'as of right'. The House of Lords concluded that simply because a landowner encourages an activity does not mean that it takes place only by virtue of his revocable permission. Lord Rodger noted at para 60 that:

> The mere fact that a landowner encourages an activity on his land does not indicate, however, that it takes place only by virtue of his revocable permission. In brief, neither cutting the grass nor constructing and leaving the seating in place justifies an inference that the owners of the Sports Arena positively granted a licence to local residents and others, who were then to be regarded as using the land by virtue of that licence, which the owners could withdraw at any time.

12.88   Under s 12 of the Inclosure Act 1857, any person who wilfully does any injury or damage to any fence of a town or village green or wilfully and without lawful authority leads or drives any cattle or animal on to it, or does any other acts to the injury of the green, or to the interruption of its use or enjoyment as a place of exercise and recreation, is guilty of an offence and is liable, on summary conviction, to pay a maximum penalty of a £250 fine and/or any damages that may arise.

12.89   The impact of a town or village green registration may be significant. Martin Edwards (39 Essex St, 2004) has noted any encroachment on or enclosure of a town or village green made otherwise than with a view to its better enjoyment is deemed, under s 29 of the Commons Act 1876, to be a public nuisance. Further, under s 34(1) of the Road Traffic Act 1984 it is an offence without lawful authority to drive a mechanically propelled vehicle onto or upon a town or village green. Perhaps most important of all the use of town or village green registration can be used to stymie development when other, more conventional legal avenues have failed.

G   PRODUCT LIABILITY

Introduction

Environmental harm may arise through unsafe or defective products. While much of the   **12.90**
law on product liability relates to personal injury and property damage, the significance for
environmental harm and the environmental aspects of defective goods should not be
ignored. For example, selling a car with a faulty exhaust system that emits excessive levels of
nitrogen oxides and particulates will cause harm locally by increasing levels of air pollution,
and globally as emissions of greenhouse gases contribute to global warming, and so climate
change.

A claim for defective or unsafe products may give rise to a claim in contract or tort, or attract   **12.91**
criminal liability. The example above of the faulty exhaust, could be either:

* a contractual complaint brought by the purchaser of the car against the seller;
* a negligence claim against the seller or even a nuisance claim against the latest owner; or
* an offence under reg 61(5) of the Road Vehicles (Construction and Use) Regulations 1986
  (SI 1986/1078) as amended, see Chapter 3: Air.

Each legal area is outlined below.

Contract

The main areas of contractual protection for harm are statutory under the Sale of Goods   **12.92**
Act 1979 (as amended) (SGA 1979). This consolidated earlier legislation including the Sale
of Goods Act 1893.

Implied term that goods correspond with description

There is an implied term that in a sale of goods by description, those goods will match the   **12.93**
description given. Section 13 of the SGA 1979 provides that:

(1)   Where there is a contract for the sale of goods by description, there is an implied term that
      the goods will correspond with the description . . .
(2)   If the sale is by sample as well as by description it is not sufficient that the bulk of the goods
      correspond with the sample if the goods do not also correspond with the description.

In *Pinnock Bros v Lewis & Peat Ltd* [1923] 1 KB 690 copra cake (a cattle feed) was imported by   **12.94**
the defendants and bought, via dealers, by the claimant. The cake made the claimant's cattle
ill and it was discovered that the cake contained a high quantity of castor beans, which were
poisonous to cattle. The court held that a contractual clause limiting liability did not help
the defendant because the copra cake mixed with castor beans could not properly be
described as copra cake. However, in *Christopher Hill Ltd v Ashington Piggeries Ltd* [1972]
AC 440 the House of Lords held that contaminated herring meal that was toxic to mink but
not to other animals was still herring meal and the claim failed. In *Jewson Ltd v Boyhan* [2003]
EWCA Civ 1030 the Court of Appeal, at para 54, cited *Christopher Hill Ltd* as authority for the
proposition that reliance may only be partial, where mink farmers had asked a compounder
of animal foods to make up mink food to a supplied formula, it was held that there was
reliance as to the suitability of the ingredients only.

Implied term as to quality

12.95 The SGA 1979 implies certain terms as to quality and fitness for purpose. Section 14(2) provides that: 'Where the seller sells goods in the course of a business, there is an implied term that the goods supplied under the contract are of satisfactory quality.'

12.96 The implied term only applies when selling is in the course of business although this may include sales that are incidental to the business such as a farmer selling his tractor. Subsections (2A) to (2C) define what is meant by satisfactory quality including fitness for all purposes for which the goods are commonly used, and taking into account appearance and finish, freedom from minor defects, safety, and durability. The Privy Council in *Grant v Australian Knitting Mills Ltd* [1936] AC 85 held that the duty to supply goods of satisfactory quality was strict and that there is no defence to state that all care was taken. In *Grant* the claimant contacted dermatitis from a woollen garment, which, when purchased, was in a defective condition due to excess chemicals used in its manufacture.

12.97 In terms of safety, dangerous goods may be made safe if there are clear instructions as to operation and use or warnings provided. When these are present but are ignored, no liability may be attached. In *Wormell v RHM Agricultural (East) Ltd* [1987] 3 All ER 75 the claimant used a weed killer without regard to the instructions and there was no finding of liability.

Fitness for purpose

12.98 Section 14(3) of the SGA 1979 provides that for sales in the course of business there is an implied term that the goods supplied are reasonably fit for any particular purpose the buyer may have made known to the seller, except where the buyer does not rely on the skill or judgement of the seller. Examples of cases where goods have been found not to be reasonably fit for purpose include:

- *Kendall (Henry) v William Lillico* [1969] 2 AC 31 in which animal food was held to be poisonous to turkeys;
- *Bristol Tramways etc. Carriage Co v Fiat Motors Ltd* [1910] 2 KB 831 where a bus and six chassis bought for heavy traffic in a hilly district in and around Bristol were found to be unsuitable and not fit for purpose; and
- *Vacwell Engineering Co Ltd v BDH Chemicals Ltd* [1971] 1 QB 88 in which a label warning that a chemical emitted a harmful vapour was held to be inadequate when it failed to warn that the chemical would also react violently with water.

12.99 For further consideration of contractual liability for products see *Chitty on Contracts* (29/e, Sweet & Maxwell, 2004).

Tort

12.100 The leading case for product liability is *Donoghue v Stevenson* [1932] AC 562 in which Lord Atkin held at 599 that:

> A manufacturer of products which he sells in such a form as to show that he intends them to reach the ultimate consumer in the form in which they left him with no reasonable possibility of intermediate examination, and with the knowledge that the absence of reasonable care in the preparation or putting up of the products will result in an injury to the consumer's life or property, owes a duty to the consumer to take reasonable care.

The principle in *Donoghue v Stevenson* applies to all products including chemicals, the con- **12.101** tainers and labels and buildings. However, in *Murphy v Brentwood DC* [1991] 1 AC 398 the House of Lords dismissed a claim that the local authority negligently approved plans for foundations, a number of the speeches confirmed that buildings did fall within Lord Atkin's principle. In *Grant v Australian Knitting Mills Ltd* the Privy Council found for the claimant in negligence as well as contract. *Donoghue v Stevenson* is considered further in Chapter 17: Civil law practice and procedure.

In *Barnes v Irwell Valley Water Board* [1939] 1 KB 21 residents in the defendant's locality **12.102** suffered lead poisoning after water had passed through lead pipework not owned by the defendants. The local authority was held liable despite supplying water that was considered pure and wholesome; the court held that they were under a duty at common law to use reasonable care to ensure that the water should be pure and wholesome at the point that it was received by the claimants; they knew that the water would stand unused in the lead pipe for some time where it would absorb some of the lead from the pipe.

In *Tutton v Walker Ltd* [1986] QB 61 the defendant farmer sprayed his oilseed rape crop with **12.103** insecticide against the advice of central government that it could kill insects such as bees if used when the crop was in flower. The defendant was found liable in negligence. See also Section F on Pesticides in Chapter 6: Fishing, farming, and animal health.

Consumer Protection Act 1987

The Consumer Protection Act 1987 (CPA 1987), as amended, was enacted to comply with EU **12.104** Directive 85/374/EEC on the approximation of the laws, regulations, and administrative provisions of the Member States concerning liability for defective products. The CPA 1987 helped to overcome the need to prove fault on behalf of the defendant, which remains the case with common law negligence. Section 2(1) of the CPA 1987 provides that, subject to exceptions: 'where any damage is caused wholly or partly by a defect in a product, every person to whom subs (2) applies shall be liable for the damage.'

The definition of a product under s 1 of the CPA 1987 is wide including goods or electricity, **12.105** component parts, and raw materials. It also includes, following the CPA 1987 (Product Liability) (Modification) Order 2000 (SI 2000/2771), game and agricultural products. Under s 45 'goods' includes substances, growing crops and things comprised in land by virtue of being attached to it, and any ship, aircraft, or vehicle.

Person liable

Where any damage is caused wholly or partly by a defect in a product every person that falls **12.106** within s 2(2) of the CPA 1987 shall be liable for the damage, i.e.:

(a) the producer of the product;
(b) any person who has held himself out to be a producer of the product; or
(c) any person who has imported the product into a Member State in the course of any business of his, to supply it to another.

Defect

Under s 3 of the CPA 1987 there is a 'defect' in a product if the safety of the product is **12.107** not such as persons generally are entitled to expect. Safety relates to damage to property, personal injury, or death. Under s 3(2), the standard of expectation is based upon the manner for which the product is marketed, what may reasonably be expected to be done with the product, and the time the product was supplied by the producer. Section 5(2) provides that there is no liability under Pt I of the CPA 1987 for the loss of or any damage to the product itself.

Defences

12.108   Section 4(1) of the CPA 1987 provides six defences to a claim under the Act including:

(a)   that the defect is attributable to compliance with an EU obligation;

(b)   that the defendant did not at any time supply the product to another;

(c)   that the only supply was otherwise than in the course of a business and s 2(2) does not apply;

(d)   that the defect did not exist at the relevant time, i.e. at the time of supply to another;

(e)   that the state of technical and scientific knowledge at the relevant time was not such that the defect might be expected to have been discovered; or

(f)   that the defect constituted a defect in a product in which the product in question had been comprised; and was wholly attributable to the design of the subsequent product or to compliance by the producer with instructions from the producer of the subsequent product.

12.109   Section 5(4) of the CPA 1987 provides that no claim can be made for any loss of or damage to property if the amount does not exceed £275. Further, s 6(4) provides that the Law Reform (Contributory Negligence) Act 1945 and s 5 of the Fatal Accident Act 1976 (contributory negligence) apply.

Civil remedies

12.110   The usual civil law remedies will apply to contract and tort claims. These are considered in Chapter 17: Civil law practice and procedure. However, there are additional provisions under the Stop Now Orders (EC Directive) Regulations 2001 (SI 2001/1422), which transposes EU Directive 98/27/EC on injunctions for the protection of consumers' interests. The Regulations apply to any act contrary to a provision in certain EU consumer protection directives as transposed into the legal order of a Member State and that harm the collective interests of consumers. The acts are defined as 'Community infringements'. The ten relevant directives are listed in Sch 1 of the Regs. There is also a non-exhaustive list of UK legislation, which, in terms of Community infringement, is to be regarded as transposing the relevant EU Directives into UK law. Directives relevant to environmental protection and harm may include:

- Directive 84/450/EEC relating to the approximation of the laws, regulations and administrative provisions of the Member States concerning misleading advertising;
- Directive 92/28/EEC on the advertising of medicinal products for human use;
- Directive 93/13/EEC on unfair terms in consumer contracts; and
- Directive 1999/44/EC on certain aspects of the sale of consumer goods and associated guarantees.

Criminal liability

Criminal liability for products is contained in a range of legislation including the Food and   **12.111**
Environmental Protection Act 1985, the Food Safety Act 1990, and The Control of Pesticides
Regulations 1986 as amended (SI 1986/1510) (considered in Chapter 6: Fishing, farming,
and animal health).

Consumer safety

Part II of the CPA 1987 provides for consumer safety, using criminal sanctions for protection.   **12.112**
Section 10(1) of the Act provides that a person shall be guilty of an offence if he:

(a) supplies any consumer goods that fail to comply with the general safety requirement;
(b) offers or agrees to supply any such goods; or
(c) exposes or possesses any such goods for supply.

Under s 10(2) goods fail to comply with the general safety requirement if they are not   **12.113**
reasonably safe having regard to all the circumstances including the way the goods are
marketed, any safety standards, and the existence of any means by which, on a cost-benefit
analysis, it would have been reasonable for the goods to have been made safer.

Safe, in relation to any goods, is defined under s 19 as such that there is no, or minimal, risk   **12.114**
that the goods, their keeping or consumption, any emission or leakage, or any reliance or
any measurement will (whether immediately or after a definite or indefinite period) cause
the death of, or any personal injury to, any person whatsoever. In *P & M Supplies (Essex) Ltd v
Walsall MBC* [1994] Crim LR 580 the court held that an absolute standard of safety was
not to be applied when considering whether goods were reasonably safe, but that all the
circumstances must be considered including any specialist or trade evidence as to the risks
involved.

Section 10(7) of the CPA 1987 provides that consumer goods are those that are ordinarily   **12.115**
intended for private use or consumption, but excluding growing crops or things comprised
in land, water, food, feeding stuff or fertiliser, gas, aircraft or motor vehicles, controlled drugs
or licensed medicinal products, or tobacco. A person guilty of an offence under s 10 shall be
liable on summary conviction to a maximum penalty of £5,000 and/or six months'
imprisonment.

Under s 11 of the CPA 1987 the Secretary of State may make safety regulations. Numerous   **12.116**
regulations have been made such as:

• Gas Appliances (Safety) Regulations 1992 (SI 1992/711) and 1995 (SI 1995/1629);
• Dangerous Substances and Preparations (Safety) (Consolidation) Regulations 1994, as
  variously amended (SI 1994/2844);
• Cosmetic Products (Safety) Regulations 1996, as variously amended (SI 1996/2925); and
• Tobacco Products (Manufacture, Presentation and Sale) (Safety) Regulations 2002
  (SI 2002/3041).

Section 12(1) of the Act provides that where any safety regulations prohibit a person from   **12.117**
supplying or offering or agreeing to supply any goods or from exposing or possessing any
goods for supply, that person shall be guilty of an offence if he contravenes the prohibition.

Under s 12(5) a person guilty of an offence under s 12 shall be liable on summary conviction to a maximum penalty of a £5,000 fine and/or six months' imprisonment.

12.118　A number of deaths have arisen from carbon monoxide poisoning through faulty gas appliances and other domestic equipment. In *Drummond-Rees v Dorset CC* (1996) 162 JP 651 the court held that it is an offence if a landlord at the start of a tenancy provides defective equipment under the safety regulations.

Prohibition, suspension, and notice to warn

12.119　Under ss 13 and 14 of the CPA 1987, the Secretary of State has the power to serve a prohibition notice, suspension, or notice to warn on any person that is supplying, offering to supply, agreeing to supply, or exposing for supply, any relevant goods that the Secretary of State considers are unsafe. A person who contravenes any notice shall be guilty of an offence and liable on summary conviction to a fine of £5,000 and/or six months' imprisonment. Any person that has been served with a suspension notice that is in force may appeal to the magistrates' court under s 15, for an order setting aside the notice. Schedule 2 of the Act sets out the procedure for the service of notices.

Pesticides

12.120　One of the common environmental concerns is the use of pesticides on farms and in residential gardens. The regulatory control of pesticides is considered in Chapter 6: Fishing, farming, and animal health.

Restriction of Hazardous Substances in Electrical Equipment Directive

12.121　The Restriction of Hazardous Substances in Electrical Equipment Directive (RoHS Directive) bans from EU markets new equipment containing more than agreed levels of certain chemicals including: lead, cadmium, mercury, hexavalent chromium, polybrominated biphenyl, and polybrominated diphenyl ether flame retardants (the banned products). The Directive has been transposed by the Restriction of the Use of Certain Hazardous Substances in Electrical and Electronic Equipment Regulations 2005 (draft) (RoHS Regs 2005 (draft)).

12.122　The RoHS Regs 2004 implement the ban on placing on the EU market new electrical and electronic equipment (EEE) containing more than the set levels of banned products from 1 July 2006. There are a number of exempted applications for these substances. Manufacturers will need to ensure that their products — and the components of such products — comply with the requirements of the Regulations by the relevant date in order to be placed on the Single Market. The Regulations will also have an impact on those who import EEE into the EU, those who export to other Member States, and those who rebrand other manufacturers' EEE as their own. The main requirement of the RoHS Regs 2004 is that from 1 July 2006 a producer (as defined in the Regulations) may not place new EEE containing the banned products, in amounts exceeding the set maximum concentration values, on the market in the EU. Responsibility for the enforcement of the RoHS Regs 2004 will lie with the Secretary of State for Trade and Industry, who may act through a third party. The DTI has produced guidance on the implementation of the RoHS Regs 2004. There are also related regulations in relation to waste electronic equipment contained in the Waste Electrical and

Electronic Equipment (Producer Responsibility) Regulations 2005 (draft) (WEEE Regs 2005 (draft)). These are considered further in Chapter 14: Waste.

H   EMISSIONS TRADING

Introduction

Emissions trading is a mechanism, or tool, which aims to reduce greenhouse gas emissions. **12.123**
The UK first introduced a national emissions trading scheme in 2002 as part of the UK
Climate Change Programme and to further the principles of the UN Framework Convention
on Climate Change 1992 (the Climate Change Convention) and the Kyoto Protocol 1997.
The Protocol established three international mechanisms:

(1)   joint implementation,
(2)   clean development mechanism, and
(3)   emissions trading.

Emissions trading allows countries that have achieved emission reductions over and above **12.124**
those required by their Kyoto target to sell the excess to countries finding it more difficult or
expensive to meet their commitments. The UK and the more recent EU emissions trading
scheme operate on a domestic and commercial level with large organizations, rather than
states, operating in the emissions trading market. There are similar emissions trading
schemes operating in the United States. Defra is the government department promoting
emissions trading in the UK. It has produced guidance on its operation, which is available
from its website: www.defra.gov.uk/environment/climatechange/trading/.

The UK and EU emissions trading schemes compared

There are a number of differences between the UK and EU emissions trading schemes: **12.125**

* the UK scheme is pilot scheme, which began in 2002 and is scheduled to run until 2006,
  whereas the EU scheme operates without a formal closing date;
* the UK scheme encourages voluntary participation, while the EU scheme is compulsory
  for certain types of operations; and
* many of the participants in the UK scheme are in business sectors that do not fall within
  the EU scheme.

In view of the intended limited duration of the UK scheme, further discussion focuses on the **12.126**
EU emissions trading scheme.

The EU emissions trading scheme

EU Directive 2003/87EC establishing a scheme for greenhouse gas emission allowance trading **12.127**
within the Community and amending Council Directive 96/61/EC (the Emissions Trading
Directive 2003) furthers the EU's commitment to the Climate Change Convention, helping
it to meet its commitment to reduce aggregate anthropogenic emissions of greenhouse gases
by 8% compared to 1990 levels in the period 2008 to 2012. The EU emissions trading scheme
began operating on 1 January 2005. Climate change is considered in Chapter 3: Air.

12.128   Member States were required to transpose the Emissions Trading Directive by 31 December 2003. The Greenhouse Gas Emissions Trading Scheme Regulations 2005, (SI 2005/925) (the Emissions Trading Regs 2005), made under section 2(2) of the European Communities Act 1972, provide the framework for the EU greenhouse gas emissions trading scheme. Importantly, the Regulations control emissions of carbon dioxide from any of the activities listed in Sch 1 to the Regulations. Part 2 of Sch 1 sets out rules for the interpretation of Pt 1 of Sch 1.

12.129   The trading scheme began operating on 1 January 2005. Article 1 of the Directive provides that:

> This Directive establishes a scheme for greenhouse gas emission allowance trading within the Community . . . in order to promote reductions of greenhouse gas emissions in a cost-effective and economically efficient manner.

12.130   Under Art 2(1) the Directive applies to the six greenhouse gases under the Protocol, listing these in Annex II. Unlike the voluntary UK scheme, the Emissions Trading Directive requires Member States to ensure that all installations undertaking any activity listed in Annex I shall hold a greenhouse gas emissions permit. These include certain installations operating in the following areas:

- energy activities including combustion installations with a rated thermal input exceeding 20 MW, mineral oil refineries, and coke ovens, but excluding hazardous or municipal waste incinerators;
- the production and processing of ferrous metals;
- installations in the mineral industry, e.g. for the production of cement clinker, and the manufacture of glass; and
- other activities, which includes the production of pulp from timber, paper, and board.

12.131   The Directive does not cover installations used for research development or testing of new products or processes. Also, under Art 27, Member States can apply for certain installations to be temporarily excluded from the scheme subject to a financial penalty. Commission Decision 29/X/2004 concerning the temporary exclusion of certain installations by the UK from the Community emissions trading scheme allowed 63 UK installations to opt out of the trading scheme for two years between 1 January 2005 and 31 December 2006. Paragraph (5) of the Decision notes that the UK confirmed that the installations would be subject to the financial penalty of £30 for each tonne of CO_2 equivalent emitted by that installation.

Operation of the EU trading scheme

Operator's permit from the competent authority

12.132   The Directive requires Member States to ensure that no installation undertakes any activity listed in Annex I unless its operator holds a permit issued by a competent authority or unless the installation is temporarily excluded under Art 27. An operator is defined under Art 3(a) as:

> any person who operates or controls an installation or, where this is provided for in national legislation, to whom decisive economic power over the technical functioning of the installation has been delegated;

Member States must designate a competent authority as defined by Art 18 of the Emissions **12.133** Trading Directive. Article 6 provides that the competent authority shall issue an emissions permit authorizing the emissions from all or part of the installation providing it is satisfied that the operator is capable of monitoring and reporting on emissions.

Under Art 5, an operator must obtain a permit by an application that includes a description **12.134** of the installation (with a non-technical summary), the raw and auxiliary materials likely to lead to greenhouse gas emissions, the sources of those emissions, and the monitoring and reporting measures to be used. The competent authorities in the UK are referred to as regulators and include:

- the Environment Agency for installations in England and Wales;
- the Scottish Environmental Protection Agency;
- the Northern Ireland Department of Environment; and
- the Department of Trade and Industry for all offshore installations covered by the scheme.

If the competent authority is satisfied the operator is capable of monitoring and reporting **12.135** the emissions from the installation, it will issue an emissions trading permit to the operator which will include, under Art 6(2) of the Directive:

(a) the name and address of the operator;
(b) a description of the activities and emissions from the installation;
(c) monitoring requirement, specifying monitoring methodology and frequency;
(d) reporting requirements; and
(e) an obligation to surrender allowances equal to the total emissions of the installation in each calendar year, as verified in accordance with Art 15, within four months following the end of the year.

Article 7 of the Emissions Trading Directive requires that the operator must inform the **12.136** competent authority of any changes in the nature or function of the installation that may require updating of the permit.

Allowances and trading

Once a permit has been granted to an operator the competent authority will issue a certain **12.137** number of allowances to that operator. An allowance is defined in Art 3(a) of the Emissions Trading Directive as:

> an allowance to emit one tonne of carbon dioxide equivalent during a specified period, which shall be valid only for the purposes of meeting the requirements of this Directive and shall be transferable in accordance with the provisions of this Directive;

Allowances are central to the emissions trading scheme. It is the allowances that are traded **12.138** on the emissions trading market. The principle may be explained, in a simplified way as follows:

- An operator that has been granted a permit is allocated 10,000 allowances, and it is therefore entitled to emit 10,000 tonnes of carbon dioxide (CO_2) equivalent.
- Because of good environmental management and performance, it only emits 9,000 tonnes of CO_2 equivalent, during the specified allocation period.

- It has then used up only 9,000 allowances and it is then entitled to sell or otherwise trade the remaining 1,000 allowances on the market.
- If, however, through poor environmental management, it had emitted 11,000 tonnes of CO_2 equivalent during the specified allocation period, it would have to purchase a further 1,000 allowances. In effect being penalized for generating too much CO_2 equivalent.

Allocation of allowances

12.139   The allocation of allowances to operators must be carried out in accordance with the national allocation plan (NAP) that each Member State must prepare under Art 9 of the Emissions Trading Directive. The Directive sets the boundaries for NAPs, e.g. under Art 10 that at least 95% of allowances must be allocated for free in the first three-year period of the plan, with at least 90% being allocated for free in the following five-year period. Although, the Greenhouse Gas Emissions Trading Scheme (Amendment) Regulations 2004 (SI 2004/ 3390) amends the earlier regulations to provide a subsistence charge to be payable to the regulator to cover the costs of administering the scheme. Annex III also provides further criteria such as, under para 8: 'the plan shall contain information on the manner in which clean technology, including energy efficient technologies, are taken into account.'

12.140   The Communication from the Commission (COM (2003) 830 final) assists in the development of NAPs. The purpose of the Communication is to:

(a)   assist Member States in drawing up their NAPs, by indicating the scope of interpretation of Annex III of the Emissions Trading Directive criteria that the Commission deems acceptable;

(b)   support the Commission assessment of notified NAPs, pursuant to Art 9(3); and

(c)   describe the circumstances under which *force majeure* is demonstrated.

12.141   Paragraph 114 of the Communication provides that a *force majeure* may include natural disasters, war and threats of war, terrorist acts, revolution, riot, sabotage, and acts of vandalism. The presence of *force majeure* must be demonstrated at installation level on a case-by-case basis. The UK National Allocation Plan 2005–7 is published by Defra in collaboration with, among others, the Welsh Assembly Government, the Scottish Executive, and the Northern Ireland Department of Environment.

Using allowances

12.142   Articles 11 to 13 of the Emissions Trading Directive provides for the use, transfer, surrender, or cancellation of allowances. The allowances that are either used as allocated or gained through trading must be surrendered to the competent authority when used. They are cancelled on surrender to the authority. The may also be cancelled on request of the operator at any time and they will be automatically cancelled if not surrendered at the end of the three-year or five-year compliance period.

Enforcement of the EU trading scheme in the UK

12.143   Under the Directive, Member States must lay down rules on penalties for infringement of the Emissions Trading Scheme. Regulation 7 of the Emissions Trading Regs 2003 creates a general prohibition by stating that: 'No person shall carry out a Sch 1 activity resulting in specified emissions after 1 January 2005, except under and to the extent authorised by a greenhouse gas emissions permit.'

Parts 4, 5, and 7 of the Regulations cover enforcement, appeals, and offences respectively. **12.144**

Part 4: enforcement

Regulation 22 provides that it shall be the duty of the regulator to take such action under **12.145**
the Regulations as may be necessary for the purpose of ensuring that the monitoring and reporting conditions are complied with. If a regulator is of the opinion that an operator is contravening such a condition it may, under reg 23, serve an enforcement notice. Further, under reg 16, the regulator may at any time revoke a greenhouse gas emissions permit, in whole or in part, by serving a revocation notice on the operator.

Part 5: appeals

Under reg 26, an operator may appeal against: **12.146**

(a)   the refusal of a grant, variation, transfer, or surrender of a permit; or
(b)   a variation, enforcement, or revocation notice;

Regulation 28 and Sch 2 of the Emissions Trading Regs 2003 set out the appeals procedure. **12.147**

Part 7: offences and civil penalties

Regulation 32(1) of the Emissions Trading Regs 2003 creates a number of offences such as **12.148**
contravening the general prohibition under reg 7, failing to comply with an enforcement notice, and intentionally making a false entry in any record required to be kept under a permit condition. A defence may be available to certain offences, e.g. reg 32(1)(e) provides a defence of reasonable excuse for failing to comply with any requirement imposed by certain notices.

A person guilty of an offence under reg 32(1) shall be liable, on summary conviction to a **12.149**
maximum penalty of a fine of £5,000 or three months' imprisonment, and an unlimited fine and/or two years' imprisonment for conviction on indictment. If the offence is committed by a company with the consent or connivance of any director, manager, secretary, or other similar officer, that person as well as the company shall be guilty of the offence.

Regulations 33 and 34 of the Emissions Trading Regs 2003 create civil penalties for failing to **12.150**
comply with a condition that results in excess emissions and for the understatement of reportable emissions.

Further EU guidance

Further formal guidance on the emissions trading has been produced by the EU including: **12.151**

• Commission Decision 280/2004/EC concerning a mechanism for monitoring Community greenhouse gas emissions and for implementing the Kyoto Protocol establishing guidelines for the monitoring and reporting of greenhouse gas emissions pursuant to Directive 2003/87/EC; and
• Commission Regulation 2216/2004 for a standardized and secured system of registries pursuant to Directive 2003/87/EC and Decision 280/2004/EC.

KEY DOCUMENTS AND MATERIALS

Law of Property Act 1925
National Parks and Countryside Act 1949
Planning (Listed Buildings and Conservation Areas) Act 1950
Occupiers Liability Act 1957
Commons Registration Act 1965
Compulsory Purchase Act 1965
Unfair Contract Terms Act 1977
Sale of Goods Act 1979
Occupiers Liability Act 1984
Consumer Protection Act 1987
Environmental Protection Act 1990
The Compulsory Purchase by Non-Ministerial Acquiring Authorities (inquiries Procedure) Rules 1990 (SI 1990/512)
The Compulsory Purchase by Ministers Inquiries Procedure) Rules 1994 (SI 1994/3264)
The Countryside and Rights of Way Act 2000
The Greenhouse Gas Emissions Trading Scheme Regulations 2003, as amended (SI 2003/3311) Commons Registration (New Land) Regulations 1969 (SI 1969/1843)
Compulsory Purchase of Land (Written Representations Procedure) (Ministers) Regulations 2004 (SI 2004/2595)

EU Directive 2003/87EC establishing a scheme for greenhouse gas emission allowance trading within the Community and amending Council Directive 96/61/EC (the Emissions Trading Directive)
EU Directive 2004/35/EC on environmental liability with regard to the prevention and remedying of environmental damage

Clerk & Lindsell on Torts. Sweet & Maxwell: London
Defra (2004). UK National Allocation Plan 2005–2007
Gray and Gray (2001). *Elements of Land Law*. Butterworths: London
Hellawell, T (2002). *Environmental Law Handbook*. 5/e. The Law Society: London
Law Society (2001). *Contaminated Land Warning Card*. Law Society: London
ODPM: Circular 06/2004: *Compulsory Purchase and the Crichel Down Rules*
Rogers, W (2002). *Winfield and Jolowicz on Tort*. Sweet & Maxwell: London
Envirosearch: www.landmark-information.co.uk
Groundsure: www.groundsure.com.

13

RADIATION

A INTRODUCTION

Defining radiation

'Radiation' is a general term for the emission or transfer of energy as waves or particles **13.01** through the air or other substances. Common forms of radiation are the sun's rays, radiation waves in microwave ovens, and radio waves from mobile phones and telecommunications masts.

For the purpose of regulation and control there are two categories of radiation: **13.02**

(1) ionizing radiation, and
(2) non-ionizing radiation.

13.03   The difference between ionizing and non-ionizing radiation is the frequency at which the radiation wave travels. Non-ionizing radiation frequencies travel at very low hertz (Hz) or cycles/second, e.g. electricity operates at 50 Hz, televisions at 20 kHz and mobile phones at around 2.5 GHz. The frequencies continue to operate more quickly and at the ultra violet band (between 7.7×10^{14} to 3×10^{17} Hz), the radiation can ionize the surface it impacts, which means shifting the electrical charge of physical matter. X-rays operate at around 10^{18} Hz and have sufficient energy to pass through tissue and damage organs and DNA. On this basis, non-ionizing radiation may be regarded as less harmful than ionizing radiation.

Ionizing radiation

13.04   Ionizing radiation is caused by the disintegration of the nucleus, a constituent part of an atom. There are different properties of ionizing radiation:

- Alpha radiation has little penetrating powering. It is generally harmless to the human body unless it enters the body through inhalation or swallowing.
- Beta radiation can penetrate the skin by up to 2 cm and may harm internal organs on entering the body.
- Gamma radiation can penetrate deep into a body and can seriously harm organs.
- X-rays are similar in nature to gamma radiation.
- Cosmic radiation is high energy particle radiation from outer space and it hits earth nearly at the speed of light.

13.05   Ionizing radiation often occurs naturally and human exposure is most commonly carrying on what may be regarded as conventional activities such as drinking and eating and being outdoors. For example, radon is produced by uranium decaying deep in bedrock that rises to the earth's surface. It is widespread but certain geographical areas produce higher quantities than others, e.g. south-west England. Cosmic radiation comes from the sun and other extra-terrestrial bodies. Energy generation, particularly nuclear power but also burning fossil fuels, causes radiation. Radiation can also be produced synthetically through nuclear reaction and other man-made processes. If the absorbed dose of ionizing radiation is significant then it is has greater potential for harm compared to non-ionizing radiation.

Non-ionizing radiation

13.06   Non-ionizing radiation derives largely from man-made sources such as electric cables, mobile phones and mobile phone masts, television sets, and computer screens. In *Network Rail Infrastructure Ltd v Morris* [2004] EWCA 172 an electromagnetic field generated from a railway signalling circuit caused interference in the claimant's nearby sound recording studio, leading to what was claimed was £60,000 of lost business. It was accepted that the railway signalling system caused electromagnetic emissions and that they could interfere with certain other equipment. However, the Court of Appeal held that any interference in the studio would not be reasonably foreseeable when installing the railway track circuit.

Radiation and nuclear installations

13.07   Nuclear or atomic power, weapons, and other nuclear matter produce radiation. A simplified explanation (adapted from Health Protection Agency (HPA) website) is set out below:

- The core of an atom (which has little of the volume but contains much of the mass and holds electric charge) is called a nucleus.
- Nuclear fission is where a nucleus is split into two or more nuclei and energy is released and nuclides or radionuclides are produced.
- A nuclear reactor is a device in which nuclear fission can be maintained by a chain reaction involving neutrons.
- Nuclear power is the power obtained from nuclear reactors; a nuclear weapon is the explosive device deriving its power from fission or fusion of nuclei.
- The generation of nuclear power using nuclides produces ionizing radiation.
- Radioactivity is the property of radionuclides of spontaneously emitting ionizing radiation.

Concerns about radiation

Harm to humans, flora, and fauna can arise from radiation but it depends upon the amount **13.08** of radiation, the form of radiation, e.g. alpha, beta, or gamma etc., the sensitivity of the skin and body tissue, whether the radiation source is internal or external, and the duration of the exposure to the radiation.

Cancer, and in particular, leukaemia has been linked to radiation. Investigations have found **13.09** clusters of childhood leukaemia around nuclear power and processing plants such as Sellafield in Cumbria, Dounreay in Scotland, and Le Hague in Northern France, although there is no conclusive causal link. While numerous studies have been undertaken there remains uncertainty about all forms of radiation and successive governments have taken a precautionary approach to ionizing radiation activities. There are other uncertainties about the emissions of radiation from mobile phones, telecommunications masts, and power lines. This is considered further in Section D: Telecommunications.

Advisory and regulatory bodies

Regulatory bodies

The regulation of radiation activities is carried out by: **13.10**

- Nuclear Installations Inspectorate, part of the Health and Safety Executive (HSE), which is responsible for safety, site licensing, and permits for the nuclear installations;
- the Environment Agency, which controls all matters relating to radioactive substances and waste;
- the HSE, responsible for ionizing radiation in the workplace; and
- local authorities that are responsible for controlling the development of mobile phone masts.

Government departments, companies, and advisory bodies

The DTI is responsible for the energy sector including nuclear energy as well as developing **13.11** the telecommunications industry. Defra is responsible for radioactive waste. The various companies and advisory bodies include:

- the UK Atomic Energy Authority (UKAEA), which is responsible for the decommissioning of nuclear reactors and other radioactive facilities;

- British Energy plc and British Nuclear Fuels plc operate the nuclear power stations;
- UK Nirex Ltd, which manages facilities to dispose of radioactive waste;
- Cogent Sector Skills Council (CSSC), licensed in 2004 to advise on the nuclear, chemical, gas, oil, and petroleum industries;
- The Committee on Medical Aspects of Radiation in the Environment (COMARE), which is an independent expert advisory committee on the health effects of ionizing and non-ionizing radiation;
- the Radioactive Waste Management Advisory Committee that advises Defra on radioactive waste;
- the International Commission on Radiological Protection (ICRP), which is an independent organisation that provides guidance on safety and other matters relating to radiation;
- the HPA, which includes the former National Radiological Protection Board (NRPB), which carries out similar functions as ICRP on a domestic level. NRPB was created by statute to provide advice and technical support to the Government; and
- the Independent Expert Group on Mobile Phones (IEGMP), which has produced a number of reports including the *Stewart Report on Mobile Phones and Health* (2000) (the *Stewart Report*).

B   NUCLEAR INSTALLATIONS

13.12   There are 12 nuclear power stations operating in the UK producing around 21% of the country's electricity needs. There is also the Sellafield Nuclear Reprocessing Plant, which reprocesses spent radioactive materials for reuse.

Outline of relevant legislation

13.13   There is a range of legislative powers, duties, and controls on nuclear installations. The Atomic Energy Act 1946 places a duty on the Secretary of State for Trade and Industry to promote the development of atomic energy. The UK Atomic Energy Authority Act 1954 created the UKAEA and there has been further UKAEA-related legislation introduced since then.

13.14   The Nuclear Installations Act 1965 (NIA 1965) is the primary source of legislation covering the operation of installations including nuclear power stations and waste processing plants. It incorporates the UN Convention on Third Party Liability in the Field of Nuclear Energy 1960 (the Paris Convention) and has been amended on a number of occasions, e.g. by the NIA 1965 (Repeals and Modifications) Regulations 1990 (SI 1990/1918).

Operating nuclear installations

13.15   The regulation of nuclear installations is based on prohibitions, i.e. operation of such an installation is banned unless the operator has a site licence and for certain activities a further permit to operate. Criminal liability attaches to any breach of prohibition and to any conditions that may be attached to a licence.

The HSE grants licences and must consult the Environment Agency before granting a   **13.16**
site licence. The HSE may also direct that the applicant for a licence should serve notice
on certain other bodies including any local authority, a water undertaker or fisheries
committee, or any other public body that an application has been made.

Criminal liability

Section 1 of the NIA 1965 prohibits the use of any site for the purpose of installing or   **13.17**
operating a nuclear reactor or other installation unless the HSE have granted a nuclear site
licence. Section 1(1)(b) of the NIA 1965 refers to a nuclear reactor or installation subject to
restrictions or licensing as:

> an installation designed or adapted for:
>
> (i)   the production or use of atomic energy;
> (ii) the carrying out of any process which is preparatory or ancillary to the production or use
>   of atomic energy and which involves or is capable of causing the emission of ionising
>   radiations; or
> (iii) the storage, processing or disposal of nuclear fuel or of bulk quantities of other radio-
>   active matter, being matter which has been produced or irradiated in the course of the
>   production or use of nuclear fuel.

Under s 1(3) of the NIA 1965, any person who contravenes s1 shall be guilty of an offence. A   **13.18**
person found guilty of an offence shall be liable, on summary conviction, to a maximum
penalty of £5,000 fine on summary conviction or an unlimited fine and/or two years'
imprisonment for conviction on indictment under s 33(3) of the Health and Safety at Work
etc. Act 1974.

Once a site licence has been granted an operator may still be prohibited from certain   **13.19**
activities without a permit. Section 2 of the NIA 1965 provides that no person other than the
UKAEA shall use any site except and in accordance with the terms of a permit:

> (a) for any treatment of irradiated matter which involves the extraction there from of
>   plutonium or uranium; or
> (b) for any treatment of uranium such as to increase the proportion of the isotope 235 con-
>   tained therein.

Section 2(2) provides that any person who contravenes s 2(1) shall be guilty of an offence   **13.20**
and be liable, on summary conviction, to a fine not exceeding £5,000 and/or three months'
imprisonment or to an unlimited fine and/or five years' imprisonment for conviction on
indictment.

Section 3 of the NIA 1965 covers the grant and variation of licences. While s 4 relates to the   **13.21**
attachment of conditions and s 5 to the revocation and surrender of a nuclear site licence.
A breach of either s 4 or s 5 is an offence, where someone found guilty will be liable on
summary conviction to a fine not exceeding £500.

Civil liability

There are also certain duties created by the Act. Section 7 provides that it is the duty of   **13.22**
the licensee of a licensed site to ensure that no injury or damage to property arises from toxic,
explosive or hazardous properties, or from ionizing radiation emissions. Sections 8 to 11

extend that duty in certain circumstances to the UKAEA, certain foreign operators, and carriers of nuclear matter.

13.23   Section 12 of the NIA 1965 provides a right to compensation under the Act. It states that where any injury or damage has been caused in breach of a duty imposed by ss 7, 8, 9, or 10 of the Act then, subject to certain grounds of exclusion or reduction, compensation in respect of the injury or damage shall be payable in accordance with s 16 of the Act. Under s 15, claims for compensation must be brought within 30 years of the date of the occurrence that gave rise to the claim or, where the occurrence was a continuing one, 30 years from the date of the last event in the course of the occurrence.

13.24   Section 16 caps the compensation payable under the Act to an aggregate sum of £140 million or £10 million in the case of licensees of such sites as may be prescribed. Sections 18 to 21 require persons that may be liable to pay compensation to secure insurance cover for such a claim. Section 19(5) creates an offence of not securing special cover for liability under s 19(1) whereby the licensee if found guilty shall be liable on summary conviction to a maximum penalty of £5,000 and/or three months' imprisonment or to an unlimited fine and/or two years' imprisonment for conviction on indictment.

13.25   In *Merlin v British Nuclear Fuels plc* [1990] 2 QB 557 a claim for loss in value of the claimant's home resulting in radioactive contamination from the Sellafield nuclear installation was dismissed on the basis that the blight caused on the property fell outside the provisions of the NIA 1965. The court concluded that the claimant's home was still habitable and therefore the loss did not arise from damage to property and was purely economic loss. However, in *Blue Circle Industries plc v Ministry of Defence* [1999] Env LR 22 the Court of Appeal upheld a claim for damages for the devaluation in property caused by land contaminated by radioactivity. In *Blue Circle* the defendant owned a site at Aldermaston, the atomic weapons establishment. After heavy rain, water from ponds on the defendant's site overflowed onto the claimant's land. When the claimant tried to sell its land it found that it was contaminated with radioactive material that exceeded acceptable levels. The sale failed and the defendant carried out remediation work on the land. The claimant then claimed £5 million compensation for the devaluation in property.

13.26   In *Reay v British Nuclear Fuels Plc* [1994] Env LR 320 children living close to Sellafield claimed personal injury for leukaemia arising from paternal irradiation. The claim was dismissed after technical and evidentiary barriers were not overcome.

Nuclear installations and land use planning

13.27   The development of nuclear installations falls under the land use planning system (governed largely by the Town and Country Planning Act 1990 (TCPA 1990)). Under the Act, an application for permission will almost certainly require an environmental statement in support. This is governed by the TCP (Environmental Impact Assessment) (England and Wales) Regulations 1999, as amended (SI 1999/293). A nuclear power station will be regarded as a major infrastructure project, which will need to be referred to the Secretary of State for determination. See Chapters 8: Land use planning and 24: Environmental assessment.

C   RADIOACTIVE SUBSTANCES

The Radioactive Substances Act 1993 (RSA 1993) regulates the keeping, use, and disposal **13.28**
of radioactive matter. It operates by prohibiting the use and accumulation or disposal of
radioactive waste without registration or authorization to do so. The Environment Agency
is the regulatory authority, although under ss 23 to 25 the Secretary of State has the power
to give directions, require that certain applications be determined by him, and restrict the
knowledge of certain applications. Under ss 41 and 42 of the Environment Act 1995, the
Environment Agency may make charging schemes for the environmental licences and
approval schemes. The Charging Scheme for Radioactive Substances Act Regulation 2004/05
allows the Environment Agency to charge fees to applicants wishing to obtain an authorization or registration.

Defining radioactive material and waste

The preliminary section provides certain definitions including: **13.29**

s 1   radioactive material means anything that, not being waste, is either a substance
specified in Sch 1 (e.g. actinium, lead, radium, radon, uranium etc.) or an article
made wholly or partly from such a substance, or a substance possessing radioactivity
that is wholly or partly attributable to a process of nuclear fission or other process of
subjecting a substance to bombardment;

s 2   radioactive waste means waste that consists wholly or partly of a substance or article
that, if it were not waste, would be radioactive material or a substance or article that
has been contaminated in the course of the production, keeping, or use of radioactive
material, or by contact with or proximity to other waste; and

s 3   mobile radioactive apparatus means any apparatus, equipment, appliance, or other
thing that is radioactive material.

Registration to use radioactive material

Sections 6 to 12 of the RSA 1993 cover the use of radioactive material and mobile radioactive **13.30**
apparatus. Under s 6 of the Act, no person shall keep, use, cause, or permit radioactive
material on any premises, knowing or having reasonable grounds for believing it to be
radioactive material unless he is registered under s 7, exempt from registration, or the radioactive material consists of mobile radioactive apparatus registered under s 10. Under s 6, the
prosecution must prove that the defendant has the required knowledge. In *Gaumont British
Distributors Ltd v Henry* [1939] 2 KB 711 the court held that the defendant should not be
found guilty of the offence of knowingly making a record without the consent of the performers, unless the court is satisfied not only that he knowingly made the record, but also
that he knew that the consent in writing of the performers had not been obtained. However,
in *James & Son v Smee* [1955] 1 QB 78 the court held that knowledge may be imputed where
someone clearly turns a blind eye to the obvious.

Under s 7 of the RSA 1993 an application for registration for use shall be made to the **13.31**
Environment Agency; on receipt of an application, a copy shall be sent to the local

authority. On considering the application the Agency may register the applicant, register an application in part, or refuse an application. Under s 7(6) the Agency may impose conditions on a registration. Section 8 provides for certain exemptions such as under s 8(1) if a nuclear site licence is in force under the NIA 1965. Sections 9 to 11 of the RSA 1993 provide similar prohibitions, registration procedures, and exemptions for mobile radioactive apparatus. While s 12 provides that the Agency may cancel or vary a registration at any time.

13.32 In *R v BBGR Ltd* (2002) Env Times Vol 8.3 p 43 the defendant was convicted of failing to register a radioactive material, polonium 210, some of which was later lost at its Salford premises. The defendant was fined £3,000 and ordered to pay costs of £1,377.

Authorization of disposal and accumulation of radioactive waste

13.33 Section 13(1) of the RSA 1993 provides, subject to s 15, that no person shall, except in accordance with an authorization granted for the purpose:

> dispose of any radioactive waste on or from any premises which are used for the purposes of any undertaking carried on by him or cause or permit any radioactive waste to be so disposed of, if he knows or has reasonable grounds for believing it to be radioactive material.

13.34 Similar prohibitions apply under s 14 of the RSA 1993 to the accumulation of radioactive waste. While s 15 provides for further exemptions from ss 13 and 14 granted by order of the Secretary of State. Orders, among others, include:

- The Radioactive Substances (Uranium and Thorium) Exemption Order 1962 (SI 1962/2649); and
- The Radioactive Substances (Hospitals) Exemption Order 1990 (SI 1990/2512).

13.35 Under s 17 the Environment Agency may revoke or vary an authorization granted under ss 13 or 14 at any time.

13.36 In *R v Inspectorate of Pollution ex p Greenpeace Ltd (No 2)* [1994] 4 All ER 329 Greenpeace challenged the Inspectorate's decision to vary an existing authorization held by British Nuclear Fuel Ltd (BNFL) to discharge liquid and gaseous radioactive waste into the Irish Sea from its thermal oxide reprocessing plant (THORP) on the basis that there had been a failure to adequately justify the releases under Art 6 of Directive 80/836/Euratom. In *R (Friends of the Earth Ltd) v Secretary of State for the Environment, Food and Rural Affairs* [2002] Env LR 612 the Court of Appeal dismissed a claim challenging the Secretary of State's decisions that the proposed manufacture of mixed oxide fuel (MOX) at THORP was justified under Directive 96/29/Euratom on the basis that the initial application to vary the discharge authorizations was not made until £300 million had been spent on building the MOX plant. The court considered that to incorporate the development costs in this instance would be a fiction.

Contaminated land

13.37 Section 78YC of the EPA 1990 excludes the use of Pt IIA of the Environment Protection Act (EPA 1990) for the remediation of contaminated land in relation to harm or pollution of controlled waters from radioactivity, although it enables the Secretary of State to make further regulations on this if required. Any land contaminated by radioactive substances falls within the RSA 1993.

Appeals and enforcement

Section 21 of the RSA 1993 provides that if the Environment Agency is of the opinion that **13.38** a person to whom a registration or authorization relates is failing to comply with any limitation or condition or is likely to do so then it may serve an enforcement notice on that person. Similarly, under s 22, if the Agency is of the opinion that the carrying on of an activity involves the imminent risk of pollution of the environment or of harm to human health, it may serve a prohibition notice on that person.

Appeals

Section 26 of the RSA 1993 provides that where the Environment Agency: **13.39**

(a)   refuses an application for registration or authorization,
(b)   attaches any limitations or conditions to an authorization, or
(c), (d) varies, cancels, or revokes an authorization,
the person may appeal to the Secretary of State.

An appeal to the Secretary of State may also be available to someone served with either **13.40** an enforcement or prohibition notice. Although s 26(3) provides that no appeal shall lie in respect of any decision taken by the Agency in pursuance of a direction of the Secretary of State. The procedure on appeals is set out under s 27, with further information prescribed under the Radioactive Substances (Appeals) Regulations 1990 (SI 1990/2504).

Enforcement

Under s 32 of the RSA 1993 any person who contravenes one of the prohibitions in the act **13.41** shall on being found guilty of an offence, be liable on summary conviction to a maximum penalty of a £20,000 fine and/or six months' imprisonment, or an unlimited fine and/or five years' imprisonment for conviction on indictment.

Section 33 creates an offence for contravention of obligations relating to documents under **13.42** ss 19 and 20, whereby a person found guilty shall be liable on summary conviction to a maximum penalty of a £5,000 fine and/or three months' imprisonment, or an unlimited fine and/or two years' imprisonment for conviction on indictment. There are also offences relating to the disclosure of trade secrets under s 34 and, under s 35, offences of making false or misleading statements or false entries.

Section 36 of the RSA 1993 provides that where a company commits an offence, and the **13.43** offence is proved to have been committed by a director, manager, or key officer, then the person shall be guilty as well as the company.

In *R v Nationwide Crash Repairs* (2002) Env Times Vol 8.1 p 48, the defendant was convicted **13.44** after failing to provide information on the source of the radioactive material and also for the loss of a paint spray gun. It was fined £21,000 plus costs of £2,080. Similarly, in *R v Ford Motor Company* (2003) Environment Action 10 (July 2003) the defendant company was convicted for the loss of a radioactive source, a paint spray gun containing polonium 210, from one of its sites. It admitted two offences under the RSA 1993, was fined £42,000 and ordered to pay costs of nearly £3,959.

13.45 Further, s 37 provides that where the act or omission of person A results in person B committing an offence, then person A may be convicted of the offence, regardless of whether
proceedings are taken against person B who actually committed the offence. See also
Chapter 19: Criminal law practice and procedure.

D TELECOMMUNICATIONS

Introduction

13.46 By far the biggest concern about non-ionizing radiation is that produced through radio-
frequency (RF) emitted from mobile phones, mobile phone masts, and other telecommunications systems. RF is electromagnetic radiation found in the electromagnetic
spectrum at longer wavelengths than infrared radiation. The rapid expansion of the
mobile phone market — there are now around 50 million mobile phones in use in the
UK — has meant that many operators have sought to erect mobile phone masts across
the UK.

Concerns about mobile phones and masts

13.47 The potential health impacts of mobile phones and masts are probably the primary
reason why people oppose their development and use. However, the impact on the landscape is also a common concern; there are expected to be up to 50,000 mobile phone
masts across the country by the end of 2007. The Government actively supports the
telecommunications industry, but does this without the conclusive evidence of the seriousness or otherwise of the long-term health impacts of mobile phones and mobile phone
masts.

13.48 In 2000, the *Stewart Report* concluded that:

> The balance of evidence to date suggests that exposures to RF radiation below NRPB and ICNIRP
> guidelines do not cause adverse health effects to the general population. . . . There is now
> scientific evidence, however, which suggests that there may be biological effects occurring at
> exposures below these guidelines.

> We conclude therefore that it is not possible at present to say that exposure to RF radiation, even
> at levels below national guidelines, is totally without potential adverse health effects, and that
> the gaps in knowledge are sufficient to justify a precautionary approach.

> We recommend that a precautionary approach to the use of mobile phone technologies be
> adopted until much more detailed and scientifically robust information on any health effects
> becomes available.

13.49 In 2005, the NRPB published a review of 26 recent reports on mobile phones: *A Summary of
Recent Reports on Mobile Phones and Health (2000–2004)*. It concluded that, overall, the reports
acknowledged that exposure to low-level radio frequency fields may cause a variety of subtle
biological effects on cells, animals, or humans, particularly on brain activity during sleep,
but the possibility of exposure causing adverse health effects remains unproven. A further
study: *Mobile Phones and Health 2004* by the NRPB reviewed the *Stewart Report* and concluded

that the main conclusions reached were still relevant and that a precautionary approach to the use of mobile phones should continue to be adopted.

The law relating to mobile phones is based upon consumer and product safety. The develop- **13.50** ment of mobile phone masts is controlled through the land use planning system, which is covered in Chapter 8: Land use planning, with areas of particular relevance considered below.

Mobile phone operators and regulators

The companies wishing to erect or develop mobile phone masts are the phone operators, **13.51** e.g. O_2 and Orange. There are also some public body operators including the police, who are developing the Tetra mast system, and Network Rail. Under the Telecommunications Act 1984 (as amended by the Communications Act 2003) the companies are referred to as Electronic Communication Code System Operators, and each one must obtain an operating licence. The operators are regulated by the Government Agency, OFCOM, and are granted certain rights to use public highways and other land in line with other public service pro- viders of water, gas, and electricity, e.g. for laying cables. Much of this activity will fall under the permitted development rights granted to statutory undertakers.

In recent years, telecommunications has been the focus for a number of national groups and **13.52** campaigns, many of which provide information and advice to people concerned about development. CPRE have produced *Telecommunications Development* (2004) available from www.cpre.org.uk. There is also Mast Action UK and Planning Sanity, both of which provide support and advice via the Internet.

Planning policy on telecommunications

Government planning policy on mobile phone masts is contained in PPG 8: *Telecom-* **13.53** *munications* (2001). This gives guidance to local planning authorities (LPAs) on what they should take into account as they prepare their development plans and documents and what may be regarded as material to decisions in individual applications for planning permission, prior approval, and appeals. PPG 8 is in two parts:

(1) the planning policy itself; and
(2) guidance on the policy, the prior approval procedure, and on technical developments within the telecommunications industry.

PPG 8 explains some points of general policy such as: **13.54**

para 4   while LPAs are encouraged to respond positively to telecommunications develop- ment proposals, they should take account of the advice on the protection of urban and rural areas in other guidance notes;

para 5   material considerations include the significance of the proposed development as part of a national network. In making an application for planning permission or prior approval, operators may be expected to provide evidence regarding the need for the proposed development; and

para 6   LPAs should not seek to prevent competition between different operators and should not question the need for the telecommunications system that the proposed development is to support.

Applying for planning permission

13.55   The basic principle with all development is s 57 of the TCPA 1990, i.e. that planning permission is required for the carrying out of any development of land. As such, a proposal to develop a mobile phone mast will require planning permission determined by the LPA following the submission of a planning application. However, certain development, such as the smallest phone antennas, may not constitute development because it is so minor or because it does not materially affect the external appearance of the building on which it is to be installed. If so, it falls outside the land use planning regime. Other development is automatically granted if it falls within development defined as permitted development under the TCP (General Permitted Development) Order 1995, as variously amended (SI 1995/418) (GPDO 1995). This is considered below.

13.56   If, however, the proposed mast does not fall within the minor development category or permitted development, the determination of the application will be subject to the general principles of publicity and entitlement of third parties to make representations, the right to know the reasons of a decision, and the applicant's right of appeal to the Secretary of State (in practice, the Planning Inspectorate) against a determination, a failure to determine an application, or certain conditions that have been applied to the grant of permission. Third parties are not entitled to appeal, although they may challenge decisions by way of a claim for judicial review.

Permitted development for certain mobile phone masts

13.57   Schedule 2, Pt 24 of the GPDO 1995 enables certain mobile phone masts to be granted planning permission automatically for:

> Development by or on behalf of a telecommunications code system operator for the purpose of the operator's telecommunications system in, on, over or under land controlled by that operator or in accordance with his licence.

13.58   Part 24 then provides details of telecommunications development that is not permitted, including, among others, under para A.1(a) if the installation or apparatus (other than on a building or other structure), excluding any antenna, would exceed a height of 15 metres above ground, and under para A(1)(i) in the case of development on any Art 1(5) land or any land that is, or is within, a site of special scientific interest.

Prior approval procedures relating to permitted development rights

13.59   Under para 2(4)(a) of Pt 24 of the GPDO 1995, certain development permitted for telecommunications masts is conditional upon the operator securing prior approval from the LPA. The conditions are contained in para A.3 and enable the LPA to consider, within 56 days, the siting and appearance of the proposed development. Guidance on the operation of the prior approval procedure is contained in Annex 1 of PPG 8, which notes that an application for prior approval is neither a notification nor an application for permission. It adds that:

> Where permission is granted under Pt 24 subject to a condition that a prior approval application to the LPA is required, failure to comply in full with that condition will mean that the development is not authorised under the GPDO, and may be subject to enforcement action by the LPA.

The public consultation requirements for the LPA under the 56-day prior approval procedure **13.60** are the same requirements as for development requiring applications for planning permission, including that LPAs should take into account any relevant representations received in determining whether to give or refuse approval for a proposed development. Annex 1 of PPG 8 advises that an LPA may wish to discuss with the developer possible modifications to the proposed development to mitigate the concerns raised by particular consultees. If an LPA fails to provide a decision within 56 days then the mast may be erected.

Withdrawal of permitted development rights

Article 4(1) of the GPDO 1995 enables the LPA, in certain circumstances, to disapply the **13.61** permitted development rights under Art 3. Paragraph 46 of PPG 8 provides that, in terms of rights under Pt 24:

> permitted development rights should not be withdrawn unless there is a real and specific threat
> to the locality in which the development is to take place. . . . But where a particular rural or
> urban location seems likely to attract obtrusive or inappropriate telecommunications develop-
> ment which would seriously threaten amenity, the Secretary of State will give sympathetic
> consideration to directions submitted for approval.

Health considerations in determining planning applications

In *R (Nunn) v First Secretary of State & ors* [2005] EWCA Civ 101, the local authority failed **13.62** to serve notice on the developer T-Mobile refusing prior approval for the erection of a mobile phone mast within the 56-day time limit under Pt 24 of the GPDO 1995 (as amended). This meant that planning permission was, in effect, granted. The authority issued an enforcement notice after T-Mobile erected the mast and the Planning Inspector allowed the appeal against the enforcement notice. The claimant challenged the Inspector's decision on the basis that it had breached her Art 6 right under the European Convention on Human Rights, the right to be heard by an independent and impartial tribunal. The Court of Appeal held that Dr Nunn's rights had been infringed but that her only remedy lay in a claim for damages against the local authority and the developer was entitled to keep the mast.

PPG 8 notes, at paras 29 to 31, that health considerations and public concern can in **13.63** principle be a material consideration in determining applications for planning permission and approval, although whether such matters are material in a particular case is ultimately a matter for the courts. It is for the decision-maker to determine what weight to attach to such considerations in any particular case.

In *Trevett v Secretary of State & ors* [2002] EWHC 2696 Admin the High Court upheld an **13.64** Inspector's decision to grant planning permission for three masts. The Inspector had properly taken into account the policy set out in PPG8: *Telecommunications* and because the proposal complied with guidelines for exposure to electro-magnetic fields it was unnecessary for the LPA to consider the health effects further. However, in the light of *Skelt v First Secretary of State & ors* [2003] No. CO/2466/2003 in which the Government conceded the claim by consent, telecommunications operators are now required to carry out a more detailed appraisal of estimated radiation levels from a proposed mast.

Perception or fear of health impacts

13.65 In *Newport CBC v Secretary of State for Wales & anor* [1997] EWCA Civ 1894 the Court of Appeal held that fear or perception of adverse health effects of a proposal may be a material planning consideration. Aldous LJ noted that:

> A planning authority may properly take into account the perceived fears of the public when deciding whether proposed developments would affect the amenity of an area ... perceived fears of the public are a planning factor which can amount (perhaps rarely) to a good reason for refusal of planning permission ... even though the factual basis for that fear has no scientific or logical reason.

Health and Safety legislation

13.66 Operators have obligations under the Health and Safety at Work etc. Act 1974 and the Management of Health and Safety at Work Regulations 1999 (SI 1999/3242) under which they must assess any risk to health and safety that may arise, including the risk from exposure to electro-magnetic fields. PPG 8 recognizes the requirements under the health and safety regime but notes that it is not for the LPA to duplicate health and safety controls through the planning system. HSE do not need to be consulted on individual planning applications except where required under Art 10 of the TCP (General Development Procedure) Order 1995 (SI 1995/419).

Alternative sites, sharing, and mast design

13.67 As part of the information to be supplied by the developer in support of a planning application (under reg 3 of the TCP (Applications) Regulations 1988 (SI 1988/1812)), para 74 of PPG 8 advises that the LPA should ensure that it has before them all the relevant planning information, including details of any related mast proposals and of how the proposal is linked to the network, to enable applications to be properly considered. Other aspects of mast development include:

- *Schools*. PPG 8 advises that it is important that the operator discusses the proposal with the school before submitting an application. In *Phillips v First Secretary of State* [2003] EWHC 2415 the High Court quashed a permission granted to develop a mast close to a school. The court held that where there were two similar mast sites, but one was a sensitive location such as a school, then this may be adequate grounds to refuse the application.
- *Environmental considerations*. Paragraph 64 of PPG 8 provides that high priority should be given to protecting high quality landscapes and quality in urban areas and the need to safeguard areas of particular environmental importance.
- *Mast and site sharing*. To limit intrusion the Government attaches considerable importance to keeping the numbers of masts to a minimum and, in para 66 of PPG 8, the sharing of masts and sites is strongly encouraged.
- *Siting and design*. Paragraph 75 notes that in some cases LPAs may conclude that prior approval or planning permission ought to be refused because of siting or appearance, but that they should seek to understand the constraints the operator faces, e.g. whether there are technical limitations or if there is a legal duty to provide a service.

Use of land under the Communications Act 2003

Under the Communications Act 2003, an operator can, in certain circumstances, apply to **13.68** the county court for an order that requires a landowner to allow an operator to develop a mast on their land. This helps ensure that appropriate land is made available for operators to provide effective coverage. However, the power under the Act does not place any obligation on an LPA considering a planning application for a mast. In *St-Leger-Davey & James Harrison v First Secretary of State* [2004] EWCA Civ 1612 the Court of Appeal dismissed an appeal following earlier challenges to quash a Planning Inspector's decision to grant the defendant permission to erect a monopole and equipment cabin. The appellants lived and attended a school about 300 metres from the mast. The claim focused on whether the Inspector took account of and correctly considered the effect of the power granted by the code contained in the Telecommunications Act 1984 under which rights and obligations relate to operators such as the interested party in this case, Orange. The court held that when an LPA considers an application for planning permission to develop a mobile phone mast it does not require that authority to conduct an analysis of how a county court is likely to react to an application for an order on sites other than the site that is the subject of the planning application.

KEY DOCUMENTS AND MATERIALS

Nuclear Installations Act 1965
Radioactive Substances Act 1993
Town and Country Planning (General Permitted Development) Order 1995, as amended
    (SI 1995/418)
Communications Act 2003

CPRE (2004). *Telecommunications Development*
NRPB (2000). *Stewart Report on Mobile Phones and Health*. NRPB: Oxford
PPG 8: *Telecommunications* (2001)

International Commission on Radiological Protection: www.icrp.org
National Radiological Protection Board: www.nrpb.org
Mast Action UK: national campaign for the sensible siting of masts: www.mastaction.co.uk

14

WASTE

A INTRODUCTION

14.01 Dealing with waste cuts across many of the other environmental areas covered in this book. For example, many of the permits issued under the Pollution Prevention and Control (PPC) regime will cover the operation of landfill sites and incinerators. While the management and control of waste as an environmental concern is covered predominantly in this chapter it is also relevant to other areas such as air, contaminated land, human health, PPC, and water (Chapters 3, 5, 7, 11, and 15 respectively).

The problem with waste

14.02 The problem of waste is not new. The accumulation of refuse in medieval towns and cities encouraged vermin and, in turn, disease. The total waste produced in the UK is about 450 million tonnes per year. Around 8% is municipal waste, which includes household waste, and 20% is from agriculture. Figures from Defra's online digest of environmental statistics state that the largest single source of waste is from mining and quarrying, which generates about 27%. The remaining 45% comes from a variety of sources including; sewage sludge, dredged spoils, commercial, industrial, demolition, and construction.

14.03 Waste disposal is now one of the most acute environmental problems in the UK, made worse by annual increases in household waste. Today, every household generates, on average, over half a tonne of waste. This is partly because we are now in the absurd position that every single tonne of consumer goods or products generates around 10 tonnes of waste. The more we consume the greater the problem. Recycling of waste provides a short-term fix, but ultimately, consumption patterns will have to change and the production of waste must be cut. In the meantime, something has to be done with the waste arisings.

14.04 The vast majority of household waste is disposed of in landfill: on average only 10% is recycled and a further 5% incinerated. The present disposal situation is critical with pressure from local communities concerned about disposal of waste nearby, an increasing lack of usable landfill sites, and pressure from the EU stating that the UK must significantly reduce its level of landfill and increase its recycling rates. To comply with EU legislation, most notably the EU Directive 1999/31/EC on the landfill of waste (the Landfill Directive 1999), the UK has targets to recover 40% of municipal waste by 2005.

14.05 There has been a steady increase in the costs of disposing of waste and in the demand to create a financial incentive to find alternative, less polluting ways, of disposing or reusing waste. While this pressure may be encouraging and may be regarded as implementing the polluter pays principle it is also resulting in an increase in fly-tipping and abandonment of vehicles and other rubbish. Further, 25% of farms in England and Wales have experienced fly-tipping in the last 5 years (equivalent to around 44,000 farms). Waste also covers litter and general refuse, see Chapter 4: Anti-social behaviour, housing, and local concerns.

What is waste?

There has been much debate and considerable case law on the definition of waste. Often, **14.06** the intention is to exclude certain matter from the need to comply with the waste management regime. Section 75 of the Environmental Protection Act 1990 (EPA 1990) provides a definition, but this should not be solely relied upon; there have been amending provisions under para 88, Sch 22 of the Environment Act 1995 incorporating the EU definition of waste due to enter into force on 'a date to be appointed' for around ten years. The commonly referred to definition of waste is contained in Art 1(a) of the EU Directive 75/442/EEC on waste (the Waste Framework Directive 1975), which provides that:

> 'waste' shall mean any substance or object in the categories set out in Annex 1 which the holder discards or intends or is required to discard. The Commission . . . will draw up a list of waste belonging to the categories listed in Annex 1.

The Annex 1 categories of waste were provided by EU Directive 91/156/EEC amending **14.07** Directive 75/442/EEC on waste and include:

Q1   Production or consumption residues not otherwise specified below
Q2   Off-specification products
Q3   Products whose date for appropriate use has expired
Q4   Materials spilled, lost, or having undergone other mishap, including any materials, equipment, etc., contaminated as a result of the mishap
Q5   Materials contaminated or soiled as a result of planned actions (e.g. residues form cleaning operations, packing materials, containers, etc.)
Q6   Unusable parts (e.g. reject batteries, exhausted catalysts, etc.)
Q7   Substances that no longer perform satisfactorily (e.g. contaminated acids, contaminated solvents, exhausted tempering salts, etc.)
Q8   Residues of industrial processes (e.g. slags, still bottoms, etc.)
Q9   Residues from pollution abatement processes (e.g. scrubber sludges, baghouse dusts, spent filters, etc.)
Q10 Machining/finishing residues (e.g. lathe turnings, mill scales, etc.)
Q11 Residues from raw materials extraction and processing (e.g. mining residues, oil filed slops, etc.)
Q12 Adulterated materials (e.g. oils contaminated with PCBs, etc.)
Q13 Any materials, substances, or products whose use has been banned by law
Q14 Products for which the holder has no further use (e.g. agricultural, household, office, commercial, and shop discards, etc.)
Q15 Contaminated materials, substances, or products resulting from remedial action with respect to land
Q16 Any materials, substances, or products that are not contained in the above categories

The lists of wastes for each category required under Art 1(a) of the Waste Framework **14.08** Directive are provided by EU Decision 2000/532/EC as amended by Decision 2001/573/EC. However, not all forms of waste are covered by the Directive definition and the supporting provisions, e.g. the regulation of hazardous and radioactive waste is provided for under separate legislation and is exempt from the Waste Framework Directive. These two distinct areas are considered separately, the following sections consider waste under the Waste Framework Directive.

Judicial interpretation of the meaning of waste

14.09   The definition of waste has been contemplated by the domestic courts and the European Court of Justice (ECJ) on a number of occasions. In *Inter-Environnement Wallonie ASBL v Region Wallonie* [1998] Env LR 623 the scope of the Waste Framework Directive was considered in some detail. The applicant company 'Inter' sought to annul parts of a regulation made by the Wallonie Regional Executive. The Belgian Conseil d'Etat referred aspects of the claim to the ECJ for a preliminary ruling which held that, among other things:

- the Waste Framework Directive applied to the disposal and recovery of waste by the undertaking that produced them, at the place of production as well as specialist undertakings;
- the Directive could apply to disposal or recovery operations forming part of an industrial process even though they did not appear to constitute a danger to human health or the environment;
- it had already held that the definition of waste did not exclude substances that were capable of economic utilisation, e.g. in Case C-224/95 *Tombesi & ors* [1997] ECR 1-3561; and
- substances forming part of an industrial process may constitute waste under Art 1(a) although there must be a distinction between waste recovery and normal industrial treatment of products. However, a substance was not excluded from the definition of waste simply because it directly or indirectly formed part of an industrial process.

14.10   The Advocate-General at pp 640 to 644 approved the OECD discussion document: *Discussion Paper on Guidance for Distinguishing between Waste and Non-waste* ENV/EPOC/WMP(96)1, which set out a non-exhaustive set of questions evaluating the material in question and assists in determining whether a substance is waste or not. (See also Chapter 20: Public law, in relation to the role of the Advocate-General in the ECJ).

14.11   In *ARCO Chemie Nederland Ltd v Minister van Volkshuisvesting* [2003] Env LR 40, a case concerned with the use of by-products as fuel for the cement industry, the court held that the term 'waste' turned on the meaning of the word 'discard' and that this term must be interpreted in light of the aim of the Directive and the precautionary and preventative principles. It followed that the concept of waste could not be interpreted restrictively. The relevance of 'discard' was also considered in the *Wallonie* judgment and is considered in Chapter 20: Public law.

14.12   In *Attorney-General's Reference (No. 5 of 2000)* [2001] EWCA Crim 1077 the defendant had been prosecuted for breach of the waste duty of care under s 34(1) of the EPA 1990 while operating a rendering plant that produced a nitrogenous condensate as a by-product. The Crown Court held that the condensate was not capable of being controlled waste and the Attorney-General referred this and other points to the Court of Appeal, which held that the condensate was capable of being waste and that whether any material was waste had to depend on its qualities, not on the qualities of storage.

In *Palin Granit Oy v Vehmassalon* Case C-90/00 ECJ the court held that leftover stone from   **14.13**
quarrying was waste even though some of the stone may be reused. The court held that
consideration of by-products as non-waste:

> should be confined to situations in which the re-use of the goods, materials or raw materials is
> not a mere possibility but a certainty, without any further processing prior to re-use as an
> integral part of the production purpose.

In *Van de Walle, Texaco Belgium SA & ors* [2004] 16 ELM 4, p 263 the ECJ provided a pre-   **14.14**
liminary ruling that land contaminated by petrol spills could be regarded as waste even if
the spill was accidental. The decision could have a potentially significant impact in the
operation of the waste regime across the EU, particularly in relation to the role of clean up
and recovery of contaminated land under Pt IIA of the EPA 1990 and also whether an
occupier of contaminated land could be liable for keeping controlled waste without a
licence.

The judicial decisions have not sought to draw together the complexities of the definition of   **14.15**
waste contained in the Waste Framework Directive, instead, they have considered specific
categories or a particular substance from these. It is likely given the increasing pressures on
disposal, reuse, and recycling and the cost of carrying this out that the refinement of the
waste definition will continue.

A challenge to the EU definition of waste, on the basis that its uncertainty breached Art 7 of   **14.16**
the European Convention on Human Rights (ECHR) that there should be no punishment
without lawful authority, was dismissed in *R (Paul Rackham Ltd) v Swaffham Magistrates'
Court and the Environment Agency* [2004] 1417 (Admin). The court was not persuaded that the
meaning of waste was so vague as to contravene Art 7(1). It added that it was generally
undesirable that criminal proceedings should be held up by collateral damages noting that:

> Questions about what led the Environment Agency to bring the prosecution may arise during
> the trial, but ... it would be wrong for the trial process to be delayed. The district judge's
> decision to refuse a stay was therefore not only justifiable but was the only decision properly
> open to him.

In *Environment Agency v Armstrong Environmental Services Ltd* [2005] EWHC 633 (Admin)   **14.17**
the defendant company had been convicted of causing waste to be deposited on land
following evidence by the agency's environment protection officer that a large pile of timber
waste had been held on the land. The Crown Court allowed an appeal against conviction on
the basis that the wood was to be reduced to chips for making chipboard, bedding for
animals and for fuel. The Crown Court stated a case for appeal to the High Court. The High
Court dismissed the appeal affirming that the chipping activity for the wood was outside the
intention of the legislators and that such activity should not fall within the waste regime.

B   WASTE POLICY

Options for waste: prevent, reuse, recycle

Underpinning waste policy and law is the recognition that society is producing too much   **14.18**
waste and the problem of trying to dispose of it may be resolved by producing less. However,

countering the concern is the modern trend for packaging. Manufacturers and sellers want society to buy more goods and packaging. They are uninterested in its long-term value; in fact, the shorter the better. Ultimately, the waste problem is unlikely to be resolved effectively without addressing the root cause of the problem, i.e. over-production and excess consumption. This is recognized in the simple hierarchy of waste management of: prevention, reuse of materials, recycling, incineration, and, when all other options have been exhausted, final disposal by landfill. This is set out below.

Figure 14.1 Hierarchy of waste management

....

Prevention

Reuse

Recycle

Incineration

Landfill

....

14.19 The five methods of waste management are referred to throughout this chapter. They provide the rationale for many of the actions and decisions to use matter and to deal with waste arisings in a particular way. There are no formal definitions for each of the methods of waste control, although the following may assist:

- *Prevention*. The EU *Community Strategy for Waste Management* (COM (96) 399) provides that prevention of waste includes the promotion of clean technologies and products and the reduction of the hazardousness of waste. More simply, prevention of waste should mean avoiding generating the matter that causes the waste in the first place.
- *Reuse*. Encouraging the reuse of objects that may appear to be finished, e.g. the reuse of glass bottles or carrier bags. The unnecessary production of goods wastes energy and resources.
- *Recycling*. This can take various forms. In essence, the matter or substance remains, although it may change form (e.g. plastic continues to be plastic but it may be remoulded). For example, recycling paper will involve reducing scrap paper and card-board to a pulp and then preparing fresh sheets. With aluminium cans, the aluminium will be smelted down and new aluminium is prepared.
- *Incineration*. Burning waste is, at times, described as recycling in that the latent energy in the matter being disposed of is being released and reused. In practice, it is not an effective form of disposal. It may also release toxic substances.
- *Landfill*. Burying waste in landfill is by far the most common form of waste disposal, although landfill sites are becoming increasingly rare in the UK. There is little environ-mental benefit from landfill.

European Union policy

14.20 Waste management has been a prominent part of EU policy and law for over 30 years. The Waste Framework Directive enacted in 1975 has been amended and refined. There have also been numerous waste policy documents providing overarching principles as well as more specific guidance and advice.

The current strategic document is the *Community Strategy for Waste Management* (COM (96) **14.21**
399). This is supported by other cross-cutting policy programmes including the 6th
Environmental Action Plan (2001–2010) (6th EAP), which is one of a series of rolling
environmental action plans that aim to address contemporary environmental concerns.
The 6th EAP includes the sustainable use of natural resources and management of waste
as one of its priority areas. The objective is to ensure that consumption of renewable and
non-renewable resources does not exceed the carrying capacity of the environment. It is
also to achieve a decoupling of resource use from economic growth through significantly
improved resource efficiency, dematerialization of the economy, and waste prevention.
Waste volumes are predicted to continue rising unless remedial action is taken. Waste prevention will be a key element of an integrated product policy approach. Further measures are
needed to encourage recycling and recovery of wastes. The EU is also developing a *Thematic
strategy on the prevention and recycling of waste* to provide further guidance for Member States
on preventing waste arisings and on how to ensure waste targets are set.

UK strategy

Under s 44A of the EPA 1990, the Secretary of State is required to publish a national waste **14.22**
strategy. It has published *Waste Strategy* (2000) for England and Wales, which remains the
main policy document for England. Wales has since published *Wise about Waste: the National
Strategy for Wales* (2002), which replaces the 2000 document in relation to Wales.

Waste Strategy (2000)

A key message of the *Waste Strategy* (2000) was that in 1999, England and Wales pro- **14.23**
duced 106 million tonnes of commercial, industrial, and municipal waste; most of which
was sent to landfill. The strategy sets targets for better waste management to recover value
from:

- 45% of municipal waste by 2010, at least 30% through recycling or composting;
  and
- two-thirds of municipal waste by 2015, at least half of that through recycling and
  composting, and to go beyond this in the longer term.

The *Strategy* states that, together with guidance to planning authorities on the siting of **14.24**
facilities, it implements the requirement within the Waste Framework Directive to produce
waste management plans. The requirement for waste management plans under the Directive
is implemented under s 44A of the EPA 1990. It is also a strategy for dealing with waste
diverted from landfill in England and Wales, as required by the Landfill Directive.

In *Derbyshire Waste Ltd v Blewett* [2004] EWCA Civ 1508 the Court of Appeal had to consider **14.25**
the weight to be given to the concept of Best Practicable Environmental Option (BPEO),
contained in the *Waste Strategy* (2000). The High Court had held that planning permission
for a landfill site should only be granted if it is the BPEO for any given waste stream, the
Court of Appeal supported this decision and affirmed that some form of BPEO is required
under the strategy when determining planning applications for waste sites. It also held that
the waste objectives contained in *Waste Strategy* must be given substantial weight rather than
regarded simply as material considerations.

Wise about Waste: the National Strategy for Wales (2002)

14.26   The *Strategy* sets out how the Welsh Assembly, in partnership with local government and other stakeholders, will manage waste in Wales. The *Strategy* establishes a ten-year programme of change. It is designed to move Wales from over-reliance on landfill. It also includes tackling litter and illegal waste practices. The strategy meets the requirements of the Waste Framework Directive (i.e. covering waste from household, commercial, industrial, and agricultural premises, mines and quarries and sewage treatment operations), but does not cover radioactive wastes.

C   WASTE MANAGEMENT

Introduction

14.27   Part II of the EPA 1990 provides for a system of waste disposal for controlled and special waste. It has been amended by the Environment Act 1995 (the EA 1995). It is also expanded by secondary legislation including:

- the Controlled Waste Regulations 1992 (SI 1992/3240) (the Controlled Waste Regs 1992); and
- the Waste Management Licensing Regulations 1994 (SI 1994/1056) (the Waste Licensing Regs 1994).

14.28   Part 5 of the Clean Neighbourhoods and Environment Act 2005 (CNEA 2005) has amended a number of the provisions relating to waste including increasing maximum penalties for offences. The waste provisions will enter into force by commencement order.

14.29   The main organizations involved in waste management include:

- Defra, the Government department responsible for preparing and implementing policy and promoting legislation;
- the Environment Agency which, under s 30(1) of the EPA 1990, is the waste regulation authority in England and Wales;
- under s 30(2), waste disposal authorities including the county council, the metropolitan counties, London waste disposal authorities, and, in Wales, the county borough;
- under s 30(3), the waste collection authorities which are the district councils, London boroughs, and any county or county borough in Wales; and
- under s 30(4), a waste disposal contractor meaning a person who in the course of business collects, keeps, treats, or disposes of waste.

14.30   Under the Controlled Waste Regs 1992, controlled waste includes household, industrial, and commercial waste, although certain types of waste arising from these categories are excluded such as sewage, scrap metal, and any waste that is not Directive waste (Directive waste is any substance or object in the categories in Pt II, Sch 4 of the Waste Management Licensing Regs 1994).

14.31   Special waste is broadly defined by the Environmental Protection (Special Waste) Regulations 1996, as amended (SI 1996/972), as any waste on the European Hazardous Waste List that has one or more of 14 defined hazardous properties.

Prohibitions and obligations for controlled waste

The waste management regime under Pt II of the EPA 1990 provides for two distinct legal **14.32** requirements. It prohibits anyone from handling or dealing with controlled waste unless they have a licence to do so. It also places a duty of care on any person that is entitled to handle waste. Both requirements are underpinned by criminal sanctions.

Prohibition on unauthorized or harmful depositing, treatment, or disposal of waste

Section 33(1) of the EPA 1990 provides that, subject to exceptions, a person shall not: **14.33**

(a) deposit controlled waste, or knowingly cause or knowingly permit controlled waste to be deposited in or on any land unless a waste management licence authorising the deposit is in force and the deposit is in accordance with the licence;

(b) treat, keep or dispose of controlled waste, or knowingly cause or knowingly permit controlled waste to be treated, kept or disposed of:
  (i) in or on any land, or
  (ii) by means of any mobile plant,
  except under and in accordance with a waste management licence;

(c) treat, keep or dispose of controlled waste in a manner likely to cause pollution of the environment or harm to human health.

The exceptions referred to in s 33(1) include, under s 33(2), dealing with household waste **14.34** from a domestic property that is dealt with within the curtilage of the dwelling by or with the permission of the occupier; and under s 33(3) that s 33(1) provisions do not apply further to any regulations made by the Secretary of State.

Under s 33(6) of the EPA 1990 a person who contravenes s 33(1) or any condition of a waste **14.35** management licence commits an offence.

It is a defence under s 33(7) to prove that the person accused: **14.36**

(a) took all reasonable precautions and exercised all due diligence to avoid the commission of the offence;

(b) that he acted under instructions from his employer and neither knew or had reason to believe that his acts constituted an offence; or

(c) that the acts alleged to constitute the contravention were done in an emergency in order to avoid danger to human health where;
  (i) all steps taken were reasonably practicable in the circumstances for minimising pollution and harm to human health, and
  (ii) particulars of the acts were furnished to the Environment Agency as soon as reasonably practicable after they were done.

A person who commits an offence under s 33 shall be liable on summary conviction to a **14.37** maximum fine of £20,000 and/or six months' imprisonment, and to an unlimited fine and/ or two years' imprisonment for conviction on indictment. If the offence relates to special waste the maximum penalty on indictment increases to an unlimited fine and/or five years' imprisonment. Section 33 offences are one of the most common forms of environmental crime. By way of example, in *R v Panther Tyres Ltd* [2003] the defendant was convicted of breaching s 33 of the EPA 1990 by storing over 5,000 scrap tyres including piles of burnt tyres without waste management licence. The defendant company was fined £19,000 on summary conviction. In *R v North Britte Metal Company Ltd* (2005) Env Times (website

27.4.05) magistrates ordered the scrap metal company and its director to pay £19,000 in fines plus £10,000 costs for operating an illegal waste site without a waste management licence.

14.38   Sections 35 to 54 of the CNEA 2005 amend a number of the offence provisions relating to waste management. Section 40(1) of the Act deletes the defence under s 33(7)(b) of the EPA 1990 while s 41 increases the maximum penalties on conviction under s 33 of the EPA 1990 to a £50,000 fine and/or 12 months' imprisonment on summary conviction and an unlimited fine and five years' imprisonment for conviction on indictment. The amendments do not apply until commencement by order of the Secretary of State.

Duty of care etc. as respects waste

14.39   Section 34(1) of the EPA 1990 provides that (with the exception of an occupier of domestic property relating to household waste on the property) it shall be the duty of any person who imports, produces, carries, keeps, treats, or disposes of controlled waste or, as a broker, has control of such waste, to take all such measures applicable to him in that capacity as are reasonable in the circumstances:

(a)   to prevent any contravention by any other person of s 33;

(aa) to prevent any contravention by any other person of reg 9 of the Pollution Prevention and Control (England and Wales) Regulations 2000 or of a condition of a permit granted under reg 10 of those Regulations;

(b)   to prevent the escape of the waste from his control or that of any other person; and

(c)   on the transfer of the waste, to secure:

   (i)   that the transfer is only to an authorised person or to a person for authorised transport purposes; and

   (ii) that there is transferred such a written description of the waste as will enable other persons to avoid a contravention of that section [or any condition of a permit granted under reg 10 of those Regulations] and to comply with the duty under this subs as respects the escape of waste.

14.40   The authorized persons referred to in s 34(1)(c) include, among others, a waste collection authority and a holder of a waste management or disposal licence. Under s 34(5) of the EPA 1990 the Secretary of State may make regulations imposing requirements on any person who is subject to the duty imposed by subs (1). They include the Environmental Protection (Duty of Care) Regulations 1991 as amended (SI 1991/2839) and the Special Waste Regulations 1996 as variously amended (SI 1996/972).

14.41   Section 34(6) of the EPA 1990 provides that any person who fails to comply with the duty imposed by subs (1) or any regulations made by the Secretary of State shall be liable on summary conviction to a maximum fine of £5,000 and to an unlimited fine for conviction on indictment. In *R v McIntyre* [2003] 15 ELM 1 p 32 the defendant was convicted under s 34 of transferring 20,000 tyres to an unauthorized person and was fined £3,000 plus £2,500 costs.

Waste management licences

General provisions of waste licences

14.42   Section 35(1) of the EPA 1990 provides that a waste management licence is a licence granted by the Environment Agency authorizing the treatment, keeping, or disposal of any specified description of controlled waste in or on specified land, or the treatment or disposal of any specified description of controlled waste by means of specified mobile plant. A licence may be granted to the occupier of land relating to the waste activities or the operator of mobile plant. A licence shall be granted subject to appropriate terms and conditions. The conditions attached to a licence may be obligations or limitations. There may also be requirements to act in a way which the licence holder may not normally be entitled. Section 35(4) provides that:

> Conditions may require the licence holder to carry out works or do other things even though he is not entitled to carry out those works ... and any person whose consent would be required shall grant, or join in granting, the holder of the licence such rights in relation to the land as will enable the licence holder to comply with any requirements imposed upon him by the licence.

A licence may not be surrendered except in accordance with s 39 of the EPA 1990. Nor is a **14.43** licence transferable by the holder, although the Environment Agency may transfer it to another person. A licence shall cease to have effect if and to the extent that the treatment or keeping or disposal of waste authorized by the licence is authorized by a permit under s 2 of the Pollution Prevention and Control Act 1999.

The general licence provisions include an obligation to keep records. Section 35(7A) of the **14.44** EPA 1990 provides that where an entry is required to be made as to the observance of any condition of a licence, and the entry has not been made, that fact shall be admissible as evidence that the condition has not been observed. Under s 35(7B) any person who intentionally makes a false entry in any record, or with intent to deceive, forges or uses a licence in such a way, shall be guilty of an offence and is liable on summary conviction to a fine of £5,000 and to an unlimited fine and/or two years' imprisonment for conviction on indictment.

Grant of licences

Section 36 of the EPA 1990 provides that an application for a waste management licence is **14.45** made to the Environment Agency on the prescribed form with such supporting information as required and the fee prescribed by the charging scheme. The Agency may refuse to consider the application if insufficient information is provided. Also it must not issue a licence unless planning permission or an established use certificate is in force. A licence must also not be issued unless the Agency has consulted with the local planning authority (LPA), the Health and Safety Executive (HSE), and, if appropriate, a nature conservancy body. These statutory consultees have 28 days to make representations. Under s 36(3) the Agency must not reject an application if it is satisfied that the applicant is a fit and proper person, unless rejection is necessary for the purpose of preventing:

(a) pollution to the environment;
(b) harm to human health; or
(c) serious detriment to the amenities of the locality.

Under s 36(9) of the EPA 1990, if the application has not been determined after four months **14.46** from the date the Agency received the application it may be assumed that the application has been rejected.

14.47   Section 36A of the EPA 1990 states that the Environment Agency must carry out basic consultation with any person that has an interest in land or is required to grant consent to the
licence holder under s 35(4).

Supervision of licensed activities

14.48   The Environment Agency has a duty under s 42 of the EPA 1990 to supervise waste management operations to ensure that the licensed activities do not cause pollution, harm to
human health, or become seriously detrimental to the amenities of the locality, and also to
ensure that licence conditions are complied with. An Agency officer may carry out work on
the land or in relation to plant or equipment on the land to which the licence relates. Under
s 42(5), if the Agency considers that a condition of a licence is not being complied with, or is
likely not to be complied with, then without prejudice to proceedings under s 33(6) of the
Act, the authority may serve a notice to that effect on the licence holder.

14.49   Under s 44 of the EPA 1990, a person who in purported compliance with a requirement to
furnish any information imposed under Pt II of the EPA 1990 or for the purpose of obtaining
for himself or another any grant of a licence, any modification of the conditions of a licence,
any acceptance of the surrender of a licence, or any transfer of a licence, makes a statement
that he knows to be false or misleading in a material particular, or recklessly makes any
statement that is false or misleading in a material particular, commits an offence.

Variation, suspension, revocation, and surrender of licences

14.50   The Environment Agency has power under Pt II of the EPA 1990 to vary, suspend, or revoke a
waste management licence. The licencee may also apply to vary or surrender its licence.

Variation of licence

14.51   Section 37 of the EPA 1990 provides that the Agency may, on its own initiative, modify the
conditions of a licence to any extent it considers desirable and unlikely to require unreasonable expense to the licence holder. Further, the Agency must modify licence conditions if it
believes that such action is necessary for preventing pollution, harm to human health, or
serious detriment to the amenities of the locality. If conditions are to be modified it must
serve notice on the licence holder stating the time when the modification is to take effect.
Under s 37A certain variations require consultation to take place prior to modification.

14.52   The licence holder may also apply to the Environment Agency for a variation of his licence.
The application to vary must be accompanied by a fee prescribed by the charging scheme
under s 41 of the EA 1995. If the Agency has not determined the licence variation application within two months of the date of receipt it shall be deemed to have been rejected.

Revocation and suspension of licences

14.53   The Environment Agency may suspend or revoke a waste management licence. Section 38 of
the EPA 1990 provides that if the Agency considers that the licence holder has ceased to be a
fit and proper person by being convicted of a relevant offence or that the continuation of the
licence activities would cause pollution, harm to human health, or serious detriment to local
amenities, and these circumstances cannot be avoided by modifying the conditions, the
Agency may revoke the licence under subs (3) and (4) or suspend the licence under subs (6).

Where a licence is suspended the Agency may, under s 38(9) of the EPA 1990, require the licence holder to take such measures to deal with or avert the pollution or harm as it thinks necessary. Section 38(12) requires that any revocation, suspension, or requirement during suspension must be effected by a notice served on the licence holder

Section 38(10) of the EPA 1990 provides that a person who, without reasonable excuse, fails **14.54** to comply with any s 38(9) requirement shall be liable on summary conviction to a maximum fine of £5,000 or an unlimited fine and/or two years' imprisonment for conviction on indictment. However, if the waste is special waste s 38(11) provides that the maximum penalty increases on summary conviction to a £5,000 fine and/or six months' imprisonment or an unlimited fine and/or five years' imprisonment for conviction on indictment.

Surrender and transfer of licences

A waste management licence may be surrendered by the licence holder, but only if the **14.55** Environment Agency accepts the surrender. This is required because the licence is likely to contain obligations for clean up and long-term maintenance of any waste site. Section 39 of the EPA 1990 provides that an application to surrender a licence must be made to the Agency. If it is satisfied that the condition of the land is unlikely to cause pollution or harm to human health, it shall accept the surrender. Where surrender is accepted, it shall issue a certificate of completion.

Under s 40 of the EPA 1990, a licence holder may apply to the Environment Agency for **14.56** the transfer of a waste management licence to another person. If, on such an application, the Agency is satisfied that the proposed transferee is a fit and proper person then it shall affect the licence transfer. If after two months of receiving the application, the Agency has not made a determination, then it shall be deemed to have rejected the application.

An appeal renders any modification or revocation of a licence ineffective until the appeal is **14.57** dismissed or withdrawn. However, an appeal has no effect on a suspension and it remains in place during the appeal process.

Appeals

Appeal against magistrates' court decisions

Section 73(1) of the EPA 1990 provides that an appeal against any decision of a magistrates' **14.58** court e.g. against conviction of a s 33 EPA 1990 offence, shall lie to the Crown Court at the instance of any party, see Chapter 19: Criminal law practice and procedure.

Appeal against variation etc. of licences

There is a right of appeal against most of the waste management licence decisions. Section **14.59** 43(1) of the EPA 1990 provides that, except in the case of a direction by the Secretary of State, a licence holder or applicant (as the case may be) may appeal against:

(a)   an application for a licence or a modification of the conditions of a licence if rejected;
(b)   a licence granted subject to conditions;
(c)   the modification of licence conditions;
(d)   suspension of a licence;

(e) revocation of a licence;

(f) rejection of an application to surrender a licence; or

(g) rejection of an application to transfer a licence.

14.60 In the cases of (a), (c), (f), and (g) above, the applicant may appeal against deemed refusal if no decision has been made by the Agency within the relevant time period under the relevant sections.

14.61 The Secretary of State has delegated the appeal functions to the Planning Inspectorate. Guidance on making an appeal is available from the Planning Inspectorate website: www.planning-inspectorate.gov.uk. The guidance explains that an appeal can be made via written representations, informal hearing, or public inquiry and is dealt with in the spirit of the Town and Country Planning Procedure Regulations, see Chapter 8: Land use planning. An appeal must be made within six months of the date of the decision (or six months from the date a decision should have been made) and should be sent to the Planning Inspectorate. There is no charge for lodging an appeal but the following must be provided.

(a) written notice of appeal (the completed and signed appeal form);

(b) a statement of the grounds of appeal, which should explain why the appeal is being made describing those aspects of the decision that are sought to be changed and how that change should be effected;

(c) a copy of the relevant application and supporting documents;

(d) a copy of the waste management licence (if any);

(e) any relevant decision, notice, planning permission/established use/lawful use certificate, any other documents that are the subject matter of the appeal, and any other correspondence between the parties; and

(f) a statement indicating whether the appeal is to be dealt with by the written representation procedure or be heard by an Inspector. A hearing or inquiry will be held if the appellant or the Agency requests this or if the Inspector or the Secretary of State decides to hold one.

Special waste and non-controlled waste

14.62 Under s 62 of the EPA 1990, the Secretary of State may make regulations for any controlled waste that may be so dangerous or difficult to treat, keep, or dispose of that special provision is required. The Special Waste Regulations 1996 as variously amended (SI 1996/972) (Special Waste Regs 1996) transpose the requirements of the EU Directive 91/689/EEC on Hazardous Waste, which sets out requirements for the controlled management of hazardous (special) waste. The Regulations set out procedures to be followed when disposing of, carrying, and receiving hazardous waste. Special waste is defined as any controlled waste to which a six-digit code is assigned in the Pt 1, Sch 2 list in the Regulations (this reproduces the list of hazardous waste annexed to Council Decision 94/904/EC) and which displays any of the properties specified in Pt II of that Schedule.

Offences under the Special Waste Regulations 1996

14.63 Under reg 18(1) of the Special Waste Regs 1996 it is an offence for a person (other than a member, officer, or employee of an Agency who is acting as authorized by that Agency) to fail to comply with any of the Regulations insofar as that provision imposes any obligation or requirement upon him.

It shall be a defence for a person charged with an offence under reg 18(1) to prove that he **14.64** was not reasonably able to comply with the provision in question by reason of an emergency or grave danger and that he took all steps as were reasonably practicable in the circumstances for minimizing any threat to the public or the environment and ensuring that the provision in question was complied with as soon as reasonably practicable after the event.

Regulation 18(3) provides that a person who, in purported compliance with a require- **14.65** ment imposed by or under any of the regulations to furnish any information, makes a statement, which he knows to be false or misleading in a material particular, or recklessly makes any statement that is false or misleading in a material particular, commits an offence.

Under reg 18(4) a person who intentionally makes a false entry in any record or register **14.66** required to be kept by virtue of any of the foregoing provisions of these Regulations commits an offence. Under regs 18(5) and (6), the provisions relating to offences due to the fault of another person and liability of company managers and directors apply to the Special Waste Regs, see Chapter 19: Criminal law practice and procedure.

Publicity

The Environment Agency is required under s 64(1) of the EPA 1990 to maintain a register **14.67** containing particulars relating to waste management licences including:

- applications for licences;
- modifications, revocation, or suspension of licences, and any appeals relating to these;
- convictions of licence holders;
- directions given by the Secretary of State;
- matters relating to the treatment, keeping, or disposal of waste in the Agency's area or any pollution that may have arisen; and
- any other document or information required to be kept under any provision of the EPA 1990.

Each waste collection authority must maintain a register containing the information con- **14.68** tained in s 64(1) as it relates to the treatment, keeping, or disposal of controlled waste in the area. Certain information may be excluded from the register on the grounds of national security under s 65(1) or for purposes of confidentiality under s 66.

Guidance and revised Special Waste Regulations

Defra has produced a series of guidance documents on waste management including: **14.69**

- *Applying for a Waste Management Licence* (2000)
- *Waste and your duty of care* (2003)
- *Waste Management Paper Nos 4* and *4a* (rev. 2000)

- *Guidance for Amendments to Special Waste Regulations* (2001)
- *Hazardous Waste Regulations — Interim Guidance on Premises Notification* (2005)

Revision of the Special Waste Regulations

14.70   In 2002, changes to the EU Hazardous Waste List were made and incorporated into the European Waste Catalogue. The Special Waste Regs 1996 must take account of these changes. In particular, the revised EU list classifies more waste as hazardous. The proposed changes to the Regulations include, among other things:

- that the term 'special waste' should be replaced by 'hazardous waste' as defined in the Hazardous Waste Directive and the revised European Waste Catalogue;
- a requirement that the Environment Agency inspects hazardous waste producers, and in particular the sites where hazardous waste is produced, which should help to improve the 'cradle to grave' audit control of hazardous waste as required by the Directive;
- that all but the lowest risk sites where hazardous waste is produced be notified to the Environment Agency;
- that revised regulations include more specific offences and fixed penalty notices would be issued for more minor offences;
- that variable fees should be implemented, based on the different costs to the Agency of processing notifications and consignee returns made by different methods; and
- that there is an increased focus by the Environment Agency on compliance, enforcement activities, and advice to businesses.

Civil liability under Part II

14.71   Sections 73(6) to (9) of the EPA 1990 give rise to civil liability for damage caused by waste deposited on land. Under s 73(6) where any damage, including death, injury, disease, or any impairment of physical or mental conditions, is caused by waste that has been deposited in or on land, any person who deposited it, or knowingly caused or knowingly permitted it to be deposited, committed an offence under s 33(1) (prohibition relating to controlled waste) or s 63(2) (an offence of depositing waste that would be special waste, if it fell within the definition of controlled waste) is liable for the damage. An exception is where the damage is due to the fault of the person who suffered it or it was suffered by a person who voluntarily accepted the risk of the damage being caused. The defences contained in s 33(7) of the Act may also be proved by way of defence to a civil action.

Transport of waste

14.72   In addition to the controls under Part II of the EPA 1990, the carriers of controlled waste must be registered with the Environment Agency in accordance with the provisions of the Control of Pollution (Amendment) Act 1989 (CPAA 1989). Section 1(1) of the Act provides that it shall be an offence for any person who is not a registered carrier of controlled waste, in the course of any business of his or otherwise with a view to profit, to transport any controlled waste to or from any place in Great Britain. There are certain defences contained in the Act, e.g., under s 1(2) it is not an offence if the transportation of the waste is between different places within the same premises. Under s 1(5) of the CPAA 1989, a person guilty of an offence is liable to a maximum fine of £5,000 on summary conviction.

An application for registration is made to the Environment Agency under the Waste **14.73** (Registration of Carriers and Seizure of Vehicles) Regulations 1991 (SI 1991/1624) as variously amended (Waste Carriers Regs 1991). Under these regulations the Environment Agency is required to maintain a register of registered carriers. Under s 3 of the CPAA 1989, the Agency can only refuse to grant an application for registration if there has been contravention of the requirements of the Waste Carriers Regs 1991 or if the applicant or another relevant person has been convicted of a prescribed offence and, in the opinion of the Agency, it is undesirable for the applicant to be authorized to transport controlled waste. The applicant may appeal against the Agency's failure to determine an application within two months or its decision on the application. Regulation 16 of the Waste Carriers Regs 1991 provides that the time limit for bringing an appeal is 28 days.

Section 35 to 39 of the CNEA 2005 has amended the waste transport provision of the CPAA **14.74** 1989, including deleting the defence under para 1(4)(c) of acting under instructions of an employer. It has also increased the enforcement powers of the Agency adding the powers of stop and search to s 5 of the CPAA 1989 and the power to seize vehicles. The new provisions will enter into force by commencement order on a date to be appointed.

D OPTIONS FOR WASTE DISPOSAL

Collection, disposal, and treatment of controlled waste

Section 45 of the EPA 1990 provides that it shall be the duty of each waste collection **14.75** authority to arrange for the collection of household waste in its area (except waste situated at a place that in the opinion of the authority is so isolated or inaccessible that the cost of collecting it would be unreasonably high) and as to which the authority is satisfied that adequate arrangements for its disposal have been or can reasonably be expected to be made by a person who controls the waste. Further, the authority must, if requested by the occupier of premises in its area to collect any commercial waste from the premises, arrange for the collection of the waste. Under s 48, the waste collection authorities are under a duty to deliver for disposal all waste that is collected by the authority to such places as the waste disposal authority for its area directs.

Under s 49 of the EPA 1990, each waste collection authority must prepare and implement a **14.76** waste recycling strategy. There are further powers under s 55 conferred upon collection authorities to carry out recycling, e.g. under s 55(3) a waste collection authority may buy or otherwise acquire waste with a view to recycling it.

Recycling and recovery

Recycling waste is generally preferable to landfill and incineration, although the environ- **14.77** mental benefit and advantage has to be considered by taking into account all aspects of the production, consumption, and disposal process. For instance, while recycling used cardboard may prevent it from being disposed of in landfill or incinerated, the energy used in the collection and reproduction of the new cardboard should be taken into account. If the recycling process uses too much energy or water and generates another toxic waste material, then it may be more appropriate to apply some other disposal method to the cardboard waste such as composting. In contrast, producing aluminium from recycled materials saves 95% of the energy needed to make aluminium from virgin materials, and recycling steel saves up to 75% of energy consumption. The Environment Agency notes that recycling metal in the UK is high because of its economic value and that of the 5.3 billion aluminium cans consumed in the UK in 2001, 42% were recycled.

Producer responsibility for packaging

14.78 One emanation of the polluter pays principle are the regulations that place the onus of packaging recovery and recycling onto the producer; the Producer Responsibility Obliga- tions (Packaging Waste) Regulations 1997 (SI 1997/648) as amended (the PROPW Regs 1997). Regulation 2 sets out a number of definitions. 'Packaging materials' means materials used in the manufacture of packaging and includes raw materials and processed materials prior to their conversion into packaging. Recovery is defined by reference to Annex IIB of the Waste Framework Directive and lists recovery operations as they occur in practice. It notes that waste must be recovered without endangering human health or the environment. Examples include:

R1   Used principally as a fuel or other means to generate electricity
R2   Solvent reclamation/regeneration
R6   Regeneration of acids or bases
R9   Oil re-refining or other reuses of oil

14.79 Under reg 2, recycling is defined as: 'reprocessing in a production process of the waste materials for the original purpose or for other purposes including organic recycling but excluding energy recovery.'

Level of obligation

14.80 The PROPW Regs 1997 place an obligation on organizations with a turnover of £1 million and more and that handle 50 tonnes of packaging a year to recover and recycle a percentage of their packaging waste. The level of recovery/recycling is set out in the schedules to the regulations and according to the class of supply (Sch 1) and the type of organization. For example, under para 3(1) of Sch 2, the following type of producers must recover/recycle the corresponding percentages of waste:

(a) manufacturer	6%
(b) convertor (a person who modifies packaging materials)	9%
(c) packer/filler	37%
(d) seller	48%
(e) secondary provider	85%

14.81 Paragraph 3(2) of Sch 2 also provides that importers are responsible for the equivalent per- centage levels of recovery/recycling according to what stage the product they import enters the production cycle. This could be as much as 100% of the obligation if the manufacturer's, converter's, packer's, and seller's obligations are aggregated.

Level of recovery and recycling

The level of recovery/recycling has steadily increased over recent years to comply with EU **14.82**
targets. The increases have been incorporated into the PROPW Regs 1997 by amending
regulations. EU Directive 2004/12/EC provides the latest targets, which include:

• recovery of all packaging waste	65%	rising to 70% by 2008
• glass recycling	49%	rising to 71% by 2008
• aluminium recycling	26%	rising to 35.5% by 2008

Details of recycling rates and new targets are provided by Defra at www.defra.gov.uk. **14.83**

Operation of the packaging waste obligations

Under Pt III of the PROPW Regs 1997, a relevant producer is required to be registered with **14.84**
the Environment Agency. An application for producer registration should be in writing and
follow the requirements of regs 6 and 7. There is a registration fee. The Agency can refuse or
cancel a registration and, if so, the company is in breach of the Regulations. Producers can
comply with the packaging obligations in person or under regs 12 to 17 join a registration
scheme, whereby a collective scheme secures compliance with the packaging obligations
on behalf of its members who pay a subscription to be part of the scheme. In both cases,
the Environment Agency requires estimates of the packaging handled, certificates of compliance, and returns. Part IV provides a right of appeal against refusal or cancellation of a
registration scheme.

Environment Agency powers and duties

The Environment Agency must monitor compliance with the Regulations and the registra- **14.85**
tion by producers. Under reg 26 it must also maintain a public register of registered
producers and schemes. The Agency has powers of entry and inspection to assist it in carrying out its functions under the PROPW Regs 1997. Regulation 28 refers to the powers granted
under s 108 of the EA 1995. Defra has published *A User's Guide to the Packaging Regulations*
(2/e, 2003).

Enforcement and penalties

Regulation 34 of the PROPW Regs 1997 provides that: **14.86**

(1) & (2) a producer who contravenes his registration obligations under reg 3(5) is guilty of
an offence;
(3) a person who either furnishes a certificate of compliance under reg 23 or fails to
furnish any information knowingly or recklessly giving false or misleading information in a material particular; or fails, without reasonable excuse, to maintain a
record or furnish any return, is guilty of an offence; and
(4) a person who intentionally delays or obstructs an Environment Agency officer or
authorized person is guilty of an offence.

A person guilty of an offence under paras 1 to 4 above shall be liable on summary conviction **14.87**
to a fine not exceeding £5,000 and to an unlimited fine for conviction on indictment. There
have been a number of prosecutions by the Agency under the PROPW Regs 1997. In *R v Grove*

International (UK) Ltd (2003) Env Times Vol 9.3 p 32 the defendant was convicted of avoiding almost £10,000 in waste handling costs by not complying with the waste packaging regulations. It was fined £9,000 plus costs of £667. In *R v Stationery Box Ltd* (2002) (unreported but summarised in Env Action) the defendant failed to comply with PROPW Regs 1997, handling 242 tonnes of packaging waste during 2001. It had saved £7,600 by non-compliance and was fined £36,000 plus £1,000 costs. In *R v Go Foods Ltd* [2003] Env Times Vol 9.2 p 31 the defendant was found to have handled packaging of 118 tones during 2001 and had saved itself £1,967 by not registering under the PROPW Regs 1997. It was fined £6,000 plus £600 costs.

End of life vehicles

14.88   There are over 30 million motor vehicles in use in the UK. The average lifespan of a vehicle is about 13 years and approximately 2 million vehicles, cars, and vans are no longer used through old age or crashes. The problem of disposal of cars has become acute with many car parts being either toxic or unrecoverable; although up to 98% of the metal in cars is recycled by the vehicle shredding industry. However, less steel is being used in vehicle manufacturing and so a significant proportion of waste from vehicles (over 30%) is ending up in landfill or being incinerated. The End of Life Vehicles Regulations 2003 (SI 2003/2635), which partially implement EU Directive 2000/53/EC on end-of-life vehicles, aim to reduce the level of non-recoverable materials.

Design and information requirements

14.89   Part III of the Regulations sets design requirements for new vehicles sold after November 2003. For instance, reg 6 provides that a producer shall ensure that materials and components of vehicles put on the market do not contain lead, mercury, cadmium, or hexavalent chromium except in the cases listed in Sch 1. Under reg 10, breach of certain regs, including reg 6, is an offence. Regulation 1 provides for liability of persons other than the principal offender and that managing officers may be charged if a company has been found guilty of an offence. Regulation 12 provides that it shall be a defence for a person charged under reg 10 to show that he took all reasonable steps and exercised all due diligence to avoid committing the offence. Under reg 11, a person guilty of an offence shall be guilty on summary conviction to a fine not exceeding £5,000 and an unlimited fine for conviction on indictment.

14.90   Part IV of the Regulations introduces information requirements whereby a producer is required to use material and component coding standards to assist the identification of those materials and components that are suitable for reuse and recovery.

Destruction of vehicles

14.91   Part V of the Regulations introduces the Certificate of Destruction (CoD). Under reg 27, when an authorized treatment facility (generally a site licence holder under Pt II of the EPA 1990) receives an end-of-life vehicle for disposal, the facility may issue a CoD. Regulation 28 prohibits the facility from charging the last owner for the certificate. Under reg 30, any person contravening regs 27 or 28 shall be guilty of an offence and shall be liable on summary conviction for a £1,000 fine.

Part VI of the Regulations prevents a treatment facility from charging the last holder or **14.92** owner of a vehicle brought for disposal providing that vehicle was put on the market after 1 July 2002 and contains the essential vehicle components of engine, transmission, coach-work, catalytic converter, and wheels. Again, it is an offence to contravene the Pt VI regulations where a defendant will on summary conviction be subject to a maximum fine of £5,000 and an unlimited fine for conviction on indictment.

Part VII of the Regulations provides that all existing site licences that enable the keeping or **14.93** treatment of waste motor vehicles it currently authorizes shall be modified to comply with the Regulations.

Waste electrical and electronic equipment

The EU has introduced two related pieces of legislation aimed at controlling the impact of **14.94** electrical and electronic equipment:

(1) Directive 2002/96/EC on waste electrical and electronic equipment (WEEE Directive); and
(2) Directive 2002/95/EC on the Restriction of the Use of Certain Hazardous Substances in Electrical and Electronic Equipment (the RoHS Directive).

The WEEE Regulations 2005 (draft)

The WEEE Directive aims to minimize the impact of electrical and electronic equipment **14.95** on the environment during its lifetime and once it becomes waste. It encourages and sets criteria for the collection, treatment, recycling, and recovery of waste electrical and electronic equipment. It makes producers responsible for financing many of the activities, while householders will be able to return waste equipment free of charge. The Directive was due to be transposed by the Waste Electrical and Electronic Equipment (Producer Responsibility) Regulations 2005 (draft) (the WEEE Regs 2005 (draft)). The Department of Trade and Industry (DTI) has produced non-statutory guidance notes on the regulations.

Distributor and producer obligations

Part III of the WEEE Regs 2005 (draft) requires distributors of electrical equipment to accept **14.96** old electronic equipment on a one-to-one basis when supplying new equipment, providing the returned equipment is of equivalent type and has fulfilled the same function as the supplied equipment. Distributors may discharge the obligation through a distributor's scheme, providing this has been registered. Part IV requires producers to provide by August 2005 at least for the financing of the collection, treatment, recovery, and environmentally sound disposal of the proportion of WEEE from private households deposited at collection facilities. Details of financing are contained in Pt VI.

Producers are being set recovery targets for certain appliances including, e.g. under reg 27 at **14.97** least 80% recovery by an average weight per appliance and at least 75% reuse and recycling of components, materials, and substances by an average weight per appliance. Producers are required to keep records for the purpose of calculating targets and to report on compliance with targets.

Enforcement of the WEEE Regulations

14.98 The Environment Agency is the regulatory authority for the WEEE Regs 2005 (draft) and they are required to monitor distributor and producer compliance under the Regulations. The Secretary of State must maintain a public register containing information relating to producer registration although this is likely to be delegated. The Environment Agency has powers of entry and inspection for the purpose of carrying out its functions.

14.99 Under reg 53 of the WEEE Regs 2005 (draft), a distributor, producer, or scheme operator who fails to comply with their obligations is guilty of an offence. There is a defence of reasonable excuse in relation to the offence of failing to furnish information. A person found guilty of an offence under the Regulations is liable on summary conviction to a maximum fine of £5,000 and an unlimited fine for conviction on indictment.

Restriction of Hazardous Substances Regulations 2005

14.100 The RoHS Directive bans new equipment containing more than agreed levels of certain chemicals from EU markets including: lead, cadmium, mercury, hexavalent chromium, polybrominated biphenyl, and polybrominated diphenyl ether flame retardants (the banned products). The Directive has been transposed by the Restriction of the Use of Certain Hazardous Substances in Electrical and Electronic Equipment Regulations 2005 (draft) (the RoHS Regulations 2005 (draft)). These are discussed in Chapter 12: Property and land rights.

Incineration of waste

14.101 Incineration is the burning of materials and substances, including waste, at very high temperatures in order to reduce those materials to ashes. There are around 7,000 incinerators in England and Wales. Of these, 12 burn municipal waste, over 60 burn chemical and clinical waste as well as sewage sludge, and ten are cement kilns or power stations co-incinerating waste. Some waste incineration is regarded as energy recovery, whereby the heat generated produces electricity. In 2002 about 8% of municipal solid waste was incinerated with energy recovery. Some of the new energy recovery plants are referred to as Co-generation (Cogen) plants, which mix waste with other fuels to produce energy to be used for local heating and power. However, as part of the national waste strategy, the Government and the National Assembly do not expect incineration with energy recovery to be considered before the opportunities for recycling and composting have been explored.

Regulating incineration

14.102 The Environment Agency is responsible for regulating all major incinerators, i.e. those that fall within the Pollution Prevention and Control (IPC/PPC) regime as Part A processes. There are around 100 of these across England and Wales. Local authorities are responsible for managing the remaining 6,900 incinerators under the Local Authority-Pollution prevention and Control (APC/LA-PPC) framework. PPC is considered further in Chapter 11: Pollution prevention and control. Specific reference to the regulation of waste incineration under the PPC regime is found in s 1.1, Pt 1, Sch 1 of the Pollution, Prevention and Control (England and Wales) Regulations 2000 as amended (SI 2000/1973) (PPC Regs 2000), which provides that a Part A(1) activity involves:

(a) Burning any fuel in an appliance with a rated thermal input of 50 megawatts or more.

(b) Burning of any of the following fuels in an appliance with a rated thermal input of 3 megawatts or more but less than 50 megawatts unless the activity is carried out as a Part A(2) or B activity:

 (i) waste oil,

 (ii) recovered oil;

 (iii) any fuel manufactured from, or comprising, any other waste.

The emphasis in s 1.1 is on combustion activities within the energy industries and covers waste as an incidental fuel that may be used in combustion. In contrast s 5.1, Pt 1, Sch 1 of the PPC Regs 2000 focuses on waste by incineration and sets out a series of activities that fall within the Part A(1), A(2), and B categories. For instance; Part A(1) activities include, among others: **14.103**

(a) The incineration of any waste chemical or waste plastic arising from the manufacture of a chemical or the manufacture of a plastic; and

(c) Unless falling within Part B, the incineration of (any other) hazardous waste in an incineration plant other than specified hazardous waste in an exempt incineration plant.

The other categories of waste regulation under PPC are considered below.

The Waste Incineration (England and Wales) Regulations 2002 (SI 2002/2980) transpose the EU Directive on the incineration of waste. These require that all existing incineration plants had applied for PPC permits by 31 March 2005. They also detail the information required for an application, particularly in relation to design, heat, and residues. The Regulations prohibit certain installations from being put into operation until a PPC permit application has been determined. They also contain offences and penalties for breach of the prohibition. **14.104**

Health concerns

There is concern that emissions from incinerators can have adverse health effects from dioxins and other gases emitted during the incineration process. The Environment Agency notes on its website that no evidence has been found of damage to human health of people living and working near to incinerators and that any risks have been greatly reduced by the substantial cuts in emissions over the last decade. It notes that evidence to date suggests that waste management has only a very small impact on health and that this far outweighs the potential impacts if waste is not managed. For example, **14.105**

• municipal solid waste by incineration accounts for less than 1% of UK emissions of dioxins, while domestic sources such as cooking and burning coal for heating account for 18% of emissions;

• less than 1% of UK emissions of nitrogen oxides come from municipal solid waste management, while 42% come from road traffic.

A report from the Committee on Carcinogencity: *Cancer Incidence Near Municipal Solid Waste Incinerators in Great Britain* (2000) considered this in some detail. Also Defra commissioned the report: *Review of Environmental and Health Effects of Waste Management: Municipal Solid Waste and Similar Wastes* (2004). **14.106**

Challenging waste policy

14.107   In *Watson v Essex CC* [2002] EWHC 669 Admin, the claimant made an application to quash Policy W7G of the Essex and Southend Waste Local Plan relating to proposals for the incineration of waste. The High Court dismissed the application on a number of grounds including that simply because a policy is difficult to apply does not mean it is unlawful and that the interests of the claimant were not substantially prejudiced by the failure to comply with the relevant requirements.

Landfill

14.108   Landfill remains by far the most common form of disposal with around 100 million tonnes of rubbish dumped in large sites and buried. It is the cheapest option of waste disposal, but this does not take into account the adverse environmental impact and that often there is a waste of valuable resources. Perhaps, more importantly, there are simply far fewer sites being made available to bury waste. The number of working landfills fell from around 3,400 in 1994 to 2,300 in 2003, although many of the sites increased in size. Because of the level of waste dumped in landfill, they are one of the most common activities controlled under the waste management regime.

14.109   About two-thirds of waste buried in landfill is biodegradable organic waste from households. This decomposes in landfill and releases methane, a potent greenhouse gas. Landfill sites have been linked to birth defects, cancers, and respiratory illnesses including asthma. Tiredness, sleepiness, and headaches have also been linked to people living near to landfill sites.

Limiting landfill

14.110   There have been legislative and financial mechanisms imposed in recent years to limit the use of landfill and encourage alternative means of disposal. EU legislation requires tough controls on landfill from Member States through the enactment of the Landfill Directive and Decision 2003/33/EC establishing criteria and procedures for the acceptance of waste at landfills. UK compliance with the Landfill Directive has been met through the enactment of primary and secondary implementation, which is outlined below.

Removing certain categories of waste from landfill

14.111   Landfill (England and Wales) Regulations 2002 (SI 2002/1559) (the Landfill Regs 2002) as amended by the Landfill (England and Wales) Regulations 2004 (SI 2004/1375). Regulation 7 of the Landfill Regs 2002 provides that the Environment Agency must classify landfills under three categories:

   (a)   hazardous waste;
   (b)   non-hazardous waste; and
   (c)   inert waste as defined.

14.112   Under reg 9 of the Landfill Regs 2002, liquid waste (except sludges), dangerous waste, some clinical and research waste, tyres, and other waste that does not meet the acceptance criteria set out in Sch 1 are banned from disposal in landfill from 16 July 2006. The Landfill Regs 2004 introduced a new waste acceptance criteria and procedure and a new Sch 1. An example of the Sch 1 criteria is that under para 1(2) waste many only be accepted at a landfill where its acceptance would not:

(a) result in unacceptable emissions to groundwater, surface water, or the surrounding environment;

(b) jeopardize environment protection systems (such as liners, leachate, and gas collection and treatment systems) at the landfill;

(c) put at risk waste stabilization processes (such as degradation or wash out) within the landfill; or

(d) endanger human health.

The Environment Agency has published a series of guidance on landfill, which is available from www.environment-agency.gov.uk. It includes a series of regulatory guidance notes (RGNs) such as: **14.113**

RGN 1   classification of sites

RGN 4   defining existing landfill sites

RGN 8   guidance for pet cemeteries and pet crematoria

RGN 17   the ban on landfilling of whole used and shredded used tyres in accordance with the requirement of the Landfill Regs 2002

Waste and Emissions Trading Act 2003

Part 1 of the Waste and Emissions Trading Act 2003 (WET Act 2003) tackles the targets set in Art 5(2) of the Landfill Directive in relation to the reduction of biodegradable municipal waste (BMW) being sent to landfill. The targets are to reduce: **14.114**

• by 2010, landfilled BMW to 75% of 1995 levels;

• by 2013, landfilled BMW to 50% of 1995 levels; and

• by 2020; landfilled BMW to 35% of 1995 levels.

These targets are currently contained in *Waste Strategy* (2000). Section 1 of the WET Act 2003 provides that the Secretary of State must specify the maximum amounts allowed by regulations. In addition to the requirements of the Landfill Directive, the Secretary of State may, under s 2, specify further targets, e.g. those relating to recovery and recycling of municipal waste contained in *Waste Strategy* (2000) including: **14.115**

• by 2005, to recover value from 40% of municipal waste and to recycle at least 25%;

• by 2010 to recover value from 45% of municipal waste and to recycle at least 30%; and

• by 2015 to recover value from 67% of municipal waste and to recycle at least 33%.

The WET Act 2003 further provides a framework for landfill allowance trading schemes, which is designed to be a cost-effective way of meeting the Art 5(2) targets by allowing WDAs to retain control over planning for the disposal of municipal waste and to trade and transfer allowances allocated by the Government with other authorities. See the Landfill Allowances and Trading Scheme Regulations 2004 and 2005 (SI 2004/3212 and 2005/880).   **14.116**

Landfill tax

Although introduced prior to the Landfill Directive, ss 39 to 71 of the Finance Act 1996 provides for a landfill tax that generates a progressive increase in the cost of disposal at landfill according to the weight of the waste being disposed. The main aim of the Act was to   **14.117** use financial incentive to discourage the use of landfill. It also begins to incorporate the polluter pays principle into waste disposal, assuming that the person disposing of the waste passes the cost of disposal on to the person who originally generated the waste. The current tax is:

- £2 per tonne for inert waste (e.g. construction waste);
- £15 per tonne for active waste.

14.118 Revenue from the landfill tax has been paid into a landfill tax trust, Entrust, which provides grants for local environment projects that are related to waste provision or reduction.

14.119 Other avenues remain open to waste collection authorities, for instance, by promoting waste reduction programmes under the well-being power contained in s 2 of the Local Government Act 2000 or by using existing powers such as s 9 of the Agriculture (Miscellaneous Provisions) Act 1954, whereby a local authority can collect kitchen and other waste in their area for use as animal feeding stuffs.

E ADDITIONAL REGULATORY WASTE CONTROL

Waste and the pollution prevention and control regime

14.120 The pollution, prevention and control regime under the EPA 1990 and the Pollution Prevention and Control Regs 1999 cover a number of waste disposal activities including landfill and incineration. Chapter 5 of Sch 1 of the PPC Regs 2000 contains the sections set out below.

s 5.1 Disposal of waste by incineration

14.121 Part A(1) processes under s 5.1 include the incineration of any waste chemical or waste plastic arising from the manufacture of a chemical or plastic; the incineration, other than incidentally in the course of burning other waste, of any waste chemical being, or comprising bromine, cadmium, chlorine, fluorine, iodine, lead, mercury, nitrogen, phosphorus, sulphur, and zinc. Also covered are certain methods of incineration of hazardous waste, municipal waste, animal remains, and the cleaning of metal chemical containers by burning out their residue. Part B processes cover smaller hazardous and non-hazardous waste plants and the cremation of human remains (see e.g. paras 14.99–14.102 and Chapter 11).

s 5.2 Disposal of waste by landfill

14.122 Section 5.2 covers the disposal of waste in a landfill receiving more than ten tonnes of waste in any day or with a total capacity of more than 25,000 tonnes, excluding disposals in landfills taking only inert waste.

s 5.3 Disposal of waste other than by incineration or landfill

14.123 There are only Part A1 processes covered by s 5.3 and these include the disposal of hazardous waste or waste oils (other than by incineration or landfill) in a facility with a capacity of more than ten tonnes per day and disposal of non-hazardous waste in a facility with a capacity of more than 50 tonnes per day.

s 5.4   Recovery of waste

Section 5.4 covers Part A.1 processes only and includes recovering oil or organic solvent by **14.124** distillation, cleaning, or regenerating carbon, charcoal, or ion exchange resins, and recovering hazardous waste in plants with a capacity of more than ten tonnes per day by various specified means providing it is not covered as part of any other Part A activity.

s 5.5   Production of fuel from waste

Section 5.5 covers making solid fuel (other than charcoal) from waste by any process involv- **14.125** ing the use of heat.

Other waste-related activities, e.g. combustion activities, may be covered in different **14.126** sections. The practice and procedure of the PPC regime is covered in detail in Chapter 11: Pollution prevention and control.

Land use planning

Planning permission is required for the development or the material change of use of land. **14.127** The deposit of waste on land will normally be regarded as a change of use. Section 55(3)(b) of the Town and Country Planning Act 1990 provides that for the avoidance of doubt:

> the deposit of refuse or waste materials on land involves a material change in its use, notwithstanding that the land is in a site already used for that purpose.

In *Bilboe v Secretary of State for the Environment* [1980] P&CR 495, a planning enforcement **14.128** notice was served on JF Bilboe for tipping unapproved material in an inert waste tip. The Court of Appeal part allowed the defendant's appeal that no enforcement action could be taken through being time-barred, but agreed that, in principle, planning permission was required for what amounted to a change of use of the land.

Many waste disposal sites will be large projects that require an environmental statement **14.129** to be submitted in support of the application. In addition reg 5 of the Landfill Regs 2002 provides that before planning permission is granted for a landfill site, the authority must take into account the matters contained in para 1(1) of Sch 2 of the Regulations including:

- the distance from the boundary of the site to residential and recreational areas, waterways, water bodies, and other agricultural or urban sites;
- the existence of groundwater, coastal water, or nature protection zones in the area;
- the geological or hydrogeological conditions in the area;
- the risk of flooding, subsidence, landslides, or avalanches on the site; and
- the protection of natural or cultural heritage in the area.

Contaminated land

Waste being disposed of on, in, or under land is likely to contaminate land to some extent. **14.130** The contaminated land regime under Pt IIA of the EPA 1990 is extensive and provides local authorities and the Environment Agency with enforcement and clean-up powers. However, the provisions do not, in general, apply to land covered by a site licence under Pt II of the EPA 1990 and if a breach of a waste management licence granted under Pt II of the EPA 1990 causes land to be contaminated, then remediation and sanctions should be pursuant to Pt II.

Also, land contamination from unlawful waste deposits should be dealt with under s 59 of the EPA 1990 (see Section E).

Radioactive waste

14.131 Radioactive waste falls outside the Pt II waste management licensing regime. Section 78 of the EPA 1990 provides that, except as provided for by regulations, nothing in Pt II applies to radioactive waste within the meaning of the Radioactive Substances Act 1993. This is considered in Chapter 13: Radiation.

Transfrontier shipment of waste

14.132 EU Regulation (EEC) 259/93 on the supervision and control of shipments of waste within, into, and out of the European Community, as amended by Regulation 120/97 (Regulation 259/93) and the Waste Framework Directive cover the transfrontier shipment of waste between EU Member States and between EU states and third countries. The Transfrontier Shipment of Waste Regulations 1994 (SI 1994/1137) set out national requirements in implementing Regulation 259/93. For example under reg 7(1) no person shall ship waste into or out of the UK unless a certificate has been issued by the Environment Agency in relation to the shipment. Also, on a request by the Environment Agency a customs officer may, under reg 10(1) detain a shipment for up to three working days.

14.133 Regulation 12 creates an offence if a person breaches a provision of Regulation 259/93. Regulation 14 provides the defence of due diligence and inability to reasonably comply with a condition on the grounds of an emergency. Penalties for breach of an offence include on summary conviction a maximum fine of £5,000 and an unlimited fine and/or two years' imprisonment for conviction on indictment.

14.134 Transfrontier movement of hazardous waste is further controlled by the UK ratification of the UN Convention on the Control of Transboundary Movements of Hazardous Wastes and their Disposal 1989 (the Basle Convention), which entered into force in 1992 and aims to protect, by strictly controlling, human health and the environment against the adverse effects that may result from the generation, transboundary movement, and management of hazardous and other wastes. Further objectives include: reducing transboundary movements of wastes to a minimum consistent with their environmentally sound and efficient management and controlling any permitted transboundary movement under the terms of the Convention; minimizing the amount of hazardous wastes generated and ensuring their environmentally sound management; and assisting developing countries in environmentally sound management of the hazardous and other wastes they generate.

F   UNLAWFUL DISPOSAL

Powers to require the removal of waste unlawfully deposited

14.135 The Environment Agency and waste collection authorities have the power to deal with controlled waste that has been unlawfully deposited (fly-tipping) within their areas. Section

59(1) of the EPA 1990 provides that if any controlled waste is deposited in or on any land in the area of the Environment Agency or waste collection authority in contravention of s 33(1) of the Act, the Agency or authority may, by serving notice, require the occupier to either:

(a) remove the waste from the land within a specified period not less than 21 days beginning with the service of the notice; and/or

(b) take within such a period specified steps with a view to eliminating or reducing the consequences of the deposit of the waste.

Appeal against s 59 notice

Section 59(2) provides that a person served with a notice under s 59(1) may appeal to the **14.136** magistrates' court within 21 days by way of summary application. If the court is satisfied that the appellant neither deposited nor knowingly caused nor knowingly permitted the deposit of the waste; or if there was a material defect in the notice, it may quash the notice. In any other case, the court shall either modify the requirement under the notice or dismiss the appeal.

Non-compliance with s 59 notice

Section 59(5) of the EPA 1990 states that if a person fails, without reasonable excuse, to **14.137** comply with a requirement imposed by s 59(1) he shall be liable on summary conviction to a fine not exceeding £5,000 and a further fine of an amount equal to £500 for each day on which the failure continues after conviction of the offence. Under s 59(6), the enforcing authority may, if the person fails to comply with the requirement under s 59(1), carry out the work that the person was required to do and may recover from him any expenses reasonably incurred in doing so.

Section 59(7) provides that, in addition to the powers to serve a notice and to carry out works **14.138** under s 59(1), an enforcing authority may remove any waste from land or take other steps to eliminate or reduce the consequences of the deposit in order to remove or prevent pollution or harm to human health.

G WASTE AND THE COMMON LAW

Common law claims for waste arise infrequently with a highly regulated system to control **14.139** and dispose of waste. Even so, there may still be some instances when a private civil law claim for unlawful disposal may be appropriate. A claim is likely to arise in nuisance, trespass and possibly negligence. These are discussed in Chapter 17: Civil law practice and procedure.

Nuisance

The most likely circumstances where a private, civil claim relating to waste will arise are in **14.140** instances of one-off escape and a nuisance claim for the unlawful interference with use or enjoyment of land. The starting point will be *Rylands v Fletcher* (1868) LR 3 HL 330, which although quite narrowly defined after the House of Lords Decision in *Transco plc v Stockport*

Metropolitan Borough Council [2003] UKHL 61 still has some limited role to play. See also *Tenant v Goldwin* (1704) 2 Ld Raym 1089 and *Johnson (t/a Johnson Brothers) v BJW Property Developments Ltd* [2002] EWHC 1131 at 47–51.

Trespass

14.141 Trespass will arise if someone deliberately disposes of waste on land owned by another. In *Kynoch Ltd v Rowlands* [1912] 1 Ch 527 the Court of Appeal dismissed an appeal against judgment for the claimants who had sought to restrain the defendant from tipping earth and rubbish upon their land and against their wall. In *Konskier v B Goodman Ltd* [1928] 1 KB 421 the claim was in negligence and trespass against the defendant building company leaving rubbish at a site that was subsequently rented to the claimants. Following heavy rain, the claimant's basement flooded due to the rubbish blocking a gully. The Court of Appeal held that the defendants were not liable in negligence, because they owed no duty to the claimants. However, in allowing the rubbish to remain beyond a reasonable time after their work had finished they were guilty of trespass.

KEY DOCUMENTS AND MATERIALS

Control of Pollution (Amendment) Act 1989
Environmental Protection Act 1990
Controlled Waste Regulations 1992 (SI 1992/3240)
Waste Management Licensing Regulations 1994 (SI 1994/1056)
The Transfrontier Shipment of Waste Regulations 1994 (SI 1994/1137)
The Special Waste Regulations 1996 (SI 1996/972)
Producer Responsibility Obligations (Packaging Waste) Regulations 1997 (SI 1997/648)
Waste Incineration (England and Wales) Regulations 2002 (SI 2002/2980)
Landfill (England and Wales) Regulations 2002 (SI 2002/1559)
End of Life Vehicles Regulations 2003 (SI 2003/2635)
Waste and Emissions Trading Act 2003
Waste Electrical and Electronic Equipment (Producer Responsibility) Regulations 2005
    (draft)
Clean Neighbourhoods and Environment Act 2005

Directive 75/442/EEC on waste
Directive 91/156/EEC amending Directive 75/442/EEC on waste
Directive 1999/31/EC on the landfill of waste
Directive 2000/53/EC on end-of-life vehicles
Directive 2002/96/EC on waste electrical and electronic equipment

Committee on Carcinogencity (2000). *Cancer Incidence Near Municipal Solid Waste Incinerators in Great Britain*
Defra (2003). *A User's Guide to the Packaging Regulations*. Defra: London
Defra (2000). *Waste Strategy*. Defra: London
National Assembly for Wales (2002). *Wise about Waste: the National Strategy for Wales*

15

WATER

A INTRODUCTION

15.01 Early water legislation included the Public Health Act 1875 and the penalty for causing water to be corrupted by gas washings and the unauthorized building over sewers. The precedent case of *Rylands v Fletcher* (1868) LR 3 HL 330 related to the escape of large quantities of water onto a neighbour's land.

Defining water

15.02 'Water' is defined in *Chambers Science and Technology Dictionary* (Chambers, 1988) as a colourless, odourless, tasteless liquid comprising the chemical elements of hydrogen and oxide. It forms a large proportion of the earth's surface and occurs in all living organisms and, besides being essential for life, it has a unique combination of solvent power, thermal capacity, chemical stability, permittivity, and abundance.

Defining a watercourse

15.03 There is frequent reference to watercourses in the law relating to water. For the purpose of the main regulatory regime, the Water Resources Act 1991 (as amended) (WRA 1991), watercourse is defined in s 221 as including, subject to exceptions:

> all rivers, streams ditches, drains, cuts, culverts, dykes, sluices, sewers, and passages through which water flows, except mains and other pipes which (a) belong to the Authority or water undertaker; or (b) are used by a water undertaker or any other person for the purpose only of providing a supply of water to any premises.

15.04 This does not cover all legislation and a different definition may arise elsewhere, e.g. under statutory nuisance.

The water cycle

15.05 To gain a greater understanding of how the various legal controls of water are brought together it is useful to outline natural water movement. The water cycle is the continuous movement of water between the land, the sea, and the atmosphere. There are some basic but important aspects of the water cycle, such as:

- *Precipitation.* Water is released from clouds by precipitation that includes rain, snow, hail, sleet, and fog.
- *Interception and surface run-off.* Following precipitation, water may collect where it falls on hard surfaces, such as roads or roofs. This is called interception. It may collect purposefully in very large quantities in reservoirs. It may also shift or flow across land causing

surface run-off, which may be in a channel, e.g. a river, or by flowing over land across a field or road.

- *Infiltration*. The process of water soaking through soil is infiltration. Following infiltration, water may percolate into rocks and reach groundwaters.
- *Groundwater* is the underground collection of water in the water table. The water table is the upper level of saturated ground, which rises during long periods of rainfall.
- *Evaporation and transpiration*. Surface water flows downhill towards the sea. Along its route and once in the sea, heat by the sun causes water to evaporate and rise into the atmosphere. Transpiration is the loss of water from plants where, again, it evaporates and returns to the atmosphere.
- *Condensation* is when the water vapour cools and turns to water droplets to form clouds. At the point that the water droplets become too heavy to be held in the atmosphere, they fall through precipitation.

Water is a valuable resource that requires protection and conservation. It can also be a source **15.06** of pollution, e.g. in cases of flooding. For the purpose of regulation and review there is a distinction between the provision of water and the protection of watercourses; between marine and coastal waters and freshwater systems. This chapter considers the main aspects of water including abstraction, water quality, pollution, flooding, and the marine environment.

B WATER POLICY

International and EU policy and law

Water policy and law is heavily influenced by international and EU law. International legis- **15.07** lation includes the Convention for the Prevention of Pollution from Ships (the MARPOL Convention) and related laws on oil pollution and protection of the seas. Many water quality standards are set by the EU. The most comprehensive piece of water legislation enacted is Directive 2000/60/EC establishing a framework for Community action in the field of water policy (the Water Framework Directive). The Directive sets out the organizational and procedural aspects of water management aiming to bring about the coordinated and sustainable management of water resources. Its primary purpose is to establish a framework for the protection of inland surface waters, transitional waters, coastal waters, and groundwater that:

- prevents further deterioration and protects and enhances the status of aquatic ecosystems;
- promotes sustainable water use based on a long-term protection of available water resources;
- aims at enhanced protection and improvement of the aquatic environment;
- ensures the progressive reduction of pollution of groundwater and prevents its further pollution; and
- contributes to mitigating the effects of floods and droughts.

The Water Framework Directive was transposed into UK law in 2003 and is being imple- **15.08** mented progressively according to a timetable approved by the EU.

National policy and law

15.09   Defra and the National Assembly for Wales (NAW) are responsible for all aspects of water policy in England and Wales, including water supply and resources and the regulatory systems for the water environment and the water industry. These include:

- drinking water quality;
- the quality of water in rivers, lakes and estuaries, coastal and marine waters;
- sewage treatment; and
- reservoir safety.

15.10   The Environment Agency manages water resources and enforces water quality standards while the Office of Water Services (Ofwat), to be superseded by the Water Service Regulation Authority, is responsible for economic regulation of the water industry. Defra and NAW coordinate policy for the coastal and marine environment, including international agreements on the North East Atlantic and the North Sea and policy on inland waterways. Both primary and secondary legislation covers areas such as water supply, sewage, flood defence, and water protection measures.

Implementing the Water Framework Directive

15.11   The *Regulatory Impact Assessment of the Water Framework Directive* (2003) carried out by Defra states that earlier EU water legislation has been integrated into the Water Framework Directive allowing the earlier Directives to be repealed in a phased approach. The legislation concerned is listed in Art 22 of the Directive. It is not intended to replace more recent pieces of legislation and it will complement the Directive 91/271/EEC on urban waste water treatment, Directive 91/676/EEC concerning the protection of waters against pollution caused by nitrates from agricultural sources (the Nitrates Directive) and Directive 96/61/EC on integrated pollution prevention and control (IPPC). Measures taken under these Directives will in many cases form an important part of the programme of measures in each river basin district.

15.12   The existing framework of primary legislation including the Environmental Protection Act 1990 (EPA 1990), the WRA 1991, the Water Industry Act 1991 (WIA 1991), and the Water Act 2003 provide many of the powers needed to implement the Water Framework Directive. For example, the WRA 1991 establishes that the discharge of polluting matter to controlled waters without permission is an offence. This enables the Environment Agency to set standards for discharges. Tighter standards for certain discharge consents might be required to meet water objectives and so this aspect of the Directive could be met through the setting of revised control measures under existing powers. Local authorities and the Agency also have duties under the EPA 1990 to secure the remediation of contaminated land where its condition is causing pollution of controlled waters such as groundwater. Another example is the Catchment Abstraction Management Strategies, which the Environment Agency now uses on a six-yearly cycle to review the sustainability of licensed water abstractions in England and Wales. These reviews, which the Agency have begun implementing, will be used to inform decisions about any need to revoke or modify licenses on sustainability grounds. This decision-making process is similar to that which will be required under river basin management plans.

The Water Environment (Water Framework Directive) (England and Wales) Regulations **15.13** 2003 (SI 2003/3242) (the Water Framework Regs 2003) implement the Water Framework Directive by establishing a series of river basin districts within England and Wales and by setting up a new strategic planning process for the purposes of managing, protecting, and improving the quality of water resources. They are the initial stage in implementing the Directive and provide a strategic base within which successive implementation steps will be taken. In some areas of water quality, most notably diffuse pollution, new regulatory powers are expected to be required to implement the provisions of the Directive.

Water Framework Directive Regulations 2003

Under reg 3 of the Water Framework Regs 2003, general responsibility for implementing the **15.14** Directive is with the Secretary of State and the NAW as the appropriate authorities and the Environment Agency. The Agency must, under regs 5 and 9, carry out detailed monitoring and analysis in relation to each river basin district and the appropriate authority must ensure that appropriate economic analysis is also carried out (reg 6). Certain waters used for the abstraction of drinking water must be identified (reg 7) and a register must be established of those waters and certain other protected areas (reg 8).

This analytical and preparatory work must then inform the preparation by the Agency **15.15** of proposals for environmental objectives and programmes of measures in relation to each river basin district (reg 10). Those objectives will translate the generic environmental objectives set out in the Directive to the particular situation in each river basin district. The preparation of such proposals must include public involvement, and proposals themselves are subject to approval by the appropriate authority.

The results of the Agency's technical work, the environmental objectives and proposals **15.16** for programmes of measures, must be brought together in the preparation of a river basin management plan for each river basin district (regs 11 to 15). The Agency must prepare draft plans after public involvement (regs 11 and 12). Those plans must contain details of the results of the prior technical and planning work that will have been done, along with the environmental objectives and programmes of measures proposed for each district. Plans are subject to approval by the appropriate authority and must be periodically reviewed (regs 13 to 15).

The Environment Agency may also prepare supplementary plans, which are not subject to **15.17** approval by the appropriate authority (reg 16). The Secretary of State, the Assembly, the Agency, and other public bodies are required to have regard to river basin management plans and to any supplementary plans in exercising their functions in relation to river basin districts (reg 17). The Regulations also make supplementary provision in respect of the publication of information, the provision of information and assistance, and the giving of guidance or directions for the purpose of giving effect to the Directive (regs 18 to 20).

C WATER SUPPLY

Despite being an apparently replaceable and abundant resource, water use is strictly con- **15.18** trolled. Securing an adequate supply of quality potable (drinkable) water for society's needs is not simple, involving substantial financial investment, energy use, and manpower. Water supply and use is regulated by the WRA 1991 with frequent reference to the WIA 1991. Water supply in the UK was privatized in 1989 and is secured by regional water undertakers acting under the WIA 1991. The Water Act 2003 has amended the WRA 1991 and WIA 1991, e.g. in relation to compensation for removal of a water abstraction licence. The Water Act 2003 is being introduced in stages and so relevant parts should be checked to see whether they are currently in force.

15.19   One of the primary water regulators is the Environment Agency. Part II of the Water Act 2003 establishes the Water Service Regulation Authority to replace the Director General of Water Services and the Consumer Council for Water. The provision of water is by statutory undertakers provided for under the WIA 1991. There are also powers and obligations in relation to water conferred upon the Secretary of State for Environment, Food and Rural Affairs, Defra, the relevant government department, and local authorities.

Duties of the Environment Agency

15.20   Section 6(1) of the Environment Act 1995 (EA 1995) provides that it shall be the duty of the Agency, to such extent as it considers desirable, generally to promote:

    (a)   the conservation and enhancement of the natural beauty and amenity of inland and coastal waters and of land associated with such waters;

    (b)   the conservation of flora and fauna which are dependent on an aquatic environment; and

    (c)   the use of such waters and land for recreational purposes;

       and it shall be the duty of the Agency, in determining what steps to take in performance of the duty imposed by para (c) to take into account the needs of persons who are chronically sick or disabled.

15.21   Under s 6(2) of the EA 1995 it is the duty of the Agency to take all action it considers necessary or expedient to conserve, redistribute, or otherwise augment water resources and to secure the proper use of those resources. Although this does not relieve a water undertaker from any obligation to develop water resources. Section 15(1) of the WRA 1991 provides that:

    It shall be the duty of the Agency, in exercising any of its powers under any enactment, to have particular regard to the duties imposed, by virtue of the provisions of Parts II to IV of the Water Industry Act 1991, on any undertaker or sewerage undertaker which appears to the Agency to be or to be likely to be affected by the exercise of the power in question.

15.22   A water undertaker is not defined under legislation although s 6 of the WIA 1991 covers the appointment of relevant undertakers and provides that they must be a limited company or a statutory undertaker or a statutory water company.

Water abstraction

15.23   Water abstraction and impounding is restricted by a licensing system under Pt II of the WRA 1991. Section 24 of the Act provides that, subject to exceptions, no person shall abstract water from any source of supply, or cause or permit any other person to do so without a licence. Under s 221(1) of the WRA 1991 abstraction includes anything where water is removed from a source of supply, whether temporarily or permanently for the purpose of being transferred to any other source of supply. Source of supply is defined as any inland waters except discrete waters such as lakes, ponds, and reservoirs. Section 25 states that no person shall construct any impounding works in any inland waters without a licence. Impound is to be understood to withhold or contain any water. Under s 25(8) impounding works includes, any dam, weir, or works where water is impounded. Exceptions to the abstraction restrictions include, under s 27, where the quantity of water taken does not exceed five cubic metres or 20 cubic metres if it is extracted with the consent of the Environment Agency under s 30. However, in certain circumstances the Agency may serve a conservation notice requiring the person to conserve water in a way specified in the notice. There are also miscellaneous rights to abstract water under s 32 of the WRA 1991.

Applying for an abstraction licence

Section 35 of the WRA 1991 provides that an application for an abstraction licence will only be considered by the Agency if made by an occupier of the land adjoining the inland waters or by someone that has a right of access to the land. The applicant must carry out certain basic publicity requirements under s 37 of the Act. **15.24**

There is an obligation on the Agency to have regard to existing rights and privileges relating to the proposed application. There is also an obligation under s 40 of the WRA 1991 to take into account physical constraints such as the river flow. When considering the application the Agency must have regard to any written representations made and the reasonable requirements of the applicant. The decision of the Agency is to grant a licence, refuse a licence, or grant a licence with conditions. Under s 41, the Secretary of State has the power to call in applications and determine a licence as he considers appropriate. **15.25**

The determination and further provisions relating to an application are made according to the Water Resources (Licences) Regulations 1965 (SI 1965/534) as amended (the Water Resources Licences Regs 1965). These include that a licence application must be determined within three months. Applications for large abstraction or impounding projects must be supported by an environmental statement prepared under the Water Resources (Environmental Impact Assessment) (England and Wales) Regulations 2003 (SI 2003/164), see Chapter 24 for environmental assessment generally. **15.26**

Appeal against a licence decision

Under s 43 of the WRA 1991, an applicant may appeal to the Secretary of State if he is dissatisfied with an Agency decision on an application for an abstraction licence or if the Agency has failed to determine the application within the three months time limit. Under reg 12 of the Water Resources Licences Regs 1965, the notice of appeal must generally be served within one month of receipt of the Agency's decision. The notice of appeal should be supported by a copy of the licence application, all relevant maps and particulars submitted to the Agency, the notice of the decision, and all relevant correspondence. **15.27**

Section 43 of the WRA 1991 covers the determination of appeals. The Secretary of State may allow or dismiss the appeal or reverse or vary any part of the decision of the Agency, whether the appeal relates to that part of the decision or not, and may deal with the application as if it had been made to him in the first instance. The appeal may be heard by an informal hearing or local inquiry. In determining the appeal the Secretary of State must take into account any **15.28** further representations received within 21 days from the date on which the copy of the notice of appeal is served on the person making the representations.

15.29 Section 43(7) of the WRA 1991 provides that the Secretary of State's decision shall be final. However, s 69(2) of the Act provides that in the case of an appeal or reference any party may within six weeks of the appeal decision question the validity of the Secretary of State's decision by an application to the High Court on the grounds that:

(a) the decision is not within the powers of the Act; or

(b) that any requirements or regulations applicable to the appeal have not been complied with.

15.30 If the High Court is satisfied that the decision was not within the powers of the Act or that the interests of the person making the application have been substantially prejudiced by a failure to comply with any relevant requirement then it may quash the decision.

Form of abstraction licence

15.31 Every licence to abstract water must state how much water is authorized to be abstracted and how quantities are to be measured. Section 48 of the WRA 1991 provides that the general effect of an abstraction or impounding licence grants a right to the holder to abstract water to the extent provided for in the licence. It adds that holding a licence provides, subject to exceptions, a defence against any action of otherwise unlawful abstraction. Under s 49 of the Act, the licence may pass with the land.

15.32 A licence holder may apply to modify the abstraction licence under s 51 of the WRA 1991. Also, a person with fishing rights may make an application for modification of an abstraction licence. Under s 57, the Environment Agency may undertake an emergency variation of an abstraction licence related to spray irrigation. There are remedies, including compensation, for the modification of a licence under s 60 of the WRA 1991.

Offences

15.33 The prohibitions on water abstraction and impounding contained in ss 24 and 25 of the WRA 1991 include that no person shall:

- abstract water from any source of supply or cause or permit any other person so to abstract any water (s 24(1));
- begin or cause or permit any other person to begin to construct or extend any well, borehole, or other work by which water may be abstracted from those strata, or install or modify machinery to abstract additional quantities of water (s 24(2)); and
- begin, or cause or permit any other person to begin, to construct or alter any impounding works in any inland waters (s 25(1));

without a licence or in excess of conditions contained in a licence.

15.34 Any person found guilty of an offence under ss 24 or 25 is liable on summary conviction to a maximum fine of £5,000 and an unlimited fine for conviction on indictment.

15.35 Section 70 of the WRA 1991 provides that the restrictions imposed under ss 24, 25, and 30 do not confer a right of civil action, affect any restriction imposed by any other enactment, or derogate from any right of action or other remedy in other proceedings.

Reservoirs

The construction and operation of reservoirs are contained in the Reservoirs Act 1975.   **15.36**
A reservoir means a reservoir for water but does not include a mine or quarry lagoon or a
canal. The Act requires, among other things, the registration, periodic inspection, and
supervision of construction of large raised reservoirs (i.e. reservoirs of over 25,000 m³
holding water above the natural level of the adjoining land). It also regulates their operation,
discontinuance, and abandonment of reservoirs.

Drought

The Environment Agency, the Secretary of State, and water undertakers are empowered to   **15.37**
take action to restrict water use during periods of water shortage. The Secretary of State may
grant ordinary and emergency drought orders under s 73 of the WRA 1991. Drought orders
may cover abstractions from and discharges into water and may allow water undertakers
to limit certain water uses. The Agency has the power to issue a drought permit, which
authorizes a water undertaker to take water from specified sources. It is permissive rather
than prohibitive. It may also temporarily restrict the use of spray irrigation licences. Under s
76 of the WIA 1991, water undertakers may, whenever there is a serious deficiency of water,
impose hosepipe bans in their area. A person who contravenes a hosepipe ban while it is in
force is guilty of an offence and is liable on summary conviction to a maximum £1,000 fine.

In *Scott-Whitehead v National Coal Board & anor* [1987] P&CR 263 the first defendant dis-   **15.38**
charged chlorine into a local watercourse during a drought. The second defendant, a
regional water authority, was held to be negligent for failing to advise the claimant farmer
that the water he abstracted downstream to irrigate his potato crop was heavily chlorinated
and therefore damaged his crop.

Maintaining and regulating water supply

Duties of the water undertakers

Part III of the WIA 1991 sets out the duties of water undertakers in supplying water. Section   **15.39**
37(1) of the Act provides that:

> It shall be the duty of every water undertaker to develop and maintain an efficient and eco-
> nomical system of water supply within its area and to ensure that all such arrangements have
> been made for (a) providing supplies of water to premises in that area and for making such
> supplies available to persons who demand them; and (b) for maintaining, improving and
> extending the water undertaker's water mains and other pipes, as are necessary for securing that
> the undertaker is and continues to be able to meet its obligations under this Part.

The undertaker's area is defined on its appointment. There are 13 water companies operating   **15.40**
in England and Wales. Most of these will be responsible for water provision and sewage;
some will only have one responsible function as a water undertaker. Examples of large water
companies are Thames Water and Anglian Water. There are further specific duties of water
undertakers contained in Ch 2, Pt III of the WIA 1991 such as, under s 37A, the preparation
and maintenance of water resources management plans (introduced by the Water Act 2003),
the provision of water mains and to make connections from the mains to premises under
ss 41 and 45 of the WIA 1991 respectively.

Local authority functions

15.41   Local authorities have obligations under the WIA 1991 in respect of water supplied to premises in their areas. Section 77(1) of the Act provides that:

> It shall be the duty of every local authority to take all such steps as they consider appropriate for keeping themselves informed about the wholesomeness and sufficiency of water supplies provided to premises in their area, including every private supply to any such premises.

15.42   Other local authority duties include, under s 77(2), complying with any direction made by the Secretary of State, to notify any water undertaker of anything to suggest that any water supply has become unwholesome or insufficient for domestic purposes, and to provide water for domestic purposes where piped supplies are insufficient or unwholesome. There are also provisions relating to water treatment, and further functions of local authorities in relation to water quality.

Quality of supplied water

15.43   Chapter 3, Pt III of the WIA 1991 covers the quality and sufficiency of water supplies. Section 67 provides that the Secretary of State may make regulations relating to standards of wholesomeness of water. The Water Supply (Water Quality) Regulations 2000, as amended (SI 2000/3184) and the Water Supply (Water Quality) Regulations 2001 (SI 2001/3911(W323)) relating to Wales (the Water Supply Regs 2000/1) are the main regulations enacted under s 67. They also implement Art 2 of EU Directive 98/83/EC to protect human health from the adverse effects of any contamination of water intended for human consumption by ensuring that it is wholesome and clean. For instance, reg 4 of the Water Supply Regs 2000/1 provides that:

(1)   Water supplied (a) for such domestic purpose as consist in or including, cooking, drinking, food preparation or washing; or (b) to premises in which food is produced, shall, subject to paras (4) and (5), be regarded as wholesome . . .;

(2)   The requirements of this paragraph are that:

    (a)   the water does not contain (i) any micro-organism (other than a parameter) or parasite; or (ii) any substance (other than a parameter) at a concentration or value which would constitute a potential danger to human health;

    (b)   that the water does not contain any substance (whether or not a parameter) at a concentration or value which, in conjunction with any other substance it contains (whether or not a parameter) would constitute a potential danger to human health;

    (c)   that the water does not contain concentrations or values of the parameters listed in Sch 1 Tables in excess of or, as the case may be, less than, the prescribed concentrations or values;

    (d)   that the water satisfies the [nitrate] formula set out.

15.44   The parameters referred to in reg 4 are specified in the Schedules to the Water Supply Regs 2000/1. The regulations also make provision for monitoring, investigation, authorization, and departures from obligations in relation to water supply.

Water supply offences

15.45   Section 70 of the WIA 1991 creates an offence of supplying water unfit for human consumption, providing that where a water undertaker supplies water by means of pipes to any premises and that water is unfit for human consumption, the undertaker shall be guilty of an offence and liable on summary conviction to a maximum fine of £5,000 and an unlimited fine and/or two years' imprisonment for conviction on indictment.

There are also criminal sanctions for wasting water during abstraction. Under s 71(1) of the   **15.46**
WIA 1991, a person is guilty of an offence if he causes or allows any underground water to run to waste from any well, borehole, or other work, or he abstracts water in excess of his reasonable requirements. Section 71(2) provides a defence for any waste that is caused following testing, cleaning, sterilizing, examining, or repairing the well, borehole, or other work. A person guilty of an offence under s 71(1) shall be liable on summary conviction to a maximum £1,000 fine. On conviction, the court may also order that the well, borehole, or other work may be sealed or order any other work that may be necessary to prevent the waste of water.

Section 72 of the WIA 1991 provides that a person is guilty of an offence if he is guilty of any   **15.47**
act or neglect whereby the water in any waterworks that is used or is likely to be used for human consumption or domestic purpose; or for manufacturing food or drink for human consumption is polluted or likely to be polluted. There is a specific defence in relation to the reasonable use of oil or tar for highway maintenance. A person guilty of an offence under s 72(1) shall be liable on summary conviction to a maximum fine of £5,000 and a further fine of up to £50 per day for each day the offence continues after conviction. There is a maximum penalty of an unlimited fine and/or two years' imprisonment for conviction on indictment.

Finally, s 73 of the WIA 1991 creates offences relating to contaminating, wasting, and mis-   **15.48**
using water intentionally or negligently by the owner or occupier of premises to which a water supply is provided by a water undertaker. This includes leaving any water fitting or pipe in need of repair or inadequately constructed. Any person found guilty for an offence under s 73 is liable on summary conviction to a maximum £1,000 fine.

Fluoridation

Fluoride is a generic term for fluorine when combined with another chemical element,   **15.49**
e.g. fluorine + calcium = calcium fluoride. The fluoride that occurs naturally at low levels in water is relatively insoluble and, in small doses, passes relatively harmlessly through the body. Fluoridation of water supply aims to artificially increase the level of fluoride in mains supplied drinking water in order to counter incidents of tooth decay. The Water (Fluoridation) Act 1985 allows health authorities to consider fluoridation. If a health authority decides in favour it makes a formal approach to the water undertaker who may then fluoridate the supply. Excess fluoridation in water is not universally popular and too much fluoride can cause fluorosis. This is a permanent condition where the effects range from barely visible white patches, to rust-coloured staining or pitting of the teeth.

Section 87 of the WIA 1991 provides that where a health authority has applied in writing to a   **15.50**
water undertaker for the water supplied in an area to be fluoridated, that undertaker may, while the application remains in force, increase the fluoride content of the water supplied in that area. However, a water undertaker has no power to fluoridate a water supply unless and until a health authority has made an application.

Under s 89(2) of the WIA 1991, any health authority that proposes to make or withdraw a   **15.51**
fluoridation application must, at least three months before implementing their proposal,

publish details of the proposal in one or more newspapers circulating within the area and give notice of the proposal to every local authority whose area falls wholly or partly within that area.

15.52 The Secretary of State may, with the consent of the Treasury, agree to indemnify any water undertaker in respect of any liability incurred by increasing the fluoride content of any water and any costs or expenses incurred in connection with any proceedings brought by any person in relation to fluoridation.

D SEWAGE

Regulating sewerage services

15.53 The provision of sewerage services and systems is carried out in England and Wales by ten water and sewerage companies known as sewerage undertakers that cover different regions. There is over 10 million tonnes of waste water collected and managed through over 350,000 kilometres of sewers. There is no formal definition of a sewerage undertaker, although s 6 of the WIA 1991 provides that a sewerage undertaker must be a limited company. The Environment Agency regulates the sewerage undertakers.

Duties of the sewerage undertakers

15.54 Part IV of the WIA 1991 sets out the regulatory regime for sewerage provision. Section 94(1) provides that it shall be the duty of every sewerage undertaker to:

(a) provide, improve, and extend such a system of public sewers (whether inside its area or elsewhere) and so to cleanse and maintain those sewers as to ensure that the area is and continues to be effectually drained; and

(b) make provision for the emptying of those sewers and such further provision (whether inside its area or elsewhere) as is necessary from time to time for effectual dealing, by means of sewage disposal works or otherwise, with the contents of those sewers.

15.55 Section 94(2) of the WIA 1991 provides that a sewerage undertaker, in carrying out its duties, must have regard to its existing and likely future obligations to allow for the discharge of trade effluent into its public sewers; and to the need to provide for the disposal of trade effluent. Under s 98 of the Act, each sewerage undertaker is under a duty to provide a public sewer to be used for the drainage for domestic purposes of premises in a particular locality in its area if the undertaker is served with a notice by persons entitled to required provision of the public sewer; these include the owner or occupier of premises in the locality, the local authority, the Commission, or development corporation for a new town, and an urban development corporation. Further, s 106 provides that any owner or occupier of premises or of a private sewer is entitled to be connected to the public sewer.

Trade effluent

15.56 The occupier of trade premises in an area may discharge any trade effluent into a public sewer providing this is with the consent of the sewerage undertaker. Section 119 of the WIA

1991 states that an application to a sewerage undertaker for a consent to discharge trade effluent into a public sewer shall be by notice served on the undertaker by the owner or occupier of the premises. The notice should state the nature or composition of the trade effluent; the maximum quantity of the trade effluent proposed to be discharged on any one day; and the highest rate at which it is proposed to discharge the trade effluent.

Certain discharges will be regarded as special category effluent. Section 120 of the WIA 1991 **15.** requires that an application for these must be referred to the Environment Agency to assess whether the discharge should be prohibited and, if not, what conditions, if any, should be imposed. If the undertaker fails to refer a special category effluent matter to the Environment Agency it shall be guilty of an offence under s 120(9) of the Act and liable on summary conviction to a maximum £5,000 fine and an unlimited fine for conviction on indictment.

The conditions of a special category consent are provided under s 121 of the WIA 1991 and **15.58** include under subs (2):

(a) the exclusion from the trade effluent of all condensing water; and
(f) the provision of testing and maintenance of meters to measure the volume and rate of discharge of any trade effluent;

Any person aggrieved by the refusal of a sewerage undertaker to provide consent may, under **15.59** ss 122 and 123 of the WIA 1991, appeal to the Director of the undertaker.

Under s 124 of the WIA 1991, a sewerage undertaker may vary the consents granted relating **15.60** to the discharge of trade effluent. An owner and occupier may appeal against a variation to the Director. Similarly, the Environment Agency may, under s 127 of the Act, review any consents relating to special category effluent. Further provisions under Pt IV relate to procedures on review including, e.g., s 136, evidence from meters.

Many of the problems and proceedings from sewerage provision relate to the pollution of **15.61** watercourses. However, sewerage undertakers are entitled to discharge a significant volume of sewage into watercourses as part of the licence conditions. For instance, from evidence given to the Government's Environmental Audit Committee in October 2004 (TSO, 2005), Thames Water Utilities Ltd is entitled to pump up to 20 million tonnes of raw sewage into the River Thames annually through 50 sewerage overflows, due to the nature of the Victorian sewerage system in London. To overcome this, it is proposed that a very large underground sewerage pipe is installed underneath the Thames.

E POLLUTION OF WATERCOURSES

Water pollution cases represent the highest proportion of the serious offences prosecuted **15.62** by the Environment Agency. It reports that in 2003, 94 pollution incidents had a major environmental impact on the waters of England and Wales, 17 had a major impact on land and six incidents had a major impact on air. Most water pollution incidents arise through lack of awareness and ignorance of consequence rather than intent. For example, washing vehicles in a road, car park of a small business, or indeed anywhere close to a rainwater drain is likely to result in some polluting substance entering the surface water drains and

then into a watercourse. Detergents and washing liquids may appear harmless but can cause significant problems upon entering a freshwater stream.

15.63   The regulatory control of pollution of watercourses is underpinned by criminal sanctions and, most particularly, Pt III of the WRA 1991. However, there are numerous other statutory offences and sanctions as well as common law liability. Each is considered below.

Part III of the WRA 1991

15.64   The control of pollution of water resources is contained in Pt III of the WRA 1991. Chapter I sets out the water quality objectives for England and Wales. Section 84(1) of the WRA 1991 provides that it shall be the duty of the Secretary of State and the Environment Agency to exercise the powers conferred upon them in such manner that ensures, as far as reasonably practicable, that water quality objectives are achieved at all times. The principal offences under Pt III are set out in ss 85 to 90 of the WRA 1991. The most frequently prosecuted offence is s 85, which states that a person contravenes this section if he causes or knowingly permits:

(1)   any poisonous, noxious, or polluting matter or any solid waste matter to enter any controlled waters.

(2)   any matter, other than trade effluent or sewerage effluent, to enter controlled waters by being discharged from a drain or sewer in contravention of a prohibition imposed under s 86 below.

(3)   any trade effluent or sewerage effluent to be discharged (a) into any controlled waters; or (b) from land in England and Wales, through a pipe, into the sea outside the seaward limits of controlled waters.

(4)   any trade effluent or sewerage effluent to be discharged, in contravention of any prohibition imposed under s 86 below, from a building or from any fixed plant (a) on to or into any land; or (b) into any waters of a lake or pond that are not inland freshwaters.

(5)   any matter whatever to enter any inland freshwaters so as to tend (either directly or in combination with other matter that he or another person causes or permits to enter those waters) to impede the proper flow of the waters in a manner leading, or likely to lead, to a substantial aggravation of: (a) pollution due to other causes; or (b) the consequences of such pollution.

15.65   Each of the offences in s 85 of the WRA 1991 relate to pollution or discharges into controlled waters. Section 104(1) of the Act states that controlled waters relate to the following classes:

(a)   relevant territorial waters, i.e. waters that extend seaward for three miles from the baselines from which the breadth of the territorial sea adjacent to England and Wales are measured [cf. the 12 nautical mile limit for territorial waters in other instances see e.g. para 121];

(b)   coastal waters, i.e. any waters that are within the area that extends landward from those baselines as far as (a) the limit of the highest tide; or (b) in the case of the waters of any relevant river or watercourse, the freshwater limit of the river or watercourse together with the waters of any enclosed dock that adjoins waters within that area;

(c)   inland freshwaters, i.e. the waters of any relevant lake or pond or of so much of any relevant river or watercourse as is above the freshwater limit;

(d)   ground waters, i.e. any waters contained in underground strata.

Chapter 19: Criminal law practice and procedure considers the principles of environmental **15.66** offences including the meaning of 'causing' and 'knowingly permitting' pollution. However, many of the cases defining the scope of these principles are water pollution cases including, e.g., *Alphacell Ltd v Woodward* [1972] AC 284 in which a stream was polluted after pumps in a settling tank became blocked, the tank overflowed and entered the watercourse, and the court considered that there should be a common-sense approach to the word 'causing'. In *Environment Agency v Empress Car Co (Abertillery) Ltd* [1999] AC 22 the House of Lords held that an operator's acts may be a 'cause' of pollution without being the most immediate cause. The court must consider whether a third party act or intervening event was a normal fact of life or something extraordinary. In *Empress Cars* the defendant company kept a diesel tank in a yard, which drained directly into the River Ebbw Fach. The tank had an outlet tap, which had not been locked. The tank was opened by an unknown person and the entire contents of the tank emptied into the yard and passed through the drain into the river. The House of Lords found the defendant company had 'caused' the pollution, even though it was not the direct cause.

In *FJH Wrothwell Ltd v Yorkshire Water Authority* [1984] Crim LR 43 the court held that the **15.67** defendant had caused the pollution even though he did not know that after he had poured chemicals into a drain it flowed directly into controlled waters. In *R v CPC (UK) Ltd* [1995] Env LR 131 it was held that it was unnecessary to highlight a single isolated pollution incident and that simply because another party may have caused pollution does not mean that the defendant can avoid liability.

With regard to knowingly permitting, in *Rochford RDC v Port of London Authority* [1914] 2 KB **15.68** 916, the defendant sanitary authority were found guilty of 'causing or suffering' sewage to flow or pass into Little Creek. The case involved the contravention of s 94 of the Thames Conservancy Act 1894 and the court held that although the defendant had not caused the sewage to enter the creek, it had 'suffered' the flow or passage of sewage and that was sufficient.

Penalties

Section 85(6) of the WRA 1991 provides that a person who contravenes s 85 or the condi- **15.69** tions of any consent given under Chapter 2 (Pollution Offences) of the WRA 1991 shall be guilty of an offence. There are various defences to the s 85 offences including in respect of authorized discharges, under s 88 of the WRA 1991, where a person shall not be guilty of an offence in respect of matter entering any waters or any discharge if it occurs in accordance with:

(a)   a consent granted under Ch 2 (Pollution Offences);
(aa) a permit granted under s 2 of the Pollution Prevention and Control Act 1999;
(b)   an authorization under Pt 1 of the Environmental Protection Act 1990;
(c)   a waste management or disposal licence;
(d)   a licence granted under Pt 2 of the Food and Environmental Protection Act 1985;
(e)   s 163 of WRA 1991 or s 165 of the WIA 1991 (discharges for works purposes);
(f)   any local statutory provision or statutory order which confers power to discharge effluent into water; or
(g)   any prescribed enactment.

15.70　Further, under s 89 of the WRA 1991, there are a number of more generic defences including under s 89(1)(a) if the entry or discharge into controlled waters was caused, permitted, or made in an emergency in order to avoid danger to life and health; and under s 89(1)(b) that the accused took all such steps as were reasonably practicable in the circumstances for minimizing the extent of the entry or discharge and its polluting effects. The accused is liable on summary conviction to a maximum fine of £20,000 and/or three months' imprisonment, and an unlimited fine and/or two years' imprisonment for conviction on indictment.

15.71　There is also a defence contained in s 87(2) of the WRA 1991 whereby a sewerage undertaker will not be guilty of a s 85 offence if the contravention is attributable to a discharge that another person caused or permitted to be made into a sewer or works, the undertaker was not bound to receive the discharge, and it could not reasonably have been expected to prevent the discharge into the sewer or works. In *National Rivers Authority v Yorkshire Water Services Ltd* [1995] 1 AC 444 the defendant sewerage undertaker received, involuntarily, a large volume of chemical matter into its treatment works, which it was unable to treat. As a result it discharged the chemical into controlled waters causing pollution. The court held that Yorkshire Water could rely upon the s 87(2) type defence. See also *R v Anglian Water Services* [2003] Crim 2243, Chapter 19: Criminal law practice and procedure.

15.72　In *R v Rhondda Cynon Taff CBC* [2003] Env Times, Vol 9.2 p 30, a land reclamation scheme included surface water discharge consents into a river. However, the defendant had been discharging other liquids into the watercourse, which had an adverse impact on the aesthetic quality of the river and resulted in the closure of a local business water inlet. The defendant was fined £2,000 plus £1,000 costs. In *R v Evans & McArthur* [2003] Env Times Vol 9.2 p 30 the defendants let cattle feed flavouring spill into controlled waters killing over 300 fish, some of which were rare and regarded as vulnerable under the Habitats Directive. They were convicted and fined £750 plus £2,500 costs.

15.73　In *R v Wessex Water Services Ltd* [2003] Env Times Vol 9.2 p 31, the defendant spilt crude sewage from a blocked sewer into a stream that runs along a SSSI valley, and which is also designated a Special Protection Area, Special Area of Conservation, and a Ramsar site. The stream flows to the sea, which is an EU Bathing Water. The defendant was convicted under s 85 and fined £5,000 plus £1,043 costs. In *R v Attwells Ltd* [2005] unreported (Environment Agency website 19.5.05) the defendant company pleaded guilty to causing trade effluent to enter a brook in contravention of s 85 of the WRA 1991. The problem arose out of the company's practice of spreading waste on land. The company was fined £5,000 plus £1,477 costs. See also Chapter 6: Fishing, farming and animal health.

Offences relating to deposits and vegetation in rivers

15.74　Part III of the WRA 1991 protects watercourses where there may not have been any polluting activity but the bottom or bed of the watercourse has nevertheless been affected in some way. Section 90 of the Act provides that a person shall be guilty of an offence if, without the consent of the Agency, he removes any part of the bottom, channel, or bed of any inland freshwaters or a deposit accumulated by reason of any dam, weir, or sluice holding back the waters; and does so by causing the deposit to be carried away by the waters. Section 90(2) then provides that a person shall be guilty of an offence if without consent he causes or permits a substantial amount of vegetation to be cut or uprooted in any inland freshwaters, or to be cut or uprooted so near to any such waters that it falls into them, and fails to take reasonable steps to remove the vegetation from those waters. A person guilty of either offence shall be liable on summary conviction of a maximum £2,500 fine.

Anti-pollution works and operations

The Environment Agency is granted certain land and works powers under Pt VII of the **15.75** WRA 1991. Under s 161 of the Act, where it appears to the Agency that any poisonous, noxious, or polluting matter or any solid waste matter is likely to enter, or to be present in, any controlled waters, it is entitled to carry out various works and operations such as:

(a) preventing the matter from entering the controlled waters; or
(b) where the matter is present in the water, to remove or dispose of the matter, remedy or mitigate any pollution, or so far as is reasonably practicable to do so, restore the waters to their state immediately before the matter became present in the water.

Under s 161(3) of the Act, where the Agency carries out such works, operations, or any **15.76** investigations required, it shall, subject to exceptions, be entitled to recover the expenses reasonably incurred in doing so from any person who may have caused or knowingly permitted the matter to enter, or was likely to enter the controlled waters.

Anti-pollution works notice

Under s 161A of the WRA 1991, the Agency may serve an anti-pollution works notice on any **15.77** person who has caused or knowingly permitted a pollutant to enter controlled waters, including from contaminated land, requiring them to carry out such works as specified in the notice.

Section 161B may require a person to carry out works in relation to land he is not entitled to **15.78** carry out those works or operation on. Section 161B(2) provides that any consent required shall be granted to enable works to be carried out. Although a person granting consent may claim compensation from the person who has been served with the works notice. A person served with a s 161A works notice may appeal against the notice to the Secretary of State within 21 days of service.

Failure to comply with works notice

Section 161D of the WRA 1991 provides that if a person served with a works notice fails to **15.79** comply with any requirement, he shall be guilty of an offence. A person found guilty of an offence under s 161D(1) shall be liable on summary conviction to a maximum fine of £20,000 and/or three months' imprisonment, and an unlimited fine and/or two years' imprisonment for conviction on indictment. If a person fails to implement the requirements of a works notice, the Agency may do what was required and recover from that person any costs or expenses reasonably incurred in doing so. Further, if the Agency is of the opinion that proceedings for an offence would be ineffectual, it may take proceedings in the High Court for the purpose of securing compliance with the notice.

15.80   The Anti-Pollution Works Regulations 1999 (SI 1999/1006) prescribe the contents of works notices, the procedure for appeals against a notice and the compensation for the rights of entry in connection with anti-pollution works paid under s 161B of the WRA 1991. The Environment Agency has published the following guidance: *Use of Anti-Pollution Works Notices*. This is available from www.environment-agency.gov.uk.

F   MISCELLANEOUS WATER REGULATION

15.81   There is a collection of laws, some held over from near-repealed legislation and others where the courts have found legislative gaps and sought to patch this through judicial interpretation. The miscellaneous laws cover pollution of watercourses and water as a pollutant.

Other offences relating to water pollution

15.82   There are a number of different parts of legislation that prohibit pollution and give rise to an offence as a result such as:

- the control of pesticides under Pt III of the Food and Environment Protection Act 1985, which applies to the control of organisms with harmful or unwanted effects on water systems;
- the Control of Pollution (Anti-fouling Paints and Treatments) Regulations 1987 as amended (SI 1987/783);
- Part I of the EPA 1990 and the need to gain an authorization to pollute under the integrated pollution control regime. Section 1(10) provides that a substance is released into any environmental medium whenever it is released directly into that medium and release includes, among other things, in relation to water, any entry (including any discharge) of the substance into water;
- the Groundwater Regulations 1998 (SI 1998/2746) were enacted under s 2(2) of the European Communities Act 1972 and complete the implementation of EU Directive 80/68/EEC (the Groundwater Directive) by supplementing reg 15 of the Waste Management Licensing Regulations 1994 (SI 1994/1056) and existing water pollution legislation. The Regulations require an authorization of the disposal or tipping of list I or II substances under Pt II of the EPA 1990 where a waste management licence is not already required and procedures for prohibiting or regulating by notice other activities in or on land that pose an indirect threat to groundwater from list I or II substances;
- the Pollution Prevention and Control Act 1999 that regulates activities capable of causing any environmental pollution (which means pollution of the air, water, or land); and
- s 4 of the Salmon and Freshwater Fisheries Act 1975, which provides that causing or knowingly permitting the release of liquid or solid matter that causes water to become poisonous or injurious to fish is an offence.

Nitrate vulnerable zones

The Protection of Water Against Agricultural Nitrate Pollution (England and Wales) Regula-   **15.83**
tions 1996 (SI 1996/888) aim to ensure that measures are taken to reduce and prevent nitrate
pollution from agricultural sources. It provides a framework for action to reduce nitrate
levels in the catchments of rivers and groundwater sources affected by such pollution. The
Regulations transpose the requirements of EU Directive 91/676/EEC and the requirement
to designate nitrate vulnerable zones where the measures required by the Directive are
not to be applied across the whole national territory. Some non-agricultural sources of
nitrate pollution are addressed by the Urban Waste Water Treatment (England and Wales)
Regulations 1994 (SI 1994/2841).

Statutory nuisance

Statutory nuisance is covered in Chapter 18. Section 79(1) of the EPA 1990 provides a series   **15.84**
of circumstances which, if found to exist, constitute a statutory nuisance. Within s 79(1)
there are two subsections that may, indirectly, relate to water. Section 79(1)(e) of the EPA
1990 provides that: 'any accumulation or deposit which is prejudicial to health or a nuisance
constitutes a statutory nuisance'.

In *R v Carrick DC ex p Shelly* [1996] Env LR 273 sewage-related debris on a beach was held to   **15.85**
come within s 79(1)(e). Strictly speaking, it was not water that was the nuisance, nor that
water was polluted. In *Carrick* it was the sewerage system that was the vehicle giving rise to
the nuisance. The case highlights that, as with most legal and particularly environmental
problems, it is important not to attempt to compartmentalize concerns too rigidly. In practice, if someone has a sewage-related nuisance problem, s 79(1)(e) may offer an opportunity
to take action to resolve the problem.

Section 79(1)(h) of the EPA 1990 provides that a statutory nuisance includes 'any other   **15.86**
matter declared by any enactment to be a statutory nuisance'. There are also two pieces of
water related legislation from the Public Health Act 1936 (PHA 1936).

Domestic water supply

Section 141 of the PHA 1936 provides that a statutory nuisance includes: **15.87**

> any well, tank, cistern or waterbutt used for the supply of water for domestic purposes which is
> so placed, constructed or kept as to render the water in it liable to contamination or otherwise
> prejudicial to health.

Statutory nuisance under s 141 of the PHA 1936 is based upon the state of a domestic water   **15.88**
supply, i.e. the contamination of the water, rather than the water causing any harm or
damage. An example is where water remains unused for some time and becomes stagnant.

Watercourses, ditches, and ponds

Section 259(1) of the PHA 1936 states that the following matters shall be statutory nuisances   **15.89**
for the purposes of Pt III of the EPA 1990, i.e.:

> (a) any pond, pool, ditch, gutter or watercourse which is so foul or in such a state that is
> prejudicial to health or a nuisance is a statutory nuisance;

(b)   any part of a watercourse, not being a part ordinarily navigated by vessels employed in the carriage of goods by water, which is so choked or silted up as to obstruct or impede the proper flow of water and thereby to cause a nuisance, or give rise to conditions prejudicial to health:

Provided that in the case of an alleged nuisance under paragraph (b) nothing in this subsection shall be deemed to impose any liability on any person other than the person by whose act or default the nuisance arises or continues.

15.90   There are two forms of nuisance under s 259(1). The first is that the water itself becomes the nuisance due to its state. The second is where the water is harmed by obstructions to its flow. Ultimately a state of affairs arising from s 259(1)(b) could lead into a problem under s 259(1)(a). In *Neath RDC v Williams* [1951] 1 KB 115 the court held that a landowner had no duty to clear obstructions occurring naturally in a watercourse and so the 'act or default' requirement relating to s 259(1)(b) is something more than doing nothing.

15.91   'Watercourse' for the purpose of a statutory nuisance is not the same as that contained in s 211 of the WRA 1991 set out above. It has been partially defined in s 108(1) of the Transport Act 1968, which provides that subject to exceptions, any inland waterway in England or Wales comprised in the undertaking of the Waterways Board, which is not a commercial waterway or cruising waterway, shall be deemed to be a watercourse for the purposes of s 259 of the PHA 1936. The meaning of watercourse was also considered in *R v Falmouth and Truro Port Health Authority ex p South West Water Ltd* [2000] Env LR 658 where the nuisance arose from sewage discharges. The court accepted that the word was capable of different meanings but declined to clarify it in relation to the PHA 1936 and held that it did not include estuarine waters and tidal areas where rivers flow into the sea.

15.92   In *Sefton Metropolitan BC v United Utilities Water Ltd* [2001] EWCA CIV 1284 the case arose over liability for repair under Pt II of the PHA 1936. The court considered whether a culverted watercourse had been transformed into a sewer and if so, whether the liability following its collapse had been transferred from the local authority to the water company. The Court of Appeal held that at the time that responsibility for all sewage matters transferred from the local authority to the water company in 1974, the collapsed watercourse was not a sewer, and as a result liability remained with the local authority for its repair. The relevance of the case was, for the purpose of the PHA 1936, that a watercourse does not include a sewerage system.

Common law

15.93   Water pollution at common law means doing something that changes the natural qualities or properties of water. In *John Young & Co v Bankier Distillery Co* [1893] AC 691, Lord MacNaghten held at 698 that every riparian proprietor is entitled to 'the water of his stream, in its natural flow, without sensible diminution or increase and without sensible alteration in its character or quality. A pollution claim in common law could arise from the infringement of certain rights and in particular riparian rights. It may also arise under nuisance, negligence, or trespass. See Chapter 17: Civil law practice and procedure.

Infringing riparian rights

An owner of land adjoining a stretch of water whether it is a river, stream, lake, or the sea, is   **15.94**
referred to as a riparian owner. Riparian ownership is a private proprietal right and does not
require ownership of the river bed or other water. The fouling of water flowing past a riparian
owner's land is an infringement of his property rights and could form the basis of a breach
of property rights. In *Pride of Derby and Derbyshire Angling Association Ltd v British Celanese
Ltd* [1953] Ch 149 the claimants alleged that a local authority had caused a nuisance by
discharging insufficiently treated effluent into the river Derwent. Denning LJ said, at p 190,
that the claimants:

> have a perfectly good cause of action for nuisance, if they can show that the defendants created
> or continued the cause of the trouble; and it must be remembered that a person may 'continue'
> a nuisance by adopting it, or in some circumstances by omitting to remedy it: see *Sedleigh-
> Denfield v O'Callaghan* [1940] AC 880.

Private nuisance

A person with riparian rights may begin private nuisance proceedings against a person who   **15.95**
has caused, inherited, or permitted a nuisance to continue, if it can be proved that there is or
has been interference with the flow or an alteration to the character or quality of the water.
Outlined below are cases relevant to water use and pollution, see also Chapter 17: Civil law
practice and procedure.

In *John Young & Co v Bankier Distillery Co* the court noted that interference with the right   **15.96**
to water is treated as equivalent to damage to land. In *Nicholls v Ely Beet Sugar Factory* [1936]
Ch 343 the Court of Appeal held that a private nuisance included interference with the right
to fish. In *Rylands v Fletcher* the House of Lords considered the escape of a large quantity of
water held from the defendant's land onto the claimant's neighbouring land. If the matter
brought on to the land (in the *Rylands* case, water) is likely to cause mischief then liability for
that escape is absolute, although liability may be excluded by statute.

In *Sedleigh-Denfield v O'Callaghan* the respondents re-positioned a grate across a drain pipe   **15.97**
that had originally been put in place by an unknown trespasser. During a heavy rainstorm it
became choked causing water to overflow onto the claimant's premises. The House of Lords
held that the respondents must be taken to have had knowledge of the existence of the
unguarded pipe on their land, even though it was placed there by a trespasser. They were
consequently liable for the damage caused by its existence and for the grating placed over it.
Lord Atkin at 899 commented that there was:

> . . . sufficient proof of the knowledge of the defendants both of the cause and its probable effect.
> What is the legal result of the original cause being due to the act of a trespasser: In my opinion
> the defendants clearly continued the nuisance for they come clearly within the terms I have
> mentioned above, they knew the danger, they were able to prevent it and they omitted to
> prevent it.

In common law, a landowner has a right to take underground water beneath his land, and   **15.98**
has a right of action against another landowner who pollutes the groundwater. However,
this right of action is qualified by the need to show foresight of harm. In *Cambridge Water Co
v Eastern Counties Leather plc* [1994] 2 AC 264 the defendant company who operated a
tannery close to a water abstraction point operated by the claimant had caused chemical

spills to drain through their floors for some time. The spills percolated through the ground and eventually contaminated the groundwater abstracted by the claimant water company. The House of Lords held that to recover damages in nuisance the defendant must have foreseen that harm would have arisen from the spills. The case is considered further in Chapter 17: Civil law practice and procedure.

15.99   The law in terms of nuisance and sewage was affirmed in *Marcic v Thames Water Utilities Ltd* [2003] UKHL 66. Mr Marcic had experienced regular and severe flooding of his garden and home from the overflow of foul and surface water sewers owned by Thames Water. He had tried to protect his property but the problem had increased over the years as increasing pressure was placed on the sewage system by the obligation to provide connections to the system for new homes and development. The House of Lords ultimately dismissed the claim. It held that neither nuisance nor human rights was an appropriate form of redress and that the claimant should have pursued a complaint against the statutory undertaker. If, on taking this route, the sewage undertaker acted unlawfully then judicial review proceedings would be the appropriate remedy for this. Lord Hope summarized the position by stating that the Court of Appeal (who had decided in favour of Mr Marcic) summed the matter up as:

> The reality is that the provisions of s 18 [of the WIA 1991] provide a procedure for striking the necessary balance in the case of those who claim that they are being denied the benefits that Thames is required to provide to them under the statute. They provide no answer to a claim such as Mr Marcic's.

However, in concluding that this was wrong, he added at para 77:

> In my opinion this approach does not give sufficient weight to the fact that Parliament has decided that the most appropriate method of achieving a fair balance between the competing interests of the individual and the community is by means of a statutory scheme administered by an independent expert regulator, whose decisions are subject to judicial review if there is a doubt as to whether the necessary balance has been struck in the right place. The role of the director on the one hand, and that of the court in judicial review on the other, form an important part of the scheme which has been laid down by the statute. The opportunity to test how effective this scheme might prove to be in Mr Marcic's case was not taken. The judge found that no approach was made by Mr Marcic or on his behalf to bring his problem to the attention of the Office of Water Services, although his solicitors were informed by the Department of the Environment, Transport and the Regions that customer service committees had been set up by the director to assist him in his role of protecting customers' interests and investigating complaints: [2002] QB 929, 938, para 15. So the effectiveness of the scheme must be considered by examining its content.

15.100   In *Kiddle v City Business Properties* [1942] 1 KB 269 the claimant suffered damage to stock in his shop following the overflow of rainwater from guttering due to the accumulation of rubbish in the gutter. The court dismissed the claim on the basis that the claimant had, as a result of renting the shop from the defendant, consented to the conditions relating to the rainwater gutters and, without any proof of negligence on behalf of the defendant, there could be no finding of nuisance. Goddard LJ held at 275 that:

> So here it was obvious that the water would run off the roof towards the plaintiff's shop. The gutters and pipes were there to carry it off, and the plaintiff has a right to require the defendants

to use reasonable care to prevent the gutters and pipes becoming choked. But the defendant's duty is not absolute. It is only to use reasonable care, and for the misfortune that has happened in this case they are not liable. There must be judgment for the defendants, with costs.

Nuisance and the common enemy

The common enemy rule in nuisance is specific to flooding. It provides that it is lawful for a landowner to erect a barrier on his land to protect it from flooding even though that may result in flooding of someone else's land. In effect, the floodwaters are the common enemy. In *Arscott & ors v Coal Authority* [2004] EWCA (Civ) 892 the claimants suffered flooding from flood defences put in place by the defendant. The Court of Appeal held that although the original common enemy rule had operated only for watercourses it was also appropriate to transfer to the case of a floodplain. However, the rule could not be used where water was already on someone's land and that water is then diverted or transferred to another's land. The case concluded by the Court of Appeal affirming that the damage suffered by the claimants was not reasonably foreseeable at the time when the defendant carried out the flood prevention work.

15.101

Negligence

Personal injury from polluted water may arise particularly in the supply of contaminated water. Human health is discussed in Chapter 7 and negligence in Chapter 17: Civil law practice and procedure.

15.102

Trespass

A claim in trespass may be available if the discharge or escape of water onto the claimant's land had resulted in a deposit on that land. In *Jones v Llanrwst UDC* [1911] 1 Ch 393 the owner of a river bed claimed in trespass for the deposit of solid wastes. The court held that a riparian owner on the banks of a natural stream, whether he is or is not the owner of any part of the bed of the stream, is entitled to the flow of the water past his land in its natural state of purity. Further, anyone that turns sewage into a river in a way that it is carried on to his neighbour's land is guilty of a trespass.

15.103

Common law defences

The defence of easement may be possible to prove against a claim by a riparian owner. However, following *Scott-Whitehead v National Coal Board* (1985) P&CR 263, it is not possible to acquire a prescriptive right where the act relied upon is illegal, something that is almost certainly to be the case under Pt III of the WRA 1991.

15.104

Radioactive substances and water pollution

Section 98 of the WRA 1991 provides that nothing in Pt III of the Act (Control of Pollution of Water Resources) shall apply in relation to radioactive waste within the meaning of the Radioactive Substances Act 1993.

15.105

G   FLOODING

15.106   Significant water leakage overflow or other forms of escape can cause immense property damage, personal injury, and on occasion loss of life. Water undertakers, the Environment Agency and landowners may each be liable for any loss or harm caused. If the damage is due to extreme adverse weather conditions, it is likely that insurers, if policies are in place, will cover the cost of clean-up. However, some buildings suffering repeated flood damage are now becoming uninsurable.

15.107   National land use planning policy highlights that around 8% of the total land area in England is at risk from river flooding, including tidal rivers and estuaries. Approximately 30% of the coastline is developed and some 2,500 km^2 of land is at risk of direct flooding by the sea. It notes that the experience of recent years suggests that the incidence of problems due to river flooding may be getting worse, both in frequency and in scale. This arises from changes in river hydrology due to human activity, changes in land management, variations in the intensity of rainfall, and the increase in development in areas at risk. In addition, climate change is expected to increase the risk of both coastal and river flooding as a result of sea-level rise and more intense rainfall. On both a national and global scale, it is already the case that damage from flooding is greater than that from any other natural disaster. Outlined below are the main areas of flood liability.

Legislative liability for the escape of water

15.108   Under s 209 of the WIA 1991 water undertakers may be liable for the escape of water from a pipe owned by the undertaker, although liability will not arise if the escape was due to the fault of the person suffering the loss or damage or by the Environment Agency. Similarly, s 208 of the WRA 1991 provides that the Agency may be liable for an escape of water from a pipe owned by the Agency, but is limited if there was fault by the person experiencing the harm or by the water undertaker.

Liability under the common law

Nuisance

15.109   Liability for holding or containing water may well attract strict liability. If the water held on the land is an unnatural use of the land, the rule in *Rylands v Fletcher* applies in certain circumstances. It states that:

> a person who brings something onto his land that may cause harm or mischief if it escapes is strictly liable for all damage that is the natural consequence of its escape.

15.110   The rule was clarified and to an extent restricted by the House of Lords in *Transco plc v Stockport MBC* [2003] UKHL 61 but it still has some relevance on the point that an isolated escape could give rise to liability. In *Transco* the claimant gas company had suffered loss following a large escape of water from a block of flats owned by the Council. The Council was held not to be liable.

15.111   The principle does not apply to things naturally on the land. Also, there is no liability for an escape of water held on land if the damage arising is due to an act of God, the act of a stranger not under the control of the land owner or occupier, or the act was by the person suffering the damage. In *Nichols v Marsland* (1876) 2 Ex D 1 CA the Court of Appeal held that an exceptionally heavy burst of rain constituted an act of God. However, this is the only case to have done so. All others considering heavy rain falls have not been regarded as so exceptional. Further, with extreme weather patterns being ever more closely linked with human-induced climate change, it is unlikely to do so in the future. In *Rickards v Lothian* [1913] AC 263, a case involving the overflow of water from a toilet in an upper floor, the Privy Council held that the defendant was not responsible unless either he instigated the act or ought reasonably to have prevented it. They added that having a proper and reasonable supply of water was an ordinary and proper use of his house, and that although he was bound to exercise all reasonable care he was not responsible for the damage not due to his own default, whether caused by inevitable accident or the wrongful acts of third persons (although, contrast this with the strict liability imposed by s 85(1) of the WRA 1991 following *Empress Cars*). Further, in *Whitmores (Edenbridge) Ltd v Stanford* [1909] 1 Ch 427 the court noted at 438 that an owner of land will not be liable for the consequences of water collected on his land by and for the benefit of another person. Although an escape of water attracts strict liability, there may be a defence of statutory authority if a person causing the escape is a water undertaker or the Environment Agency and there is no evidence of negligence on their part.

If, however, water held naturally on land escapes due to the nuisance action, negligence, or wilful act of the owner or occupier then liability may arise. In *Foster v Warblington UDC* [1906] 1 KB 648 the claimant had farmed oysters in oyster ponds at sea. The defendant local authority significantly increased the level of sewage being discharge from a nearby sewage outlet and created a nuisance to the oyster farming. The Court of Appeal held that the claimant, as occupier of the oyster ponds, was entitled to maintain an action for trespass to the same by wrongdoers and that the defendant authority, not having any right to discharge sewage into the sea that amounted to a nuisance were wrongdoers. **15.112**

Also, if a person alters the natural flow of a watercourse and as a result of defective construction water escapes then liability is likely to arise. In *Corporation of Greenock v Caledonian Railway Co* [1917] AC 556 the House of Lords held that it was the duty of anyone who interferes with the course of a stream to see that the works that he substitutes for the channel are adequate to carry off the water brought down even by extraordinary rainfall, and if damage results from the deficiency of the substitute he will be liable. **15.113**

In contrast to the escape of water onto a neighbour's land is where an owner or occupier abstracting groundwater from his own land also withdraws water from his neighbour's land and causes the land to subside. In this instance, the neighbour has no common law right to support from the groundwater. In *English v Metropolitan Water Board* [1907] 1 KB 588 the defendants owned a well and pumping station and indirectly caused water in a nearby stream to reduce. The court held that because the defendants did not appropriate any of the water of the stream by pumping it up through their pipes, but merely caused it to sink a short distance into the ground, the damage to the stream gave no cause of action. **15.114**

Land use planning and flood risk

15.115   The role of land use planning is fundamental to flooding and flood risk. With increasing pressure on land available for development there has been considerable construction on floodplains. Planning Policy Guidance Note (PPG) 25: *Development and Flood Risk* (2001) emphasizes that local authorities should bear these considerations in mind in framing planning policy and in determining planning applications. It provides that:

- the susceptibility of land to flooding is a material planning consideration;
- the Environment Agency has the lead role in providing advice on flood issues, at a strategic level and in relation to planning applications;
- policies in development plans should outline the consideration that will be given to flood issues, recognizing the uncertainties that are inherent in the prediction of flooding and that flood risk is expected to increase as a result of climate change;
- planning authorities should apply the precautionary principle to the issue of flood risk, using a risk-based search sequence to avoid such risk where possible and managing it elsewhere;
- planning authorities should recognize the importance of functional flood plains, where water flows or is held at times of flood, and avoid inappropriate development on undeveloped and undefended flood plains
- developers should fund the provision and maintenance of flood defences that are required because of the development; and
- planning policies and decisions should recognize that the consideration of flood risk and its management needs to be applied on a whole-catchment basis and not restricted to flood plains.

H   FLOOD DEFENCE AND LAND DRAINAGE

15.116   There is a common law obligation on landowners to drain and protect land from flooding. However, perhaps more relevant today are the additional statutory obligations placed upon drainage bodies under the WRA 1991 and the Land Drainage Act 1991 (LDA 1991). The drainage bodies include:

- the Environment Agency;
- internal drainage boards;
- local authorities; and
- any body with power to make or maintain land drainage.

Environment Agency flood defence obligations

15.117   Section 6(4) of the Environment Act 1995 provides that:

> Subject to s 106 of the 1991 Act (obligation to carry out flood defence functions through committees) the Agency shall in relation to England and Wales exercise a general supervision over all matters relating to flood defence.

Part IV of the WRA 1991 covers flood defence. Section 105(2) provides that for the purpose of   **15.118**
carrying out its flood defence functions the Agency must from time to time carry out surveys
of its areas. It must carry out its functions through flood defence committees. The activities
relating to flood defence are only in relation to main rivers. A main river is defined as a
watercourse that is shown as such on a main river map and includes any structure or
applicant for controlling or regulating the flow of water into, in, or out of the channel. The
Agency has further powers and functions relating to flood defence. For instance, s 107 of the
WRA 1991 defines the permissive powers that are available to the Agency in respect of main
rivers, and deals with maintenance, improvement works, and construction. Section 109 gives
power to the Agency to control the erection, alteration, and repair of structures in, over, or
under main rivers. While s 165 of the Act gives powers to the Agency, in connection with
main rivers and for the purpose of defence against sea water or tidal water, to maintain and
improve existing works and construct new works. Further, the Agency must be consulted by a
local planning authority on the flood defence implications of a planning application.

The powers of the Agency under the WRA 1991 also include, under s 161, the general power   **15.119**
to carry out flood defence and drainage works including, e.g. in connection with a main river
to cleanse, repair, or otherwise maintain in a due state of efficiency any existing watercourse
or any drainage work. There is also, under s 166, the power to carry out works for the purpose
of providing a flood warning system and the power to dispose of soil in connection with
flood defence works (s 167).

District authority flood defence powers

Section 14 of the LDA 1991 confers powers on local authorities and others, similar to those   **15.120**
given to the Agency and the internal drainage boards in relation to the prevention, mitigation, and remedying of flood damage. Local authorities have powers to maintain and
improve existing 'ordinary' watercourses and to construct new works. Under s 25, local
authorities may serve notice on persons requiring them to carry out necessary works to
maintain the flow of 'ordinary' watercourses. Sections 17 and 26 of the Act require local
authorities, among others, to obtain the consent of the Agency before the exercising of any
of its land drainage powers. Section 66 of the LDA 1991 enables a local authority to make
bye-laws to secure the efficient working of the drainage system in its area.

I   THE MARINE ENVIRONMENT

The law relating to the marine environment may be considered in two parts: **15.121**

(1)   the national laws relating to coastal waters; and
(2)   the international obligations on states and agreements between states.

Estuaries and coastal waters

In accordance with international practice the territorial waters around the UK includes   **15.122**
the sea for up to 12 nautical miles from points set by Order in Territorial waters. The

International Convention on the Territorial Sea and the Contigious Zones 1965 provides that territorial sea is a belt of sea adjacent to the coast of a state lying beyond its land territory and its internal waters. Internal waters include waters that lie to the landward side of the baseline from which the territorial sea is measured. In some instances the extent of territorial waters may be reduced. The Territorial Sea (Limits) Order 1989 (SI 1989/482) provides separate seaward distances for certain water including parts of the English Channel and the sea around the Isle of Man. The sovereignty over territorial waters must respect the rights of others including, e.g., the right of innocent passage for vessels.

15.123 Defra in collaboration with other bodies, such as the Marine Environment Monitoring Group, is undertaking an extensive integrated assessment of the state of UK seas. The report Marine Environment Quality presents information on the current status of marine environmental quality in the UK, in relation to human activities. It covers fish and fisheries, aquaculture, nutrients and eutrophication, hazardous substances, microbiological contamination, oil and oil-based contaminants, radioactivity, construction and aggregate extraction, litter, navigation dredging and dredged material relocation, shipping impacts, and non-indigenous species. The report notes that one of the biggest concerns is over-fishing whereas other problems such as chemical input into waters is not yet at critical levels stating that:

> In principle, human interference with the nitrogen and phosphorus cycles presents a widespread threat to the marine environment. However, despite the level of nutrient enrichment in some UK waters, there is evidence that undesirable disturbance to the balance of organisms and to water quality has not occurred.

15.124 It also notes that in 2003, 98% of UK identified bathing waters met the mandatory standards and 74% met guideline standards, an increase in compliance of 21% and 45% respectively, since 1990. This largely reflects investment in improvements in sewage treatment and infrastructure. Continuing failures of bathing water mandatory standards are seen at a small number of sites in Yorkshire, Cornwall, and Lancashire.

International protection of the sea

15.125 The *Global Environmental Outlook Yearbook 2004/05* (UNEP, 2005) states that of the 66 major water areas of the world there were very few that are relatively free of impact with among the worst areas affected including the Gulf of Mexico (especially the Rio Grande and the Mississippi sub-units) and the Caribbean sea, as well as the Black, Aral and Caspian Seas. Some of the main concerns were loss of eco-systems and overexploitation of fisheries. The concern of degradation of the marine environment is recognized by many governments across the world and their support for the United Nations (UN) and the United Nations Environment Programme (UNEP) in developing international legislation.

UN Convention on the Law of the Sea 1982

15.126 The UN Convention on the Law of the Sea 1982 (UNCLOS 1982) provides a general framework for all areas of marine protection. Its preamble notes that the objective of UNCLOS is:

> to establish a legal order for the seas and oceans which will facilitate international communication, and will promote the peaceful uses of the seas and oceans, the equitable and efficient

utilisation of their resources, the conservation of their living resources, and the study, protection and preservation of the marine environment.

Part XII of UNCLOS provides general provisions for states such as: **15.127**

Art 192	a general obligation to protect and preserve the marine environment;
Art 193	the right to exploit natural resources pursuant to their environmental policies and Art 192 obligations;
Art 194	measures to prevent, reduce, and control pollution; and
Art 195	a duty not to transfer damage or hazards or transform one type of pollution into another.

Further specific provisions are provided in s 5, Pt XII including the requirement that states   **15.128**
take measures, including the adoption of laws and regulations to prevent, reduce, and
control pollution from:

Art 207	rivers, estuaries, pipelines, and outfall structures;
Art 208	seabed activities subject to national jurisdiction;
Art 209	activities in the Area;
Art 210	dumping;
Art 211	vessels; and
Art 212	activities that cause releases into the atmosphere.

Part XV of the UNCLOS 1982 provides for the settlement of disputes and the obligation   **15.129**
under Art 279 on party states to settle any dispute between them by peaceful means. If
this is not achieved then either party may refer the matter to the court of tribunal having
jurisdiction under s 2 of Pt XV.

Regional seas programmes

UNCLOS 1982 recognizes the wide variation in marine environments across the world and   **15.130**
the various regional seas programmes that have been developed to protect these unique
ecosystems. Regions are not defined under UNCLOS 1982 but tend to be defined by reference
to political and geographical considerations. There are about 20 marine environment treaties that may be regarded as regional in nature and are devised, enacted, and implemented by
the states in each. Some of the European regional seas programmes include:

- the North Sea and North East Atlantic;
- the Mediterranean and the Black Sea, and
- the Baltic Sea.

The prominent piece of legislation for the North Sea and North East Atlantic is the Paris   **15.131**
Convention for the Protection of the Marine Environment 1992 (the OSPAR Convention)
covering pollution from land-based and offshore sources as well as dumping. There is also
the Helsinki Convention for the Protection of the Marine Environment of the Baltic Sea Area
1992 (the Helsinki Convention), which aims to promote restoration and preservation of the
Baltic Sea eco-systems. The Mediterranean and the Black Sea regional seas programme is
supported by two conventions: the Convention for the Protection of the Marine Environment and the Coast Region of the Mediterranean 1995 and the Convention on the Protection of the Black Sea Against Pollution 1992. Many of the Conventions are framework

conventions with a number of protocols to the respective conventions implemented to provide the detail.

Pollution from ships

15.132   Patricia Birnie and Alan Boyle in *International Law and the Environment* (2/e, OUP, 2002) note that pollution from ships is, in general, either:

- operational, which is a function in the way that ships operate; or
- accidental, e.g. arising from collisions.

15.133   They add that neither problem should be exaggerated and that the major sources of marine pollution emanate from land-based causes, not from floating sea-borne vessels. That said, the ever greater reliance on oil for energy use coupled with the reduction in local reserves means that more and more oil is being shipped across greater distances, and increasingly regular shipping incidents involving oil tankers have resulted in large oil spills. In 1978, The *Amoco Cadiz* ran aground off the coast of Brittany, France and 68 million gallons of oil spilled into the sea; the *Exxon Valdez* spill in 1989 resulted in 11 million gallons of crude oil entering the Prince William Sound, Alaska; and the break up of the *Prestige* in 2002 off the north-west coast of Spain caused 77,000 tonnes of heavy fuel oil to spill into the Atlantic and be washed ashore in Portugal, Spain, and France.

15.134   The regulation of shipping is by the International Maritime Organisation (IMO). The Safety of Life at Sea Convention 1974 covers the construction and equipment of ships and general standards of seaworthiness. The International Convention for the Prevention of Pollution by Ships 1973, as amended (the MARPOL Convention 1973) controls the discharge from ships including oil escapes. Annex I of the MARPOL Convention 1973 relates to oil pollution and Annex II chemicals. All parties are bound by these Annexes; the remaining Annexes are non-mandatory. The UK has transposed Annex I by the enactment of the Merchant Shipping (Prevention of Oil Pollution) Regulations 1996 as amended (SI 1996/2154) and Annex II through the Merchant Shipping (Dangerous or Noxious Liquid Substances in Bulk) Regulations 1996 as amended (SI 1996/3010)

15.135   The Oil Pollution Liability Convention 1992 aims to cover the cost of clean-up of oil spill from vessels. This is primarily through the maintenance of the International Oil Pollution Convention Fund (the IOPC Fund) whereby any person suffering loss, damage, or harm directly from an oil spill may make a claim to the Fund, which provides up to €250 million. The IOPC Fund is largely financed by contributions from oil companies based in IOPC member states. Explanation of claims to the fund are set out in the *International Oil Pollution Compensation Fund, Claims Manual* (IOPC, 2002). In *RJ Tilbury & Sons (Devon) Ltd v International Oil Pollution Compensation Fund 1971 & ors* [2003] 15 ELM 24 in a claim relating to the grounding of the *Sea Empress* oil tanker in Milford Haven, the Court of Appeal held that only direct loss can be claimed from the fund.

15.136   Although the regulation of ships and sea vessels is largely left to the flag state, i.e. the country in which the vessel is registered, there are certain rights held by the country that controls its own coastal areas. This can present difficulties. In the case of the *Prestige*, the Spanish coastal authorities refused to allow the crippled tanker into port and consequently contributed to the rapid deterioration and break up of the vessel in the storm.

KEY MATERIALS AND DOCUMENTS

Water Resources (Licences) Regulations 1965 as amended (SI 1965/534)

Environmental Protection Act 1990

Land Drainage Act 1991

Water Industry Act 1991 (WIA 1991)

Water Resources Act 1991

Protection of Water Against Agricultural Nitrate Pollution (England and Wales) Regulations 1996 (SI 1996/888)

Anti-Pollution Works Regulations 1999 (SI 1999/1006)

The Water Supply (Water Quality) Regulations 2000, as amended (SI 2000/3184)

United Nations Environment Programme (UNEP)

Water Act 2003

Water Resources (Environmental Impact Assessment) (England and Wales) Regulations 2003 (SI 2003/164)

Water Environment (Water Framework Directive) (England and Wales) Regulations 2003 (SI 2003/3242)

Directive 2000/60/EC establishing a framework for Community action in the field of water policy (the Water Framework Directive)

Convention for the Protection of the Marine Environment and the Coast Region of the Mediterranean 1995

Convention on the Law of the Sea 1982 (UNCLOS 1982)

Convention on the Protection of the Black Sea Against Pollution 1992

Convention on the Territorial Sea and the Contigious Zones 1965

Helsinki Convention for the Protection of the Marine Environment of the Baltic Sea Area 1992 (the Helsinki Convention)

International Convention for the Prevention of Pollution by Ships 1973, as amended (the MARPOL Convention 1973)

Oil Pollution Liability Convention 1992

Paris Convention for the Protection of the Marine Environment 1992 (the OSPAR Convention)

Birnie, P and Boyle, A. *International Law and the Environment 2/e* (OUP, 2002)

Environment Agency. *Use of Anti-Pollution Works Notices*. Environment Agency: Bristol

IOPC (2002). *International Oil Pollution Compensation Fund, Claims Manual*

Planning Policy Guidance Note (PPG) 25: *Development and flood risk*

UNEP (2005). *Global Environmental Outlook Yearbook 2004/05*

International Maritime Organisation (IMO): the UN agency concerned with the safety of shipping and cleaner seas: www.imo.org

www.environment-agency.gov.uk

16

WILDLIFE AND NATURE CONSERVATION

A   INTRODUCTION

16.01   A common starting point when considering wildlife and nature protection and preservation is to consider the range of prohibitions underpinned by criminal sanctions when contravened. It is an area of environmental law where the police have a prominent enforcement role and are supported by committed private prosecutors such as the Royal Society for the Protection of Birds (RSPB) and other government bodies such as English Nature and local authorities. The Environment Agency is primarily responsible for protection of freshwater and fish and the prosecution of offences relating to them, while HM Customs and Excise play a key role in investigating and prosecuting international wildlife crime including the control of trade in endangered species. The main government body, Defra, coordinates many of these organizations including the development of the Partnership for Action Against Wildlife Crime (PAW).

Defining wildlife crime

16.02   The Environmental Audit Committee's report: *Wildlife Crime 12th Report of Session 2003–04* concluded that there was no agreed definition of wildlife crime among the prosecuting bodies or across government departments. It noted that it may be generally defined as any action that contravenes current legislation governing the protection of flora and fauna. It noted however, that: 'the absence of an accepted definition of wildlife crime has . . . had a direct and negative impact on the public's perception of wildlife crime.'

16.03   This confusion is compounded by the inconsistent approach of the Police in pursuing offences to the point where it does not regard many wildlife crimes as crimes at all. It only recognizes them as offences and does not need to record them for the purposes of Home Office statistics.

The legal framework

16.04   The enforcement provisions referred to above are supported by the ability of government and its agencies to designate areas of land and water as sites requiring increased protection. Many of the designated sites will influence and often restrict the way the land may be used. Section F outlines the main types of specially designated sites. Wildlife and habitat legislation also influences distinct legal sectors such as land use planning, water and marine law ensuring compliance with EU obligations.

16.05   These are amended from time to time as species become endangered or in need of protection. Section B below covers the protection of wild birds, animals, and plants. There is also protection for specific species under domestic and EU legislation, considered in Section C.

EU Habitats Directive

16.06   EU Directive 92/43/EEC on the conservation of natural habitats and of wild fauna and flora, as amended (the Habitats Directive) aims to contribute towards ensuring bio-diversity through the conservation of natural habitats and of wild fauna and flora in the European territory of the Member States to which the Treaty applies. Measures taken under the Directive must be designed to maintain or restore, at favourable conservation status, natural habitats and species of wild fauna and flora of Community interest. They should also take account of economic, social, and cultural requirements and regional and local characteristics. Appropriate assessments of plans and projects are required under the Directive. These are considered in Chapter 24: Environmental assessment.

The Conservation (Natural Habitats, etc.) Regulations 1994

The Conservation (Natural Habitats, etc.) Regulations 1994 (SI 1994/2716) (the Habitat **16.07** Regs 1994) make provision for implementing the Habitats Directive. Regulation 3(2) states that the Secretary of State and the nature conservation bodies (the Countryside Agency and the Countryside Council for Wales) must exercise their functions under the enactments relating to nature conservation to secure compliance with the requirements of the Habitats Directive. Those enactments include:

- Pt III of the National Parks and Access to the Countryside Act 1949;
- s 15 of the Countryside Act 1968 (areas of special scientific interest);
- Pt I and ss 28 to 38 of the Wildlife Conservation Act 1981 (WCA 1981);
- ss 131 to 134 of the Environmental Protection Act 1990 (EPA 1990); and,
- the Habitat Regs 1994 themselves.

Under reg 3(3) and in relation to marine areas any competent authority (any Minister, **16.08** government department, public or statutory undertaker, public body of any description, or person holding a public office) having functions relevant to marine conservation shall exercise those functions so as to secure compliance with the requirements of the Habitats Directive. This applies, in particular, to functions under:

- the Sea Fisheries Acts within the meaning of s 1 of the Sea Fisheries (Wildlife Conservation) Act 1992;
- the Dockyard Ports Regulation Act 1865;
- s 2(2) of the Military Lands Act 1900 (provisions as to use of sea, tidal water, or shore);
- the Harbours Act 1964;
- Pt II of the Control of Pollution Act 1974;
- ss 36 and 37 of the WCA 1981 (marine nature reserves),
- the Water Resources Act 1991;
- the Land Drainage Act 1991; and
- the Habitat Regs 1994.

Part II of the Habitat Regs 1994 provides for the conservation of natural habitats and habitats **16.09** of species. In particular:

- regs 7 to 15 cover the selection, registration, and notification of sites to be protected under the Directive ('European sites');
- regs 16 and 17 require management agreements for European sites;
- regs 18 to 27 provide for the control of damaging operations and for special nature conservation orders for European sites;
- regs 28 to 32 allow bye-laws and compulsory purchase orders for European sites; and
- regs 33 to 36 provide for the protection of European marine sites.

16.10   Part III of the Habitat Regs 1994 covers the protection of certain wild animals and plants including:

reg 39   which, subject to exceptions, creates an offence to deliberately capture, kill, or disturb those animals or to trade in them;

reg 43   which, subject to exceptions, makes it an offence to pick, collect, cut, uproot, or destroy those plants or to trade in them; and

reg 44   the grant of licences for certain purposes including scientific and educational, conserving wild animals, and preserving public health or public safety, or other imperative reasons of overriding public interest including those of a social or economic nature and beneficial consequences of primary importance for the environment.

16.11   In *R (Newsum) v Welsh Assembly Government* [2004] EWCA Civ 1565 the Court of Appeal affirmed the Welsh Assembly's refusal to grant a licence under reg 44(2)(e) of the Habitats Regs 1994 (overriding public interest). The claimant, representing the Trustees of the Duke of Westminster's Estate, had sought to work a quarry and required the licence for the trans-location of a population of great crested newts, but had not shown that there was an 'imperative reason of overriding public interest'.

16.12   There is a considerable degree of overlap between the Habitat Regs 1994 and the WCA 1981. However, in implementing the Directive, the Regulations provide slightly greater protection by covering deliberate disturbance of animals, whereas disturbance under the WCA 1981 relates to when animals are under shelter.

16.13   Part IV of the Habitats Regulations makes provision for the adaptation of planning and certain other controls for the protection of European sites:

- regs 48, 49, and 54 require the effect on a European site to be considered before a grant of planning permission and, subject to certain exceptions, restrict the grant of planning permission where the integrity of the European site would be adversely affected (see Chapter 24: Environmental assessment);
- regs 50, 51, and 55 to 58 require planning permissions granted before the date on which a site becomes a European site (or if later, the commencement of these Regulations) to be reviewed and in certain circumstances revoked where the integrity of the site would be adversely affected. Equivalent provision for the requirement to consider the effect on a European site and for review is made as respects the construction or improvement of highways, roads, or cycle tracks (regs 69 and 70), consents under the Electricity Act 1989 (regs 71 to 74), authorizations under the Pipe-lines Act 1962 (regs 75 to 78), orders under the Transport and Works Act 1992 (regs 79 to 82), authorizations and licences under the EPA 1990 (regs 83 and 84) and discharge consents under water pollution legislation (reg 85). Regulations 60 to 67 make special provision as respects general and special development orders, simplified planning zones, and enterprise zones.

EU Birds Directive

16.14   Article 1 of the EU Directive 79/409/EEC on the conservation of wild birds (the Birds Directive) states that it relates to the conservation of all species of naturally occurring birds in the wild state in the European territory of the Member States to which the Treaty applies. It covers the protection, management and control of these species and lays down rules for their exploitation. It applies to birds, their eggs, nests, and habitats.

Article 2 of the Birds Directive provides that Member States shall take the requisite measures   **16.15** to maintain the population of the species referred to in Art 1 at a level that corresponds in particular to ecological, scientific, and cultural requirements, while taking account of economic and recreational requirements, or to adapt the population of these species to that level. Article 3 adds that in the light of the requirements referred to in Art 2, Member States shall take the requisite measures to preserve, maintain, or re-establish a sufficient diversity and area of habitats for all the species of birds referred to in Art 1. The Directive provides for more specific measures such as special conservation measures for species in danger of extinction and species vulnerable to habitat change. It provides for prohibition of deliberate killing or disturbance and keeping of certain species. The WCA 1981 is the main legislative vehicle for implementing the Birds Directive.

B   THE WILDLIFE AND COUNTRYSIDE ACT 1981

The legislative protection of wildlife is dominated by the WCA 1981, which has been sig-   **16.16** nificantly amended by primary and secondary legislation including the Countryside and Rights of Way Act 2000 (CRoW Act 2000). Part I of the WCA 1981 sets out a series of restrictions and prohibitions relating to wild birds, wild animals, and plants. Many of the offences under Pt I are regarded as serious enough to be recognized as arrestable offences under the Police and Criminal Evidence Act 1984 (PACE) Sections 19 to 21 of the WCA 1981 provide for enforcement, investigation, and penalties. Each Pt I category has a corresponding schedule, which are published in Appendix 2.

Protection of wild birds

Protection of wild birds, their nests, and eggs

The protection of wild birds, their nests, and eggs is provided under s 1(1) of the WCA 1981   **16.17** stating that:

> if any person intentionally
> (a) kills, injures or takes any wild bird;
> (b) takes, damages or destroys the nest of any wild bird while that nest is in use or being built, or
> (c) takes or destroys an egg of any wild bird,
> he shall be guilty of an offence.

Unlike many environmental offences, those under s 1(1) require intention. They are also   **16.18** subject to the exceptions contained in s 2 of the WCA 1981 (see below). In *Robinson v Everett and W & FC Bonham & Son Ltd* [1988] Crim LR 699 the court held that 'takes' for the purpose of Pt I means 'captures'. 'Wild bird' is defined in s 27(1) of the Act as any bird of a kind that is ordinarily resident in or is a visitor to Great Britain in a wild state but does not include poultry or, except in ss 5 and 16, any game bird. The s 1(1) offence is listed in Sch 1A of PACE as an arrestable offence.

16.19   Section 1(2) of the WCA 1981 provides that if any person has in his possession or control any live or dead wild bird or any part of, or anything derived from such a bird; or an egg of a wild bird or any part of such an egg, he shall be guilty of an offence. The court in *Robinson v Everett* considered that a golden eagle, which had been stuffed and mounted, should still be regarded as a 'dead wild bird' for the purposed of this Part.

16.20   In *Kirkland v Robinson* [1987] Crim LR 643 the court affirmed that the s 1(2) offences of possession and control are of strict liability in nature. They are, however, subject to s 1(3), which states that a person will not be guilty of an offence under subs (2) if he can show that the bird or egg had not been killed or taken or had been killed or taken otherwise than in contravention of the provisions of Pt I of the Acts (or the Protection of Birds Acts 1954 to 1967 and orders made under those Acts, which were repealed under s 73 of the WCA 1981). Importantly, it is for the defendant to show that the offences committed were otherwise than in contravention of the provisions referred to.

16.21   Section 1(5) of the WCA 1981 provides that if any person intentionally or recklessly disturbs any wild bird listed in Sch 1 of the Act while it is building a nest or is in, on, or near a nest containing eggs or young; or disturbs dependent young of such a bird, he shall be guilty of an offence. An offence under s 1(5) is based upon intent or recklessness and is listed in Sch 1A of PACE as an arrestable offence.

Offences in areas of special protection

16.22   Section 3 of the WCA 1981 enables the Secretary of State to increase the protection available to wild birds in certain areas by enacting an order that a specified local area is defined as an area of special protection. Within such a designated area any person who, at any time or during any period so specified, intentionally:

(a)   kills, injures, or takes any wild bird or bird so specified;

(b)   takes, damages, or destroys the nest of such a bird while that nest is in use or being built;

(c)   takes or destroys an egg of such a bird;

(d)   disturbs such a bird while it is building a nest or is in, on, or near a nest containing eggs or young; or

(e)   disturbs dependent young of such a bird

shall be guilty of an offence under this section.

16.23   An authorized person will not be liable under s 3. In *R v Secretary of State for the Environment ex p RSPB* [1997] QB 206 the court held that when making a special protection area order the Secretary of State must not take into account economic considerations.

Prohibition on certain methods of killing or taking wild birds

16.24   Section 5 of the WCA 1981 prohibits certain types of killing or taking of wild birds, e.g. using an article placed in order to cause bodily injury to any wild bird including any trap, gin, snare, electrical device, or poison. There are defences contained in subs (4) and (4A) for specific offences. These include taking or killing in the interest of public health, etc., and carrying out such activities with all reasonable precautions to prevent injury to wild birds.

Sale of birds etc.

Under s 6 of the WCA 1981 any person who sells, offers, or exposes for sale, has in his **16.25** possession or transports for sale, or shows in a competition any live wild bird other than a bird included in Pt 1, Sch 3, or an egg, or part of an egg, of a wild bird or publishes any advertisement to do so, is guilty of an offence. The s 6 offences are listed in Sch 1A of PACE as arrestable offences.

Registration of certain captive birds

Any bird included in Sch 4 of the WCA 1981 must be registered in accordance with **16.26** regulations made under s 7 of the Act. Failure to do so is an offence. The Wildlife and Countryside (Registration and Ringing of Certain Captive Birds) Regulations 1982, as amended (SI 1982/1221) have been enacted for the purpose of s 7. It is also an offence under s 17 to intentionally or recklessly make a false statement when obtaining registration.

Protection of captive birds

Under s 8(1) of the WCA 1981, if any person confines any bird in any cage or other recep- **16.27** tacle, which is not sufficient in height, length, or breadth to permit the bird to stretch its wings free, he shall be guilty of an offence. Although this offence does not apply to poultry, when the bird is being transported for certain activities such as to be sold, going to a competition, or visiting a vet.

Exceptions to the wild bird offences

The exceptions to the offences in s 1 largely relate to killing or attempting to kill any wild **16.28** bird listed in Pts I and II, Sch 2 of the WCA 1981 outside the close season. Although the exceptions only apply to certain scheduled birds with respect to authorized persons; who include under s 27(1) the owner or occupier, or person authorized by them, or someone authorized in writing by the local authority; the Countryside Agency, the Environment Agency, or a water undertaker.

Further exceptions to the offences under ss 1 and 3 are provided by s 4 including anything **16.29** done in pursuance of a requirement by the Secretary of State for Environment, Food and Rural Affairs; to help the recovery of a disabled bird or to kill a seriously disabled bird that has no chance of recovery; or if the act was incidental to a lawful operation that could not reasonably have been avoided. There are exceptions under s 4(3) if any act was:

(a) to preserve public safety:
(b) prevent the spread of disease; or
(c) prevent serious damage to livestock or their food, crops, vegetables, fruit, timber, fisheries, or inland waters.

However, an authorized person may not rely on the defence under s 4(3)(c) if he should have **16.30** reasonably obtained a licence to carry out the otherwise unlawful activities.

Protection of wild animals

The WCA 1981 provides protection to certain wild animals. There are also specific Acts to **16.31** protect particular species, e.g. seals and badgers, which are considered separately. Sections 9 to 12 of the WCA 1981 provides for the protection of certain wild animals, and in similar fashion to the wild bird offences, there are a series of offences with some specific exceptions.

Protection of certain wild animals

16.32   Under s 9(1) of the WCA 1981, any person who intentionally kills, injures, or takes any wild animal included in Sch 5 of the Act shall be guilty of an offence. The offence is listed in Sch 1A of PACE as an arrestable offence. Other s 9 offences include:

s 9(2)   having the possession or control of any live or dead wild animals included in Sch 5 or any part of, or anything derived from them;

s 9(4)   intentionally or recklessly damaging or destroying or obstructing access to any structure or place that any wild animal included in Sch 5 uses for shelter or protection;

s 9(4A)   intentionally or recklessly disturbing any wild animal included in Sch 5 as (a) a dolphin or whale, or (b) a basking shark;

s 9(5)   selling, offering, or exposing for sale etc. any live or dead wild animal included in Sch 5 or publishing or advertising to buy or sell any of those things.

16.33   Under s 9(6) of the Act, in any proceedings for an offence under subs (1)(2) or (5)(a), the animal in question shall be presumed to have been a wild animal unless the contrary is shown.

Prohibition on certain methods of killing and taking wild animals

16.34   Section 11 of the WCA 1981 prohibits certain types of killing or taking of wild animals. This section is similar in style and content to that under s 5 for birds, e.g. using an article placed in order to cause bodily injury to any wild animal including any trap, gin, snare, electrical device, or poison. Again, any animal relating to the prohibition is presumed to be a wild animal and there are defences contained in subs (6) and (7) for specific offences. These include taking or killing in the interest of public health, etc., and carrying out such activities with all reasonable precautions to prevent injury to wild animals.

Introduction of new wild animal species

16.35   Under s 14(1) of the WCA 1981, if any person releases or allows to escape into the wild any animal that is:

(a)   a kind which is not ordinarily resident in and is not a regular visitor to Great Britain in a wild state; or

(b)   is included in Pt I of Sch 9,
       he shall be guilty of an offence.

16.36   The offences are arrestable offences under Sch 1A of PACE. Section 14(3) of the Act provides a defence to a charge of committing an offence under s 14(1) or (2) to prove that the accused took all reasonable steps and exercised all due diligence to avoid committing the offence. Although, where this defence involves the allegation that the offence was due to the act or default of another person, under s 14(4) the person charged shall not, without leave of the court, be entitled to rely on the defence unless, within seven days before the hearing, he has served on the prosecutor a notice identifying that other person.

Exceptions to the wild animal offences

Section 9(3) of the WCA 1981 provides a person shall not be guilty of an offence under s 9(2) **16.37** if he shows (a) that the animal had not been killed or taken etc. otherwise than in contravention of the relevant provisions; or (b) that the animal or other thing in his possession or control had been sold otherwise than in contravention of the provisions.

Section 10 provides further exceptions to the s 9 offences such as anything done in pur- **16.38** suance of a requirement of the Secretary of State under s 98 of the Agriculture Act 1947 (taking steps for the prevention of damage by pests) or the Animal Health Act 1981, killing an animal if it was seriously disabled, or killing or injuring an animal to prevent serious damage to livestock, foodstuffs, crops, vegetables, fruit, timber, other forms of property, or fish.

Protection of wild plants

Section 13(1) of the WCA 1981 provides that if any person: **16.39**

(a) intentionally picks, uproots, or destroys any wild plant included in Sch 8; or
(b) not being an authorized person, intentionally uproots any wild plant not included in that Schedule,
     he shall be guilty of an offence.

Further, under s 13(2) of the Act, if any person (a) sells, offers, or exposes for sale, or has in his **16.40** possession or transports for the purpose of sale, any live or dead wild plant included in Sch 8, or (b) advertises that he intends to buy or sell any of those things, he is guilty of an offence. In any proceedings relating to s 13(2)(a) the plant in question is presumed to have been a wild plant unless the contrary is shown. Offences under s 13(1)(a) and (2) are arrestable offences under PACE.

Introduction of new wild plant species

Section 14(2) of the WCA 1981 provides that if any person plants or otherwise causes **16.41** to grow in the wild any plant that is included in Pt II of Sch 9 he shall be guilty of an offence.

Exceptions to the wild plant offences

Section 13(3) of the WCA 1981 provides that a person shall not be guilty of an offence under **16.42** s 13(1) if he shows that the act was an incidental result of a lawful operation and could not have been reasonably avoided.

Licences to carry out activities

Licences for wild birds

Section 16(1) of the WCA 1981 provides that the wild bird offences under Pt 1 do not apply **16.43** to the range of activities listed in the section providing these are carried out in accordance with the terms of any licence granted by the appropriate authority. These include:

(a)   scientific, research, or education purposes;

(d)   the purpose of protecting any collection of wild birds; or

(j)   the purpose of preventing the spread of disease

16.44   The appropriate authority is either the relevant Nature Conservancy Council (i.e. the Countryside Agency or the Countryside Commission for Wales) or the Secretary of State. The activities listed in s 16(1) are exhaustive and any licence issued will only authorize the activities specified in the licence. In *RSPCA v Cundey* [2001] EWHC Admin 906 the court held that a s 16 licence will not authorize an activity listed in subs (1) if the licence held does not cover the particular activity relating to the offence. As with registration, it is an offence to intentionally or recklessly make a false statement when applying for a licence.

Licences for wild animals

16.45   It is possible to obtain a licence to lawfully carry out certain acts in relation to wild animals (as with wild birds). Section 16(3) of the WCA 1981 provides that the wild animal offences under ss 9(1), (2), (4), (4A), 11(1), (2), and 13(1) do not apply, among other things, to:

(a)   scientific, research, or education purposes;

(c)   the purpose of conserving wild animals or wild plants or introducing them to particular areas; or

(e)   the purpose of preventing the spread of disease.

Enforcement

16.46   The enforcement provisions under Pt 1 of the WCA 1981 include powers of entry, investigation, and the penalties for offences applying to wild birds, animals, and plants.

Attempting to commit an offence

16.47   Section 18 of the WCA 1981 provides that any person who attempts to commit an offence under Pt I shall be guilty of an offence and punishable in like manner as for the offence itself. Similarly, if a person has in his possession anything capable of being used for committing the offence, he shall be punished in a similar fashion.

Powers of investigation

16.48   Part 1 of the WCA 1981 empowers two types of enforcement officers, the police and wildlife inspectors, to help protect birds. The powers also cover the protection of animals and plants. Under s 19(1) of the Act if a constable suspects with reasonable cause that any person is committing or has committed an offence under Pt 1, he may without warrant:

(a)   stop and search that person if the constable suspects with reasonable cause that evidence of the commission of the offence is to be found on that person;

(b)   search or examine any thing which that person may then be using or have in his possession if the constable suspects with reasonable cause that evidence of the commission of the offence is to be found on that thing; or

(d)   seize and detain for the purposes of proceedings under Pt 1 any thing which may be evidence of the commission of the offence or may be liable to be forfeited under s 21.

Section 19(2) of the WCA 1981 confers the powers of entry under s 25 of PACE on the police   **16.49**
officer. Under s 19(3), a constable may seek a warrant to enter and search premises from the
magistrates' court.

Wildlife inspectors may be authorized to operate under s 19ZA of the WCA 1981 by the   **16.50**
Secretary of State, although they may be subject to limitations and conditions. Section 19ZA
confers powers of entry to and inspection of premises in certain specified situations. Section
19ZA(7) creates offences for the intentional obstruction of inspectors and failing, without
reasonable excuse, to give assistance to an officer. Under s 19ZA(8) any person, who, with
intent to deceive, falsely pretends to be a wildlife inspector shall be guilty of an offence. (This
is one of the few wildlife offences that is recognized as a crime for Home Office recording.)

Under s 19ZB constables and, in certain circumstances, wildlife inspectors, have the power to   **16.51**
take blood and tissue samples in order to identify any specimen.

Prosecution and penalties

Section 20 of the WCA 1981 provides a time limit on prosecuting wildlife offences in   **16.52**
summary proceedings. Under s 20(2) summary proceedings may be brought within six
months from the date on which evidence sufficient in the opinion of the prosecutor to
warrant proceedings came to his knowledge, but no such proceedings shall be brought more
than two years after the commission of the offence. Section 20(3) requires a prosecutor
to complete and sign a certificate confirming the date when evidence first came to his
knowledge.

The penalties for conviction of offences under Pt 1 are contained in s 21 and vary according   **16.53**
to the relevant section creating the offence. The most serious wild bird penalty is under
s 21(1), which provides that, subject to subs (5), a person guilty of an offence under any of
ss 1 to 13 or s 17 shall be liable on summary conviction to a maximum £5,000 fine and/or six
months' imprisonment. For other more general offences, the offence may be triable either
way and the sentence more severe. For example, a person found guilty under s 21(4C) for
falsely pretending to be a wildlife officer (s 19ZA(8)) is liable on summary conviction to
maximum £5,000 fine and/or six months' imprisonment, and an unlimited fine and/or two
years' imprisonment for conviction on indictment.

The RSPB publishes an annual report on wild bird offences: *Birdcrime*. This noted that in   **16.54**
2003 there were 67 wild bird prosecutions in England and Wales, of which 32 were taken
by the Crown Prosecution Service, 24 by RSPB, and 11 by the Police. The penalties under the
WCA 1981 included:

- 220 hours community service order for taking a wild bird under s 1(1)(a);
- a £100 fine for the possession of a live wild bird under s 1(2)(a); and
- a £750 fine for the possession of items capable of being used to commit an offence under
  s 18(2).

Due to their summary nature, most wildlife offences go unreported although the RSPB   **16.55**
investigations newsletter, *Legal Eagle*, summarizes some key decisions. In *R v Cripps* (Jan
2004) unreported, the defendant gamekeeper was convicted at Buxton Magistrates' Court of
destroying goshawk eggs in their nest. He was sentenced to three months' imprisonment
suspended for two years. He was also given a one-month concurrent suspended sentence for

recklessly disturbing the goshawk and for possession of climbing irons. In *R v Berry* (Sept 2004) unreported, Southampton Crown Court convicted the owner of the New Forest Owl Sanctuary for offences involving theft of a saker falcon and licensing breaches, he was also convicted of other animal offences and was sentenced to a total of 240 hours' community service. In *R v D'cruze* (September 2002) unreported, the defendant was sentenced to six months in prison for the taking and possession of rare bird eggs.

C   SPECIES PROTECTION UNDER OTHER LEGISLATION

Seals

16.56   The Conservation of Seals Act 1970 (the Seals Act 1970) provides for protection of seals in addition to the protection under the Habitat Regs 1994. Section 1 of the Act provides that if any person poisons or kills with certain firearms any seal, he shall be guilty of an offence. Under s 15, firearms and ammunition have the same meaning as in the Firearms Act 1968. Further, under s 2 if any person kills or injures or takes a seal during the close season for grey seals, he shall be guilty of an offence. The Secretary of State may, by order, enact further measures to prohibit the killing of seals, e.g. through the Conservation of Seals (England) Order 1999 (SI 1999/3052) although this was the subject of a review during 2003.

16.57   There are general exceptions to the prohibitions contained in s 9 of the Seals Act 1970, including taking any seal that is disabled or the unavoidable killing of a seal incidental to a lawful action. Also, the Secretary of State may grant a licence under s 10 to any person authorizing that person to kill seals for scientific, educational, or other purposes (including the reduction of a population surplus of seals) set out in the section. A licence may be subject to conditions and to revocation at any time.

16.58   Under s 5 of the Seals Act 1970 a person found guilty of an offence under the Act shall be liable on summary conviction to a fine not exceeding £2,500. Further, a court may order the forfeiture of any seal or seal skin relating to the offence or any seal, skin, firearm, ammunition, or poisonous substance in the defendant's possession at the time of the offence. Section 7 of the Act provides that where the offence is committed on the coast or at sea, the place of the commission of the offence shall, of the purposes of the jurisdiction of the court, be deemed to be any place where the offender is found or to which he is first brought after the commission of the offence. However, s 17(2) of the Seals Act 1970 provides that nothing done outside the seaward limits of the territorial waters adjacent to Great Britain shall constitute an offence under the Act.

Badgers

16.59   Badgers are given protection over and above that contained in the WCA 1981 and the Habitats Regs 1992 through the Protection of Badgers Act 1992 (the Badgers Act 1992). In similar fashion to the other bird and animal protection legislation, badgers are protected by a series of prohibitions with exceptions to those prohibitions and the option to obtain a licence to carry out certain activities according to the conditions of the licence. By way of example, s 1(1) of the Badgers Act 1992 provides that:

A person is guilty of an offence if, except as permitted by or under this Act, he wilfully kills, injures or takes, or attempts to kill, injure or take, a badger.

Section 1(2) of the Act provides that if, in any proceedings for an offence under subs (1), **16.60** there is evidence from which it could reasonably be concluded that at the material time the accused was attempting to kill, injure, or take a badger, he shall be presumed to have been attempting to kill, injure, or take a badger unless the contrary is shown. Under s 1(3), a person is guilty of an offence if, except as permitted by or under this Act, he has in his possession or under his control any dead badger. However, s 1(4) provides that a person is not guilty of an offence under s 1(3) if he shows that:

(a) the badger had not been killed, or had been killed otherwise than in contravention of the provisions of this Act; or

(b) the badger or other thing in his possession or control had been sold (whether to him or any other person) and, at the time of the purchase, the purchaser had had no reason to believe that the badger had been killed in contravention of any of those provisions.

Section 2 of the Badgers Act 1992 creates an offence of cruelty to badgers, s 3; of interfering **16.61** with badgers sets, and s 4 of selling and possession of live badgers. A series of exceptions to the offences are contained in ss 6 to 9 and the granting of licences is provided under s 10. A person guilty of an offence under the Act is liable on summary conviction to a maximum penalty of a £5,000 fine and/or six months' imprisonment, with certain offences attracting a lesser maximum penalty. If a dog was used in the commission of certain offences, the court may, on conviction, order the destruction or disposal of the dog, or order that the offender be disqualified from having custody of a dog.

Animal Health Act 1981

Section 1 of the Animal Health Act 1981 (as amended by the Animal Health Act 2002) (AHA **16.62** 1981) gives general powers to the Secretary of State to make orders and authorize regulations. Over 65 pieces of secondary legislation have been enacted under s 1, many of these relate to animal disease and slaughter. However, certain regulations are relevant to wild birds and animals, e.g. the Welfare of Animals (Transport) Order 1997, as variously amended (SI 1997/1480), which makes general provision for the welfare of animals in transport including the means of transport or receptacles used, the amount of space available to each animal and the fitness of animals to travel. It requires animals that fall ill or are injured in the course of transport to be treated. Article 21 of the Order provides that a contravention of any provision constitutes an offence under s 75 of the AHA 1981, which provides for a maximum penalty of a £5,000 fine.

Miscellaneous legislation protecting wild animals

Protection of Animals Act 1911

The Protection of Animals Act 1911 relates to wild birds and animals and is considered **16.63** further in Chapter 6: Fishing, farming, and animal health.

Food and Environmental Protection Act 1985

16.64   Part III of the Food and Environmental Protection Act 1985 covers the control of pesticides. Under s 16(12) of the Act, a person who, without reasonable excuse, contravenes any regulations made under the Act shall be guilty of an offence. This is considered in Chapter 6: Fishing, farming, and animal health.

Wild Mammals (Protection) Act 1996

16.65   Section 1 of the Wild Mammals (Protection) Act 1996 provides that if, save as permitted by this Act, any person mutilates, kicks, beats, nails or otherwise impales, stabs, burns, stones, crushes, drowns, drags, or asphyxiates any wild mammal with intent to inflict unnecessary suffering, he shall be guilty of an offence. Under s 2 a person shall not be guilty of an offence under this Act by reason of, among other things, an act of mercy, the killing was reasonably swift and humane and that the mammal had been injured or taken during lawful shooting, hunting, etc., or the lawful use of any poisonous or noxious substance on any wild mammal. Under s 3 'wild mammal' means any mammal that is not a domestic or captive animal within the meaning of s 15 of the Protection of Animals Act 1911. A person guilty of an offence shall be liable on summary conviction to a maximum £5,000 fine and/or six months' imprisonment. The court, on conviction, may order the confiscation of any vehicle or equipment used in the commission of the offence.

Other general criminal activities

16.66   In addition to specific animal related legislation, more general offences such as theft under the Theft Act 1968 or common law offences such as attempting to pervert the course of justice may be relevant to offences against wild birds and animals.

D   INTERNATIONAL WILDLIFE TRADE

16.67   In its memorandum to the Government inquiry on Wildlife Crime 2004, TRAFFIC noted that global wildlife trade is huge, with an annual turnover estimated in billions of dollars and involving hundreds of millions of individual plants and animals every year. It added that most of the trade is legal but a significant portion is not. Illegal trade in wildlife presents a serious threat to the survival of many endangered species. It is estimated that in the UK, around half of those prosecuted for wildlife crimes had previous convictions for other serious offences including drugs and firearms.

CITES

16.68   Wildlife crime has been recognized as a global problem for some time. The Convention on International Trade in Endangered Species of Wild Fauna and Flora 1973 (CITES) has over 165 state parties and was ratified by the UK in 1976. Its aim is to ensure that international trade in specimens of wild animals and plants does not threaten their survival. It is implemented in the UK through European and national legislation.

16.69   CITES operates by controlling international trade in specimens of selected species. All import, export, re-export, and introduction from the sea of species covered by the

Convention are regulated through a licensing system. The species covered under CITES are contained in Appendices and categorized according to the protection required. Article 2 of CITES sets out certain fundamental principles including that:

- Appendix I shall include all species threatened with extinction that are or may be affected by trade. Trade in specimens of these species must be subject to particularly strict regulation in order not to endanger further their survival and must only be authorized in exceptional circumstances.
- Appendix II shall include: (a) all species that although not necessarily now threatened with extinction may become so unless trade in specimens of such species is subject to strict regulation in order to avoid utilization incompatible with their survival; and (b) other species that must be subject to regulation in order that trade in specimens of certain species referred to in subparagraph (a) of this paragraph may be brought under effective control.
- Appendix III shall include all species that any party identifies as being subject to regulation within its jurisdiction for the purpose of preventing or restricting exploitation, and as needing the cooperation of other parties in the control of trade.

The CITES Secretariat provides details on the Convention. It advises that each signatory **16.70** state must designate one or more management authorities in charge of administering the licensing system and one or more scientific authorities to advise them on the effects of trade on the status of the species. A specimen of a CITES-listed species may be imported into or exported (or re-exported) from a State party to the Convention only if the appropriate document has been obtained and presented for clearance at the port of entry or exit. There is some variation of the requirements from one country to another and it is always necessary to check on the national laws. The CITES Secretariat can be contacted via www.cites.org.

EU Regulation 338/97

The EU Regulation 338/97 on the protection of species of wild fauna and flora (as amended) **16.71** (the Principal CITES Regulation) implements CITES within the European Union while introducing certain additional stricter measures concerning European species and stricter import, housing, and transport conditions for live specimens. Commission Regulation No 939/97 (the Subsidiary Regulation) implements the Principal CITES Regulation. As EU Regulations they have direct effect without the need for transposing legislation by Member States. In *Tridon (Federation Departementale des chasseurs de l'Isere & anor)* Case C-510/99 ECJ, 23 October 2001, the European Court of Justice (ECJ) held that the purpose of the Regulations was to ensure the conservation of animal and plant species, and hence the protection of the life and health of those species.

National control of trade in endangered species

The Control of Trade in Endangered Species (Enforcement) Regulations 1997 (SI 1997/1372) **16.72** (COTES) make provision for the enforcement of the EU's Principal CITES Regulation and the Subsidiary Regulation. COTES provides for criminal offences relating to breach of requirements of the Principal Regulation including:

reg 3   which creates a number of offences relating to the making of false statements or the furnishing of false information for the purpose of obtaining a permit or certificate under the Principal CITES Regulation or Subsidiary Regulation;

reg 4   which provides for offences relating to the misuse of such permits or certificates;

reg 5   which refers to the powers of persons commissioned or authorized by the Commissioners of Customs and Excise to require proof of lawful import or export of a specimen;

reg 6   which creates an offence for any person to contravene any condition or requirement of a permit or certificate issued in accordance with the Principal Regulation or Subsidiary Regulation;

reg 7   which creates an offence to move a live specimen listed in Annex A of the Principal CITES Regulation from the address specified in the import permit or in any other certificate relating to that specimen or to keep such a specimen at a different address without prior authorization;

reg 8   which creates a number of offences relating to a range of activities including the purchase and sale of specimens listed in Annex A of the Principal Regulation or of specimens listed in Annex B, which have been imported or acquired unlawfully;

16.73 Regulations 9 and 10 of COTES provide for powers of entry, including the power to take samples from specimens, and seizure for the purposes of enforcement of the Principal CITES Regulation. While reg 11 provides for forfeiture of specimens and other things upon a conviction. Regulation 12 provides for the liability of corporations. HM Customs and Excise are primarily responsible for managing illegal trade although the police provide further support.

16.74 In addition to COTES and the implementation of CITES, s 170 of the Customs and Excise Management Act 1979 (CEMA 1979) covers the fraudulent evasion of duty and the creation of offences in relation to actions carried on with intent to evade tax payments.

16.75 In *R v Sissen* [2000] All ER (D) 2193 (8 December 2000, CA) the defendant was imprisoned for 30 months for importing three Lear's macaw. Following his imprisonment the defendant took judicial review proceedings of the HM Customs and Excise seizure of 144 birds from the claimant's home. The High Court dismissed the claim taking into account the claimant's record of illegal importation. In *R v Humphrey* (2002) T 2001/0105, unreported, a case prosecuted under CEMA 1979, the court recognized the serious nature of damage in an illegal wildlife trade case. The offender was charged with trafficking in endangered birds of prey from Thailand. The birds had been packed in plastic tubes and many did not survive their journey. In addition, the defendant had also smuggled into the UK a golden-cheeked gibbon, which is endangered in the wild with fewer than 1,000 individuals remaining. The trial resulted in a custodial sentence of six-and-a-half years.

16.76 In *R v Secretary of State for the Environment, Food & Rural Affairs ex p White* [2001] 14 ELM 1 p 14 the claimant challenged the impounding of non-permitted caviar following incompatibility of CITES export permits. The claim was dismissed with Forbes J, noting that there was: 'fundamental public interest in the preservation of endangered species.'

E TREES AND HEDGEROWS

The protection of trees and hedgerows arises in a number of ways in land use planning. PPS **16.77**
12: *Development Plans* (2004) provides that plans and policies should be designed to secure
the enhancement of the natural beauty and amenity of land including tree and hedgerow
protection and planting.

Trees

The Government: *Tree Preservation Orders: A Guide to the Law and Good Practice* (2000) states at **16.78**
para 5.5 that the presence of trees and woodlands has always been recognized as an important material consideration in determining planning applications. Further, s 197 of the Town
and Country Planning Act 1990 (TCPA 1990) places a duty on local planning authorities
(LPAs) to ensure that, whenever appropriate, adequate provision is made for trees when
granting planning permission. This may be achieved by conditions for preservation or
planting.

Sections 198 to 214D of the TCPA 1990 provide powers for LPAs to make provision for the **16.79**
preservation of trees or woodlands through tree preservation orders (TPOs) and for trees in
conservation areas. A TPO can prohibit the cutting down, topping, lopping, uprooting, or
wilful damage or destruction of a tree, group of trees, or woodlands. The maximum penalty
for non-compliance with a TPO is a £20,000 fine on summary conviction and an unlimited
fine on indictment. Sections 211 to 214 provide further protection to trees in conservation
areas. LPA powers to protect trees include a right of entry to land with or without a warrant
and, under s 214A, to apply for an injunction to restrain an offence under ss 210 or 211.

In defining a tree, Phillips J suggested in *Bullock v Secretary of State* (1980) 40 P&CR 246 that **16.80**
for the purposes of the Act: 'anything that ordinarily one would call a tree is a "tree" . . .'

Forestry Act 1967

The Forestry Act 1967 provides the legal basis for the Forestry Commission and its Com- **16.81**
missioner. The Act requires the Commission to promote the interests of forestry, the
development of afforestation, the production and supply of timber, and the establishment and maintenance of adequate reserves of growing trees. Under s 46 of the Act, the
Commissioners have the power to make bye-laws relating to land under their management
and control and to which the public have, or may have, access.

The Commission is given wide powers to control tree-felling. The term 'felling' is defined **16.82**
under s 35 of the Act to include wilfully destroying by any means. Section 9 of the Forestry
Act 1967 covers unlawful tree-felling. It states that, subject to exceptions, a felling licence is
required for the felling of any growing tree. The Forestry (Felling of Trees) Regulations 1979,
as amended by SI 1987/632 and SI 2002/226 (SI 1979/791), prescribes the procedure for
applying for a felling licence.

Section 17 of the Forestry Act 1967 provides that anyone who fells a tree without a felling **16.83**
licence shall be guilty of an offence and liable on summary conviction to a maximum
penalty of a fine of £2,500 or twice the sum that appears to the court to be the value of the

tree, whichever is the higher. In *Forestry Commission v Frost & Thompson* (1989) 154 JP 14 the court held that the term 'anyone' in the Act is not confined to someone with an estate or interest in the land in question and who is entitled to apply for a licence under the Act. Proceedings for an offence under s 17 may be instituted within six months from the first discovery of the offence, with a bar on commencing proceedings more than two years after the offence.

16.84   As well as preventing tree-felling, the Forestry Commission under s 24 of the Forestry Act 1967 is empowered to direct the owner of growing trees to fell them within a specified period (not less than three months). Failure to comply with any directions, or with the conditions of a felling licence is an offence. A person guilty of an offence under s 24 is liable on summary conviction to a maximum penalty of a £5,000 fine.

16.85   The prosecuting authority is the Forestry Commission for offences under the Act. An officer of the Commissioners or any other person authorized by them is, under s 48 of the Forestry Act 1967, given powers of entry to survey any land for the purpose of ascertaining whether it is suitable for afforestation or the purpose of inspecting any timber on the land.

Hedgerows

16.86   The main protection for hedgerows, other than their consideration as a matter of general planning principles, is under the Hedgerows Regulations 1997 (SI 1997/1160) (enacted by the Secretary of State under s 97 of the Environment Act 1995). Government guidance: *The Hedgerows Regulations: A Guide to the Law and Good Practice* (1997) suggests that a hedgerow is: 'a row of bushes forming a hedge, with trees, etc., growing in it'.

16.87   The Regulations only cover *important* hedgerows, which are growing on, or adjacent to: common land, protected land, land used for agriculture or forestry, or land used for keeping or breeding horses, ponies, or donkeys. To be protected they are also required to be either at least 20 metres in length, to meet another hedgerow or to be part of such a hedgerow. The Regulations do not apply to hedgerows within or on the boundary of a dwellinghouse.

16.88   The protection for important hedgerows under reg 5 of the Regulations is that the LPA must be informed of a proposal to remove part or all of the hedgerow unless the activity relates to minor works. The LPA may then take further action including issuing a hedgerow retention notice. Regulation 7 creates an offence of intentionally or recklessly removing a hedgerow in contravention of reg 5. The maximum penalty is a £5,000 fine on summary conviction or an unlimited fine for conviction on indictment, LPAs also have powers to require replacement and to apply for an injunction to restrain an actual or apprehended offence.

F   NATURE CONSERVATION AREAS

16.89   One of the more effective ways to protect wildlife is by designated special conservation sites, in particular in restricting land use planning. Annex A of Planning Policy Guidance

(PPG) 9: *Nature Conservation* (1994) describes the range of designations. Each of these is outlined below

Sites of Special Scientific Interest

Sites of Special Scientific Interest (SSSIs) are designated and managed by English Nature **16.90** under ss 28 to 28R of the WCA 1981. All sites of national and international importance on land including National Nature Reserves, Nature and Geological Conservation Review sites, Special Protection Areas, Special Areas of Conservation, and Ramsar sites are notified as SSSIs. In *R (Fisher) v English Nature* [2004] EWCA Civ 633 the claimant challenged a decision by English Nature to designate over 13,000 hectares of land in East Anglia as an SSSI on the basis that, among other things:

- the decision to designate was beyond the reasonable range of meanings open to it under s 28 of the WCA 1981;
- English Nature had failed to carry out adequate investigations and had failed to ask itself the right questions and to take reasonable steps to acquaint itself with the relevant information to enable it to properly designate the land a SSSI;
- the decision was irrational because it proceeded on the basis of flawed logic regarding special scientific interest (and national importance) without understanding the different focus of the 1981 Act from the relevant European legislation. These recurring flaws in the decision-making process reveal an error of law; and
- English Nature had acted in breach of Art 1 of the first Protocol to the European Convention on Human Rights, which provided that everyone is entitled to the peaceful enjoyment of their possessions. Article 1 required a fair balance to be struck between the interests of the state and the rights of the individual.

The Court of Appeal concluded that there was no irrationality in the decision-making **16.91** process and no procedural irregularity in the decision-making process. It concluded that English Nature was entitled both to notify and confirm the farmland as an SSSI. There had been no infringement of the claimant's Art 1 rights.

Areas listed as SSSIs are protected under Pt II of the WCA 1981. In *R v Saccombe Estates* (2005), **16.92** unreported, the company was fined £7,500 plus costs of £6,787 after pleading guilty to damaging heather moorland in North Yorkshire. The damage was caused by unauthorized building works. The magistrates also made a restoration order to remedy the damage done. In *R v Ennstone Breedon Ltd* (2004), unreported, (16.2.04 — English Nature) the defendant company was fined £13,000, ordered to pay £6,000 in costs and subjected to a restoration order after pleading guilty to causing damage to an internationally important wildlife site. The damage was caused by waste material from a quarry being tipped close to the bank of the De Lank River harming over 1,700 square metres of bankside vegetation and polluting the river.

Limestone Pavement Orders

Limestone Pavement Orders (LPOs) are identified as a priority habitat in the Habitats **16.93** Directive and are of particular physiographical and biological interest, particularly in the north of England. They have been vulnerable to rock extraction for use in domestic gardens.

Under s 34 and Sch 11 of the WCA, the Secretary of State or LPAs may make an LPO to protect areas. The removal of stone from land subject to an LPO requires an application under Pt III of the TCPA 1990.

National Nature Reserves

16.94 National Nature Reserves (NNRs) are areas of national importance owned or leased by English Nature or managed by landowners according to Nature Reserve Agreements.

Special Protection Areas and Special Areas of Conservation

16.95 Special Protection Areas (SPAs) and Special Areas of Conservation (SACs) are intended to protect the habitats of threatened wildlife species and arise from the Birds Directive and the Habitats Directive. One of the key cases relating to a SPA is *R v Secretary of State for the Environment ex p RSPB* [1997] QB 206. The case concerned Lappel Bank, an internationally important mudflat on the Medway Estuary, which supports an average of 53,900 wintering waders and wildfowl. The Bank itself supported average peak numbers of 1,700 birds. In 1989 Medway Ports Authority sought and received planning permission for the reclamation of Lappel Bank for a car and cargo park. The permission was not immediately implemented. In 1993, the Secretary of State for the Environment designated the Medway Estuary and Marshes as a SPA, but decided to exclude Lappel Bank on the grounds that the economic need not to impair the future expansion of the port outweighed the site's nature conservation value. The RSPB challenged this decision on the grounds that the Birds Directive did not allow economic considerations to be taken into account in the designation of a SPA. RSPB challenged the Secretary of State's decision by judicial review. The matter was eventually referred by the House of Lords to the ECJ who ruled that the UK Government had acted illegally to withhold Lappel Bank from the SPA designation for economic reasons. This decision underlined that economic considerations cannot be used to exclude areas of habitat from designation as SPA. Unfortunately, during the course of the litigation the planning permission had been implemented and the site destroyed. The ECJ ruling left the UK Government with an obligation to compensate for the habitat loss in order to maintain the coherence of the Natura 2000 network. The Government has now announced a site that could be used for this compensation.

Ramsar sites

16.96 Ramsar sites are listed by the Secretary of State in accordance with the Convention on Wetlands of International Importance Especially of Waterfowl Habitat 1971 (the Ramsar Convention). The Convention requires signatory states to promote the wise use of wetlands and to designate alternative sites should the development of any designated sites become necessary in the urgent national interest.

Biogenetic reserves

16.97 Biogenetic reserves tend to be sites already designated as SSSIs or NNRs but that are also identified under a Council of Europe programme for the conservation of heathlands and grasslands. Designation is by the Secretary of State with assistance from English Nature.

Marine Nature Reserves (MNRs) are designated under the WCA to conserve marine flora, **16.98** fauna, geological or physiographical features, or to allow study of such features. The Secretary of State may designated an area as an MNR following an application by English Nature. English Nature or local authorities may make bye-laws to control activities on the foreshore and other parts of an MNR within their boundaries.

Areas of Special Protection for Birds

The Secretary of State may designate Areas of Special Protection for Birds (AOSPs) under the **16.99** WCA 1981 to provide sanctuary to particularly vulnerable groups of birds.

Local Nature Reserves

Local authorities may establish Local Nature Reserves (LNRs) under the National Parks **16.100** and Access to the Countryside Act 1949. The purpose is to provide nature conservation and also the opportunity for the public to learn and enjoy wildlife locally.

KEY MATERIALS AND DOCUMENTS

Conservation of Seals Act 1970
Animal Health Act 1981
Wildlife and Countryside Act 1981
Conservation (Natural Habitats, etc) Regulations 1994 (SI 1994/2716)
Protection of Badgers Act 1992
Control of Trade in Endangered Species (Enforcement) Regulations 1997 (SI 1997/1372)
    (COTES)
Countryside and Rights of Way Act 2000 (CRoW Act 2000)

EU Directive 79/409/EEC on the conservation of wild birds (the Birds Directive)
EU Directive 92/43/EEC on the conservation of natural habitats and of wild fauna and flora,
    as amended
EU Regulation 338/97 on the protection of species of wild fauna and flora (as amended)

Convention on International Trade in Endangered Species of Wild Fauna and Flora 1973
    (CITES)

Defra (1997). *The Hedgerows Regulations: A Guide to the Law and Good Practice*
Defra (2000). *Tree Preservation Orders: A Guide to the Law and Good Practice*
Planning Policy Guidance (PPG) 9 *Nature Conservation*
Environmental Audit Committee report: *Wildlife Crime 12th Report of Session 2003–04*

Countryside Agency: The statutory body working to conserve and enhance the English
    countryside and to promote social equity and economic opportunity for the people who
    live there: www.countryside.gov.uk.

Countryside Commission for Wales is the Government statutory adviser on sustaining
   natural beauty, wildlife and the opportunity for outdoor employment in Wales:
   www.ccw.gov.uk
Royal Society for the Protection of Birds: UK charity working to secure a healthy
   environment for birds and wildlife: www.rspb.org
WWF-UK: works on global and local environmental issues. www.WWF.org.uk

PART III
PRACTICE AND PROCEDURE

17

CIVIL LAW PRACTICE AND PROCEDURE

A   INTRODUCTION

17.01 The number of claims being issued in the civil justice system has fallen sharply in recent years. In 1996 there were 2.3 million claims issued in the county courts; in 2003 there were 1.57 million. However, the pursuit of compensation remains high with a much higher proportion of matters settling before formal proceedings commence. There is still reliance on the civil justice system but the civil justice reforms coupled with the increased cost of litigation are persuading parties to settle before issuing claims. Whether this analysis can be applied to environmental law claims in the civil courts is uncertain. Research supported by Defra in 2003 entitled: *Civil Law Aspects of Environmental Justice* was unable to find any pattern emerging among environmental claims in the civil courts, but equally, nothing to suggest that the general trend was not replicated with environmental civil claims. There clearly remains a need to appreciate the court practice and procedure to ensure that any claim is pursued or defended in an appropriate and professional manner.

Purpose of the civil justice system

17.02 The primary purpose of the civil justice system is to resolve disputes between two or more parties. The main remedy is to receive compensation in an attempt to put someone in the position they would have been if an agreement had been concluded successfully. It is also possible to obtain an injunction to either prevent someone from doing something or to force an action to be carried out. Claims arising out of nuisance, negligence, and trespass are pursued within the civil justice system. Each of these is referred to as a tort, which is commonly defined as a 'civil' wrong. It aims to provide a remedy to a person or their property that has been, or may potentially be, harmed by the conduct of another. And while there is now a highly regulated system of environmental protection throughout England and Wales, there remains the need to use the private civil law to resolve disputes and to claim compensation for harm that has arisen.

B   OUTLINE OF CIVIL PROCEDURE

Pre-action procedure and considerations

17.03 If, on taking initial instructions and advising on the merits of a case, the client wishes to pursue or resist a claim, there must be consideration of legal procedure, which is, for civil claims, governed by the Civil Procedure Rules 1998 (CPR 1998). The rules are also supplemented by Practice Directions. Both the Rules and the Practice Directions are subject to regular review, amendment, and revision. Where they are relevant to environmental cases, they are considered in outline below.

Civil Procedure Rules 1998

Rule 1.1 of the CPR 1998 states that the overriding objective of the Rules is enabling the court to deal with cases justly, which, under r 1.1(2), includes so far as is practicable: **17.04**

(a) ensuring that the parties are on an equal footing;
(b) saving expense;
(c) dealing with the case in ways which are proportionate (i) to the amount of money involved, (ii) the importance of the case, iii) to the complexity of the issues, and iv) to the financial position of each party;
(d) ensuring that it is dealt with expeditiously and fairly; and
(e) allotting to it an appropriate share of the court's resources, while taking into account the need to allot resources to other cases.

That the court only has to deal with a case justly, so far as is reasonably practicable, has meant that a court cannot prevent a party from instructing the legal representatives or experts of their choice, even though, this in practice may result in parties being on an unequal footing. However, following *Maltez v Lewis* (1999) The Times, 4 May 1999 the court may order a larger firm to prepare court bundles or let a smaller firm have more time to prepare. The CPR 1998 and the latest Practice Directions are available at the Department of Constitutional Affairs' website at www.dca.gov.uk. **17.05**

Limitation periods

The main purpose of limitation periods is to avoid a defendant having the indefinite threat of a claim. The Limitation Act 1980 (as amended) covers limitation periods for most environmental claims, although judicial review is covered under r 54.5 of the CPR 1998 and is discussed in Chapter 20: Public law. Sections 2 and 5 of the Act state that for contract and tort claims (including nuisance and trespass) the limitation period is six years. Important exceptions to this include, among other things: under s 11 of the Act, the special time limit for claims in respect of personal injuries, and s 11A claims in respect of defective products under the Consumer Protection Act 1987. Under s 190 of the Merchant Shipping Act 1995, claims for personal injury or damage to vessel, cargo, or property at sea have a limitation period of two years and under s 7(5) of the Human Rights Act 1998, human rights claims are subject to a limitation period of one year. **17.06**

The general rule in tort is that the time starts to run in calculating the limitation period from the date the act or omission occurred, not the date of knowledge. For personal injury actions s 11(4) of the Limitation Act 1980 provides that time runs from the date the cause of action accrued or, if later, the date of the claimant's knowledge. For other, non-personal injury negligence claims, ss 14A and 14B provide that the starting date is the earliest date the claimant knew that the damage was sufficiently serious to justify proceedings, that it was attributable to the alleged negligence, and the defendant's identity. It will be important to check the legislation and any Limitation Act 1980 provision that may relate specifically to the environmental concern, e.g. housing, statutory nuisance, etc. **17.07**

Pre-action protocols

17.08   The Civil Procedure Rules 1998 Practice Direction on Protocols provides at para 1.4 that the objectives of pre-action protocols are:

- to encourage the exchange of early and full information about the prospective legal claim;
- to enable parties to avoid litigation by agreeing a settlement of the claim before the commencement of proceedings; and
- to support the efficient management of proceedings where litigation cannot be avoided.

17.09   Paragraph 2.1 of the Practice Direction adds that r 3 of the CPR 1998 enables the court to take into account compliance or non-compliance with an applicable protocol when giving directions for management of proceedings, while r 44.3(5) can take such matters into account when making orders for costs. At present, the main pre-action protocol relevant to environmental claims is the Personal Injury Protocol, however, the Practice Direction provides at paras:

   4.1   In cases not covered by any approved protocol, the court will expect the parties, in accordance with the overriding objective and matters referred to in CPR 1998 1.1(2)(a), (b) and (c), to act reasonably in exchanging information and documents relevant to the claim and generally in trying to avoid the necessity for the start of proceedings.

   4.2   Parties to a potential dispute should follow a reasonable procedure, suitable to their particular circumstances, which is intended to avoid litigation. The procedure should not be regarded as a prelude to inevitable litigation.

17.10   For personal injury and property damage from road incidents, there is compulsory insurance under s 145 of the Road Traffic Act 1988, and providing a claimant gives a defendant's insurer notice of proceedings before or within seven days after proceedings begin, the insurer must satisfy any judgment obtained.

Commencing proceedings

17.11   County courts and the Queen's Bench Division of the High Court usually hear environmental claims in civil law; they both have jurisdiction. However, unless the claim is a particularly complex one of very high value, then the matter should begin in the county court. Also, Art 5 of The High Court and County Courts Jurisdiction Order 1991 (SI 1991/724) provides that for personal injury claims where the claimant does not expect to recover more than £50,000, the claim must be commenced in a county court.

Issuing and serving a claim

17.12   Part 7 of the CPR 1998 explains how to start proceedings. Claim form N1 is the general form that must be completed. This and many other court forms can be downloaded from www.hmcourts-service.gov.uk. Part 7.2 of the CPR 1998 states that proceedings are started when the court issues the claim form at the request of the claimant. A claim form is issued on the date entered on the form by the court. It must then be served on the defendant within four months (Pt 7.5 of the CPR 1998) together with the particulars of claim, forms for either defending or admitting the claim, and the acknowledgement of service. If the particulars of claim are not served with the claim form, they must be served within 14 days.

The circumstances of any particular case may also determine what other actions should **17.13** be taken on issuing and serving a claim. For example, whether there is a need to apply for an injunction to restrain or prevent a trespass, or to apply for an interim possession order in relation to anti-social behaviour by a tenant.

Responding to a claim

A defendant who wants to challenge a claim must, within 14 days from the date of service, **17.14** reply to the claim form by filing an acknowledgement of service and/or a defence at court. Under r 10.2 of the CPR 1998 if a defendant fails to file an acknowledgement of service or defence, the claimant may obtain default judgment under Pt 12. An extension of time for filing a defence may be agreed up to a period of 28 days. Defended claims may also find that the case is transferred to the defendant's local court or to the High Court in particular circumstances.

A defendant, in addition to submitting a defence, may wish to make a Pt 20 claim. Rule **17.15** 20.2(1) provides that a Pt 20 claim is any claim other than a claim by a claimant against a defendant and includes:

(a) a counterclaim by a defendant against the claimant or against the claimant and some other person;
(b) a claim by a defendant against any person (whether or not already a party) for contribution or indemnity or some other remedy; and
(c) where a Pt 20 claim has been made against a person who is not already a party, any claim made by that person against any other person (whether or not already a party).

The purpose of Pt 20 of the CPR 1998 is to enable any counterclaims or other claims to be **17.16** managed in the most convenient and effective manner. Rule 20.4 (1) states that a defendant may make a counterclaim against a claimant by filing particulars of the counterclaim either without the court's permission if he files it with his defence, or at any other time with the court's permission. The Civil Liability (Contribution) Act 1978 provides that a defendant who is liable to a claim in negligence or any other tort can recover from someone else that he believes is also responsible. It is not strictly a defence but it can significantly reduce the financial liability of a defendant.

Statements of case

Rule 2.3(1) of the CPR 1998 defines a 'statement of case' to include: **17.17**

(a) a claim form, particulars of claims where these are not included in a claim form, defence, Part 20 claim or a reply to a defence; and
(b) includes any further information given in relation to them voluntarily or by court order under r 18.1; . . .

Rule 22.1(1) of the CPR 1998 provides that a statement of truth must verify a statement of **17.18** case. Parties are allowed to serve documents in support of the statement of case. These may include expert and medical reports and any written agreements.

Amendment of case

Part 17 of the CPR 1998 governs the procedure for amending a statement of case. It can be **17.19** amended without permission any time before it is served, with the written consent of the parties at any stage of the proceedings, or with the permission of the court. Part 17 provides details relating to amendments in specific circumstances, e.g. to disallow amendments made without permission and those after the end of a relevant limitation period.

Track allocation and case management

17.20 Part 26 provides for the automatic transfer of some defended cases between courts and the allocation of defended cases to case management tracks. There are three case management tracks:

- small claims track;
- fast track; and
- multi-track.

17.21 Once a defence has been filed, the court will serve allocation questionnaires (form N150) on all parties (or, if appropriate, dispense with the need for questionnaires). However, if an application for default or summary judgment is made, or if there is a stay in the proceedings then the matter will not be allocated but be dealt with accordingly.

17.22 Rule 26.3(6) of the CPR 1998 states that each party must file the completed allocation questionnaire no later than the date specified in it, which shall be at least 14 days after the date when it is deemed to be served on the party in question. The claimant must file an allocation fee (currently £200) when returning the completed questionnaire.

17.23 Cases are allocated, in general, on the financial value of the claim. Rule 26.6 sets the criteria for each track.

Rule 26.6(1): small claims track

17.24 The small claims track is the normal track for any claim, subject to certain exclusions, which has a financial value of not more than £5,000 except personal injury claims where the pain, suffering, and loss of amenity element exceeds £1,000. Hearings of small claims are generally given a time estimate of between one and three hours.

Rule 26.6(4), (5): fast track

17.25 Rule 26.6(4) provides that the fast track is the normal track for any claim for which the small claims track is not the normal track and that has a financial value of not more than £15,000. The fast track is the normal track for the claims referred to in para (4) only if the court considers that the trial is likely to last for no longer than one day; and oral expert evidence at trial will be limited to one expert per party in relation to any expert evidence in two expert fields.

Rule 26.6(6): multi-track

17.26 Rule 26.6(6) provides that the multi-track is the normal track for any claim for which the small claims track or the fast track are not the normal track.

Progressing the proceedings

17.27 There are a number of matters that may arise during the course of proceedings depending on how the case progresses. These include, among other things, seeking further information, joining parties to proceedings, applying for summary judgment, striking out, or discontinuing the claim.

Further information

If the statement of case provided by a party to proceedings is unclear or the other side **17.28**
requires further information then they may apply to the court for an order under Pt 18.
Rule 18.1 (1) states that:

> The court may at any time order a party to:
> (a) clarify any matter which is in dispute in the proceedings; or
> (b) give additional information in relation to any such matter,
> whether or not the matter is contained or referred to in a statement of case.

Joining parties, group litigation, and consolidation

Part 19 of the CPR 1998 allows review and amendment to the parties in an action. Rule 19.1 **17.29**
states that any number of claimants or defendants may be joined as parties to a claim. Under
r 19.11 the court may make a Group Litigation Order (GLO) where there are or are likely
to be a number of claims giving rise to the GLO issues. A GLO is defined in r 19.10 as: 'an
order made under r 19.11 to provide for the case management of claims which give rise to
common or related issues of fact or law (the GLO issues).'

The Civil Procedure Volume 1 (the *White Book*) gives examples at para 19.10.0 of circum- **17.30**
stances in which the handling of claims involving multiple parties may be assisted by group
litigation. These include:

> (1) personal injury claims, arising from e.g. (a) sudden disaster, (b) industrial disease or
> accident, (c) medical investigation or treatment, or (d) taking of medicines or (e) use
> of defective products; and . . .
> (3) damage to property, arising from e.g. a) landlord's failure to repair properties with multiple
> tenants, b) nuisance or diminution of value of business or residential premises arising from
> a common cause.

It adds that since the decision in *Lubbe & ors v Cape Plc* [2000] 1 WLR 1545 it is clear that **17.31**
proceedings, including group actions, can be brought in the UK against parent companies of
multinational corporations arising from action in other jurisdictions on *forum conveniens*
grounds, i.e. the most appropriate forum, but only when the claimants could be denied
justice in their own jurisdictions. Further, *Afrika v Cape Plc* [2001] EWCA Civ 2017 CA
is an important decision on cost sharing in group litigation, in particular that the determination of costs payable by claimants who discontinue proceedings should wait until the
determination of the relevant common issues.

A list of current GLOs in the Queen's Bench Division is available at www.hmcourts- **17.32**
service.gov.uk. Rule 19.13 of the CPR 1998 provides that directions by the management
court may include appointing the solicitor of one or more parties to be the lead solicitor for
the claimants or defendants.

Consolidation of closely connected claims may also be ordered under r 3.1(2)(g) of the CPR **17.33**
1998 as part of the court's case management powers. The distinction between consolidation

and group litigation is that for consolidation two or more claims are brought together under one claim and the matter proceeds as one claim thereafter. Under a GLO a number of distinct proceedings are brought together but are not merged. They are simply managed collectively but remain distinct sets of proceedings. Either consolidation or group litigation may often be appropriate in environmental claims, and in particular disease-related cases, where a number of claimants have suffered injury out of either the same or similar sets of facts.

Summary judgment

17.34   The court may give summary judgment against a claimant or defendant on the whole claim or on a particular issue if, under r 24.2:

   (a)   it considers that (i) that claimant has no real prospect of succeeding on the claim or issue; or (ii) that defendant has no real prospect of successfully defending the claim or issue; and

   (b)   there is no other compelling reason why the case or issue should be disposed of at a trial.

17.35   The difference between default and summary judgment is that default judgment (under Pt 12) may be given when the defendant fails to file an acknowledgement of service and/or a defence) whereas summary judgment is where the court considers on the application of one of the parties that the claim, defence, or issue has no real prospects of success.

Striking out the statement of case

17.36   Rule 3.4(2) of the CPR 1998 states that the court may strike out a statement of case if it appears to the court:

   (a)   that the statement of case discloses no reasonable grounds for bringing or defending the claim;

   (b)   that the statement of case is an abuse of the court's process or is otherwise likely to obstruct the just disposal of the proceedings; or

   (c)   that there has been a failure to comply with a rule, practice direction or court order.

17.37   Two key distinctions between summary judgment and an order to strike out under r 3.4(2) are that, such an order applies to cases where there is non-compliance with a rule, practice direction, or court order and summary judgment can include the summary disposal of pre-liminary issues rather than the whole claim. However, to strike out a claim solely on the claimant's delay where there is a reasonable prospect of success is likely to breach Art 6(1) of the European Convention of Human Rights: see *Arrow Nominees Inc v Blackledge* (1999) The Times, 8 December 1999.

Discontinuance

17.38   Rule 38.2(1) of the CPR 1998 enables a claimant to discontinue all or part of a claim at any time. In general, the claimant does not require permission of the court although r 38.1(2) includes some instances where the court's permission is required, e.g. the claimant wishes to discontinue all or part of a claim where an interim injunction has been granted or where any party has given an undertaking to the court. Under r 38.6, a claimant is liable for the costs of the defendant incurred on or before the date on which notice of discontinuance was served, unless the court orders otherwise.

Settlement

A settlement is often reached between the parties before the claim is heard at trial by the **17.39** court. Settlement may also arise at the start or even part way through a trial. There are various ways to record a settlement; these range from concluding the matter by consent order to reaching settlement between counsel for the parties with settlement terms being endorsed on counsel's brief, which is the most informal approach and most difficult to enforce.

Paragraph 4.1 of Practice Direction 39 provides that where an offer to settle a claim is **17.40** accepted, a settlement is reached, or a claim is discontinued, which disposes of the whole of a claim for which a date or 'window' has been fixed for the trial, the parties must ensure that the listing officer for the trial court is notified immediately. Paragraph 4.2 adds that if an order is drawn up giving effect to the settlement or discontinuance, a copy of the sealed order should be filed with the listing officer.

Stay on proceedings

There may be occasions when effective case management requires that a case should be **17.41** stayed pending a related outcome or event. Rule 3.1(2)(f) provides that the court may stay the whole or part of any proceedings either generally or until a specified date or event. There are also a number of specific rules to enable a stay including, under r 26.4, to allow for settlement of the case or a reference to the European Court of Justice under Pt 68.

There are instances where proceedings have been stayed to secure compliance with pro- **17.42** cedural rules, e.g. in *Dunn v British Coal Corporation* (1993) The Times, 5 March 1993, a stay was ordered for the disclosure of medical records.

There may also be a stay of one of a number of similar proceedings where it is more efficient **17.43** to hear all the claims together but where consolidation of the claims is not appropriate. In this instance, one or more case may be stayed to allow for others to 'catch up': see *Slough Estates Ltd v Slough BC* [1968] Ch 299. In instances where there are concurrent criminal and civil proceedings the court may stay the civil proceedings until the outcome of the criminal matter, taking into account the defendant's right to silence in those proceedings. In *Barnet LBC v Hurst* [2002] EWCA Civ 1009 the judge, upon the defendant giving an undertaking, adjourned the hearing of the council's committal application for breach of an anti-social behaviour order until the completion of criminal proceedings against the defendant.

Reference to European Court of Justice

With much of environmental law derived from the EU, there are, on occasions, matters **17.44** that need to be clarified by reference to the European Court of Justice (ECJ). Under Pt 68 of the CPR 1998 the court may refer a question to the ECJ for a preliminary ruling under:

(a) Art 234 of the EU Treaty;
(b) Art 150 of the Euratom Treaty;
(c) Art 41 of the ECSC Treaty;
(d) the Protocol of 3.6.71 on the interpretation by the European Court of the Convention of 27.9.68 on Jurisdiction and the Enforcement of Judgments in Civil and Commercial Matters; or

(e) the Protocol of 19.12.88 on the interpretation by the European Court of the Convention of 19.6.80 on the Law applicable to Contractual Obligations.

17.45 An order may be made at any stage of the proceedings by the court of its own initiative or on application by a party. Where an order is made, unless the court orders otherwise, the proceedings will be stayed until the ECJ has given a preliminary ruling on the question referred to it.

Interim orders

17.46 Either party may apply to the court for an interim order prior to the full hearing and any judgment given. In particular there may be interim payments and interim remedies.

Interim remedies

17.47 Under r 25.1(1) the court may grant a wide range of interim remedies such as:

    (a) an interim injunction;
    (b) an interim declaration;
    (c) an order for, [among other things, detention, custody, preservation or inspection of relevant property];
    (d) an order authorising a person to enter any land or building for carrying out an order under (c) . . .
    (h) an order (referred to as a 'search order') under s 7 of the Civil Procedure Act 1997 (order requiring a party to admit another party to premises for the purpose of preserving evidence, etc.); [also known as an *Anton Pillar* order] . . .

17.48 Under r 25.2(1) an order for an interim remedy may be made at any time including before proceedings are started and after judgment has been given. This is subject to any rule, practice direction, or other enactment providing otherwise; and that the matter must be urgent or that it is otherwise necessary to do so in the interests of justice; and that, unless the court otherwise directs, a defendant may not apply for any order before filing an acknowledgement of service or a defence.

17.49 The more common form of interim remedy is an interim injunction. An application for an interim injunction in the county court is by way of form N16, which should include the order sought and the date, time, and place of the hearing. Many applications are made to secure urgent protection and the application is made pre-action and often without notice to the other side. The application is likely to be heard at a hearing, although in extremely urgent cases, an application can be made by telephone. Any order granted by the court will only be effective once it is served on the other party. Paragraph 5.1 of Practice Direction 25 states that unless the court orders otherwise, any order made without notice must contain an undertaking by the applicant to the court to serve on the respondent the application notice, evidence in support, and any order made as soon as practicable, and a return date for a further hearing at which the other party can be present.

17.50 In *American Cyanamid v Ethicon Ltd* [1975] AC 396 the House of Lords suggested that the following guidelines should be followed when seeking to order an interim prohibitory (rather than mandatory) injunction:

- that there must be a serious question to be tried;
- that damages would be an inadequate remedy;
- that an undertaking in damages could be provided by the applicant for the injunction;
- that there was a balance of convenience that had to be applied between the parties;
- that the status quo should be maintained; and
- that there may be special factors to take into account.

Interim payments

One element of r 25.1(1) in subpara (k) is referred to as an order for interim payment which **17.51**
is: 'an order . . . under r 25.6 for payment by a defendant on account of any damages, debt or
other sum (except costs) which the court may hold the defendant liable to pay.'

In contrast to an application for an interim injunction, an interim payment order may **17.52**
only be applied for after the end of the period provided for filing of acknowledgement of
service.

Evidence

General principles

In civil claims it is, in general, for the claimant to prove on a balance of probabilities **17.53**
(more than 50%) that the point at issue is proved in the affirmative. If this is done then the
claimant has a case and the defendant will have to challenge the assertion.

Evidence to support a case may be direct evidence, e.g. a witness giving oral evidence on **17.54**
oath, or as is now usual in civil matters, a witness statement being admitted as evidence and
the statement maker being cross-examined on the statement. Under s 1 of the Civil Evidence
Act 1995 (CEA 1995) hearsay evidence may be used in civil proceedings. Hearsay is defined
in s 1(2)(a) as a statement made otherwise than by a witness from the witness box. A
party seeking to rely on hearsay must comply with the requirements of the CEA 1995
including giving advance notice to all other parties that hearsay evidence intends to be used.
Finally, circumstantial evidence may be used to prove a fact. *Cross & Tapper on Evidence*
(Butterworths, 2004) defines circumstantial evidence as any fact from the existence of which
the judge or jury may infer the existence of a fact in issue (the principal fact). In gathering
evidence it may well be possible and indeed, necessary, to rely upon the Environmental
Information Regulations 2004 (SI 2004/3391) to secure such information, see Chapter 2:
Environmental rights and principles. Pugh (LexisNexis, 2004) suggests that there may
be four categories of evidence that establish causation in a personal injury pollution
case: historical, toxicological, medical, and epidemiological evidence. Each is outlined
below.

Historical evidence

Historical evidence will include the claimant's history of what has occurred, the symptoms **17.55**
of the injury, and the impact on the claimant and others. Important information will
include any diary notes or records made and any other correspondence with relevant
organizations. Other organizations and public bodies may well have valuable information to
build up a complete picture in particular organizations such as the police, local authority
health officers, and the fire brigade.

Toxicological evidence

17.56 Toxicology is the science of poisons and so toxicological evidence should aim to assess the relationship between any disease, injury, or illness and the exposure to any hazardous substance or poison.

Medical evidence

17.57 Any medical evidence should aim to provide an initial and then subsequent diagnosis of injury, a history and then programme of treatment, and a prognosis.

Epidemiological evidence

17.58 Epidemiology is the study of the distribution and determinants of disease in human populations. Any evidence of this nature will look at general causation and, for example, whether or not the particular environmental impact or effect is capable of causing the disease, injury, or illness concerned. In *Reay v British Nuclear Fuels plc* [1994] Env LR 320 the court set out the criteria for adopting epidemiological evidence in a claim including:

- the strength of association found by the study;
- the consistency of the dose-response relationship, e.g. whether the risk of disease rises with increasing exposure;
- temporal relationships, and in particular that the exposure must precede the onset of the disease;
- the consistency of the study results with other similar studies concerned with the same subject matter;
- whether it is plausible that the substance can cause the relevant illness; and
- experimental evidence, e.g. have laboratory tests been used in support.

Section 11 of the Civil Evidence Act 1968

17.59 Section 11(1) of the Civil Evidence Act 1968 provides that:

> In any civil proceedings the fact that a person has been convicted of an offence by or before any court in the UK or by a court-martial there or elsewhere shall . . . be admissible in evidence for the purpose of proving, where to do so is relevant to any issue in those proceedings, that he committed that offence, whether he was so convicted upon a plea of guilty or otherwise and whether or not he is a party to the civil proceedings, but no conviction other than a subsisting one shall be admissible in evidence.

17.60 In *Edgson v Vickers Plc* [1994] ICR 510 the widow of a man who contracted mesothelioma sought damages from his former employer for his death. The court held that there was a breach of the health and safety regulations and so a breach of their duty of care; see Chapter 7: Human health.

Use of evidence

17.61 Judgment is given after taking all the evidence from the parties. Part 32 of the CPR 1998 relates to evidence. Rule 32.1(1) states that the court may control the evidence by giving directions as to:

(a) the issues on which it requires evidence;

(b)   the nature of the evidence which it requires to decide those issues; and

(c)   the way in which the evidence is to be placed before the court.

Under r 32.1(2) the court may use its power under this rule to exclude evidence that would **17.62** otherwise be admissible. It may, under r 32.1(3) limit cross-examination.

Disclosure

Disclosure is defined under r 31.2 of the CPR 1998 as 'stating that a document exists or has **17.63** existed.'

There is no provision for automatic disclosure; the duty to disclose arises upon the court **17.64** ordering so. This will often be as directions made at the track allocation stage. Rule 31.6 provides that standard disclosure requires a party to disclose only those documents on which he relies; and the documents that adversely affect his own case, adversely affect another party's case, or support another party's case, and the document that he is required to disclose by a relevant practice direction.

The procedure for standard disclosure is under r 31.10(2) that each party must make and **17.65** serve on every other party, a list of documents in the relevant practice form. The list must identify the documents in a convenient order and manner and as concisely as possible. The list must indicate the documents in respect of which the party claims a right or duty to withhold inspection as well as those documents that are no longer in the party's control and what has happened to those documents. Certain documents may be subject to legal professional privilege such as communications between a solicitor and client.

Inspection of documents can be either personal inspection or by each party supplying **17.66** copy documents on the undertaking that the other side pay the reasonable copy charges.

Experts

Environmental claims will often require the evidence of professional and expert witnesses **17.67** providing opinion on scientific and technical matters such as the environmental effects of a pollution incident. This is largely due to the complex relationship between pollution, the environment, and human beings. Expert evidence will generally be based upon a report.

Part 35 of the CPR 1998 governs experts and assessors. Under r 35.3 expert witnesses have an **17.68** overriding duty to the court to help the court on the matters within their expertise. However, no party can call an expert or put in evidence an expert's report without the court's permission. Rule 35.4(2) states that when a party applies for permission he must identify the field in which he wishes to rely on expert evidence and, where practicable, the expert in that field on whose evidence he wishes to rely. If permission is granted it shall only be in relation to the expert named or the field identified. Rule 35.7(1) provides that where two or more parties wish to submit expert evidence on a particular issue, the court may direct that the evidence on that issue is to be given by one expert only.

In personal injury claims it is likely that the defendant's medical experts will need to **17.69** examine the claimant although the court cannot order the claimant to be examined by the defendant party. To assist the defendant in obtaining medical evidence, the court can order a stay of proceedings if the claimant refuses a reasonable request for a medical examination undertaken on behalf of the defendant. In *Starr v National Coal Board* [1977] 1 WLR 63 the court held that when considering whether to stay proceedings in this instance, the defendant's examination request must be reasonable and the claimant's refusal or resistance must be such as to prevent the just determination of the claim.

17.70   The *Code of Guidance on Expert Evidence: A Guide for Experts and those Instructing them for the Purpose of Court Proceedings* (2001) aims to help experts and those instructing them in all cases where the CPR 1998 apply. It is intended to facilitate better communication and dealings both between the expert and the instructing party and between the parties. Many professional bodies also have certain requirements in acting as an expert witness, e.g. The Royal Institution of Chartered Surveyors requirements are set out in *Acting as Expert Witnesses: Practice Statements* (2001).

Witnesses and witness statements

17.71   Rule 32.2 provides that the general rule to witness evidence is that any fact that needs to be provided by the evidence of witnesses is to be proved at trial, by their oral evidence given in public, and, at any other hearing, by their evidence in writing.

17.72   Witness evidence at trial used to be given orally, but more recently witness statements exchanged before trial stand as evidence in chief, with the other party able to cross-examine the witness on these at the trial. The most common form of written evidence is the witness statement, which includes a statement of truth at the end, although other forms of written evidence may be used including:

- witness summaries; informal documents summarizing what the witness is expected to say at trial (they may be used if there has been some difficulty in arranging the witness's signature of a full statement);
- affidavits and affirmations; not used so frequently since the introduction of witness statements.

Witness summons

17.73   If a witness is unwilling to attend trial, r 34.2(1) provides that a witness summons is a document issued by the court requiring a witness to attend court to give evidence; or produce documents to the court. It must be in the relevant practice form. A party must obtain permission from the court where he wishes to have a summons issued less than seven days before the date of trial, or to have a summons issued for a witness to attend court to give evidence or to produce documents on any date except the date fixed for the trial or to attend any hearing except the trial.

17.74   Securing evidence of the many components of nuisance will be critical. There will need to be evidence of standing, of harm, and of reasonableness. In *Piper v Clifford Kent Ltd* [2003] EWCA Civ 1692 the Court of Appeal held that a judge who, after a site visit, concluded that there was no continuing nuisance from a specified date (refusing injunctive relief but awarding damages) had overlooked the fact that the nuisance was never said to be a continuous nuisance but was of an intermittent character. Proving that a smell did not exist on one day did not prove that it did not exist on others. The matter was remitted back to the county court for further investigation.

Trial

Listing and pre-trial reviews

Listing for trial varies according to the type of case management track: **17.75**

- small claims trial dates are often fixed when the court allocates the case to this track;
- fast track claims aim to be heard within 30 weeks of allocation and are either fixed or provided with a trial window of up to three weeks, during which the case is likely to be heard.
- for multi-track claims the court on allocation of the case gives, under r 29.2(1), directions for the management of the case and sets a timetable for the steps to be taken between the giving of directions and the trial; or fixes either a case management conference or a pre-trial review, or both.

Pre-trial reviews are generally only used for multi-track claims. They are likely to be con- **17.76**
ducted by the trial judge a few weeks before trial. Rule 29.8 provides that as soon as practicable after each party has filed a completed pre-trial checklist, the court has held a listing hearing, or the court has held a pre-trial review the court will:

(i)   set a timetable for the trial unless a timetable has already been fixed, or the court considers that it would be inappropriate to do so;

(ii) fix the date for the trial or the week within which the trial is to begin (or, if it has already done so, confirm that date); and

(iii) notify the parties of the trial timetable (where one is fixed under this rule) and the date of the trial period.

The general rule is, under r 39.2 of the CPR 1998, that the trial is to be in public although **17.77**
this does not require the court to make special arrangements for accommodating the public. However, it may be in private if, e.g. publicity would defeat the object of the hearing, or the court considers this necessary in the interests of justice. This meets the requirements of Art 6 of the ECHR, which provides that:

> in the determination of his civil rights and obligations . . . everyone is entitled to a fair and public hearing . . . Judgment shall be pronounced publicly but the press and public may be excluded from all or part of the trial in the interest of morals, public order or national security.

Documentation

For fast track and multi-track claims, trial bundles containing all documents to be referred **17.78**
to should be filed by the claimant not more than seven but not less than three days before the start of the trial. Paragraph 3 of Practice Direction 39 states that, unless the court orders otherwise, the trial bundle should include a copy of:

(1) the claim form and all statements of case;

(2) a case summary and/or chronology where appropriate;

(3) requests for further information and responses to the requests;

(4) all witness statements to be relied on as evidence;

(5) any witness summaries;

(6) any notices of intention to rely on hearsay evidence under r 32.2;

(7) any notices of intention to rely on evidence (such as a plan, photograph, etc.) under r 33.6, which is not (a) contained in a witness statement, affidavit, or expert's report, (b) being given orally at trial, (c) hearsay evidence under r 33.2;

(8) any medical reports and responses to them;

(9) any experts' reports and responses to them;

(10) any order giving directions as to the conduct of the trial; and

(11) any other necessary documents.

17.79   In cases being tried in the Queen's Bench Division, the claimant must lodge with the trial bundle a reading list for the judge who will conduct the hearing, an estimated length of reading time, and an estimated length for the hearing.

Rights of audience

17.80   Under s 27(2) of the Courts and Legal Services Act 1990, a number of persons currently have rights of audience at trial including:

(a) counsel and solicitors, subject to the terms of their authorized body;

(b) persons given a right of audience under statute, e.g. a local authority officer in certain proceedings;

(c) where a right of audience has been granted by the court; and

(d) a litigant in person.

Procedure at trial

17.81   It is likely that the judge would have had an opportunity to read the papers in the trial bundle before the trial and often the claimant's opening speech can be dispensed with. If so, evidence, e.g. witnesses on behalf of the claimant, will be called. Following confirmation of the witness statement a witness may be cross-examined by the defendant. Any matter raised in cross-examination may be re-examined by the claimant's representative. The trial judge can seek clarification from the witnesses during evidence.

17.82   After all the evidence from the claimant, the defendant may make a submission of no case to answer, although in practice this is uncommon. Usually, the defence will call evidence in the same way as a claimant, with the defendant's evidence being cross-examined by the claimant. Following the defence evidence, there is a closing speech by the defendant. The trial concludes by a closing speech from the claimant.

Failure to attend trial

17.83   Rule 39.3(1) of the CPR 1998 states that the court may proceed with a trial in the absence of a party but:

(a) if no party attends the trial it may strike out the whole of the proceedings;

(b) if the claimant does not attend, it may strike out his claim and any defence to counter-claim; and

(c) if a defendant does not attend, it may strike out his defence or counterclaim (or both).

17.84   Under r 39.3(2), where the court strikes out proceedings, or any part of them, it may subsequently restore the proceedings, or that part. And, under r 39.3(3) where a party does not attend and the court gives judgment or makes an order against him, the party who failed to attend may apply for the judgment or order to be set aside. However, an application under subs (2) and (3) must be supported by evidence. The court may grant the application only if the applicant acted promptly when he found out that the court had exercised its power to strike out or to enter judgment, had a good reason for not attending the trial, and has a reasonable prospect of success at trial.

Part 36 offers

A Part 36 offer and Part 36 payment are an offer to settle the claim and a payment into court **17.85** respectively, made in accordance with the provisions of Pt 36 of the CPR 1998. Part 36 applies to claims, counterclaims and other additional claims made under Pt 20 of the CPR 1998. They are a means of putting pressure on the other party to settle by creating the risk of having to pay the costs of the other side for the proceedings after the date of the offer or payment into court, if any final award by the court is not greater than the value of that payment into court.

Judgments and orders

The judgment in a case is, in general, the conclusion to the substantive proceedings and is **17.86** given at the end of the trial. For more complex cases, the judgment may be reserved for a later date. In addition or instead of the judgment there may be a court order. Rule 40.7(1) of the CPR 1998 states that a judgment or order takes effect from the day when it is given or made, or such later date as the court may specify. The judgment or order will be drawn up by the court unless either the court orders a party to draw it up, a party, with the court's permission, agrees to draw it up, the court dispenses with the need to draw it up, or it is a consent order.

Orders that may be made by the court include: **17.87**

- an award of damages;
- an injunction order or an undertaking to the court, given by one or more of the parties;
- a consent order, which is effectively a contract between the parties;
- a Tomlin order, where terms of compromise of the claim are agreed and intend to stay the claim, following the Practice Note [1927] WN 290 made by Tomlin J who stated that the claimant and defendant:

> . . . having agreed to the terms set forth in the schedule hereto, it is ordered that all further proceedings in this claim be stayed, except for the purpose of carrying such terms into effect. Liberty to apply as to carrying such terms into effect.

Damages

Damages is a legal term defined in *Halsburys Laws of England* 4/e as: '. . . the recompense **17.88** given by process of law to a person for the wrong that another has done him.'

Injunctions

Injunctions are an important aspect of environmental protection under the civil law. They **17.89** are a discretionary remedy where the court will consider a range of factors particular to the case. A key principle on which an injunction is likely to be granted is if the harm caused from the defendant's behaviour is of such a nature that an award of compensation would not be an adequate remedy for the claimant.

The courts are reluctant to grant injunctions. Lord Justice A L Smith in *Shelfer v City of London* **17.90** *Electrical Lighting Co.* [1895] 1 Ch 287 stated that the good working rule in considering whether or not to grant an injunction was that:

(1) if the injury to the plaintiff's legal right is small;

(2) is one that is capable of being estimated in money;

(3) is one that can be adequately compensated by a money payment; and

(4) the case is one in which it would be oppressive to the defendant to grant an injunction;

then damages in substitution for an injunction may be given.

17.91 This approach has been followed in some cases including *Kennaway v Thompson* [1981] QB 88 but not in others, e.g. *Colls v Home and Colonial Stores Ltd* [1904] AC 179 (see para 17.160).

17.92 An injunction may, in an emergency, be granted without notice to the defendant, although the injunction will not be effective until it is served upon him. A without notice injunction order will usually be drafted to remain in force for a short period. The date of expiry will coincide with a return hearing date where the matter will be heard on notice giving the defendant an opportunity to defend the claim. An application for an injunction on form N16A cannot be applied for on its own merit but must be in support of a substantive claim for damages on form N1.

17.93 Under s 222 of the Local Government Act 1972, a local authority may bring, defend, or appear in proceedings for the promotion or protection of the interests of inhabitants of their area. Under s 91 of the Anti-social Behaviour Act 2003, if the court grants an injunction that prohibits conduct that is capable of causing nuisance or annoyance to a person it may, if the conduct includes the use or threatened use of violence, or if there is a significant risk of harm to that person, attach a power of arrest to any provision of the injunction.

17.94 The House of Lords in *South Bucks DC v Porter* [2003] UKHL 26 upheld the Court of Appeal decision that a court should not grant an injunction unless it was prepared to commit the defendants to prison for breach of that injunction. The county court had earlier granted injunctions to the local planning authority to require gypsies living in mobile homes in breach of planning control to move off the site. In this case the injunction was not a proportionate remedy. However, ultimately it is for the court to decide whether it was just and appropriate to grant relief. In *Tonbridge and Malling BC v Davis* [2004] EWCA Civ 194 the Court of Appeal upheld the grant of an injunction to a local authority to restrain a group of travelling showmen from continuing to occupy a green belt site in breach of planning control.

Appeals

17.95 There may be an opportunity to appeal an order or judgment if that decision was, under r 52.11(3) (a) wrong, or (b) unjust because of a serious procedural or other irregularity in the proceedings. Part 52 and Practice Direction 52 cover the appeal process. Important aspects of appeal relate to: seeking permission to appeal, timing, and choosing the appeal court.

Permission to appeal

17.96 Rule 52.3(1) provides that an appellant or respondent requires permission to appeal where it is from a decision of a judge in a county court or the High Court, except where the appeal is against, among other things, a committal order; or as provided by the relevant practice direction. The claimant (or his/her representative) will often seek permission to appeal at the end of the hearing that is the subject of appeal. If permission is refused, a further application for permission may be made to the appeal court. If the appeal is to the Court of Appeal, then permission is required from that court. Permission to appeal will only be given where:

(a)   the court considers that the appeal would have a real prospect of success; or

(b)   there is some other compelling reason why the appeal should be heard.

Under r 52.5, a respondent may file and serve a respondent's notice. Although, under **17.97** subpara 52.5(2), this is required if a respondent is seeking permission to appeal from the appeal court or wishes to ask the appeal court to uphold the order from the lower court for reasons different from or additional to those given by the lower court.

Timing

Rule 52.4 provides that where an appellant seeks permission from the appeal court it must be **17.98** made in the appellant's notice. The appellant must file the notice within 14 days of the date of the decision of the lower court, unless the lower court directs otherwise. An appeal notice must then be served on each respondent as soon as practicable, and in any event not later than seven days after it has been filed. Time starts to run from the date when the judge makes his decision, not on the date the order is drawn: see *Sayers v Clarke Walker* [2002] EWCA Civ 645.

Appellant's notice and appeal documents

If permission has not already been granted by the lower court at the end of the hearing, an **17.99** appeal must be made by an appellant's notice by way of form N161. Paragraph 5.6 of the Practice Direction states that the following documents must be filed with form N161:

(1)   an additional copy of the appellant's notice for the appeal court; and

(2)   one copy of the appellant's notice for each of the respondents;

(3)   one copy of the appellant's skeleton argument

(4)   a scaled copy of the order being appealed;

(5)   any order giving or refusing permission to appeal, together with a copy of the reasons for that decision;

(6)   any witness statements or affidavits in support of any application included in the appellant's notice; and

(7)   a bundle of documents in support of the appeal including copies of documents referred to in paragraphs 1 to 6 and any other documents that the appellant reasonably considers necessary to enable the appeal court to reach its decision on the hearing of the application or appeal.

Granting permission to appeal

If the appellant is granted permission to appeal, it will send the permission order and other **17.100** directions to the parties. It will also send either notification of the period when the appeal is likely to be heard or, for the Court of Appeal, a date by which the appeal will be heard. The Court of Appeal will also send an appeal questionnaire.

Hearing of appeals

17.101 Rule 52.11 of the CPR 1998 provides that every appeal will be limited to a review of the decision of the lower court unless:

(a) a practice direction makes a different provision for a particular category of appeal; or

(b) the court considers that in the circumstances of an individual appeal it would be in the interests of justice to hold a re-hearing.

17.102 Under r 52.11(2), the appeal court, unless it orders otherwise, will not receive oral evidence or evidence that was not before the lower court.

17.103 Rule 52.10 provides that the appeal court has all the powers of the lower court and, under subpara (2), also has the power to:

(a) affirm, set aside or vary any order or judgment made or given by the lower court;

(b) refer any claim or issue for determination by the lower court;

(c) order a new trial or hearing;

(d) make an order for the payment of interest;

(e) make a costs order.

Enforcement

17.104 Obtaining judgment may not be an end of the matter and any award or order by the court may need to be enforced to ensure that what is due is actually received. Parts 71 to 75 cover the enforcement of judgment debts. The judgment creditor can apply for one of the following actions:

- execution of goods through a warrant of execution in the county court and a writ of *fieri facias* in the High Court;
- an administration order;
- a third party debt order;
- a charging order (only usually available in the county court);
- an attachment of earnings order; and
- committal for breach of an injunction order or undertaking.

Costs

17.105 The cost of litigation is always high. For many, and despite the attempts of the civil justice system, it is often prohibitively expensive for those who may otherwise have pursued a claim that may well have had a reasonable prospect of success. For those that are able to afford the cost of litigation there are a number of general principles relating to costs, including that a client will always be responsible for his or her own solicitor's costs through the original terms of instruction, even though, ultimately they may be paid by someone else such as the other party, or for those with public funding, the Community Legal Service. The cost of funding litigation is considered in Chapter 21: Funding civil and public law litigation. The costs rules following court proceedings are outlined below.

17.106 Part 44 of the CPR 1998 sets out the general rules about costs including two key principles under r 44.3, which are:

(1) that the court has discretion as to whether costs are payable by one party to another, the amount of those costs and when they are paid; and

(2) If the court decides to make an order about costs the general rule is that the unsuccessful party will be ordered to pay the costs of the successful party [i.e. that costs follow the event]; but that the court may make a different order.

In deciding what order, if any, to make about costs the court must, under r 44.3(4), have regard to all the circumstances, including: **17.107**

(a) the conduct of the parties;

(b) whether a party has succeeded on part of his case, even if he has not been wholly successful; and

(c) any payment into court or admissible offer to settle made by a party, which is drawn to the court's attention.

The general principles and circumstances set out above are expanded in r 44.3 of the CPR 1998 where any costs award may also be influenced by: **17.108**

- the recoupment of benefits in claims involving personal injury;
- where a claimant has been awarded only nominal damages;
- under r 44.3(5)(a), the extent to which the parties followed any relevant pre-action protocol; and
- whether the claim was wrongly started in the High Court.

Part 45 of the CPR 1998 sets the amount of fixed costs in certain cases, e.g. where judgment in default is obtained. Costs in small claims cases are limited to the court fees paid by the successful party, a fixed sum covering the claimant's solicitor's costs in issuing the claim, and limited witness expenses and expert's fees, the general principle is that each party pays their own costs. Costs in the fast track and multi-track are also restricted but do follow the general principle that costs follow the event, e.g. advocates' trial fees in fast track cases are under r 46.2 of the CPR 1998, limited according to the value of the claim. **17.109**

In *Andrews v Reading BC* [2005] JPL 129 the High Court held that a small claim could give rise to important issues, which would inevitably mean that the costs of litigation exceeded the value of the claim and that sometimes that could be dealt with by an order that a public body, with a genuine interest in establishing a point of importance, should pay costs above an amount proportionate to a small claim. **17.110**

Detailed assessment of costs in civil proceedings

The detailed assessment of costs is the process of examining and, if necessary, reducing a party's bill of costs. 'Costs' may include the solicitor's, barristers', and experts' fees. *Judicial Statistics 2003* (DCA, 2004) notes that the purpose of a detailed assessment is: **17.111**

(a) to determine how much costs a successful party in litigation is entitled to recover from his unsuccessful opponent;

(b) in publicly funded cases, to determine the amount that a solicitor or barrister is to be paid out of public funds; and

(c) under the Solicitors' Act 1974, to determine how much a client may have to pay his solicitor.

17.112 The office responsible for assessing costs depends on the case and whether it is publicly funded. The Supreme Court Costs Office deals mainly with costs relating to all proceedings in the Chancery and Queen's Bench Divisions of the High Court, the Court of Appeal (Civil Division), and the London County Court Group. It also deals with costs in matters involving the Court of Protection, various tribunals and assessments transferred from county courts and district registries. Additionally, it deals with appeals against the determination of costs in the Crown Court. The Privy Council, House of Lords, Lands Tribunal, and, except as above, district registries and county courts are responsible for the detailed assessment of costs in their respective courts.

C   NUISANCE

Introduction

17.113 Nuisance is one of the oldest forms of legal action and provides the basis for much of modern environmental law. There are three types of nuisance:

(1) private nuisance: balancing competing rights of neighbours in using their property. It protects rights and interests and the ability to enjoy them;

(2) public nuisance: a crime that protects public rights, albeit with availability of civil ancillary relief, e.g. an injunction. This is discussed in Chapter 19: Criminal law practice and procedure; and

(3) statutory nuisance: which assists public authorities in protecting the environment and human health. It is quasi-criminal in nature, starting off as a civil process but turning to the criminal courts for enforcement. This is discussed in Chapter 18: Statutory nuisance.

17.114 Due to the development of regulation and statutory control of environmental impacts, private nuisance is used relatively infrequently today, although it continues to require judicial clarification and provides important principles from which other aspects of environmental protection seek clarity; in particular the statutory nuisance regime. It has been the subject of a number of key House of Lords decisions in recent years including *Cambridge Water Co. v Eastern Counties Leather* [1994] 1 All ER 53, *Hunter v Canary Wharf* [1997] AC 655, *Transco plc v Stockport MBC* [2003] UKHL 61, and *Marcic v Thames Water Utilities Ltd* [2003] UKHL 66.

Defining private nuisance

17.115 The legal definition of private nuisance is more restrictive than what may be regarded as a nuisance in modern language. In *Read v Lyons & Co.* [1947] AC 156 nuisance was defined as: 'the unlawful interference with a person's use or enjoyment of land or some right over, or in connection with it.'

17.116 This was affirmed in *Miller v Jackson* [1977] QB 966 when the court noted that the essence of a private nuisance is the unreasonable use of a person's land to the detriment of his neighbour. The case illustrates that deciding nuisance cases involves a balance of competing interests. Often in environmental matters it will be pollution and environmental harm that is incidental to economic interests competing against an interest in a clean environment or amenity. In *Miller v Jackson* the nuisance of playing cricket was considered by Lord Denning MR to be of benefit to the community as a whole and had to be balanced with the risk of physical or property damage by stray cricket balls landing in or on land adjoining the cricket green.

The short definition, the unlawful interference with use or enjoyment of land, has a number **17.117** of components and it is necessary to analyse and satisfy each to establish a nuisance claim. The components include:

• material interference or harm suffered by the claimant;
• that the claimant has an interest in the land harmed;
• that there is an appropriate defendant;
• unreasonable use of neighbouring land by the defendant; and
• reasonable foreseeability of the harm by the defendant.

Each of these components is considered below. There is also consideration in relation to **17.118** certain specific environmental concerns in the relevant chapters, e.g. in Chapter 10: Noise.

Material interference or harm

There must be an act or default of the defendant that is a material interference with the **17.119** claimant's property or personal comfort. Lord Evershed in *Thompson-Shwab v Costaki* [1956] 1 WLR 335 affirmed that a private nuisance may be and usually is caused by a person doing, on his own land, something that he is lawfully entitled to do. His conduct only becomes a nuisance when the consequences of his act are not confined to his own land but extend to the land of his neighbour by:

• causing an encroachment on his neighbour's land, when it closely resembles trespass;
• causing physical damage to his neighbour's land, building, works, or vegetation upon it; or
• unduly interfering with his neighbour in the comfortable and convenient enjoyment of his land, often referred to as injury to amenity.

Encroachment onto land

Encroachment on a neighbour's land includes rainwater run-off from a building extension **17.120** that protrudes into a neighbour's garden caused by a building extension following the facts in *Fay v Prentice* (1845) 1 CB 828; and roots from a tree in the highway damaging property as in *Delaware Mansions Ltd v Westminster CC* [2002] 1 AC 321. In both instances, the nuisance action involved an actual intrusion onto the neighbour's land resembling trespass, although the distinction between trespass and encroachment nuisance is that the former is direct while encroachment will be indirect.

Physical damage

Physical damage to property must be something more than nominal. In *St Helen's Smelting* **17.121** *Co v Tipping* [1865] 11 HLC 642, a case in which the damage was to trees and shrubs caused by emissions from a copper smelting works, the court emphasized that there should be material injury to property. Cases of physical damage without encroachment have included enduring smuts on curtains for a number of years (*Halsey v Esso Petroleum* [1961] 1 WLR 683);

where blocked drains cause flooding of a neighbour's land (*Sedleigh-Denfield v O'Callaghan* [1940] AC 880, but see *Marcic v Thames Water Utilities* [2003] UKHL 66); and keeping materials next to a neighbour's land causing damp to develop (*Maberley v Peabody & Co.* [1946] 2 All ER 192).

Injury to amenity

17.122   Lord Hoffman described undue interference with comfort and enjoyment of land in *Hunter v Canary Wharf* as 'injury to amenity'. It was considered in *St Helen's Smelting* to include:

> the personal inconvenience and interference with one's enjoyment, one's quiet, one's personal freedom, anything that discomposes or injuriously affects the senses or nerves.

17.123   In *Walter v Selfe* (1851) 64 ER 849 the Vice Chancellor implied at 852 that nuisance should involve:

> inconvenience materially interfering with the ordinary comfort physically of human existence, not merely according to elegant or dainty modes and habits of living, but according to plain and sober and simple notions among the English people.

17.124   In *Dennis v Ministry of Defence* [2003] EWHC 793 (QB) the court awarded a sum of £950,000 for noise nuisance and blight on property value, loss of commercial use, and loss of amenity and without allocating specific sums suggested that an award of less than £50,000 would not do justice to the serious loss of amenity. Perhaps less exceptionally, in *Farley v Skinner* [2002] 2 AC 732, the court viewed an award of £10,000 for the discomfort of suffering aircraft noise as high and at the very top of an appropriate bracket.

17.125   Interference with enjoyment, personal freedom, or injuriously affecting the senses or nerves does not extend to personal injury. The right to recover for personal injuries caused by a public nuisance has been criticized for some time. In *Hunter v Canary Wharf* Lord Goff suggested that personal injury should be excluded from nuisance claims. This was recently affirmed in *Transco v Stockport MBC*.

Level of interference

17.126   The House of Lords in *Cambridge Water Company v Eastern Counties Leather* affirmed that an essential component of a private nuisance claim is that the claimant should have experienced some damage by the acts or omissions alleged. The Lords noted that:

> It is not to be forgotten that both nuisance and negligence are historically actions on the case, and accordingly in neither case is the tort complete, so that damages are recoverable, unless and until damage has been caused to the plaintiff.

17.127   In *Anglian Water Services v Crawshaw Robbins & Co* [2001] BLR 173 found no action in nuisance for an inability to cook for a short period of time following the loss of a gas supply. The interference requires more than nominal interference.

Claimant's interest in land

17.128   Lord Goff, in *Hunter v Canary Wharf*, affirmed that a claimant requires some legal interest in the land affected to pursue a nuisance claim stating that ordinarily:

a person can only sue if he has the right to exclusive possession of the land, such as a freeholder or tenant in possession, or even a licensee with exclusive possession. Exceptionally however, as [*Foster v Warblington UDC* [1906] 1 KB 648] shows, this category may include a person in actual possession who has no right to be there; and in any event a reversioner can sue in so far his reversionary interest is affected. But a mere licensee on the land has no right to sue.

In *Pemberton v Southwark LBC* [2001] Env LR 96 the court held that a former secure tenant who remained in the defendant's home as a 'tolerated trespasser' under Pt IV of the Housing Act 1985 had sufficient interest to make a private nuisance claim. While in *McKenna v British Aluminium Ltd* [2002] Env LR 30, in an application under CPR 1998 r 3.4, the court refused to strike out the nuisance aspect of a claim by claimants who had no proprietary interest in their homes, adding that it was arguable that requiring such an interest would not be compliant with the European Convention on Human Rights. The claim in *McKenna* was that emissions, noise pollution, and invasion of privacy from the defendant's neighbouring factory had caused mental distress and physical harm relating to the claimants' occupation and/or enjoyment of the home. **17.129**

Appropriate defendant

Action can be brought against the 'polluter' and those allowing or authorizing the pollution to arise. In *Sedleigh-Denfield v O'Callaghan* the House of Lords held that an occupier of land 'continues' a nuisance if, with knowledge of its existence, he fails to take reasonable means to bring it to an end when he has ample time to do so; and he 'adopts' it if he makes any use of the erection or artificial structure that constitutes the nuisance. Lord Wright at 903 noted that: 'the ground of responsibility is the possession and control of the land from which the nuisance proceeds.' **17.130**

A nuisance action can be brought against: **17.131**

- the creator of the nuisance whether or not he or she is the occupier of the land at the time (*Thompson v Gibson* (1841) 7 M&W 456);
- the occupier of the premises if (a) (s)he creates the nuisance, or (b) the nuisance is caused by his/her servant or agent. Although, in *Leakey v National Trust for Places of Historic Interest or Natural Beauty* [1980] QB 485 where the nuisance is not being created by the occupier (s)he is only expected to do what is reasonable in the individual circumstances to prevent or minimize the known risk to his or her neighbour; or
- a landlord, although as a general rule a landlord will not be liable, unless he has authorized the nuisance. In *Smith v Scott* [1973], Ch 314 Pennycuick VC stated that: 'In general, a landlord is not liable for nuisance committed by his tenant, but to this rule there is, so far as now in point, one recognised exception, namely, that the landlord is liable if he has authorized his tenant to commit the nuisance. . . . The exception is squarely based in the reported cases as express or implied authority.' In *Which & anor v Mid-Bedfordshire DC* ELM 14 [2002] 5 p 299 the Council were found to be occupiers of the land where it had granted a licence to occupy to gypsies. Consequently, they were liable for the nuisance caused by the gypsies, which included starting fires, dumping rubbish, causing noise and smoke, and racing cars. The Council were held to have sufficient control of the gypsies through their eviction procedures. By contrast, in *Calvert v Gardiner* ELM 14 [2002] 3 p 156 a Bishop was not liable for nuisance caused by a bell-ringing vicar.

The vicar had security of tenure and bell-ringing was the province of the vicar not the Bishop.

Unreasonable use of land

17.132 The defendant's use of neighbouring land must be unreasonable to give rise to a claim in nuisance. In *Saunders-Clark v Grosvenor Mansions* [1900] 2 Ch 373 Buckley J at 375–6 emphasized the importance of reasonableness in stating that:

> the court must consider whether the defendant is using his property reasonably or not. If he is using it reasonably, there is nothing which at law can be considered a nuisance; but if he is not using it reasonably . . . then the plaintiff is entitled to relief.

17.133 Reasonableness involves a number of factors that need to be collectively considered. The unreasonable use of land, something necessary to establish in nuisance, involves weighing up competing interests in land use. The factors to consider include:

- locality;
- continuing wrong;
- sensitivity of the claimant;
- intention of the defendant; and
- the utility of the defendant's conduct.

Locality

17.134 The term, 'locality' may be regarded as synonymous with the local environment. In *Sturges v Bridgman* Thesiger LJ held at 865 that whether anything is a nuisance or not is a question to be determined in reference to its circumstances and that: 'what would be a nuisance in Belgrave Square would not necessarily be so in Bermondsey'.

17.135 More recently, in *Gillingham BC and CV Medway (Chatham) Dock Co* [1993] QB 343 the court suggested that the grant of planning permission to reopen the docks for commerce, effectively changed the character of the neighbourhood to the extent that a nuisance action had to be considered in the light of the existing environment, not one in the past. However, the Court of Appeal accepted in *Wheeler & anor v JJ Saunders Ltd* [1995] 2 All ER 61 that planning permission may change the local environment, but did not agree that such permission authorized any nuisance that arose from it. Further, and although not a point for the House of Lords on appeal, Lord Hoffman and Lord Cooke in *Hunter v Canary Wharf* confirmed that compliance with planning control was not in itself a defence to a nuisance action while both Lordships agreed with the proposition that planning permission may be relevant indirectly. Further, in the Court of Sessions case (Scotland) of *Maguire & ors v Charles M'Neil Ltd* [1922] SC 174 the court held that the establishment of an industrial process may amount to a nuisance notwithstanding that similar processes are characteristic of the locality.

Continuing wrong

17.136 Nuisance is normally a continuing wrong, i.e. it arises with the actions or a state of affairs that continuously or repeatedly cause the escape of noxious things onto a neighbour's land or interfere with use of a potential claimant's land. An isolated incident is not generally regarded as a nuisance although there is no reason in principle why not. For a number of years the need for continuance meant relying on what was regarded as the rule in *Rylands v Fletcher* (1868) LR 3 HL 330. This arose from the statement in the case that:

> the person who for his own purposes brings on his land and collects and keeps there anything likely to do mischief if it escapes, must keep it in at his peril, and, if he does not do so, is *prima facie* answerable for all the damage which is the natural consequence of its escape.

However, in *Cambridge Water v Eastern Counties Leather* the House of Lords reiterated that the **17.137** rule in *Rylands v Fletcher* was not a distinct tort but instead a development of the law of nuisance, which enabled a remedy, exceptionally, to be provided for an isolated escape as opposed to a continuous state of affairs. In *Transco v Stockport MBC* the House of Lords believed that the rule did have some role to play as an aspect of nuisance, but that its scope was limited to the use of land creating an extraordinary risk to neighbouring property. In *Transco* the Council were not found liable for causing damage to the claimant's gas equipment and services following a large escape of water from a block of flats owned by the Council and, although a large amount of water had accumulated, it had not been the defendant Council that had caused this.

Clift v Welsh Office (1998) The Times, 24 August 1998 affirms that harm caused by temporary **17.138** building work is not actionable, is confined to mere inconvenience, and does not extend to actual physical damage to property: see also *Hunter v Canary Wharf* above.

Sensitivity of the claimant

In contrast to negligence actions (discussed below), where the defendant broadly takes the **17.139** victim as they find him or her, if a claimant is hypersensitive then a nuisance claim is unlikely to succeed. In *Robinson v Kilvert* (1889) 41 Ch D 88 the court held that:

> a man who carries on an exceptionally delicate trade cannot complain because it is injured by his neighbour doing something lawful on his property, if it is something which would not injure anything but an exceptionally delicate trade.

In *Network Rail Infrastructure Ltd v Morris* [2004] EWCA Civ 172 the claim was for £60,000 in **17.140** compensation for loss caused by interference with the claimant's recording studio from the defendants' replacement track circuit. The Court of Appeal held that it was difficult to say, in the modern era, that a sound recording studio was so unusual as necessarily to disqualify the claimant from the protection of the law of nuisance. With this particular relationship between the studio and the defendant as a main line railway operator, the question of sensitive use was no longer apt (although the claim was dismissed on the basis that the nuisance claimed was unforeseeable by the defendant, see para 17.144).

Intention of the defendant

If a defendant intends to cause the nuisance this will lower the threshold of what constitutes **17.141** a nuisance. In *Hollywood Silver Fox Farms v Emmet* [1936] 2 KB 468 the claimant, who bred silver foxes, was able to point to the defendant's malice in deliberately shooting his rifle along the boundary of the fox farm with the knowledge that this was likely to cause vixens to abort. In *Hunter v Canary Wharf* it was said that the malicious erection of a structure designed to interfere with television reception should be actionable in nuisance whereas the same structure erected without malice would not be regarded as a nuisance.

Utility of the defendant's conduct

17.142 The benefit to society and the whole community that the interference provides will be a factor in reasonableness. In essence, the more social value the activity provides, the more the interference will be regarded as reasonable and not constitute a nuisance. However, community benefit is only one factor and not a conclusive one, in *Elliot v Islington LBC* [1991] 10 EG 145 the Court of Appeal upheld an injunction order for the removal of an ancient tree, rejecting that the tree should be preserved as a valuable local amenity and granting compensation for its encroachment. See also: *Shelfer v City of London Electric Co.* [1895] 1 Ch 287 in which an injunction to prevent noise was upheld, albeit on very limited grounds, whereas in *Kennaway v Thompson* [1981] QB 88 there was a finding in nuisance but damages were awarded in lieu of an injunction.

Foreseeability

17.143 In the *Cambridge Water* case the court emphasized that it was a requirement of nuisance that the damage arising from the interference was foreseeable by a reasonable person in the position of the defendant at the date the incident complained of occurred. In *Arscott & ors v Coal Authority* [2004] EWCA (Civ) 892 the claimants suffered flooding as a result of flood defences put in place by the defendant. The Court of Appeal held that when the flood defence scheme was developed it was not reasonably foreseeable that such a scheme would cause flooding elsewhere. The court relied on the doctrine of common enemy and that a landowner could protect his land from flooding (the common enemy) even though it may result in flooding of someone else's land (see Chapter 15: Water). The High Court had noted that, in terms of reasonableness, the flood defence scheme was a reasonable use of land by the defendant.

17.144 In *Network Rail Infrastructure Ltd v Morris* the claim for damages for interference with the recording studio failed because it was not foreseeable that the magnetic radiation from the defendant rail operator's replacement track circuit would cause interference with the recording activities at the claimant's studio.

Defences

17.145 There is a range of purported defences against a claim for nuisance, some more effective than others and some not actually defences at all.

Statutory authority

17.146 The House of Lords in *Department of Transport v North West Water Authority* [1984] AC 336 set out when the defence of statutory authority would be available in nuisance. Lord Fraser at 359 noted that:

- In the absence of negligence, a body is not liable for a nuisance which is attributable to the [performance] by it of a duty imposed by statute.
- A body is liable for a nuisance by it attributable to the exercise of a power conferred by statute, even without negligence, if by statute it is expressly either made liable, or not exempted from liability, for nuisance.

In *Manchester Corporation v Farnworth* [1930] AC 171 the defendant claimed that they were **17.147** empowered to set up a power station by s 32 of the Manchester Corporation Act 1914 and that this provided a defence to a claim for an injunction and damages for the emission of fumes from the power station. The House of Lords dismissed an appeal against an injunction and award of damages. Viscount Sumner at 195 concluded that the defendant corporation had:

> failed to show that they have used all reasonable diligence and taken all reasonable steps and precautions to prevent their operations from being a nuisance to their neighbours, and this for two reasons. (1) At the time of the erection their responsible officers never directed their minds to the prevention of the nuisances, which it was quite obvious might occur, but (2) they were under the impression that, for all practical purposes, so long as their plant was efficiently and successfully conducted, the neighbours must endure their consequent injuries with such stoicism as they could muster.

In *Allen v Gulf Oil Refinery Ltd* [1981] AC 1001 the House of Lords rejected a claim by local **17.148** residents who sought to stop noise nuisance from the defendant's oil refinery. The Lords considered that the Act authorizing the construction of the refinery gave the defendant immunity if they could prove that the nuisance was inevitable despite using all reasonable care. Statutory authority does not extend to the grant of planning permission see *Wheeler v Saunders* and *Gillingham BC v Chatham Dock Co* para 29 (see 17.135).

Prescription

In certain circumstances, a right to commit a private nuisance may be acquired by prescrip- **17.149** tion as an easement and so provide a defence to a nuisance claim. Prescription generally requires 20 years' continuance of an action. However, there must be certainty and knowledge of the nuisance and so a secret discharge of pollutants will not provide a defence because the claimant was unaware that the action was a nuisance. Also, if the action shifts from being a nuisance at some times and not others then the continuance is interrupted. Also, the nuisance proposed must be capable of becoming an easement.

In *Sturges v Bridgman* the court suggested that there could be no action if the nuisance had **17.150** continued for more than 20 years, although the claimant must know that the state of affairs had run from the beginning of the 20-year period.

Care and precaution to prevent the nuisance

It is no defence to a nuisance claim that care and precaution has been taken to prevent the **17.151** nuisance or that activities have been carried on in a reasonable manner. In *Read v J Lyons & Co Ltd* [1947] AC 156 the claimant, an inspector at the defendant's explosives factory, suffered personal injury when an explosion killed one man and injured several others, including herself. There was no assertion of negligence. On appeal, the House of Lords commented that if someone commits a nuisance: 'it is no answer to his injured neighbour that he took the utmost care not to commit it. There the liability is strict, and there he alone has a lawful claim.'

The defence of best practical means available in statutory nuisance does not apply in private **17.152** nuisance. Veale J, in *Halsey v Esso Petroleum Co. Ltd* [1961] 2 All ER 145, held that:

> the making or causing of such a noise as materially interferes with the comfort of a neighbour, when judged by the standard to which I have referred constitutes an actionable nuisance, and it

is no answer to say that the best known means have been taken to reduce or prevent the noise complained of, or that the cause of the nuisance is the exercise of a business or trade in a reasonable and proper manner.

Coming to the nuisance

17.153   It is no defence to argue that the claimant came to the nuisance. In *St Helens Smelting Co.* the claimant bought an estate neighbouring an existing copper smelting works and successfully sued. However, the assumption in *Sturges v Bridgman* that there was no answer to the assertion that the claimant brought the trouble on his own head by moving close to the nuisance neighbour was challenged in *Miller v Jackson* [1977] QB 966, when the court noted that:

> it does not seem just that a long established activity, in itself innocuous, should be brought to an end because someone else chooses to build a house nearby and so turn an innocent pastime into an actionable nuisance.

17.154   Nevertheless, in *Miller v Jackson* the court reluctantly held that there was a nuisance although declined to award an injunction instead awarding compensation for any past and future damage that could arise.

Nuisance caused by many

17.155   It is no defence to state that the defendant was simply one of a number of persons all carrying on similar activities and that the nuisance was a result of those collective activities. The defendant's conduct is not considered in isolation. In *Polsue & Alfieri Ltd v Rushmer* [1907] AC 121 the House of Lords dismissed an appeal by a printer who had been restrained from working printing machinery throughout the night despite the fact that other similar activities operated at that time, and that by itself the noise from the operation was not great.

Utility of conduct

17.156   The utility or public benefit from the defendant's conduct is not a defence, although it may be a factor to consider when assessing reasonableness: see para 17:132. In *Adams v Ursell* [1913] 1 Ch 269 a defendant who ran a fried fish shop argued unsuccessfully that an injunction to prevent him running his business would cause hardship to his customers who were poor.

Consent of the claimant

17.157   Where the claimant has consented, either expressly or implicitly, to the nuisance the defendant cannot be liable, unless there is some negligence. In *Kiddle v City Business Properties* [1942] 1 KB 269 the court held that in the absence of negligence, the defendants were not liable to the claimant in an action for nuisance for allowing rainwater to escape on to his premises as:

- the claimant's shop formed part of a larger building belonging to the defendant and the claimant had rented the shop as it was (and had therefore by implication consented to the situation); and
- that arrangements for the collection and carrying away of water from the roof to the cellar was for the benefit of the claimant and defendant.

Contributory negligence

Where the claimant may have contributed to the harm by his own actions, any damages **17.158** may be reduced by the level of involvement. Section 4 of the Law Reform (Contributory Negligence) Act 1945 provides that fault includes negligence, breach of statutory duty or other act or omission that gives rise to liability in tort.

Remedies

There are two common remedies available in a nuisance claim; an injunction to prevent it **17.159** occurring and damages to compensate for any harm caused. The courts have been reluctant to grant injunctions. Instead, if there has been a finding of nuisance, they will try to compensate the claimant for past, and sometimes, future damage, although injunctions have been granted on occasions.

Injunctions

The rule in *Shelfer v City of London Electrical Lighting Co.* (see para 17:90) was approved by **17.160** the House of Lords in *Colls v Home and Colonial Stores Ltd* when Lord Lindley, at 212, held that the general rule is that where a legal right is continuously infringed an injunction to protect that right should be granted, subject to qualifications. In *Colls*, however, the Lords dismissed the claim for an injunction to prevent building works encroaching on a right to light.

In *Halsey v Esso Petroleum Ltd* [1961] 1 WLR 683 an injunction was granted to reduce noise, **17.161** smuts, and dust arising from the defendant's use of on-site boilers and road tankers coming and going from its Fulham refinery. In *Leakey v National Trust for Places of Historic Interest or Natural Beauty* [1980] QB 485 the National Trust had to abate the nuisance from a serious fall of soil by way of an interlocutory injunction. While in *Stannard v Charles Pitcher Ltd* [2003] Env LR 10 a mandatory injunction was awarded requiring the installation of appropriate floor coverings with acoustic barriers in order to reduce unreasonable noise penetrating through ceilings. However, in *Goode v Owen* 14 [2002] 1 ELM p 25 golf balls regularly landing on a farmer's land created a nuisance but did not justify a mandatory injunction order for the construction of a 40-feet high fence to prevent the balls entering the land. Compensation was awarded instead.

In *Manchester Corporation v Farnworth* an injunction was granted on appeal to stop the **17.162** defendant company emitting poisonous fumes that had destroyed the claimant's fields. The House of Lords varied the order by declaring that the injunction be suspended for one year and that the claimant receive damages for that period and further, that the defendant could apply for the injunction to be dissolved after all reasonable efforts to abate the nuisance had been exhausted.

Damages

St Helens Smelting Co v Tipping held that compensation may be claimed for property and **17.163** chattel damage as well as land. In *Blue Circle Industries plc v Ministry of Defence* [1999] Env LR 22 compensation of £5 million was awarded for diminution in land value plus consequential losses incurred in running the estate contaminated by the defendant's radioactive leakage, together with the costs associated with clean up. In *Delaware Mansions Ltd v Westminster City*

Council, where roots from a tree in the highway damaged the claimant's property prior to sale, the claimant could recover the reasonable remedial expenditure incurred. In *Dennis v MoD* the overall sum of £950,000 for noise nuisance, blight on property value, loss of commercial use, and loss of amenity was regarded as extreme and 'unlikely to add to the growing compensation culture'. It does, nevertheless, require the claimant's interest in land to be of sufficient significance to justify claiming such a loss. In *Hunter v Canary Wharf* Lord Hoffman noted that a claimant would be:

> entitled to loss of profits which are the result of inability to use the land for the purposes of his business. Or, if the land is flooded, he may also be able to recover damages for chattels or livestock as a result.

17.164 In *LE Jones (Insurance) v Portsmouth CC* ELM 14 [2002] 6 p 362 the insurance company successfully claimed the cost of repairing and making good damage to their offices arising from tree roots and subsidence as a result of the Council's inaction in keeping the highway in good order. The Court of Appeal dismissed an appeal based on the fact that it was not the highway authority (although it had accepted those delegated responsibilities from the County Council) and that it had not been given sufficient time to abate the nuisance (the Court of Appeal believed otherwise).

Abatement

17.165 Abatement of a nuisance is, on occasion, recognized as a self-help remedy, although the courts do not encourage this.

Summary

17.166 There are pros and cons when considering advising on pursuing a nuisance claim. Often a nuisance claim can provide a more effective remedy than, say, negligence because there is almost strict liability and because injunctive relief is available, see e.g. *Stannard v Charles Pitcher Ltd*. The availability of damages is useful, in particular to carry out remediation of the environmental damage. It remains useful for certain litigants, e.g. community associations, environmental organizations, and user groups, e.g. fishing associations who may find that there is no relief under statute. Some harm may be reasonably straightforward to prove and involve a small claim limited to property damage. For example, insurance companies find it useful in claiming back funds paid in insurance payouts, e.g. in subsidence cases.

17.167 However, often such action will fall outside the small claims regime where each party pays their own costs, and so costs implications will be a significant factor. It may be difficult to establish the source of pollution or environmental harm and then to establish a causal link between the pollution and the damage caused. Gaining and producing evidence is often expensive and may be disproportionate to any potential damages. However, note *Dennis v MoD*.

17.168 Injunctions granted by the court in nuisance remain a minority remedy and a claim more often provides a potential cure rather than prevention. Also, because of its more common retrospective approach whereby a claimant is only likely to take action after damage has been done it tends to provide environmental protection on an *ad hoc* basis only. Statutory regulation of the environment is often more effective at preventing pollution and taking appropriate action, including legal action, when appropriate. This was affirmed in *Hunter v Canary Wharf*, in that it is for Parliament to extend the law to cover environmental protection. The introduction of foreseeability by the *Cambridge Water* case will limit the claims of historic pollution although see now the contaminated land regime covered in Chapter 5: Contaminated land.

The judicial trend in private nuisance has been to accommodate the polluter and polluting activity rather than those suffering harm or damage to property. Further, human rights provisions such as Art 8 and Art 1 of Protocol 1 of the European Convention on Human Rights have not particularly assisted environmental protection and remediation in nuisance claims with the courts referring to the balancing of the competing interests of private individuals and society as a whole. This is considered both in *Dennis v MoD* and *Marcic v Thames Water*, which found the regular flooding of the claimant's home and garden from an overloaded public sewage system operated by the defendant had to be balanced with the need of users of the sewage system and that, in the circumstances, the claim failed. The Lords also stated that the common law was not, in Mr Marcic's case, an appropriate form of redress when a statutory scheme of protection was available, which could, if necessary, be underpinned by judicial review (see also Chapter 15: Water).   **17.169**

D NEGLIGENCE

Introduction

In law, negligence can refer to: **17.170**

- an independent tort; and
- the mental state of someone that is accused of committing a crime, e.g. manslaughter, which requires the proof of gross negligence by the accused, and the mental element in tortuous liability outside of the tort of negligence, e.g. in breach of certain statutory duties.

In this section negligence is considered as an independent area of tort law. It has developed over many years from a large number of judicial statements and opinions. Many of these must be considered in building the complete picture of negligence in law. In summary it may be defined as: 'the breach of a duty of care, owed by the defendant to the claimant that results in damage to the claimant.'   **17.171**

To establish negligence there are at least four components that should be considered: **17.172**

- a duty of care;
- a breach of that duty; and
- causation and the remoteness of harm.

If negligence has been found to exist it will then be necessary to consider: **17.173**

- any defences, including the extent of any negligent action by the claimant that may have contributed to the harm; and
- the remedies available.

17.174 There is a lot of overlap between the components and between the elements that make up each component. It should also be noted that considering the aspects of negligence, ultimately the court might simply not wish to extend the law in a particular way. Lord Denning MR in *Lamb v Camden LBC* [1981] QB 625 commented that:

> it is not every consequence of a wrongful act which is the subject of compensation. The law has to draw a line somewhere. Sometimes it is done by limiting the range of persons to whom a duty is owed. Sometimes it is done by saying that there is a break in the chain of causation. At other times it is done by saying that the consequence is too remote to be a head of damages. All these devices are useful in their way. Ultimately, it is a question of policy for judges to decide.

Duty of care

17.175 Lord Atkin, in *Donoghue v Stevenson* [1932] AC 562, believed that there was a general principle of relations that would give rise to a duty of care:

> [That] you must take reasonable care to avoid acts or omissions which you can reasonably foresee would be likely to injure your neighbour. . . . [My neighbours are] persons who are so closely and directly affected by my act that I ought reasonably to have them in contemplation as being so affected when I am directing my mind to the acts or omissions which are called in question.

17.176 *Donoghue v Stevenson* concerned a compensation claim for illness arising from drinking ginger beer from a bottle that was contaminated by a decomposed snail. Under Lord Atkin's principle, the manufacturer should have reasonably contemplated that someone may buy a bottle of ginger beer to be drunk by a friend as well as the purchaser (as was the case) and so, even though there was no direct contractual relationship between Mrs Donoghue and the defendant, she was still able to bring a claim. See also Chapter 12: Property and land rights.

17.177 In *Caparo Industries Plc v Dickman* [1990] 2 AC 605 Lord Bridge provided what is regarded to be the present position in relation to duty of care in that:

> in addition to the foreseeability of damage, necessary ingredients in any situation giving rise to a duty of care are that there should exist between the party owing the duty and the party to whom it is owed a relationship characterised by the law as one of 'proximity' or 'neighbour-hood'; and that the situation should be one in which the court considers it fair, just and reasonable that the law should impose a duty of a given scope on the one party for the benefit of the other.

17.178 This is a three-part test in finding a duty of care, which is:

(1) ensuring that there is sufficient proximity between the parties;

(2) that it must be just, fair and reasonable to impose a duty of care; and

(3) that injury to the claimant must be reasonably foreseeable.

Sufficient proximity

17.179 Proximity may be equated with Lord Atkin's neighbourhood principle. Geographical proximity may be a factor but it is not essential, see e.g. *Home Office v Dorset Yacht Co Ltd* [1970] AC 1004 where the damaged property was in the vicinity of a detention centre run by the defendant. See also *Muirhead v Industrial Tank Ltd* [1986] QB 507 at 528. In *Caparo v Dickman* Lord Oliver noted that proximity was:

> an expression used not necessarily as indicating literally 'closeness' in a physical or meta-phorical sense but merely . . . a convenient label to describe circumstances from which the law will attribute a duty of care.

Just, fair, and reasonable

Even if there is sufficient proximity between the claimant and the defendant, a duty of care **17.180** may not arise because to do so would not be just, fair, and reasonable. In *Mulcahy v Ministry of Defence* [1996] QB 732 the Court of Appeal struck out a claim by a soldier for deafness, which, it was alleged, was caused during artillery fire during the Gulf War. In *Mulcahy*, the defendants accepted that there was proximity and foreseeability of harm.

Reasonable foresight

Consideration of reasonable foresight at an early stage of negligence is to establish a notional **17.181** duty of care. It may be considered again to see whether the defendant acted carelessly and finally in the assessment of remoteness of harm, i.e. whether the result was foreseeable. Reasonable foresight is based upon the knowledge that someone in the defendant's position would be expected to possess. The greater the awareness of potential harm; the more likely this test will be satisfied.

There is a high level of flexibility for the courts in considering whether a particular outc- **17.182** ome was reasonably foreseeable. This is convenient when the courts may need to take policy decisions in ensuring that a claim does not result in something wholly adverse to public interest. It was explained in *McKew v Holland & ors* [1969] 3 All ER 1621 at 1623 in that:

> It only leads to trouble if one tries to graft on to the concept of foreseeability some rule of law to the effect that a wrongdoer is not bound to foresee something which in fact he could readily foresee as quite likely to happen.

Public policy

Public policy is relevant in whether a duty of care arises. For instance, while it is appropriate **17.183** that many negligent acts should be compensated, it is also important to ensure that bodies carrying out public functions do not lead to those functions being carried out in a defensive and accordingly, less effective, manner. In *Harris v Evans* [1998] 3 All ER 522 an HSE inspector advised the claimant to take steps to ensure that his bungee jumping operation was safe for the public. The claimant later discovered that the advice was contrary to HSE policy and claimed compensation for economic loss as a result of that advice. The court held that the inspector did not owe a duty of care to the bungee jumping operator. However, in *Stovin v Wise* [1993] 3 All ER 467 a highway authority failed to take action to remove a bank of land adjacent to a road that obstructed vision of road users. It was held liable for the personal injury of a claimant who was injured in a road incident because they owed a duty of care to road users to progress steps to remove the obstruction.

There is no general duty of care imposed on a failure to act. In *East Suffolk Rivers Catchment* **17.184** *Board v Kent* [1941] AC 74 the House of Lords held that the Rivers Board was not liable for flooding as a result of their ineffective repairs to the sea wall because they were under no duty to repair the sea wall in the first place.

Breach of duty

17.185   In *Blyth v Birmingham Waterworks Co* (1856) 11 Exch 781 negligence was defined as:

> the omission to do something which a reasonable man, guided upon those considerations which ordinarily regulate the conduct of human affairs, would do, or doing something which a prudent and reasonable man would not do.

17.186   The significance of this definition is the emphasis placed on the 'reasonable man' enabling a degree of flexibility when considering any given case. The factors to be considered by the court when considering whether the defendant has acted reasonably are:

- that reasonableness is considered objectively;
- the likelihood of harm;
- the seriousness of the harm;
- the utility of the conduct; and
- the cost-benefit analysis of avoiding the risk.

17.187   Further, where precautionary steps should be taken, the standard of care that may be reasonably expected in taking them will vary according to the magnitude of risk, i.e. the likelihood of harm multiplied by the seriousness of the harm, as well as the purpose (utility) of the defendant's activity and the practicability (cost-benefit analysis) of the precautions.

Objective reasonableness

17.188   The test as to what is a reasonable man is objective and does not take account of the particular nature of a particular defendant. And so where someone carries on an activity that requires a certain level of skill, they will be judged by the standard of a person who is reasonably competent in exercising that skill. In *Nettleship v Weston* [1971] 2 QB 691 the Court of Appeal held that a learner driver must exercise the care of a reasonably experienced driver stating that:

> the learner driver may be doing his best, but his incompetent best is not good enough. He must drive in as good a manner as a driver of skill, experience and care, who is sound in mind and limb, who makes no errors of judgement, has good eyesight and hearing, and is free from any infirmity. . . . Morally the learner driver is not at fault; but legally she is liable because she is insured and the risk should fall on her.

17.189   Yet while the test of reasonableness is objective. The standard relating to particular activities will vary according to those activities. In considering the negligent polluting of a watercourse by a car repair business, the test will be of a car repair garage with the professional skill and care of any similar business carrying out its business properly. Where dangerous products are involved the standard of care should be objective, and relatively high. In *Dominion Natural Gas Co v Collins and anor* [1909] AC 640 the court stated that:

> What that duty is will depend on the subject matter of the things involved. It has, however, again and again been held that in the case of articles dangerous in themselves, such as loaded firearms, poisons, explosives and other things . . . there is a particular duty to take precautions

imposed upon those who send forth or install such articles when it is necessarily the case that other parties will come within their proximity.

However, a defendant is not required to anticipate future developments in their field and is judged according to the accepted state of knowledge at the date that the act causing the harm occurred. In *Roe v Ministry of Health* [1954] 2 QB 66 an anaesthetist was not held liable for harm caused by contaminated equipment when it was not known that contamination in the circumstances could arise. **17.190**

Likelihood of harm

In *Bolton v Stone* [1951] AC 850 at 886 the Lords held that the likelihood of the claimant being struck by a cricket ball that had been hit out of the ground and over a seven-foot fence was slight and so the cricket club was not negligent in allowing cricket to be played without further precautions such as increasing the height of the fence. **17.191**

Seriousness of the harm

The level of precaution required by a defendant may increase where the risk to the claimant is higher than normal. In *Paris v Stepney BC* [1951] AC 367 the House of Lords considered that the seriousness of the loss of sight for a one-eyed claimant was much greater than for someone with vision in both eyes. The defendant should have provided the claimant with goggles to protect his eye whereas his colleagues may not necessarily have needed these. The magnitude of the risk of total blindness was far greater for the claimant and in assessing magnitude, it is according to the individual claimant. **17.192**

Utility of the conduct

In *Watt v Hertfordshire CC* [1954] 2 All ER 368 the claimant was injured when a lifting jack slipped as a result of not being properly secured in transit. It was held that, because the fire brigade were trying to get the jack to an emergency where someone was trapped under a bus, they were not held liable for not using a specially designed vehicle, which was unavailable, to transport the jack. The benefit from transporting the jack in this way outweighed the risk of exposing the claimant to injury. **17.193**

The cost-benefit analysis

The cost-benefit analysis means that the risk involved in any action must be balanced against the precautionary measures necessary in order to eliminate this. In *Smith v Little-woods Organisation Ltd* [1987] AC 241 the defendants were not liable for vandals entering a disused cinema and causing a fire that damaged the claimant's property. Full-time security at the cinema was not regarded as a realistic response to the potential risk. However, contrast this with the analysis of causation in criminal cases and the case of *Environment Agency v Empress Car Co (Abertillery) Ltd* [1999] 2 AC 22 where the defendant was liable for oil pollution of a watercourse after vandals had turned on a tap on an oil tank, even though the defendant was not the immediate cause of the polluting incident. **17.194**

Res ipsa loquitur

The maxim *res ipsa loquitur* (the thing speaks for itself) may be raised by the claimant, which asks the court to make an initial finding of negligence where the claimant is unable to **17.195** explain how the accident happened. In *Scott v London & St Katherine Docks Co* (1865) 3 H&C 596 the court held that to rely upon the maxim, three conditions must be met:

(1) that the thing causing the harm must be under the management of the defendant;
(2) that the accident could not have happened if management is carried out with proper care; and
(3) that, in the absence of explanation, the accident arose through want of care.

17.196   To conclude that the defendant has management or control of the thing or situation, the test is whether external interference was likely. In *Easson v London & North East Railway Co* [1944] KB 421 the four-year-old claimant fell through a door in the corridor of the train. The claimant raised *res ipsa loquitur*, but the court held that the defendant did not have sufficient control over the door for the maxim to apply. In *Barkway v South Wales Transport Co Ltd* [1950] 1 All ER 392 the cause of the accident was known and so the maxim, although raised by the claimant, did not apply.

Causation and remoteness of harm

Causation in fact: 'but for . . .'

17.197   A difficulty in using the civil justice system to protect the environment or claim compensation for harm suffered is the need to prove causation. In finding liability for an act of harm the claimant must show that the harm suffered was, as a matter of fact, caused by the defendant's breach of his duty of care. This is commonly explained as the 'but for' test set out in *Barnett v Chelsea & Kensington Hospital Management Committee* [1969] 1 QB 428 in which Denning LJ commented:

> If the damage would not have happened but for a particular fault then that fault is the cause of the damage; if it would have happened just the same, fault or no fault, the fault is not the cause of the damage.

17.198   In *Kuwait Airways Corp v Iraqi Airways Co (Nos. 4 & 5)* [2002] UKHL 19 Lord Nicholls held that there is no uniform causal requirement for liability in tort and, at para 73, that the 'but for' test:

> cannot be expected to set out a formula whose mechanical application will provide infallible threshold guidance on causal connection for every tort in every circumstance. In particular, the 'but for' test can be over-exclusionary.
>
> . . . This may occur where more than one wrongdoer is involved. The classic example is where two persons independently search for the source of a gas leak with the aid of lighted candles. According to the simple 'but for' test, neither would be liable for damage caused by the resultant explosion. In this type of case, involving multiple wrongdoers, the court may treat wrongful conduct as having sufficient causal connection with the loss for the purpose of attracting responsibility even though the simple 'but for' test is not satisfied.

17.199   However, if the claimant is unable to prove that a particular breach of duty caused the harm it is may be sufficient to show that it made the harm more likely to arise. In *McGhee v National Coal Board* [1973] 1 WLR 1 medical evidence could not demonstrate that the lack of showers at the defendant's brick kilns caused dermatitis. However, it could show that if there were showers available at the works, using them would have reduced the risk of the skin disease.

The courts do accept that causation may be proved if the claimant can establish that the **17.200** defendant's acts were a material contribution to the harm arising. In *Bonnington Castings v Wardlaw* [1956] 1 All ER 615 the claimant suffered lung disease following exposure to dust in the defendant's workplace even though the claimant could not prove 'but for' the exposure he would not have developed the disease, the exposure had made a material contribution to the disease and the claimant was entitled to be compensated in full.

If two separate incidents cause or worsen the harm complained of, then the first should be **17.201** regarded as the cause: see *Baker v Willoughby* [1970] AC 467, although in *Jobling v Associated Dairies Ltd* [1981] 2 All ER 752 the court considered that if the second incident was a natural cause entirely unrelated to the first, a defendant responsible for the harm caused from the first incident would only be liable to compensate for the period between the two.

Remoteness of harm

The concept of remoteness, or foreseeability, of harm sets a boundary in civil claims, beyond **17.202** which the harm arising is not regarded as being caused, in law, by the defendant's breach of duty. Put another way, the claimant must show that the kind of harm caused was not so unforeseen or remote that the law will deny liability. In *The Wagon Mound* [1961] AC 388 a large volume of oil leaked from the defendant's ship into the harbour. The claimants were aware of the polluted waters but were advised that it was safe to continue their welding activities. Shortly after, the polluted water caught fire and damaged two ships. However, according to expert evidence, it was unforeseeable that waters would ignite and so the fire damage from the incident was regarded as not being reasonably foreseeable and the defendants were not liable for the fire damage to the ships.

However, in *Hughes v Lord Advocate* [1963] AC 837 the defendant was liable for severe **17.203** burning to an eight-year-old boy from an explosion at an unattended open manhole with paraffin lamps close by. In the circumstances, the court held that the explosion was foresee-able, in itself, even though burns to a young boy from such a scenario were not. If the kind of harm and its occurrence are reasonably foreseeable, it does not matter that the harm is greater than one would expect: *Vacwell Engineering Co Ltd v BDH Chemicals Ltd* [1971] 1 QB 88. However, in *Carslogie Steamship Co Ltd v The Royal Norwegian Government* [1952] AC 292 the defendants were not liable for storm damage to a ship arising while on a voyage to repair damage originally from the defendant's negligence. The storm was an intervening event occurring independently of the original acts of the defendant.

The 'egg-shell skull' rule

The 'egg-shell skull' rule means that defendants causing harm must take their victims as **17.204** they find them and if a claimant is particularly susceptible or hyper-sensitive to an incident then so be it. For example, in *Smith v Leech Brain & Co.* [1962] 2 QB 405 the claimant employee suffered a burn on his lip arising from inadequate health and safety provision at the defendant's factory. The burn activated a pre-malignant condition and the claimant later died from cancer. Lord Parker CJ held at p 414 that the defendant company was liable, noting that it had: 'always been the law of this country that a tortfeasor takes the victim as he finds him.'

Defences

Contributory negligence

17.205   Contributory negligence is where the claimant in some way contributes to the seriousness of the harm. A simple example of this is where the car driver crashes in an incident that is entirely the result of the negligence of the defendant, but where the harm caused would have been less severe if the claimant had been wearing a seat belt: see *Froom v Butcher* [1976] 2 QB 286. In *O'Connell v Jackson* [1972] 1 QB 270 the Court of Appeal reduced the damages awarded to a motorcyclist injured in a crash by 15% because less harm would have arisen if the claimant had been wearing a crash helmet.

17.206   Section 1 of the Law Reform (Contributory Negligence) Act 1945 provides:

> (1)   Where any person suffers damage as the result partly of his own fault and partly of the fault of any other person or persons, a claim in respect of that damage shall not be defeated by reason of the fault of the person suffering the damage, but the damages recoverable in respect thereof shall be reduced to such extent as the court thinks just and equitable having regard to the claimant's share in the responsibility for the damage; . . .
>
> (2)   Where damages are recoverable by any person by virtue of [subs (1) . . .] the court shall find and record the total damages which would have been recoverable if the claimant had not been at fault . . .

17.207   The contributory action caused must be within the boundaries of a main negligent act; causation and blameworthiness are related but remain distinct, e.g. someone may be very careless but that may be irrelevant to the harm suffered. In *Jones v Livox Quarries* [1952] 2 QB 608 the claimant argued that the risk of injury from his action was irrelevant to actual harm caused. The Court of Appeal declined to accept this, holding that by acting the way he did, i.e. riding on the tow bar of a construction vehicle, the claimant had exposed himself to the risk of being crushed by another vehicle. However, In *Jones v Boyce* (1816) 1 Stark 493 the claimant jumped from a stagecoach he believed was about to crash and was injured. The court held that he had acted reasonably in the circumstances in trying to avert a more serious danger and did not contribute to the negligent act.

17.208   If the defendant is going to rely on the defence of contributory negligence, then it must be specifically pleaded. In *Fookes v Slaytor* [1979] 1 All ER 137 it was held that the court could not raise the issue of contributory negligence on its own motion. There can also be contributory negligence apportioned among defendants under the Civil Liability (Contribution) Act 1978.

Consent (*volenti non fit injuria*)

17.209   The defence of consent, often referred to as *volenti non fit injuria*, means that a defendant may not be liable in negligence if the claimant voluntarily accepted the risk of harm involved in carrying out any particular activity. However, the claimant will be taken to voluntarily agree to accept the consequences of the risk initially created by the defendant, only where the claimant has full knowledge of the nature and extent of the risk. In *Smith v Charles Baker & Sons* [1891] AC 325 the court rejected the *volenti* defence where the claimant was injured from falling stones. The claimant had knowledge of the risk but had complained to the defendant employer about the dangers of the act; he was not acting voluntarily. However, in

Rathcliff v McDonnell & anor (1998) The Times, 3 December 1998, a trespasser, knowing the risk, voluntarily accepted it as his own.

Remedies

The only remedy generally available in negligence is compensation. The main principle **17.210** behind this is that the claimant should be fully compensated for the loss and be restored, as best as money can accommodate, to the position he would have been in if the negligence had not been committed. In personal injury claims, the compensation can include damages for pain, suffering, and loss of amenity, financial loss such as loss of wages and future lost earnings, and the cost of care. Personal injury is discussed in Chapter 7: Human health.

In *AB v South West Water Service Ltd* [1993] QB 507 aluminium sulphate was introduced into **17.211** the drinking water system at a treatment works operated by the defendant. The claimants (around 180 of the defendant's customers) brought actions under the Water Act 1989 alleging nuisance, negligence, and breach of statutory duty and by a master statement of claim sought compensation for injuries arising from drinking the contaminated water as well as exemplary and aggravated damages for the alleged conduct of the defendants following the incident. The Court of Appeal allowed the defendant's appeal against a High Court order dismissing a summons to strike out the claim. The Court held that exemplary and aggravated damages were not available on the facts.

Summary

Although claims for environmental harm based upon a negligence action are less common **17.212** than nuisance, disease-related claims will be personal injury matters. There are also some other negligence claims in terms of product liability and land use. The cases are covered in other chapters including: *Scott-Whitehead v National Coal Board & anor* [1987] P&CR 263, Chapter 15: Water; *Tutton v Walker Ltd* [1986] QB 61, Chapter 12: Property and land rights; and *AB v South West Water Service Ltd* [1993] QB 507 and *Reay v British Nuclear Fuels Plc* [1994] Env LR 320, Chapter 7: Human health. As often arises in environmental law, there may be a conflict between promoting the environment and access to open spaces and liability for accidents that may arise when offering this: see Chapter 12 for further discussion.

E TRESPASS TO LAND

Defining trespass to land

Trespass to land is the unjustifiable intrusion or interference with land. It includes being **17.213** physically present on the land, removing part of it, leaving waste and rubbish, or digging up and destroying plants. Coleridge CJ, in *Ellis v Loftus Iron Co* [1874] LR 10 CP noted at 12 that:

> If the defendant places a part of his foot on the plaintiff's land unlawfully, it is in law as much a trespass as if he walked half a mile on it.

In *League Against Cruel Sports Ltd v Scott* [1986] QB 240 a houndmaster was liable for the **17.214** entry of a pack of dogs onto private land. While in *McDonald v Associated Fuels* [1954]

3 DLR 775 it was held that blowing carbon monoxide into a house was trespass. In *Gregory v Piper* (1820) 9 B&C 591 the defendant dumped rubbish on public land and some fell against the claimant's wall causing trespass. Blocking the highway itself is trespass, see *Randall v Tarrant* [1955] 1 WLR 255. Finally, in *Jones v Llanrwst UDC* [1911] 1 Ch 393 sewage accidentally released into a river that polluted the claimant's land downstream was held to be trespass.

Trespass without harm to the land

17.215 It is unnecessary to show that there is any harm done to the land for trespass. *Clerk & Lindsell on Torts*, para 17-08 suggests that the reason trespass is actionable *per se* seems to be that acts of direct interference with another's possession are likely to lead to breaches of the peace and that the policy of the law therefore demands that that the claimant be relieved from the requirement of proving damage. It adds that where entry is merely threatened, a *quia timet* injunction is the appropriate remedy.

Continuing trespass

17.216 Trespass will continue for the time that the person that entered remains on the land, or the things placed on the land remain on that land. In *Holmes v Wilson* (1839) 10 A&E 50 the highway authority built a road by unlawfully placing buttresses on the claimant's land. The claimant was awarded compensation and then claimed once again when the authority failed to remove the objects, see *Konskier v Goodman Ltd* [1928] 1 KB 421.

Trespass *ab initio*

17.217 Where a person has entered land with lawful authority and then abuses that authority he becomes a trespasser *ab initio* and his conduct renders his original entry unlawful.

17.218 It is important to note the distinct tort of trespass to the person, which covers assault, battery, and false imprisonment and is unlikely to relate to any aspect of environmental law, except perhaps, where environmental protesters may be unlawfully held or harmed.

Parties to a trespass claim

Claimant

17.219 A claim for trespass may be brought by someone who is in possession of the land in question, including an owner and a tenant, although most landlords cannot sue if the tenant has some right of exclusive possession. This does not extend to a lodger where the possession remains with the landlord.

The claimant's land

17.220 The claimant's land includes any subsoil and building. In *Rawson v Peters* (1972) 225 EG 89 CA the Court of Appeal held that the owner of an exclusive right of fishing claimed trespass against someone polluting and interfering with the fishing right. While in *Harrison v Duke of Rutland* [1893] 1 QB 142 interfering with the claimant's subsoil constituted trespass. The claimant's land also includes, to a limited extent, the airspace above land. In *Bernstein v Skyviews and General Ltd* [1978] QB 479 it was held that flying over private property at a reasonable and safe height was not a trespass. Also, s 76 of the Civil Aviation Act 1976 provides that no civil action may be taken against civil aircraft unless there is some negligent act see: Chapter 10: Noise.

Defendant

To define someone as a trespasser requires consideration of that person's willingness to **17.221** enter the land. Providing that the entry onto land is voluntary it is irrelevant that the trespasser entered with intention, through negligence, or by mistake. However, if entry to the land is involuntary then this will not constitute trespass. In *Smith v Stone* [1647] Sty 65 the defendant was carried on to the claimant's land involuntarily by other people and the court considered that the party that carried the defendant trespassed not the defendant himself.

Defences

Licence

A licence for the purpose of trespass was described by Sir Frederick Pollock in *Torts* (15th ed) **17.222** as: 'that consent which, without passing any interest in the property to which it relates, merely prevents the acts to which consent is given from being wrongful.'

A licence enables a person to be on land without being a trespasser until that licence is **17.223** revoked.

Justification

An act or state of affairs that would otherwise be trespass may be prevented from being so by **17.224** a legally justified reason. For instance, a right of entry onto private land may be conferred by legislation. Section 60 of the National Parks and Access to the Countryside Act 1949 provides that:

> where an access agreement or order is in force as respects any land a person who enters upon land, comprised in the agreement or order for the purpose of open-air recreation without breaking or damaging any wall, fence, hedge or gate, or who is on such land for that purpose after having so entered thereon, shall not be treated as a trespasser on that land or incur any other liability by reason only of so entering or being on the land.

The police and other local authority officers have a number of rights and powers of entry **17.225** onto land, e.g. s 293 of the Highways Act 1980 provides a power of entry to enter land for purposes connected with certain orders relating to footpaths and bridle ways. Environment Agency officers also have power to enter premises at any reasonable time under s 108 of the Environment Act 1995.

In *Monsanto v Tilly & ors* [1999] Env LR 313 the defendants raised the defence of necessity **17.226** in a claim by the large biotechnology company to prevent protesters uprooting GM crops. Lord Justice Pill commented at 338 that:

> In exceptional circumstances necessity may justify trespass to land or to goods, but it is impossible to conclude from the nature of the matters which these defendants wish to establish at trial that the necessity defence has any real prospect of success in this case. The defence is only available to the individual in cases of emergency where it is necessary for the private citizen to

act in the face of immediate and serious danger to life or property and the citizen acts reasonably in all the circumstances.

17.227 The regulation of GM crops is considered in Chapter 6: Fishing, farming, and animal health.

Remedies

17.228 Remedies for trespass include securing land by a possession order, obtaining an injunction forbidding further acts of trespass, and damages to compensate for the harm done to the land as a result of the trespassing activity.

Possession proceedings

17.229 Part 55 of the CPR 1998 makes provision for a possession claim against trespassers. Rule 55.1(b) states that:

> a possession claim against trespassers means a claim for the recovery of land which the claimant alleges is occupied only by a person or persons who entered or remained on the land without the consent of a person entitled to possession of that land.

17.230 The matters under Pt 55 are concluded without a full trial on the basis that the defendants, as trespassers, have no defence. Rule 55.3 covers the procedure for starting the claim. Proceedings must start in the county court for the district in which the land is situated unless there is justification for bringing the matter in the High Court including, under para 1.3 of Practice Direction 55, that:

(1)   there are complicated disputes of fact;

(2)   there are points of law of general importance; or

(3)   the claim is against trespassers and there is a substantial risk of public disturbance or of serious harm to person or property, which properly require immediate determination.

17.231 The proceedings require a special claim form (Form N5). Under r 55.3(4) where the claimant does not know the name of a person in occupation or possession of the land, the claim must be brought against 'persons unknown' in addition to any named defendants.

17.232 In *Dutton v Manchester Airport Plc* [1999] 2 All ER 675 the claim was against trespassers who were protesting against the construction of a second runway at Manchester Airport. The National Trust owned the land and airport operators had been given a licence to fell some trees in order to assist the runway's construction. The court held that an order for possession did not interfere with the rights of the National Trust. In *Secretary of State for Transport v Haughian & ors* [1997] Env LR 59, a case involving the construction of the Newbury bypass, Hutchinson LT commented that:

> All that we are concerned with is the simple question whether the applicants have an arguable defence to claims for possession. They cannot, in my judgment, by asserting or admitting that the motive for their presence is to protest as against the implementation of the scheme, convert their status as mere trespassers into something conferring rights or entitling them to maintain their right to remain against the claim by the Secretary of State whose title is undoubtedly, in my view, sufficient to maintain these claims against them.

Injunction

A claimant may also apply for an injunction which prohibits a trespasser to enter land or to cause any damage to that land. **17.233**

Damages

A claimant may be entitled to damages even though there is no harm caused. This sum will be assessed on the price a reasonable man would be prepared to pay for the right to use the land. Where harm has occurred, the level of compensation will be the diminution in the value of the land after the trespass and harm has occurred, although the cost of reparation may be claimed provided the claimant is proposing to carry out that work, see: *Perry v Sidney Phillips & Son* [1982] 1 WLR 1297. **17.234**

Trespass as a crime

Despite the common landowner's sign 'trespassers will be prosecuted', trespass is, in general, a civil claim and such a sign has been described as a 'wooden falsehood' arising from an ancient right that was finally abolished in 1694. However, a number of statutory provisions create offences relating to trespass. Part II of the Criminal Law Act 1977 creates a number of offences relating to entering land including: **17.235**

s 6   without lawful authority, using or threatening violence to secure entry;

s 7   remaining on residential premises, having entered as a trespasser and after being required to leave by order; and

s 8   having, as a trespasser, without lawful authority or reasonable excuse, an offensive weapon.

Section 39 of the Public Order Act 1986 creates an offence if a senior police officer has asked two or more persons to leave land that he believes they are residing on as trespassers. While s 68 of the Criminal Justice and Public Order Act 1994 creates an offence of aggravated trespass if a person trespasses on land in the open air and does anything that is intended to have the effect of intimidating, obstructing, or disrupting lawful activity. **17.236**

The commentary in the Environmental Law Report [2000] 341, following the case of *Monsanto v Tilly* noted that there had been a number of cases dealing with the legal issues surrounding environmental interest groups, campaigning, and protests including: *Manchester Airport v Dutton* [1999] 3 WLR 524 (CA) relating to ecological trespassers resisting the development of a second runway at Manchester Airport, *Secretary of State for Transport v Haughian* relating to the construction of the Newbury bypass, and *The Mayor and Burgesses of the LB of Bromley v Susanna & ors* [1999] Env LR D13 concerning the development of Crystal Palace park and *Huntingdon Life Sciences v Curtin* [1998] Env LR D9. It added: **17.237**

> in each of the above cases, the court's final decision centred around a strict legalistic interpretation of the relevant provisions. Accordingly there was either an explicit or implicit judicial rejection of the values or arguments which the protest groups were putting forward.

F   BREACH OF STATUTORY DUTY

17.238 Where there is a breach of a statutory or regulatory provision, e.g. that constitutes an offence under an Act, and, in addition to the criminal nature of the act, someone suffers harm or loss, the breach of duty may also give rise to a claim in civil law.

Express provision

17.239 There are a few statutory provisions that expressly provide for a civil remedy in environmental matters. For example, s 73(6) of the Environmental Protection Act 1990 provides that:

> where any damage is caused by waste which has been deposited in or on land, any person who deposited, or knowingly caused or knowingly permitted it to be deposited so as to commit an offence under sections 33(1) or 63(2) is liable for the damage caused.

17.240 Section 60 of the Water Resources Act 1991 provides that damages are available where the Environment Agency has granted water abstraction rights that impair the existing rights of third parties. Section 18 of the Water Industry Act 1991 (WIA 1991) enables the Secretary of State or the Director-General of Water Services to make an enforcement order to secure compliance with certain provisions contained within that section. Section 22(1) of the WIA 1991 provides that the obligation to comply with an enforcement order shall be a duty owed to any person who may be affected by a contravention of the order. While s 22(2) provides that: 'Where a duty is owed under subs (1), any breach of the duty which causes that person to sustain loss or damage shall be actionable at the suit of that person.'

17.241 In *AB v South West Water Service Ltd* [1993] QB 507 a group action involving 80 litigants brought a claim in public nuisance and breach of statutory duty under the Water Act 1989 against the water supplier for damages suffered after their drinking water became contaminated with aluminium sulphate. Express provision for a civil remedy may be regarded as a tort in its own right.

Implied provision

17.242 In most instances of civil liability under statute the Act does not expressly provide for a civil remedy, instead it is for the court to interpret the relevant statute and to determine whether or not a remedy is available. This has not always been easy and there has been some inconsistency in judicial interpretation. In *X (Minors) v Bedfordshire CC* [1995] 2 AC 633 Lord Browne-Wilkinson stated at 731 that:

> The principles applicable in determining whether [a] statutory cause of action exists are now well established, although the application of the principles in any particular case remains difficult. The basic proposition is that in the ordinary case a breach of statutory duty does, by itself, give rise to any private law cause of action. However a private law cause of action will arise if it can be shown, as a matter of construction of a statute, that the statutory duty was imposed for the protection of a limited class of the public and that Parliament intended to confer on members of that class a private right of action for breach of a duty. . . . If the statute provides no other remedy for its breach and the Parliamentary intention to protect a limited class is shown,

that indicates that there may be a private right of action. . . . If the statute does provide some other means of enforcing the duty that will normally indicate that the statutory right was intended to be enforceable by those means and not by private right of action. . . . However, the mere existence of some other statutory remedy is not necessarily decisive. It is still possible to show that on the true construction of the statute the protected class was intended by Parliament to have a private remedy. Thus the specific duties imposed on an employer in relation to factory premises are enforceable by an action for damages, notwithstanding the imposition by the statute of criminal penalties for any breach.

In *Issa v Hackney LBC* [1997] 1 WLR 956 the Court of Appeal held that a claim for breach of **17.243** statutory duty was not available in respect of a breach of Pt III of the Public Health Act 1936 on the basis that the legislation provided a complete procedure that included the abatement of a statutory nuisance and the means for enforcement. If there is an alternative common law remedy it is unlikely that the court will rely on a breach of statutory duty. In *Phillips v Britannia Hygienic Laundry Co Ltd* [1923] 2 KB 832 the court concluded that the breach of regulations governing the condition of motor cars did not give rise to a civil action.

Establishing liability for breach of statutory duty

If it can be implied that a breach of statutory duty gives rise to a civil claim then the elements **17.244** that make up the tort are similar to those in negligence including having to establish that:

- the defendant owed the claimant a duty;
- the defendant was in breach of that duty;
- there was harm of a type that the relevant Act aims to prevent; and
- that the breach of duty caused or materially contributed to the harm.

The defendant may also rely upon the defences of *volenti non fit injuria* and contributory **17.245** negligence. For further analysis see paras 17.158 and 17.205 to 17.208.

G   ENVIRONMENTAL LIABILITY DIRECTIVE 2004/35/EC

Directive 2004/35/EC on environmental liability with regard to the prevention and remedy- **17.246** ing of environmental damage (Environmental Liability Directive) entered into force in April 2004. The main purpose of the Directive is to ensure that an operator whose activity has caused environmental damage or the imminent threat of such damage is held financially liable. This is in order to encourage operators to adopt measures and develop practices to minimize the risks of environmental damages so that their exposure to financial liability is reduced.

The Directive is narrow in scope and use. It does not cover all aspects of the environment but **17.247** is limited to specific areas by defining 'environmental damage' under Art 2(1) as:

(a) damage to protected species and natural habitats, which is any damage that has significant adverse effects on reaching or maintaining the favourable conservation status of such habitats or species. . . .;

(b) water damage, which is any damage that significantly adversely affects the ecological, chemical and/or quantitative statues and/or ecological potential, as defined in Directive 2000/60/EC (the Water Framework Directive), of the waters concerned . . .; and

(c)   land damage, which is any land contamination that creates a significant risk of human health being adversely affected as a result of the direct or indirect introduction, in, on or under land, of substances, preparation, organisms or micro-organisms.

17.248   Damage itself is defined under Art 2(2) of the Directive as a measurable adverse change or impairment of a nature resource service, which may occur directly or indirectly. Where environmental damage has occurred the operator is obliged under Art 6(1) of the Directive to: 'take all practicable steps . . . to limit or to prevent further environmental damage and adverse effects on human health or further impairment of services and the necessary remedial measures.'

17.249   The competent authorities will determine which remedial measures should be taken in accordance with Art 7 and Annex II of the Directive.

17.250   The Environmental Liability Directive does not consider the relationship between a victim of a pollution incident and a polluter (whether public or private), but requires the competent authority to take action to prevent or remedy environmental damage, although Arts 11 and 12 of the Directive confer the right on any natural or legal person affected or likely to be affected by environmental harm to request the competent authority to take action. Environmental protection non-governmental organizations will be deemed to have sufficient interest or to have rights capable of being impaired. In effect, despite its name in creating civil liability, in the UK, any remedy for private individuals is likely to be under public law in securing enforcement action by a competent authority. Member States must transpose the Directive into national law by 30 April 2007.

KEY DOCUMENTS AND MATERIALS

Law Reform (Contributory Negligence) Act 1945
Limitation Act 1980 (as amended)
Civil Procedure Rules 1998 and supporting Practice Directions

Directive 2004/35/EC on environmental liability with regard to the prevention and remedying of environmental damage (Environmental Liability Directive)

Civil Procedure Volumes 1 and 2 (the *White Book*) (2005) Sweet & Maxwell: London
Code of Guidance on Expert Evidence: A guide for experts and those instructing them for the purpose of court proceedings (2001)

The Court Service at www.hmcourts-service.gov.uk

18

STATUTORY NUISANCE

A   INTRODUCTION

18.01 The present statutory nuisance regime has its foundations in the public health statutes of the mid-nineteenth century. It was developed under the various Public Health Acts 1848 to 1936, which were enacted to control matters that were thought to affect public health. During 1844–5, Friedrich Engels wrote about Manchester in *The Condition of the Working Class in England* commenting that:

> The view from [Ducie] bridge . . . is characteristic for the whole district. At the bottom flows, or rather stagnates, the Irk, a narrow, coal-black, foul-smelling stream, full of debris and refuse, which it deposits on the shallower right bank. In dry weather, a long string of the most disgusting, blackish-green, slime pools are left standing on this bank, from the depths of which bubbles of miasmatic gas constantly arise and give forth a stench unendurable even on the bridge forty or fifty feet above the stream. But besides this, the stream itself is checked every few paces by high weirs, behind which slime and refuse accumulate and rot in thick masses. Above the bridge are tanneries, bone mills, and gasworks, from which all drains and refuse find their way into the Irk, which receives further the contents of all the neighbouring sewers and privies . . .

Statutory nuisance covers all activities that Parliament has determined is a nuisance **18.02** for the purpose of protecting human health and the environment. The main aim of the legislation is to provide a quick and simple remedy to stop nuisance occurring. It was most recently consolidated under Pt III of the Environmental Protection Act 1990 (EPA 1990) and has subsequently been amended to accommodate the latest nuisances of modern life by the insertion of new activities such as audible car alarms. Some of the case law relating to statutory nuisance is based upon earlier legislation but nevertheless remains relevant.

An important distinction between private and statutory nuisance is that the primary **18.03** purpose of statutory nuisance is to protect people, not property. Its name derives from the fact that only nuisances that are defined by statute are covered. For instance, the EPA 1990 expressly excludes a number of activities which could popularly be regarded as nuisance on the basis that there are other, more effective, forms of statutory control of such activities.

B OUTLINE OF RELEVANT LEGISLATION

There is one piece of legislation that dominates statutory nuisance; Pt III of the EPA 1990. **18.04** However, a number of other legislative provisions remain in force and are set out below. There is a thorough analysis of the law in McCracken *et al*, *Statutory Nuisance* (Butterworths, 2001) to which reference is made in this chapter.

Part III of the Environmental Protection Act 1990

Section 79(1) of the EPA 1990, as amended, states that the following matters constitute **18.05** statutory nuisances:

(a) any premises in such a state as to be prejudicial to health or a nuisance;
(b) smoke emitted from premises so as to be prejudicial to health or a nuisance;
(c) fumes or gases emitted from premises so as to be prejudicial to health or a nuisance;
(d) any dust, steam, smell or other effluvia arising on industrial, trade or business premises and being prejudicial to health or a nuisance;
(e) any accumulation or deposit which is prejudicial to health or a nuisance;
(f) any animal kept in such a place or manner as to be prejudicial to health or a nuisance;
(fa) any insects emanating from relevant industrial, trade or business premises and being prejudicial to health or a nuisance;
(fb) artificial light emitted from premises so as to be prejudicial to health or a nuisance;
(g) noise emitted from premises so as to be prejudicial to health or a nuisance;
(ga) noise that is prejudicial to health or a nuisance and is emitted from or caused by a vehicle, machinery or equipment in a street;
(h) any other matter declared by any enactment to be a statutory nuisance.

Sections 101–103 of the Clean Neighbourhoods and Environment Act 2005 (CNEA 2005) has **18.06** introduced two new forms of statutory nuisance in relation to insects and artificial lighting. It has also introduced various amending provisions. The relevant sections will enter into force by commencement order. Section 80 of the EPA 1990 provides for summary proceedings for statutory nuisance, while ss 81, 81A, and 81B cover supplementary provisions and matters relating to recovery of expenses. Section 82 of the EPA 1990 covers summary proceedings by a person aggrieved.

Statutory Nuisance Appeals Regulations 1995

18.07 Regulation 2 of the Statutory Nuisance Appeals Regulations 1995 (SI 1995/2644) (Appeal Regs 1995) provides that any person served with an abatement notice by a local authority under s 80(3) of the EPA 1990 may appeal against the notice. Regulation 3 states that, subject to exceptions, any appeal has the effect of suspending any abatement notice until the appeal has been abandoned or decided by the court.

Miscellaneous public health provisions

Public Health Act 1936

18.08 The Public Health Act 1936 (PHA 1936) provides two categories of statutory nuisance not covered in Pt III of the EPA including, under s 141, any well, tank, cistern, or waterbutt for domestic water supply that is prejudicial to health and, under s 259, any pond, pool, or watercourse in a state to be prejudicial to health or a nuisance.

Housing

18.09 Sections 189 to 208 of the Housing Act 1985 enable local authorities to serve a housing repair notice on any dwellinghouse or house in multiple occupation that is unfit for human habitation. Other landlord and tenant obligations are considered in Chapter 4: Anti-social behaviour, housing and local concerns.

Noise

18.10 The Noise Act 1996, as amended by the Anti-social Behaviour Act 2003, provides that a local authority may, if they receive a complaint by an individual present in a dwelling between 11.00 pm and 7.00 am that excessive noise is coming from another dwelling, arrange for an officer of the authority to take reasonable steps to investigate the complaint.

18.11 See also the regulatory sanctions in criminal law that aim to control nuisances and that may be specifically excluded from the statutory nuisance regime such as:

- PPC and IPC sanctions that cover activities operating in contravention of licence/permit regime under Pt I of the EPA 1990 and the Pollution Prevention and Control Act 1999 (Chapter 11: Pollution prevention and control);
- Part II of the EPA 1990 in relation to unlawful disposal of waste (Chapter 14: Waste);
- the removal of abandoned vehicles under the Refuse Disposal (Amenity) Act 1978 (Chapter 14: Waste);
- defective and dangerous premises including those that have collapsed or may have drainage problems under the Building Act 1984; and
- dog fouling under the Dogs (Fouling of Land) Act 1996.

C KEY PRINCIPLES OF STATUTORY NUISANCE

What is prejudicial to health?

Section 79(7) of the EPA 1990 includes a number of definitions for the purposes of Pt III. **18.12** It defines prejudicial to health as 'injurious, or likely to cause injury, to health'. The court in *Coventry CC v Cartwright* [1975] 1 WLR 845 clarified this by stating that it is health rather than personal injury. For example, risk of injury from broken glass would not be prejudicial to health for the purposes of statutory nuisance but could cause personal injury. In *County CC v Cartwright* the court held that a pile of builder's rubble was not a statutory nuisance and could only cause personal injury if someone walked over it or into it in some way. The court noted that: 'the general purpose of the Act is to stop accumulations which have a public health consequence, which tend to create smell or smoke or other emanations.'

In *Betts v Penge UDC* [1942] 2 KB 154 the court held that in order to sustain a conviction for **18.13** statutory nuisance on premises it was sufficient to prove that, by the defendant's act or default, the premises were in such a state as to interfere with the personal comfort of the occupiers, without necessarily being injurious to health.

Prejudicial to health can include indirect effects such as sleeplessness. The section protects **18.14** anyone that is put at risk and the test of what is prejudicial to health is objective. In *R (Anne) v Test Valley BC* [2002] Env LR 538 the court affirmed that the correct test for 'prejudicial to health' was not simply whether the claimant's health was or had been prejudiced but whether the average person's health would have been prejudiced. In *R (Anne) v Test Valley BC*, the claimant had been affected by mould spores developing as a result of insects nesting in a tree next to her home. She was considered to have a hypersensitive reaction, which the average person would not have suffered. Thus, in certain cases, expert evidence may be necessary to help clarify whether the nuisance complained of would be prejudicial to the health of the average person.

In *Birmingham City Council v Oakley* [2001] Env LR 37 the House of Lords considered a claim **18.15** that a council property without a washbasin in the WC was a statutory nuisance, noting that any danger to health arose from the absence of a washbasin in the vicinity of the toilet. Lord Slynn held that:

> There must be a factor which in itself is prejudicial to health. I do not think that the arrangement of the rooms otherwise not in themselves insanitary so as to be prejudicial to health falls within section 79(1)(a).

See also *R v Bristol CC ex p Everett* [1999] Env LR 589 considered below at paras 18.30 **18.16** and 18.89.

What is a nuisance under the Act?

Nuisance is the unacceptable interference with the personal comfort or amenity of **18.17** neighbours or the nearby community. In *Baxter v London Borough of Camden* [2000] Env LR 112 Lord Millet stated that:

The governing principle is that of good neighbourliness, and this involves reciprocity. A landowner [or anyone else using land] must show the same consideration for his neighbour as he would expect his neighbour to show for him.

18.18 In *National Coal Board v Thorne* [1976] 1 WLR 543 the court considered that statutory nuisance should be interpreted in line with civil or public nuisance. The court felt that it was not possible to claim statutory nuisance if the interference came from the same property rather than a neighbouring one, although subsequent decisions have appeared to relax this. See *Carr v LB of Hackney* [1995] Env LR 372 and *Calvert v Gardiner* ELM 14 [2002] 3 p 156.

Premises

18.19 The state or use of premises is relevant to a number of the statutory nuisances contained in s 79(1). Under s 79(7) of the EPA 1990 premises includes land and any vessel. Contaminated land that falls within Pt IIA of the EPA 1990 is expressly excluded from the definition of statutory nuisance by s 79(1A) and (1B). Section 268(1) of the PHA 1936 (a predecessor of Pt III) provides that house includes tents, vans, sheds, and other structures for human habitation. In *Stevenage BC v Wilson* [1993] Env LR 214 the High Court dismissed an appeal based upon the defendant arguing that her garden did not come within the definition of dwelling; a term used in the abatement notice. Section 343(1) of the PHA 1936 uses the definition of vessel contained in the Merchant Shipping Act 1995 of 'every vessel used in navigation'; although s 79(12) of the EPA 1990 states that a vessel powered by steam reciprocating machinery is not a vessel to which Pt III applies.

18.20 In *East Riding of Yorkshire Council v Yorkshire Water Services Limited* [2001] Env LR 7 the court affirmed that public sewers did not constitute 'premises' within the meaning of s 79(1)(a), developing the decision in *R v Parlby* (1889) 22 QBD 520 that sewage treatment works were not included in the expression 'premises'.

18.21 In *Pollway Nominees Ltd v LB of Havering* (1989) 21 HLR 462 the defendant company was landlord of a flat that was suffering from dampness caused by a defective external wall. The defendant argued that the outside wall was not part of the demised premises and that the abatement notice should have been served on the owner of the wall. The court rejected the argument holding the term 'premises' referred to the premises which were prejudicial to health which, in this case, was the flat itself even though the concern arose from an external wall owned by someone else.

18.22 Section 101 of the CNEA 2005 further defines premises for the purpose of Pt III of the EPA 1990 by inserting four new subsections. Subsections 79(7A) and (7B) clarify railway premises, while subs 79(7C) excludes a number of premises from the meaning of industrial trade and business purposes. These include:

   (a)   land used as arable, grazing, meadow, or pasture land,
   (b)   land used as osier land, reed beds, or woodland,
   (c)   land used for market gardens, nursery grounds, or orchards,
   (d)   land forming part of an agricultural unit, not being land falling within any of paragraphs (a) to (c), where the land is of a description prescribed by regulations made by the appropriate person, and

(e)   land included in a site of special scientific interest (as defined in s 52(1) of the Wildlife and Countryside Act 1981),

and excluding land covered by, and the waters of, any river or watercourse, that is neither a sewer nor a drain, or any lake or pond.

Subsection 79(7D) of the EPA 1990 then clarifies this further by explaining that 'agricultural' **18.23** has the same meaning as in s 109 of the Agriculture Act 1947, 'agricultural unit' means land that is occupied as a unit for agricultural purposes, and that 'drain', 'lake or pond', and 'sewer' have the same meaning as the Water Resources Act 1991.

Balancing factors

Statutory nuisance relies on a number of aspects of private nuisance in determining whether **18.24** a statutory nuisance exists. These include the concepts of reasonableness and the need to balance a number of competing factors such as locality, continuance, and utility. These factors are considered in some detail in Chapter 17: Civil law practice and procedure. In *Budd v Colchester BC* [1997] Env LR 128 Schiemann LJ at 134 commented that:

in nuisance cases there is always an element of judgement in a continuum between a mildly irritating activity to something which is intolerable and positively criminal if it affects a large enough number of people.

Locality

The locality in which the nuisance arises may be material in balancing whether or not a **18.25** nuisance exists. Noise emanating from a nightclub in the city centre is likely to be less of a nuisance compared to a similar level of noise in a quiet village. In *Sturges v Bridgman* (1879) 11 Ch D 852 the court noted that a nuisance in Belgrave Square would not necessarily be so in Bermondsey.

When nuisance arises and for how long

When the nuisance occurs will be a factor in assessing whether a nuisance exists. For **18.26** example, playing the drums or another loud musical instrument may be acceptable on a Saturday afternoon but is unlikely to be so first thing on a Sunday morning. Nuisance should generally be something more than temporary. Occasional incidents can be a nuisance, but only where the activity causing the nuisance is a continuing use, e.g. a factory that through its operation gives rise to occasional emissions of fumes. Regular noisy parties every other week day will not be acceptable, whereas an occasional party held at a weekend may well be.

Utility, convention, and difficulty in preventing the nuisance

In *Leenan v Montagu* [1936] 2 All ER 1677 it was held that the existence of common usage will **18.27** be influential. A factory may emit noise and odours but also provide employment for local residents while noise from a school playground will be justified and hard to avoid.

In summary, when considering the balancing factors in statutory nuisance and, as indicated **18.28** above, what constitutes a nuisance, reference should be made to private nuisance under the common law: see Chapter 17: Civil law practice and procedure.

D CATEGORIES OF NUISANCE

18.29 Section 79(1) of the EPA 1990 provides for ten specific categories of statutory nuisance and one category of residual legislation. Importantly, if a polluting incident or matter of environmental harm falls outside the scope of the definitions it cannot be classed as a statutory nuisance and anyone suffering the harm cannot be assisted by the regime having, instead, to turn to alternative remedies such as the PPC regime, Clean Air Act 1993 (CAA 1993) provisions, or common law private nuisance, any of which may assist depending on the circumstances. Each of the categories listed in s 79(1) and regarded as a statutory nuisance is considered below.

Premises in a poor state

18.30 Section 79(1)(a) provides that a statutory nuisance includes: 'any premises in such a state as to be prejudicial to health or a nuisance'.

18.31 This category has regularly been used by tenants of rented accommodation trying to force landlords to improve living conditions, where conventional breach of tenancy agreements may not be helpful, e.g. for breach of repair, see Chapter 4. In *Issa v London Borough of Hackney* [1997] 1 All ER 999 it was held that houses with condensation and mould could fall within the statutory nuisance regime. This was affirmed in *R (Islington LBC) v Inner London Crown Court* [2003] EWHC 2500 Admin. Contrast this with Lord Clyde's comments in *Birmingham City Council v Oakley* that:

> Whether the law should require washbasins to be installed near lavatories is a matter for Parliament, but the Public Health Acts are not a suitable vehicle. They are concerned with the state of premises and not their physical layout or the facilities to be provided in them.

18.32 In *R v Bristol CC ex p Everett* the Court of Appeal dismissed an appeal on the basis that the state of premises could not amount to a statutory nuisance by reason that they created a likelihood of accident causing personal injury, in this case a steep staircase. The case reaffirmed the position that although the statutory provisions may be capable of embracing accidental physical injury, it was reasonably clear that they were not intended to be so wide in scope and that that kind of problem fell outside the legislative purpose.

Smoke from premises

18.33 Under s 79(1)(b) of the EPA 1990 a statutory nuisance includes, 'smoke emitted from premises so as to be prejudicial to health or a nuisance'.

18.34 The definition of smoke in s 79(7) includes soot, ash, grit, and gritty particles emitted in smoke. It adds that any expressions used in Pt III have the same meaning as the Clean Air Act 1993 and that the definition of dark smoke in s 3 of that Act shall apply. Also, many smoke emissions from business premises or land are excluded from the statutory nuisance regime on the basis that they are controlled more effectively under the CAA 1993 and PPC/LA-PPC legislation. These are discussed in Chapters 3: Air and 11: Pollution prevention and control respectively. Also, see Chapter 3: Air for a practical analysis of smoke and its composition.

This sub-section covers garden bonfires and barbecues (providing that they comply with the **18.35** regularity and frequency principles) and burning of tyres on domestic land. However, s 79(3) excludes smoke from either a private dwelling within a smoke control area or a railway locomotive steam engine and dark smoke from industrial or trade premises or from a chimney of a building or serving a furnace or boiler (all of which fall under the CAA 1993).

Under s 79(1)(b), smoke extends to the smell of smoke. In *Griffiths v Pembrokeshire County* **18.36** *Council* [2000] EWHC Admin 319 the defendant continued to burn animal carcasses in contravention of an abatement notice, he argued that although there may have been the smell of smoke that would not amount to smoke as a statutory nuisance. The High Court dismissed an appeal by way of case stated and held that the term 'smoke' could apply to the smell of smoke.

Fumes or gases emitted from premises

Section 79(1)(c) of the EPA 1990 provides that a statutory nuisance includes, 'fumes or gases **18.37** emitted from premises so as to be prejudicial to health or a nuisance'.

Section 79(4) of the EPA 1990 limits s 79(1)(c) to private dwellings. As with s 79(1)(b), the **18.38** restriction is based upon more effective controls being available under the PPC/LA-PPC regime and the CAA 1993 for business premises. The definitions in s 79(7) provide that fumes mean any airborne solid matter smaller than dust; and gas includes vapour and moisture precipitated from vapour. There is no definition of vapour although a common definition is that it is particles of liquid suspended in air. McCracken *et al* in *Statutory Nuisance* suggests that this section may be used to address problems caused by exhaust gases emitted from the flue of a central heating boiler in a neighbour's home and that offensive odours from home cooking, soap or candle making may also fall within this category.

Dust, steam, smell or other effluvia from business premises

Under s 79(1)(d) of the EPA 1990 a statutory nuisance includes: 'any dust, steam, smell or **18.39** other effluvia arising on industrial, trade or business premises and being prejudicial to health or a nuisance'. Section 79(1)(d) does not cover residential property and s 79(7) provides that dust does not include dust emitted from a chimney as an ingredient of smoke. There is no statutory definition of steam, smell, or effluvia. In common use effluvia means unpleasant smells or exhalation from gas or decaying matter. In *Malton Board of Health v Malton Farmer's Manure Company* (1879) 4 Ex D 302 it was held to include the vapours arising from the production of manure.

Accumulations and deposits

Under s 79(1)(e) of the EPA 1990 a statutory nuisance includes: 'any accumulation or deposit **18.40** which is prejudicial to health or a nuisance'.

The terms 'accumulation' or 'deposit' are not defined under Pt III of the Act, although **18.41** McCracken *et al* advises that an accumulation is the result of a series of deposits whether by man, beast, nature, or machine, whereas a deposit is the result of a single instance. The decision in *Coventry CC v Cartwright* considered above affirmed that any accumulation or deposit must be capable of causing disease rather than physical injury. In *R v Carrick DC ex p Shelley* [1996] Env LR 273 sewage discharge on a beach was found to be a statutory nuisance under this provision.

Keeping of animals

18.42 Section 79(1)(f) of the EPA 1990 provides that a statutory nuisance includes: 'any animal kept in such a place or manner as to be prejudicial to health or a nuisance'.

18.43 This category of nuisance does not seem to add anything to those set out in ss 79(1)(a) and (g) although cases will always be unique on their facts and there would not be any value in removing the category. There is some early case law, e.g. *Steers v Manton* (1893) 57 JP 584 relating to the keeping of pigs. In *Galer v Morrissey* [1955] 1 WLR 110 the court held that noise from animals did not fall within this category whereas in *Coventry CC v Cartright* they suggested that it did and the best approach has to be to include subs (f) in any claim. In local authority areas that have implemented the provisions under the Dogs (Fouling of Land) Act 1996, this may be a more effective means of control, although only certain areas are designated areas where the provisions apply, and it may be that s 79(1)(f) could be relevant where dog fouling is a persistent problem.

Insects

18.44 Section 101 of the CNEA 2005 amends s 79(1) of the EPA 1990 by inserting a new subs (fa) which provides that the following constitutes a statutory nuisance: 'any insects emanating from relevant industrial, trade or business premises and being prejudicial to health or a nuisance.'

18.45 The CNEA 2005 clarifies the scope of insects that fall within the regime by inserting a new subs 79(1)(5A) of the EPA 1990, which provides that the relevant subsection does not apply to insects that are wild animals included in Sch 5 of the Wildlife and Countryside Act 1981 (animals that are protected), unless they are included in respect of s 9(5) of that Act only. The Government consultation document *Clean Neighbourhoods* (Defra, 2004) explained that the purpose of the new section is to prevent nuisance from unwelcome insects from premises where activities were likely to provide fertile breeding grounds where this was prejudicial to health or a nuisance. This would, one assumes, include nuisance flies and cockroaches.

18.46 There have been a number of civil claims relating to maggot and cockroach infestation. In *Southwark LBC v Long* [2002] EWCA Civ 403, the Court of Appeal allowed a private nuisance claim by a tenant following maggot infestation, smells, and noise from tenants using a chute and leaving rubbish in the common parts. The award of £13,500 general damages was upheld. In *Dolan v Sefton MBC* [2001] LAB 27, the county court awarded damages of £16,000 for personal injury following a property affected by severe cockroach infestation for three years. Other claims may arise out of a breach of covenant to repair: see Chapter 4.

Lighting

Section 102 of the CNEA 2005 amends s 79(1) of the EPA 1990 by inserting a new subs (fb) **18.47**
which provides that the following constitutes a statutory nuisance: 'artificial light emitted
from premises so as to be prejudicial to health or a nuisance; . . .' The new artificial lighting
statutory nuisance does not apply to premises occupied for defence purposes as excepted by
s 79(2) of the EPA 1990. Further, a new s 79(5B) provides that s 79(1)(fb) does not apply to
artificial light emitted from airports, harbours, railway and tramway premises, bus stations
and public service vehicle operating centres, goods vehicle centres, lighthouses, and prisons.
Light pollution is discussed in Chapter 9: Light.

Noise from premises

Section 79(1)(g) of the EPA 1990 provides that a statutory nuisance includes: 'noise emitted **18.48**
from premises so as to be prejudicial to health or a nuisance'.

Under s 79(7) of the EPA 1990 noise includes vibration but provides no further definition. In **18.49**
short, noise is sound that is unwanted by the recipient. It is the most common form of
complaint to environmental health officers and gives rise to a relatively large number
of statutory nuisance claims. The legislative and judicial approach to noise and statutory
nuisance are considered further in Chapter 10: Noise.

Noise from a vehicle, machinery, or equipment in a street

Under s 79(1)(ga) of the EPA 1990 a statutory nuisance includes: 'noise that is prejudicial **18.50**
to health and is emitted from or caused by a vehicle, machinery or equipment in a
street'.

Section 79(1)(ga) of the EPA 1990 was inserted by the Noise and Statutory Nuisance Act **18.51**
1993. It applies to individual vehicles. Under s 79(7) equipment includes a musical instrument. Section 79(6A) of the EPA 1990 provides that subsection (ga) does not apply to noise
made by:

(a) traffic;
(b) any naval, military or air force; or
(c) a political demonstration or those supporting or opposing a cause or campaign.

This category is considered further in Chapter 10: Noise.

Any other matter declared by any enactment

Section 79(1)(h) of the EPA 1990 provides that a statutory nuisance includes: 'any other **18.52**
matter declared by any enactment to be a statutory nuisance'. This is a residual category that
covers statutory nuisances arising from any earlier or subsequent legislation. Some of the
main provisions still in force are outlined below.

Public Health Act 1936

The PHA 1936 provides three categories of statutory nuisance relating to water including: **18.53** s 141(1)   any well, tank, cistern, or waterbutt used for the supply of water for domestic purposes that is so placed, constructed, or kept as to render the water in it liable to contamination or otherwise prejudicial to health.

s 259(1)(a)   any pond, pool, ditch, gutter, or watercourse that is so foul or in such a state that is prejudicial to health or a nuisance is a statutory nuisance;

s 259(1)(b)   any part of a watercourse, not being a part ordinarily navigated by vessels employed in the carriage of goods by water, which is so choked or silted up as to obstruct or impede the proper flow of water and thereby to cause a nuisance, or give rise to conditions prejudicial to health.

These are considered in Chapter 15: Water.

18.54 Under s 268(2) of the PHA 1936 a tent, van, shed, or similar structure used for human habitation:

(a) which is in such a state, or so overcrowded, as to be prejudicial to health of the inmates; or

(b) the use of which, by reason of the absence of proper sanitary accommodation or otherwise, gives rise, whether on the site or on other land, to a nuisance or to conditions prejudicial to health,

shall be a statutory nuisance, and the expression 'occupier' . . . shall include any person for the time being in charge thereof.

18.55 Section 268(2) supplements the type of premises contained in s 79(1)(a) of the EPA 1990. Section 268(3) provides a defence for an occupier of land who did not authorize the structure to be stationed or erected on the land.

Section 151(2) of the Mines and Quarries Act 1954

18.56 There are two categories of statutory nuisance under s 151(2) of the Mines and Quarries Act:

(a) a shaft or outlet of an abandoned mine, or of a mine which has not been worked for 12 months, being a shaft or outlet the surface entrance to which is not provided with a properly maintained efficient enclosure, barrier plug or other device so designed and constructed as to prevent any person from accidentally falling down the shaft or entering the outlet; . . .

(c) a quarry (whether in the course of being worked or not) which is not provided with an efficient and properly maintained barrier so designed and constructed as to prevent any person from accidentally falling into the quarry, and which, by reason of its accessibility from a highway or place of public resort, constitutes a danger to the public.

Other related areas of statutory protection

18.57 Sections 189 to 208 of the Housing Act 1985 enables local authorities to serve a housing repair notice on any dwellinghouse or house in multiple occupation that is unfit for human habitation, see Chapter 4. Under the Noise Act 1996 a local authority may, following complaints about residential night-time noise, take reasonable steps to investigate the complaint. For further discussion see Chapter 10: Noise.

London Local Authorities Act 1996

Section 24 of the London Local Authorities Act 1996 provides, for the purposes of London **18.58** boroughs, a statutory nuisance under s 79(1)(gb) of the EPA 1990, for smoke, fumes, or gases emitted (except from its exhaust) from any vehicle, machinery, or equipment on a street so as to be prejudicial to health or a nuisance other than from any vehicle, machinery, or equipment being used by the fire brigade. The aim of the section is to tackle emissions from food stalls or chip vans.

E ACTION TO ABATE A NUISANCE

Local authority duties under the EPA 1990

Section 79(1) of the EPA 1990 provides that: **18.59**

> it shall be the duty of every local authority to cause its area to be inspected from time to time to detect any statutory nuisances which ought to be dealt with under s 80 below or 80A below and, where a complaint of a statutory nuisance is made to it by a person living within its area, to take such steps as are reasonably practicable to investigate the complaint.

Many local authorities do have civic wardens that travel around their area with a role in **18.60** identifying nuisances and other anti-social activities that may be occurring, and this could satisfy the duty under s 79(1) to inspect their area from time to time for statutory nuisances. If a local authority fails to inspect an area, the Secretary of State may order it to inspect or transfer the function to himself under para 4, Sch 3 of the EPA 1990. Failure to inspect may also give rise to a claim for judicial review, see Chapter 20: Public law. The court in *Meade v LB Haringey* [1979] 1 WLR 637 held that a single inspection was unlikely to be sufficient.

In practice, most cases of statutory nuisance follow a complaint from a person within their **18.61** area. On receiving a complaint, s 79(1) provides that a local authority must take reasonably practicable steps to investigate the complaint. In *R (Anne) v Test Valley BC* the claimant argued that the local authority had failed to adequately investigate the statutory nuisance, however the court held that the investigation had been properly carried out and the conclusions reached were neither unreasonable nor irrational.

Human rights

Any action taken by the local authority should be compliant with the provisions of the **18.62** Human Rights Act 1998. Section 6(1) of the Act makes it unlawful for local authorities to act in a way that is incompatible with a right set out in the European Convention on Human Rights (ECHR). In cases where an abatement notice is being considered, relevant human rights may include Art 8 of the ECHR: the right to private life and the home and Art 1 of Protocol 1: the right to peaceful enjoyment of possessions. Further, there should be consideration of whether the procedure in issuing an abatement notice is compliant with Art 6: the right to a fair and public hearing. However, all of these rights are qualified rights and authorities will need to balance the public interest in abating the nuisance with the private interests of the individual causing the nuisance. Human rights are considered in Chapter 2: Environmental rights and principles.

The abatement notice

Duty to issue an abatement notice

18.63 Under s 80(1) of the EPA 1990 where a local authority is satisfied that a statutory nuisance exists or is likely to occur or recur it must issue an abatement notice. In *R v Carrick DC ex p Shelley* a local authority was held not to have discharged its duty where it decided to monitor the situation rather than to take action.

18.64 McCracken *et al*, in *Statutory Nuisance*, suggest that the duty to issue an abatement notice may be defeated by a recipient appealing against the notice under s 80(3) of the EPA 1990 on the grounds of best practical means. If so, an alternative approach may be to restrict rather than abate the nuisance to a level that corresponds to best practice.

Restriction on proceedings relating to IPC or PPCs

18.65 In some instances where a nuisance arises from an activity or installation regulated under either the Integrated Pollution Control (IPC) or Pollution Prevention Control (PPC) regimes proceedings cannot begin if action to control the nuisance may commence under the relevant regime. Section 79(10) of the EPA 1990 provides that:

> A local authority shall not without the consent of the Secretary of State institute summary proceedings under this Part in respect of a nuisance falling within para 79(1)(b), (d), (e) or (g) if proceedings in respect thereof might be instituted under Part I or under regulations under s 2 of the Pollution Prevention and Control Act 1999.

Preliminary action

18.66 There is no obligation to issue a letter before action or serve what is sometimes referred to as a 'minded to act' notice. There is clearly a duty to issue an abatement notice: there is no duty to consult prior to issue following consideration of this point in *R v Falmouth and Truro PHA ex p South West Water Ltd* [2000] Env LR 658. It may be appropriate to contact the person(s) causing or responsible for a nuisance or potential nuisance before the abatement notice is issued, but it is suggested by McCracken *et al* in *Statutory Nuisance* that any formal correspondence should be taken cautiously, although where a best practical means defence is likely to be raised, the authority may consider writing to a proposed recipient highlighting that best practical means are required in carrying out their activities.

18.67 If preliminary action such as informal written correspondence, a site visit, or telephone correspondence is undertaken, a record of these should be kept on the case file. If any informal negotiation is successful, the duty required under s 80(1) falls away because a statutory nuisance will no longer exist. In practice, it is very likely that an environmental health officer will make a site visit prior to issuing an abatement notice and, when doing so, discuss the matter with someone responsible for the nuisance. If the outcome of any discussion results in the cessation of a nuisance, this avoids the need for any further action.

Form and content of the notice

18.68 There is no prescribed form of abatement notice although s 80(1) of the EPA 1990 states that an abatement notice shall impose all or any of the following requirements:

(a) requiring the abatement of the nuisance or prohibiting or restricting its occurrence or recurrence,

(b) requiring the execution of such works, and the taking of such other steps, as may be necessary for any of those purposes,

and the notice shall specify the time or times within which the requirements of the notice are to be complied with.

However, some informality, defect, or error in the notice is a ground of appeal under reg 2(2)(b) of the Appeal Regs 1995 and there have been a number of decisions on this. In particular, whether an abatement notice needs to set out any steps to be taken or any work to be carried out or whether it can simply state that the nuisance be abated. **18.69**

The specification of works or means to abate the nuisance was considered in some detail in the Court of Appeal case of *R v Falmouth and Truro PHA*. Simon Brown LJ at 686 held that: **18.70**

I would, therefore, overrule *Kirklees* and hold that in *all* cases the local authority can if it wishes leave the choice of means of abatement to the perpetrator of the nuisance. If, however, the means of abatement *are* required by the local authority, then they must be specified;

Lady Justice Hale concluded on the same point at 707 that: **18.71**

the local authority may, if it wishes, leave the choice of means of abatement to the perpetrator, and need only specify the works required if it chooses to require them. Indeed, that view will often be in the interests, not only of the local authority, but also of the perpetrator.

The requirement and subsequent specification of means of abatement stated by LJ Simon Brown in *R v Falmouth and Truro PHA* may appear unclear. It was clarified when the case was discussed and followed in *Lambie v Thanet DC* [2001] Env LR 397. In *Lambie* Langley J summarized at 401 what he thought had been established: **18.72**

(1) A local authority which serves an abatement notice can, if it wishes, leave the choice of means of abatement to the perpetrator of the nuisance.
(2) If, however, it chooses to require works to be executed or steps to be taken under s 80(1)(b) to abate the nuisance, then they must be specified and specified with sufficient clarity.
(3) What is 'sufficient clarity' must, I think, be a matter for consideration in the particular circumstances of each case, but the context is that the addressee of the notice must know with reasonable certainty what is required of him.

Lambie v Thanet DC further held that the local authority could specify steps to be taken by someone other than the recipient of the abatement notice, e.g. the local authority itself. The case is considered further in Chapter 10: Noise. **18.73**

Regulation 3(3) of the Appeal Regs 1995 operates to help ensure that suspension of an abatement notice on appeal does not arise in certain situations. Importantly, under reg 3(3) the abatement notice should include a statement that reg 3(2) of the Appeal Regs 1995 applies if this is the case. Regulation 3(2) provides that if the nuisance to which the abatement notice relates is injurious to health, or is likely to be of a limited duration such that suspension of the notice would render it of no practical effect; or if any expenditure incurred in complying with the notice is not disproportionate to the public benefit to be expected from compliance, then the abatement notice need not be suspended on appeal providing a statement to that effect is contained in the notice itself. Grounds of appeal against an abatement notice including suspension are considered in Section F. **18.74**

18.75 Model notices and practical guidance on drafting an abatement notice is provided by McCracken *et al* in *Statutory Nuisance* and include:

- where abstention from or ordinary care in undertaking an activity will resolve the problem then the notice need only, and generally should only, describe the nuisance, require its abatement, and prohibit its recurrence;
- where the terms of the notice require steps to be taken or works undertaken to abate the nuisance, the notice must specify them clearly;
- where the notice or accompanying documentation imply that works or steps will be required, the works or steps must be specified;
- if in doubt, leave works and steps out; simply require the abatement and prohibit the recurrence of the nuisance; and
- decide whether the notice will or should be suspended.

18.76 Only a local authority is authorized to issue and serve an abatement notice, although they may delegate this to either a committee or officer acting on their behalf, however any delegation must be formalized. The local authority must sign an abatement notice.

Serving the notice

18.77 On deciding whether or not to serve a notice the local authority is entitled to have regard to three possible situations. These are, following the judgment of Pill LJ in *R v Crown Court at Knightsbridge ex p Cataldi* [1999] Env LR 62 at 71:

1. that there is an existing statutory nuisance,
2. that a statutory nuisance is likely to occur, and
3. that there is not, on that date, a statutory nuisance, but there has been such a nuisance in the past and it is likely to recur.

18.78 If one of these three situations exists on the date the notice is served then the local authority is entitled to serve the notice and the notice will be justified.

18.79 There is no prescribed form of service of an abatement notice. More generally, s 160(2) of the EPA 1990 provides that any notice to be served under the Act may be served or given by delivering it to the recipient, by leaving it at the recipient's proper address, or by sending it by post to him at that address. Section 80(2) of the EPA 1990 provides that that abatement notice shall be served on either:

(a) the person responsible for the nuisance;

(b) on the owner of the premises (where the nuisance arises from any defect of a structural character; or

(c) where the person responsible for the nuisance cannot be found or the nuisance has not yet occurred, on the owner or occupier of the premises.

18.80 The person responsible mentioned in s 80(2) is defined in s 79(7) as:

(a) for a statutory nuisance, the person to whose act, default, or sufferance the nuisance is attributable;

(b) for vehicles, the registered keeper or driver of the vehicle; and

(c) for equipment, the operator of the equipment.

18.81 In most cases it will be clear who the person responsible for the nuisance is. However, in *Network Housing Association v Westminster CC* [1995] Env LR 176, a case arising from noise between flats, the person responsible was the landlord for failing to provide adequate insulation between flats, rather than the person occupying the neighbouring flat. Where a number of people are responsible for the nuisance, the abatement notice may be served on one or more of those responsible.

In *Camden LBC v Gunby* [1999] 4 All ER 602 the word 'owner' included a managing agent **18.82** who received rack rent for the premises giving rise to the nuisance.

Supplementary matters

Section 81 and Sch III of the EPA 1990 include supplementary provisions relating to further **18.83** procedural matters and conferring certain powers on local authorities in respect of statutory nuisance. Certain provisions are considered elsewhere, see e.g. para 18:96 on local authority abatement, others are set out below.

Cumulative nuisance

Section 81(1) of the EPA 1990 provides that, subject to exceptions: **18.84**

> where more than one person is responsible for a statutory nuisance s 80 above shall apply to each of those persons whether or not what any of them is responsible for would by itself amount to a nuisance.

This subsection appears to provide for what may be regarded as a cumulative nuisance **18.85** whereby the act or default of one person will not constitute a statutory nuisance but the acts of a number of people, collectively, may do so. An example of this may be a row of neighbours each regularly lighting bonfires.

Powers of entry

Paragraph 2, Sch 3 of the EPA 1990 provides that any person authorized by a local authority **18.86** may, on production (if required) of his authority, enter any premises at any reasonable time to ascertain whether or not a statutory nuisance exists, or to take any action, or execute any work, authorized or required by the Act. If there is an emergency (defined in para 2(7)), entry into premises can be demanded at any time.

Warrant for entry

If admission to any premises is refused, the local authority may, under para 2(3), Sch 3 of the **18.87** EPA 1990 apply to the magistrates' court for an entry warrant. Paragraph 3(1), Sch 3 provides that any person who wilfully obstructs an entry acting under the powers in para 2 is liable on summary conviction to a maximum fine of £1,000.

Protection from personal liability

Paragraph 5, Sch 3 of the EPA 1990 provides protection from personal liability to local **18.88** authorities, its members, and officers in relation to the implementation of Pt III of the Act providing they acted in good faith, although liability remains under ss 17 or 18 of the Audit Commission Act 1998.

Action by recipient of an abatement notice

18.89   If a local authority decides that a statutory nuisance exists and then issues an abatement notice the recipient of that notice can either:

- comply with the notice;
- ignore the notice; or
- challenge the notice.

Complying with the notice

18.90   If the recipient complies with the abatement notice there should be no further action necessary by the local authority. However, abatement will often not be immediately possible. One of the grounds of appeal against an abatement notice is that the time period for compliance with the notice is not reasonably sufficient for the purpose. In *Thomas v Nokes* (1894) 58 JP 672 the court held compliance with the notice should be within a reasonable time. The circumstances of the case will usually determine the most appropriate time period for compliance. If the nuisance is severe and impacts on a significant number of people then there should be a greater urgency in securing compliance.

18.91   Section 80(1) of the EPA 1990 provides that the notice shall specify the time or times within which the requirements of the notice are to be complied with. However, in *R v Tunbridge Wells Justices ex p Tunbridge Wells BC* [1996] Env LR D7 the court affirmed that a failure to state a time limit for compliance did not nullify the notice.

18.92   In *R v Birmingham Justices ex p Guppy* (1998) 152 JP 159 it was held that a notice prohibiting as opposed to abating a nuisance, e.g. not to play loud music, should continue indefinitely. The duration of an abatement notice was considered in *Battersea BC v Goerg* (1906) 71 JP 11, where a nuisance was stopped upon service of an abatement notice and recurred two years later. On appeal, the court regarded the later nuisance as new and not a breach of the original abatement notice. Similarly in *Greenwich BC v London CC* (1912) 76 JP 267 six months passed between the service of abatement notice and a recurrence of the nuisance, and was regarded as a fresh matter.

Ignoring the abatement notice

18.93   A common, but often unwise, response to receiving an abatement notice is for the recipient to simply ignore the notice. If so, the local authority has a number of options:

- do nothing;
- suspend the notice and consult;
- abate the nuisance itself;
- take injunction proceedings; or
- commence criminal proceedings to enforce the abatement notice. This is considered in the following section.

Do nothing

18.94   The local authority is not under any obligation to take further action following service of the abatement notice. If it takes this decision then any persons aggrieved may take summary proceedings under s 82 of the EPA 1990. This is considered in Section H below.

Suspend the notice and consult

The local authority can suspend an abatement notice once service has taken place and this **18.95** can arise automatically in certain appeal cases. If so, the authority may wish to negotiate with the recipient to abate the nuisance. However, as noted above, *R v Falmouth and Truro PHA* confirms that there is no duty on the local authority to consult with the person causing the nuisance to remedy the problem. In *R v Bristol CC ex p Everett* the court held that the local authority has an implied power to withdraw an abatement notice after it has been served. Richards J commented:

> It seems senseless that an authority should be unable to withdraw an abatement notice which, for whatever reason, it no longer considers to be appropriate. It is particularly unsatisfactory that the recipient of the notice should remain subject to it . . . A power of withdrawal is there-fore consistent with, and serves to promote rather than to undermine, the legislative scheme. I see no difficulty in implying such a power.

Local authority abatement

Regardless of whether or not the local authority decides to prosecute the person causing the **18.96** nuisance, it may, under s 81(3) of the EPA 1990, abate the nuisance itself or do whatever may be necessary in execution of the notice. Section 81(4) provides that any expenses reasonably incurred by a local authority in abating, or preventing the recurrence of, a statutory nuisance under subs (3) may be recovered from the nuisance maker and, where that person was the owner of the premises, from any person who is the owner for the time being of the premises. If more than one person is responsible for the nuisance the court may apportion liability between them as the court considers fair and reasonable.

Injunction proceedings

The local authority may, in certain circumstances, choose to issue civil proceedings, **18.97** including injunctive relief, against the person responsible for the nuisance where they consider that criminal proceedings for breach of an abatement notice would be ineffective. Section 81(5) of the EPA 1990 provides that:

> If a local authority is of the opinion that proceedings for an offence under s 80(4) above would afford an inadequate remedy in the case of any statutory nuisance, they may subject to subs (6) [relating to construction site defences under the Control of Pollution Act 1974] below take proceedings in the High Court for the purpose of securing the abatement, prohibition or restriction of the nuisance, and the proceedings shall be maintainable notwithstanding the local authority have suffered no damage from the nuisance.

Section 222 of the Local Government Act 1972 enables a local authority to sue in its **18.98** own name, including taking civil proceedings under s 81(5). However, the House of Lords in *Stoke on Trent CC v B&Q (Retail) Ltd* [1984] AC 754 held that the sanctions avail-able in civil proceedings should be capable of being more onerous than a criminal penalty. The local authority must conclude that criminal proceedings are inadequate. In *Vale of White Horse DC v Allen & Partners* [1997] Env LR 212 the Court dismissed the originating summons for an injunction and costs to prevent nuisance arising from keeping pigs. This was because the claimant had not formed the opinion that proceedings under s 80(4) would afford an inadequate remedy; the council resolution to issue pro-ceedings could not allow such an inference to be drawn. The decision to take High Court proceedings was invalid on the grounds of *Wednesbury* unreasonableness, see Chapter 20: Public law.

18.99   By contrast, the court in *Hammersmith LBC v Magnum Automated Forecourts Ltd* [1978] 1 All ER 401 considered that the remedy for injunctive relief is in addition to those available summarily; a local authority may seek an injunction even though the statutory appeal procedure has not been exhausted.

Challenging the abatement notice

18.100   If the recipient of the abatement notice decides to challenge or resist the notice then he or she has a number of options such as:

- challenging the lawfulness of the local authority by making a claim for judicial review, see Chapter 20: Public law;
- submitting a complaint to Local Government Ombudsman, outlined in Chapter 22: Extra-legal options; or
- appealing against the notice to the magistrates' court under s 80(3) of the EPA 1990: Section F.

F   APPEALING AGAINST THE ABATEMENT NOTICE

18.101   Section 80(3) of the EPA 1990 provides that a person served with an abatement notice may appeal against the notice to a magistrates' court within 21 days from the date on which he was served with the notice.

Grounds of appeal

18.102   There are several grounds of appeal contained in reg 2(2) of the Statutory Nuisance (Appeals) Regulations 1995 (SI 1995/2644) (the Appeal Regs 1995) including:

(a)   that the abatement notice is not justified by s 80 of the EPA 1990;

(b)   that there has been some informality, defect, or error in, or in connection with, the abatement notice, or in, or in connection with, any copy of the abatement notice served under s 80A(3);

(c)   that the authority has refused unreasonably to accept compliance with alternative requirements, or that the requirements of the notice are otherwise unreasonable in character or extent, or are unnecessary;

(d)   that the time[s] within which the requirements of the notice are to be complied with is not reasonably sufficient for the purpose;

(e)   that (for nuisances under s 79(1)(a), (d), (e), (f) or (g) arising from industrial, trade or business premises; nuisances under s 79(1)(b) and smoke emitted from a vehicle; and nuisance within s 79(1)(ga) which is noise emitted from a vehicle, machinery, or equipment from industrial, trade or business purposes) the best practical means were used to prevent, or to counteract, the effects of the nuisance;

(f) & (g)   that, for noise cases, the requirements imposed by the notice are more onerous than those already in force from a notice issued under the Control of Pollution Act 1974 or the Noise and Statutory Nuisance Act 1993;

(h), (i), & (j)   that the notice should have been served on some other person instead of and/or as well as, the appellant, and (for (i) and (j)) it would have been equitable for it to have been so served.

Each of the grounds of appeal is considered below. However, it is important to note that the court, when considering an appeal, should consider the facts at the time of service of the abatement notice. This approach was approved by the Divisional Court in *Surrey Free Inns plc v Gosport BC* [1999] Env LR 1, and affirmed by the Court of Appeal in *R v Knightsbridge Crown Court ex p Cataldi* [1999] Env LR 62, which also applied the same approach for local authorities when considering whether or not to serve an abatement notice in the first place.   **18.103**

Ground (a) the notice is not justified

Appealing on ground (a), that the abatement notice is not justified by s 80, will require argument that either the alleged nuisance act or omission did not exist in the first place, or if it did, was not sufficient for it to amount to a statutory nuisance, or that there is no evidence to suggest that any nuisance act is likely to occur or recur. In *Budd v Colchester BC* [1997] Env LR 128 the Divisional Court stated that the burden was on the local authority to justify its notice. In *Surrey Free Inns plc v Gosport BC* the Court of Appeal considered an appeal under grounds (a) and (e). In *Godfrey v Conwy CBC* [2001] Env LR 674 the Divisional Court heard an appeal that had been dismissed by the Crown Court and the magistrates' court beforehand following an appeal against an abatement notice on appeal grounds (a) and (b).   **18.104**

Ground (b) informality, defect, or error

An appeal on ground (b) that there has been some informality, defect, or error in the abatement notice is qualified by reg 2(3) of the Appeal Regs 1995, which states that: **18.105**

> If and so far as an appeal is based on the ground of some informality, defect or error in, or in connection with the abatement notice, or in, or in connection with, any copy of the notice served under s 80A(3), the court shall dismiss the appeal if it is satisfied that the informality, defect or error was not a material one.

Budd v Colchester BC related to an appeal on ground (b). In *Sevenoaks DC v Brands Hatch Leisure Group Ltd* [2001] Env LR 86 the defendant challenged the validity of the abatement notice. The magistrates' court dismissed the appeal, finding the notice valid, the Crown Court allowed an appeal contending that the notice failed to adequately specify steps and the Queen's Bench Division allowed the appeal finding again that the notice was valid and that there was no unfairness to the defendant.   **18.106**

In *Lowe & Watson v South Somerset DC* [1998] Env LR 143, a case arising from noise from cockerels and waterfowl, the appellants complained that, among other things, the abatement notice should state whether the noise was either 'prejudicial to health' or a 'nuisance' and that in any event the noise from cockerels is no more than should be expected in a country area. The High Court dismissed the appeal noting that Pt III of the EPA 1990 did not require a notice to set out precisely whether the nuisance alleged was prejudicial to health, a common law nuisance, or both. What was important was that the acts constituting the   **18.107** nuisance were sufficiently alleged that the person served with the notice knew what was required to abate it. The court added that there was nothing to suggest that the case had been conducted with any procedural unfairness.

Ground (c) unreasonableness in the notice or in compliance by alternative means

18.108 Appeal on ground (c) has two parts relating to the reasonableness of the local authority in either the steps required in abating the nuisance or in accepting compliance with the notice by alternative means to those specified in the notice. To rely on this ground, there should be some evidence that the recipient offered options or schemes to the local authority to abate the nuisance, prior to the issue of the abatement notice. It will be for the justices to determine what is unreasonable in the circumstances of the case. It is now settled that in many instances, the local authority does not need to set out how the nuisance is to be abated, see paras 18.70 to 18.73. If it chooses not to, then it is likely to avoid an appeal of unreasonableness based on requirements in the abatement notice.

Ground (d) insufficient time for compliance

18.109 An appeal on ground (d) is that the recipient needs more time than has been allowed in the notice to abate the nuisance. The time limit stated in the notice should be reasonable. However, if time is the only basis for an appeal then the recipient has accepted that at some stage the nuisance should be abated. In practice, by the time an appeal is heard it is unlikely that this ground will succeed on its own unless there are other grounds of appeal and the notice has been suspended. In which case it may be legitimate to argue this ground on the basis that time does not run while the notice has been suspended by the appeal proceedings. Further, if the notice specifies three months, an appeal is heard after six months from the date of the notice and the recipient argues that nine months is a reasonable time in the circumstances, then the appeal on ground (d) may well be justified.

Ground (e) best practicable means

18.110 An appeal on ground (e) that the best practicable means (BPM) were used in trying to prevent or counteract the effects of a nuisance is only available in the circumstances provided for in reg 2(3)(e), e.g. industrial, trade, or business premises in such a state as to be prejudicial to health of a nuisance. BPM is a concept used in other areas of environmental legislation such as the Control of Pollution Act 1974 (CoPA 1974). Section 79(7) of the EPA 1990 states that 'best practicable means' is to be interpreted by reference to the following provisions:

(a) 'practicable' means reasonably practicable having regard among other things to local conditions and circumstances, to the current state of technical knowledge, and to the financial implications;

(b) the means employed include the design, installation, and maintenance and manner and periods of operation of plant and machinery, and the design, construction, and maintenance of buildings and structures;

(c) the test is to apply only so far as compatible with any duty imposed by law;

(d) the test is to apply only so far as compatible with safety and safe conditions, and with the exigencies of any emergency or unforeseeable circumstances;

and, in circumstances where a code of practice under s 71 of CoPA 1974 (noise minimization) is applicable, regard shall also be had to guidance given in it.

In *East Devon DC v Farr* [2002] Env LR 735 the respondents to an appeal by way of case stated **18.111** to the High Court had successfully appealed against an abatement notice on the following grounds; reg 2(2)(a) of the Appeal Regs 1995 that the notice was not justified; under reg 2(2)(c) that the authority had unreasonably refused to accept compliance with alternative requirements; and under reg 2(2)(e) that BPM had been used. Elias J held at 741 that, in relation to reg 2(2)(e):

> The justices have in terms said that the respondent had taken all reasonable and practical steps to reduce the effect of the noise. As I have indicated, in determining that question under s 79(9) they are entitled to have regard to the local conditions and circumstances, as well as to the financial implications. . . . It seems to me that the justices have concluded that the best practical means were used to counteract the effects of the nuisance . . . I do not consider that the failure specifically to refer to the statutory provision invalidates that determination.

The BPM employed in *Farr* were taken in an effort to reduce the noise levels from the **18.112** respondent's metal polishing business when, in hot weather, they used to open the front doors of the workshop. It had been held by the magistrates that other options such as extraction equipment and air conditioning could increase the noise and the efficiency of air conditioning was questionable due to the emission of fine dust particles. Also, that the cost of either equipment could be prohibitive.

Grounds (f) and (g) notice requirements too onerous

An appeal on either ground (f) or (g) relates to other legislation that provides notice of **18.113** restrictions or limitations and that the requirements imposed by the abatement notice go beyond the notice or consent already in place.

Grounds (h), (i), and (j) service of notice on another person

An appeal on grounds (h), (i), and (j) arises if the appellant considers that the notice should **18.114** have been served on some other person instead of or, in the case of ground (j), as well as the appellant. If grounds (i) and (j) are relied upon, reg 2(4) of the Appeal Regs 1995 provides that:

> the appellant shall serve a copy of his notice of appeal on any other person referred to, and in the case of any appeal to which these regulations apply he may serve a copy of his notice of appeal on any other person having an estate or interest in the premises, vehicle, machinery or equipment in question.

Suspension of the abatement notice

Under reg 3(1) of the Appeal Regs 1995, where an appeal is brought against an abatement **18.115** notice, the notice may, in certain circumstances, be suspended until the appeal has been abandoned or decided by the court. Suspension will operate if either:

(i) compliance with the abatement notice would involve any person in expenditure on the carrying out of works before the hearing of the appeal, or

(ii) in the case of a nuisance under s 79(1)(g) or (ga), the noise to which the abatement notice relates is noise necessarily caused in the course of the performance of some duty imposed by law on the appellant, and

either paragraph (2) does not apply, or it does apply but the requirements of paragraph (3) have not been met.

18.116　Regulation 2(2) states that a notice will not be suspended where:

    (a)　the nuisance is (i) injurious to health or (ii) is likely to be of limited duration, and suspension of the notice would mean that the notice would have no practical effect; or

    (b)　the costs in complying with the abatement notice before any appeal has been decided would not be disproportionate to the public benefit to be expected in that period from such compliance.

18.117　The Court of Appeal in *Wycombe DC v Jeffways and Pilot Coaches* (1983) 81 LGR 662 held that in carrying out their obligations under Pt III for noise nuisance a local authority must consider the interest of all residents in the area and, on appeal, magistrates must decide whether the local authority was reasonable in its consideration of balancing the competing interests of the community.

18.118　Regulation 3(3) states that where para (2) applies the abatement notice:

    (a)　shall include a statement that paragraph (2) applies, and that as a consequence it shall have effect notwithstanding any appeal to a magistrates' court which has not been decided by the court, and

    (b)　shall include a statement as to which of the grounds set out in paragraph (2) apply.

18.119　In *Cambridge CC v Douglas* [2001] Env LR 715 the appellant local authority had served an abatement notice relating to noise that included a statement that para 3(2) of the Appeal Regs 1995 applied. The defendant appealed against the abatement notice and the magistrates, while finding a statutory nuisance existed, allowed the appeal on the grounds that the notice was defective by not specifying exactly where the noise emanated from, was ambiguous, and was unreasonable in not setting out acceptable sound levels. The Divisional Court quashed the magistrates' court decision and remitted the matter back with a direction to dismiss the appeal holding that, among other things, there was no reason why the suspension provisions pending appeal under reg 3 of the Appeal Regs 1995 should apply only to notices under s 80(1)(b). They added that even if the noise was not in breach of a public entertainment licence, such a licence could not permit a nuisance.

Appeal procedure

18.120　The procedure for commencing an appeal is contained in para 1(2), Sch 3 of the EPA 1990, which provides that an appeal shall be by way of complaint for an order and the Magistrates' Courts Act 1980 (MCA 1980) shall apply to the proceedings.

Time limit for appeal

18.121　The 21-day time limit for making a complaint under s 80(3) of the EPA 1990 is absolute. There is no statutory extension of time or discretion conferred to the magistrates to extend the period. This is so, even though the recipient of the notice may not be aware that it exists, e.g. if service was by post to the recipient's last known address and the recipient had not attended that address in recent times.

Complaint and issue of summons

18.122　The complaint to the magistrates' court can be made orally, but it is almost always in writing. The prescribed form of complaint is on Form 98 and can be found in the

Magistrates' Court (Forms) Rules 1981 (SI 1981/553). It should include the grounds of appeal on which the appellant seeks to rely. If the court is satisfied that it has jurisdiction, under s 52 of the MCA 1980, to issue the summons and that the complaint has been made in time, it issues a summons. The court will then serve the summons on the local authority directing it to appear before the court to answer the complaint.

Regulation 2(4) of the Appeal Regs 1995 refers to serving a notice of appeal on other interested parties. The complaint may be regarded as the notice of appeal.   **18.123**

Progressing the proceedings

Following service of the summons the matter will proceed to trial. There are no formal rules **18.124** governing disclosure and case management. However, in more complex cases, it is common for the court to order a pre-trial review in order to clarify certain matters, e.g. any evidential matters. McCracken *et al* in *Statutory Nuisance* note that there are no formal court powers available to make an order for directions but recommend sending a pre-trial questionnaire with the summons in order to clarify matters. They refer to the comment by Sedley LJ in *Sovereign Rubber Ltd v Stockport MBC* [2000] Env LR 194 at 198:

> The principal object of the statutory appeal against an abatement notice is plainly to relieve the person served of the need to await a prosecution and to risk a conviction before being able to contest the need for the contents of the notice. Precisely because an appeal under s 80(3) is therefore not a criminal proceeding it is reasonable to expect some sensible co-operation between the person served and the local authority in producing an intelligible and workable abatement notice, unless it really is arguable that no statutory nuisance existed or was likely to occur or recur at the date of the notice. There is no call for the kind of arm's length confrontation which occurred in this case and has bedevilled the appeal too.

Evidence

Proceedings commenced in the magistrates' court by way of complaint are civil proceedings **18.125** where the civil rules of evidence, including hearsay, apply. Thus, the standard of proof is the civil standard that requires the appellant (the complainant) to prove, on a balance of probabilities (i.e. more than 50%) that the point at issue is proved in the affirmative. If this is done then the appellant has a case and the defendant will have to challenge the assertion.

The Magistrates' Court (Hearsay Evidence in Civil Proceedings) Rules 1999 (SI 1999/681 as **18.126** amended by SI 2001/615) made under the Civil Evidence Act 1995 are applicable, including e.g. that a party wishing to give hearsay evidence must, at least 21 days before the date fixed for the hearing, serve a hearsay notice on every other party.

Withdrawing an appeal

If, after an appeal has been made, the parties negotiate and reach agreement on how to abate **18.127** or control the nuisance they will then aim to avoid further legal proceedings and the costs incurred. Neither the provisions under the EPA 1990 nor the court rules provide for withdrawal of appeal proceedings. In the circumstances, an option may be an application to the court that each party provides appropriate undertakings to the court. If the court does not approve this, the matter will have to proceed and the parties can ask the court if it is willing to make an order according to terms agreed by the parties. If this is not acceptable to the court, then the matter will have to proceed and the court will have to hear evidence from the parties. Alternatively, the local authority may seek to withdraw the abatement notice or the appellant may wish to simply abandon the appeal, although this is likely to result in the appellant being liable for the local authority's costs in defending the appeal.

The hearing

18.128 The procedure at the hearing of an appeal is governed by s 53 of the MCA 1980 and 14 of the Magistrates' Court Rules 1981 (SI 1981/552): Order of evidence and speeches: complaint. Section 53 provides that: 'on the hearing of a complaint, the court shall, if the defendant appears, state to him the substance of the complaint.'

18.129 Rule 14 further provides that:

(1) On the hearing of a complaint . . . the complainant [the appellant] shall call his evidence, and before doing so may address the court.

(2) At the conclusion of the evidence for the complainant the defendant may address the court, whether or not he afterwards calls evidence.

(3) At the conclusion of the evidence, if any, for the defence, the complainant may call evidence to rebut that evidence.

(4) At the conclusion of the evidence for the defence and the evidence, if any, in rebuttal, the defendant may address the court if he has not already done so.

(5) Either party may, with the leave of the court, address the court a second time, but where the court grants leave to one party it shall not refuse leave to the other.

(6) Where the defendant obtains leave to address the court for a second time his second address shall be made for the second address, if any, of the complainant.

Powers of magistrates on appeal

18.130 Regulation 2(5) of the Appeal Regs 1995 provides that on the hearing of an appeal the court may:

(a) quash the abatement notice to which the appeal relates, or

(b) vary the notice in favour of the appellant in such manner as it thinks fit, or

(c) dismiss the appeal;

and an abatement notice that is varied under reg 2(5)(b) shall be final and shall have effect, as if made by the local authority.

18.131 The outcome of the magistrates' decision in subs (a) and (c) is straightforward. Under subs (b) the abatement notice may only be varied in favour of the appellant, i.e. the court cannot impose requirements that are more strict than the existing notice, it can simply apply less onerous provisions. The court may also, under regs 2(6) and (7) of the Appeals Regs 1995 and in relation to any work to be executed and the cost of that work, make any order it thinks fit.

Challenging the magistrates' court decision

18.132 Paragraph 1(3), Sch 3 of the EPA 1990 further provides that an appeal against any decision of a magistrates' court shall lie to the Crown Court at the instance of any party to the proceedings in which the decision was given. In this case, the Crown Court hears the matter as a fresh matter and has the same powers as the magistrates' court. It hears questions of fact and law.

If there has been some unlawfulness in the procedure of the magistrates' court then it is open **18.133** for any party to make a claim for judicial review of the procedure under Pt 54 of the Civil Procedure Rules 1998: see Chapter 20: Public law.

Costs

Section 64(1) of the MCA 1980 states that on the hearing of a complaint, a magistrates' court **18.134** shall have power in its discretion to make such order as to costs:

(a) on making the order for which the complaint is made, to be paid by the defendant to the complainant;

(b) on dismissing the complaint, to be paid by the complainant to the defendant,

as it thinks just and reasonable.

In considering what is just and reasonable, *R v Highgate Justices ex p Petrou* [1954] 1 All ER 406 **18.135** noted that any costs awarded should not be in excess of the proper costs incurred: it should not be a penalty in disguise of costs. It is recommended that a breakdown of each party's costs be submitted to the court before the end of the hearing. Discretion is with the court. Unlike civil and public law matters, there is no presumption that costs follow the event. An application for costs by either party should be considered when appropriate.

Similarly costs relating to an appeal in the Crown Court will be up to the discretion of that **18.136** court. Rule 12(2) of the Crown Court Rules 1982 (SI 1982/1109) provides that the Crown Court may make such order for costs as it thinks just.

G CRIMINAL PROCEEDINGS FOR BREACH OF AN ABATEMENT NOTICE

If the recipient of the abatement notice ignores it and continues to cause the nuisance, the **18.137** local authority may begin criminal proceedings for a breach of the notice. Section 80(4) of the EPA 1990 provides that:

> If a person on whom an abatement notice is served, without reasonable excuse, contravenes or fails to comply with any requirement or prohibition imposed by the notice, he shall be guilty of an offence.

Elements of the offence

The offence requires the prosecution to prove that: **18.138**

- the defendant who caused the nuisance was correctly served with the notice;
- the defendant breached one or more of the requirements stated in the abatement notice; and
- if the defence assert that they had a reasonable excuse not to comply with the notice, that the excuse was not reasonable.

18.139   In *AMEC Building Ltd v LB of Camden* [1997] Env LR 330 the court held that the notice requirements under s 160 of the EPA 1990 and s 233 of the Local Government Act 1972 did not allow service other than directly on the relevant person or body. In this case, the local authority had served a sister company at the same address. See Chapter 19, for further discussion on this.

What constitutes a breach?

18.140   Defining what constitutes a contravention or failure to comply with any requirement or prohibition will depend upon the text of the abatement notice. If it provides that the person responsible should simply abate a nuisance, then contravention will be failing to abate the nuisance. If it prohibits certain activities, e.g. playing loud music, then doing so will be the contravention.

18.141   The offence is the breach of the notice, rather than a continuing nuisance. For example, if a statutory nuisance was found to exist following complaints from neighbours about persistent smoky bonfires and an abatement notice was served prohibiting bonfires, then igniting one would be an offence, even though the smoke had blown away from the neighbours and there were no further complaints. If the abatement notice requires certain steps, then a failure to take those steps will be an offence.

Progressing the proceedings

18.142   The criminal proceedings for breach of an abatement notice broadly follow conventional criminal proceedings. The following sections deal with matters specific to statutory nuisance proceedings under s 80(4), but reference should also be made to the criminal law procedure in Chapter 19.

Parties to proceedings

18.143   The parties to the proceedings should be straightforward. For a prosecution under s 80(4) of the EPA 1990, the prosecution will be the local authority that investigated the nuisance claim, determined that a statutory nuisance existed, and then served the abatement notice. The defendant will be the person on whom the abatement notice was served.

Investigation

18.144   The prosecuting authority will carry out investigation of the offence, in general by the environmental health officers who have managed the case from the outset. Criminal investigations must comply with the Police and Criminal Evidence Act 1984 and, in particular, Code C of the Codes of Practice, and the Criminal Procedure and Investigations Act 1996 relating to disclosure.

Evidence

18.145   The relevance to statutory nuisance is highlighted above, in particular that in order to progress a prosecution there must be evidence of a breach of the abatement notice and not necessarily that of a further nuisance or act that was prejudicial to health.

The prosecution case

Importantly, the prosecution will need to prove the elements of the offence (see para **18.146** 18.138). If the prosecution does not provide evidence in respect of one or more elements of the offence then the defendant may be acquitted following an application by the defence of no case to answer. Importantly, if a defence of reasonable excuse is raised and there is sufficient evidence to discharge the evidential burden it will be for the prosecution to prove that the reasonable excuse was inadequate.

The defence case

A number of the defences set out in Chapter 19 may apply to statutory nuisance **18.147** prosecutions such as:

- reasonable excuse (qualifying an element of the offence);
- best practical means (under s 80(7));
- defence to certain noise nuisances under s 80(9) of the EPA 1990; and
- invalid notice.

Reasonable excuse and best practical means are considered in Chapter 19, defences to certain **18.148** noise nuisance activities and invalid notice are set out below.

Section 80(9) of the EPA 1990

Section 80(9) of the EPA 1990 provides that in proceedings in respect of a statutory nuisance **18.149** relating to noise under s 79(1)(g) and (ga) it is a defence to prove:

(a) that the alleged offence was covered by a notice served under s 60 or a consent given under ss 61 or 65 of the Control of Pollution Act 1974 (construction sites, etc.); or
(b) where the alleged offence was committed at a time when the premises were subject to a notice under s 66 of that Act (noise reduction notice) that the level of noise emitted from the premises at that time was not such as to constitute a contravention of the notice under that section; or
(c) where the alleged offence was committed at a time when the premises were not subject to a notice under s 66 of that Act, and when a level fixed under s 67 of that Act (new buildings liable to abatement order) applied to the premises, that the level of noise emitted from the premises at that time did not exceed that level.

Section 80(10) of the EPA adds that subs (9)(b) and (c) apply whether or not the relevant notice **18.150** was subject to appeal at the time when the offence was alleged to have been committed.

Invalid notice

The defendant must have been served with the notice; see *AMEC Building Ltd v Camden LBC* **18.151** above for the requirement of proper service on companies and where the notice was not directed to the defendant and therefore had not been properly served. If it has not been served on the person responsible, then it is likely that he does not know that the notice exists. If so, it could be difficult to appeal against the notice under s 80(3) of the EPA 1990 within 21 days. In these circumstances the validity of the abatement notice should provide the basis for a defence, despite the statement in *Lambert Flat Management Ltd v Lomas* [1981] 1 WLR 898. See also *Hewlings v McLeans* [2000] EGCS 1000.

18.152   In *Sterling Homes (Midlands) Ltd. v Birmingham CC* [1996] Env LR 121 the court held that the abatement notice was too vague to prosecute an offence and make a conviction. In *Camden LBC v Easynet Ltd* ELM 15 [2003] 1, p 29 an abatement notice was held to be invalid because the letter accompanying the notice when served specified certain works to be carried out but the notice itself did not. The court stated that a straightforward solution would be for local authorities simply to draft a covering letter in general terms without seeking to modify or explain the terms of the abatement notice. The remedy for the local authority was to re-serve the abatement notice, in simple terms, requiring abatement of the nuisance.

Sentencing

18.153   Section 80(5) of the EPA 1990 provides that, on summary conviction, the defendant is liable to a maximum penalty of a £5,000 fine and a further fine of up to 1/10 of that level for each day the offence continues after conviction. For discussion of daily fines see Chapter 19: Criminal law practice and procedure.

18.154   For offences committed on industrial, trade, or business premises, s 80(6) provides a maximum penalty of a £20,000 fine, without the ability of imposing a daily fine for nuisance continuing after conviction. Under s 157 of the EPA 1990 where a company has committed an offence it is possible to prosecute any consenting, conniving, or negligent managing officer.

Compensation

18.155   A compensation order may be made in addition to any fine that is imposed by the court, see Chapter 19 generally. In *R v Crown Court at Liverpool ex p Cooke* [1996] 4 All ER 589 the court held that compensation for statutory nuisance should only be awarded for injury, loss, or damage arising after the final date set for compliance with the abatement notice until the date of the hearing. This compensation period is subject to a maximum of six months.

Post conviction

18.156   Matters such as costs, enforcement, and appeals against a conviction or sentence are considered in Chapter 19: Criminal law practice and procedure.

H   SUMMARY PROCEEDINGS BY PERSONS AGGRIEVED

18.157   If the local authority has decided not to take proceedings for breach of an abatement notice, there is no obligation for it to do so. In short, prosecution for breach of an abatement notice is a power available to the local authority, not a duty that It must comply with. However, under s 82 of the EPA 1990 it is open for a person suffering from the adverse impacts of a statutory nuisance to commence summary proceedings in the magistrates' court against the person responsible. The proceedings are similar to a local authority prosecution except that what is being sought from the court is an abatement order that the defendant must comply with, whereas a local authority prosecution is for the breach of an abatement notice.

Parties to proceedings

Person aggrieved

Section 82 of the EPA 1990 provides that: **18.158**

> A magistrates' court may act under this section on a complaint made by any person on the ground that he is aggrieved by the existence of a statutory nuisance.

One of the objectives of s 82 is to provide a simple, relatively cheap, remedy. In *Hall v*   **18.159**
Kingston upon Hull CC [1999] 2 All ER 609, Lord Justice Rose noted that the s 82 proceedings should be a system that is, 'operable by people who may be neither very sophisticated nor very articulate and who may not in some cases have the benefit of legal advice.'

Person responsible

The person responsible for the nuisance will be the defendant in the proceedings; this may   **18.160**
be the local authority if they are responsible for the nuisance. Where another person is responsible and the local authority has decided not to take action to abate the nuisance, the court can order the local authority to take action to abate the nuisance.

Commencing proceedings

Written notice of intention to start proceedings

Section 82(6) of the EPA 1990 provides that before instituting proceedings for an order under   **18.161**
s 82(2) against anyone, the person aggrieved by the nuisance shall give to that person such notice in writing of his intention to bring the proceedings. The intention notice should be served at least 21 days before proceedings commence, unless the nuisance is noise, which requires at least 3 days' notice. In *R v Dudley Magistrates' Court ex p Hollis* [1998] Env LR 354 Moses J stated at p 360 that:

> The only requirement imposed upon an aggrieved person who wishes to issue a complaint pursuant to s 82(1) is to give written notice of an intention to bring proceedings which must specify the matter complained of (subsection 6) and to give a minimum period of notice of 21 days (subsection 7). He is, thus, under no obligation to heed requests for a longer period within which to undertake work or to wait after the expiry of 21 days to see whether any promises are honoured, before issuing a complaint.

The notice should state the name and address of the complainant and recipient, the address   **18.162**
of premises that is the subject of complaint and a clear description of the complaint. It would also be good practice to state that the notice is a formal notice under s 82 of the EPA 1990 and specify the date after which proceedings may be commenced.

Making a complaint or laying an information?

Section 82(1) of the EPA 1990 provides that a magistrates' court may act on a complaint,   **18.163**
which, as can be noted from the appeal process under s 80(3) of the EPA 1990, is a civil

process. However, in *Botross v Hammersmith and Fulham LBC* (1994) 27 HLR 179 and *East Staffordshire BC v Fairless* [1999] Env LR 525 the court has held that s 82 proceedings are criminal in nature. On this basis, laying an information is the correct way to commence criminal proceedings. Accordingly, in s 82 proceedings, the standard of proof required on the prosecution to prove the case is the criminal standard; beyond reasonable doubt.

18.164   On laying the information the court will assess the materials and, if appropriate, issue a summons and serve this on the defendant. In *R v Highbury Corner Magistrates' Court ex p Edwards* [1995] Crim LR 65 the chief clerk refused to issue the summons on the grounds that the authority was in breach of covenants in the tenancy agreement and that civil proceedings cover the same ground as the proposed criminal proceedings and as they had begun first they should continue. The High Court allowed the claim for judicial review of the magistrates' court decisions, holding that the law as it stands recognizes that an applicant may obtain an order for work to be done for the abatement of a statutory nuisance that could not be required of a landlord under a contractual or other statutory duty. On the material before the clerk he had no choice but to issue the summons.

18.165   Following issue of the summons, proceedings under s 82 of the EPA 1990, continue along similar lines to a conventional prosecution in the magistrates' court.

Defences

18.166   There are no statutory defences to an allegation of nuisance under s 82 of the EPA 1990. However, McCracken *et al* in *Statutory Nuisance* suggests that the wording of s 82 allows for the following defences:

- that the notice given for the purpose of s 82(6) of the EPA 1990 was not sufficiently detailed as in *East Stafford BC v Fairless*, or that it was served on the wrong person (*Leeds v LB Islington* [1998] Env LR 665);
- that the complainant is not a 'person aggrieved' by the alleged statutory nuisance (*Birmingham DC v McMahon* (1987) 151 JP 709);
- that the defendant is not the person responsible for either the nuisance, the owner or occupier of the relevant premises, or the person responsible for the vehicle, machinery, or equipment, see *Carr v Hackney LBC* and *Quigley v Liverpool Housing Action Trust Anglia Ltd* [1999] EGCS 94;
- that, in the case of an owner or occupier who is prosecuted under s 82(4)(c) of the EPA 1990 relating to premises unfit for human habitation, the person responsible for the nuisance can be found; and
- that the nuisance alleged in the complaint (or information) does not exist at the date of trial and is not likely to recur, see *R v Dudley Magistrates' Court ex p Hollis* [1999] 1 WLR 642.

18.167   There is uncertainty whether the BPM defence can be raised in the proceedings for an order. It is available in certain circumstances following a breach of the abatement order made by the court on conviction. The defence of prior consent for construction site noise and noise arising in noise abatement zones is expressly excluded. Section 61(9) of the CoPA 1974 provides that a prior consent to carry out specified construction site work shall contain a statement that the consent does not of itself constitute any ground of defence against proceedings instituted under s 82 of the EPA 1990. Similarly, under s 65(8) of the CoPA 1974 consent to exceed noise levels within an abatement zone does not provide a defence.

Court orders under s 82 of the EPA 1990

Nuisance order

Section 82(2) of the EPA 1990 provides that if the magistrates' court is satisfied that the **18.168** alleged nuisance exists, or that although abated it is likely to recur on the same premises (or street, if relevant), the court shall make an order (nuisance order) for either or both of the following purposes:

(a) requiring the defendant to abate the nuisance, within a time specified in the order, and to execute any works necessary for the purpose;

(b) prohibiting a recurrence of the nuisance, and requiring the defendant, within a time specified in the order, to execute any works necessary to prevent the recurrence;

and may also impose on the defendant a fine not exceeding £5,000.

Further, s 82(3) of the EPA 1990 enables the court to prohibit the use of premises unfit for **18.169** human habitation. Subsections 82(4) to 82(5B) provide further clarification to the main orders in subs (2) and (3).

The courts powers under s 82 of the EPA 1990 are to make an order that is comparable to an **18.170** abatement notice. The nuisance order is a form of sentence and certainly the ability to impose a fine in addition to the order is a criminal conviction. However, the main aim of the order is not to punish but to prevent further harm or nuisance.

McCracken *et al* in *Statutory Nuisance* sets out some key differences between an abatement **18.171** notice under s 80(1) of the EPA 1990 and an order under s 82:

- s 80(1)(a) allows the local authority to restrict a nuisance rather than require its abatement or prohibition whereas a nuisance order must require the abatement or prohibition of the nuisance completely;
- s 80(1)(a) allows the abatement notice to require the taking of steps to abate the nuisance, while s 82(2) provides that a nuisance order can require steps but does not refer to a requirement of steps;
- s 80 allows the local authority abatement notice to impose 'all or any' of the statutory requirements in s 80(1)(a) and (b), whereas the court under s 82 must make an order for either or both statutory sentences in s 82(2)(a) or (b); and
- there is a right of appeal against an abatement notice on grounds which address the terms of the notice itself, however there is not similar right of appeal against a nuisance order.

Examples of proceedings being taken under s 82 of the EPA 1990 include *R (Islington LBC) v* **18.172** *Inner London Crown Court* [2003] EWHC 2500 Admin, in which proceedings were commenced by a mother and daughter on the basis that their home was unfit for human habitation, and *Nichols, Albion and Lainson v Powergen Renewables Ltd and Wind Prospect Ltd* South Lakeland Magistrates' Court, 20 January 2004. In this latter case a group of residents claimed that noise from a wind farm constituted a statutory nuisance and commenced proceedings under s 82 of the EPA 1990. The magistrates concluded that the defendants were not causing a statutory nuisance. Stephen Tromans, commenting in JPL [2004] 1023–127 (Sweet &

Maxwell, 2004) noted that, as well as being the first case on noise nuisance from wind farms, there was some debate about whether the proceedings were correctly brought under s 82 of the EPA 1990.

Orders against local authorities

18.173 If the proposed defendant to s 82 proceedings cannot be found, the court may order the local authority to abate the nuisance. Section 82(13) of the EPA 1990 provides that:

> If it appears to the magistrates' court . . . that neither the person responsible for the nuisance nor the owner or occupier of the premises or (as the case may be) the person responsible for the vehicle, machinery or equipment can be found the court . . . after giving the local authority in whose area the nuisance has occurred an opportunity of being heard, [can] direct the authority to do any thing which the court . . . would have ordered that person to do.

Breach of a nuisance order

18.174 It is an offence to breach a nuisance order granted by the court. Section 82(8) of the EPA 1990 provides that: 'A person who, without reasonable excuse, contravenes any requirement or prohibition imposed by an order under subs (2) above shall be guilty of an offence'.

Proceedings

18.175 Proceedings for breach of a nuisance order follow conventional criminal proceedings in a magistrates' court, see Chapter 19: Criminal law practice and procedure. It may be assumed that the prosecutor will be the person aggrieved, or possibly the local authority, providing it has not been made a party to the proceedings in any way.

Defences

18.176 The defence of reasonable excuse is available as an aspect of the offence under s 82(8) of the EPA 1990. This is discussed in Chapter 19. Section s 82(9) provides that it shall be a defence to prove that BPM were used to prevent or to counteract the effects of the nuisance, but is unavailable for the following types of nuisance under s 79(1):

    (a) those under paras (a), (d), (e), (f) or (g) except where the nuisance arises on industrial, trade or business premises;

  (aa) those under para (ga) except where the noise is emitted from or caused by a vehicle, machinery or equipment being used for industrial, trade or business purposes;

    (b) those under para (b) except where the smoke is emitted from a chimney;

    (c) those under para (c) or (h); and

    (d) those which are such as to render the premises unfit for human habitation.

Best practical means is discussed in paras 18.110 to 18.112 and in Chapter 19.

Sentencing

18.177 A defendant guilty of an offence under s 82(8) is liable on summary conviction to a fine not exceeding £5,000 together with a further fine of a £500 for each day on which the offence continues after the conviction. It should be assumed that the principles of daily fines relevant to conventional offences apply to a breach of a nuisance order, i.e. that despite the wording of s 82(8) of the EPA 1990, the daily amount due is up to 1/10 of £5,000 as is the case with sentencing on breach of an abatement notice: see *Canterbury CC v Ferris* [1997]. Env LR D 14 and Chapter 19.

Post conviction

Matters such as costs, enforcement, and appeals against a conviction or sentence are **18.178** considered in Chapter 19.

I COSTS IN STATUTORY NUISANCE CRIMINAL PROCEEDINGS

Section 80 proceedings

Costs in s 80 proceedings follow the general principles of costs in criminal proceedings and **18.179** are discussed in Chapter 19.

Section 82 proceedings

Costs for the aggrieved person

Section 82(12) of the EPA 1990 provides an aggrieved person who brings proceedings with a **18.180** statutory right to claim costs against the defendant if any claim is successful. Section 18 of the Prosecution of Offences Act 1985 (POA 1985) also applies whereby the court may order that the convicted defendant or unsuccessful appellant pay prosecution costs that are just and reasonable. Under s 82(13) of the EPA 1990, where the accused cannot be found, the court may make an order that the local authority pay the prosecutor (the person aggrieved) compensation.

Costs of the successful defendant

Section 16(1) of the POA 1985 provides that a successful defendant may be awarded his costs **18.181** by the court out of central funds. There is no general power to award costs against the s 82 prosecutor (person aggrieved) personally. However, under s 19A of the POA 1985, a court may exceptionally order a party's legal or other representative to personally pay some or all of the costs of the other side to the extent that the representative has acted unreasonably, negligently, or improperly and costs have been incurred. But while this provision applies to representatives of a party it is not apt to encompass a litigant acting in person.

KEY DOCUMENTS AND MATERIALS

Environmental Protection Act 1990
Statutory Nuisance Appeals Regulations 1995 (SI 1995/2644)
Clean Neighbourhoods and Environment Act 2005

Defra (2004). Clean Neighbourhoods consultation documents
McCracken, R, Jones, G, Pereira, J, Payne, S (2001). *Statutory Nuisance*.
  Butterworths: London

19

CRIMINAL LAW PRACTICE AND PROCEDURE

A   INTRODUCTION

Environmental protection and criminal law

19.01   Criminal law supports environmental protection by:

(1)   providing direct criminal sanctions for environmental harm, damage, or injury; and

(2)   in a subsidiary role underpinning regulatory systems of control.

It is more commonly used in the second way. This is primarily because, until very recently, the main purpose of the criminal law has been to punish readily identified wrongs, and ensure that wrongdoers get their 'just deserts'. Yet, in relation to many environmental matters, it is often impossible to identify wrongful acts without reference to other factors, e.g. that society demands industrial and manufacturing processes, which often produce pollution. The polluting activities are controlled and often licensed, and it is when the conditions of those licences are exceeded that the criminal law, ultimately, steps in to sanction the exceedences. At present, most members of society accept some pollution, whether through prioritizing other societal goals, such as economic progress, because the pollution is not directly and immediately affecting them, or because of ignorance. Until all forms of pollution are regarded as unacceptable, there will need to be a controlling, regulatory regime that has some means of force.

19.02   Concerns in relation to environmental justice in criminal law are that prosecution is costly, that many crimes go unpunished, that those crimes that are prosecuted are not punished severely enough and that, on occasions, sentences that are high are significantly reduced in the Court of Appeal. Further, there is concern that the deterrent nature of environmental crimes is ineffective and that it is often cheaper to pollute and pay a fine than to comply with a regulatory regime or to avoid pollution incidents altogether.

19.03   There was also concern for some years that environmental protection was ineffective without the ability to take enforcement action against those who pollute or carry out unlawful trade, such as illegal trade in wildlife. Successive governments have legislated to provide protection and enforcement powers to executive bodies and agencies. International environmental law and principles have been transposed into national law to ensure compliance with state commitments such as the Convention on International Trade in Endangered Species of Wild Fauna and Flora (1973) (CITES) incorporated into national law through the Customs and Excise Management Act 1979 and the Control of Trade in Endangered Species (Enforcement) Regulations 1997 (COTES).

19.04   Environmental crime is not codified and incorporated into a single Act or legislative framework unlike, for example, the Environmental Protection and Biodiversity Conservation Act 1999 of Australia or even the Employment Rights Act 1996 in the UK. Instead, it is found in specific sections of a variety of Acts of Parliament. Nevertheless, a great deal of the more frequently used environmental penalties and sanctions can be found in the Environmental Protection Act 1990 (as amended) (EPA 1990). This includes waste, the early integrated pollution control regime, contaminated land, and statutory nuisances including noise and certain air emissions. Water pollution is largely covered by the Water Resources Act 1991

(WRA 1991); air pollution by the Clean Air Act 1993 (CAA 1993) and the most polluting activities by the Pollution Prevention and Control Act 1999 (PPCA 1999).

Analysis of environmental crime data

There are between 5,000 and 10,000 environmental prosecutions in England and Wales **19.05** every year. The variance depends on how an environmental crime is classified and the data used to determine a prosecution. The Department for Constitutional Affairs (DCA) does not recognize environmental crime as a discrete legal area and does not collect data specific to this area. In contrast there is detailed analysis by the DCA of other crimes such as burglary, assault and criminal damage.

A report by the Environmental Justice Project (a collaboration between the Environmental **19.06** Law Foundation, Leigh Day & Co Solicitors, and WWF-UK) in *Environmental Justice* (EJP, 2004) included data from a range of organizations involved in environmental prosecutions. A summary of average annual prosecutions taken from the report is set out below and provides an illustration of environmental offences. The study found limited data on certain offences, e.g. oil pollution of coastal waters and in ports.

Table 19.1 Summary of annual environmental prosecutions

Type of prosecution	Prosecuting body	Average prosecutions/year
Air pollution (CAA 93)	Local authorities	899
CITES	Customs & Excise	6
Fisheries, navigation, flood defences	Environment Agency	16
Health & safety	Health & Safety Executive	1902
Litter	Local authorities	488
Noise (CoPA not s.79)	Local authorities	65
Obstruction etc. (EA 95)	Local authorities + Environment Agency	7
Process industry	Environment Agency	7
Radioactive substances	Environment Agency	10
Statutory nuisance	Local authorities	2424
Waste	Environment Agency	436
Water quality	Environment Agency	227
Water resources	Environment Agency	13
Wildlife	Police & others, e.g. RSPB	378
	total:	6878

The Environment Agency produces an annual report on company performance that sets out **19.07** key data on prosecutions and fines: *Spotlight on the Business Environmental Performance*. The 2004 report concluded that during 2003 the Agency prosecuted 266 companies.

The present statistics from the *Environmental Justice* report did not cover a range of crimes **19.08** that impact on the environment but may be prosecuted by the police and other agencies under more traditional criminal powers and law. In particular, graffiti and vandalism under the Criminal Damage Act 1971 and the breach of anti-social behaviour orders secured by local authorities. These may not be regarded as traditional environmental crimes but, it is suggested, have a very real impact on a local neighbourhood and its environment: see Chapter 4.

19.09 Compared to conventional criminal prosecutions, the number of environmental crimes is small. For instance, there were 1.93 million offenders proceeded against in the year 2002–3 with 33,000 for burglary alone. This would suggest that in comparative terms prosecutions of environmental crime should be given less attention. However, this does not take into account the uniqueness of environmental crime, protection, and improvement.

The uniqueness of environmental crime

19.10 Environmental crimes have some similar characteristics to conventional crimes. For instance, the motivation for committing the crime may often be based on financial gain, particularly with waste offences. Other cases may be based upon a lack of respect for a neighbourhood. However, environmental crime and justice may be regarded as distinct from most other areas of law because of:

(a) the impact of any given incident on a wide population of people, wildlife, and habitats; and

(b) the role of intra-generational and inter-generational equity in environmental matters and in achieving sustainable development.

19.11 The wider effects of adverse environmental impacts are not widely understood and, it is submitted, not properly addressed in environmental prosecutions and convictions. Legislation has attempted to tackle this with the majority of environmental offences enabling magistrates to award maximum sentences up to four times the level of standard magistrates court sentencing powers (at present limited to a £5,000 fine and/or six months' imprisonment) with certain offences attracting maximum fines of even greater sums, e.g. the maximum £50,000 fine for certain waste offences introduced under the clean Neighbour-hoods and Environment Act 2005. Legislation also provides that many offences are of strict liability so that once a defendant has been found to have caused the offence, the prosecution has no need to prove fault or guilty knowledge. This assists prosecutors in securing a conviction but has been said to reduce sentences by 'mischievous mitigation' whereby the defence argues that the crime was not a 'true crime' with blameworthiness and so should not be punished so severely.

Categories of environmental crime

19.12 Environmental offences can be said to fall into the following categories:

- Causing pollution
- Knowingly permitting pollution
- Breach of licence conditions
- Failure to comply with notices
- Breach of statutory duty
- Contravention of prohibitions

Causing pollution

Pollution has been defined by the courts. In *R v Dovermoss Ltd* [1995] Env LR 258 it was held **19.13** that the term 'pollute' should be given its ordinary dictionary meaning of: 'to make physically impure, foul, or filthy; to dirty, stain, taint or befoul.' In *Express Dairies Ltd v Environment Agency* [2004] EWHC 1710 (Admin) it was held this did not require evidence of harmful effects. Section 1(3) of the EPA 1990 provides that 'pollution of the environment' means:

> pollution of the environment due to the release (into any environmental medium) from any process of substances which are capable of causing harm to man or any other living organisms supported by the environment.

Causing pollution is an offence under a number of statutory provisions. For example, **19.14** it is an offence to 'knowingly cause' controlled waste to be deposited under s 33(1)(a) of the EPA 1990. To cause pollution requires some positive act, but not necessarily an intention to pollute or to be negligent. It is sufficient that there is a direct, although not necessarily immediate, relationship between the activities of the defendant and the offence complained of. Any break in the chain of causation may be enough to avoid liability.

In *Alphacell Ltd v Woodward* [1972] AC 284 the House of Lords held that there was no need to **19.15** prove negligence or fault in relation to causing an offence but that the causing 'must involve some active operation or chain of operations involving as the result the pollution of the stream'. They warned that the operator of an installation from which pollutants escape into a watercourse may not escape liability for 'causing' pollution, merely because the immediate cause of the escape was an act of vandalism by a third party.

Causation was considered at length in *Environment Agency v Empress Car Co (Abertillery) Ltd* **19.16** [1999] AC 22. The House of Lords held that the operator's acts may be a 'cause' of the pollution without being the most immediate cause; but the court must consider whether the third party act or intervening event was a normal fact of life or something extraordinary. Lord Hoffman stated at p 36 that:

> If it was in the general run of things a matter of ordinary occurrence, it will not negative the causal effect of the defendant's acts, even if it was not foreseeable that it would happen to that particular defendant or take that particular form. . . . the distinction between ordinary and extraordinary is one of fact and degree to which the [court] must apply common sense and knowledge of what happens in the area.

In the *Empress Cars* case it was considered that, as a first step, the prosecution should **19.17** identify what it says the defendant did to cause the pollution, which was not necessarily the immediate cause, maintaining a tank full of polluting matter would be enough, even if the immediate cause was different. Once the prosecution had identified this act, the court must then decide whether the act had caused the pollution. If the act created a situation whereby pollution could occur, but there was also either a third party act or natural event, then there must be consideration of whether that intervening event was unusual enough to break the chain of causation. The Lords felt that an 'act of God' or other natural event may break the chain of causation leading from the accused's initial act if it was not reasonably foreseeable and if it was also the sole immediate cause of the consequence in question.

The event must be 'of so powerful a nature that the conduct of the defendant was not a cause at all, but was merely a part of the surrounding circumstances.' In *Southern Water Authority v Pegrum* [1989] Crim LR 442 the court considered that foreseeable natural events, such as seasonal floods or cold winter nights, could not have such an effect.

Knowingly permitting pollution

19.18   Some statutes provide a separate offence of 'knowingly permitting' pollution. For example, s 85(1) of the WRA 1991 creates the offence of knowingly permitting poisonous, noxious, or polluting matter to enter controlled waters. 'Permitting' may apply to passive situations whereas 'causing' does not. In *Price v Cromack* [1975] 2 All ER 113 it was held that 'knowingly permitting' involves a failure to prevent pollution, although there has to be knowledge of the circumstances. Knowingly permitting pollution can be regarded as taking a passive response to an incident. In *Rochford RDC v Port of London Authority* [1914] 2 KB 916 the defendant sanitary authority was found guilty of 'causing or suffering' sewage to flow or pass into Little Creek, and the court considered the passive role of 'suffering' the flow of sewage. Darling J noted at 992–3 that:

> if a person is in a situation where he might, without committing any legal wrong, prevent a stream from flowing in a particular direction, and he does not prevent it, he 'suffers' it to flow in that direction; but he cannot be said to 'suffer' it if he is not in a position either physically to prevent it or if by law he ought not to prevent it. In my opinion the present appellants were in a position in which they physically could, and legally might, have stopped this sewage from flowing into Little Creek.

Breach of licence conditions

19.19   It is not an offence to pollute air, land, or water in many circumstances providing the polluting activity has been authorized or permitted by the relevant regulatory authority such as the Environment Agency or the local authority Environmental Health Department. However, it will be an offence not to comply with any conditions imposed on the authorization or permit. Section 23 of the EPA 1990 makes it a criminal offence not to comply with the conditions of an Integrated Pollution Control (IPC) authorization granted under Pt 1 of the Act, while under s 33(6) it is an offence to contravene the conditions of a Waste Management Licence.

Failure to comply with notices

19.20   The Environment Agency and local authorities have the power to serve a variety of notices in order to either prevent a nuisance occurring, to prohibit a polluting activity or to require remedial work to take place. A common example is the statutory nuisance abatement notice served under Pt III of the EPA 1990. This is discussed in Chapter 18: Statutory nuisance.

Breach of statutory duty

19.21   An environmental offence that is committed quite frequently is a breach of the statutory duty of care in relation to the handling of waste under s 34 of the EPA 1990. All waste holders are subject to the duty of care irrespective of whether or not they require a Waste Management Licence.

Contravention of prohibitions

Some environmental legislation simply prohibits specified activities and contravening that **19.22** activity is an offence, e.g. s 1 of the Wildlife and Countryside Act 1981 provides that, among other things, any person intentionally killing, injuring, or taking any wild bird shall be guilty of an offence. Also, s 33(1)(c) of the EPA 1990 provides that, subject to exceptions, a person shall not treat, keep or dispose of controlled waste in a manner likely to cause pollution of the environment or harm to human health.

B KEY PRINCIPLES OF ENVIRONMENTAL CRIME

Strict liability

The majority of environmental offences are strict liability. The offences do not require proof **19.23** of the *mens rea* in respect of one or more elements of the *actus reus*. It has been said that these offences are not 'real' crimes but mere civil matters prohibited under a penalty see: *Sherras v De Rutzen* [1895] 1 QB 918.

The defence may stress in mitigation that, because the defences are of strict liability, they **19.24** should not attract any moral culpability and that the sentence should reflect the fact that no deliberate offence has been committed and they should not be 'blamed'. This has been described as 'mischievous mitigation', although often there will be a genuine sense of grievance that a company or individual finds itself in court for an incident they were as anxious as anyone else to avoid.

The degree of carelessness will be relevant to the sentence and certainly any element of **19.25** intention, e.g. the calculated cutting of corners will be a serious aggravating factor. The purpose of strict liability offences is to ensure that those who carry out, and profit from business activities where there is a risk of environmental damage also ensure that the best possible management systems are implemented and proper precautions are taken to minimize risk of harm.

Liability is strict, not absolute. There are a number of defences to many environmental **19.26** offences. These are discussed in Section C.

Corporate liability

Many environmental offenders will be companies. An incorporated company is a legal per- **19.27** son under company law and can therefore be liable for strict liability offences. In *Alphacell Ltd v Woodward* a company that owned a factory from which pollution entered a river had its conviction under the Rivers (Prevention of Pollution) Act 1951 upheld by the House of Lords. Many of the offences refer to the person responsible and, unless there is expression to the contrary, e.g. by referring to an individual rather than person, then it should be assumed that person has a broad meaning, i.e. under s 5 and Sch 1 of the Interpretation Act 1978 that unless the contrary intention appears: ' "Person" includes a body of persons incorporate or unincorporated'.

Company directors and managers

19.28 Despite the separate legal personality of corporate bodies, a number of statutory provisions may find senior management liable if it can be proved that the manager responsible was a directing mind of the company. Section 157 of the EPA 1990 provides that:

> where an offence under the Act has been committed by a company or other corporate body and it is proved to have been committed with the consent or connivance of, or to have been attributable to any neglect on the part of, any director, manager, secretary or any similar officer of the company etc . . . he, as well as the company, shall be guilty of the offence and liable to be proceeded against and punished accordingly.

19.29 Similar provisions exist under s 217 of the WRA 1991, s 52 of the Clean Air Act 1993 and reg 32 of the Pollution Prevention and Control (England and Wales) Regulations 2000 (SI 2000/1973) (the PPC Regs 2000). In *R v Barker* (1997) ENDS Report 273 p 45 the owner of a milk bottling business was the first person to be imprisoned for a water pollution offence after polluting a stream and pond with gas oil. He was sentenced to two months in prison. In 2003, the courts convicted 11 company directors for environmental crimes prosecuted by the Environment Agency. However, not all company officers will be liable under the officer liability provisions. In *Tesco Supermarkets v Nattrass* [1972] AC 53 Lord Reid, when considering management liability for a false trade description, noted that:

> the board never delegated any part of their functions. They set up a chain of command through regional and district supervisors, but they remained in control. The shop managers had to obey their general directions and also take orders from their superiors. The acts or omissions of shop managers were not acts of the company itself. . . . It must be a question of law whether, once the facts have been ascertained, a person in doing particular things is to be regarded as the company or merely as the company's servant or agent.

19.30 In *R v Boal* [1992] 3 All ER 177 the Court of Appeal held that, on a charge under the Fire Precautions Act 1971, a temporary manager in charge of a shop for a week was not a 'manager' of the company. Under the EPA 1990 and related legislation, a manager is some-one who is part of the 'controlling' mind of the company, similarly a 'secretary' is the company secretary required under s 283 of the Companies Act 1985, as opposed to the general understanding of a secretary carrying out purely administrative functions in an organization. In *Huckerby v Elliot* [1970] 1 All ER 189, Ashworth J noted at 194 that: 'It would seem that where a director consents to the commission of an offence by his company, he is well aware of what is going on and agrees to it.'

Vicarious liability

19.31 The general rule is that criminal liability is personal, not vicarious, see *Huggins* (1730) 2 Ld Raym 1574. However, vicarious liability is usually, but not always, imposed in the case of strict liability offences. In *Mousell Brothers Ltd v London and North-Western Railway Co* [1917] 2 KB 836 Atkin J noted that:

> while *prima facie* a principal is not to be made criminally responsible for the acts of his servants, yet the legislature may prohibit an act or enforce a duty in such words as to make the pro-hibition or the duty absolute; in which case the principal is liable if the act is in fact done by his servants. To ascertain whether a particular Act of Parliament has that effect or not regard must

be had to the object of the statute, the words used, the nature of the duty laid down, the person upon whom it is imposed, the person by whom it would in ordinary circumstances be performed, and the person upon whom the penalty is imposed.

An exception to this principle is highlighted at para A4.4 of *Blackstone's Criminal Practice* **19.32** *2005*, which notes that s 100 of the Merchant Shipping Act 1995 imposes a duty on a ship owner to ensure that the ship is operated and managed safely. Failing to do so is an offence of strict but not vicarious liability, because (a) a wide range of omissions could constitute a failure to take reasonable steps and (b) a wide range of persons might make an omission. In *Seaboard Offshore Ltd v Secretary of State for Transport* [1994] 1 WLR 541 this exception along with the contextual evidence led the court to conclude that liability under the Act was limited to the owner.

Offence due to another's fault

Some environmental offences are supported by provisions that enable a person to be **19.33** charged even though, strictly speaking, the offence was committed by another person. For example, s 217(3) of the WRA 1991 provides that:

> where the commission of the offence under the water pollution provisions of this Act is due to the act or default of some other person, that other person may be charged with and convicted of the offence whether or not proceedings for the offence are taken against the first-mentioned person.

Section 37 of the Radioactive Substances Act 1993 has similar provisions. Thus, where the act **19.34** of person A results in person B committing an offence, then person A may be convicted of the offence, regardless of whether proceedings are taken against person B who actually committed the offence.

In *Express Dairies Ltd v Environment Agency*, one of the offences prosecuted was under s 217(3) **19.35** of the WRA 1991. The defendant argued that s 217(3) could not apply because it was not under a duty to act and that the offence was not one of strict liability. The Court disagreed and found the defendant guilty. Kennedy LJ held that if a landowner permits an operation on his land that gives rise to a risk of pollution, then in order not to breach s 85(1):

> he must carry out a risk assessment and respond to what the assessment reveals. Otherwise if pollution does occur it may be impossible for him to say that the offence committed by those using his land is not due to one or more of his acts or defaults.

C OUTLINE OF CRIMINAL PROCEDURE

Parties to proceedings

Prosecutors

There are at least ten different environmental prosecuting authorities each of which special- **19.36** izes in different areas of environmental crime. These include:

• Centre for Environment, Fisheries and Aquaculture Science (CEFAS) who prosecute freshwater and marine fisheries offences;

- Department for Environment, Food and Rural Affairs (Defra) covering animal welfare offences, GMOs, nitrate vulnerable zones, pesticides and fertilizers, and uncultivated land
- English Nature prosecuting SSSIs, SACs, and Ramsar sites;
- the Environment Agency who prosecute certain contaminated land, PPC, radioactive substances, water pollution, and waste management and fly-tipping offences.
- the Health & Safety Executive (HSE) who prosecute health and safety matters including those with environmental impacts.
- HM Customs & Excise who control the import of waste, banned materials, and endangered species and taxation of the environment;
- Local authorities who cover air emissions, contaminated land, noise and vibration, planning and development, pollution, prevention and control (LA-PPC) (smaller operations), waste management and fly-tipping;
- the Police in collaboration with the Crown Prosecution Service (CPS) who cover wildlife offences, trade in endangered species, and criminal damage, e.g. graffiti;
- Royal Society for the Protection of Birds (RSPB) who prosecute wild bird offences; and
- Water companies covering water abstraction, use, and discharges to sewers.

19.37 Many of these organizations such as the Environment Agency, HSE, and local authorities, have in-house prosecutors. Others work with partner organizations. For example, the Police, working with the CPS and RSPB, often instruct specialist lawyers to carry out prosecutions on their behalf. The CPS, on occasions, assigns the conduct of cases to barristers and solicitors in private practice under s 5 of the Prosecution of Offences Act 1985.

19.38 All environmental prosecutors must comply with the Code for Crown Prosecutors published by the CPS and available at www.cps.gov.uk. The Code notes in its introductory paragraph that:

> The decision to prosecute an individual is a serious step. Fair and effective prosecution is essential to the maintenance of law and order. The CPS [and other prosecutors] should apply the Code for Crown Prosecutors so that it can make fair and consistent decisions about prosecutions.

19.39 The Code lists, under para 6, common public interest factors in favour of and against prosecution such as whether there is evidence that the offence was pre-meditated (para 6.4(f) in favour), and whether the defendant has put right the loss or harm caused (para 6.5(g) against prosecution).

Defendants

19.40 The defendants who are alleged to have carried out environmental offences vary according to the crimes committed. Many water pollution cases arise from water companies discharging sewage effluent from water treatment works or from farmers causing toxic substances to drain through the soil and into the watercourse. Noise pollution commonly arises from residential premises and fly-tipping offences are often carried out by small one or two partner organizations, although this does not underestimate the impact of more organized gangs of fly-tippers. The Environment Agency's *Spotlight 2003* reported that 'small and medium-sized enterprises are responsible for up to 80% of all pollution incidents and more than 60% of the commercial and industrial waste produced in England and Wales.' In some instances of criminal damage such as graffiti, the defendant is a juvenile (under 18 years of age).

Investigation

The investigation of an environmental offence often begins following a member of the   **19.41**
public reporting a pollution incident or as a result of a site inspection. To bring a case to
court an inspector must determine whether an offence has been committed and gather
evidence necessary to secure a conviction.

Powers of investigation

The Environment Agency, local authority, and other environmental enforcement and   **19.42**
investigation officers have wide-ranging powers of investigation. For example, s 108 of the
Environment Act 1995 (EA 1995) provides a comprehensive set of powers of entry and
investigation that apply to all enforcing authorities exercising pollution control functions
at central and local level. An Agency inspector may gather information, ask questions, and
enter premises, which he has reason to believe it is necessary to enter. In *Hicks v Faulkner*
(1878) 8 QBD 67 'reason to believe' meant:

> a reasonable and *bona fide* belief in the existence of such a state of things as would amount to
> a justification of the course pursued. . . . It is not essential in any case that facts should be
> established . . . as evidence (for) a jury.

Under s 108(7), if entry is refused, or expected to be refused, a warrant must be obtained from   **19.43**
a magistrate. Once on the premises, the inspector may make such examination and investigation, including measurements and photographs, as may be necessary. Other powers of
an inspector include requiring the production of records and taking copies of them and
requiring a person who may be able to help his inquiries to answer his questions and sign
a declaration of truth as to the answers. In *R v Hertfordshire CC ex p Green Environmental
Industries Ltd* [2000] 2 AC 412 the House of Lords held that the powers to request entry under
s 71 of the EPA 1990 were valid.

PACE Codes of Practice

Section 67(9) of the Police and Criminal Evidence Act 1984 (PACE) states that: **19.44**

> persons other than police officers who are charged with the duty of investigating offences or
> charging offenders shall in the discharge of that duty have regard to the relevant provisions
> of any [Codes of Practice].

PACE provides powers for police and investigation officers to carry out the detection and   **19.45**
enforcement of the law. Section 66 of PACE provides that the Secretary of State shall issue
codes of practice in connection with policy officers' statutory powers, the detention, treatment, questioning, and identification of persons, searches of premises, and the seizure of
property. Revised Codes A to E came into force in April 2003 and are available from
www.homeoffice.gov.uk. All environmental enforcement and investigation officers must
comply with the Codes. In *Dudley MCC v Debenhams* (1994) The Times, 19 August 1994,
the court held that the Codes apply to routine inspections to establish compliance with
legislation as well as to the investigation of specific regulatory breaches.

An important code is C10.6 where officers must, before interviewing a potential defendant,   **19.46**
caution that person in the following terms: 'You do not have to say anything. But it may

harm your defence if you do not mention when questioned something which you later rely on in court. Anything you do say may be given in evidence.'

19.47   Failure to caution a defendant may result in the evidence gained during any interview being excluded by the court under s 78 of PACE because it may have an adverse effect on the fairness of the proceedings. Also, the provisions of the European Convention on Human Rights limit the powers of an inspector where arbitrary use may result in the fettering of the right to a fair trial under Art 6(1) of the Convention, or the right to respect for private life under Art 8.

19.48   Investigating officers must take into account the provisions of the Criminal Procedure and Investigations Act 1996 (CPIA 1996), as amended by the Criminal Justice Act 2003 (CJA 2003), and the matters relating to disclosure of evidence. Importantly s 26(1) of the CPIA 1996 provides that local authorities should have regard to any relevant provision in the act.

Enforcement policies

19.49   Prosecutors will need to follow any relevant guidance such as the HELA Circular for Local Authorities and the Environment Agency's prosecution and enforcement policy, which is available at www.environment-agency.gov.uk.

Evidence

19.50   It is, in general, for the prosecution to prove, beyond reasonable doubt, that the defendant was guilty of the offence. Until this is proved, he is considered to be innocent. In *Ferguson v The Queen* [1979] 1 WLR 94 Lord Scarman suggested that the jury should be satisfied beyond reasonable doubt so that you feel sure of the defendant's guilt. However, the evidential test necessary in order to commence proceedings is set out in the Code for Crown Prosecutors. Paragraph 5.1 states that: 'Prosecutors must be satisfied that there is enough evidence to provide a "realistic prospect of conviction" against each defendant on each charge.'

19.51   For environmental offences, vital evidence will be gained from witness accounts, employee interviews, samples, and tests. A key rule of evidence is that, subject to the exclusionary rules, all evidence that is sufficiently relevant to the facts in issue is admissible, and all evidence that is irrelevant, or insufficiently relevant to the facts, should be excluded. As an offence of strict liability involves no proof of *mens rea*, evidence of motive, intention, or knowledge is inadmissible, being irrelevant to what the prosecution must prove and merely prejudicial to the accused. Lord Simon of Glaisdale in *DPP v Kilbourne* [1973] AC 729 said that:

> Evidence is relevant if it is logically probative or disprobative of some matter which requires proof. I do not pause to analyse what is involved in 'logical probativeness', except to note that the term does not of itself express the element of experience which is so significant of its operation in law, and possibly elsewhere. It is sufficient to say, even at the risk of etymological tautology, that relevant (i.e., logically probative or disprobative) evidence is evidence which makes the matter which requires proof more or less probable.

19.52   Regardless of the need to prove intention, it remains necessary to secure sufficient evidence to prove causation and, importantly, to provide evidence of the extent of environmental harm for the purpose of sentencing. Any samples and subsequent analysis have to stand up in court. Any sample taken must be of a quantity and quality to be capable of analysis by the use of ordinary equipment and ordinary skill by a reasonably competent analyst; whether or not it was so capable of being a question of fact, see *Smith v Cole* [1971] 1 All ER 200.

Evidence is not limited to inspectors using their powers but can also be obtained by simple analysis or photographic evidence. For example, in a water pollution case analysis of water samples, pictures of dead fish or eye witness accounts as to the state of watercourses will be of value. However, following *Trent River Board v Wardle* [1857] Crim LR 196 it will remain necessary to show that the water pollution was caused by the defendant. Investigation may be exercised by someone specifically authorized to do so by the prosecuting agency for the purpose of complying with a requirement to prepare a report or assessment on a serious incident or a situation that may give rise to one in relation to the incident. **19.53**

Where a discharge can be shown to be polluting it will be for the defendant to prove that it was made under a consent or licence and in accordance with any conditions attached to it. For summary trials, s 101 of the Magistrates' Court Act 1980 as amended (MCA 1980) provides that: **19.54**

> Where the defendant to an information or complaint relies for his defence on any exception, exemption, proviso, excuse or qualification, whether or not it accompanies the description of the offence or matter of complaint in the enactment creating the offence on which the complaint is founded, the burden of proving the exception, exemption, proviso, excuse or qualification shall be on him, and this notwithstanding that the information or complaint contains an allegation negativing the exception, exemption, provision, excuse or qualification.

For trial on indictment, the Court of Appeal in *R v Edwards* [1975] 1 QB 27 affirmed the common law in similar fashion stating that: **19.55**

> Over the centuries the common law, as a result of experience and the need to ensure that justice is done both to the community and to defendants, has evolved an exception to the fundamental rule of our criminal law that the prosecution must prove every element of the offence charged. . . . It is limited to offences arising under enactments which prohibit the doing of an act save in specified circumstances or by persons of specified classes or with specified qualification or with the licence or permission of specified authorities. Whenever the prosecution seeks to rely on this exception, the court must construe the enactment under which the charge is laid. If the true construction is that the enactment prohibits the doing of acts, subject to provisos, exceptions and the like, then the prosecution can rely upon the exception.

If it is within the powers of the prosecutor to adduce reliable evidence about the discharge he should do so; under the *Code for Crown Prosecutors* it is the duty of prosecutors to ensure that all relevant facts are given to the court. **19.56**

Witnesses

Interviewing witnesses and taking statements will often be one of the early forms of evidence gathering for environmental offences. Statements should be taken on approved s 9 Statement forms (under s 9 of the Criminal Justice Act 1967). The witness may provide exhibits that should form part of the statement. These may include photographs or documentary evidence such as a diary of polluting events or activities. **19.57**

19.58   Section 53(1) of the Youth Justice and Criminal Evidence Act 1999 provides that: 'at every stage in criminal proceedings all persons are (whatever their age) competent to give evidence.'

19.59   Exceptions include, under s 53(3), that a person is not competent if it appears to the court that he will not understand questions put to him as a witness, and give answers that can be understood. Also, under s 53(4) a defendant may not be called as a witness for the prosecution, although he may, but is not compelled to, be a witness for his own defence. Any witness that is unwilling to be interviewed or attend court may be required to attend by service of a witness summons, preferably before the trial begins.

19.60   After taking statements from witnesses and following up other investigations, e.g. taking samples and measurement of polluting activity, it will be appropriate to interview the defendant.

Expert evidence

19.61   Both sides may seek to rely on expert evidence to prove aspects of their case. Generally, witnesses are not allowed to give opinion evidence. However, expert opinion evidence is admissible where the ability to provide an opinion has been acquired by a special study or experience. Moreover, a court will only admit expert evidence if it is on a subject that is outside the experience or knowledge expected in a judge or jury. In *R v Ward* (1992) The Times, 8 June 1992, the Court of Appeal noted that the expert's duty was to the court not the side instructing him. The duty is 'to act in the cause of justice'.

19.62   For summary trials, r 3(1) of the Magistrates' Courts (Advanced Notice of Expert Evidence) Rules 1997 (SI 1997/705) provides that:

> Where a magistrates' court proceeds to trial in respect of an alleged offence and the person charged with that offence pleads not guilty in respect of it, if any party to the proceedings proposes to adduce expert evidence (whether of fact or opinion) in the proceedings (otherwise than in relation to sentence) he shall as soon as practicable after the person charged has so pleaded, . . .
>
> (a)   furnish the other party or parties with a statement in writing of any finding or opinion which he proposes to adduce in evidence; and
>
> (b)   where requested, provide that party with a copy of the record of any observation, test, calculation or other procedure in respect of which any such procedure has been carried out.

19.63   There are similar provisions under the Crown Court (Advance Notice of Expert Evidence) Rules 1987, i.e. that an expert intending to produce a report at trial must send a copy to the other side as soon as practicable.

Options on commission of an offence

19.64   If a prosecuting body suspects that an offence has been committed they may have one of the following options:

- do nothing;
- formally caution the alleged offender;

- for juveniles — issue a reprimand or warning;
- for certain offences — issue a fixed penalty notice; or
- prosecute the offence.

Do nothing

This may be an appropriate response in the light of the Code for Prosecutors and other   **19.65**
prosecutors' guidance.

Formal caution

For clarity, a distinction has been made between a caution given by an investigating officer   **19.66**
before asking questions and a formal caution where there is a written acceptance by an
offender that they have committed an offence and that the prosecutor is deciding to deal
with the offence in this way. The Home Office *Circular on Cautioning 18/94* and the *National
Standards for Cautioning* provide guidance to prosecutors on cautioning. *Blackstone's Criminal
Practice 2005* cites at D1.63 that there are three preconditions to be met if an offence is to be
dealt with by way of formal caution:

(a)   that the evidence is sufficient to have warranted a prosecution;
(b)   that the offender admits his guilt; and
(c)   that the person cautioned agrees to such a disposal, having been made aware that,
      among other things, the caution may be cited in court in the event of future offending.

The following factors relating to cautions should be noted: **19.67**

- that while an admission of guilt is a requirement for a caution, following *R v Commissioner
  of Police for the Metropolis ex p Thompson* [1997] 1 WLR 1519, this should not be actively
  sought from the prosecuting officer;
- that issuing a caution does not prevent subsequent prosecution of the same matter,
  including a private prosecution, although in *Haytor v L* [1998] 1 WLR 854 the defendant
  applied for and obtained an order that the prosecution be stayed.

Reprimands and warnings for juveniles

Sections 65 and 66 of the Crime and Disorder Act 1998 replaces cautions with reprimands   **19.68**
and warnings for juveniles where, in certain circumstances, a juvenile may be issued with a
reprimand for a first offence, with a warning for a second, and then prosecuted for a third.
If the juvenile has been previously convicted of any offence the reprimand/warning option
is not available.

Environment Agency Enforcement and Prosecution Policy

The Environment Agency has adopted an *Enforcement and Prosecution Policy* that includes the   **19.69**
principles on which the Agency will make enforcement and prosecution decisions. Under
the policy, the Agency has adopted a Common Incident Classification Scheme (CICS) for
assessing response level and categorizing incidents that come to the attention of the Agency
and which may have an environmental and/or operational impact. CICS classifies incidents
into four categories and is used to guide the enforcement response where an offence has
been committed:

- for a Category 1 impact, or potential impact, prosecution will be the normal response;
- for a Category 2 impact, or potential impact, prosecution or a formal caution will be the normal response;
- for a Category 3 and 4 impact, or potential impact, a warning will be the normal response unless other factors make a firmer response necessary. A warning may be either a warning letter or a recorded site warning by the investigating officer.

19.70 The Environment Agency has published *Guidance for the Enforcement and Prosecution Policy version 8* (2004) to explain how the enforcement policy will be put into practice, to denote normal enforcement action, and to secure a consistent approach to enforcement across all the Agency's activities.

Prosecution

19.71 Any prosecution is at the discretion of the prosecutor and although the courts are reluctant to interfere with this decision, it may be subject to a claim for judicial review. In *R v Sevenoaks DC ex p Palley* [1995] JPL 915 the court quashed a local planning authority decision to prosecute before taking other non-criminal enforcement proceedings. See also *R v Kebilene* [2000] 2 AC 326.

19.72 Criminal proceedings can begin in two ways:

(1) by charging a suspect with an offence; or
(2) by laying an information before the magistrates' court.

19.73 Only the police and the CPS may charge a suspect, whereas laying an information can be done by the police and all other prosecutors, including the public by way of private prosecution. Thus, environmental offences, with the exception of some wildlife crimes, will commence by laying an information.

Laying an information

19.74 An information can be put before the court orally or in writing although, in practice, laying an information orally is unusual. Rule 100 of the Magistrates' Courts Rules 1981 (SI 1981/552) (MCR 1981) sets out the form in which an offence may be stated in documents, including an information:

(1) Every information, summons, warrant, or other document laid, issued or made for the purposes of, or in connection with, any proceedings before a magistrates' court for an offence shall be sufficient if it describes the specific offence with which the accused is charged, or of which he is convicted, in ordinary language avoiding as far as possible the use of technical terms and without necessarily stating all the elements of the offence, and gives such particulars as may be necessary for giving reasonable information of the nature of the charge.
(2) If the offence charged is one created by or under any Act, the description of the offence shall contain a reference to the section of the Act, or, as the case may be, the rule, order, regulation, byelaw or other instrument creating the offence.

19.75 Under r 100(2) of the MCR 1981, if the offence is a statutory offence, e.g. under s 85 of the WRA 1991, then the information must at least refer to the statute and the relevant section. In *Atterton v Browne* [1945] KB 122 the defendant was charged with selling milk with added water. The summons contained no reference to s 83(3) of the Food and Drugs Act 1938, the relevant statute. The court held that since the summons omitted vital particulars it was so defective and inaccurate as to be misleading. Viscount Caldecote CJ at page 126 commented that: 'I cannot see why . . . it should not be incumbent on the prosecution to state in the summons the material legislation which constitutes the offence charged.'

Progressing the proceedings

All proceedings begin in the magistrates' court. As they progress they may remain in the magistrates' court, e.g. for summary trial, or be transferred to the Crown Court either for trial on indictment or for sentencing. Before any evidence is heard, the mode of trial must be determined. This requires asking the defendant whether he pleads guilty or not guilty.

19.76

Time limits

Under s 127(1) of the MCA 1980, subject to exceptions, a magistrates' court shall not try an information or hear a complaint unless the information was laid, or the complaint made, within six months from the time when the offence was committed or the matter of complaint arose. The intention is that prosecutions are progressed early. In *R v Brentford Justices ex p Wong* [1981] QB 445 the High Court approved of magistrates acquitting the defendant without hearing evidence following the prosecution's delay. Section 127(2) of the MCA 1980 provides that subs (1) does not apply to an indictable offence whether triable exclusively on indictment or triable either way.

19.77

Pleas

If the defendant pleads guilty then the matter may be adjourned for sentencing or referred to the Crown Court for sentencing under s 3 of the Powers of the Criminal Courts (Sentencing) Act 2000 (PCCSA 2000) (although note the new limited provisions under s 3 and 3A of the PCCSA 2000, introduced under Sch 3 of the CJA 2003 and due to come into force in December 2005). Due to the relatively high proportion of strict liability environmental crimes, many environmental offenders plead guilty at the earliest opportunity. This is particularly so with many larger corporate defendants, e.g. water companies.

19.78

The Court of Appeal in *R v Friskies Petcare UK Ltd* (2000) Case No. 99/5226/W5 set out important guidelines for prosecutors, defendants, and the sentencing court in the event of a guilty plea. It recommended that the salient facts of the case, together with the aggravating and mitigating features, should be presented to the sentencing court in the form of schedules (now known as *Friskies* schedules), which should, if possible, be agreed in advance. There should therefore be no doubt about the basis on which sentence is passed and any higher court dealing with an appeal against sentence will have the relevant facts at its fingertips.

19.79

If the defendant pleads not guilty, the matter will proceed to trial either by way of summary trial or, if the defendant elects trial on indictment, on transfer to the Crown Court (NB: again, note the new provisions under the CJA 2003).

19.80

Mode of trial

For the purpose of determining the mode of trial, there are three types of offence:

19.81

(1) summary offences, which are tried only in the magistrates' court;

(2) offences tried only on indictment, which are tried only in the Crown Court; and

(3) offences triable either way, which can be tried in either court depending on whether the defendant elects to choose a summary trial or trial on indictment with a judge and jury.

19.82 Paragraph 51 of *Practice Direction (Criminal Proceedings: Consolidation)* [2002] 1 WLR 2870 sets out the National Mode of Trial Guidelines, which aim to help magistrates decide whether or not to commit either way offences to the Crown Court and include general considerations such as reference to s 19 of the MCA 1980 as well as specific reference to common either way offences.

19.83 After consideration of the mode of trial, the proceedings are adjourned to a further hearing or transferred to the Crown Court as appropriate. Magistrates' courts hear 95% of all criminal cases, while the Crown Court hears the remaining, more serious, criminal matters. It is only the very simplest of cases, e.g. straightforward motoring offences, which will be concluded in one hearing. Environmental crime matters that proceed to summary trial are most likely to remain in the magistrates' court, at least until sentencing.

Bail and remand

19.84 With most environmental crimes being summary/triable either way offences, often committed by corporate defenders, and of strict liability in nature it is unlikely that a defendant who pleads not guilty will need to be placed on remand or that he will be granted bail with the need to provide sureties before being released for adjournment of proceedings.

Committal for trial by indictment

19.85 If the defendant has elected for trial by indictment, the magistrates must hold committal proceedings where they assess the evidence before the court to see whether there is a *prima facie* case. If so, the defendant is committed to the Crown Court for trial; if not, the defendant is discharged.

Prosecution case

19.86 The obligation to pursue a prosecution only where there is enough evidence to provide a realistic prospect of conviction (para 6.2 of the *Code for Crown Prosecutors*) means that, prior to the commencement of proceedings, the prosecution should have gathered sufficient evidence to progress their case. Following the plea hearings and decision as to the mode of trial the prosecution should then progress the case by disclosing evidence to the defence.

Disclosure

19.87 There is a duty under the CPIA 1996 for the prosecution to disclose the evidence it will rely on to the defence. The Magistrates' Courts (Advance Information) Rules 1985, as amended (SI 1985/601), supplement the CPIA 1996 but do not apply to summary only proceedings. The defendant, in turn, must provide a statement setting out the defence and highlighting those parts of the prosecution case that are at issue. Section 3(1) of the CPIA 1996 states that the prosecutor must:

(a) disclose to the accused any prosecution material that has not previously been disclosed to the accused and that might reasonably be considered capable of undermining the case for the prosecution against the accused or of assisting the case for the accused, or

(b) give to the accused a written statement that there is no material of a description mentioned in paragraph (a).

A Code of Practice on Disclosure has been issued as required under s 23 of the CPIA 1996. **19.88** This details the obligations for prosecutors and the defence. For example, under para 5.1 of the Disclosure Code: 'The investigator must retain material obtained in a criminal investigation which may be relevant to the investigation.'

Section 26 of the CPIA 1996 provides that those people, other than police officers, charged **19.89** with the duty of conducting criminal investigations must have regard to the Code's provisions. This will include all environmental investigation and enforcement officers. To assist, the Health & Safety and Local Authority association (HELA) has published guidance supporting the code: *The HELA Circular for Local Authorities* No. 45/16. There is also the *Attorney-General's Guidelines: Disclosure of Information in Criminal Proceedings* published in 2000, which emphasize the right to a fair trial and the role that fair disclosure plays in that.

Section 1(1) of the CPIA 1996 provides that the disclosure requirements cover summary **19.90** proceedings where the court proceeds to summary trial and the defendant pleads not guilty and all trials on indictment. However, the obligations on summary trial are less onerous, in particular because the defence are not required to serve a defence statement on the prosecution following primary disclosure. In summary the procedure is:

• primary prosecution disclosure (sometimes referred to as advance information or disclosure) by the prosecution; followed by
• defence disclosure (not obligatory in summary trial); followed by
• secondary prosecution disclosure (at times referred to as availability disclosure) providing there has been defence disclosure.

The disclosure provisions include a number of limitations and other options for disclosure. **19.91** For example, s 8 of the CPIA 1996 enables the defendant to apply to the court for an order on disclosure if he reasonably believes evidence that may assist his case has not been disclosed, although s 8(5) enables the prosecutor to obtain public interest immunity for certain evidence where appropriate. Also, the prosecution are under a continuing duty to review evidence and disclosure under s 9 of the CPIA 1996, e.g. if there is material that may undermine the prosecution case. The defendant may seek evidence being held by a third party. If that third party is unwilling to forward the evidence, the defendant may apply for a witness summons for the evidence to be brought to court.

Defence case

If the trial is proceeding on indictment then the defence will be obliged, following primary **19.92** prosecution disclosure, to serve a written defence statement on the prosecution. The defence may choose to provide this at summary trial although this option is often not taken up on the basis that certain evidence or lines of further inquiry may be raised in a defence statement, or that further secondary prosecution evidence may be introduced that may weaken the defence case.

19.93   While many environmental offences are of strict liability, they often expressly provide defences or can rely on exemptions provided elsewhere in the CPIA 1996 that can operate as a defence. However, there is no consistent approach to defences and it is necessary to check the statute creating the offence to see whether it has a corresponding defence. Some examples of the main statutory defences to environmental crimes are set out below, but see also the relevant chapters for more detail.

Acting under instructions from an employer

19.94   It is a defence for a person charged with an offence relating to the prohibition of unauthorized or harmful depositing, treatment, or disposal etc. of waste under s 33(7)(b) of the EPA to prove: 'that he acted under instructions from his employer and neither knew nor had reason to suppose that the acts done by him constituted a contravention'.

As far as (reasonably) practicable

19.95   The health and safety legislation qualifies many of the obligations of employers and organizations by the fact that they must be met so far as is reasonably practicable, or so far as practicable. For example s 2(1)(a) of the Health and Safety at Work etc. Act 1974 places a general duty on employers so far as is reasonably practicable to ensure the health, safety, and welfare at work of all their employees.

Best practicable means

19.96   The use of best practicable means (BPM) in controlling pollution was introduced under the Alkali Act 1863 and has been retained in some statutory provisions as a form of defence. Section 80(7) of the EPA 1990 provides that in any proceedings relating to a statutory nuisance on industrial, trade or business premises it is a defence to prove that the BPM were used to prevent, or counteract the effects of, the nuisance. Under s 60 of the Control of Pollution Act 1974 (CoPA 1974) the local authority shall have regard to the need for ensuring that the BPM are employed to minimize noise, while s 68 of the Act states that it will be a defence to any contravention that the means used for reducing noise were not less effective than the means required by the regulations. BPM is usually defined and adopts a similar style in the relevant Acts, e.g. s 72 of CoPA 1974 and s 79(9) of the EPA 1990 as a defence to a breach of a statutory nuisance abatement notice.

19.97   Section 80(7) of the EPA 1990 provides that in any proceedings for an offence of breach of an abatement notice it shall be a defence to prove that the BPM were used to prevent, or to counteract the effects of, the nuisance. This involves determining if the technological means for the control of the nuisance exist and, if so, were the BPM used. While 'reasonably practicable' allows for a balance of risk against the cost and difficulty of the control, BPM is based more on acknowledgement of technological limitations with less weight being permitted to the cost aspect. For the purpose of statutory nuisance, BPM is defined in s 79(9) of the EPA 1990 as:

(a) 'practicable' means reasonably practicable having regard among other things to local conditions and circumstances, to the current state of technical knowledge, and to the financial implications;

(b) the means employed include the design, installation, and maintenance and manner and periods of operation of plant and machinery, and the design, construction, and maintenance of buildings and structures;

(c) the test is to apply only so far as compatible with any duty imposed by law;

(d) the test is to apply only so far as compatible with safety and safe conditions, and with the exigencies of any emergency or unforeseeable circumstances;

and, in circumstances where a code of practice under s 71 of CoPA 1974 (noise minimization) is applicable, regard shall also be had to guidance given in it.

Newman J in *Manley v New Forest DC* [1999] PLR 36 commented that BPM was developed as **19.98** a means of pollution control and that an important part of the concept had always been that it allowed for flexibility to cater for local and individual circumstances. He noted that: 'Its introduction reflected a conciliatory and co-operational approach, so that the method of enforcement would not place an undue burden on manufacturing industry and on businesses.'

In *Wivenhoe Port v Colchester BC* (1985) JPL 175 the defendant argued that to prevent **19.99** dust nuisance arising from certain machinery was not practicable because it would render the activity unprofitable. The Crown Court accepted that profitability may be a relevant factor in considering BPM, but increased expense was not sufficient, by itself, to establish a defence of BPM. In *Tewkesbury BC v Deacon* [2003] EWHC 2544 the BPM defence was held not to be sufficient when a compressor to limit noise levels was not set at the correct level. BPM is also discussed in relation to appeals against abatement notices in Chapter 18: Statutory nuisance.

Emergency actions

Emergency actions can provide a defence to certain offences. Under s 33(7)(c) of the EPA **19.100** 1990 it is a defence to a charge relating to the prohibition on unauthorized or harmful depositing, treatment, or disposal etc. of waste, if the defendant can prove:

that the acts alleged to constitute the contravention were done in an emergency in order to avoid danger to human health in a case where:

(i) he took all such steps as were reasonably practicable in the circumstances for minimising pollution of the environment and harm to human health; and

(ii) particulars of the acts were furnished to the waste regulation authority as soon as reasonable practicable after they were done.

Section 89(1)(a) of the WRA 1991 provides that a person shall not be guilty of an offence **19.101** under s 85, i.e. causing or knowingly permit pollution to enter controlled waters, if the entry is caused or permitted, or the discharge is made, in an emergency in order to avoid danger to life or health. In *Express Ltd v Environment Agency* [2003] Env LR 29 the High Court, on appeal from the magistrates' court, allowed an appeal by the defendant following conviction for polluting a watercourse with milk. The court held that the emergency defence was available to a driver who, following a tyre blow out on a milk tanker pulled over onto the hard shoulder of a motorway to avoid danger to life or health on the road. The blow out on the tyre had broken a milk delivery pipe causing the milk to enter the watercourse.

Reasonable excuse

19.102 The defence of reasonable excuse often arises as part of the elements of an offence. For example, reg 32(1)(e) of the PPC Regs 2000 provides that is an offence to fail, without reasonable excuse, to comply with any requirement of a notice requiring information and service by the Secretary of State or the regulator under the PPC Regs 2000. If the defendant raises the reasonable excuse he has the evidential burden of proving that such a state of affairs existed. *Cross & Tapper on Evidence* (9/e, Butterworths 1999), at p 139, provides that:

> When the accused bears the evidential burden alone, it is necessary for there to be only such evidence as would, if believed and uncontradicted, induce a reasonable doubt in the mind of a reasonable jury as to whether his version might be true.

19.103 Once the defence has discharged the evidential burden of proving that he had reasonable excuse to carry out the act that is the subject of the offence. It is for the prosecution to prove, beyond reasonable doubt, that defendant did not have a reasonable excuse. For example, s 80(4) of the EPA 1990 provides that: 'If a person on whom an abatement notice is served, *without reasonable excuse*, contravenes or fails to comply with any requirement or prohibition imposed by the notice, he shall be guilty of an offence.'

19.104 In *Polychronakis v Richards & Jerrom Ltd* [1998] Env LR 346 the justices sought, by way of case stated, an opinion of the High Court on whether they had been correct in finding that the burden was on the defendant to prove the defence of reasonable excuse in breach of an abatement notice. The High Court held that once the defendant had laid the proper evidential basis for the contention of a reasonable excuse it was for the prosecution to satisfy the court to the criminal standard or proof that the excuse was not a reasonable one.

19.105 In *Wellingborough BC v Gordon* [1993] Env LR 218 the court held that the defence of reasonable excuse is unavailable for the deliberate and intentional contravention of an abatement notice. In *Saddleworth UDC v Aggregate and Sand* (1970) 114 SJ 931 lack of finance was held not to be a reasonable excuse. However, in *Hope Butuyuyu v LB Hammersmith & Fulham* [1997] Env LR D13 the significance of personal circumstances was taken into account when assessing whether a reasonable excuse existed. In *A Lambert Flat Management Ltd v Lomas* [1981] 1 WLR 898 the court held that a defendant was not entitled to raise matters that could have been raised on appeal or matters that were covered by other statutory defences such as BPM.

Reasonable precaution (due diligence)

19.106 It is a statutory defence that reasonable precaution or care (also referred to as due diligence) has been taken. It is for the defendant to show that they acted with such care. Examples of the reasonable precaution defence include: s 33(7)(a) of the EPA 1990, which states that for an offence relating to the prohibition of unauthorized or harmful depositing, treatment, or disposal etc. of waste: 'It shall be a defence for a person charged with an offence under this section . . . to prove that he took all reasonable precautions and exercised all due diligence to avoid the commission of the offence'.

19.107 Under s 87(2) of the WRA 1991, a sewerage undertaker shall not be guilty of a s 85 offence of polluting controlled waters if the contravention is attributable to a discharge that another person caused or permitted; the undertaker was bound to receive the discharge into the sewer and the undertaker could not reasonably have been expected to prevent the discharge into the sewer or works.

Defences specific to certain offences

There are a number of defences that are unique to an offence created under statute. For **19.108** example, a defendant charged with an offence in relation to contravention of a Tree Preservation Order under s 210 of the Town and Country Planning Act 1990 may rely on a number of exemptions provided in s 198 of that Act for example in cutting down, uprooting, topping, or lopping any trees that are dying or dead or have become dangerous.

Also, under s 78M(2) of the EPA 1990 it is a defence to a charge of failing to comply with a **19.109** contaminated land remediation notice to show that the reason the notice was not complied with was because a joint polluter could not or would not pay his allocated share of the cost of compliance.

Trial

Because many environmental offences are of strict liability they do not often proceed to **19.110** trial. If they do almost all cases will be tried in the magistrates' court because all environ-mental crimes are either summary offences or triable either way. It is very rare that an environmental offence is tried on indictment. It is therefore sensible to outline summary trial procedure, rather than trial on indictment. It is recommended that *Blackstone's Criminal Practice* or *Stone's Justices Manual* is considered for detailed consideration of both summary trial and trial on indictment.

Summary trial

The MCA 1980 covers much of the summary trial procedure. The magistrates' court must **19.111** comprise either two or (usually) three magistrates. If a defendant does not appear for trial, then the magistrates may, under s 11 of the MCA 1980, proceed without him, entering a plea of not guilty on his behalf. Under s 12 a defendant may plead guilty by post, although this procedure is only available for summary offences with a maximum penalty of three months' imprisonment (Note: s 308 of the CJA 2003 will remove this limitation). If the prosecution do not appear for trial, the magistrates can either dismiss the information or adjourn the hearing.

At the start of the trial, the clerk will put the information to the accused and he must plead **19.112** either guilty or not guilty. If the defendant pleads guilty, pre-sentence proceedings may begin. If he pleads not guilty, then the prosecution can begin their case, often, but not necessarily, by making an opening speech.

After any opening speech, prosecution witnesses may be called. Written statements under **19.113** s 9 of the CJA 1967 may be used instead of undertaking a full examination in chief. After a prosecution witness has given evidence in chief, he may be cross-examined by the defend-ant, and then, if required, subjected to re-examination and questions from the magistrates.

Following all evidence from the prosecution, the defence may make a submission of no case **19.114** to answer. If so, the decision whether to reject the submission should be based upon whether a reasonable tribunal might convict on the evidence heard so far, see the judgment of Lord Lane CJ in *R v Galbraith* [1981] 1 WLR 1039, which provides a two-stage test for trial on indictment:

(1) If there is no evidence that the crime alleged has been committed by the defendant, the judge will stop the case.

(2) If there is some evidence, but it is of a tenuous nature then (a) the judge should consider whether the prosecution evidence, taken at its highest, is such that no jury properly directed could convict, if so, then upon submission he should stop the case; (b) where however, the prosecution case is such that its strength is on the view of a witness or some other matter, then the judge should allow the matter to be tried by the jury.

19.115 The defence case follows a similar pattern of calling defence witnesses who are subject to examination in chief, cross-examination, re-examination, and any questions from the magistrates. The defence has the option of making either an opening or closing speech. It is almost always best to opt for a closing speech.

Verdict

19.116 Following all submissions, the magistrates are likely to retire to consider a verdict. They may seek the advice from their legal adviser (formerly the justice's clerk), although this should only be on matters relating to law not fact. Following consideration of the case, the magistrates will return to court and give a verdict of either convicting the defendant on the charge or acquitting them. There is no option, unlike a jury in a Crown Court trial, to convict of a lesser offence, although in practice, the prosecution may lay an alternative lesser charge against the defendant, which the magistrates may opt for.

Trial on indictment

19.117 Indictment is the mode of trial for the more serious offences. It is in the Crown Court with a single judge and a jury of 12 members of the public. The procedure at trial, in principle, follows that in the magistrates' court with the prosecution case being followed by the defence case. However, the rules of court are more complex and importantly, the jury decides issues of fact while the judge decides issues of law. The jury also decides whether to convict a defendant on all the evidence presented before the court. Following conviction, the judge determines the sentence.

19.118 If the court convicts, then the matter proceeds to sentencing. If the court acquits then the matter is closed and the offence cannot be re-prosecuted. Thus, a defendant would in any potential subsequent proceedings for the same matter be entitled to rely upon the defence of *autrefois acquis*.

Sentencing procedure

19.119 Sentencing is one of the most important aspects of environmental crime, where the seriousness of environmental harm must be put before the court in order to ensure that, among other things, the true cost of the crime to society and the environment is reflected in the sentence. The principles of and approach to environmental sentencing are covered in Section D. Outlined below is the court procedure.

Pre-sentencing procedure

Following a conviction by the court or a guilty plea by the defendant, the court will proceed **19.120** to sentencing. To do this, the court often requires a sentencing report. In the Crown Court, sentencing is the role of the judge. In the magistrates' court, sentence is decided by a majority of the bench.

If there has been a trial the court will have heard the full facts of the case and will not need to **19.121** revisit these for the purpose of sentencing. However, if the defendant pleaded guilty, the court will need to know the facts of the case, which are summarized by the prosecution. The summary should be objective without suggesting any particular sentence. If a compensation, confiscation, or forfeiture order is appropriate, the prosecution should apply for this. Also, the prosecution should, if appropriate, provide a 'victim impact statement' following the guidelines set out in *R v Perks* [2001] 1 Cr App R(S) 66 and para 28: Personal Statement of Victims, of *Practice Direction (Criminal Proceedings: Consolidation)* [2002] 1 WLR 2870 that:

(a) a sentencer must not make assumptions, without evidence, about the effects of an offence on the victim;

(b) if an offence had had a particularly damaging effect upon the victim, the court should be informed and it should be taken into account when passing sentence;

(c) evidence of the effects of an offence on the victim must be in a proper form as a witness statement, an expert report, or otherwise, and served upon the defendant;

(d) evidence of the victim alone should be approached with care, particularly if it covered matters that the defence could not realistically be expected to investigate; and

(e) the opinions of the victim and the victim's close relatives on the level of sentence should not be taken into account.

'Newton' hearing

If, following a guilty plea, there remains a dispute about certain facts of the offence that will **19.122** impact on sentence, following Lord Lane's statement in *R v Newton* (1982) 77 Cr App R 13, the court has three options:

(1) obtain the answer from a jury;

(2) hear evidence from each party and come to his own conclusion, acting as jury on the issue that is the root of the problem; or

(3) hear submission of counsel and then come to a conclusion.

Option 2 above, is now referred to as a *Newton* hearing. Following *Gardner* [1994] Crim LR **19.123** 301, counsel are under a duty to inform the court when a *Newton* hearing is appropriate. The court may also decide to hold such a hearing, even if opposed by the defendant.

Following a summary of the facts, the court will hear evidence of the defendant's character **19.124** and antecedents in a form prescribed by para 27 of the *Practice Direction (Criminal Proceedings: Consolidation)* [2002]. The court should then consider any pre-sentence reports prepared by probation officers, medical and psychiatric reports, and any assessment on the suitability of community service.

The court will hear any submissions of mitigation by the defendant. In *Gross v O'Toole* (1982) **19.125** 4 Cr App R (S) 283 the Divisional Court, on appeal, set out the principles relating to mitigation:

if an advocate is going to put forward in mitigation something which is, on the face of it, quite inconsistent with the other information that the magistrates have so far as sentence is concerned, e.g. the list of previous convictions, it really is for the defending advocate to indicate that he wishes to make good the submission . . . he takes the chance himself if he does not offer to call evidence. . . . I do not think [the magistrates] were obliged to tell the defending advocate that they did not accept his mitigation, because I do not think anyone in court, least of all the defending advocate, could have supposed for a moment that they would accept his mitigation.

19.126   There is concern that a defendant who is not legally represented when hearing mitigation on sentencing may be disadvantaged and not gain what could amount to a justifiably lighter sentence than is given. Section 83(1) of the PCCSA 2000 provides that a court shall not pass a sentence of imprisonment on a person who is not legally represented and has not previously been sentenced to that punishment by a court in any part of the UK, unless he was granted a right to representation as part of the Criminal Defence Service (CDS) but the right was withdrawn or, having been informed of his right to representation, he refused or failed to apply.

19.127   Finally, the court may be asked to take into consideration other offences that the defendant has admitted to, which are within the general type of offence as the main conviction. While this could, in theory, increase the defendant's sentence significantly, in practice this does not occur and has the advantage for the defendant that the matter can be closed rather than have the risk of prosecution for that offence at a later date.

Sentencing

19.128   After considering any evidence, reports, or legal representations the court may pass sentence. Magistrates are, generally, subject to exceptional statutory maxima, limited to passing sentences of fines up to the standard level 5, currently £5,000 under s 37 of the Criminal Justice Act 1982, compensation of £5,000 (under s 131 of the PCCSA 2000) and imprisonment of six months for each offence (under s 78 of the PCCSA 2000), subject to a maximum of 12 months for two or more consecutive sentences. Section 155 of the CJA 2003 will, when it enters into force at the end of 2005, increase the maximum term running consecutively from 12 months to 65 weeks. Section D: Environmental sentencing covers the factors to take into account when determining sentence.

19.129   If the court considers that the sentence passed does not reflect the offence then it may, within 28 days of passing sentence, vary or rescind a sentence under s 155 of the PCCSA 2000 and s 142 of the MCA 1980. Variation will often involve a reduction in sentence, but the court is not limited to this. Under s 1 of the PCCSA 2000, the court may defer passing sentencing for up to six months so that the court may have regard to:

(a)   the defendant's conduct after conviction (including, where appropriate, the making by him of reparation for his offence); or

(b)   any change in his circumstances.

19.130   Deferment is only available where the defendant consents and if the court were satisfied that it would be in the interests of justice to exercise the power. In *R v George* [1984] 1 WLR 1082 Lord Lane CJ gave guidance on deferment including that the court must make it clear to the defendant the purpose of the deferment and the kind of conduct expected of him during the deferment period.

Appeals

Appeals are considered more fully in Sprack's *A Practical Approach to Criminal Procedure* (OUP, **19.131**
2004). In outline, under s 108 of the MCA 1980, a defendant convicted in the magistrates'
court may appeal to the Crown Court against his conviction (if he pleaded not guilty) and
sentence. A defendant tried or sentenced in the Crown Court may appeal against his conviction and sentence to the Criminal Division of the Court of Appeal under s 1 of the Criminal
Appeal Act 1968 (CAA 1968). While a guilty plea is, in general, a bar to an appeal against
conviction, there are limited exceptions to the rule where the defendant may argue that his
guilty plea was equivocal and not a genuine admission of guilt, see e.g. *R v Forde* [1923]
2 KB 400. Also, any person aggrieved by a court's decision may appeal to the Divisional
Court by way of case stated or make a claim for judicial review to the Administrative Court.

Time limits on appeal

Rule 7 of the Crown Court Rules 1982 provides that an appeal from the magistrates' court to **19.132**
the Crown Court must be made within 21 days of the date of conviction. Notice of appeal
from the Crown Court to the Court of Appeal under s 18(2) of the CAA 1968 must be filed
within 28 days. Under s 111(2) of the MCA 1980, an application for appeal by way of case
stated must be made to the magistrates' court within 21 days of the date on which the court
sentences or otherwise deals with the offender. A claim for judicial review must be made
under Pt 54 of the Civil Procedure Rules 1998 within three months and in any event
promptly and is discussed further in Chapter 20: Public law.

Appeal from the magistrates' court

Section 48 of the Supreme Court Act 1981 sets out the powers of the Crown Court on appeal **19.133**
from the magistrates' court. These include:

- s 48(1), correcting any error or mistake in the order or judgment, provided that the order
  or judgment is incorporated in the decision appealed against;
- s 48(2)(a), confirming, reversing, or varying any part of the decision appealed against;
- s 48(2)(b), remitting the matter back to the magistrates' court with its opinion; and
- s 48(2)(c), making any such order that seems just, including increasing any sentence
  appealed against.

The Crown Court, following *Dutta v Westcott* (1987) 84 Cr App R 103 DC, can also amend **19.134**
any sentence that may have been imposed at the same time as the sentence appealed against.

Appeal from the Crown Court

Section 1 of the CAA 1968 states that a person convicted of an offence on indictment may **19.135**
appeal against his conviction or sentence with leave of the Court of Appeal or if the judge of
the trial court grants a certificate of appeal, although, in practice, a certificate is granted very
rarely. Section 2(1) of the CAA 1968 (as amended by the Criminal Appeal Act 1995) provides
that the Court of Appeal: 'shall allow an appeal against conviction if they think that the
conviction is unsafe; and shall dismiss an appeal in any other case.'

Under s 2(2) of the CAA 1968 if the conviction is unsafe, the Court of Appeal must quash the **19.136**
appellant's conviction. The court may then order a retrial. If not, the defendant is regarded
as being acquitted.

Appeal by way of case stated

19.137 An appeal by way of case stated can be made on a point of law. Section 111(1) of the MCA 1980 provides that:

> Any person who was a party to the proceeding before a magistrates' court or is aggrieved by the conviction, order, determination or other proceeding of the court may question the proceeding on the ground that it is wrong in law or is in excess of jurisdiction by applying to the 'magistrates' to state a case for the opinion of the High Court on the question of law or jurisdiction involved.

19.138 A person aggrieved includes the prosecution and the defendant.

Application for judicial review

19.139 The principles and procedure on judicial review are considered in Chapter 20: Public law.

Costs

19.140 The general costs principle that the loser pays the winner's costs is, to a limited extent, followed in criminal proceedings. However, Pt II of the Prosecution of Offences Act 1985 (POA 1985) confers powers to the court to award costs in proceedings. The court also has a discretion to award costs as it thinks fit. Further, many defendants will be in receipt of public funding, which, in practice, means that one public body, the prosecutor, will simply be taking from another public body, the Legal Services Commission.

Public funding

19.141 The Access to Justice Act 1999 (AJA 1999) established the Legal Services Commission and the Criminal Defence Service CDS. Section 12(1) of the AJA 1999 provides that the purpose of the CDS is to ensure that: 'individuals involved in criminal investigations or criminal proceedings have access to such advice, assistance and representation as the interests of justice require.'

19.142 The service is provided largely through solicitors in private practice who must secure a General Criminal Contract in order to carry out publicly funded criminal defence work.

19.143 Regulations 6 to 10 of the CDS (General No. 2) Regulations 2001 (SI 2001/1437) set out the procedure for a defendant to apply for a representation order, which can be made in any criminal court. There is no means test, contribution, or payment required for representation, although a court (other than a magistrates' court) may make an order that an individual repay some or all of the cost of any such representation under the CDS (Recovery of Defence Costs Orders) Regulations 2001 (SI 2001/856).

19.144 Public funding under the CDS is only available to individuals, so corporate defenders must secure private funding for legal representation.

Part II of the Prosecution of Offences Act 1985

19.145 Part II of the POA 1985 contains the main costs rules in criminal cases. Section 16 covers the defendant's costs orders paid out of central funds, where for example, an information is not proceeded with, a defendant is acquitted after trial on any count or a defendant convicted in the magistrates' court appeals and his conviction is set aside or is awarded a less severe punishment. In *R (Harry A Coff Ltd) v Environment Agency* [2003] EWHC 1305 (Admin) the Administrative Court held that a court was wrong to decline a defendant's costs order on the ground that the amount sought was unreasonable on its face. What had been requested was an assessment of costs and so it would be for the costs assessor to determine whether the defendant's costs were excessive.

Section 17 of the POA 1985 empowers the court to order that the prosecution is paid out of central funds such amount of its costs as it considers it reasonably necessary to be compensated for any expenses properly inccurred in the proceedings. **19.146**

Under s 18 of the POA 1985, the court may order that the convicted defendant or unsuccessful appellant pay prosecution costs that are just and reasonable. The prosecution should be able to provide the court with details of the costs incurred at each stage in the proceedings. In *R v Associated Octel* [1997] Crim LR 144, a case prosecuted by the HSE, the Court of Appeal held that prosecution costs could include investigation as well as legal costs. **19.147**

In *Northallerton Magistrates' Court ex p Dove* [1999] Crim LR 760 the High Court gave guidance on prosecution costs paid by the defendant including that: **19.148**

- costs orders should never exceed the amount the defendant was able to pay and which was reasonable to pay, having regard to the defendant's means and any other financial order made;
- the sum should not exceed the amount the prosecutor had actually and reasonably incurred;
- the purpose of an order was to compensate the prosecutor and not punish the defender;
- any costs ordered should not be disproportionate to any fine imposed and, where the fine and costs exceeded the sum that the offender could reasonably be ordered to pay, the costs, rather than the fine, should be reduced; and
- an offender facing a fine or costs order should inform the court of his financial position, giving him a fair opportunity to adduce any relevant financial information, so that they could assess what could reasonably be paid.

Section 19 of the POA 1985 enables the court to make an order that a party guilty of improper acts or omission in the course of proceedings pay any costs thrown away by the other side, while s 19A allows the court to make an order against legal representatives **19.149**

D   ENVIRONMENTAL SENTENCING

Introduction

With a number of common environmental offences attracting strict liability, many defendants will plead guilty and the courts then proceed to sentencing. Environmental sentencing is consistent with other sentencing in that it should punish offenders appropriately, but it should also ensure that the polluter pays the price for the environmental harm caused and also that an offender does not profit from the offence, even after being sentenced. **19.150**

19.151   There has been criticism for some time of the level of environmental sentencing. The Environmental Audit Committee Inquiry report *Environmental Crime and the Courts (Sixth Report of Session 2003–04)* (May 2004) expressed concern that the general level at which fines were imposed neither reflected the gravity of environmental crimes, nor deterred or adequately punished offenders. Reasons in the report for the low level of environmental sentencing were that:

- environmental cases came before the courts relatively infrequently;
- there was a perception that environmental crime was not as serious as other crimes in which a victim and the harm suffered may be more readily identifiable; and
- the courts were unable to properly assess the seriousness of environmental crimes if accurate information about the environmental impact of an offence had not been submitted to the court.

However, written evidence from the Environment Agency to the Inquiry noted that: 'prosecutors are reporting a perception of a greater confidence, understanding and awareness by sentencers of the applicable factors when handling such cases.'

19.152   As indicated above, magistrates' courts deal with the vast majority of environmental cases, although for offences triable either way there is the option of referring a case to the Crown Court for sentencing.

Options on environmental sentencing

19.153   To date, environmental sentences have tended to focus on fines as the main form of punishment. Indeed, this is partly due to the advice given by the Sentencing Advisory Panel in 2000: *Advice to the Court of Appeal on Environmental Sentencing*, which noted that the starting point for environmental sentences should be a fine. For corporate offenders, this is often the extent of the sentence, although see paras 19.28 to 19.30, and the potential liability for directors and managers. For non-corporate offenders, the court may have a number of sentencing options appropriate for environmental cases including:

- imprisonment and suspended sentences;
- community orders;
- fines;
- conditional and absolute discharges; and
- compensation, forfeiture, and confiscation orders.

Each of these is considered briefly below.

Imprisonment

19.154   Many environmental offences provide for a maximum prison term of five years, e.g. s 111 of the EPA 1990 provides that someone importing, acquiring, releasing, or marketing genetically modified organisms without consent is liable on summary conviction to a maximum six months' imprisonment and five years' on indictment. And, while it remains relatively unusual, a custodial sentence for an environmental offence remains a real possibility. In *R v Sissen* [2000] All ER (D) 2193 CA the defendant was convicted of the illegal import of three Lear's macaw, one of the world's most endangered bird species (with around 150 left in the wild). He was imprisoned for 30 months by the Crown Court.

If a defendant is convicted of two or more offences then the court may order that the prison **19.155** terms run either concurrently (at the same time) or consecutively (one immediately after the other). If an offender is already in prison serving another sentence, the court can order that the latest sentence runs either concurrently or consecutively.

In *R v Higgins* [2003] Env Times Vol 9.2, p32, the defendant was convicted, under s 33 of the **19.156** EPA 1990, of dumping hundreds of car tyres in the countryside using a bogus tyre disposal company to collect and be paid for the disposal. Magistrates sentenced the defendant to three months' imprisonment, taking into account 12 other offences including theft.

Suspended sentences

In exceptional circumstances the court may suspend a prison sentence. However, a **19.157** suspended sentence cannot be granted for a defendant under 21 and the total sentence, aggregating all the offences concurrently, cannot be suspended for more than two years. Section 118(4) of the PCCSA 2000 provides that:

> A court shall not deal with an offender by means of a suspended sentence unless it is of the opinion (a) that the case is one in which a sentence of imprisonment would have been appropriate even without the power to suspend the sentence; and (b) that the exercise of that power can be justified by the exceptional circumstances of the case.

Custody plus

Sections 181 and 182 of the CJA 2003 introduce a new sentence entitled a 'custody plus **19.158** order' that will eventually replace all prison terms of under 12 months for 18 to 21 year olds. The order will include a two-stage sentence whereby part 1 is custodial and part 2 involves being released on licence under certain conditions including requirements to carry out unpaid work and other activities, curfews, prohibitions, and exclusions. The new provisions are to be introduced in 2006.

Community orders

The CJA 2003 revised various community-based sentences and brought them together under **19.159** the umbrella of a community order. Section 177(1) provides that where a person over 16 is convicted of an offence, the court may make a community order imposing on him, among other things:

(a) an unpaid work requirement;
(b) an activity requirement;
(c) a programme requirement;
(d) a prohibited activity requirement;

One of the consequences of the community order is that it will allow a court to impose a **19.160** single order with a combination of any requirement, where it was previously only capable of imposing one or other distinct orders. In *R v Gath Drums & Jones* (1998) ENDS Report 281 p 50, June 1998, the director of a Yorkshire drum cleaning company was the first individual to be prosecuted under the Integrated Pollution Control regime. The director was ordered to undertake 60 hours' community service.

In *R v David Power* (2002) Env Times, Vol 8.1 p 42, the defendant was found guilty of his **19.161** workmen removing asbestos roof sheets from a building in Wimborne, Dorset. He had failed to comply with the waste duty of care regime under s 34 of the EPA 1990 and had not completed the required consignment notes for the transfer and disposal of the special waste. The defendant was sentenced to 100 hours' community punishment plus costs of £2,000.

Fines

19.162   Fines are, for all offences, by far the most common form of sentence for summary and either way offences. They are, currently, the only sentence available to courts for convicted corporate offenders. For many environmental offences, Parliament has provided exceptional statutory maxima financial penalties for magistrates with most set at four times the maximum standard scale (currently £5,000) at £20,000. Others include a maximum fine on summary conviction of £50,000 under s 139 of the Merchant Shipping Act 1995 for failing to comply with directions of an authorized person following a marine accident, and a maximum £250,000 for discharge of oil from a ship into certain UK waters contrary to s 131 of the Merchant Shipping Act 1995.

19.163   The court in determining the size of any fine will need to consider any aggravating and mitigating factors. A fine may be combined with a custodial sentence, a community sentence or a compensation order. The court is often obliged to give the defendant time to pay, although under s 82 of the MCA 1980 they may refuse time to pay when the offence is imprisonable and the defendant appears to have the money to pay, the defendant is of no fixed abode, or is likely to leave the UK, or he is already serving a custodial sentence or is given such a sentence at the same time as the fine.

19.164   There is no formal guidance on the level of fine beyond where any statutory offence provides a maximum penalty. However, in *R v F Howe & Son (Engineers) Ltd* [1999] 2 All ER 249 the court set out important principles relating to fines. The company had pleaded guilty to offences under the Health and Safety at Work etc. Act 1974 of, among others, failing to ensure so far as was reasonably practicable the safety at work of its employees, following the death by electrocution of an employee during a cleaning session. The company had been fined £48,000 and ordered to pay £7,500 in costs. The company appealed on the grounds that the total fine was excessive. The Court of Appeal allowed the appeal and reduced the total financial burden on the company to £22,500. As part of the appeal the court made the following points:

- that fines on companies need to be large enough to make an impact on shareholders — past fining levels were far too low;
- a company is presumed to be able to pay any fine the court is minded to impose unless financial information to the contrary is available to the court before the hearing; and
- a deliberate breach of the legislation by a company or an individual with a view to profit seriously aggravates the offence.

Continuing daily fines post-conviction

19.165   Many offences provide for daily fines for non-compliance with regulations post-conviction, e.g. continuing non-compliance with a contaminated land remediation notice under s 78M of the EPA 1990 and continuing non-compliance with an abatement notice post-conviction under s 80(5) of the EPA 1990. In *Canterbury CC v Ferris* [1997] Env LR D14 the High Court held that the amount set for a daily fine following conviction was a maximum penalty and that magistrates were entitled to impose a daily fine below the statutory amount. This would seem sensible and an approach that should be adopted with all environmental sentences that provide for daily fines. If not, the unusual position could arise where a conviction on sentence could be less than the daily fine imposed for non-compliance after conviction. Indeed, certain offences provide that a continuing fine will not be in excess of a fixed sum. For example, an offence under the Agriculture (Poisonous Substances) Act 1952 provides that if a contravention of a provision continues after conviction the defendant: 'shall be guilty of a further offence and liable in respect thereof to a fine *not exceeding* £10 for each day on which the contravention is so continued.'

Examples of environmental fines

In *R v Milford Haven Port Authority ('Sea Empress')* [2000] JPL 943 erroneous navigation by the **19.166** pilot caused the oil tanker 'Sea Empress' to become grounded losing a total of around 70,000 tonnes of crude oil. Milford Haven Port Authority was responsible for the pilots and the port was prosecuted by the Environment Agency under s 85(1) of the WRA 1991 and under common law for the offence of causing a public nuisance. The Port Authority pleaded guilty to the WRA offence (the public nuisance offence being left on the file) and the judge ordered a fine of £4 million plus an agreed £825,000 towards the costs of the prosecution. The defendant appealed to the Court of Appeal who reduced the fine to £750,000.

In *R v Yorkshire Water Services Ltd* [2001] EWCA 2635 Yorkshire Water Services (YWS) faced a **19.167** total of 33 counts of breaches of s 70(1) of the Water Industry Act 1991 and pleaded guilty to 17 counts (the remainder being left on the file). YWS were fined a total of £119,000 plus prosecution costs of £125,599. YWS appealed against the fines and costs and the Court of Appeal reduced the fine to £80,000. It did not disturb the costs award.

In *R v Anglian Water Services Ltd* [2003] Crim 2243 the defendant pleaded guilty to an offence **19.168** under s 85(3) of the WRA 1991 of causing sewage effluent to be discharged into the River Crouch. The magistrates committed the case to the Crown Court for sentence on the basis that the maximum sentence they could impose (£20,000) was insufficient. Crown Court fined the defendant £200,000 plus costs of £9,579.58. The Court of Appeal reduced this to £60,000.

In *R v Ferrybridge Recovery Ltd* [2003] Env Times Vol 9.2, p31, magistrates convicted the **19.169** defendant company of contravening the waste obligations under s 33 of the EPA 1990 when scrap motor vehicles, plastics, rubber, and other combustible materials were found buried and smouldering at a car breaker's yard. The fire brigade and a JCB exposed waste and hosed down smouldering scrap. The defendant was fined £5,000 and ordered to pay costs of £1,009.

Fines are imposed on the person convicted of the offence. It is unlawful for another person **19.170** to pay the fine on behalf of the defendant.

Conditional and absolute discharges

Section 12 of the PCCSA 2000 provides that where a court is of the opinion that it is **19.171** inexpedient to inflict punishment on an offender the court may make an order either discharging him absolutely or subject to the condition that he commits no offence during such period, not exceeding three years, ordered by the court. Following *R v Sanck* (1990)

12 Cr App R (S) 155, a discharge cannot, in general, be combined with a custodial sentence, community sentence, or a fine. However, under s 12(7) of the PCCSA 2000 it can be combined with a compensation, deprivation, or restitution order. Also, if an offender has been convicted of a number of offences, the court may discharge the defendant for one or more of the offences while passing another form of sentence on the remaining convictions.

19.172 In *CPC (UK) v National Rivers Authority* [1995] Env LR 121 the defendant was convicted under s 85 of the WRA 1991 of causing 168 gallons of cleaning liquid to escape and enter a water-course through a storm drain after a pipe in its milk processing plant fractured. The company was given an absolute discharge and ordered to pay the prosecution's costs.

Compensation orders

19.173 Under s 130 of the PCCSA 2000 a court, instead of or in addition to dealing with a defendant in any other way, may, on an application or otherwise, make an order requiring the defendant to pay compensation for, among other things, personal injury, loss, or damage resulting from that offence, or any other offence which is taken into consideration by the court in determining sentence. Any compensation paid shall be of an amount that the court considers appropriate, having regard to any evidence and to any representations that are made by or on behalf of the defendant or the prosecutor.

19.174 Scarman LJ stated in *R v Inwood* (1974) 60 Cr App R 70:

> Compensation orders were not introduced into our law to enable the convicted to buy them-
> selves out of the penalties of crime. [They were introduced] as a convenient and rapid means of
> avoiding the expense of resort to civil litigation when the criminal clearly has means which
> would enable the compensation to be paid.

19.175 Section 130(12) of the PCCSA 2000 states that where it is appropriate to order a fine and make a compensation order, but the offender has insufficient means to pay both, the court shall give preference to compensation. The *Magistrates' Court Sentencing Guidelines* (Magistrates' Association 2004), pp 89–90 provide information on calculating compensation. Compensation orders, together with an absolute or conditional discharge, are not intended to be punitive sentences and, under s 131(1) of the PCCSA 2000, are limited to a maximum award of £5,000. In *Davenport v Walsall MBC* [1997] Env LR 24 the court held that the normal principles applicable to compensation orders applied to statutory nuisance cases including that such orders should be confined to simple, straightforward cases. It also held that the potential difficulty in making a civil claim should have been borne in mind by the justices when exercising their discretion to make a compensation order, although the lack of civil remedy does not automatically mean that a compensation order should be made.

Deprivation orders

19.176 The court has the power, under s 143 of the PCCSA 2000, to make a deprivation (forfeiture) order where a person is convicted of an offence and the court is satisfied that any property that has been lawfully seized, or that was in his possession or under his control at the time when he was apprehended or when the summons was issued was used for the purpose of committing or facilitating the offence.

Confiscation orders

The Proceeds of Crime Act 2002 (PCA 2002) enables the Crown Court to make an order **19.177** confiscating the assets of offenders if they have been convicted of an offence in proceedings in the Crown Court. Under s 6 of the PCA 2002, the court must consider whether the defendant has a criminal lifestyle, as defined in s 75 and Sch 2. If so, the court must then decide, under s 6(4)(b), whether the defendant has benefited from his general criminal conduct. If not, the court must decide whether he has benefited from his particular criminal conduct. If the defendant has benefited from his criminal conduct then it must:

(a) decide the recoverable amount; and
(b) make a confiscation order requiring him to pay that amount.

The court must consider the criminal lifestyle provisions if the prosecutor requests this, or **19.178** if the court believes that it is appropriate. A magistrates' court does not have the power to make a confiscation order, although it may commit an offender to the Crown Court where the prosecutor requests this.

Determining sentence

Sprack's *A Practical Approach to Criminal Procedure* sets out what the court should consider **19.179** when determining sentence. It notes that, as can be seen above, the court has a number of sentencing options and that, in almost every case, it will also be influenced by:

* the type of offence (e.g. whether it is imprisonable or not); and
* by the offender (e.g. his age, his financial circumstances, whether it is a company).

It suggests that although precedent plays a role and is most often set in the Court of Appeal, **19.180** it is qualified by the following:

* that every case should turn on its own facts and that no two offenders or offences will be the same; thus, if a legal representative is assisting the court in any way it should be in general terms rather than pointing to what a court has stated in a particular case;
* that the Court of Appeal is reluctant to interfere with a sentencing court's broad discretion, and will only do so if a sentence is outside the range of sentences appropriate to the gravity of the offence after allowing for mitigating circumstances; and
* that if the defendant appeals the Court of Appeal has no power to increase sentence, although they may at times imply that they would have imposed a harsher sentence

Thresholds for custodial and community sentences

The PCCSA 2000 sets criteria or thresholds for imprisonment and community sentences. **19.181** Section 35(1) of the PCCSA 2000 states that a court shall not pass a community sentence unless it is of the opinion that the offence, or the combination of offences, was serious enough to warrant such a sentence. Under s 79 of the Act, a custodial sentence must only be given if either the offence (or combination of offences) was so serious that only a custodial sentence is justified; or it is a violent or sexual offence, and only a custodial sentence would be adequate to protect the public from the offender.

19.182   The seriousness of the offence is the sole criterion when deciding community sentences and the primary criterion in deciding whether a custodial sentence is appropriate. It also plays a significant role in determining the level of fines.

Seriousness of the offence

19.183   The Court of Appeal in *R v Howells* [1998] Crim LR 836 set out factors influencing offence seriousness that sentencers should consider for cases around the custody threshold. These include, among other things, the nature and extent of the defendant's criminal intention and of any injury or damage caused to the victim; whether the offence was premeditated or spontaneous; any provocation to which the offender was subjected; any personal injury or mental trauma suffered by the victim, particularly if permanent; any previous convictions of the offender and failure to respond to previous sentences; and whether the offence was committed on bail. It went on to set out mitigating factors such as previous good character, physical and mental disability, and whether the offender had served a custodial sentence before. Seriousness of the offence is most recently defined by s 143 of the CJA 2003, which provides that:

> In considering the seriousness of any offence, the court must consider the offender's culpability in committing the offence and any harm which the offence caused, was intended to cause or might foreseeably have caused.

Protection of the public

19.184   Although it is, hopefully, unlikely to be relevant to environmental crime, the court may rely on s 79(2) of the PCCSA 2000 to pass a custodial sentence if the offence is a violent or sexual offence, and that only such a sentence would be adequate to protect the public from harm.

Aggravating factors

19.185   There is considerable emphasis on aggravating and mitigating factors in sentencing legislation, e.g. s 81(4)(a) provides that in deciding whether to pass a custodial sentence and, if so, the length of that sentence, a court shall: 'take into account all such information as is available to it about the circumstances of the offence . . . including any aggravating or mitigating factors'.

19.186   There will be a wide number of aggravating factors to consider in any given case. Knowledge and expertise will be relevant: in *R v Duckworth* (1995) 16 Cr App Rep (S) 529 the defendant chartered surveyor was convicted of unlawful demolition of a listed building contrary to ss 7 and 9 of the Planning (Listed Buildings and Conservation Areas) Act 1990 (see Chapter 8: Land use planning). His professional experience and knowledge of matters relating to historic buildings was held to be an aggravating factor. Also, any financial benefit from committing the crime will be relevant; see *R v Jo Sims Ltd* [1993] Env LR 323.

Mitigating factors

19.187   Mitigating factors will include the defendant's means and ability to pay any fine. Section 128(1) of the PCCSA 2000 provides that before fixing the amount of any fine to be imposed on an offender who is an individual, a court shall inquire into his financial circumstances. Section 128(3) adds that:

In fixing the amount of any fine to be imposed on an offender (whether an individual or other person), a court shall take into account the circumstances of the case including, among other things, the financial circumstances of the offender so far as they are known, or appear, to the court.

This requirement often leaves sentencing courts in the unenviable position of seeking to impose what may be regarded as an appropriate fine for an offence, but being obliged to take account of the impecunious offender. Further examples of aggravating and mitigating factors in relation to environmental offences are contained in the extract from the Magistrates' Association publication: *Costing the Earth* (2002) set out in para 19.193 below.   **19.188**

Magistrates' Court Sentencing Guidelines (2004)

The *Magistrates' Court Sentencing Guidelines* (2004) published by the Magistrates Association   **19.189** set out the structure to be used for determining sentences. It states that magistrates must always start the sentencing process by taking full account of all the circumstances of the offence and making a judicial assessment of the seriousness category into which it falls and that it is important that the court makes clear the factual basis on which the sentence is based. It notes that in every case, the Criminal Justice Act 1991 (CJA 1991) requires sentencers to consider:

- is a discharge or a fine appropriate?
- is the offence serious enough for a community penalty?
- is it so serious that only custody is appropriate?

The format of the sentencing guidelines are: **19.190**

(a) Consider the seriousness of the offence: magistrates must always make an assessment of seriousness.

(b) Consider aggravating and mitigating factors: if the offence was racially or religiously aggravated, the court must treat that fact as an aggravating factor under s 153 of the PCCSA 2000.

(c) Take a preliminary view of seriousness then consider offender mitigation: when an initial assessment of the seriousness of the offence has been formed, consider the offender. Any offender mitigation that the court accepts must lead to some downward revision of the provisional assessment of seriousness, although this revision may be minor.

(d) Consider your sentence: the law requires the court to consider reducing the sentence for a timely guilty plea. Credit for a timely guilty plea may result in a sentencing reduction of up to one-third but the precise amount of credit will depend upon the facts of each case and a last minute plea of guilty may attract only a minimal reduction.

(e) Decide your sentence: remember that magistrates have a duty to consider the award of compensation in all appropriate cases, and to give reasons if compensation is not awarded.

Environmental sentencing guidelines

There is a wide range of sentencing guidance; all of which aims to ensure that environmental   **19.191** sentencing is appropriate. In 2000, the Sentencing Advisory Panel issued Advice to the Court of Appeal on Environmental Sentencing. In *R v Milford Haven Port Authority* the Court of Appeal concluded that it could not usefully do more than draw attention to factors laid down in the earlier health and safety case of *R v Howe*. Further guidance was provided by the Court of Appeal in *R v Friskies Petcare*.

19.192   In May 2001, the Magistrates' Association produced guidelines entitled: *Fining of Companies for Environmental and Health and Safety Offences* to supplement the Court of Appeal decisions in *R v Howe* and *R v Friskies Petcare*. The guidelines were approved by the Court of Appeal in *R v Anglian Water Services Ltd* and are set out in full in Appendix 4. The Magistrates' Association issued further guidelines in November 2002 entitled: *Sentencing for Wildlife Trade and Conservation Offences*.

Costing the Earth; guidance for sentencers

19.193   The Magistrates' Association also publishes extensive training and guidance on environmental sentencing entitled: *Costing the Earth* contains general principles on environmental sentencing as well as over 50 case studies that consider those principles. It is regularly updated and is fully available online at www.magistrates-association.org.uk. Sections 3 and 4 of the guidance, excluding footnotes, are reproduced below.

COSTING THE EARTH: GUIDANCE FOR SENTENCERS

3 ASSESSING THE SERIOUSNESS OF ENVIRONMENTAL OFFENCES

The next two sections of this guidance analyse and elaborate on some of the principles set out in the *Fining of Companies* guidelines (see section 20). There are two critical parts in determining a defendant's sentence in environmental cases:

- assessing the seriousness of the offence (discussed in this section), and
- considering other sentencing criteria e.g. ability to pay fine (section 4).

There will be areas of overlap in the two stages and it may well be necessary to review seriousness when analysing other sentencing criteria. As the *Fining of Companies* guidelines suggest, an early assessment of seriousness must be carried out to determine key factors such as whether the matter should be committed to the Crown Court for sentencing and what type of sentence should be decided upon. Any analysis should also be consistent with the approach taken in the *Magistrates' Court Sentencing Guidelines* updated in January 2004 which is to:

- consider the seriousness of the offence;
- consider aggravating and mitigating factors;
- take a preliminary view of seriousness, then consider offender mitigation;
- consider the sentence; and finally
- decide the sentence.

Assessing seriousness of environmental offences requires a detailed analysis of the direct and immediate harm as well as the wider environmental consequences, potential impacts and, in some instances the risk of harm arising from an offence.

Environmental impacts will not only include direct impacts e.g. water pollution, loss of species or contamination of land, but also indirect impacts including those that may be more readily identified as social or economic impacts e.g. health problems from air pollution, the decline in local amenity through litter, fly-posting, graffiti and other vandalism, loss of work due to ill health and commercial advantage by non-compliance.

The culpability of the defendant should also be assessed e.g. the extent of involvement in crime, motivation and co-operation with regulatory authorities. Highlighting the aggravating and mitigating circumstances will help clarify the seriousness of an environmental offence. However, it is important to ignore the now outdated assertion that environmental offences are not 'real crimes' due to their strict liability nature (see section 3.8).

3.1 The immediate and direct impact of environmental crime

Section 143(1) of the Criminal Justice Act 2003 (CJA) provides that in considering the seriousness of any offence, the court must consider . . . any harm the offence caused, was intended to cause or might foreseeably have caused. This can be assessed in terms of the core environmental, social and economic aspects of sustainable development. The actual harm arising may have included:

- **Environmental impact (protection and use of resources).** This could include dead fish poisoned from polluted water; loss of threatened or endangered species or their habitats that may be irreplaceable; contamination of land, air or water by a pollutant; and poor plant health due to air pollution.

  It is important to determine the extent of damage. How many fish were killed? Did the pollution travel far downstream? Were invertebrates and other wildlife affected?
- **Social impact.** Consider the link between abandoned vehicles and neighbourhood effect. There is a tendency for offences such as graffiti, fly-posting and vandalism to attract similar offences and result in a downward spiral in the quality of the local environment and neighbourhood. This is the 'broken windows' theory: that one broken window leads to many more.

  Consider also the impact of nuisance and the mental health of victims, food poisoning and physical health problems, air pollution and health problems, polluted waters and an inability to fish, the pollution effect on amenity values, difficulty in remediation of blighted areas, the impacts of graffiti decreasing aesthetic value, regeneration, renovation, poverty and concentration of factors that cause environmental deterioration.
- **Economic impact.** Replenishing fish stocks, effect on businesses and employment, the cost of crop damage by air pollution, the impact on tourism, costs of clean-up, cost of loss of time at work due to health impacts, re-offending and the savings from not carrying out the work activities necessary to prevent the crime occurring in the first place.

3.2 The wider effects in environmental, social and economic terms

Consider all the effects in environmental, social and economic terms including the bigger picture, diffuse impact, cumulative effects and long-term effects.

- **Bigger picture (global, transboundary).** Is there a link between a fishing offence and the global fishing problem of extinction of species and loss of fishing stocks? Consider threatened species and global status of species. Is there a link between water pollution from pesticides or oil and the contamination of global waters; or air emissions and transboundary air pollution and global warming?
- **Diffuse impact.** Air pollution can have a small impact over a large area, so too can water pollution in rivers, the sea and on beaches, including the use of pesticides leaching into watercourses. Radioactivity is likely to have a diffuse effect.
- **Cumulative effects.** These can include the impact on health from multiple sources of pollution such as a high number of factories in one area, fly-tipping encouraging others to dump waste in the locality.
- **Long-term effects.** Health impact from radiation or asbestos, persistent pesticides in soil, irretrievable loss of natural resources (unsustainable fishing by over-harvesting, over abstraction of water, loss of habitat by the destruction of micro organisms, loss of groundwater through a pollutant).

3.3 Human fatality, serious injury or ill health

Take into account any human fatality, serious injury or ill health as a consequence of the defendant's actions e.g. loss of limb or loss of sight or persistent respiratory problems from air pollution, carcinogens, ease of access (inadequate security) to toxic chemicals or the spread of disease.

3.4 Health of flora and fauna

Has animal health or flora health been adversely affected? Were endangered species killed, injured by the offence? Were they poisoned by pesticides? Has air pollution affected crops and plants or has there been destruction of trees and woodland?

3.5 Assessing the potential harm and risks taken

It is important to assess the potential harm and the risks taken by the defendant. Section 143(1) of the CJA provides that seriousness should include the harm intended to be caused or might foreseeably have been caused. Lack of actual damage does not render the offence merely technical, it may still be serious if there has been risk. In considering risk of harm also consider:

- **Negligence.** Has there been a risk of harm to workers, the local community or local environment through negligent action?
- **Characteristics of pollutant.** Is the pollutant highly toxic? Consider, for example, radioactivity and the potential impact on human and environmental health. High toxicity and pervasiveness means there is a larger risk and potential harm to be aware of, possibility of the spread of disease in plants, animals or humans.

3.6 State of mind of the defendant

Section 143(1) of the CJA provides that in considering the seriousness of any offence, the court must consider, among other things, the culpability of any offence caused. It is therefore important to take account or consider the state of mind of the defendant, even for strict liability offences. For instance, was the offence the result of:

- **Intentional action.** Was there a deliberate breach of the law e.g. by deliberately disposing of a pollutant in river; collecting wildlife specimens (rare species, bird eggs) for personal pleasure and no regard for conservation implications; fly-tipping waste; or joyriding and then burning out vehicles.
- **Recklessness.** Has the defendant's behaviour lead to the offence e.g. by not preventing pollutant run off from entering a water body.
- **Carelessness/lack of awareness (mitigates offence)** e.g. being unaware that discharge is polluting a water course.

Environmental offences of strict liability

Most environmental offences are strict liability offences. The prosecution has no need to prove fault or guilty knowledge. This is quite deliberate and is due, in part, to the heavy obligation on operators due to the inherent risks in the processes and materials they handle. It is also to re-enforce the seriousness of the offence and the potential to cause long-term and irreparable harm.[1] In the Court of Appeal case of *Environment Agency v Milford Haven Port Authority (The Sea Empress)* [2000] 2 Cr App R (S) 423 Lord Bingham CJ noted that:

---

[1] The relevance of strict liability and its relationship with environmental crimes is considered by Dr Carolyn Abbot (2004) in *Friend or foe? Strict liability in English environmental licensing regimes*. Environmental Law and Management, Vol. 16, issue 2. Lawtext Publishing: Witney, Oxon.

'Parliament creates an offence of strict liability because it regards the doing or not doing of a particular thing as itself so undesirable as to merit the imposition of criminal punishment on anyone who does or does not do that thing irrespective of that party's knowledge, state of mind, belief or intention.'

The extent of the blameworthiness can increase or decrease depending on any mitigating and aggravating circumstances, however any attempt by the defendant to assert that strict liability environmental crimes are not 'real crimes' should be ignored. In *R v Anglian Water Services* [2003] EWCA 2243 a case involving significant water pollution from a sewage discharge, Lord Justice Scott Baker commented that:

'We would not categorise breaches of section 85(3) [of the Water Resources Act 1991] of the nature that occurred in this case as being of a non-criminal character, albeit the offence is one of strict liability. The environment in which we live is a precious heritage and it is incumbent on the present generation to preserve it for the future. . . . Parliament has imposed on people like the appellant a heavy burden to do everything possible to ensure that they do not cause pollution.'

3.7 Relationship with regulatory authorities and attitude to regulation

What is the defendant's attitude towards, and co-operation with the regulatory authorities, regulatory regimes or his/her own workforce?

- **Advice from enforcing authority.** Has there been complete disregard when an enforcing authority advises how to abate pollution?
- **Warnings from enforcing authority.** Has there been a failure to take notice when warned of committing an offence?
- **Warnings from workforce.** Have the workforce notified the employer of unsafe work methods on previous occasions?
- **Disregarding an abatement notice.** Has the polluter taken steps to abate the pollution once an abatement notice has been served?
- **Lack of co-operation.** Has there been a failure to turn up for interviews, or to court? Is there a bad attitude towards regulatory authority?
- **Ignorance/disregard of environmental standards.** How far below the relevant statutory environmental standard has the defendant's behaviour actually fallen?

3.8 Licensing

What is the defendant's licensing status?

- **Breach of Licence.** Has the defendant been carrying on activities outside his or her licence conditions?
- **No licence.** Is there a requirement for a licence for carrying out the offending activities?
- **Fraudulent papers.** Has the defendant been operating on fraudulent licences or other papers such as a stolen driving licence.

3.9 Economic gain for the defendant

Consider the economic gain to the defendant such as:

- **Profit.** This may include demolishing a listed building and profiting from the development; charging a fee for collecting waste and then dumping it illegally, illegally trading in wildlife specimens.
- **Cost saving.** Has the defendant illegally disposed of his/her own waste to avoid disposal costs.
- **Neglecting preventative methods.** This may include inadequate training for workers handling toxic substances; failing to install telemetry technology which could have detected equipment failure, failing to use preventative equipment when necessary e.g. air filters, noise insulation or protective gear.

- **Avoiding licence fees.** Carrying out an act that requires a licence without obtaining one or not operating within the conditions imposed by such a licence.
- **Tax and Duties evasion.** Import and/or export duties that have been avoided.

3.10 Offence pattern

Section 143(2) of the CJA provides that when assessing seriousness of an offence a court must take into account relevant previous convictions as an aggravating factor, or if the offence was committed while on bail. It is therefore important to consider the defendant's offence pattern and whether there is there evidence of:

- **Re-offending.** Previous conviction for the same offence e.g. repeat conviction of fly-tipping.
- **Repeat offending.** Where the defendant has broken the law at least once but has not received a formal sanction from the court.
- **Unrelated previous offences.** Have there been other non-environmental, but possibly anti-social offences committed by the defendant?
- **Isolated incident.** Was the offence a one-off incident?

3.11 Abatement and reparation

Seriousness should consider the need for any reparation, clean up and restoration work necessary to be undertaken either by the regulatory authority, the defendant or any other party, such as the emergency services. For example, the resources used to clean up contaminated land or water or the cost to replenish fish stock. Alternatively, it may have been necessary to call the fire brigade to a dangerous incident. The actual cost should also be considered later in setting any sentence or level of fine. The cost of abatement and reparation will also need to be considered when determining and deciding the type of sentence to hand down and the level of any fine.

3.12 Mitigation

Are there any mitigating circumstances?

- **Isolated incident.** Is there a good past record of the defendant? Was this a one-off offence or is there evidence of repeat offending?
- **Awareness.** Did the defendant genuinely and reasonably lack awareness or understanding of the regulations specific to the activity in which he was engaged.
- **Guilty plea.** Was there a timely plea of guilt by the defendant?
- **Co-operation.** Has there been co-operation with the enforcing authority.
- **Role in the offending activity.** Did the defendant play a relatively minor role in the offence.
- **Personal position.** Is the defendant suffering genuine hardship or adverse social/personal circumstances?
- **Tackling the problem.** Were steps taken to remedy the problem as soon as possible?

4 SENTENCING CRITERIA FOR ENVIRONMENTAL OFFENCES

Many environmental offences carry maximum summary penalties of £20,000. A few offences, such as failure to comply with directions of authorised persons following a marine accident (s 139 of the Merchant Shipping Act 1995) have a maximum penalty of £50,000. And, exceptionally the discharge of oil from a ship into certain UK waters has a maximum summary penalty of £250,000 under s 131 of the Merchant Shipping Act 1995 (as amended).

The second stage of environmental sentencing builds on the assessment of seriousness. When deciding on the sentence for an environmental crime there are a range of criteria to consider such as the seriousness of the offence, the purpose of sentencing, the defendant's ability to pay, any economic gain, the polluter pays principle, any abatement and prosecution costs, whether a fine is the most appropriate sentence and the ability of referral to the Crown Court. Each of these is considered below.

4.1 Seriousness

The extent of the damage, risk and culpability, etc of the defendant should be reflected in the level of any fine. Seriousness is considered in detail in section 3 above.

4.2 Refer to Crown Court?

Magistrates may commit for sentence to the Crown Court if they feel that their sentencing provisions are insufficient. The *Fining of Companies* guidelines suggest that, when dealing with an either way offence, one of the first questions to be asked is whether the seriousness of the offence is such that the matter should be committed to the Crown Court where many environmental offences attract an unlimited fine and/or a custodial sentence e.g. in *R v Humphrey* (2002), a case prosecuted in Isleworth Crown Court under the Customs and Excise Management Act 1979, the court recognised the serious nature of damage in trafficking endangered birds of prey. The trial resulted in a custodial sentence of over 6 years.

4.3 Statutory purpose of sentencing

Under the proposed s 142(1) of the CJA, any court dealing with an offender in respect of his offence must have regard to the following purposes of sentencing:

(a)   the punishment of offenders,
(b)   the reduction of crime (including its reduction by deterrence),
(c)   the reform and rehabilitation of offenders,
(d)   the protection of the public, and
(e)   the making of reparation by offenders to person affected by their offences.

For environmental sentences, this may have shifted the focus of the earlier approach of seeking 'just deserts' by emphasising the role of reduction (prevention by deterrence) and the protection of the public. The preventative, precautionary and polluter pays principles are considered in section 2.

4.4 Type of sentence

The Sentencing Advisory Panel in its advice to the Court of Appeal (2000) suggested that when determining sentences for environmental crimes, the starting point should usually be a fine. However, in the light of the greater options for community orders under the Criminal Justice Act 2003, it is important to consider whether another form of sentencing, rather than a financial penalty, is more appropriate? For example, a custodial sentence, a discharge or community service. Should compensation be considered?

In *R v Sissen* [2000] All ER (D) 2193, Mr Justice Ouseley stated that:

> '. . . the law is clear as to where the interests of conservation lie. These are serious offences. An immediate custodial sentence is usually appropriate to mark their gravity and the need for deterrence.'

4.5 Economic gain

The revenue gained or cost saved from the crime should be reflected in the sentence. An offender should not profit from the crime. For example, avoiding landfill tax and dumping the waste illegally should be punished so that the sentence is higher than the landfill tax otherwise lawfully paid. If not, there is no deterrent because it is cheaper to dump the waste illegally and run the risk of paying the fines.

4.6 Ability to pay

The fine imposed should reflect the means of the individual or company concerned. A fine for a multinational company with a multi-million pound turnover will not have the same economic impact as it will on a small local company or an individual.

The criteria for sentencing laid down in *R v Howe & Son (Engineers) Ltd* [1999] 2 AER 249 and discussed in detail in the Magistrates' Association *Fining of Companies* guidelines (see section 20) is important. It emphasises that fines need to be large enough to bring the message home not only to the management of an organisation but also to its shareholders. The adverse publicity accompanying substantial fines may also help to change corporate behaviour. Under *Howe*, magistrates are entitled to conclude that a company is able to pay any fine imposed unless it has supplied financial information to support any representations to the contrary before the hearing. The *Howe* guidelines also provide that a deliberate and/or regular breach of legislation with a view to profit seriously aggravates the offence.

In the case of a large company, the fine should be substantial enough to have a real economic impact and certainly be higher than the cost of complying with the requirements. For small companies, the fine must be higher than the cost of complying with the requirements. However, it is necessary to bear in mind that a large fine could make it difficult to improve conditions in order to comply with the law. Or, the company may have to close down which would lead to unemployment and affect the local economy.

The closure of a company should be avoided unless it seems as the only way to stop what is already a track record of serious repeat offending. Should a re-offending company be in business at all, bearing in mind that prosecutions are there to protect employees as well as the public and the environment?

4.7 The Preventative and Polluter Pays principles

Emphasis should be given to the preventative and polluter pays principles (section 2.3) above. In particular, that the full cost of abatement, restoration, reparation is covered in the overall sentence/costs award. For example, the resources used to clean up contaminated land or water or the cost to replenish fish stock.

4.8 Prosecution costs

The level of the fine should reflect the process of negotiation and discussion, repeated requests to abate and site visits are all costly to the public purse. It is important to reflect this as part of the Polluter Pays Principle. An uncooperative defendant increases the costs of the enforcing authority. The general rule that prosecution costs should be proportionate to the sentence[2] will not cause concern, if the full severity of the offence is demonstrated to the court.

4.9 Useful guidance and legal advice

Finally, it is important to note that the prosecution can draw the court's attention towards guideline cases. There is now a developing body of summary environmental case decisions in regular publications such as the *Environment Times*, which publishes over 100 environmental sentencing case summaries on waste, water and air pollution matters in each edition.[3] As suggested in *Fining of Companies*, magistrates should seek the advice of their legal advisers on sentencing options and guidelines in all cases.

---

[2] *R (Dove) v Northallerton Magistrates' Court* [1999] EWHC Admin 499
[3] *Environment Times* is published by Beckhouse Media Ltd: Chorley, Lancs.

Proposed statutory purpose of sentencing

The proposed statutory purpose of sentencing contained in the CJA 2003, and due to enter **19.194** into force in 2006, expands on the traditional purpose of criminal punishment and seeking 'just deserts'. Section 142(1) of the Act provides that any court dealing with an offender in respect of his offence must have regard to the following purposes of sentencing:

(a) the punishment of offenders;
(b) the reduction of crime (including its reduction by deterrence);
(c) the reform and rehabilitation of offenders;
(d) the protection of the public; and
(e) the making of reparation by offenders to persons affected by their offences.

Each of these purposes is likely to be relevant for many environmental crimes.

E   REMEDIATION

One of the primary concerns with pollution offences is the environmental harm that is **19.195** caused. Many of the statutory offences provide for the remediation of a site or activity, to help ensure that the environment is returned to an acceptable state after the polluting activity has occurred.

IPC

Under s 26 of the EPA 1990, where a defendant has been convicted of an offence and the **19.196** court considers it within its power to remedy the harm done, the court has the power to order him to take specified steps, within a certain time, to carry out the remedial work.

Waste

Under s 59 of the EPA 1990 where waste has been unlawfully deposited the Environment **19.197** Agency or local authority may require the land to be cleaned up.

Contaminated land

Under s 78E of the EPA 1990, once a site has been identified as contaminated land the **19.198** relevant authority is under a duty to prepare a 'remediation notice'. However, this is prior to any prosecution, which only arises on a failure to comply with the remediation notice itself.

Statutory nuisance

Under s 81(3) of the EPA 1990, where an abatement notice has not been complied with a **19.199** local authority, whether or not they take proceedings for the offence, may abate the nuisance and do whatever may be necessary in execution of the notice. Section 81(4) provides that any expenses reasonably incurred may be recovered from the person causing the nuisance.

GMOs

Under s 161 of the EPA 1990, the Secretary of State has power to order works to be done to **19.200** remedy any harm caused by unlawful GMO releases.

Water

19.201   Under s 161 of the WRA, the Environment Agency can require works to be done to deal with any poisonous, noxious, or polluting material that either has entered, or appears to it to be likely to enter, controlled waters. A works notice will be served on the person who caused or knowingly permitted the matter to enter the waters.

F   PRIVATE PROSECUTIONS

19.202   If a prosecutor does not wish to prosecute an environmental offence, then it is open for an individual or organization to bring a private prosecution. Section 6(1) of the POA 1985 provides that: 'nothing in this Part shall preclude any person from instituting any criminal proceedings or conducting any criminal proceedings'.

19.203   However, under s 6(2) of the POA 1985, the Director of Public Prosecutions (DPP) may take over the conduct of the proceedings at any time either to pursue the case more efficiently or to discontinue the proceedings. In *R v DPP ex p Duckenfield* [2000] 1 WLR 55 the court held that the DPP policy to only take over conduct of a case to discontinue proceedings on evidential grounds where there was clearly no case to answer complied with s 6(1) of the POA 1985. The case of *R v Anglian Water Services Ltd* was a private prosecution.

G   A–Z OF ENVIRONMENTAL CRIMES

19.204   There is a wide range of environmental crimes that are currently included in *Costing the Earth*. This section aims to highlight the extent of regulatory control of the environment through the criminal law. This is not an exhaustive list and many of the offences are considered in detail elsewhere in the book.

Air quality

19.205   Section 2 of the Clean Air Act 1993 prohibits dark smoke from industrial/trade premises with a maximum penalty of a £20,000 fine on summary conviction. Section 6(1) of the EPA 1990 provides that no person shall carry on a prescribed process except under an authorization granted by the enforcing authority. Under s 23 of the EPA 1990, it is an offence to contravene s 6(1) with a maximum penalty on summary conviction of a £20,000 fine and/or three months' imprisonment, and unlimited fine and/or two years' imprisonment following conviction on indictment.

Animal health

19.206   Under the Products of Animal Origin (Import and Export) Regulations 1996 no person shall import any product of animal origin except at a border inspection post. There is a maximum penalty on summary conviction of a £5,000 fine and/or three months' imprisonment, and an unlimited fine and/or two years' imprisonment following conviction on indictment.

Fisheries

Section 2(4) of the Salmon and Freshwater Fisheries Act 1975 creates offences of unlawful **19.207** fishing, disturbing spawning fish, and obstruction of a water bailiff. There are various maximum penalties including on summary conviction a £5,000 fine and/or three months' imprisonment and an unlimited fine and/or two years' imprisonment on indictment

Council Regulation (EEC) 2847/93 and the Sea Fishing (Enforcement of Community Control **19.208** Measures) Order 2000 (SI 2000/51) contain offences relating to unlawful sea fishing and false landing declarations with a maximum penalty on summary conviction of a £50,000 fine and an unlimited fine following conviction on indictment.

Genetically Modified Organisms

Section 111 of the EPA 1990 provides that no person shall import, acquire, release, or market **19.209** GMOs except with the Secretary of State's consent. Contravention attracts a maximum penalty on summary conviction of a £20,000 fine and/or six months' imprisonment or an unlimited fine and/or five years' imprisonment following conviction on indictment.

Health and Safety

Section 15(1) of the Health and Safety at Work etc. Act 1974 (HSWA 1974) enables the **19.210** Secretary of State to make health and safety regulations. Section 33 of the HSWA 1974 provides that it is an offence to contravene any health and safety regulations with a maximum penalty on summary conviction of £5,000 fine and an unlimited fine and/or two years' imprisonment following conviction on indictment

Section 2(1) of HSWA 1974 provides that it is the duty of every employer to ensure, so far as is **19.211** reasonably practicable, the health, safety, and welfare of all his employees with a maximum penalty on summary conviction of £20,000 fine, and an unlimited fine and/or two years' imprisonment following conviction on indictment

Section 16(2) of the Food and Environmental Protection Act 1985 empowers ministers **19.212** to make regulations under the Act. Under s 16(12) a person, who, without reasonable excuse, contravenes any regulations made under the Act shall be guilty of an offence with a maximum penalty on summary conviction of a £5,000 fine and an unlimited fine on indictment.

Land use and public space

Under s 3(1) of the Dogs (Fouling of Land) Act 1996, if a dog defecates at any time on **19.213** designated land and a person in charge of the dog at that time fails to clear it up that person is guilty of an offence with a maximum penalty on summary conviction of a £1,000 fine.

Under Pt VII of the Town and Country Planning Act 1990 (TCPA 1990): it is, among other **19.214** things, an offence to fail to comply with a notice served by a planning authority that relates to unauthorized development or breach of planning conditions with various maximum penalties on summary conviction of up to £20,000 fine and an unlimited fine following conviction on indictment.

Sections 197 to 214 of the TCPA 1990 cover Tree Preservation Orders (TPO). A TPO is a means **19.215** by which individual trees, groups of trees, or woodlands may be protected from damage.

Under s 210 of the Act any person who, in contravention of a TPO and without consent of the local planning authority, cuts down, uproots, or wilfully destroys a tree commits an offence with a maximum penalty on summary conviction of a £20,000 fine and an unlimited fine following conviction on indictment.

Pollution prevention and control

19.216   Part I of the EPA 1990 governs the system of Integrated Pollution Control (IPC) and the related system of Local Authority Air Pollution Control (LA-APC), although this is due to be fully repealed and superseded by the Pollution Prevention and Control regime introduced by the Pollution Prevention and Control Act 1999. The aim is to have the new regime in place by 2007. See further Chapter: 11: Pollution prevention and control.

19.217   Section 6(1) of the EPA 1990 provides that no person shall carry on a prescribed process except under an authorization granted by the enforcing authority. Under s 23 of the EPA 1990, it is an offence to contravene s 6(1) with a maximum penalty on summary conviction of a £20,000 fine and/or three months' imprisonment, and unlimited fine and/or two years' imprisonment following conviction on indictment.

Public nuisance

19.218   It is a common law offence, triable either way, for a person to cause public nuisance. The maximum penalty on summary conviction is a £5,000 fine and/or three months' imprisonment. The sentence on indictment is at the discretion of the court although it should not be disproportionate to the offence.

19.219   Public nuisance covers a wide range of activities such as selling food unfit for human consumption or as in *R v Shorrock* [1994] QB 279 using land for an acid-house party. In *Attorney-General v PYA Quarries Ltd* [1957] 2 QB 169 the Court of Appeal expressed approval of the definition of public nuisance found in *Stephen's Digest of Criminal Law* that:

> A common nuisance is an act not warranted by law or an omission to discharge a legal duty which act or omission obstructs or causes inconvenience or damage to the public in the exercise of rights common to all of His Majesty's subjects.

19.220   Usually it is local authorities who, under s 222 of the Local Government Act 1972, may start proceedings in their own name in the interests of the inhabitants of their areas. In *Wandsworth LBC v Railtrack plc* [2001] Env LR 441 the local authority successfully claimed damages for the nuisance caused by pigeons roosting under a railway bridge owned by the defendant. The Attorney-General can also bring proceeding on behalf of the public. Private individuals do not, as a general rule, have standing in proceedings in respect of a public nuisance, unless they have suffered special damage over and above other members of the public: see *Gouriet v Union of Post Office Workers* [1978] AC 435. There is a requirement in public nuisance that the damage should be suffered by a section of the community. However, in *A-G v PYA Quarries* Romer LJ stated that

> It is not necessary, in my judgment, to prove that every member of the classes has been injuriously affected; it is sufficient to show that a representative cross-section of the class has been so affected for an injunction to issue.

It is possible for the same set of circumstances to be both a public and private nuisance, **19.221** although there is no direct link between the two. However, despite its criminal nature, public nuisance remedies may include an injunction to prevent harm or damage arising and damages may be awarded to a particular person in the community that has suffered damage over and above the other inhabitants.

The Licensing Act 2003 introduces a completely new regime for liquor licensing, transferring **19.222** the primary responsibility for determining and granting licences from the magistrates' court to local authorities. The Act sets four objectives to be pursued by local authorities in carrying out their licensing functions. Section 4(2) of the Licensing Act 2003 states that the licensing objectives for local authorities are:

• the prevention of crime and disorder;
• public safety;
• the prevention of public nuisance; and
• the protection of children from harm.

There is no definition of public nuisance in the Act. When debating the Bill it was argued **19.223** that public nuisance should follow its common law meaning, although this was criticized by some members in the House of Lords.

The Anti-social Behaviour Act 2003 creates a range of new offences that attempt to tackle **19.224** anti-social behaviour. The Home Office publication: *A Guide to the Anti-Social Behaviour Orders and Acceptable Behaviour Contracts* (2003) defines anti-social behaviour as any behaviour that causes or is likely to cause harassment, alarm, or distress to one or more people not in the same household as the perpetrator and can take the form of: graffiti, abusive and intimidating language, excessive noise, litter, drunken behaviour, and dealing drugs. Part 6 of the Act relates to the environment. Section 40 provides that in the closing of noisy premises the chief executive officer of the relevant local authority may make a closure order in relation to premises to which this section applies if he reasonably believes that: 'a public nuisance is being caused by noise coming from the premises; and the closure of the premises is necessary to prevent that nuisance.'

As with the Licensing Act 2003 there is no definition of public nuisance. **19.225**

Radioactive substances

Section 6 of the Radioactive Substances Act 1993 provides that no person shall keep or **19.226** use radioactive material unless he is registered or exempt from registration. Under s 7(6) of the Act, any person who contravenes s 6 shall be guilty of an offence with a maximum penalty on summary conviction of a £20,000 fine and/or six months' imprisonment, and an unlimited fine and/or five years' imprisonment following conviction on indictment.

Statutory nuisance

Part III of the EPA 1990 codifies the law on statutory nuisances including smoke, dust, smell, **19.227** accumulations, etc., which are a health or pollution risk. If a local authority is satisfied that a statutory nuisance exists the local authority shall serve an abatement notice. Section 80(4) of the EPA 1990 provides that if a person on whom an abatement notice is served, contravenes or fails to comply with any requirement or prohibition imposed by the notice, without reasonable excuse, he shall be guilty of an offence with a maximum penalty on summary conviction of a £20,000 fine, see Chapter 18: Statutory nuisance.

Waste

19.228   Part II of the EPA 1990 covers the regulation of waste and provides waste-related offences. The waste management licensing regime was introduced by the Waste Management Licensing Regulations 1994. Section 33(1) of the EPA 1990 provides that a person shall not treat, keep, dispose of, or deposit controlled waste except under and in accordance with a waste management licence. Under s 33(6) of the Act, a person who contravenes s 33(1) or any condition of a waste management licence commits an offence with a maximum penalty on summary conviction of a £20,000 fine and/or six months' imprisonment, and an unlimited fine and/or two years' imprisonment following conviction on indictment. Note also the new provisions under the CNEA 2005.

19.229   Section 3 (1) of the Prevention of Damage by Pests Act 1949 provides that an occupier of land must notify the authority in writing if he becomes aware of rats or mice infestation. Under s 3(4) of the Act, failure to give notice is an offence with a maximum penalty on summary conviction of a £250 fine.

19.230   Section 79(1)(e) of the EPA 1990 (the statutory nuisance provisions) provides that accumulations or deposits that are prejudicial to health or a nuisance, constitute a statutory nuisance. Under the provisions there is a maximum penalty on summary conviction of a £20,000 fine, see Chapter 18: Statutory nuisance.

19.231   Section 89(1) of the EPA 1990 states that there is a duty on specified authorities and persons to ensure that their land is, so far as practicable, kept clear of litter and refuse. Under s 91 of the Act, members of the public may take legal action to have litter removed from certain public areas. If magistrates are satisfied that a complaint has been made out, they may make a litter abatement order. Failure to comply, without reasonable excuse, with a s 91 order is an offence with a maximum penalty on summary conviction of a £2,500 fine and 1/20 of the fine daily thereafter if the offence continues after conviction.

19.232   Under reg 3(5) of the Producer Responsibility Obligations (Packaging Waste) Regulations 1997 (SI 1997/648), a producer has, in respect of any year, obligations to take reasonable steps to recover and recycle packaging waste and furnish a certificate of compliance. It is an offence to contravene reg 3(5) with a maximum penalty on summary conviction of a £5,000 fine, and an unlimited fine following conviction on indictment. See further Chapter 14: Waste.

Water

19.233   Under s 85(1) of the WRA 1991, a person who knowingly permits or causes any polluting matter or solid waste to enter any controlled water shall be guilty of an offence with a maximum penalty on summary conviction of a £20,000 fine and/or three months' imprisonment, and an unlimited fine and/or five years' imprisonment following conviction on indictment.

19.234   Section 118 of the Water Industry Act 1991 states that it is an offence for an occupier of trade premises to discharge trade effluent into public sewers without or in breach of a sewage undertaker's consent as to the nature and composition, the quantity and rate of the discharge, and identification of the sewers into which the discharge can be made. Conviction of an offence under the act carries a maximum penalty on summary conviction of a £5,000 fine and an unlimited fine following conviction on indictment.

Wildlife

The Wildlife and Countryside Act 1981 (WCA 1981), as amended by the Countryside and Rights of Way Act 2000, contains key nature conservation legislation. Part I of the Act provides for the protection of specific species and Pt II considers the protection of eco-systems such as SSSIs or Ramsar sites. Under ss 1(2) and 7(1) of the WCA 1981, taking, keeping, and possessing wild-caught birds is an offence while s 6(1) of the Act provides that any person that sells birds other than a bird included in Pt 1, Sch 3 shall be guilty of an offence. The Act provides for a maximum penalty on summary conviction of a £20,000 fine and/or six months' imprisonment.   **19.235**

Regulation 8(1) of the Control of Trade in Endangered Species (Enforcement) Regulations 1997 (SI 1997/1372) provides that selling and offering for sale specimens in Annex A of the Regulations without a certificate is an offence with a maximum penalty on summary conviction of a £5,000 fine and/or three months' imprisonment and an unlimited fine and/or two years' imprisonment following conviction on indictment.   **19.236**

H ENVIRONMENTAL CRIME AND HUMAN RIGHTS

Prosecutors must take into account the Human Rights Act 1998 when prosecuting. Art 6(1) of the European Convention on Human Rights provides that: 'Everyone is entitled to a fair and public hearing within a reasonable time by an independent and impartial tribunal established by law.'   **19.237**

One area that has the potential to cause a breach is where there is delay in prosecuting a case and then progressing that case once a summons has been issued. The *Attorney General's Guidelines* suggest that areas where some potentially justifiable delay may arise is where: **19.238**

- there are a large number of complex inquiries;
- there is complexity in the number of legal and evidential issues;
- there is strong public interest in prosecuting cases involving serious criminal misconduct, which may take more time to prepare; and
- expert evidence is required.

In *Bell v DPP of Jamaica* [1985] AC 937 the Privy Council set out guidelines for deciding whether delay would lead to an unfair trial. These included consideration of: **19.239**

- the length of delay;
- the prosecution's reasons to justify the delay;
- the accused's efforts to assert his rights; and
- the prejudice caused to the accused.

The question of significant delay should not arise in environmental cases that proceed by laying an information because proceedings must commence within six months of the offence occurring.   **19.240**

KEY DOCUMENTS AND MATERIALS

Magistrates Court Act 1980

Prosecution of Offenders Act 1985

Environmental Protection Act 1990

Criminal Procedure and Investigations Act 1996

Powers of the Criminal Courts (Sentencing) Act 2000

Criminal Justice Act 2003

Circular on Cautioning 18/94 Home Office

Crown Prosecution Service (1999). *Code for Crown Prosecutors*, available at www.cps.gov.uk.

Environment Agency (2003). *Spotlight on the business environmental performance*. Environment Agency: Bristol

Environment Agency (2004). *Enforcement and Prosecution Policy*. Environment Agency: Bristol

Environment Agency *Guidance for the Enforcement and Prosecution Policy* December 2004

Environment Times, quarterly journal published by Beckhouse Media Ltd, Chorley, Lancs

Environmental Audit Committee (2004). *Environmental Crime and the Courts (Sixth Report of Session 2003–04)*. TSO: London

Environmental Justice Project (2004). *Environmental Justice*. Environmental Law Foundation, Leigh Day & Co, and WWF-UK: London

HELA Circular for Local Authorities No. 45/16

Home Office (2003). *A Guide to the Anti-Social Behaviour Orders and Acceptable Behaviour Contracts*. TSO: London

Magistrates' Association (2001). *Fining of Companies for Environmental and Health and Safety Offences*. Magistrates' Association: London

Magistrates' Association (2002). *Sentencing for Wildlife Trade and Conservation Offences*. Magistrates' Association: London

Magistrates' Association (2002). *Costing the Earth: Guidance for Sentencers*. Environmental Law Foundation/Magistrates' Association: London

Magistrates' Association (2004). *Magistrates' Court Sentencing Guidelines*. Magistrates' Association: London

Attorney-General's Guidelines: Disclosure of Information in Criminal Proceedings Murphy *et al* (2005). *Blackstone's Criminal Practice*. OUP: Oxford

National Standards for Cautioning

PACE Codes of Practice

Practice Direction (Criminal Proceedings: Consolidation) [2002] 1 WLR 2870

Sentencing Advisory Panel (2000) *Advice to the Court of Appeal on Environmental Sentencing*.

Sprack, J (2004). *A Practical Approach to Criminal Procedure*. OUP: Oxford

www.environment-agency.gov.uk

20

PUBLIC LAW

A INTRODUCTION TO JUDICIAL REVIEW

Judicial review is the control of public bodies as they act and take decisions on behalf of   **20.01**
society. It operates to supervise the approach of public bodies in their functions and can

correct unlawful activity. Claims are heard by the Administrative Court section of the High Court. Judicial review is not primarily concerned with the merits of the decision, act, or omission upon which review is sought but with the decision-making process. The court does not operate as certain appeal courts, hearing the matter *de novo* (anew) and then, if it chooses, substituting its own opinion and decision in place of the lower court. It is limited to ensuring that decision-making is carried out in a lawful manner. Sedley J, in *R v Secretary of State for Transport ex p LB Richmond (No. 3)* [1995] Env LR 409, said at 415 that 'the purpose of judicial review is to ensure that government is conducted within the law.'

20.02   Because public bodies, on behalf of society, carry out so much environmental protection, judicial review plays a prominent role in environmental law. In particular, for communities and individuals who may have no other legal option available. It is also available where other legal avenues have been used but decisions, e.g. by magistrates or the Secretary of State, have been made unlawfully.

20.03   Part 54 of the Civil Procedure Rules 1998 (CPR 1998) governs the procedure for judicial review. It is supplemented by the Pt 54 Practice Direction. Part 54 and the Practice Direction are available from the Department of Constitutional Affairs (DCA) website: www.dca.gov.uk and set out in full at Appendix 5.

20.04   Part 54.1(2)(a) of the CPR 1998 provides that a claim for judicial review means a claim to review the lawfulness of:

(a)   an enactment; or
(b)   a decision, act, or failure to act in relation to the exercise of a public function.

20.05   The following sections outline the scope, set out the practice and procedure, and consider the remedies available for judicial review. For a comprehensive analysis of judicial review read Michael Fordham's Judicial Review Handbook 4/e (Hart Publishing Ltd 2005).

B   SCOPE OF JUDICIAL REVIEW

20.06   Judicial review may only be used in public law matters. For example, in land use planning it may be used to challenge a decision of the Local Planning Authority (LPA), the Secretary of State, the Planning Inspectorate, or the Local Government Ombudsman. It is a remedy of last resort, and so other options of challenge should be exhausted before considering a claim. In land use planning it will often be the only option for residents and other interested groups (i.e. groups other than the developer or the LPA/Secretary of State) to challenge unlawful planning decisions.

20.07   Because the court is, in general, not concerned with whether the decision or action under challenge was good or bad (although such matters often do form the backdrop to the challenge and cannot be completely overlooked), it is not unusual for judges to say that they would not have reached that decision themselves but the decision under challenge was lawful or was reached by a lawful procedure. Although in cases in which there may be a violation of human rights the courts have to look more closely at the substance of the decision itself.

The claimant: who can use judicial review?

Section 31(3) of the Supreme Court Act 1981 (SCA 1981) provides that someone must have **20.08** 'sufficient interest' in the matter to which the claim relates to use judicial review. Deciding what comprises sufficient interest is a mixed question of fact and law (see *R v Inland Revenue Commissioners ex p National Federation of Self Employed & Small Businesses* [1982] AC 617). It has included parents, neighbours, parish councils, non-governmental organizations, and the developer (although all other options including the appeal provisions and statutory review should be considered before resorting to judicial review). In *R v Inspectorate of Pollution ex p Greenpeace Ltd (No. 2)* [1994] 4 All ER 329 Greenpeace challenged the Inspector's permission granted to British Nuclear Fuels Ltd (BNFL), the operators of the THORP nuclear reprocessing plant, to discharge radioactive waste. On considering whether Greenpeace had sufficient interest to bring review proceedings Otton J stated:

> if I were to deny standing to Greenpeace, those it represents might not have an effective way to bring the issues before the court. There would have to be an application either by an individual employee of BNFL or a near neighbour. In this case it is unlikely that either would be able to command the expertise which is at the disposal of Greenpeace. Consequently, a less well-informed challenge might be mounted which could not afford the court the assistance it requires in order to do justice between the parties. Further, if the unsuccessful Applicant had the benefit of legal aid it might leave the respondents and BNFL without an effective remedy in costs. Alternatively, the individual (or Greenpeace) might seek to persuade Her Majesty's Attorney General to commence a relator action which (as a matter of policy or practice) he may be reluctant to undertake against a government department. Neither of these courses of action would have the advantage of an application by Greenpeace, who, with its particular expertise in environmental matters, its access to experts in relevant realms of science and technology (not to mention the law), is able to mount a carefully selected, focused, relevant and well-argued challenge.

Examples of other environment-related groups or representatives have included national **20.09** groups such as CPRE and Friends of the Earth, see e.g. *R v Secretary of State for the Environment ex p Friends of the Earth* [1996] Env LR 326; local groups that have formed a limited company as in *R v Hammersmith & Fulham BC ex p People before Profit Ltd* (1983) 45 PLCR 364 and a single resident in *Edwards v Environment Agency* [2004] EWHC 736 (Admin). In *Edwards* the court held that there had been no abuse of process even though the claimant had not been part of the formal consultation process when the Environment Agency had been considering an application for a PPC permit.

The defendant and interested parties

The defendant

The defendant in environmental claims is likely to include local authorities (as LPAs, **20.10** local environmental health or public protection teams, and any other department taking decisions or actions in relation to the environment), the Environment Agency, the Planning Inspectorate (carrying out functions on behalf of the Secretary of State including land use planning, contaminated land, PPC and other appeal functions), and the Secretary of State itself. The list is not exhaustive; recent claims have been against English Nature and the Inland Revenue. Importantly, judicial review proceedings will be against the decision-maker or active public body, not the polluter/developer, although they may have an interest in the matter.

Interested parties or interveners

20.11 Interested parties are those persons who will be affected by a challenge to the decision. They will either be cited as interested parties by the claimant or seek permission by the court to join the proceedings. There may also be parties that can assist the court in determining the matter and are therefore permitted to intervene for this purpose. In *R (Corner House Research) v Secretary of State for Trade and Industry* [2005] EWCA Civ 192 the Public Law Project were permitted to intervene by placing before the High Court judge a substantive generic submission in relation to protective costs orders.

Grounds for review

20.12 Judicial review is only concerned with the lawfulness of the decision-making process. It cannot consider the merits of any decision. It will not interfere with the discretion of a public body unless the public body has acted unlawfully. Grounds of review were broadly classified by Lord Diplock in *Council of Civil Service Unions v Minister for the Civil Service* [1985] AC 374 as unlawfulness, unreasonableness, and unfairness.

20.13 Many other classifications have been made ranging from 'all matters falling within the ground of *ultra vires*' (Lord Steyn in *Boddington v British Transport Police* [1999] 2 AC 143 commented that: 'I see no reason to depart from the orthodox view that *ultra vires* is the central principle of administrative law') to a set of codified grounds contained in Art 230 of the EU Treaty for challenging acts of EU bodies. The Art 230 grounds include lack of competence, infringement of essential procedural requirement, infringement of the EU Treaty, or any rule relating to its application and misuse of power.

20.14 In practice, whatever classification is used there is always likely to be some degree of overlap between them. The conventional grouping of unlawfulness, unreasonableness, and unfairness is outlined below with consideration of the concept of proportionality.

Unlawfulness

20.15 Unlawfulness includes, among other things, illegality, error of law, abuse of power, and breaches of the Human Rights Act 1998 (HRA 1998). Under s 2 of the Local Government Act 2000, the powers of local authorities have been significantly widened although the principle remains that they can only do what legislation allows them to do and must do what it requires them to do. They cannot be compelled to exercise their discretionary powers in a particular way (although they are under a general duty to consider whether or not to exercise any discretionary powers that they have).

20.16 For example, under s 172 of the Town and Country Planning Act 1990 (TCPA 1990) the LPA may issue an enforcement notice where it appears to it that there has been a breach of planning control and it is expedient to issue the notice. This is a very wide discretion but if it became clear that development was taking place in breach of planning control, the LPA would be under a duty to consider whether to issue an enforcement notice.

There have been a number of significant environmental judicial review decisions on **20.17** unlawfulness. In relation to environmental impact assessments (EIAs), one of the leading cases is *Berkeley v Secretary of State for the Environment* [2000] 2 AC 603, which confirmed that an environmental statement is required to be in a complete form including a non-technical summary, that token participation in EIA cases was inadequate and that the public should be properly involved in EIA-related decisions: see also Chapter 24: Environmental assessment.

In *R v Canterbury City Council ex p Springimage Ltd* [1993] 3 PLR 5 the planning committee was **20.18** told by its planning officer that it was required simply to 'have regard' to the development plan. But, under ss 54A and 70 of the TCPA 1990 (now s 38(b) of the Planning and Compulsory Purchase Act 2004) a decision whether or not to grant planning permission should have been determined 'in accordance with the development plan, unless material considerations indicate otherwise'. The court held that the first task of the decision-maker is to determine whether the proposal is in accordance with the development plan or not; simply considering the development plan did not give effect to the statutory duty and so the decision was reached unlawfully.

In *Meravale Builders Ltd v Secretary of State* [1978] 36 P&CR 87 a local authority had powers of **20.19** compulsory purchase for the provision of housing accommodation. It tried to purchase land to construct a road unconnected with any housing purpose and it was held that the purchase order was unlawful.

Local authorities have a wide power to delegate their functions to a committee, sub- **20.20** committee, or an officer under s 101 of the Local Government Act 1972 (LGA 1972). In *R v Powys County Council ex p Andrews* [1997] Env LR 170 a council officer was delegated authority to decide whether or not an environmental statement was necessary for particular development proposals; the terms of his delegation required him to consult with (Councillors) before that decision was made; he failed to consult and therefore the subsequent grant of planning permission was liable to be quashed.

Unfairness

Unfairness includes, among other things, procedural impropriety, bias, and breach of **20.21** natural justice. A decision-maker must not be biased (or appear to be biased) and in some circumstances must provide a fair hearing. These broad principles are applied by the courts to the facts of each situation, e.g. an LPA will sometimes have an interest in the decisions that it takes such as owning the land that is the subject of a planning application. In such circumstances, the courts accept that the LPA is competent to make the decision whether or not to grant permission. However, it must be particularly scrupulous in its approach to evaluating the merits of the application. In *R v Sevenoaks DC ex p Terry* [1985] 3 All ER 226 there was no bias where the LPA granted permission for a developer to develop the Council's own land. Apparent bias was regarded as irrelevant because the decision was administrative.

In *R v Teeside Development Corpn ex p Wm. Morrison Supermarket plc* [1998] JPL 23, one of the **20.22** aims of the local authority was to secure regeneration of its area. It granted planning permission for a supermarket on land that it owned. The facts showed that the authority had allowed its aim of regenerating the land to dominate its planning functions so that there had been no objective evaluation of the merits of the application before it; the decision to grant planning permission was quashed.

20.23 What is meant by a 'fair hearing' varies depending upon the circumstances. In land use planning, there are comprehensive procedural requirements designed to ensure that there is a fair hearing for concerned parties. This is achieved by, for example, publicizing applications, through consultation, and by the consideration of objections and support for particular proposals, together with an open meeting to consider the planning application, which the public may attend.

20.24 At public inquiries, the developer and the LPA will be able to present their respective cases. Other third party objectors/supporters will usually be allowed to make their objections and ask questions of the witnesses. Usually a fair hearing will involve at least knowing what the issues are that you have to address and being given the opportunity to address them.

20.25 Procedural fairness does not necessarily mean that there must be an oral hearing or public inquiry; sometimes it is sufficient if the opportunity is given to make written representations on a particular matter.

20.26 In terms of bias the case of *Porter v Magill* [2001] UKHL 67 (which related to policies promoted by Shirley Porter in selling homes for votes while a member at Westminster City Council) was applied in *Costas Georgiou v LB Enfield & ors* [2005] JPL 62 (discussed in Chapter 8: Land use planning).

20.27 In *R v Secretary of State ex p Slot* (1997) *The Times*, 11 December 1997, a landowner applied to have a footpath diverted and the local authority received an objection. It was lawfully agreed that they would deal with the objection by way of written representations. However, the authority denied the applicant access to the objector's submissions and the chance of making representations on them. The court held that this was a breach of natural justice.

20.28 Where procedures are set out in legislation or a statutory instrument they must be followed. Particular examples include:

- publicity for planning applications;
- a duty to give reasons for certain decisions; and
- the requirements relating to EIAs.

In relation to the first two of these, the court is unlikely to quash the resulting decision unless the procedural failure made, or might have made, a difference. However, if the project is one that requires an EIA then the relevant rules and procedures must be applied; and the decision will be quashed if this has not been the case. If it has been determined that an EIA is required, then the need to produce an environmental statement and a non-technical summary is clear: see *Berkeley v Secretary of State for the Environment*.

20.29 In *R (Gavin) v Haringey London Borough Council* [2003] EWHC 2591 (Admin) the LPA failed to adequately publicize a planning application to develop a new warehouse and hire centre. The claimant lived opposite the proposal but had not been notified. Two years after the grant of planning permission the claimant became aware of the development when building works commenced. Judicial review proceedings began 32 months after the original permission had been granted. The court found that there had been unfairness to the claimant in the grant of planning permission. However, it declined to quash the permission but made a declaration that the LPA had failed to comply with its publicity and EIA obligations. Importantly, the case highlights that:

- the court, in exceptional circumstances, is willing to accept proceedings outside the time limit where a sufficient explanation and prejudice has arisen;
- despite serious breaches, the court will be reluctant to quash planning permission, because to do so after a long period would be detrimental to good administration as well as causing hardship and prejudice to the developer;
- a developer is entitled to rely upon the LPA to discharge publicity requirements and was not obliged to monitor the steps taken by the LPA to comply with them; and
- third parties are entitled to rely upon information in the planning register.

Unreasonableness

A decision may be unlawful if it is so unreasonable or irrational that no sensible person **20.30** taking the decision in question could lawfully have arrived at the decision reached. Such a decision is sometimes referred to as being 'perverse' or '*Wednesbury* unreasonable' following the statement by Lord Greene MR in *Associated Provincial Picture Houses Ltd v Wednesbury Corporation* [1948] 1 KB 223 that it is 'something so absurd that no sensible person could dream it being within the powers of the authority.'

This heading applies to decisions that have no rational justification in the context of the **20.31** legislation in question. An example would be a decision to refuse planning permission because the applicant had red hair. In *R v Hinckley and Bosworth BC ex p F L Fitchett* (1996) 74 P&CR 52 the LPA refused to take into account representations because they were received four minutes outside the statutory time limit and this was held to be perverse.

Proportionality

The proportionality is used most often in judicial review when applying or considering **20.32** matters relating to EU law and the Human Rights Act 1998. The proportionality principle was defined in *B v Secretary of State for the Home Department* [2000] UKHRR 498 in which Sedley LJ explained, at 502, that:

> a measure which interferes with a Community or human right must not only be authorised by law but must correspond to a pressing social need and go no further than strictly necessary in a pluralistic society to achieve its permitted purpose; or, more shortly, must be appropriate and necessary to its legitimate aim.

There is some uncertainty whether the concept of *Wednesbury* unreasonableness has been **20.33** superseded by the principle of proportionality. In *R (Association of British Civilian Internees (Far East)) v Secretary of State for Defence* [2003] EWCA Civ 473, Dyson LJ at paras 34 and 35 commented that:

> we have difficulty in seeing what justification there now is for retaining the *Wednesbury* test, . . . but we consider that it is not for this court to perform its burial duties. . . . The continuing existence of *Wednesbury* has been acknowledged by the House of Lords on more than one occasion.

At present, it seems that judicial review ground of *Wednesbury* unreasonableness remains.

C PROCEDURE

20.34   The basic steps in making a claim for judicial review are set out below. They derive from Pt 54 of the CPR 1998 and the Pt 54 Practice Direction (see Appendix 5). There are two fundamental points to be noted about procedure:

(1) the claimant must have sufficient interest (or standing), as discussed in paras 20.8 to 20.9 above; and

(2) the application for permission to proceed must be made promptly. (This is considered below).

Pre-action procedure and considerations

A claim for judicial review must be made promptly

20.35   Part 54.5 of the CPR 1998 provides that:

(1) the claim form must be filed: (a) promptly; and (b) in any event not later than 3 months after the grounds to make the claim first arose.

(2) The time limit in this rule may not be extended by agreement between the parties.

(3) This rule does not apply when any other enactment specifies a shorter time limit for making the claim for judicial review.

20.36   In *R v Hammersmith and Fulham LB ex p Burkett* [2002] UKHL 23 the House of Lords affirmed that the three-month time limit contained in the SCA 1981, and reiterated by Pt 54.5, could not be reduced to six weeks (and therefore be more in line with statutory review) by the courts. They also confirmed that when challenging planning permissions, the three-month time limit began from the date of the grant of permission, not the date of the resolution to grant permission. However, despite the three-month time limit, it may be possible to be refused permission to claim judicial review if the application has not been made promptly, albeit within the three-month limit.

20.37   As seen in *R (Gavin) v Haringey London Borough Council* the court will consider hearing cases outside the time limit in very exceptional cases.

The letter before action

20.38   The court will expect the claimant to have written a 'letter before action' to the body being accused of acting unlawfully. The matters that should be set out in such a letter are described in the 'Judicial Review Pre-action Protocol', which came into effect in 2002 and can be found on the DCA website: www.dca.gov.uk. The letter before action must explain how the defendant (the public body) has acted illegally. A copy of the letter should also be sent to any party interested in the decision, e.g. a developer or process operator who made the original application to which the decision relates.

Commencing proceedings

Making the claim

20.39   A judicial review claim form must be completed and delivered to the High Court together with any relevant documents that support the claim. Only copies of relevant pages of documents are necessary, although, if any key documents are omitted it is likely to undermine the case. The basic content requirements of the claim form are set out in r 8.2 of the CPR 1998 in proceedings that are unlikely to involve a substantial dispute of fact. Part 54.6 of the CPR 1998 supplements this by providing that the claim must also state:

(a) the name and address of any person he considers to be an interested party;

(b) that he is requesting permission to proceed with a claim for judicial review; and

(c) any remedy (including any interim remedy) he is claiming.

Paragraphs 5.6 to 5.10 of the Pt 54 Practice Direction set out what the claim form must **20.40** include and the things that must accompany this. Paragraph 5.3 provides that where the claimant is raising any issue under the HRA 1998, the claim form must include the information in para 15 of the Pt 16 Practice Direction. This provides, among other things, that the HRA 1998 remedy must be stated in the statement of case and that the relief sought must be specified. If the claim is based on unlawfulness of another court, details of the findings must be provided. It adds that Pt 25 of the CPR 1998 sets out how to apply for an interim remedy and that the claim form must be accompanied by the documents required in the Pt 54 Practice Direction.

Serving the claim form

Part 54.7 of the CPR 1998 states that the claim form (and other documents) must be served **20.41** on the defendant and, unless the court directs otherwise, any person the claimant considers to be an interested party within seven days from the date of issue.

Progressing the proceedings

Acknowledgement of service

Any person served with the claim form who wishes to take part in the judicial review must **20.42** file an acknowledgement of service in the relevant practice form. Rule 54.8(1) provides that any acknowledgement of service must be:

(a) filed not more than 21 days after service of the claim form; and

(b) served on the claimant and, subject to r 54.7(b), any other person named in the claim form as soon as practicable and, in any event, not later than 7 days after it is filed.

Rule 54.8(4) provides that the acknowledgement of service (a) must, where the person filing **20.43** it intends to contest the claim, set out a summary of his grounds for doing so (the summary grounds of resistance); and state the name and address of any person that the person filing it considers to be an interested party; and (b) may include or be accompanied by an application for directions. Where a person served with a claim form has failed to file an acknowledgement of service he may not take part in a hearing to decide whether permission should be given unless the court allows him to do so (r 54.9(a)); however, provided he complies with r 54.14 or any other direction of the court regarding the filing and service of detailed grounds for contesting the claim this does not prevent the defendant from taking part in the substantive hearing.

Permission to bring the judicial review

20.44   The first judicial consideration of review proceedings is at the permission stage. Paragraph 8.4 of the Pt 54 Practice Direction notes that the court will generally, in the first instance, consider the question of permission on the documents submitted and without a hearing. This is likely to be carried out after about two months of the claim form being served.

20.45   If the judge decides to grant permission to proceed with the judicial review he or she will then consider any other applications made in support of the claim for judicial review. This may include an application for an injunction to prevent any immediate threat of pollution or that the hearing should be expedited.

20.46   Paragraph 8.5 of the Pt 54 Practice Direction provides that neither the defendant nor any other interested party need attend a hearing on the question of permission unless the court directs otherwise. If so, a date will be set and both the claimant and the directly affected parties will be invited to attend.

20.47   Rules 54.10 to 54.12 of the CPR 1998 set out the procedure on giving or refusing permission. First, where permission to proceed is given the court may also give directions including a stay of proceedings to which the claim relates. The court will serve the order giving or refusing permission and any direction on the claimant, the defendant and any other person who filed an acknowledgement of service.

20.48   Where the court refuses permission or grants it subject to conditions or on certain grounds, the court will serve its reasons for this with the decision. The claimant may not appeal but may request that the decision be reconsidered at a hearing. Under r 54.12(4) the request for a hearing must be filed within seven days after service of the reasons.

20.49   The oral permission hearing should, in principle, be relatively short. The standard time allowed is 20 minutes. However, in complex cases, they have been known to take several days. Importantly, the permission hearing should not be an argument of the case itself. It is designed to weed out unmeritorious and vexatious cases. In *R v Somerset CC and ARC Southern Ltd ex p Dixon* [1998] Env LR 111 Sedley J noted at 121 that:

> Public law is not at base about rights, even though abuses of power may and often do invade private rights; it is about wrongs — that is to say misuses of public power; and the courts have always been alive to the fact that a person or organisation with no particular stake in the issue or the outcome may, without in any sense being a mere meddler, wish and be well placed to call the attention of the court to an apparent misuse of public power. If an arguable case of such misuse can be made out on an application for leave, the court's only concern is to ensure that it is not being done for an ill motive. It is if, on a substantive hearing, the abuse of power is made out that everything relevant to the applicant's standing will be weighed up, whether with regard to the grant or simply to the form or relief.

Post-permission proceedings

20.50   If permission to pursue the challenge is granted, the defendant and any other person served with the claim form who wishes to contest the claim or support it on additional grounds must file and serve within 35 days:

(a) detailed grounds contesting the claim or supporting it on additional grounds; and

(b) any written evidence.

A date for a court hearing will then be set by the court office and, unless the case has been **20.51**
expedited, this could be some months later.

Evidence and disclosure

Rule 54.16 of the CPR 1998 provides that no written evidence may be relied on unless it has **20.52**
been served in accordance with any Pt 54 rule, it is under a court direction, or the court gives
permission to do so. Under r 54.17 any person may apply for permission to file evidence or
make representations to do so. This rule may be used where individuals or organizations
who may have an interest in the matter being challenged, but are not party to the proceedings wish to assist the court in a particular area. For example, in *Corner House Research* the
Public Law Project made representations to the court in relation to protective costs orders.

Under para 15 of the Pt 54 Practice Direction, the claimant must file and serve a skeleton **20.53**
argument at least 21 working days before the hearing. The defendant and any other party
wishing to make representations must do the same at least 14 days before. Paragraph 15.3
sets out what skeleton arguments must contain including a list of issues and list of legal
points to be taken.

The hearing

Judicial review hearings are conducted using written documents and legal submissions. It **20.54**
is quite rare for anyone to actually give oral evidence. Hearings may take anything from
half a day to up to one week, although one or two days are common in most cases. At
times, judgment is given immediately, although, generally it is given a few days later. In *R v
Broadcasting Complaints Commission ex p Owen* [1985] QB 1153 the Court of Appeal considered the situation where a number of reasons had been given for a decision. It held that
if the reasons given could be separated and the court was satisfied that the decision would
have been the same, then, even though one reason was unlawful, as a matter of discretion,
the court would not intervene in the decision-making process.

Decision

The court's decision-making powers are discretionary but are limited to the remedies **20.55**
available contained in Pt 54.2 of the CPR 1998. These are considered in Section D.

Appeal

There is a right of appeal against the High Court's substantive review decision to the Court of **20.56**
Appeal and the House of Lords and the general civil procedure rules under Pt 52 apply. These
are considered in Chapter 17: Civil law practice and procedure.

D   REMEDIES

20.57   The remedies available to the court in judicial review proceedings are set out in Pt 54.2 of the CPR 1998 and include:

- (a)   a mandatory order;
- (b)   a prohibiting order;
- (c)   a quashing order; or
- (d)   an injunction under s 30 of the SCA 1981 (restraining a person from acting in any office in which he is not entitled to act).

20.58   Under Pt 54.3 it is also possible to obtain a declaration and damages. However, it is important to emphasize that all remedies are discretionary and even if the grounds for review are made out, the court may still refuse a remedy.

Mandatory order

20.59   This requires the public body to carry out a particular duty.

Prohibiting order

20.60   This order prevents a public body from acting or continuing to act unlawfully. It is similar to an injunction.

Quashing order

20.61   A quashing order has the effect of quashing (annulling) the decision being challenged. This is the most common judicial review remedy. If a claim successfully quashes a decision, then under Pt 54.19(1), the court may:

- (a)   remit the matter to the decision-maker; and
- (b)   direct it to reconsider the matter and reach a decision in accordance with the judgment of the court.

20.62   Further, where the court considers that there is no purpose to be served in remitting the matter to the decision-maker it may, subject to any statutory provision, take the decision itself (Pt 54.19(3)).

Declaration

20.63   A declaration states the law on a particular issue, although Sch 1 of the CPR 1998 provides that granting a declaration requires that the question under consideration is a real question, that the person seeking the declaration has a real interest, and that there has been proper argument.

Injunction

20.64   In judicial review proceedings an injunction has the same effect as a mandatory or prohibiting order. However, an injunction may be an interim remedy while a prohibiting order may only be granted at the conclusion of the case. In *R v Secretary of State for the Environment ex p RSPB* [1997] QB 206 the RSPB sought an interim injunction but was not prepared to give a cross-undertaking in damages for the loss resulting from delay in the proposed development.

Damages

Rule 54.3(2) of the CPR 1998 provides that a claim for judicial review may include a claim for **20.65** damages but may not seek damages alone. Damages are discretionary, i.e. there is no automatic right to compensation and they may only be claimed incidental to one of the primary remedies available under Pt 54.2. Section 31(4) of the SCA 1981 provides that a claim for damages, restitution, or the recovery of a sum may be available if the claim could have been made in a private law cause of action (e.g. breach of statutory duty, negligence, and misfeasance in public office), a claim under the HRA 1998 or any EU legislation that may provide for damages.

In *Anufrijeva v Southwark LBC* [2004] 2 WLR 605, a claim relating to immigration and **20.66** housing, the Court of Appeal considered a claim for damages relating to a breach of Art 8 of the ECHR and the right to respect of his private life and home. It held that in the breach of the human right there must be some culpability on behalf of the defendant public body, that they should only be awarded when it was necessary (i.e. that a finding of a violation would often in itself satisfy the claim), and that the level of damages paid would need to take account of the balance of interests between the individual and society more generally. However, in *Andrews v Reading BC* [2005] EWHC 256 (QB) the court awarded damages to the claimant when the significant increase in traffic noise constituted a breach of Art 8 of the ECHR (for further discussion of the facts see Chapter 10: Noise).

E COSTS

The basic civil proceedings principle on costs that the loser pays the winner's fees, applies **20.67** to judicial review proceedings. However, this starting principle is revised by the CPR 1998 and the approach of the courts to public law matters. In *McDonald v Horn* [1995] ICR 685 Hoffman LJ noted at 693 that:

> The court's jurisdiction to deal with litigation costs is based upon s 51 of the Supreme Court Act 1981, which [provides that] (1) Subject to the provisions of this or any other enactment and to rules of court, the costs of and incidental to all proceedings . . . in the High Court . . . shall be in the discretion of the court . . . (3) The court shall have full power to determine by whom and to what extent the costs are to be paid.

It is argued by some practitioners and commentators that in judicial review matters where **20.68** there are public policy considerations, the general rule 'loser pays' rule is not appropriate. See e.g. the briefing paper *Access to Environmental Justice: Making it Affordable* (Coalition for Access to Justice for the Environment, 2004).

Permission hearings

Paragraph 8.6 of the Pt 54 Practice Direction provides that where the defendant or any party **20.69** does attend a hearing, the court will not generally make an order for costs against the claimant. However, the costs of preparing summary grounds of resistance may be claimed. In *R (Leach) v Commissioner for Local Administration* [2001] EWHC Admin 445 the High Court made an order that the claimant should pay his costs of filing the acknowledgment of service. Collins J held that:

> why should the successful party, in this case the defendant, have to bear the costs of putting forward his objections to the claim, if those objections then serve to defeat the claim? Why should he be required by the rules to incur costs which he can never recover, even if he is successful as a result of what he has done? . . . if a defendant incurs costs in submitting an acknowledgement of service, as required by the rules, then he ought to be able, if he succeeds, to recover his costs of so doing.

20.70 Collins J went on to state that the amount that the defendant should be able to recover should be limited to the costs incurred in actually producing the acknowledgement, and that those will obviously depend on the circumstances.

The court's discretion

20.71 The court has a general discretion to award costs. If the claimant loses but has the benefit of public funding those costs should be covered by the public funding scheme. Sometimes, in environmental cases brought in the public interest, it may be possible to persuade the court to 'make no order' if the claimant loses.

20.72 In *Belize Alliance of Conservation Non-Governmental Organisations v Department of the Environment (1) and Belize Electricity Company Limited (2) Privy Council* [2004] Appeal No. 47 of 2003 the Privy Council held that the claim was a public interest matter and that the claimant would not be ordered to pay the costs of the Belize government, despite being unsuccessful.

Protective costs orders

20.73 In recent years, some claimants have applied to the court to obtain a protective costs order. The main purpose of a protective costs order is to allow a claimant of limited means access to the court in order to advance his case without the fear of an order for substantial costs being made against him, a fear that would dissuade him continuing with the case. The guidelines as to when a protective costs order may be made were reviewed by the Court of Appeal in *Corner House Research*, in which Lord Phillips MR stated at para 74 that:

(1) A protective costs order may be made at any stage of the proceedings, on such conditions as the court thinks fit, provided that the court is satisfied that:
   (i)   the issues raised are of general importance;
   (ii) the public interest requires that those issues should be resolved;
   (iii) the applicant has no private interest in the outcome of the case;
   (iv) having regard to the financial resources of the applicant and respondent(s) and to the amount of costs that are likely to be involved it is fair and just to make the order;
   (v)   if the order is not made the applicant will probably discontinue the proceedings and will be acting reasonably in so doing.
(2) If those acting for the applicant are doing so *pro bono* this will be likely to enhance the merits of the application for a PCO.
(3) It is for the court, in its discretion, to decide whether it is fair and just to make the order in the light of the considerations set out above.

As a concluding note Lord Phillips in *Corner House Research* endorsed the European Court of   **20.74**
Human Rights (ECtHR) in *Steel & Morris v UK* (2005) No. 68416/01 ECtHR, (considered in
Chapter 2), that even small and informal groups must be able to carry on their activities
effectively.

F   EUROPEAN COURT OF JUSTICE PROCEEDINGS

An outline of the European Court of Justice (ECJ) is provided in Chapter 1. ECJ proceedings   **20.75**
are considered below. Cases are submitted to the registry and distributed among the judges.
Each file is followed by a specific judge and advocate-general. The court may sit either in
plenary session, or in Chambers of three or five judges, depending on the importance or
complexity of the case. The court sits in plenary session when a Member State or a Community institution that is a party to the proceedings so requests, or in particularly complex
or important cases. Other cases are heard by a chamber.

Preliminary rulings

Domestic courts are under an obligation to ensure the effective application of EU law within   **20.76**
their states. This will include ruling on whether EU primary and secondary legislation (such
as Regulations, Directives, and Decisions) are implemented correctly. The ECJ may provide
preliminary rulings on cases involving EU law if national courts seek clarification on the
interpretation or validity of that law.

Procedure in preliminary rulings

To secure a preliminary ruling the domestic court submits questions concerning the inter-   **20.77**
pretation or validity of a provision of Community law, generally in the form of a judicial
decision in accordance with national procedural rules. The ECJ Registrar has the question
translated into all the Community languages, then serves it on the parties to the original
proceedings as well as the Member States, the Commission, and where appropriate, the
Council. A notice of the request is then published in the EU's Official Journal. The parties,
the Member States, and the Community institutions have two months within which to
submit their written observations to the Court.

Those parties entitled to submit written observations to the ECJ may also make oral repre-   **20.78**
sentations at the hearing. Once the Advocate-General has delivered his Opinion and the
judges have deliberated, the judgment is read in open court and sent by the Registrar to the
national court that sought the ruling.

In *R v (Thames Water Utilities Ltd) v Bromley Magistrates Court* (2005) unreported, the court   **20.79**
referred the matter of whether sewage that escapes from a sewerage network maintained by a
statutory sewerage undertaker under the Water Industry Act 1991 and EU Directive 91/272/
EEC on urban waste water amounts to 'Directive Waste' for the purpose of the EU Waste
Framework Directive 75/442/EC. The preliminary ruling is awaited, for discussion on waste
see Chapter 14.

Direct jurisdiction of the ECJ

Proceedings for failing to comply with an EU obligation

20.80 An action may be brought by the Commission, or at times by another Member State, requesting that the ECJ determine whether a Member State has failed to comply with a Treaty obligation. If the court finds that the obligation has not been fulfilled, the Member State concerned must comply without delay. If the Member State fails to comply with the judgment, further proceedings may be taken. The ECJ may, on finding a failure to comply, impose a fixed or periodic financial penalty.

Proceedings for annulment

20.81 The EU Council, Commission (on occasions), the European Parliament, or a Member State may apply to the ECJ for the annulment of all or part of an item of EU legislation. Further, individuals may seek the annulment of a legal measure that is of direct concern, although the court tends to regard its jurisdiction to hear individual applications for annulment in narrow terms. If the action is well founded, the contested measure is declared void.

Procedure in direct actions

20.82 A direct action claim commences by written application to the ECJ Registry. On receipt, it is entered in the court register. The Registrar publishes a notice of the action and the applicant's claim in the Official Journal. A Judge-Rapporteur and an Advocate-General are then appointed. The application is served on the other party, who has one month within which to lodge a defence. The claimant may submit a reply to the defence, and the defendant a rejoinder to the reply. Each stage in the proceedings has a time limit of one month, unless an extension of time for service is requested from and granted by the ECJ President.

20.83 Following close of pleadings, the Judge-Rapporteur and Advocate-General may carry out a preparatory inquiry for the court. If so, this report should be submitted to the court before the ECJ President sets the date for the public hearing. In a preparatory report for the hearing, the Judge-Rapporteur outlines the facts and argument of the parties and any interveners. The report is made public in the language of the case at the hearing. The case is then argued at public hearing for the judges and the Advocate-General to whom the case has been assigned. They may put to the parties any questions they think fit. Judgment is given in open court at a later date, with the Advocate-General also providing his Opinion to the Court.

The Advocate-General

20.84 A decision by the ECJ includes an opinion by an Advocate-General who is not a member of the Court but provides an impartial opinion to the Court. The Advocates-General deliver, in open court, opinions on the cases brought before the Court. There are no permanent Advocates-General in the Court of First Instance. The role is performed in certain cases by one of the judges. This follows the practice in many European Countries that have a civil law system rather than a common law system as in the UK and Ireland. An example of an Advocate-General's opinion is contained in the case of *Inter-Environnement Wallonie ASBL v Region Wallone* [1998] Env LR 623, which considered the meaning of waste under Art 1(a) of EU Directive 75/442/EEC on waste. At p 639, Advocate-General Jacobs stated that:

The scope of the term 'waste' therefore turns on the meaning of the term 'discard'. As I noted in my opinion in *Tombesi* [1997] ECR I-3561 (para 50), it is clear from the provisions of the directive, in particular 4, 8 to 12 and Annexes IIA and B, that the term 'discard' employed in the definition of waste in Article 1(a) has a special meaning encompassing not only the disposal of waste but also its consignment to a recovery operation.

The ECJ may rule on EU liability for damage caused by one of its institutions or servants **20.85** in the performance of their duties. It may hear appeals, on points of law only, against judgments given by the Court of First Instance. For more information on the ECJ see: www.curia.eu.int.

G   EUROPEAN COURT OF HUMAN RIGHTS PROCEEDINGS

The ECtHR provides a means of redress and enforcement of the obligations under the **20.86** European Convention on Human Rights 1950 (ECHR). The court includes a number of judges equal to that of the 45 contracting states. The court includes a Chamber and Grand Chamber that acts as an appellate court in certain cases, see e.g. *Hatton & ors v UK* [2003] 36022/97 considered in Chapters 2: Environmental rights and principles and 10: Noise. The full text of the ECHR is contained in Sch 1 of the HRA 1998 available at www.opsi.gov.uk or from the ECtHR website at www.echr.coe.int. Human rights principles and case law relating to the environment are discussed in Chapter 2.

The legal procedure for complaints to the ECtHR are contained in the Rules of Procedure of **20.87** the European Court of Human Rights (ECtHR Procedure Rules).

Preliminary matters

A complaint to the ECtHR to challenge a breach of an ECHR right may be made by: **20.88**

- any contracting state; or
- any individual alleging that they are a victim of a Convention violation by a contracting state.

Although an initial complaint does not have to be made on any special form providing key **20.89** information is provided, a formal application or complaint form must be completed to formally pursue the matter. A notice for the guidance of complaints and forms for making applications may be obtained from the ECtHR Registry. Rule 47 of the ECtHR Procedure Rules requires that applicants provide details of:

- their name, age, address, and occupation and any representative;
- the respondent country;
- a clear and concise statement of facts;
- the relevant national law and Convention provisions;
- the purpose of the complaint, i.e. what is sought from the court (e.g. reversal of a decision);
- details of all remedies pursued in the national court; and
- any judgment, decisions, or other relevant documents.

Time limits

20.90 Complaints to the ECtHR must be made within six months from the date of violation of Convention rights or a decision causing such a violation to occur. In some cases there may be a continuing violation and so this may be taken into account when considering the time limit.

Seeking alternative remedies before a complaint to the ECtHR

20.91 It is important that an individual applicant considers all options of redress within national law before making a complaint to the ECtHR. Article 35.1 of the ECHR provides that 'The Court may only deal with the matter after all domestic remedies have been exhausted, according to the generally recognised rules of international law'.

20.92 However in *Hobbs v UK* (2002) (63684/00), a taxation case in which the UK Government submitted that the applicant had failed to exhaust domestic remedies as required by Art 35.1, the ECtHR held that:

> The Government highlighted two domestic courses of action which the applicant had failed to pursue. The first was judicial review proceedings in the High Court, by which they said that the applicant could have sought an order that the responsible Government department make a payment to him equivalent to the amount of the widow's bereavement allowance which he would have received had he been a woman. The second was an appeal to the Tax Commissioners.

> The applicant argued that neither of these courses of action could have provided him with an effective remedy for his complaint. The Court recalls that the only remedies which Art 35.1 of the Convention requires to be exhausted are those that are effective and capable of providing redress for the complaint. The existence of such remedies must be sufficiently certain not only in theory but also in practice, failing which they will lack the requisite accessibility and effectiveness. It falls to the respondent State, if it pleads non-exhaustion, to establish that the various conditions are satisfied (see, e.g the *Johnston v UK* judgment of 18 December 1996, Series A No. 112, 45).

Progressing the proceedings

20.93 Judicial procedure is adversarial and any hearings are in public, unless the court rules otherwise in exceptional circumstances, although the majority of applications are considered on paper. Documents filed at the ECtHR Registry by the parties are generally open to public inspection. Litigants in person may present their own cases, but legal representation is recommended, and usually required once an application has been communicated to the respondent government. The Council of Europe operates a legal aid scheme for applicants who do not have sufficient means.

Permission stage

20.94 Each application, on receipt by the court, is assigned to either:

- a Committee who either declare that the application is inadmissible and strike it out, or declare it admissible and refer it to a Chamber for consideration; or
- a Chamber, who determines both admissibility and the merits of the case.

State applications are always examined by a Chamber.

A case may be relinquished to the Grand Chamber at any time where a case raises a serious **20.95** question of interpretation of the Convention or where there is a risk of departing from existing case law, unless one of the parties objects to such relinquishment within one month of notification of the intention to relinquish. In the event of relinquishment the procedure followed is the same as that set out below for Chambers. Decisions on admissibility must contain reasons and be made public.

Consideration of the merits

Once the application has been declared admissible the court may invite the parties to submit **20.96** further evidence and written observations, including any claims for 'just satisfaction' by the applicant. If no hearing has taken place at the admissibility stage, it may decide to hold a hearing on the merits of the case. The President of the Chamber may invite, or grant leave to, any contracting state or any person concerned who is not the applicant or party to the proceedings to submit written comments or to make representations at the hearing. A contracting state whose national is an applicant in the case is entitled to intervene as of right. During the merits proceedings, negotiations to reach an informal settlement may be proposed to the Court Registrar, although all negotiations are confidential.

Decision by the European Court of Human Rights

Chambers decide by a majority vote. Any judge who has taken part in the consideration of **20.97** the case may append to the judgment either a separate opinion concurring or dissenting or a bare statement of dissent. A Chamber's judgment becomes final after:

- three months of the decision;
- the parties announce that they have no intention of requesting a referral; or
- a decision of the panel rejecting a request for referral.

Referral to the Grand Chamber

Any party may, within three months of judgment by a Chamber, request a referral to the **20.98** Grand Chamber on a serious question of interpretation or application or an issue of general importance. A Grand Chamber panel of five judges, including the President of the Court, examines referral requests. If the panel accepts the request, the Grand Chamber renders its decision on the case in the form of a judgment. It decides by a majority vote and its judgments are final. All final judgments of the court are binding on the respondent states concerned.

Implementation of judgments lies with the Committee of Ministers of the Council of **20.99** Europe. The Committee of Ministers verifies whether violating contracting states have taken appropriate steps to comply with any judgment obligations.

Advisory opinions

The court may, at the request of the Committee of Ministers, give advisory opinions on the **20.100** interpretation of the ECHR. Advisory opinions are given by the Grand Chamber and adopted by a majority vote.

KEY DOCUMENTS AND MATERIALS

Civil Procedure Rules 1998

Access to environmental justice: making it affordable (Coalition for Access to Justice for the Environment, 2004)
Michael Fordham (2005). Judicial Review Handbook 4/e. Hart Publishing: Oxford
Official Journal
Rules of Procedure of the European Court of Human Rights

Department for Constitutional Affairs: www.dca.gov.uk
European Court of Human Rights: www.echr.coe.int
European Court of Justice: www.curia.eu.int

21

FUNDING CIVIL AND
PUBLIC LAW LITIGATION

A   INTRODUCTION

Matters of funding and costs in criminal proceedings are relatively straightforward com-   **21.01**
pared to civil and public law matters. The costs section in Chapter 19: Criminal law practice
and procedure considers funding in prosecution that has legislative control including the
Prosecution of Offences Act 1985. Also, prosecutors must act in accordance with the Code of
Prosecutors, which requires the cost of proceedings to be considered, among many other
things, when deciding whether or not to prosecute. The focus of this chapter is on funding
for civil and public law proceedings.

General information on costs

Solicitors' rates

Solicitors' charges vary enormously. The main factors are: **21.02**

• geographical, i.e. where the lawyer is based; charges are much higher in the City of
  London than more rural areas;

- the experience of the practitioner including years in practice and speciality; and
- the type of work being carried out.

21.03   The courts and the government's Department of Constitutional Affairs have developed a tariff of hourly rates, which is used to assess what parties should pay when they lose a case. The tariff rates are a guide and it is possible to recover at higher levels to reflect experience and expertise. In *R and Plymouth City Airport v Secretary of State for the Environment ex p Thomas* [2001] EWCA Civ 144 the Court of Appeal upheld that approach.

Recovering costs from a losing party

21.04   The general principle is that the loser pays the winner's costs. However, even applying that principle there are likely to be costs that will not be recovered. The other side may object to extra work caused by overlap between two fee earners, or travelling to see the client where the client might have come to visit the solicitor. Usually, any doubt is resolved by the court in favour of the paying party.

Costs exposure

21.05   The same factors affect exposure to the other side's costs. Usually, solicitors in public bodies (including the Treasury Solicitor representing central government) charge at less than commercial rates, and their bills can appear relatively modest. Sometimes, however, they will employ outside solicitors and/or senior barristers when the exposure can increase markedly, especially if London solicitors are appointed.

Second respondent's costs

21.06   In judicial review work, the claim is often against a decision-making authority. Although an interested party (e.g. a developer) who has benefited from the public body's decision may wish to make representations in court to help the authority defend its decision and to inform the court of its particular position. Interested parties are often well funded. However, they are not normally entitled to their costs from a losing party, although sometimes they may be awarded the costs of specific procedures, e.g. producing some evidence that has helped the court. The risk of possible exposure to interested parties' costs needs careful consideration. In *Berkeley v Secretary of State for the Environment Transport and the Regions (No. 2)* [2002] Env LR 378 the point was clarified where the Court of Appeal overturned a High Court ruling awarding a second set of costs against the claimant.

Barristers' costs

21.07   Barristers may charge more on an item-by-item basis, although this tends to reflect time spent. However, agreeing fees in advance can assist. It can be a lot more economical to have a barrister involved in a case at an early stage. Barristers' hourly rates can be comparable to those of solicitors depending on the level of experience of fee earners. At the hearing, the barrister will charge a fixed 'brief' fee, which reflects estimated preparation time and appearing in court for the first day. A daily 'refresher' is charged thereafter. For a one-day hearing in the High Court, one expects to pay in the region of £1,750 to £4,000 to brief a junior barrister and £6,000 for a QC. Corresponding refreshers will be around £600 to £1,000, and £1,500.

Costs of legal proceedings

Some court fees in the High Court are modest. For example, it is £50 to lodge an application **21.08** for judicial review and a further £120 if you are granted permission to proceed to a full hearing although the cost of a statutory appeal under s 288 of the Town and Country Planning Act 1990 is £400. However, fees for other types of action, e.g. nuisance cases, are higher. Fees increase in the Court of Appeal and again in the House of Lords.

Costs in public law proceedings will depend upon which stage has been reached. To reach **21.09** the permission stage in judicial review is likely to cost in the region of £2,500 to £5,000 and exceeding £6,000 is unusual. If permission is refused and an oral hearing is pursued, the costs of this will normally be in the region of £1,500 to £2,500 including counsel's fees. New rules of court make it unlikely that you will be exposed to the other side's costs even if they turn up and successfully oppose you at the oral hearing. However, you are exposed to the costs that the defending party has been put to in providing written so-called 'summary grounds for contesting the claim'. These should be relatively small but it is sensible to budget a figure in the £1,000 to £2,000 bracket (see the costs section in Chapter 20: Public law).

Non-contentious legal advice and assistance

The majority of advice and assistance provided to a client will be outside formal legal **21.10** proceedings, and, unless the case develops into litigation, this is almost always going to be costs that cannot be recovered by the other side. Also, many instances arise where legal representation will be required but the proceedings are not regarded as formal proceedings. The most common example is in land use planning, where attendance and representation at committee hearings and appeals may arise. In these situations, each party is expected to pay their own costs (although for many appeal procedures, the decision-maker often has a discretion to make a costs award).

B PRIVATE FUNDING

Many parties to proceedings will be privately funded. This is likely to be the case for most **21.11** corporate and public bodies whether acting as claimant or defendant. Many organizations will allocate part of their budget to legal or quasi-legal proceedings. For instance, many land developers, will factor in costs for lobbying local government, and preparing for and attending planning inquiries. The client will be keen to ensure that the question of costs is relevant to the proceedings but agreeing the level of fees and a charging rate will, broadly, be a matter between the legal team and the client. How this translates into any award for costs during or following litigation is a separate matter and often involves the intervention of the court.

In contrast to corporate organizations, individuals and local groups will not, to begin with, **21.12** have a separate litigation budget. Most will not even consider legal action until a local concern arises; and the cost of proceedings will often be a determining factor in whether or not to proceed with any action, regardless of whether they may have reasonable prospects of success. In the circumstances raising funds to pursue a claim is, perhaps, the greatest hurdle to overcome when considering legal action.

21.13   It is often the case that individuals aiming to resolve an environmental concern will be supported by other like-minded neighbours who may organize into a group to challenge the concern. However, specific local fundraising events can often be inefficient, taking far more effort than would be the case if the interested individuals collectively provided funds. People may or may not support environmental litigation for all sorts of reasons, but in particular, where an issue affects their house value or amenity, as is often the case, if people think in relation to the cash values at risk, it may be perfectly possible to fund cases adequately. The case should also be put into perspective. If the financial input of 20 local people is equated to the value of a couple of tanks of petrol, or the cost of an average night out, then collective litigation costs start to become far more realistic.

21.14   However, the justice system does recognize that some people are unable to afford litigation and therefore operates the public funding system discussed in Section E below. This may or may not be subject to contribution from others, depending on circumstances and according to the funding code of the Legal Services Commission (LSC).

Legal expenses insurance

21.15   Many private home and car insurers provide legal expenses insurance. For instance, the Co-operative Insurance Services Home Options insurance policy provides, via DAS Legal Expenses Insurance, for:

(a)   an event that causes death or injury to the family;

(b)   a dispute arising from a contract of employment as an employee;

(c)   a contractual dispute; and

(d)   a civil action relating to material property where there is physical damage over £100 or any nuisance or trespass.

21.16   It is always important to check whether legal expenses cover is available. This is required in certain applications for public funding.

Conditional fee agreements

21.17   Conditional fee agreements (CFAs) are agreements between a client and lawyer, which mean that the client pays less (or nothing, depending on what is agreed) if the client loses a case, but a full fee (usually with an 'uplift', again, subject to agreement) if the client wins. If successful, the client can usually recover most of his costs from the other side, including the uplift and insurance that they may have taken out to cover the costs in the event of losing.

21.18   CFAs sound simple but can be complicated. They must be in writing and the agreement must deal with various specific points, as laid down in the Conditional Fees Regulations 2000 (SI 2000/692). A potentially difficult issue is how to decide what 'success' means. It is important that the client understands what the agreement means. Success will, in practice, usually tie in with costs being ordered to be paid by the other side, but this may not necessarily be so, e.g. if the other side has secured a protective costs order.

Counsel and experts may agree also to work on a conditional basis, although any disburse- **21.19**
ments such as an insurance premium, court fees, etc. will have to be paid by the client.

Insuring the costs of litigation

The prospect of a client losing a case and having to pay an unknown amount of money to **21.20**
the other side is always a real concern for clients — however good the adviser or the client
considers the case to be. In publicly funded cases this is not usually a problem. A client's
costs are paid. As for the other side's costs, although an order for costs may be made against
the loser, it cannot be enforced without the court's permission.

It is possible to obtain insurance against losing and the liability for costs in two ways: **21.21**

(1) Litigation insurance that covers all a client's costs, i.e. his own and the other party's or
    parties' costs, up to the limit of indemnity purchased.
(2) CFA insurance which covers all the client's costs except its own solicitors fees up to the
    limit of the indemnity purchased.

Litigation insurance is more expensive; typically, the premium is 20 to 40% of the sum **21.22**
insured. The premium for CFA insurance is around 15%. It is possible to insure against loss
of the premium, although this may need to be done as a separate add-on to the main
insurance. In practice, it is all but impossible, at present, to obtain litigation insurance for
environmental claims and for matters relating to public law.

Limited companies

On occasions, local communities and neighbours group together and form a private limited **21.23**
company in order to resolve environmental concerns. This has the advantage of formalizing
a group's activity and limiting the risk of costs liability if legal proceedings are pursued. In
Hereford Waste Watchers Ltd v Hereford Council [2005] EWHC 191 Admin, the claimant company sought to quash the decision of the defendant council, which had granted planning
permission to develop a waste treatment and recycling facility in Hereford. Hereford Waste
Watchers Ltd was a company limited by guarantee that was formed specifically to challenge
the development in the case, although as noted in the judgment, the company proposed to
take an interest in, and monitor, planning applications in its area which may have an impact
on the environment. This is not uncommon, Sandwich Action Group for the Environment
(SAGE) was set up to oppose the development of an energy from waste incinerator proposed
in East Kent. The group now campaigns against all forms of incineration in the county and
lobbies Kent County Council to implement a more sustainable waste strategy.

C   PUBLIC FUNDING

Public Funding (formerly legal aid) from the LSC may be available to financially assist a **21.24**
person with their claim. It is administered by the LSC via solicitors that have contracts with
the LSC to run the scheme. The following public funding may be available for environment-
related matters:

- legal help;
- advocacy assistance; and
- legal representation.

Each of these is considered below.

Legal help

21.25   Legal help may be available in providing initial advice and assistance to a person that is on a very low income. Solicitors must be approved and have a contract to provide public law funding. The advice and assistance is generally limited to two hours' work and payment rates for legal help are very low. Since April 2005 all legal help must be carried out by firms participating in the tailored fixed fee scheme for civil (non-immigration) controlled work.

Advocacy assistance

21.26   Public funding for defendant representation is available for certain Anti-social Behaviour Order (ASBO) proceedings. Solicitors can self grant advocacy assistance, there are no defendant financial criteria, although it may not be provided where it appears unreasonable that approval for assistance should be granted or where the interests of justice test is not met: see Chapter 4.

Legal representation

21.27   Legal representation may be available for certain environmental claims but is subject to:

- the applicant's financial means; and
- the merits of the case.

Financial means

21.28   Obtaining public funding will require the client's income and savings to be below a certain limit. The income and savings of a client's partner will also be taken into account, unless the concern arises out of a dispute between the partners.

21.29   If the client is on a very low income with little capital, he or she should qualify for free representation. People on income support, income-based job seekers' allowance, or guaranteed state pension credit will qualify automatically on financial grounds, but there are different rules for different types of help. If a client's income is low, but not very low, the client may be required to contribute towards the cost of legal representation. The client's capital (e.g. savings) are also taken into account.

Merits of the claim

21.30   The LSC will want to see evidence of the merits of the case. The most common environmental claim will be based upon judicial review proceedings, and there should generally be some evidence of the client having reasonable prospects of success. The instructing solicitor will submit the application form to the LSC. There are a few specialist public and environmental law firms in England and Wales that have public funding franchises and may, if appropriate, grant emergency public funding using devolved powers. If devolved powers are used a full application for funding must be made to the LSC within 5 working days.

Public funding certificate

The LSC ultimately grant the public funding certificate regardless of whether emergency **21.31** powers have been exercised. Public funding is available in two forms:

(1) investigative help: this funding is limited to investigation of the strength of a claim; and

(2) full representation: whereby funding is provided to represent people in legal proceedings.

Both forms of funding are likely to have limitations relating to the financial expenditure and **21.32** the extent of the proceedings covered. The certificate will only enable work to be carried out to a certain level. Once the work reaches that point, a further application to extend the certificate must be made. This staged approach continues until the case concludes.

The LSC states that one of its aims is to produce consistent and justifiable decisions through- **21.33** out its regional offices and among its contracted suppliers. Decisions taken under the Access to Justice Act 1999, the Funding Code, the regulatory framework, and the Rules under the General Civil Contract often involve the exercise of discretion. The Funding Code, which was approved by Parliament under s 9 of the Access to Justice Act 1999 (AJA 1999), provides in the Procedures (in Pt A at 9.1 to 9.3) that all persons making decisions under the Funding Code shall have regard to guidance issued by the Lord Chancellor under s 23 of the AJA 1999 and to guidance issued by the LSC.

Alternative funding

Many environmental concerns affect hundreds, if not thousands, of people. For example, a **21.34** proposed waste incinerator may potentially affect the health of a whole community. In many applications for public funding, the LSC will want to see evidence of the consideration of alternative funding. The LSC considers that in many instances, public funding should be at least part-matched by private funding. As a general rule if a group wishes to challenge a decision of a public body to grant consent for a large project that clearly has the potential to cause harm to a number of people in a local community it should not expect such a challenge to be funded entirely by the LSC. The LSC may well ask for a matched contribution at the beginning of the case, and again during the case as costs rise; it is best to be prepared for this at the start.

Special Cases Unit

The Special Cases Unit (SCU) at the LSC is responsible for the administration of very high **21.35** cost cases, i.e. where costs are likely to exceed £25,000, and in litigation support cases where a CFA is in place and funding is sought for costs above £15,000 or disbursements above £5,000. Cases that are referred to the SCU are subject to an affordability test and the proposals put forward for progressing the litigation must be approved by the LSC.

Public Interest Advisory Panel

21.36   If there is alleged to be a wide public interest in a case, and the decision, act, or omission to be challenged raises arguments that could impact on everyone, the LSC will refer the application to its Public Interest Advisory Panel (PIAP), who will assess whether or not there is a wider public interest, and if so whether it is 'significant', 'significant to high', or 'high'. If the panel decides that there is a wider public interest, the LSC may take a more liberal approach to the question of whether public funding should be required, and if so how much. Summaries of cases considered by the Panel are available on the LSC website: www.lsc.gov.uk and are grouped according to subject matter. These are taken from the full reports of the Panel, but omit individual client details. In each case the Panel gives an opinion as to whether or not the case has a significant wider public interest. Cases that have a significant wider public interest are usually assessed in one of three categories, namely 'exceptional', 'high' or simply in the general category of 'significant' wider public interest. Examples of environmental cases considered by the PIAP include:

- PIAP/0026 Judicial review proceedings and the need for public enquiry into decommissioning of nuclear submarines.
- PIAP/01/33, Judicial review proceedings. Proposed challenge to a planning decision to allow the building of a waste disposal incinerator.
- PIAP/01/88 Proposed group action for nuisance relating to foul odours escaping from sewage treatment works.
- PIAP/03/209 Judicial review of the Environment Agency and a local authority concerning the modification of a waste management licence to allow the scrapping of war ships at a waste management site.

Costs indemnity

21.37   One advantage of a challenge proceeding through one individual entitled to public funding is that any other claimants are protected from any costs order against them if they lose their case. The court will not give permission unless there are exceptional circumstances such as an individual winning a large amount of money on the football pools or the lottery.

Current concerns in public funding in environmental matters

21.38   There is increasing concern about funding public interest environmental litigation. This has been raised by the legal profession on a number of occasions including the report, *Civil Aspects of Environmental Justice* (ELF, 2003) and *Environmental Justice* (EJP, 2004). The judiciary have also, on a number of occasions outside of the courts, commented on the issue. See, for example, the article by Lord Justice Carnwath in the Journal of Environmental Law (OUP, 1999) Vol. 11 No. 1 Environmental Litigation — A way through the Maze? suggesting that you had to be either very poor or very rich to use the courts to protect the environment. In 2002, Lord Justice Sedley expressed similar concerns to the Aarhus Convention Conference in London (ELF, 2002). Most recently, Lord Justice Brooke provided a four-page addendum to the judgment in *R (Burkett) v Hammersmith v Fulham LBC (2) and ors* [2004] EWCA 1342, noting that the current trend and restrictions in public funding are putting pressure on the very few specialist environmental practitioners willing to take on publicly funded work. He added that there needed further study into the matter and whether the current costs rules may be a potent factor in deterring litigation towards environmental protection.

KEY DOCUMENTS AND MATERIALS

Access to Justice Act 1999
Conditional Fees Regulations 2000 (SI 2000/692)

Legal Services Commission Funding Manual Vol. 1–3 (2004) LSC: London

Legal Services Commission: www.legalservices.gov.uk

22

EXTRA-LEGAL OPTIONS

A INTRODUCTION

There will be occasions when legal proceedings may not be pursued and an alternative non-legal resolution to an environmental problem should be considered. For example, if there is only the potential risk of environmental harm, and the aim is to prevent this arising by informal negotiation with other parties. Or there is the opportunity to influence decision-making by representations. This will be particularly so with land use planning, considered in Chapter 8: Land use planning. **22.01**

This chapter highlights some of the main options for resolution available that may be regarded as extra-legal, but may nevertheless be useful in resolving an environmental problem. Among these early options may be informal correspondence with the polluter, developer, or regulator. **22.02**

Informal correspondence

The first step in any action should be to contact the person or organization that is believed to be responsible for the environmental concern or problem and ask them to resolve that problem or to change the decision taken. This early step is now required prior to commencing many legal proceedings under pre-action protocols. A well-drafted, concise, and timely letter sent to the relevant organization, e.g. the Chief Executive of a local authority, may resolve the problem without the need for further action. **22.03**

Complaint to the Monitoring Officer

22.04 If the organization responsible for regulating, preventing, or deciding on the environmental concern is a local authority then a formal complaint to the Monitoring Officer may assist. Every local authority must appoint a Monitoring Officer who should report internally on any proposal, decision, or omission by the authority that is likely to result in mal-administration. The Monitoring Officer is a statutory appointment under s 5 of the Local Government and Housing Act 1989 (as amended). It is the Monitoring Officer's role to report on any matter relating to a local authority's legal powers, possible maladministration, impropriety, and probity. Part III of the Local Government Act 2000 extended the responsibilities of the Monitoring Officer in relation to the Conduct of Members and Standards Committees including:

- establishing and maintaining a register of council member interests and register of member gifts and hospitalities;
- investigating misconduct of councillors; and
- promoting and maintaining high standards of conduct and providing advice to council members on the interpretation of the Code of Conduct.

22.05 If a complaint to the Monitoring Officer does not resolve the concern, the next stage will be a complaint to the Local Government Ombudsman, see Section B.

B   THE OMBUDSMAN

22.06 Ombudsmen cover a number of public sector functions and investigate maladministration within a public body or institution. If the maladministration relates to certain socio-environmental concerns it may be appropriate to contact:

- the Local Government Ombudsman and the Welsh Local Government Ombudsman, in relation to local government matters;
- the European Ombudsman for maladministration in EU institutions; or
- the Parliamentary Ombudsman, who investigates complaints about central government departments, agencies, and certain other organizations.

Local Government Ombudsman

22.07 The Local Government Ombudsman (LGO) investigates complaints about local authorities and certain other bodies, including the Environment Agency in relation to flood defence and land drainage. The LGO is impartial and has the same powers as the High Court to order the production of documents or information. There is no charge for the service and investigations are carried out in private.

22.08 The LGO is unable to investigate certain categories of complaints including any concern that is older than 12 months or one that is the subject of legal proceedings. The LGO looks for maladministration by a council that has caused a complainant injustice, although he cannot question whether a council's decision or action is right or wrong simply because a complainant disagrees with it. The LGO may not investigate a complaint if he decides that the injustice is slight.

A complaint to the LGO must be in writing, preferably by using the standard complaint **22.09** form issued by the LGO's office. Once a complaint has been submitted and is being investigated, the local authority will have a chance to answer. After an investigation, the LGO will reach a decision and, if necessary, write a report. If the local authority has been at fault and there has been some injustice, the LGO will make recommendations as to how the local authority may resolve this. For details of practice and procedure and to make a complaint to the LGO, visit their website at www.lgo.org.uk. See also Chapter 8 for planning-related complaints.

Recent LGO decisions are available via the Internet, a recent example in the Planning and **22.10** Building Control section is *East Northamptonshire DC* (02/B/16418) LGO (October 2004). In this case, the LGO found that the local authority had failed to report the Town Council's views to its Planning and Licensing Committee and failed to consult English Heritage in relation to an application for residential development that affected listed buildings and a conservation area. The LGO found maladministration causing injustice and that this may be resolved if the local authority compensated the complainant for the uncertainty and inconvenience he had experienced. The local authority agreed to pay the complainant £750 by way of compensation.

In *Chester City Council* (04/C/5309) (March 2005) (*Environmental health*) it was alleged that **22.11** the Council had pursued an unreasonable and improper course of action against the complainant and his wife following an allegation by their neighbour of nuisance from cooking smells from their home. The investigation found that the Council had failed to verify its understanding of the legislation and had threatened the complainant with an abatement notice when, in fact, it had no power to do so. It failed to answer the complainant's questions and failed to investigate the allegations properly. The Ombudsman found maladministration causing injustice and the Council agreed to pay £250 compensation for the anxiety and trouble the actions of its officers caused, and to apologise for the mistakes made. The Council had already taken action to amend its guidance to officers and improve its record keeping.

While in *Derwentside District Council* (02/C/10019) and the *Environment Agency* (02/C/15789) **22.12** (August 2004) (*Planning consideration/neighbour amenity & drainage*) the complaint related to the development of seven dwellings. A condition attached to the planning permission required the new houses to be built to a minimum floor level to ensure that they would not flood. The complainants alleged that the Council did not take account of the potential effect on their land when it imposed this condition. Also, both the Council and the Environment Agency missed references in later reports which should have drawn their attention to the fact that the land was to be raised by up to one metre in places, which they believed had caused their land to be waterlogged and has been flooded in times of heavy rain. The Ombudsman found maladministration causing injustice by both the Council and the Environment Agency, and recommended that:

- a full flood risk assessment be arranged by the Environment Agency jointly funded by the Council and the Agency;

- the Council pay two thirds and the Agency one third of the cost of any works found necessary to alleviate the risk of flooding as a result of the development adjacent; and
- the Council should pay the complainants £500 and the Agency should pay £250 for their anxiety and their time and trouble in pursuing the complaint.

Parliamentary Ombudsman

22.13   The Parliamentary Ombudsman, also known as the Parliamentary Commissioner for Administration (PCA), investigates complaints about actions or inactions of central government departments. Over 200 public bodies are within the PCA's scope. A complaint must be made to an MP within 12 months from the date when the complainant was first aware of the problem. Following a complaint being referred by the MP, the PCA will assess whether the complaint falls within its scope. If so, it will then investigate the matter and come to a conclusion. Remedies available include the PCA recommending to the relevant government body that the complainant be provided with an explanation relating to the complaint, an apology, expenses to be reimbursed, and, on occasions, compensation.

European Ombudsman

22.14   The European Ombudsman investigates complaints about maladministration by the institutions and bodies of the European Community. Maladministration in this sense arises when a public body fails to act in accordance with a rule or principle that is binding upon it, e.g. if an EU institution fails to do something it should have done, if it does it in the wrong way, or if it does something it should not have done. Many of the common complaints to the European Ombudsman relate to unnecessary delay, refusal of information, and abuse of power. A complainant does not need to show that they were directly concerned by the alleged administration in order to lodge a complaint.

22.15   A complaint to the European Ombudsman must be made within two years of the date when the facts giving rise to the complaint were first known. The complaint should be made on the prescribed complaint form available from the Ombudsman or available via the Internet on www.euro-ombudsman.eu.int. It should be accompanied by any relevant documents. On receipt of a complaint, the Ombudsman aims to decide whether to open an inquiry within one month and to close an inquiry within one year. The options of resolution available to the Ombudsman include:

- encouraging the complaint to be settled by the institution, i.e. when the Ombudsman informs the relevant institution about a complaint, that institution can resolve the problem itself;
- securing a 'friendly solution' to the maladministration, if it is not resolved during the Ombudsman's investigation;
- making a draft recommendation to the institution, calling on it to take necessary steps to remedy the maladministration; or
- if the institution does not accept the recommendation, make a special report to the European Parliament.

C ALTERNATIVE DISPUTE RESOLUTION

There are a number of alternatives to court action, collectively known as alternative **22.16** dispute resolution (ADR) where parties can express and explain their concerns, describe their interest, and consider options for resolving the problem. Importantly, with ADR all parties to a dispute should have the opportunity to raise their concerns and consider their options proposed. Benefits of ADR include:

- preserving relationships between the parties;
- a wide range of settlement options;
- it can be cheaper than court action;
- it can reduce delay in reaching a conclusion; and
- a better long-term result.

The legal justice system encourages ADR. Under the Civil Procedure Rules 1998 courts may **22.17** order parties to attempt mediation or some other form of ADR, and can impose cost sanctions if a party has acted unreasonably in refusing to do so. Lord Woolf CJ noted in *Cowl v Plymouth CC* [2001] EWCA Civ 1935 that:

> even in disputes between public authorities and the members of the public for whom they are responsible, insufficient attention is paid to the paramount importance of avoiding litigation whenever this is possible. Particularly in the case of these disputes both sides must by now be acutely conscious of the contribution alternative dispute resolution can make to resolving disputes in a manner which both meets the needs of the parties and the public and saves time, expense and stress.

In certain circumstances public funding may be available to carry out ADR. Further, for **22.18** public law and personal injury claims some negotiation and pre-action correspondence is required. The main types of ADR are outlined below.

Arbitration

Arbitration is the form of ADR that is most similar to conventional litigation. It often **22.19** operates within a legal framework, even though the process and settlement are not rigidly defined.

If arbitration has been agreed, an arbitrator may be chosen by the parties or, for many formal **22.20** arbitration schemes, is appointed by the administering body, e.g. the Chartered Institute of Arbitrators (CIA). Often, arbitrators choose to use a standard set of arbitration rules, although in many instances these are revised to take account of the needs of the parties. Arbitration proceedings follow a similar process as court proceedings hearing concerns of each party. At the end, the arbitrator rules on factual issues and reaches determinations as to how the law would apply to the factual findings. The end result is an arbitral award that is binding on the parties.

Disputes in which arbitration is used includes subsidence claims or for securing repairs to **22.21** property by public sector landlords. However, some schemes may require less formal steps of resolution before arbitration takes place. For instance, the Southwark Arbitration Tribunal requires that before submitting a landlord and tenant case to arbitration, tenants must have informed its housing department, and have exhausted the three-step complaints procedure or, by consent, agreed to waive it. Some of the early significant international environmental law decisions have been based on arbitration proceedings including the *Behring Sea Fur Arbitration (GB v US)* J Moore, Int. Arb 755 (1893) and the *Trail Smelter Arbitration (US v Can)* (1941) 3 RIAA 1938.

Mediation

22.22   Mediation enables the parties to reach an agreement that is acceptable, or the least unacceptable, to them with the help of a third party mediator. It can help to clarify issues and focus on real needs, as well as help to explore appropriate settlements. Mediation is confidential and without prejudice to the parties' rights unless committed to a formal form, signed by the parties and converted into a court order. It can be inexpensive and highly effective. After the use of mediation has been agreed the parties may choose a mediator.

22.23   During mediation each party puts its case for a pre-agreed time, during which the other party remains silent. After this, the other party has its turn. During both periods, the mediator limits himself or herself to 'active listening', i.e. rephrasing what a party has said and raising questions on matters of clarity and factual chronology. The mediator does not advise on the law. After both parties have presented their case, the meeting opens into a general discussion.

22.24   The mediator does not propose solutions. It leaves this to the parties in order that they 'own' any result achieved. There are a number of local mediation providers. For more information contact the Centre for Dispute Resolution at www.cedr.co.uk or Mediation UK at www.mediationuk.org.uk.

Negotiation

22.25   Negotiation is an ADR technique in which the parties deal with each other directly, with or without representatives. It is used by everyone, every day, and is simply the means by which one person achieves a certain goal through communication with others, when the parties have shared interests. For more formal negotiation, such as ADR, each party should have a minimum expectation. This is the very least they hope to gain from the negotiation (this is often called the bottom line). Each party should also set its best alternative to a negotiated agreement (BATNA), which will help to focus the minds of the parties if negotiation breaks down. In some situations a party's BATNA may be a breakdown of relations or having to pursue litigation. However, a party's BATNA, the absolute bottom line, may shift during negotiation, demonstrating the informality and flexibility of ADR generally.

Stakeholder dialogue

22.26   Stakeholder dialogue aims to reach decisions through consensus-building. It adopts the process of 'participate–agree–implement' rather than the more conventional process of 'decide–announce–defend'. Consensus-building methods aim to include all stakeholders, i.e. people having an interest in the issue, in the decision-making process from the outset. The Environment Council is regarded as one of the leading proponents in the area of stakeholder dialogue. See www.the-environment-council.org.uk.

Using alternative dispute resolution

If ADR may be a useful way of resolving a problem the first step forward may be to contact **22.27** the other parties involved in the dispute to assess their interest in this. If a party does not respond, then a third party, e.g. a mediator or negotiator, may be asked to contact the other party(ies) to determine the level of interest in attempting to reach a non-judicial resolution.

D PETITIONING THE EUROPEAN PARLIAMENT

Any citizen or organization based within the EU has the right to petition the European **22.28** Parliament on any matter relating to the EU; including environmental protection. The petition may relate to a matter of general concern, an individual complaint, or a request for Parliament to take a position on a particular matter of public interest.

A petition may be submitted to the Petitions Committee of the European Parliament in **22.29** written or electronic form. An electronic petition may be made by completing the online form at www.europarl.eu.int/petition/petition_en.htm. A written submission does not follow a prescribed form but should include the petitioner's name, occupation, nationality, and place of residence. A group petition may be made with one lead signatory.

On receipt of the petition by the Petitions Committee, it will be assessed to ensure that the **22.30** subject matter falls within the remit of the EU. If the petition is held to fall outside of the remit of the EU, it will be declared inadmissible and the petitioner will be notified. If the subject matter of the petition is within the remit of the EU it will be considered by the Petitions Committee, informing the petitioner as soon as a decision is reached.

The Petitions Committee may take the following action: **22.31**

- ask the European Commission to provide information regarding compliance with the relevant EU legislation;
- refer the petition to other European Parliament committees for further action;
- submit a report to Parliament to be voted on in plenary; or
- draw up an opinion and ask the President of the European Parliament to forward it to the Council and/or European Commission for action. This may include calling on the Commission to refer a case to the European Court of Justice.

Petitions entered in the general register and the main decisions taken on them during the **22.32** consideration procedure are announced at plenary sessions of the European Parliament.

KEY DOCUMENTS AND MATERIALS

European Ombudsman at www.euro-ombudsman.eu.int
European Parliament at www.europarl.eu.int/petition/petition_en.htm
Local Government Ombudsman at www.lgo.org.uk
Parliamentary Commissioner for Administration (PCA) at www.ombudsman.org.uk

23

ENVIRONMENTAL MANAGEMENT

A   INTRODUCTION

23.01   The purpose of environmental management is to improve the performance of an activity, operation, or organization to ensure that its adverse environmental impacts are kept to a minimum or avoided altogether. There are a number of tools and techniques that fall within the scope of environmental management each carrying out distinct functions, each one helping to inform decision-making and action in projects and operations. One of the more common environmental management tools is environmental assessment. This has a complex legal framework with obligations in many areas of environmental law. It is considered in some detail in Chapter 24: Environmental assessment. Other management tools include auditing, life cycle assessment, risk management, and cost-benefit analysis. Each of these is outlined below, although first is an outline of environmental management systems, which often have an overarching function and rely on the other techniques for support. Reference in this chapter has been made to the University of Bath, Integrated Environmental Management Core Module Workbook 2 (University of Bath, 1995 (rev 1999)) (Bath IEM).

B   ENVIRONMENTAL MANAGEMENT SYSTEMS

The purpose of environmental management systems

23.02   The main aim of an environmental management system (EMS) is to secure continuous improvement in an organization's environmental performance. It should also ensure compliance with environmental legislation and any obligations it has to its employees, customers, and other stakeholders, e.g. the environmental aspects of health and safety legislation. An effective EMS may well reduce operating costs. For instance, a system that cuts waste arisings is likely to reduce the cost of waste disposal. The two common schemes are:

(1) ISO 14001 (set by the International Organisation for Standardisation (ISO), which is promoted in the UK by the British Standards Institute (BSI)), and

(2) the Eco-Management and Audit Scheme (EMAS) promoted under EU Regulation (EC) 761/2001 allowing voluntary participation by organizations in a Community eco-management and audit scheme (EMAS Regulation 2001).

23.03   There is also *Project Acorn* a relatively new scheme aimed at smaller businesses, which is managed by the Institute of Environmental Management and Assessment (IEMA). It encourages a step-by-step approach to developing an EMS, that can ultimately lead to full EMAS accreditation. More informal systems may be implemented according to the needs of a business.

23.04   Implementing an EMS is voluntary, although a robust and accredited system will assist operations that require a pollution permit under the pollution, prevention and control regime, see Chapter 11: Pollution prevention and control. The Environment Agency Position Statement on EMSs provides that:

The Agency formally recognises EMSs in its risk-based approach to regulation via the OPRA (Operator and Pollution Risk Appraisal) schemes. . . . The Agency strongly encourages the implementation and use of robust EMSs. A robust EMS should lead to improved environmental performance, including better and more consistent legal compliance. . . . Firms with recognised EMSs are awarded additional points in the OPRA scoring system. EMAS receives the highest number of points, followed by ISO 14001 and then companies with in-house systems.

Although EMSs are commonly used in industrial processes they are not exclusively for such **23.05** organizations. A number of local authorities are EMAS registered, e.g. London Borough of Sutton, Newcastle City Council and Lewes District Council, and many law firms are ISO 14001 accredited (see Law Society Gazette, 12 May 2005 p 25).

An EMS will include the following stages: **23.06**

- policy setting;
- initial review (also called a baseline or scoping review);
- setting objectives and targets to improve performance;
- developing a management programme to meet the objectives and targets;
- implementation of the activities in the programme;
- auditing (checking) the programme of activities;
- a review of the programme (and policy statement) to see where further improvements can be made; and
- revising the programme, which is likely to include setting new targets and revising the management programme.

Environmental management systems are iterative in nature, continuously reviewing **23.07** activities and operations, targets and objectives to ensure that overall environmental performance continues to improve and complements the development of an organization and its operations.

While the stages set out above follow a general pattern, they often overlap to meet the **23.08** demands of business and to ensure that a system does not stall through being inflexible. EMSs are cyclical in nature; they should evolve. They follow a pattern familiar to many other management systems such as Investors In People and ISO 9000. Each stage of an EMS is outlined below with reference at times to the requirements of EMAS. This is because EMAS is a more rigorous management system than ISO 14001 to the extent that compliance with EMAS will almost certainly secure compliance with ISO 14001; the converse is not necessarily the case. Annex 1 of the EMAS Regulation 2001 sets out the requirements for environmental management systems under EMAS.

The environmental policy

An environmental policy is a public commitment to protecting and improving the **23.09** environment. It should provide a clear statement of an organization's vision, together with its aims and approach to environmental protection and improvement. The policy need not specify detailed actions or targets; which will be set out in the EMS action programme.

Developing the policy

23.10   Securing senior management level commitment to an environmental policy is as important as drafting the policy itself. It is often very effective to include senior management in policy drafting. Everyone involved in the organization can contribute to the success of an EMS and so must be aware of why it should be implemented.

23.11   If an environmental policy is to state more than a general commitment to minimizing environmental impacts (which is acceptable) then preparing a draft policy, which is finalized as the EMS progresses, may be appropriate. It is important to recognize that priorities may change and that the policy could shift emphasis over time. Paragraph I A.2 of the EMAS Regulation 2001 provides that top management shall define the organization's environmental policy and ensure that it:

(a)   is appropriate to the nature, scale, and environmental impact of its activities, product, and services;

(b)   includes a commitment to continual improvement and prevention of pollution;

(c)   includes a commitment to comply with relevant environmental legislation and regulations, and with other requirements to which the organization subscribes;

(d)   provides the framework for setting and reviewing environmental objectives and targets;

(e)   is documented, implemented, and maintained and communicated to all employees;

(f)   is available to the public.

Initial review

23.12   In order to be able to manage the environmental impacts of an organization it is essential to know what the impacts are and how significant they may be. Many management initiatives, e.g. improvements in health and safety, will have an indirect reduction in environmental impacts. The initial review is arguably the most important aspect of an EMS and is often the stage where most time and attention is spent; an inadequate initial review could easily lead to inappropriate objectives and targets in the subsequent action plan. For example, if a review misses a significant adverse impact relating to energy consumption, any objectives, targets, or action carried out that do not address that impact are likely to result in the EMS not being implemented effectively.

Undertaking the review

23.13   There is usually a key person or group driving an EMS forward. They may have drafted the policy and will be keen to promote environmental good practice. Yet, however motivated they may be they will need the support of many of their colleagues in carrying the policy forward through the EMS. It is very useful to establish an EMS project team of key staff, which may consist of just two or three people or anything up to ten, depending on the size of the organization or the site being managed.

23.14   It is important to check whether the project team has the relevant skills and authority to carry out a review and propose actions to further the environmental programme. If not, then it will be necessary to train one or more of the project team to a competent level or to hire expertise from consultants operating in the field. The IEMA has over 8,000 members, many of which have expertise in implementing EMSs.

Setting the boundaries of the review

The project team should set the scope and aims of the review, e.g. will it cover just one site **23.15** or a number of different sites? Is the review going to complete within three months, six, or longer? Setting clear boundaries at the outset will assist as the review progresses. The review should cover the following areas:

- main environmental impacts (effects);
- legislative requirements;
- existing management procedures; and
- previous incidents or concerns.

Main environmental effects

Assessing the environmental impacts of the organization will take time and it is often **23.16** helpful to break the review into either geographical or operational sections, e.g. if there are a number of different sites of an organization then each site may be considered separately.

The inputs and outputs of each unit must be assessed. Inputs include use of raw materials, **23.17** water, oil, gas, and other forms of energy. Outputs will include waste, noise, smells, etc. The impact on air, land, and water will need to be highlighted. Table 23.1 is a sample issues and impacts schedule. If this is used then for all analyses the level of impact should be highlighted.

Table 23.1 Summary issues and impacts

Unit	Use or generation of:						Impact on:		
	raw	energy	water	waste	noise	odour	air	water	land
TRUMPTON SITE									
transport		high	—	—	high	med	high	—	high
office equipment	—	—	—	—	—	—	—	—	—
machinery	high	high	med	low	high	low	med	—	—
products	high	med	med	high	—	—	low	low	high
other									

The environmental impacts identified as high in the review must be considered in detail **23.18** and, in particular, how they can be minimized, reduced, or prevented completely. For example, a business that needs steam in its operating processes and electricity in operations should consider investing in a small combined heat and power plant that provides electricity and, in doing so, generates significant quantities of steam that may be used in its operations.

Annex III of the European Commission Recommendation C (2001) 2503 on guidance for **23.19** the implementation of Regulation (EC) No. 761/2001 allowing voluntary participation by organizations in a Community eco-management and audit scheme provides assistance to organizations on the identification of environmental aspects and assessment of their significance.

Reporting the findings

23.20 Once the review is complete the findings should be written up and presented to the project team and to senior management. It is important to report on the positive as well as adverse environmental impacts of the organization. There may have been genuine support for environmental management during the initial review, and it should be noted that progressing the EMS might not be as difficult as perceived. It may therefore be appropriate to inform the whole organization of the outcome of the initial review to maintain support and commitment. The initial review report should make recommendations for action, which should inform the next stage of the EMS: setting objectives and targets.

Setting objectives and targets

23.21 The objectives and targets stage is turning the outcomes and recommendations from the initial review into positive steps of action. Objectives and targets are often confused. The distinction is that:

- *objectives* are long term aims, e.g. it is the *objective* of the training programme to ensure that all employees have an appropriate level of environmental awareness; whereas
- *targets* are the clearly defined outcomes that show whether or not the objectives set are being achieved, e.g. it is a target that within 12 months from [date] 50% of all employees are using low-energy PC screens.

23.22 It is quite appropriate to set high objectives, which when achieved result in genuine change. They can be demanding but must be realistic. Targets may be described as being SMART in that they are:

- Specific: clearly stating their intention.
- Measurable: by clearly being able to be measured.
- Achievable: in that the target set can be achieved — albeit with some effort.
- Realistic: it is not unrealistic to set such a target — e.g. does it make sense?
- Time specific: there must be a clear time-scale in which to meet the target.

Developing the programme

23.23 Developing the EMS programme means taking the objectives and targets that have been set in the stage before and preparing a plan or programme as to how those objectives and targets will be achieved. Each objective should be supported by a specific action plan, detailing who is going to do what and when they are going to do it. In preparing the programme the following questions should be answered:

- What needs to be done? This will be clear from the initial review and the recommendations arising from it.
- Why does it need to be done? Again this may well be clear from the initial review.
- When does it need to be done? The targets set should include this.
- How will it be done? Clear objectives and targets should demonstrate this.
- Where will it be done? This is likely to be the business site or building that is the subject of the environmental policy.

- Who will do it? This will need to be confirmed and effectively delegated by any project team or dedicated officer.

When each of the questions is answered for all of the objectives, then the EMS programme **23.24** will be reasonably complete and positive steps to implement the plan can begin. The whole programme may be set to carry on over a year, 18 months, or even 2 years, although some parts may be concluded quite quickly.

Implementation

The most important stage of an EMS is the implementation stage, i.e. when the proposals to **23.25** minimize environmental impacts are put into action. Without implementation there will be no continuing improvement in environmental performance. Implementation will be a mix of direct practical steps taken by a number of people across an organization and indirect activities aimed at changing people's behaviour.

- Direct actions include, e.g. that all vehicle users turn their car/lorry engines off when their vehicle is stationary for anything more than a few seconds and that people use less paper when carrying out their work.
- Indirect activities include providing training and information on environmental best practice. This will not directly reduce impacts but is nevertheless important in ensuring that other people reduce theirs as they gain a greater understanding of environmental principles.

Training

Some form of training will be necessary to ensure that many of the direct actions are imple- **23.26** mented successfully. Many of the simplest, yet most effective, environmental management outcomes occur through a shift in attitude. There is also a knock-on effect that people who work in an environmentally friendly workplace begin to change their living patterns at home.

Information provision

As with training, people need to be informed about how to minimize their environmental **23.27** impacts and also what the consequences of their actions are. Information provision can vary from putting up a small poster by a light switch reminding people to turn lights off when they are the last to leave a room to providing regular environmental newsletters highlighting the progress of the environmental action within the workplace.

Documentation

To ensure that an EMS remains effective in the long term, it is necessary to document the **23.28** actions undertaken and any responses to activities at an early stage. Collecting documentation must begin from the initial review. Documentation should also provide the procedures for what happens when things go wrong. Many adverse impacts arise in the workplace through accidents. The environmental impact is likely to be minimized if effective response procedures are well known to all. Thus, documentation may include emergency plans and procedures. Documentation is most effective if it is transmitted to other people, in other words, the effective use of information provision.

23.29   Annex II of Recommendation C (2001) 2503 provides guidance to organizations on employee participation within the framework of EMAS.

Monitoring the action programme

23.30   Regular documentation of the actions carried out under the EMS assists the monitoring of the action programme. This is vital to ensure that the actions being undertaken are effective and result in genuine improvement. If certain actions are not securing improvements in environmental performance this should become clear during the monitoring process. Also, there is little point setting objectives and targets if they are not then checked to see whether they have been met.

Auditing

23.31   Auditing should be regarded as a more formal monitoring process that should aim to take place at a set time during the EMS programme. It should be made simpler by an effective continuing monitoring programme. The reason for more systematic and formal monitoring through an audit is that it helps to inform a review of the EMS and to assist the next stage of the EMS.

23.32   An experienced environmental auditor should undertake an audit. This could be someone independent of the organization, although this is not formally required under EMAS. Paragraph 2.1 of the EMAS Regulation 2001 provides that:

> Persons sufficiently independent of the activity being audited shall carry out internal audits to ensure an impartial view. They may be carried out by employees of the organisation or by external parties (employees from other organisations, employees from other parts of the same organisation or consultants).

23.33   The reason for this is that it adds weight to any findings of the audit. If this is unrealistic, then a member of the EMS project team should be trained in environmental auditing.

Review

23.34   The formal audit carried out on the EMS may well make recommendations on areas of improvement of the EMS. Any recommendations or suggestions for actions should be brought forward into the formal EMS review. In addition, the review may contain other matters that were outside the scope of the audit, such as consideration of forthcoming environmental legislation that the organization will need to prepare for. The review provides the opportunity to evaluate the success of the EMS. Paragraph I-A.6 of the EMAS Regulation 2001 provides that:

> The organisation's top management shall, at intervals that it determines, review the EMS, to ensure its continuing suitability, adequacy and effectiveness. The management review process shall ensure that the necessary information is collected to allow management to carry out this evaluation. This review shall be documented.

Revising the policy and programme

The review recommendations should be brought forward into the EMS programme and, if appropriate, the environmental policy. Revisions are likely to include setting new targets and revising any specific action required as part of the programme. A robust EMS that genuinely seeks to secure continuing improvement in environmental performance will, on review, be setting increasingly tough environmental objectives and targets. **23.35**

Report outcomes

Both ISO 14001 and EMAS recognize public reporting plays a fundamental role in an effective EMS. A public report should highlight the outcomes of your review and any steps proposed to revise the policy and programme. Annex III of the EMAS Regulation 2001 sets out the requirements for public reporting in what it refers to as the environmental statement. An environmental statement is required to be published upon first registration of the organization's EMAS and every three years thereafter. Paragraph 3.1 of Annex III provides that: **23.36**

> The aim of the environmental statement is to provide environmental information to the public and other interested parties regarding the environmental impact and performance and the continual improvement of environmental performance of the organisation.

Annex I of Recommendation C (2001) 2503 provides assistance to organizations in producing the environmental statement. **23.37**

Independent verification and requirements on implementing EMAS

The EMAS Regulation 2001 requires that all organizations accredited with EMAS be verified. The function of the verifiers (set out in para 5.4) is to check compliance with all the requirements of the Regulation including, among other things, the initial review, the audit, and the environmental statement, and to check the reliability, credibility, and correctness of the data and information in the statement and information to be validated. **23.38**

Annex IB sets out the issues to be addressed by organizations implementing EMAS. These include: **23.39**

- *Legal compliance*. Organizations must be able to demonstrate that they have identified and know the implications of all environmental legislation, can provide for legal compliance with environmental legislation, and have procedures in place that enable the organization to meet the requirements on an ongoing basis.
- *Performance*. Organizations must be able to demonstrate that the EMS and audit procedures address the actual environmental performance of the organization.
- *External communication and relations*. Organizations must demonstrate an open dialogue with the public and other interested parties including local communities and customers.
- *Employee involvement*. Employees must be involved in the process aimed at continually improving environmental performance.

C ENVIRONMENTAL AUDITING

Types of audit

23.40 An environmental audit may be defined as a systematic, documented, periodic, and objective review of an operation, site, or activity. It may be designed to verify compliance with legislation, evaluate management practices, or assess the risk from operations. There are various types of audit that fall into three broad categories:

(1) liability;
(2) management; and
(3) activities.

Liability audits

23.41 Liability auditing aims to identify areas of an operation or a site that could give rise to liability. A compliance audit should clarify whether an organization is complying with current and future legislation. An environmental risk audit considers what actual or potential risks are associated with an organization or a site. A pre-acquisition audit (sometimes referred to as a due diligence audit) will include a comprehensive site investigation and is generally carried out before the purchase of land or operations. In essence, a buyer will want to know exactly what is being bought including any liability that exists or may arise at some time in the future.

Management audits

23.42 These have been considered above under environmental management systems. In essence, a management audit is checking whether the management of an operation is acting as it should be, with correct systems in place and, in the case of EMAS, that the system is delivering environmental performance.

Activity audits

23.43 An activity audit will consider specific activities, operations, or process systems. For instance, it may check the effectiveness of clean technology, waste disposal systems, or energy management.

Undertaking an environmental audit

23.44 There are three main stages in carrying out an environmental audit: a planning stage, conducting the audit, and a reporting stage. The emphasis or level of work required in each stage will vary according to the intended purpose of the audit.

Planning stage

23.45 As with an EMS, the planning stage of an audit is perhaps the most important stage. It is vital to ensure that everyone involved in the auditing process is clear as to the purpose of the audit, i.e. what it is meant to achieve and the scope of the audit including any geographical or business boundaries.

Conducting the audit

An audit can be carried out in two main parts. A desk-top survey should be carried out in the **23.46** early stages of the audit to consider any relevant documentation and materials available. These will include checking maps and photos of a site, considering any public registers relating to pollution permits, e.g. under the pollution prevention control regime. It will also be worth checking any accident record books. The site survey should then take place, which may also include interviews with employees and occupiers of the site and, if appropriate, any neighbours. Following both the desk-top and site surveys, the information should be assessed and any gaps in the analysis reviewed and made complete. The audit should then identify any areas for concern, improvements that may be made, and recommend any course of action required.

Reporting

The scoping phase of the audit during planning will determine how the results of the surveys **23.47** are to be reported. This is likely to be by written report. A draft report will be prepared for consultation by interested parties, including the instructing client. This will then be finalized and will set out the auditor's opinion of compliance and/or performance. The report may well include a post-audit action programme highlighting work and action to be undertaken in order to resolve any concerns that may have arisen.

D LIFE CYCLE ASSESSMENT

Introduction

Life cycle assessment (LCA) is a specific environmental management tool that aims to assess **23.48** the impact of an operation, process, or product throughout its whole life. ISO 14040 defines LCA as 'the compilation and evaluation of the inputs, outputs and the potential environmental impacts of a product system throughout its entire life cycle.'

The ISO 14000 series provides further guidance or standards on LCA including ISO 14041: **23.49** *Life Cycle Inventory Analysis* and ISO 14043: *Life Cycle Assessment Interpretation*.

Carrying out a life cycle assessment

There are four key stages in LCA: **23.50**

(1) preparation and scoping;
(2) inventory analysis;
(3) impact assessment; and
(4) interpretation.

Preparation and scoping

The preparation stage of LCA should clearly set out the aims of the study. This helps **23.51** to ensure that only relevant information is collected, which is important, because when starting to consider life cycles, there can be a tendency to open up the boundaries to include every activity and impact on the planet. Clearly defining the purpose, i.e. what is hoped to be achieved, by the assessment will help set the boundaries of the study.

23.52   The boundaries of the study will be critical. ISO 14040 notes that the scope of an LCA shall clearly specify the functions of the system being studied. A functional unit is a measure of the performance of the functional outputs of the product system. A very simple analysis of what may constitute a functional unit is by considering the provision of milk by a customer. This is set out below.

Figure 23.1 What is a functional unit?

Milk may be provided to customers in at least two ways; by a milkman delivering milk to the doorstep in milk bottles, and by a supermarket selling milk in large plastic containers at one of its shops. LCA may be used to find out the overall environmental impact of each method, in short to see which method of milk delivery is more environmentally friendly.

Each assessment must be carried out separately, what LCA cannot do is merge the two systems. Also, each assessment must have consistent starting points, e.g. extraction of milk from cows and extraction of materials for the container. Each assessment should also have the same end point, i.e. final disposal of the container.

The functional unit is the boundaries to be assessed in each case, i.e. the extraction of materials for the container, the extraction of milk, the delivery of milk to the customer, and the disposal of the container.

Given this example, perhaps the most environmentally friendly form of milk delivery is by a local farmer, milking his own cows, bottling the milk produced at the farm, and delivering it to people living in the neighbourhood. The bottles will be returned, washed, and used again. Conversely the most environmentally damaging provision (which is regrettably now very quite common) will be milking cows in Eastern Europe where the milk is then delivered to a packaging plant in the UK, packaged in a plastic container, transported to a distribution centre in another region of the UK, and then distributed to a supermarket in the customer's locality. The plastic container is most likely to be buried in landfill.

Life cycle inventory analysis

23.53   In *Guidelines for Life Cycle Assessment: A Code of Practice* (1993) the Society of Environmental Toxicology and Chemistry (SETAC) defined life cycle inventory analysis as:

> an objective, data based process of quantifying energy and raw material requirements, air emissions, waterborne effluents, solid wastes, and other environmental releases incurred throughout the life cycle of a product, process, or activity.

23.54   In outline, the inventory analysis stage of LCA involves gathering information relating to the inputs into and releases out of the functional unit. To manage this task, it is likely that the functional unit will be broken down into manageable sections. For example, extraction of raw material for the central product, extraction of raw materials for the indirect activities such as transportation, any production processes, and the distribution of the product or services to users. The inventory analysis should also include the validation of any data collected and relating that to the functional unit.

Impact assessment and interpretation

Following the collection and validation of information and data relevant to the functional **23.55** unit, this has to be interpreted and assessed. ISO 14040 notes that impact assessment is 'the phase of LCA aimed at understanding and evaluating the magnitude and significance of the potential impacts of a . . . system.'

Impact assessment in LCA follows the general principles of environmental impact assess- **23.56** ment (EIA) considered in Chapter 24: Environmental assessment. Further, an EIA may need to incorporate or carry out some simplified form of LCA to ensure that the overall effects of a proposed project or development are properly understood by decision-makers.

Following the Bath IEM core module, the key stages in life cycle impact are: **23.57**

- selection and definition of impact categories;
- assignment of life cycle inventory results (also referred to as classification), which involves allocating the inventory data to relevant issue categories;
- category modelling (also known as characterization), which provides the basis for aggregating the inventory results within a category;
- assessment of the overall relevance of the impact (also referred to as normalization); and
- weighting across the impact categories (also known as valuation), which is a subjective process involving assigning relative weights (or values) to the various categories of environmental impact.

Interpretation

ISO 14043 defines life cycle interpretation as: **23.58**

a systematic procedure to identify, qualify, check, and evaluate information from the conclusions of the inventory analysis and/or impact assessment of a system, and present them in order to meet the goals and scope of the study.

It notes that it is also a process of communicating the more technical phrases of LCA in a **23.59** form that is understandable and useful to the decision-maker. The SETAC guidelines provide that an LCA report should provide a clear statement of the objectives of the study, together with an explanation of the scope and rationale for the boundaries of the functional unit. It should include flow diagrams describing the system and all important inputs, outputs, and products as well as a description of the methodology used and explanation of value judgements and assumptions. An LCA report should include the data used together with its source details on the quality of data. It should provide conclusions that will be drawn from the study; it should be objective and transparent.

E RISK MANAGEMENT

Introduction

Risk management is the means of using information gathered through risk assessment in **23.60** decision-making and then acting upon that information to control the risk as appropriate. Central to risk management is risk assessment. Petts and Eduljee in *Environmental Impact Assessment for Waste Treatment and Disposal Facilities* (Wiley, 1994) define risk assessment as:

a process in which prediction and evaluation are combined to estimate the probability or frequency of harm (risk) for a given hazard (an event which has the potential to be harmful). Manifestation of a risk requires an event, and a pathway for transport and a receptor which could be harmed at the exposure point. In essence, risk assessment provides a structured approach for ascertaining the nature and extent of the relationship between cause and effect.

23.61   The receptors referred to in the above definition may include people and populations, flora, fauna, ecosystems, buildings, agriculture, marine life, watercourses, indeed anything that may be adversely affected by harm. Bath IEM sets out the framework for risk management that is set out below.

Figure 23.2 Framework for risk management

<hr>

RISK ASSESSMENT

Risk Estimation

(1)   Clarification of intention
(2)   Identification of hazard
(3)   Identification of consequences
(4)   Estimation of magnitude of consequences
(5)   Estimation of probability of consequences
(6)   Deriving the measure of risk

Risk evaluation

Option analysis

(a)   Changing the hazard
(b)   Reducing the probability of occurrence
(c)   Diminishing the consequences
(d)   Developing the minimum acceptable strategy

Risk monitoring

<hr>

Key stages of risk assessment

23.62   Risk assessment is, by itself, an important aspect of environmental management, practice, and law. It should be included in the consideration of most major project proposals, when assessing the impacts of significant socio-environmental harm. The seven key stages in risk assessment are explained in outline below adapting the Bath IEM core module.

(1) Clarification of intention

23.63   Clarifying the intention means setting out exactly what is to be done and how it is to be achieved. One intention is to do nothing, another may be to produce a toxic substance, develop a motorway, chop down a forest, or build a nuclear power station. This is a descriptive exercise only.

(2) Identification of hazard

A hazard is a property or situation, which in particular circumstances may lead to harm.   **23.64**
Hazard identification should ask the question: where and to what extent might an operation
or process or the individual stages of one, cause harm to human health or the environment
by virtue of either their nature or through failure? Answering this question is likely to
involve considering numerous options and a variety of answers. The potential hazards
arising from one intended action will be numerous and the fault of each action could
be equally numerous based on human error, faulty equipment, vandalism, or natural
occurrences. Hazard identification is highly technical. Where a suspected hazard may be
relevant, it is appropriate to apply the precautionary principle, which provides that where
there is a lack of certainty or evidence as to whether an intention, act, omission, or decision
will cause harm, a precautionary approach should be taken.

(3) Identification of consequences

Identification of the consequences involves determining what would happen to all the   **23.65**
receptors should a hazardous event occur. The link between the hazard and the consequence
can be shown by the impact pathway. A simplified impact pathway is shown below. The
consequences of a specific hazard being realized are, by definition, harm or adverse effects on
human health and/or the environment.

(4) Estimation of magnitude of consequences

Quantifying a particular consequence requires establishing a dose-effect (sometimes referred   **23.66**
to as exposure-response or dose-response) between the consequence and the receptor.
This requires detailed knowledge of emission or release rates of the pollutant, the pathway
by which the receptors are affected, the extent of exposure of the receiving environment, and the density of the receptor. There are now a range of credible publications providing case studies of the operation of certain pollutants, e.g. impacts of air pollution on
human health, which may provide core and source materials as to the reaction of pollutants
on receptors.

(5) Estimation of probability of consequences

Probability estimates can be calculated either with prior knowledge or hindsight. Prior   **23.67**
knowledge will be based on the experience of the risk assessor based upon the relative
frequency at which a particular hazard or consequence has occurred in the past. These are
referred to as objective probabilities. Hindsight estimates are carried out based upon expert
knowledge and a subjective evaluation of similar past events. It is called subjective
probabilities and is regularly used in risk assessment. To assist, there are databases of
incidents and occurrences, which may be used to extrapolate statistics for a risk assessment.

(6) Risk estimation

Risk estimation combines the probability estimates with the estimates of magnitude of each   **23.68**
consequence for each hazard, in order to estimate the overall level of risk

(7) Evaluation of risk

Once the overall risks have been estimated the final stage is to assess the significance of   **23.69**
the risks. This will involve weighting or attaching a value to the risk. Risk weighting

requires considering aspects of the intention relating to the receptors and to the perception of the risk by those likely to be affected. For some risks public bodies have set what they regard as acceptable levels of risk, e.g. the Health and Safety Executive has set the requirement for risks to be set 'as low as is reasonably practicable' (ALARP), which very broadly provides that the acceptable level of risk in the UK is based upon one death in a million.

Perception of risk

23.70   The perception of risk can be taken into account in the evaluation of risk. The relevant perception is that of the people likely to be affected. The Bath IEM core module suggests that individuals tend to perceive exposure to involuntary risks as more significant than exposure to voluntary risks; with non-fatal carcinogenic health impacts generally being perceived to be more severe than other non-fatal health impacts. In *Newport CBC v Secretary of State for Wales & anor* [1997] EWCA Civ 1894 the Court of Appeal held that the perception or fear of adverse health effects of a proposal may be a material planning consideration.

Risk management

23.71   Risk management is the process of using the information obtained during the risk assessment and incorporating it into operational activities and decision-making. The options available to control are highlighted in Figure 23.2 above, and include changing the hazard, reducing the probability of the occurrence, reducing the consequences of the risk, and developing a plan that provides a standard at which the risk becomes acceptable. For completeness any risk management system should incorporate risk monitoring.

Figure 23.3 Human health impact for air pollution

··

Emission

↓

Transport and atmospheric chemistry
ambient air concentrations, wind speed, direction,
temperature etc

↓

Exposure
ambient air concentrations of pollutants

Mechanism of effects
e.g. irritant effects on respiratory system

Mortality/morbidity
premature death, cases of asthma, restricted activity days

··

F COST-BENEFIT ANALYSIS

Introduction

Environmental cost-benefit analysis (CBA) is an appraisal tool for assessing the relative costs **23.72** and benefits of a project, including non-financial costs and benefits to society and the environment. Abelson in *Project Appraisal and Valuation of the Environment* (Macmillan, 1996) provides that:

> CBA is designed to show whether the total benefits of a policy or project exceed the costs, including environmental benefits and costs . . . as far as possible, all effects are measured as the person affected would measure them.

Cost-benefit analysis is, in various forms, incorporated into environmental legislation. **23.73** For example, s 7 of the Environmental Protection Act 1990 (EPA 1990) provides that in any authorization there should be specific conditions, as the regulator considers appropriate, for ensuring that the best available techniques not entailing excessive costs will be used in carrying on a prescribed process. Also in considering the defence of best practicable means contained in s 79(9) of the EPA 1990, subs (a) provides that ' "practicable" means reasonably practicable having regard among other things to local conditions and circumstances, to the current state of technical knowledge and to the financial implications'.

More directly, s 39 of the Environment Act 1995 provides that the Environment Agency in **23.74** considering whether or not to exercise any power conferred upon it by or under any enactment must 'take into account the likely costs and benefits of the exercise or non-exercise of the power or its exercise in the manner in question.'

Environmental cost-benefit analysis framework

CBA can be complex, particularly when seeking to value environmental benefits and future **23.75** benefits. Bath IEM core module suggests that a basic approach to CBA divides a project into three main stages:

(1) identifying and quantifying project effects;
(2) valuing costs and benefits; and
(3) decision-making.

Identifying and quantifying project effects

The first stage involves identifying all the parties and receptors (e.g. a watercourse) that will **23.76** be potentially affected by the project and quantifying the impact of the project on those parties and receptors. Effects to be included in a project appraisal include all:

- tangible negative effects (costs) experienced by the providers and consumers of the projects' output or conclusion;
- tangible positive effects (benefits) to providers and consumers;
- intangible costs borne by third parties, the most important of which will be externalities, which are costs arising from a project that are external to a project operator's financial or other accounting systems, e.g. the cost of increased morbidity and hospital admissions as a result of air pollution from road transport will not be paid for by the driver, petrol

companies, or motor manufacturers and so may be regarded as external to their cost;

- intangible benefits to third parties, including e.g. the employment generated from the development of a power station.

Valuing costs and benefits

23.77 Valuing project costs and benefits can give rise to difficult and contentious decisions. Tangible costs and benefits can be assessed relatively easily using observed market prices, although it is important to ensure that all tangible costs and benefits are incorporated. However, intangible costs and benefits must be implied through the use of valuation techniques, which aim to secure a level of individuals' willingness to pay or willingness to accept payment for deterioration in environmental quality. The valuation techniques include:

- *Use of actual market price techniques.* The value costs and benefits that have readily observable prices should be applied to intangible costs and benefits. Techniques include: change in productivity approaches, preventative expenditure/replacement cost approaches, and shadow project approaches.
- *Surrogate market techniques.* These use market information and use the prices of substitute or complementary goods to value environmental benefits. Surrogate market methods include, property value approach, the wage differential approach, and travel cost method.
- *Survey-based techniques.* These techniques rely on responses to survey whereby individuals are asked among other things, for their willingness to pay for an environmental benefit, such as clean air. Survey-based techniques include contingent valuation method and contingent ranking.

Decision-making

23.78 Once all the costs and benefits of a project have been valued, it is possible to assess the value of the project according to economic criteria. This will involve weighting many of the costs and benefits that arise at different points in time. For example, a large project is likely to require significant initial investment and, if a CBA is based upon a short term, the costs are likely to outweigh the benefits. However, looking ahead on a project needs to take account of the fact that a £1 today may be worth £0.97 in one year's time, simply due to inflation. To adjust costs and benefits for future values there are three discounted project selection criteria used: net present value, the benefit–cost ratio, and the internal rate of return. Applying the project selection criteria to the valued costs and benefits (both tangible and intangible) enables a long-term project to be valued. A similar approach is applied when assessing personal injury compensation claims where large lump sum payments to cover loss over a lifetime are discounted on the basis that lump sums are invested and capable of producing income.

Pricing the environment

23.79 Cost-benefit analysis does enable external costs to be incorporated into decision-making but it does have its critics. It is argued that it is objectionable to put a price on the environment, and the right to a clean environment should be an absolute price and not traded. There will also be some difficulty in valuing certain externalities, e.g. the six-months premature death will be valued differently by someone aged 25 years compared to someone aged 85 years. On balance, CBA does have value but it should be used with caution, as with all environmental management techniques, it is a tool to assist decision-making and operations, but does not in itself determine the decision.

KEY DOCUMENTS AND MATERIALS

EU Regulation (EC) 761/2001 allowing voluntary participation by organisations in a Community eco-management and audit scheme

European Commission Recommendation C (2001) 2503 on guidance for the implementation of Regulation (EC) No. 761/2001 allowing voluntary participation by organisations in a Community eco-management and audit scheme

International Organisation for Standardisation: ISO 14001

ISO 14041: *Life Cycle Inventory Analysis*

ISO 14043: *Life Cycle Assessment Interpretation*

Society of Environmental Toxicology and Chemistry *Guidelines for life cycle assessment: a code of practice* (SETAC, 1993)

University of Bath, Integrated Environmental Management Core Module Workbook 2 (University of Bath, 1995 (rev 1999))

Eco-Management and Audit Scheme (EMAS)

Environment Agency Position Statement on EMSs

The Institute of Environmental Management and Assessment (IEMA)

24

ENVIRONMENTAL ASSESSMENT

A OVERVIEW OF ENVIRONMENTAL ASSESSMENT

What is environmental impact assessment?

Environmental impact assessment (EIA) is a tool to identify and predict the potential impact **24.01** of major development proposals on the environment and human health. It is designed to prevent, rather than alleviate, damage at the earliest opportunity. The conclusion of an EIA is the environmental statement (ES). An ES is not in itself a decision or conclusion. It is a report (or statement) that is prepared in support of proposals and projects and informs decision-makers about the potentially significant environmental effects of the related proposal. Any developer can prepare or commission an EIA for their own benefit. However, the majority of EIAs that are carried out in the UK are based on the need to fulfil a legal obligation to submit an ES, rather than a voluntary action.

24.02   In addition to EIAs that cover specific, albeit large, project proposals, strategic environmental assessment (SEA) is a similar environmental management tool that covers strategic plans and programmes. It aims to ensure that significant environmental effects are identified and assessed, subject to public participation, taken into account by decision-makers, and that sustainable development is promoted. SEA is considered in Section C below.

EU involvement in environmental assessment

24.03   Environmental assessment has been one of the few areas of EU legislative involvement in land use planning, that otherwise relies upon the principle of subsidiarity, and that decisions on land use are best taken at either a national, regional, or local level. National EIA legislation derives from the EU Directive 85/337/EEC on the assessment of the effects of certain public and private projects on the environment (as amended by Directive 97/11/EC (the Amending Directive) and Directive 2003/35/EC providing for public participation in drawing up certain environmental plans and programmes). Directive 85/337/EEC as amended is referred to throughout this chapter as the EIA Directive.

Projects covered by the EIA Directive

24.04   The EIA Directive covers a wide variety of projects, some of which fall outside the scope of development in terms of the land use planning system under the Town and Country Planning Act 1990 (TCPA 1990) etc (see Chapter 8: Land use planning), and while the majority of EIAs carried out in England and Wales are fulfilling requirements under the TCPA 1990 (and so considered in detail in this chapter), the following project areas also require EIA in support of proposals for approval. Further information of each project is provided in the Office of the Deputy Prime Minister (ODPM) publication *Environmental Impact Assessment: A Guide to Procedures* (2002). Summaries of the relevant parts of the guidance are provided below.

The trunk road network

24.05   Proposals for road projects in England and Wales that are the responsibility of the Highways Agency (i.e. major trunk roads and motorways) are approved under procedures in the Highways Act 1980. The Highways (Assessment of Environmental Effects) Regulations 1999 (SI 1999/369) apply to all new trunk roads and motorways subject to the smallest schemes falling outside the EIA process. Roads developed by local planning authorities (LPAs) and private developers fall within land use planning legislation.

Oil and gas pipe-lines

24.06   Oil and gas pipe-lines more than 80 cm in diameter and 40 kilometres long require an EIA under the EIA Directive. Pipe-lines below these thresholds may require an EIA, again under the Directive itself. Oil and gas pipe-lines that are 10 miles long or less are approved under the land use planning legislation.

Proposed onshore pipes more than 10 miles long require a pipe-line construction authoriza-　**24.07**
tion (PCA) under the Pipe-lines Act 1962. Assessment is required under the Pipe-line Works
(EIA) Regulations 2000 (SI 2000/1928). Companies wishing to convey gas may be licensed
as public gas transporters and are exempt from the PCA requirements, although they are
required to comply with the Public Gas Transporter Pipe-line Works (EIA) Regulations 1999
(SI 1999/672).

Offshore oil and gas projects

A licence is required from the Secretary of State for the extraction of petroleum and natural　**24.08**
gas for commercial purposes that exceeds 500 tonnes per day of petroleum and 500,000
cubic metres per day of gas. Also, consent is required for the drilling of a well and
the erection of any structure in connection with this. Relevant EIA requirements are
the Offshore Petroleum Production and Pipe-lines (Assessment of Environmental Effects)
Regulations 1999 (SI 1999/360).

Nuclear power stations, other power stations, and overhead power lines

The EIA Directive provides that the development, dismantling, and decommissioning of　**24.09**
nuclear power stations and other nuclear reactors require an EIA. For applications relating
to the development of nuclear power stations over 50 megawatts, the Secretary of State
is the decision-maker and the Electricity Works (Assessment of Environmental Effects)
Regulations 1999 (SI 1999/1927) implements the EIA Directive. This also applies to the
development of thermal power stations and overhead power lines. For power stations of
less than 50 megawatts and other buildings to house small nuclear reactors, permission to
develop is determined under the land use planning system.

Consent of the Health and Safety Executive is required for the dismantling and decom-　**24.10**
missioning of nuclear power stations and reactors. An application for consent must be
supported with an ES prepared in accordance with the Nuclear Reactors (EIA for Decommissioning) Regulations 1999 (SI 1999/2892).

Forestry projects

Anyone proposing to carry out a forestry project that is likely to have significant effects　**24.11**
on the environment must apply for consent from the Forestry Commission before starting
work. An application for consent must be supported by an EIA prepared in accordance with
the EIA (Forestry) (England and Wales) Regulations 1999 (SI 1999/2228).

Land drainage improvements

Land drainage projects fall within Annex II of the EIA Directive. New land drainage works　**24.12**
including flood defence and defences against the sea require permission under the land use
planning regime and land drainage improvement works are permitted development under
the Town & Country Planning (General Permitted Development) Order 1995 (see Chapter 8).
However, because such works may have significant environmental effects the EIA (Land
Drainage Improvement Works) Regulations 1999 (SI 1999/1783) require a drainage body to
consider whether proposed drainage works are likely to have significant environmental
impacts. If it decides that no significant environmental impacts are likely to arise then it
must publicize the proposed works. If any representations are that the proposed works may

have significant environmental effects, or that the drainage body concludes this anyway, it should prepare an ES.

Ports and harbours

24.13   Proposed development at ports and harbours down to the low water mark is subject to the Town & Country Planning EIA Regulations. For other works, the requirements are contained in the Harbour Works (EIA) Regulations 1999 (SI 1999/3445).

Marine fish farming

24.14   Onshore fish farming facilities may require planning permission under the Town and Country Planning system. Offshore facilities do not require planning permission but require a lease from the Crown Estates Commissioners. The EIA (Fish Farming in Marine Waters) Regulations 1999 (SI 1999/367) set indicative criteria, which, when triggered, require the Commissioners to screen applications to determine whether an EIA is necessary. The Scottish Executive Rural Affairs Department has issued: *A Guide to the EIA (Fish Farming in Marine Waters) Regulations 1999*.

Marine dredging for minerals

24.15   The extraction of minerals by marine dredging requires permission unless the regulator, i.e. the Secretary of State or National Assembly for Wales, has provided a written determination that the proposed dredging is not likely to have significant effects. An ES must accompany an application for permission.

Transport and Works Act 1992

24.16   The Transport and Works Act 1992 enables orders (TWA orders) to be made authorizing the construction or operation of railways, tramways, other guided transport systems, and inland waterways; and works interfering with rights of navigation. Orders may also authorize ancillary matters such as compulsory purchase and creating or extinguishing rights over land. Applicants for TWA orders may apply at the same time for a direction that planning permission is deemed to be granted. The procedures for making applications for orders under Pt 1 of the Act are contained in the Transport and Works (Applications and Objections Procedure) (England and Wales) Rules 2000 (SI 2000/2190), which also implement the EIA Directive.

Water abstraction and impounding

24.17   The Water Resources (EIA) (England and Wales) Regulations 2003 (SI 2003/164) set procedural requirements in relation to the consideration of applications or proposals for abstraction or impounding licences under Pt II of the Water Resources Act 1991 and require consent in other cases. The Environment Agency is the competent authority. Regulation 3 requires an EIA to be carried out for water management projects for agriculture including irrigation projects, which would be likely to have significant effects on the environment by virtue, among other things, of their nature, size, or location. Projects involving the abstraction of water are only included if the amounts abstracted exceed 20 cubic metres in any 24 hours. There are exceptions where the work to be carried out comes within the TCPA 1990 or the land drainage legislation, which requires an EIA independently.

As with most of the legislation enacted for the purpose of complying with the EIA Directive **24.18** the regulations set the procedure, but that procedure closely follows the requirements of the EIA Regulations to ensure compliance with the Directive.

Projects under the birds and habitats directives

Regulation 48(1) of the Conservation (Natural Habitats etc.) Regulations 1994 (SI 1994/ **24.19** 2716) (the Habitat Regs 1994) provides that a competent authority (Minister, government department, public or statutory undertaker, or public body) before deciding to undertake, or give any consent, permission, or other authorization for, a plan or project that is likely to have a significant effect on a European site (and that the plan or project is not directly connected with or necessary to the management of the site) shall make an appropriate assessment of the implications for the site in view of that site's conservation objectives. Regulation 10 states that a European site means:

(a) a special area of conservation;
(b) a site of community importance under Art 4(2) of the EU Directive 92/43/EEC on the conservation of natural habitats and of wild fauna and flora, as amended (the Habitats Directive);
(c) a site hosting a priority natural habitat type or priority species in respect of which consultation has been initiated under Art 5(1) of the Habitats Directive during the consultation period or pending a decision of the Council under Article 5(3); or
(d) an area classified pursuant to Art 4(1) or (2) of the Directive 79/409/EEC on the conservation of wild birds.

Under reg 49 of the Habitat Regs 1994 the competent authority must only agree to any **24.20** plan or project, notwithstanding a negative assessment of the implications for the site, if they are satisfied that there are no alternative solutions and that the plan or project must be carried out for imperative reasons of overriding public interest, which may be of a social or economic nature.

The distinction between any assessment under the Habitat Regs 1994 and EIAs in general **24.21** is that a habitats assessment becomes central to the decision-making process whereas an ES can only ever inform a decision-making body about the potential impacts.

In the ECJ case, *Landelijke Vereniging tot van de Waddenzee v Staatssecretaris van Landbouw,* **24.22** *Natuurbeheer en Visserij* (2004) Case C-127/02, the Grand Chamber held that mechanical cockle fishing was a plan or project for the purpose of the Habitats Directive and so required an appropriate assessment of the proposal if the activity was to be pursued on a conservation site.

Assessment of major accident hazards

The Control of Major Accident Hazard Regulations 1999 (SI 1999/743) (COMAH Regs 1999) **24.23** implements EU Directive 96/82/EC (the Seveso II Directive). In England and Wales, the COMAH Regs 1999 are implemented by the Environment Agency and Health & Safety Executive (HSE), who, together, operate as the competent authority required under the

Directive. The regulations apply to around 1,200 establishments that have the potential to cause major accidents because they use, or store, significant quantities of dangerous substances, such as oil products, natural gas, chemical, or explosives. The Planning (Control of Major Accident Hazards) Amendment Regulations 2005 (SI 2005/1088) amend the COMAH Regs 1999 in relation to land use planning. The amendments may limit future development within the vicinity of a site.

24.24 Under the COMAH Regs 1999, operators must prepare a major accident prevention policy to demonstrate that effective safety management systems are operating. Regulation 7 also places a duty on the competent authority to examine safety reports prepared by the operators proposing to operate activities that will hold large quantities of hazardous substances and to inform operators about the conclusions of its examinations. Further, the Regulations require the operator to prepare an on-site emergency plan and the local authority for the locality to prepare an off-site emergency plan. Both plans should be tested at least once every three years. The HSE has published the following guidance: *Preparing Safety Reports* (1999) and *Emergency Planning for Major Accidents* (1999). More information on the COMAH Regs 1999 is available from www.hse.gov.uk/comah.

Guidance on EIA

24.25 There is a wide range of guidance on the preparation and development of EIAs. Some of this is discussed throughout this chapter such as Circular 02/99 and the ODPM *Note on EIA for Local Planning Authorities* (2004). The Institute of Environmental Management recently published a comprehensive set of guidelines and Assessment (IEMA) entitled: *Guidelines for Environmental Assessment* (2004). This covers the principles and process of EIA and how to ensure that EIAs are carried out effectively. A detailed legal analysis may be found in Tromans and Fuller's: *EIA — Law and Practice* (LexisNexis, 2003).

B   EIA UNDER THE TOWN AND COUNTRY PLANNING SYSTEM

Introduction

24.26 Land use planning regulated under the various Town and Country Planning Acts and Regulations is considered in detail in Chapter 8. It plays the primary role in implementing the EIA Directive but has not been without some difficulty as illustrated by the comparatively large number of court cases, with decisions regularly referred to the appellate courts and to the European Court of Justice.

24.27 In an attempt to clarify some of the complexities in relation to EIA, certain government guidance has been issued to support the regulations and it is worth summarising the relevant legislation and government guidance in relation to land use planning:

- The EU Directive 85/337/EEC on the assessment of the effects of certain public and private projects on the environment amended by Directive 97/11/EC and other procedural amending directives such as Directive 2003/35/EC on public participation (the EIA Directive).

- TCPA 1990.
- The Town and Country Planning (EIA) (England and Wales) Regulations 1999 (SI 1999/ 293) as amended by, among others, the TCP (EIA) (England and Wales) (Amendment) Regulations 2000 (SI 2000/2867) (the EIA Regulations 1999).
- Circular 2/99: Environmental Impact Assessment.
- The ODPM guidance: *Environmental Impact Assessment: A Guide to Procedures* (2002).
- The ODPM: *Note on EIA for Local Planning Authorities* (19 April 2004).

Defining the environment

The environment is not expressly defined in the EIA Directive or the domestic EIA **24.28** Regulations 1999. However, both pieces of legislation set out what information should be included in the ES; the description in the Regulations being slightly wider than the Directive. Schedule 4 of the EIA Regulations 1999 is set out in full below. Paragraph 1(c), Pt 1 states that a description of the development should include in particular:

> an estimate, by type and quantity, of expected residues and emissions (water, air and soil pollution, noise, vibration, light, heat, radiation, etc) resulting from the operation of the proposed development.

Paragraph 3 of Sch 4, Pt 1 of the EIA Regulations 1999 provides that information in an **24.29** ES should include:

> A description of the aspects of the environment likely to be significantly affected by the development, including, in particular, population, fauna, flora, soil, water, air, climatic factors, material assets, including the architectural and archaeological heritage, landscape and the inter-relationship between the above factors.

Extent of EIAs under the TCPA 1990

The number of EIAs in support of planning applications for major development proposals **24.30** has increased significantly in recent years. According to ODPM statistics, during the 1990s there were around 150 statements received in support of planning applications every year under the former EIA Regulations 1988 (SI 1988/1199). By 2002, the number of ESs received had increased to 416. The EIA Regulations 1999 are the main source of EIA legislation, although this has been subject to amendment. Regulation 2 provides that an 'EIA application' means an application for planning permission for EIA development.

If it is accepted that EIA is primarily a tool for helping decision-makers make more informed **24.31** decisions on developments, then the increase in the number of EIAs should be regarded as a positive step. However, properly carrying out an EIA takes time and money and, from a financial view, the need to prepare an EIA may be regarded as an unwelcome expense.

Key stages of an EIA

Due to the nature of projects that may be subject to an EIA the decision-maker can be **24.32** either an LPA, the Secretary of State, or a planning inspector. An ES must be provided in support of the planning applications for certain major project proposals likely to have a significant impact on the environment. Statutory consultees and members of the public must be given the opportunity to comment on an ES. Importantly, reg 3 of the EIA Regulations 1999 states that the decision-maker must take into account both the ES and any representations made about the environmental effects before a planning application is determined and that they must state in their decision that they have done so. Key stages of an EIA include:

- screening, whenever necessary;
- scoping;
- carrying out the assessment;
- preparing an ES;
- submitting the planning application and ES in support;
- consultation; and
- determining the planning application.

Screening

24.33 Screening is the process carried out by the decision-maker to establish whether an EIA is required based upon the characteristics, location, and potential impacts of a proposed development. Screening is covered in Pts II and III of the EIA Regulations 1999. Under reg 5, a developer may ask the relevant LPA for a screening opinion before submitting a planning application. If a planning application is submitted without an ES, the LPA may regard the application as a request for a screening opinion (reg 7). In *Berkeley v Secretary of State for the Environment Transport and the Regions (No. 2)* [2002] Env LR 14 378 Schiemann LJ considered the EIA Directive and its EU case law and then summarized the position in relation to EIA and screening by stating that:

- The planning authority, Secretary of State and the inspector are not empowered to grant planning permission for an EIA application unless the environmental impact assessment procedures have been gone through — see Regulation 3.
- The amended Directive is not intended to prevent all development which is likely to have a significant effect on the environment, it is intended to improve the quality of the decision taking process in a group of cases.
- In relation to [Schedule 2] development the Community has 'in accordance with the subsidiarity principle' left it to Member States to identify the parameters of the group of development permission for which cannot be granted without an EIA.
- Member States are under a duty to ensure that before consent is given, projects likely to have significant effects on the environment will be subjected to an EIA.

24.34 Prior to evaluating whether a development proposal is subject to the EIA Regulations 1999. The project or proposal must be of the nature that falls within the land use planning system. In almost all cases this will be clear, the Regulations refer to any proposals as development. However, the EIA Directive refers to projects. Many projects under the EIA will be covered under other legislation (see Section A). In *Westminster City Council & ors v Mayor of London* [2002] EWHC 2440 (also discussed in Chapter 3: Air) Mr Justice Kay concluded that the London Congestion Charging Scheme could not be regarded as an urban development project under Sch 2 of the EIA Regulations 1999 and that an urban development project suggested something more in the nature of building and construction.

24.35 The EIA Regulations set out the need for an EIA for two types of proposal described in the Schedules 1 and 2:

(1) Schedule 1 development covers the largest projects; and

(2) Schedule 2 development, if it is likely to have significant effects on the environment due to its size, nature, and location.

There will also need to be an EIA for changes or extensions to both types of development.

In summary, Sch 1 development will always require an EIA, while other major development **24.36** that does not come within the descriptions in Sch 1 will only be regarded as Sch 2 development (and so require an EIA) if it is above the selection thresholds and criteria contained in Sch 2 and Sch 3. Schedules 1 to 3 of the EIA Regulations are set out, excluding footnotes, in full below.

THE TOWN AND COUNTRY PLANNING (ENVIRONMENTAL IMPACT ASSESSMENT) (ENGLAND AND WALES) REGULATIONS 1999 (SI 1999/293)

SCHEDULE 1
DESCRIPTIONS OF DEVELOPMENT FOR THE PURPOSES OF THE DEFINITION OF 'SCHEDULE 1 DEVELOPMENT'

Interpretation

In this Schedule—

'airport' means an airport which complies with the definition in the 1944 Chicago Convention setting up the International Civil Aviation Organisation (Annex 14);

'express road' means a road which complies with the definition in the European Agreement on Main International Traffic Arteries of 15 November 1975;

'nuclear power station' and 'other nuclear reactor' do not include an installation from the site of which all nuclear fuel and other radioactive contaminated materials have been permanently removed; and development for the purpose of dismantling or decommissioning a nuclear power station or other nuclear reactor shall not be treated as development of the description mentioned in paragraph 2(b) of this Schedule.

Descriptions of development

The carrying out of development to provide any of the following—

1. Crude-oil refineries (excluding undertakings manufacturing only lubricants from crude oil) and installations for the gasification and liquefaction of 500 tonnes or more of coal or bituminous shale per day.

2. (a) Thermal power stations and other combustion installations with a heat output of 300 megawatts or more; and

    (b) Nuclear power stations and other nuclear reactors (except research installations for the production and conversion of fissionable and fertile materials, whose maximum power does not exceed 1 kilowatt continuous thermal load).

3. (a) Installations for the reprocessing of irradiated nuclear fuel.

    (b) Installations designed—

    (i)   for the production or enrichment of nuclear fuel,

    (ii) for the processing of irradiated nuclear fuel or high-level radioactive waste,

     (iii) for the final disposal of irradiated nuclear fuel,

     (iv) solely for the final disposal of radioactive waste,

     (v) solely for the storage (planned for more than 10 years) of irradiated nuclear fuels or radioactive waste in a different site than the production site.

4. (a) Integrated works for the initial smelting of cast-iron and steel;

     (b) Installations for the production of non-ferrous crude metals from ore, concentrates or secondary raw materials by metallurgical, chemical or electrolytic processes.

5. Installations for the extraction of asbestos and for the processing and transformation of asbestos and products containing asbestos—

     (a) for asbestos-cement products, with an annual production of more than 20,000 tonnes of finished products;

     (b) for friction material, with an annual production of more than 50 tonnes of finished products; and

     (c) for other uses of asbestos, utilisation of more than 200 tonnes per year.

6. Integrated chemical installations, that is to say, installations for the manufacture on an industrial scale of substances using chemical conversion processes, in which several units are juxtaposed and are functionally linked to one another and which are—

     (a) for the production of basic organic chemicals;

     (b) for the production of basic inorganic chemicals;

     (c) for the production of phosphorous-, nitrogen- or potassium-based fertilisers (simple or compound fertilisers);

     (d) for the production of basic plant health products and of biocides;

     (e) for the production of basic pharmaceutical products using a chemical or biological process;

     (f) for the production of explosives.

7. (a) Construction of lines for long-distance railway traffic and of airports with a basic runway length of 2,100 metres or more;

     (b) Construction of motorways and express roads;

     (c) Construction of a new road of four or more lanes, or realignment and/or widening of an existing road of two lanes or less so as to provide four or more lanes, where such new road, or realigned and/or widened section of road would be 10 kilometres or more in a continuous length.

8. (a) Inland waterways and ports for inland-waterway traffic which permit the passage of vessels of over 1,350 tonnes;

     (b) Trading ports, piers for loading and unloading connected to land and outside ports (excluding ferry piers) which can take vessels of over 1,350 tonnes.

9. Waste disposal installations for the incineration, chemical treatment (as defined in Annex IIA to Council Directive 75/442/EEC under heading D9), or landfill of hazardous waste (that is to say, waste to which Council Directive 91/689/EEC applies).

10. Waste disposal installations for the incineration or chemical treatment (as defined in Annex IIA to Council Directive 75/442/EEC under heading D9) of non-hazardous waste with a capacity exceeding 100 tonnes per day.

11. Goundwater abstraction or artificial groundwater recharge schemes where the annual volume of water abstracted or recharged is equivalent to or exceeds 10 million cubic metres.

12. (a) Works for the transfer of water resources, other than piped drinking water, between river basins where the transfer aims at preventing possible shortages of water and where the amount of water transferred exceeds 100 million cubic metres per year;

     (b) In all other cases, works for the transfer of water resources, other than piped drinking water, between river basins where the multi-annual average flow of the basin of abstraction exceeds 2,000 million cubic metres per year and where the amount of water transferred exceeds 5% of this flow.

13. Waste water treatment plants with a capacity exceeding 150,000 population equivalent as defined in Article 2 point (6) of Council Directive 91/271/EEC.

14. Extraction of petroleum and natural gas for commercial purposes where the amount extracted exceeds 500 tonnes per day in the case of petroleum and 500,000 cubic metres per day in the case of gas.

15. Dams and other installations designed for the holding back or permanent storage of water, where a new or additional amount of water held back or stored exceeds 10 million cubic metres.

16. Pipelines for the transport of gas, oil or chemicals with a diameter of more than 800 millimetres and a length of more than 40 kilometres.

17. Installations for the intensive rearing of poultry or pigs with more than—
    (a) 85,000 places for broilers or 60,000 places for hens;
    (b) 3,000 places for production pigs (over 30 kg); or
    (c) 900 places for sows.

18. Industrial plants for—
    (a) the production of pulp from timber or similar fibrous materials;
    (b) the production of paper and board with a production capacity exceeding 200 tonnes per day.

19. Quarries and open-cast mining where the surface of the site exceeds 25 hectares, or peat extraction where the surface of the site exceeds 150 hectares.

20. Installations for storage of petroleum, petrochemical or chemical products with a capacity of 200,000 tonnes or more.

SCHEDULE 2
DESCRIPTIONS OF DEVELOPMENT AND APPLICABLE THRESHOLDS AND CRITERIA FOR THE PURPOSES OF THE DEFINITION OF 'SCHEDULE 2 DEVELOPMENT'

1. In the table below—
   'area of the works' includes any area occupied by apparatus, equipment, machinery, materials, plant, spoil heaps or other facilities or stores required for construction or installation;
   'controlled waters' has the same meaning as in the Water Resources Act 1991;
   'floorspace' means the floorspace in a building or buildings.

2. The table below sets out the descriptions of development and applicable thresholds and criteria for the purpose of classifying development as Schedule 2 development.

Column 1 *Description of development*	*Column 2* *Applicable thresholds and criteria*
The carrying out of development to provide any of the following—	
1. Agriculture and aquaculture	
(a) Projects for the use of uncultivated land or semi-natural areas for intensive agricultural purposes;	The area of the development exceeds 0.5 hectare.
(b) Water management projects for agriculture, including irrigation and land drainage projects;	The area of the works exceeds 1 hectare.
(c) Intensive livestock installations (unless included in Schedule 1);	The area of new floorspace exceeds 500 square metres.
(d) Intensive fish farming;	The installation resulting from the development is designed to produce more than 10 tonnes of dead weight fish per year.
(e) Reclamation of land from the sea.	All development.

2. Extractive industry

(a) Quarries, open-cast mining and peat extraction (unless included in Schedule 1);	All development except the construction of buildings or other ancillary structures where the new floorspace does not exceed 1,000 square metres.
(b) Underground mining;	

(c) Extraction of minerals by fluvial dredging;	All development.

(d) Deep drillings, in particular—

(i) geothermal drilling;	(i) In relation to any type of drilling, the area of the works exceeds 1 hectare; or
(ii) drilling for the storage of nuclear waste material;	(ii) in relation to geothermal drilling and drilling for the storage of nuclear waste material, the drilling is within 100 metres of any controlled waters.
(iii) drilling for water supplies;	

with the exception of drillings for investigating the stability of the soil.

(e) Surface industrial installations for the extraction of coal, petroleum, natural gas and ores, as well as bituminous shale.	The area of the development exceeds 0.5 hectare.

3. Energy industry

(a) Industrial installations for the production of electricity, steam and hot water (unless included in Schedule 1);	The area of the development exceeds 0.5 hectare.
(b) Industrial installations for carrying gas, steam and hot water;	The area of the works exceeds 1 hectare.
(c) Surface storage of natural gas;	(i) The area of any new building, deposit or structure exceeds 500 square metres; or
(d) Underground storage of combustible gases;	(ii) a new building, deposit or structure is to be sited within 100 metres of any controlled waters.
(e) Surface storage of fossil fuels;	
(f) Industrial briquetting of coal and lignite;	The area of new floorspace exceeds 1,000 square metres.
(g) Installations for the processing and storage of radioactive waste (unless included in Schedule 1);	(i) The area of new floorspace exceeds 1,000 square metres; or
	(ii) the installation resulting from the development will require an authorisation or the variation of an authorisation under the Radioactive Substances Act 1993.
(h) Installations for hydroelectric energy production;	The installation is designed to produce more than 0.5 megawatts.
(i) Installations for the harnessing of wind power for energy production (wind farms).	(i) The development involves the installation of more than 2 turbines; or
	(ii) the hub height of any turbine or height of any other structure exceeds 15 metres.

4. Production and processing of metals

(a) Installations for the production of pig iron or steel (primary or secondary fusion) including continuous casting;	The area of new floorspace exceeds 1,000 square metres.
(b) Installations for the processing of ferrous metals—	

    (i)   hot-rolling mills;

    (ii) smitheries with hammers;

    (iii) application of protective fused metal coats.

(c) Ferrous metal foundries;

(d) Installations for the smelting, including the alloyage, of non-ferrous metals, excluding precious metals, including recovered products (refining, foundry casting, etc.);

(e) Installations for surface treatment of metals and plastic materials using an electrolytic or chemical process;

(f) Manufacture and assembly of motor vehicles and manufacture of motor-vehicle engines;

(g) Shipyards;

(h) Installations for the construction and repair of aircraft;

(i) Manufacture of railway equipment;

(j) Swaging by explosives;

(k) Installations for the roasting and sintering of metallic ores.

5. Mineral industry

(a) Coke ovens (dry coal distillation);

(b) Installations for the manufacture of cement;

    The area of new floorspace exceeds 1,000 square metres.

(c) Installations for the production of asbestos and the manufacture of asbestos-based products (unless included in Schedule 1);

(d) Installations for the manufacture of glass including glass fibre;

(e) Installations for smelting mineral substances including the production of mineral fibres;

(f) Manufacture of ceramic products by burning, in particular roofing tiles, bricks, refractory bricks, tiles, stonewear or porcelain.

6. Chemical industry (unless included in Schedule 1)

(a) Treatment of intermediate products and production of chemicals;

    The area of new floorspace exceeds 1,000 square metres.

(b) Production of pesticides and pharmaceutical products, paint and varnishes, elastomers and peroxides;

(c) Storage facilities for petroleum, petrochemical and chemical products.

    (i) The area of any new building or structure exceeds 0.05 hectare; or

    (ii) more than 200 tonnes of petroleum, petrochemical or chemical products is to be stored at any one time.

7. Food industry

(a) Manufacture of vegetable and animal oils and fats;

(b) Packing and canning of animal and vegetable products;

(c) Manufacture of dairy products;

(d) Brewing and malting;

(e) Confectionery and syrup manufacture;

(f) Installations for the slaughter of animals;

(g) Industrial starch manufacturing installations;

(h) Fish-meal and fish-oil factories;

(i) Sugar factories.

The area of new floorspace exceeds 1,000 square metres.

8. Textile, leather, wood and paper industries

(a) Industrial plants for the production of paper and board (unless included in Schedule 1);

(b) Plants for the pre-treatment (operations such as washing, bleaching, mercerisation) or dyeing of fibres or textiles;

(c) Plants for the tanning of hides and skins;

(d) Cellulose-processing and production installations.

The area of new floorspace exceeds 1,000 square metres.

9. Rubber industry

Manufacture and treatment of elastomer-based products.

The area of new floorspace exceeds 1,000 square metres.

10. Infrastructure projects

(a) Industrial estate development projects;

(b) Urban development projects, including the construction of shopping centres and car parks, sports stadiums, leisure centres and multiplex cinemas;

(c) Construction of intermodal transshipment facilities and of intermodal terminals (unless included in Schedule 1);

(d) Construction of railways (unless included in Schedule 1);

(e) Construction of airfields (unless included in Schedule 1);

(f) Construction of roads (unless included in Schedule 1);

(g) Construction of harbours and port installations including fishing harbours (unless included in Schedule 1);

(h) Inland-waterway construction not included in Schedule 1, canalisation and flood-relief works;

The area of the development exceeds 0.5 hectare.

The area of the works exceeds 1 hectare.

(i) The development involves an extension to a runway; or

(ii) the area of the works exceeds 1 hectare.

The area of the works exceeds 1 hectare.

The area of the works exceeds 1 hectare.

The area of the works exceeds 1 hectare.

(i) Dams and other installations designed to hold water or store it on a long-term basis (unless included in Schedule 1);

(j) Tramways, elevated and underground railways, suspended lines or similar lines of a particular type, used exclusively or mainly for passenger transport;

(k) Oil and gas pipeline installations (unless included in Schedule 1);

    (i) The area of the works exceeds 1 hectare; or,

(l) Installations of long-distance aqueducts;

    (ii) in the case of a gas pipeline, the installation has a design operating pressure exceeding 7 bar gauge.

(m) Coastal work to combat erosion and maritime works capable of altering the coast through the construction, for example, of dykes, moles, jetties and other sea defence works, excluding the maintenance and reconstruction of such works;

All development.

(n) Groundwater abstraction and artificial groundwater recharge schemes not included in Schedule 1;

The area of the works exceeds 1 hectare.

(o) Works for the transfer of water resources between river basins not included in Schedule 1;

(p) Motorway service areas.

The area of the development exceeds 0.5 hectare.

11. Other projects

(a) Permanent racing and test tracks for motorised vehicles;

The area of the development exceeds 1 hectare.

(b) Installations for the disposal of waste (unless included in Schedule 1);

    (i)   The disposal is by incineration; or

    (ii) the area of the development exceeds 0.5 hectare; or

    (iii) the installation is to be sited within 100 metres of any controlled waters.

(c) Waste-water treatment plants (unless included in Schedule 1);

The area of the development exceeds 1,000 square metres.

(d) Sludge-deposition sites;

    (i)   The area of deposit or storage exceeds 0.5 hectare; or

(e) Storage of scrap iron, including scrap vehicles;

    (ii) a deposit is to be made or scrap stored within 100 metres of any controlled waters.

(f) Test benches for engines, turbines or reactors;

The area of new floorspace exceeds 1,000 square metres.

(g) Installations for the manufacture of artificial mineral fibres;

(h) Installations for the recovery or destruction of explosive substances;

    (i) Knackers' yards.

12. Tourism and leisure

(a) Ski-runs, ski-lifts and cable-cars and associated developments;

(i) The area of the works exceeds 1 hectare; or
(ii) the height of any building or other structure exceeds 15 metres.

(b) Marinas;

The area of the enclosed water surface exceeds 1,000 square metres.

(c) Holiday villages and hotel complexes outside urban areas and associated developments;

The area of the development exceeds 0.5 hectare.

(d) Theme parks;

(e) Permanent camp sites and caravan sites;

The area of the development exceeds 1 hectare.

(f) Golf courses and associated developments.

The area of the development exceeds 1 hectare.

13.

(a) Any change to or extension of development of a description listed in Schedule 1 or in paragraphs 1 to 12 of Column 1 of this table, where that development is already authorised, executed or in the process of being executed, and the change or extension may have significant adverse effects on the environment;

(i) In relation to development of a description mentioned in Column 1 of this table, the thresholds and criteria in the corresponding part of Column 2 of this table applied to the change or extension (and not to the development as changed or extended).

(ii) In relation to development of a description mentioned in a paragraph in Schedule 1 indicated below, the thresholds and criteria in Column 2 of the paragraph of this table indicated below applied to the change or extension (and not to the development as changed or extended):

Paragraph in Schedule 1	Paragraph of this table
1	6(a)
2(a)	3(a)
2(b)	3(g)
3	3(g)
4	4
5	5
6	6(a)
7(a)	10(d) (in relation to railways) or 10(e) (in relation to airports)
7(b) and (c)	10(f)
8(a)	10(h)
8(b)	10(g)
9	11(b)
10	11(b)
11	10(n)
12	10(o)
13	11(c)
14	2(e)
15	10(i)
16	10(k)
17	1(c)
18	8(a)

19	2(a)
20	6(c)

(b) Development of a description mentioned   All development.
    in Schedule 1 undertaken exclusively or
    mainly for the development and testing of
    new methods or products and not used for
    more than two years.

SCHEDULE 3
SELECTION CRITERIA FOR SCREENING SCHEDULE 2 DEVELOPMENT

1. Characteristics of development

The characteristics of development must be considered having regard, in particular, to—

(a) the size of the development;

(b) the cumulation with other development;

(c) the use of natural resources;

(d) the production of waste;

(e) pollution and nuisances;

(f) the risk of accidents, having regard in particular to substances or technologies used.

2. Location of development

The environmental sensitivity of geographical areas likely to be affected by development must be considered, having regard, in particular, to—

(a) the existing land use;

(b) the relative abundance, quality and regenerative capacity of natural resources in the area;

(c) the absorption capacity of the natural environment, paying particular attention to the following areas—

  (i)   wetlands;

  (ii) coastal zones;

  (iii) mountain and forest areas;

  (iv) nature reserves and parks;

  (v)   areas classified or protected under Member States' legislation; areas designated by Member States pursuant to Council Directive 79/409/EEC on the conservation of wild birds and Council Directive 92/43/EEC on the conservation of natural habitats and of wild fauna and flora;

  (vi) areas in which the environmental quality standards laid down in Community legislation have already been exceeded;

  (vii) densely populated areas;

  (viii) landscapes of historical, cultural or archaeological significance.

3. Characteristics of the potential impact

The potential significant effects of development must be considered in relation to criteria set out under paragraphs 1 and 2 above, and having regard in particular to—

(a) the extent of the impact (geographical area and size of the affected population);

(b) the transfrontier nature of the impact;

(c) the magnitude and complexity of the impact;

(d) the probability of the impact;

(e) the duration, frequency and reversibility of the impact.

Determining whether an EIA is required for Schedule 2 development

24.37   Circular 02/99 advises that the determination of whether or not an EIA is required for a particular proposal can take place at a number of stages including:

- when the developer decides that an EIA is required and submits an ES for the purpose of the Regulations with a planning application;
- when the developer, before submitting an application, requests a screening opinion from the LPA (available under reg 5 of the EIA Regulations 1999). If the developer disputes the need for an EIA, or an opinion is not adopted within the relevant period, the developer may apply to the Secretary of State for a screening direction. Similar procedures apply to permitted development;
- the LPA may determine that an EIA is required following receipt of a planning application and inform the developer of this. If the developer then disputes the need for an EIA, the developer may apply to the Secretary of State for a screening direction;
- the Secretary of State may determine that an EIA is required for an application that has been called in for his determination or is before him on appeal; or
- the Secretary of State may direct that an EIA is required at any stage prior to the grant of consent for particular development.

Requesting a screening opinion

24.38   If the developer has requested a screening opinion, it must include, under reg 5(2) of the EIA Regulations 1999:

(a)   a plan sufficient to identify the land;

(b)   a brief description of the nature and purpose of the development and of its possible effects on the environment; and

(c)   such other information or representations as the person making the request may wish to provide or make.

24.39   If the developer has requested a screening opinion from the LPA prior to submitting a planning application then the LPA must adopt an opinion within three weeks (or longer, if agreed). If the LPA fails to adopt a decision or state that an EIA is required, the developer, under reg 6, may request a screening direction from the Secretary of State. If a request to the Secretary of State has been made for a screening direction then this must also be provided within three weeks or such time as is reasonable (reg 6(4)).

24.40   For cases where an application has been received without an ES and either the LPA, the Secretary of State or, if it is a planning appeal, the Planning Inspector has informed the developer that an ES is required in support of the application then the onus is on the developer to provide an ES and, if he fails to do so the application will ultimately be regarded as refused (regs 8 and 9).

Screening beyond the three-week time period

24.41   It may be the case that an LPA will decide that an EIA is not required, or not decide at all within the initial three-week period set by the Regulations, e.g. if further information about the application comes to light as the application is being considered. The *Note on EIA for LPAs* (2004) issued by the ODPM advises that if the LPA had not issued a screening opinion and it considers that an EIA was required it could seek to persuade the applicant voluntarily to carry out an assessment and provide an ES. If the applicant was unwilling to do so, the authority can ask the Secretary of State to issue a screening direction to determine whether an EIA is required.

In *BT plc v Gloucester CC* [2001] EWHC Admin 1001 Elias J considered that the three-week **24.42** time period did not operate as a mandatory requirement after which an ES could not lawfully be required and that requesting an ES at a later stage would be akin to seeking an amendment to the original planning application. He added that:

> Provided the procedures relating to consultation are complied with, and the representations are before the planning authority when it makes its decision, neither logic nor common sense nor the public interest dictate that the courts should treat the exercise as invalid merely because the planning authority only realised the need for the statement late in the day.

In *Fernback & ors v Harrow LBC* [2000] EWHC Admin 278 the court held that a negative **24.43** screening opinion by an LPA did not determine whether a planning application was EIA development and a positive opinion was determinative only in the absence of a screening direction by the Secretary of State. However, a direction by the Secretary of State was, either way, determinative.

Identifying Schedule 2 development during screening

Paragraphs 29 to 48 of Circular 02/99 provide guidance in identifying Sch 2 development. **24.44** It states that Sch 2 development is development of the type listed in Sch 2 of the EIA Regulations 1999, which:

   (a)   is located wholly or in part in a 'sensitive area' as defined in reg 2(1); or
   (b)   meets one of the relevant criteria or exceeds one of the relevant thresholds listed in the 2nd column of the Sch 2 table.

The Circular stresses that development in a sensitive area should only be considered to be Sch **24.45** 2 development if it falls within a description of Sch 2 and that the majority of proposals such as householder and small business developments will not fall within any of the descriptions. Development below the thresholds or not meeting one of the criteria in the second column of the table in Sch 2 does not require an EIA. However, there may be circumstances in which small development may give rise to significant environmental effects and in those cases the Secretary of State can use his powers under reg 4(8) to direct that an EIA is required.

Circular 02/99 states that an LPA must screen every planning application for Sch 2 develop- **24.46** ment to determine whether or not an EIA is required and must ask 'would this particular development be likely to have significant effects on the environment?' It goes on to indicate considerations to be taken into account in answering the question and refers to the three broad selection criteria contained in Sch 3 of the EIA Regulations 1999, which are:

(1)   the characteristics of the development;
(2)   the environmental sensitivity of the location; and
(3)   the characteristics of the potential impact.

The Circular adds that it is the Secretary of State's view that, in general, an EIA will be **24.47** necessary in three main types of Sch 2 development:

   (a)   for major developments which are of more than local importance including, on some occasions, proposals that the Secretary of State may wish to exercise his power to 'call in' the application for his own determination;

(b) development in environmentally sensitive areas, including those areas defined in reg 2(1) as 'sensitive areas' and for which the thresholds/criteria requirement do not apply; and

(c) development with particularly complex and potentially hazardous effects, including those that could have complex, long-term or irreversible effects.

24.48 The Circular suggests that it is not possible to formulate standard criteria or thresholds and that each case should be considered on a case-by-case basis. However, it provides some indicative thresholds and criteria in Annex A covering agriculture, the extractive and energy industries, and infrastructure developments such as roads. In general, each application should be considered on its own merits although it identifies the opportunity to avoid an EIA by making a series of small developments that collectively may generate an overall significant effect. The requirement to carry out an EIA should not be frustrated by a number of small but related planning applications being made and the cumulative impact of the developments should be taken into account. In *R v Swale BC ex p RSPB* [1991] 1 PLR 6 the court noted that in determining whether a Sch 2 development would be likely to have significant effects on the environment by virtue of its nature, size, or location is a matter that should not be considered in isolation if, in reality, the development is properly to be regarded as an integral part of an inevitably more substantial development. Paragraph 46 of Circular 02/99 states that:

> The need of EIA (including the applicability of any indicative thresholds) must be considered in respect of the total development. . . . In this context, it will be important to establish whether each of the proposed developments could proceed independently and whether the aims of the Regulations and Directive are being frustrated by the submission of multiple planning applications.

24.49 Changes and extensions to existing or approved development may be required by an EIA if it is likely to have significant environmental effect and such proposals should be considered in the light of the general guidance in the Circular. In *Commission v Spain* (2004) Case C-227/01 the ECJ held that a 13-kilometre section of railway that had not been subject to an EIA should be considered in context and that it in fact doubled the existing track. The court recognized the objectives of the Directive, its wide scope and very broad purpose, and that these should not be undermined by splitting up a large project into a series of short sections.

24.50 The *EIA Guide to Procedures* states that development that will not usually require planning permission because of the provisions of the Town and Country Planning (General Permitted Development) Order 1995 (SI 1995/418) but is considered to be either Sch 1 or Sch 2 development, may have permitted development rights withdrawn. Similarly for Sch 1 and 2 development that falls within a Simplified Planning Zone or Enterprise Zone, an EIA will continue to be required and if so planning permission is required in the normal way.

24.51 Finally, where EIA is required for outline planning applications, the Circular advises that the requirements of the Regulations must be fully met at the outline stages since reserved matters cannot be subject to EIA. When any planning application is made in outline the LPA will need to be satisfied that they have sufficient information available on the environmental effects of the proposal to be able to determine whether or not permission should be granted in principle.

There is some clarification as to what type of proposal requires a screening opinion. There **24.52** have been a large number of legal claims relating to screening and whether an ES should support a planning proposal in the first place. In *R v Swale BC ex p RSPB* the court considered that the decision as to whether any particular development fell within the EIA regime was entirely a matter for the planning authority and for many years the courts avoided the question. However, in *R v St Edmundsbury Borough Council ex p Walton* [1999] Env LR 879 planning permission was quashed because a decision not to require an EIA was taken by an officer who did not have formal delegated authority.

In *R (Roplas) v Kingston upon Hull CC* [2002] EWHC 1364 (Admin) the LPA accepted that it **24.53** had failed to provide a screening opinion for an urban development project just over 0.5 hectares. In *R v (Prophet) v York CC* [2002] EWHC 588 (Admin) the Court agreed that a screening opinion was desirable for a development of 24 flats on a site of 0.51 hectare.

In *R (Lebus & ors) v South Cambridgeshire DC* [2002] EWHC 2009 (Admin) permission for a **24.54** large egg production unit for 12,000 'free range' chickens was quashed because the LPA felt that it should not be drawn into requiring an ES simply to get information it should expect anyway. The LPA also believed that any impacts that may arise would be insignificant because conditions imposed on any grant of permission would control these. The court disapproved of this approach believing that an EIA and subsequent ES should inform the decision-making process. It held that:

> it is not appropriate for a person charged with making a screening decision to start from the premise that although there may be significant impacts, these can be reduced to insignificance by the application of conditions of various kinds. The appropriate course in such a case is to require an environmental statement and the measures which it is said will reduce their significance.

The High Court in *Hereford Waste Watchers Ltd v Hereford Council* [2005] EWHC 191 Admin **24.55** also considered the grant of permission and conditions relating to environmental impacts. In *Hereford Waste Watchers* the claimant argued that the ES in support of a planning application for a waste treatment and recycling facility failed properly and fully to provide relevant information. As a result, it was argued that Council was unable to assess whether the effects of the proposal were significant or not and that the permission subject to conditions should not have been granted. Elias J concluded at para 51 that:

> It follows that in my view the planning permission is flawed. The information which the planning authority requires, and which it has stipulated should be made available prior to the development commencing, should have been made available prior to the planning permission being granted. It may be that the information will confirm the assessment made by the developer. But I cannot properly make that assumption, and I should not deny the claimant and any other potential consultee the possible opportunity to respond to whatever is forthcoming. I would therefore quash the planning permission on this ground.

The Court of Appeal in *R (Goodman) v Lewisham LBC* [2002] EWHC Admin 1769 held **24.56** that infrastructure, for the purpose of the EIA Directive, went far wider than the normal understanding and as quoted in the *Shorter Oxford English Dictionary*. It held that the LPA determination that a proposal to construct a storage and distribution facility was outside Sch 2.10(b) of the EIA Regulations 1999, was unreasonable, and so the planning permission was quashed and the application remitted to the LPA for reconsideration. The *Note on EIA for LPAs* comments that following *Goodman* the messages are clear:

(1) the Directive is not open to narrow interpretation;

(2) do not assume a project is excluded simply because it is not expressly mentioned; and

(3) if in doubt about whether an EIA is required seek legal advice.

24.57 In *R (Wells) v Secretary of State for Transport, Local Government and the Regions* (2004) Case C-201/02 ECJ, the European Court of Justice took a broad, purposive approach to what constituted development consent for the purpose of EIA holding that the statutory review of old mining permissions should fall within this category, and as general principle, where consent for development is granted in stages, the EIA should take place at the stage of the principal decision. However, in *R (Noble) v Thanet DC* [2004] EWHC 296 (Admin) the High Court refined the position in *Wells* dismissing a claim for judicial review challenging an outline grant of planning permission for lack of an EIA.

24.58 Formal reasons are not required for screening opinions that conclude that a proposal is not EIA development. However, any record of these may well be useful if a challenge was made to a subsequent planning determination. However, in *Younger Homes (Northern) Ltd v First Secretary of State* [2004] EWCA Civ 1060 the court held that the fact that a negative screening opinion was not in the proper form and had not been placed on the planning register did not justify quashing the planning permission and that it was a procedural flaw that could be resolved.

The scope and contents of an environmental statement

24.59 Scoping is the process of setting out the parameters, the approach to the EIA, and the contents of the ES. Under reg 10 of the EIA Regulations a developer may ask the decision-maker to provide a written opinion as to the information to be provided in the ES.

Requirements of an ES

24.60 Circular 02/99 reiterates that it is the developer's responsibility to prepare the ES. There is no prescribed form although it must contain the information specified in Pts I and II of Sch 4 of the EIA Regulations 1999 as relevant (see above). The Circular adds that while an ES should provide a full factual description, the emphasis should be on the 'main' or 'significant' environmental effects to which a development is likely to give rise. The ES should out-line the main alternative approaches to the development and encourage the nature of con-sideration of alternative sites (which may amount to a material consideration to be taken into account in determining the planning application).

24.61 The environmental aspects that may be significantly affected by a proposal are listed in para 3, Pt I, Sch 4 and include human beings, flora, fauna, soil, water, air, climate, land-scape, material assets, and the interaction between any of these. Paragraph 4 suggests that consideration should also be given to, among other things, the likely significant effects resulting from the use of natural resources, the emission of pollutants, the creation of nuisances, and the elimination of waste.

24.62 Paragraph 85 of Circular 02/99 states that the information in an ES must be summarized in a non-technical summary in accessible plain English. This is vital for ensuring that the public can comment fully on it.

Scoping

There is no obligation to consult about the contents of an ES. However, reg 10 of the EIA **24.63** Regulations 1999 enables a developer to ask an LPA to state in writing a scoping opinion as to the information to be included in an ES. To obtain a scoping opinion the developer must, under reg 10(2), provide the LPA with:

(a) a plan sufficient to identify the land;

(b) a brief description of the nature and purpose of the development and of its possible effects on the environment; and

(c) such other information or representations as the person making the request may wish to provide or make.

Regulation 10(5) of the EIA Regulations 1999 provides that an LPA must adopt a scoping **24.64** opinion within five weeks of a request or of adopting a screening opinion (if the screening and scoping opinion were requested simultaneously) unless any further period is agreed. If the LPA fails to provide a scoping opinion the developer may apply to the Secretary of State for a scoping direction (reg 10(7)). The scoping opinion must be kept publicly available on the LPA's planning register for two years. Once an LPA has been informed that the developer intends to submit an ES it must inform the relevant consultation bodies and remind them of their obligations to make available any relevant information they may have.

The courts have been reluctant to clarify the scope and therefore the potential significant **24.65** effects of a proposal. Although, in *BT Plc v Gloucester CC* [2001] EWHC 1001 the court explained that an EIA should consider all significant effects, both beneficial and adverse and to determine a screening opinion on the fact that there were no significant *adverse* effects was wrong. What may be adverse to one person may not be so to another.

Contents of an ES

The contents of an ES will be determined to an extent by the assessment that is carried out. **24.66** There is extensive guidance on how to assess projects such as the IEMA: *Guidelines for Environmental Impact Assessment 2004*. It is likely that developers will instruct consultants to undertake the assessment while the LPA and statutory consultees should be able to advise on particular local conditions. Schedule 4 of the Regulations sets out what should be included within an ES.

THE TOWN AND COUNTRY PLANNING (ENVIRONMENTAL IMPACT ASSESSMENT) (ENGLAND AND WALES) REGULATIONS 1999 (SI 1999/293)

SCHEDULE 4
INFORMATION FOR INCLUSION IN ENVIRONMENTAL STATEMENTS

Part I

1. Description of the development, including in particular—
    (a) a description of the physical characteristics of the whole development and the land-use requirements during the construction and operational phases;

    (b) a description of the main characteristics of the production processes, for instance, nature and quantity of the materials used;

    (c) an estimate, by type and quantity, of expected residues and emissions (water, air and soil pollution, noise, vibration, light, heat, radiation, etc.) resulting from the operation of the proposed development.

2. An outline of the main alternatives studied by the applicant or appellant and an indication of the main reasons for his choice, taking into account the environmental effects.

3. A description of the aspects of the environment likely to be significantly affected by the development, including, in particular, population, fauna, flora, soil, water, air, climatic factors, material assets, including the architectural and archaeological heritage, landscape and the inter-relationship between the above factors.

4. A description of the likely significant effects of the development on the environment, which should cover the direct effects and any indirect, secondary, cumulative, short, medium and long-term, permanent and temporary, positive and negative effects of the development, resulting from:

    (a) the existence of the development;

    (b) the use of natural resources;

    (c) the emission of pollutants, the creation of nuisances and the elimination of waste, and the description by the applicant of the forecasting methods used to assess the effects on the environment.

5. A description of the measures envisaged to prevent, reduce and where possible offset any significant adverse effects on the environment.

6. A non-technical summary of the information provided under paragraphs 1 to 5 of this Part.

7. An indication of any difficulties (technical deficiencies or lack of know-how) encountered by the applicant in compiling the required information.

Part II

1. A description of the development comprising information on the site, design and size of the development.

2. A description of the measures envisaged in order to avoid, reduce and, if possible, remedy significant adverse effects.

3. The data required to identify and assess the main effects which the development is likely to have on the environment.

4. An outline of the main alternatives studied by the applicant or appellant and an indication of the main reasons for his choice, taking into account the environmental effects.

5. A non-technical summary of the information provided under paragraphs 1 to 4 of this Part.

Submission of planning application and supporting ES

24.67   Regulation 13(1) of the EIA Regulations 1999 provides that if an applicant making an EIA application submits an ES in support, he shall provide the LPA with three additional copies of the ES for the Secretary of State. The developer should also provide sufficient copies as necessary to allow the LPA to send one to each consultation body and a note of everyone that has already been sent or will be sent a copy of the statement.

The procedure for the submission of an environmental statement to the LPA in conjunction   **24.68**
with a planning application is summarized in the flow chart contained below.

The LPA must send the ES to the Secretary of State within two weeks of receipt, which will   **24.69**
allow him to consider whether the proposal is likely to have significant effects on another
EU Member State or other country that has ratified the Convention on EIA in a Transboundary Context 1991 (the Espoo Convention 1991).

Figure 24.1 Submission of environmental statement to local planning authority in conjunction with
planning application

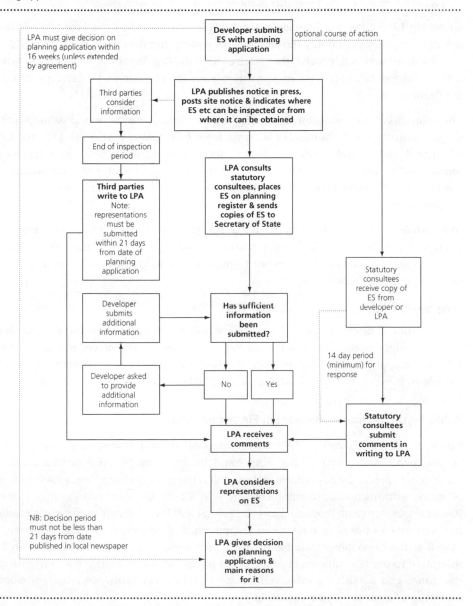

Evaluating the ES

24.70 The evaluation of the ES is, ultimately, a matter for the decision-maker. The *Note on EIA for LPAs* states that:

> The planning authority is responsible for evaluating the ES to ensure it addresses all the relevant environmental issues and that the information is presented accurately, clearly and systematically. It should be prepared to challenge the findings of these if it believes they are not adequately supported by scientific evidence. If it believes that key issues are not fully addressed, or not addressed at all, it must request further information. The authority has to ensure that it has in its possession all relevant environmental information about the likely significant environmental effects of the project before it makes its decision whether to grant planning permission. It is too late to address the issues after planning permission has been granted.

24.71 Under reg 19(1) if the decision-maker is of the opinion that these should contain additional information, they shall notify the developer in writing and the developer shall provide the additional information, which is then referred to in the Regulations as 'further information'. If the developer fails to provide enough information the decision-maker can only refuse the application.

24.72 The courts have been reluctant to interfere with the interpretation or evaluation as part of the determination for planning. In *Malster v Ipswich BC* [2001] EWCA Civ 1715 the Court of Appeal did consider environmental effects, but defined them in quite narrow terms, finding that 'severe' shadowing from the development of a football stadium on the homes of neighbouring residents should not be regarded as a significant effect on the environment.

24.73 In *R v Swale BC ex p RSPB* the court noted that the question of whether the development is of a category described in the Regulations must be answered strictly in relation to the development applied for and not by reference to the permission granted (if different) or to any development contemplated beyond that.

Time period for determining an EIA application

24.74 An LPA should determine an EIA application within 16 weeks from the date of receipt instead of eight weeks (reg 32 of the EIA Regulations 1999). The procedural stages of considering an application are illustrated in flowcharts provided as an appendix to *EIA Guide to Procedures*; these may be downloaded from the ODPM website: www.odpm.gov.uk.

Publicity and public involvement in EIA applications

24.75 Part V of the EIA Regulations 1999 covers the publicity and procedures on submission of environmental statements. Under regs 17 and 18 the developer must make a reasonable number of copies of the ES available to the public, either free of charge or at a reasonable cost reflecting printing and distribution costs. Article 8(3) of the Town and Country Planning (General Development Procedure) Order 1995 (SI 1995/418) provides particular publicity requirements for planning applications accompanied by an ES requiring a notice being displayed at the development site for at least 21 days and a local advertisement. If an ES is submitted to the LPA subsequent to the planning application the applicant must provide a site notice and publish a local advertisement (reg 14). Any further information required under reg 19 must also be advertised.

Consultation and public involvement in EIA-related applications is vital. In *Berkeley v* **24.76**
Secretary of State for the Environment [2000] 2 AC 603 the House of Lords emphasized that
token participation was not enough and that the public should be properly involved in EIA
decisions. Lord Hoffman noted that the directly enforceable right of the citizen under the
EIA Directive was:

> not merely a right to a fully informed decision on the substantive issue. It must have been
> adopted on an appropriate basis that requires the inclusive and democratic procedure
> prescribed by the Directive in which the public, however misguided or wrongheaded its views
> may be, is given an opportunity to express its opinion on the environmental issues.

Encouraging community involvement

Paragraph 105 of Circular 02/99 states that developers are encouraged to publish the non- **24.77**
technical summary (which must be included in every ES) as a separate document, and
to make copies available free of charge so as to facilitate wider public consultation. Also,
that developers and LPAs may wish to make further arrangements to make details of the
development available to the public. This approach is in line with the Government's commitment to increased community involvement in planning and set out in Planning Policy
Statement (PPS) 1: *Delivering Sustainable Development* (2005).

Early public involvement in the EIA

It should be recognized that the level of community involvement in planning required by **24.78**
legislation, i.e. to comment on the publication of the ES, is at the lower end of the public
participation spectrum. More effective ways to achieve community involvement in EIA
would be to encourage participation early on in the scoping process, inviting input into the
development of the EIA itself, and, in turn, the preparation of the ES. A number of publications and reports have emphasized the benefits of public involvement early on in the EIA
process. The EU *Guidance on Scoping 2001* suggests that there are three main groups to consult including: environmental authorities, other interested organizations, and the general
public. The guidance defines the general public as landowners, residents, general members
of the local and wider public, elected representatives, and community figures such as
religious leaders, teachers, and local community groups. It has also been suggested that early
public participation can minimize public frustration and anger and so help to avoid the
possibility of more forceful 'participation' such as legal challenges at a later stage.

Determining the planning application

When determining the planning application the decision-maker must take into account the **24.79**
ES as well as any further information. It must also take into account any comments from
consultation bodies and representations made by the public, as well as to other material
considerations. The decision-maker cannot take the view that an application is invalid
because an inadequate ES has been submitted. Any inadequacies should have been addressed
when requesting further information from the developer: see para 24.71 above. The
decision-maker may refuse permission or grant it with or without conditions.

Mitigating adverse environmental impacts

Paragraph 2, Pt II, Sch 4 of the EIA Regulations 1999 provides that an ES must include: 'A **24.80** description of the measures envisaged in order to avoid, reduce and, if possible, remedy significant adverse effects.'

24.81   Any mitigation measures contained in an ES should limit the environmental effects of the development. Circular 02/99 advises that LPAs will need to consider carefully how such measures are secured, particularly in relation to the main mitigation measures specified in the decision. It adds that conditions attached to a planning permission may include mitigation measures although a condition such as 'in accordance with the environmental statement' is unlikely to be valid unless the ES was exceptionally precise. A planning condition may require a scheme of mitigation for more minor measures to be submitted to the LPA and approved in writing before any development is carried out, although planning conditions should not duplicate other legislative controls.

24.82   Mitigation measures may also be secured by adopting planning obligations under s 106 of the TCPA 1990 and implementing environmental management systems to provide plans and objectives, and to monitor progress on mitigation: see Chapter 23: Environmental management.

24.83   In *R v Cornwall CC ex p Hardy* [2001] Env LR 473 the LPA imposed a condition requiring the developer to carry out a survey to establish whether bats were present before starting development. The court held that this information should have been included in the ES and the permission was quashed. *Gillespie v Secretary of State & Bellway Urban Renewal* [2003] EWHC 8 Admin involved the grant of planning permission by the Secretary of State of a housing development on a former gas works site. It was concluded that an EIA was unnecessary because any permission would be with conditions for detailed site examination to establish the nature, extent, and degree of the site contamination and to remediate it before development began. The Court of Appeal held that the grant of planning permission could not assume that in a complex case any remediation measures would be successfully implemented.

24.84   The *Note on EIA for LPAs* suggests that remediation measures need not be ignored when making decisions about the likely significant effects of proposed development, but care and judgement must be exercised. Uncontroversial measures such as cleaning wheels of trucks and covering lorry loads to minimize dust may well be taken into account. However, in more complex development it may be less appropriate to take proposed measures into account. It is important that the offer of remediation is not used to frustrate the purpose of the EIA Directive. See also *R (Lebus & ors) v South Cambridgeshire DC*.

Special cases of EIA

Part VII of the EIA Regulations 1999

24.85   Part VII of the EIA Regulations 1999 covers special cases of EIA including:

reg 22   Development by an LPA.

reg 23   Restriction of grant of permission by old simplified planning zone schemes or enterprise zone orders.

reg 24   Restriction of grant of permission by new simplified planning zone schemes or enterprise zone orders.

reg 25   Unauthorized development. In particular the Secretary of State shall not grant planning permission under s 177 of the TCPA 1990 in respect of EIA development that is the subject of an enforcement notice under s 172 unless he has first taken the environmental information into consideration. Many provisions similar to those for conventional EIA applications then apply to those for further information and publicity.

reg 26   Unauthorized development with significant transboundary effects.

reg 26A   Registration of old mining permission (ROMP) applications. The EIA Regulations 1999 apply to a ROMP application as they apply to a planning application.

Outline permission

In relation to an application for outline planning permission, the EIA Regulations must be **24.86** complied with at the outline stage. Development consent is defined in Art 1(2) of the EIA Directive as: 'the decision of the competent authority or authorities which entitles the developer to proceed with the project.'

The grant of outline permission is the grant of permission in principle and so any reserved **24.87** matters cannot be subject to EIA. Circular 02/99 advises that when a planning application is made in outline, the LPA will need to satisfy themselves that they have sufficient information available on the environmental effects of the proposal to enable them to determine whether or not planning permission should be granted in principle.

In *R (Barker) v London Borough of Bromley* [2001] EWCA Civ 1766 Latham LJ summarized the **24.88** position on outline planning permission when refusing an appeal by the claimant that reserved matters in relation to the development of a leisure complex in Crystal Palace Park, South London, should be subject to EIA. The case was based upon the 1988, rather than the 1999 Regulations (SI 1988/1199), but the principles on outline permission remain valid:

> In *R v Rochdale MBC ex p Tew* [1999] 3 PLR 74 [Sullivan J] concluded that an environmental statement accompanying an outline application for planning permission which contained no details so that it did not provide any information about the design and size or scale of the development, did not comply with Sch 3 of the 1988 Regulations and accordingly planning permission could not be granted.
>
> The developers extensively revised the application form to give greater detail and submitted a new environmental statement dealing with the project, together with two other full applications for planning permissions relating to the road layout. The planning authority granted permission, subject to numerous conditions. This decision was also challenged. The case ultimately came before Sullivan J again, whose judgment is reported as *R v Rochdale MBC ex p Milne* [2000] 81 P &CR 365. He dismissed the challenge. He held that whilst there was bound to be less certainty in relation to the environmental effects of proposals put forward for outline planning permissions than will be the case in proposals for full planning permission, nonetheless the planning authority is entitled to consider whether or not the information that has been provided is sufficient to give it full knowledge of its likely significant effects on the environment, and if so satisfied, it can accept an environmental statement based upon such an application as a sufficient basis for an EA for the purposes of granting permission. If it is not so satisfied, it can require further material, or refuse the application.
>
> In these two judgments, Sullivan J describes in detail and with great clarity the way in which the 1988 Regulations apply in the context of applications for outline planning permission. The premise upon which he bases his judgments is that the 1988 Regulations required the

full environmental impact of a proposed development to be capable of being identified at the time the planning authority considers the grant of permission. It may or may not be possible in any given case to define that impact in a purely outline application. If it is not, then clearly permission cannot be granted and the matter must proceed by way of an application for full permission. However, in many cases, sufficient information can be provided within an outline application to enable the planning authority to determine the impact that such a development is capable of producing and to make an EIA accordingly. The planning authority has ample powers to require further information by way of detail to enable it to carry out this task and always has the sanction of refusing permission if the material is not made available.

C STRATEGIC ENVIRONMENTAL ASSESSMENT

24.89 The EU Directive 2001/42/EC on the assessment of the effect of certain plans and programmes on the environment (the SEA Directive) required Member States to bring into force laws, regulations, and administrative provisions to implement the Directive by July 2004. There is no reference to *strategic* environmental assessment, although this is now a common term and is referred to in much of the guide such as the *Draft Practical Guide to the Strategic Environmental Assessment Directive* published by the ODPM in 2004. Under Art 2(a) environmental assessment is defined as:

> the preparation of an environmental report, the carrying out of consultations, the taking into account of the environmental report and the results of the consultations in decision-making and the provision of information on the decision; and providing information when the plan or programme is adopted and showing how the results of the environmental assessment have been taken into account.

24.90 The objective of the SEA Directive under Art 1 is:

> to provide for a high level of protection of the environment and to contribute to the integration of environmental considerations into the preparation and adoption of plans and programmes with a view to promoting sustainable development, by ensuring that, in accordance with this Directive, an environmental assessment is carried out of certain plans and programmes which are likely to have significant effects on the environment.

24.91 The SEA Directive is transposed into domestic law under s 2(2) of the European Communities Act 1972, which enables any designated Minister or department to make provision for implementing Community obligations by regulations, by enacting the Environmental Assessment of Plans and Programmes Regulations 2004 (SI 2004/1633) (SEA Regulations 2004) and the Environmental Assessment of Plans and Programmes (Wales) Regulations 2004 (SI 2004/1656). Because of the nature of the SEA Regulation 2004, in that they cover plans and programmes rather than discrete projects, it is public bodies, referred to in reg 2(1) as 'responsible authorities', who carry out the assessments. The SEA Regulations 2004 provide the scope and the procedural requirements necessary for carrying out an SEA.

Plans and programmes covered by the SEA Regulations 2004

24.92 Regulation 5 of the SEA Regulations 2004 provides that the responsible authority must carry out an SEA during the preparation of plans or programmes that are prepared for agriculture, forestry, fisheries, energy, industry, transport, waste management, water management, tele-communications, tourism, town and country planning, or land use, and sets the framework for future development consent of projects covered by the EIA Directive; or in view of the likely effect on sites, has been determined to require an assessment under Arts 6 or 7 of the Habitats Directive.

Further, the requirement for SEA also applies to other plans and programmes that set the framework for future development consent of projects if they are subject of a determination under reg 9(1) that the plan or programme is likely to have significant environmental effects (reg 5(4)). The requirements do not apply to plans and programmes whose sole purpose is to serve national defence or civil emergency, or to financial or budget plans and programmes (reg 5(5)). Further, an SEA is not required for plans or programmes that deter-mine the use of small areas at local level or a minor modification to a plan or programme (reg 5(6)). **24.93**

In contrast to the EIA provisions, the SEA Regulations 2004 are not limited to land use planning matters and the *Draft Practical Guide* provides an indicative list of plans and programmes subject to SEA including: **24.94**

Land use and spatial planning

This category includes Local Development Documents, Local Development Plans in Wales and Regional Spatial Strategies, Minerals Local Plans, Waste Local Plans, and the London Plan (the Mayor's Spatial Development Strategy). **24.95**

Other regional and local authority plans and programmes

This category includes Regional Economic Strategies, Regional and Local Transport Strategies, Regional and Local Housing Strategies, Community Strategies (in certain circum-stances), Local Air Quality Action Plans, Recreation/Sports Strategies, and Primary Care Trusts Local Delivery Plans. Some plans may not meet the criteria of being likely to generate significant environmental effects. **24.96**

Environmental protection and management

This category includes Revisions to the Waste Strategy 2000, River Basin Management Plans/ Programmes of Measures, and Salmon Action Plans although in many instances case-by-case screening will be necessary to clarify the likelihood of significant environmental effects arising. **24.97**

Plans and programmes for industrial sectors

The final category includes Offshore Oil and Gas Licensing Rounds, Offshore Windfarm Licensing Rounds, Water Company Resource plans, and Water Service Capital Works Pro-grammes (relevant to Northern Ireland). The more specific areas of activity are covered by further guidance including: **24.98**

- *The SEA Directive: Guidance for Planning Authorities* (2003), published by the ODPM and covering land use and spatial plans in England;
- *SEA — Core Guidance for Transport Plans* (2004) published by the Department for Transport and covering transport plans in England; and
- *SEA Good Practice Guidelines* (2004) published by the Environment Agency.

Screening certain plans and programmes

24.99 Regulation 9(1) provides that the responsible authority shall determine whether or not a plan, programme, or modification of a description referred to in reg 5(4) or (6) is likely to have significant effects. The criteria for determination are set out in Sch 1 below.

THE ENVIRONMENTAL ASSESSMENT OF PLANS AND PROGRAMMES REGULATIONS 2004 (SI 2004/1633)

SCHEDULE 1

Regulations 9(2)(a) and 10(4)(a)

CRITERIA FOR DETERMINING THE LIKELY SIGNIFICANCE OF EFFECTS ON THE ENVIRONMENT

1. The characteristics of plans and programmes, having regard, in particular, to—
    (a) the degree to which the plan or programme sets a framework for projects and other activities, either with regard to the location, nature, size and operating conditions or by allocating resources;
    (b) the degree to which the plan or programme influences other plans and programmes including those in a hierarchy;
    (c) the relevance of the plan or programme for the integration of environmental considerations in particular with a view to promoting sustainable development;
    (d) environmental problems relevant to the plan or programme; and
    (e) the relevance of the plan or programme for the implementation of Community legislation on the environment (for example, plans and programmes linked to waste management or water protection).

2. Characteristics of the effects and of the area likely to be affected, having regard, in particular, to—
    (a) the probability, duration, frequency and reversibility of the effects;
    (b) the cumulative nature of the effects;
    (c) the transboundary nature of the effects;
    (d) the risks to human health or the environment (for example, due to accidents);
    (e) the magnitude and spatial extent of the effects (geographical area and size of the population likely to be affected);
    (f) the value and vulnerability of the area likely to be affected due to—
        (i)   special natural characteristics or cultural heritage;
        (ii) exceeded environmental quality standards or limit values; or
        (iii) intensive land-use; and
    (g) the effects on areas or landscapes which have a recognised national, Community or international protection status.

24.100 Regulation 9(3) of the SEA Regulations 2004 provides that where the responsible authority determines that a plan, programme, or modification does not require an SEA it shall prepare a statement of its reasons for the determination. Within 28 days of the determination the responsible body shall, under reg 11, send to each consultation body a copy of the determination and, if required, a statement of reasons for not requiring an SEA. It shall also keep a copy of the determination and any statement of reasons available for public inspection and within 28 days of making the determination take steps to bring it to the attention of the public.

Preparation of environmental reports

Part 3 of the SEA Regulations 2004 covers environmental reports and consultation pro- **24.101** cedures. Regulation 12(2) provides that the report shall identify, describe, and evaluate the likely significant effects on the environment of:

(a) implementing the plan or programme; and
(b) reasonable alternatives taking into account the objectives and the geographical scope of the plan or programme

The report should, under reg 12(3), include such information referred to in Sch 2 as may be **24.102** reasonably required taking account of:

(a) current knowledge and methods of assessment;
(b) the contents and level of detail in the plan or programme;
(c) the stage of the plan or programme in the decision-making process; and
(d) the extent to which certain matters are more appropriately assessed at different levels in that process in order to avoid duplication of the assessment.

Schedule 2 of the SEA Regulations 2004 is set out below: **24.103**

THE ENVIRONMENTAL ASSESSMENT OF PLANS AND PROGRAMMES REGULATIONS 2004 (SI 2004/1633)

SCHEDULE 2

Regulation 12(3)

INFORMATION FOR ENVIRONMENTAL REPORTS

1. An outline of the contents and main objectives of the plan or programme, and of its relationship with other relevant plans and programmes.
2. The relevant aspects of the current state of the environment and the likely evolution thereof without implementation of the plan or programme.
3. The environmental characteristics of areas likely to be significantly affected.
4. Any existing environmental problems which are relevant to the plan or programme including, in particular, those relating to any areas of a particular environmental importance, such as areas designated pursuant to Council Directive 79/409/EEC on the conservation of wild birds and the Habitats Directive.
5. The environmental protection objectives, established at international, Community or Member State level, which are relevant to the plan or programme and the way those objectives and any environmental considerations have been taken into account during its preparation.
6. The likely significant effects on the environment, including short, medium and long-term effects, permanent and temporary effects, positive and negative effects, and secondary, cumulative and synergistic effects, on issues such as—

(a) biodiversity;

(b) population;

(c) human health;

(d) fauna;

(e) flora;

(f) soil;

(g) water;

(h) air;

(i) climatic factors;

(j) material assets;

(k) cultural heritage, including architectural and archaeological heritage;

(l) landscape; and

(m) the inter-relationship between the issues referred to in sub-paragraphs (a) to (l).

7. The measures envisaged to prevent, reduce and as fully as possible offset any significant adverse effects on the environment of implementing the plan or programme.

8. An outline of the reasons for selecting the alternatives dealt with, and a description of how the assessment was undertaken including any difficulties (such as technical deficiencies or lack of know-how) encountered in compiling the required information.

9. A description of the measures envisaged concerning monitoring in accordance with regulation 17.

10. A non-technical summary of the information provided under paragraphs 1 to 9.

Consultation on the environmental report

24.104 The SEA Directive requires that the public and the authorities likely to be concerned by the environmental effects of implementing the plan or programme are consulted as part of the SEA process. The intention is to encourage transparent decision-making and ensure that the information supplied for the SEA is comprehensive and reliable. In addition to the consultation required as part of the SEA screening process, reg 13 of the SEA Regulations 2004 provides that on preparation of the environmental report, the responsible authority shall:

(a) send to each consultation body a copy of any draft plan or programme and supporting environmental report;

(b) take appropriate steps to bring the preparation of the report and relevant documents to the attention of persons, who in the authority's opinion, are likely to be affected by, or have an interest in the decisions involved in the assessment and adoption of the plan or programme;

(c) inform the public consultees of the address at which relevant documents may be viewed; and

(d) invite the consultees to express their opinion on the relevant documents, specifying the address to which, and the period within which, opinions must be sent.

24.105 Regulation 14 of the SEA Regulations 2004 covers transboundary consultations. If the responsible authority considers that the plan or programme is likely to have significant effects on the environment of another Member State, it shall, as soon as reasonably practicable notify the Secretary of State and supply him with a copy of the plan or programme and supporting environmental report.

Adopting the plan or programme

The SEA Regulations 2004 do not cover the process after starting the consultation process. **24.106** However, Art 8 of the Directive requires that the environmental report and any consultation responses received from the public, consultation bodies, and any Member States, must be taken into account during the preparation of the plan or programme and before its adoption or submission to the legislative procedure.

The SEA requirements differ from the EIA provisions at the plan or programme adoption **24.107** stage. Regulation 16(1) of the SEA Regulations 2004 provides that as soon as reasonably practicable after the adoption of the plan or programme for which an SEA has been carried out, the responsible authority shall:

(a) make the plan or programme and its accompanying environmental statement available for public inspection at all reasonable times and free of charge; and

(b) take appropriate steps to bring to the public attention; the plan or programme, its date of adoption and where it may be viewed free of charge.

Under reg 16(2), the responsible authority should also inform the consultation bodies, **24.108** public consultees, and the Secretary of State. The Secretary of State should, in turn, inform any Member States involved in the consultation process.

Post-adoption requirements

The post-adoption procedures require that part of the information to be provided should **24.109** include the particulars contained in reg 16(4) and include a statement containing:

(a) how environmental considerations have been integrated into the plan or programme;

(b) how the environmental report has been taken into account;

(c) how opinions expressed in response to screening consultation under reg 13 have been taken into account;

(d) how the results of any transboundary consultations under reg 14 have been taken into account;

(e) the reasons for choosing the plan or programme as adopted, in the light of the other reasonable alternatives dealt with; and

(f) the measures that are to be taken to monitor the significant environmental effects of the implementation of the plan or programme as required under reg 17.

An important distinction between EIA and SEA is that an EIA is only required to inform the **24.110** decision making whereas SEA forms part of the plan or programme to be adopted and provides a mechanism under reg 17 to monitor the significant environmental effects with the purpose of identifying unforeseen adverse effects at any early stage and being able to undertake appropriate remedial action.

There is limited judicial opinion on SEA however, the Environment Agency provides a num- **24.111** ber of case studies setting out how they are carrying out SEAs as part of the management responsibilities. For example, the Humber estuary flood management strategy incorporates SEA with the purpose of ensuring environmental considerations and alternatives are addressed as early as possible in the flood management process and on a par with economic and social factors in the strategy development. Other case studies include wind energy, minerals replacement and the Broadland flood alleviation.

KEY DOCUMENTS AND MATERIALS

Town and Country Planning Act 1990

Town and Country Planning (EIA) (England and Wales) Regulations 1999 (SI 1999/293) as amended by the TCP (EIA) (England and Wales) (Amendment) Regulations 2000 (SI 2000/2867)

Environmental Assessment of Plans and Programmes (Wales) Regulations 2004 (SI 2004/1633)

Environmental Assessment of Plans and Programmes Regulations 2004 (SI 2004/1656)

EU Directive 85/337/EEC on the assessment of the effects of certain public and private projects on the environment amended by the 97/11/EC Directive and the Directive 2003/35/EC on public participation (the EIA Directive)

Circular 2/99: Environmental Impact Assessment

Department for Transport (2004). *SEA — Core Guidance for Transport Plans*. DfT: London

Environment Agency (2004). *SEA Good Practice Guidelines*. Environment Agency: Bristol

EC *Guidance on EIA Scoping 2001*. European Commission: Brussels

IEMA (2004). *Guidelines for Environmental Impact Assessment*. IEMA: Lincoln

ODPM (2003). *The SEA Directive: Guidance for Planning Authorities*. ODPM: London

ODPM (2004). *Draft Practical Guide to the Strategic Environmental Assessment Directive*. ODPM: London

ODPM (2002). *Environmental Impact Assessment: A Guide to Procedures*. ODPM: London

ODPM (2004). *Note on EIA for local planning authorities 19.4.04*. ODPM: London

Environment Agency: www.environment-agency.gov.uk

Office of Deputy Prime Minister: www.odpm.gov.uk

25

YOUR PRACTICE

A INTRODUCTION

As can be seen from the scope of this book, environmental law covers a wide area, which **25.01**
often finds a remedy in other discrete areas of law, e.g. a nuisance problem may be resolved
through landlord and tenant claims. Further, an environmental legal claim may be based in
either civil, public, or criminal law, and on a range of matters in each of those areas, and it is
important to have an understanding of each area to know which one is the most appropriate
to resolve a problem; particularly when the law itself is now refusing a remedy until all other
options including legal options, have been tried (see judicial review CPR Pt 54 and the
ruling in *Marcic v Thames Water* [2003] UKHL 66.

Unfortunately, in such a wide legal arena, there can be a tendency to operate within quite **25.02**
narrow specialist areas. This may be important to gain adequate expertise in a particular field
but could result in not being fully aware of a related but important aspect of work that
doesn't fit the practitioner's regular caseload. The following sections set out good sources
of environmental law and practice to assist practitioners in clarifying and advising on an
environmental concern.

Law practice management

Law firms and chambers have, on occasions, been subject to criticism about how they oper- **25.03**
ate, implying that while lawyers may have many skills and virtues, practical management

skills may not be one of them. However, the concept of continuous improvement in performance and taking an iterative approach to management, which is outlined in Chapter 23: Environmental management, in relation to environmental management can equally apply to general practice. There are, very simply, four key stages to implementing a management system:

(1) review;
(2) plan;
(3) do; and
(4) check.

25.04 After checking the activity(ies) at stage four, the aim is to then carry out a further review and continue the process from number 1 again. It is hoped that many firms may wish to carry out an EMS of their own and significant reductions can be made in adverse impacts of an office. It is widely accepted that a 10% reduction in operational costs can be achieved in implementing an EMS in the average office without the need to invest in any technological improvements or updates.

B   RESOURCES, LIBRARY AND RESEARCH MATERIALS

Government departments

25.05 Because of the highly regulatory nature of environmental law, there is considerable guidance and policy issued from central government. Important government departments and agencies include:

Department of Environment, Food and Rural Affairs (Defra)

25.06 Defra is the central government body that legislates and issues policy on environmental protection and sustainable development. There are detailed guidance notes on the IPC/PPC regulations as well as strategic documents such as the UK Sustainable Development Strategy.

Office of Deputy Prime Minister (ODPM)

25.07 The ODPM is responsible for local government, and land use planning. Planning policy and circulars are published on the website as well as consultation papers and emerging legislation.

Department for Transport (DfT)

25.08 The DfT is responsible for delivering the Government's transport strategy, making transport safe, secure, and reliable while safeguarding the environment. Consultation papers, news releases, and other publications can be obtained from their website.

Environment Agency

25.09 The Environment Agency is a public body that protects and improves the environment. It influences governmental policy and regulates major national industries. Their website has a wide selection of information, publications, and consultation papers. It also contains the

Netregs, the Internet-based information source on environmental legal compliance for small- and medium-sized businesses.

Planning Inspectorate

The Planning Inspectorate (PINS) processes planning and enforcement appeals and holds **25.10** inquiries into local development plans. The website contains some publications and press releases and links to planning decisions. The Planning Inspectorate also considers appeals for pollution control, waste management licensing, water and sewerage controls, contaminated land, hazardous substances, and hedgerows.

Department for Constitutional Affairs (DCA)

The DCA is responsible in government for upholding justice, rights, and democracy. It **25.11** covers areas such as public funding and the provision of legal services, in particular to those that are unable to afford access to justice.

The Internet

There is now a wide range of research materials and guidance on environmental law. If there **25.12** is easy access to the Internet then this is often the best place to start in finding materials, particularly government guidance on regulatory and policy matters. Obtaining broadband is essential in ensuring that Internet access is quick and efficient.

www.bailii.org

This website was set up to make UK and international case law widely available. It is provided **25.13** free for all from the above website and now extends to legislation.

www.opsi.gov.uk

The Office of Public Sector Information website provides all UK legislation from 1988 and **25.14** Statutory Instruments from 1987. If the citation or name of the legislation is known then this is a useful source of primary materials. However, it is important to note that the legislation appears as it was enacted and so any subsequent amendments or repeals are not shown.

www.hmcourts-service.gov.uk

Provides most Court of Appeal judgments, which become available as soon as they are **25.15** handed down. It also provides information on court hearings in the Royal Courts of Justice Crown Courts and selected county courts, information on a range of judicial activity and a large number of legal forms and precedents. House of Lords judgments are available from www.parliament.uk.

www.defra.gov.uk

For environmental regulation, protection, and sustainable development. Also for food and **25.16** agricultural matters.

www.europa.eu.int

The website of the European Union provides detail on all EU legislation and policy including **25.17** developing law. There are also links to the European Court of Justice judgments.

www.echr.org

25.18 The website of the European Court of Human Rights, with case law.

www.odpm.gov.uk

25.19 For planning and local government-related matters.

www.idea.gov.uk

25.20 For a list of all local government-related environmental legislation including noise, litter, waste, etc.

Practitioner's texts

25.21 There are two main updated practitioner's texts relevant to environmental law:

(1) *Garner's Environmental Law* published by LexisNexis. This six-volume work covers all aspects of environmental law.

(2) *Planning Law* published by Sweet and Maxwell, edited by M Grant.

25.22 Useful texts on environment and law include:

- NSCA: *Pollution Handbook*. NSCA: Brighton, which is updated annually and provides summarized coverage of legislation in England, Wales, Scotland, and Northern Ireland.
- IEMA (2004): *Environmental Management Handbook*. Earthscan: London. This provides a comprehensive guide to all aspects of environmental management with over 30 chapters and editing by the IEMA.

Law reports

25.23 Not all the environmental law cases will be available via the public Internet sites, although some of the subscription sites are comprehensive. There are two main sources of environmental law reports:

(1) The Environmental Law Reports, Sweet & Maxwell: London.

(2) The Journal of Planning and Environmental Law, Sweet & Maxwell: London.

Other case reports are found in Environmental Law and Management, the Environment Times and ENDS Reports: see para 25.24.

Journals and keeping up to date

25.24 To get regular updates and analysis on environmental law and policy the following journals are recommended:

- *ENDS report* and *ENDS daily*. ENDS is a regular journal with an emphasis on environmental practice, although it also covers regular legal analysis and case summaries.
- *Environment Times* published by Beckhouse Media Ltd. This provides comprehensive coverage of recent environmental prosecutions as well as articles on recent environ-

mental matters. The emphasis is on environmental practice but provides regular legal analysis.

- *Environmental Law and Management* (ELM) by Lawtext Publishing, Oxon. This provides topical articles by leading practitioners, case summaries, analysis, and legal updates. There are also a range of related publications including the Journal of Water Law, Environmental Liability, and Bio-Science Law Review.
- *Journal of Environmental Law* (JEL) published by Oxford University Press. This includes articles on current environmental law matters.
- *Journal of Planning and Environmental Law* (JPL) by Sweet & Maxwell. This provides current topics, articles, updates and a wide range of planning case reports, summaries and analysis.

Environmental law is continuing to develop at a rapid pace. The EU is still enacting a range **25.25** of legislation; the courts are committing time and resources to environmental training and guidance. It is therefore important to be cautious when considering recent developments. Many of the case reports and analysis will be about evolving law, often with first instance decisions. Any novel areas of law may well be appealed or subject to further challenge. The case of *Hatton v UK* reached the European Court of Human Rights (ECtHR) in 2002 after nearly ten years of judicial activity in the UK. The ECtHR found for the claimants and that the Government had acted unlawfully in its approach to night flights at Heathrow. The Government then appealed to the ECtHR Grand Chamber that, in the main, overturned the earlier ECtHR ruling.

C FURTHER DEVELOPMENT AND PROFESSIONAL TRAINING

There are a number of courses on environmental law. In particular many universities run **25.26** regular courses on environmental and planning law, environmental crime, and public law. The Environmental Law Foundation also holds regular seminars, conferences, and workshops on specific aspects of environmental law see: www.elflaw.org as does UKELA www.ukela.org. It is always worth following the diary dates in the Law Society Gazette and on the Bar Council website.

D USEFUL ORGANIZATIONS

Campaign to Protect Rural England (CPRE) **25.27**
128 Southwark St, London SE1 0SW
t. 020 7981 2800, www.cpre.org.uk
CPRE exists to promote the beauty, tranquillity, and diversity of rural England.

Environmental Law Foundation (ELF)
Suite 309, 16 Baldwins Gardens, London EC1N 7RJ
t. 020 7404 1030, www.elflaw.org
ELF aims to secure access to environmental justice for all.

Environment Council
212 High Holborn, London WC1V 7VW
t. 020 7836 2626, www.the-environment-council.org.uk
The Council helps people improve their environment through stakeholder dialogue.

Foundation for International Environmental Law and Development (FIELD)
3 Endsleigh Street, London WC1H 0DD
t. 020 7637 7950, www.field.org.uk
FIELD promotes international law that protects the environment.

Friends of the Earth (FoE)
26–28 Underwood Street, London N1 7JQ
t. 020 7490 1555, www.foe.co.uk
FoE promotes protection of the environment.

Greenpeace
Canonbury Villas, London N1 2PN
t. 020 7865 8100, www.greenpeace.org.uk
Greenpeace acts against environmental injustice throughout the world.

Institute of Environmental Management and Assessment (IEMA)
St Nicholas House, 70 Newport, Lincoln LN1 3DP
t. 01522 540069, www.iema.net
IEMA promotes best practice standards in environmental management, auditing, and assessment.

National Society for Clean Air and Environmental Protection (NSCA)
44 Grand Parade, Brighton BN1 1RG
t. 01273 878770, www.NSCA.org.uk
The NSCA promotes protection for the environment, improved air quality, and reduction of noise.

Royal Society for the Protection of Birds (RSPB)
The Trolge, Sandy, Bedfordshire SG19 2DL
t. 01767 680551, www.rspb.org.uk
The RSPB works to secure a healthy environment for birds and wildlife.

UK Environmental Law Association (UKELA)
Honeycroft House, Pangbourne Road, Upper Basildon RG8 8LP
t. 01491 671184, www.ukela.org.
UKELA aims to make the law work for a better environment and to improve understanding and awareness of environmental law.

World Wildlife Fund — UK (WWF-UK)
Panda House, Weyside Park, Godalming, Surrey GU7 1XR
t. 01483 426444, www.WWF-uk.org.
The WWF promotes conservation and protection of endangered species.

APPENDIX 1

UNECE Convention on Access to Information, Public Participation in Decision-making and Access to Justice in Environmental Matters

done at Aarhus, Denmark,
on 25 June 1998

The Parties to this Convention,

Recalling principle 1 of the Stockholm Declaration on the Human Environment,

Recalling also principle 10 of the Rio Declaration on Environment and Development,

Recalling further General Assembly resolutions 37/7 of 28 October 1982 on the World Charter for Nature and 45/94 of 14 December 1990 on the need to ensure a healthy environment for the well-being of individuals,

Recalling the European Charter on Environment and Health adopted at the First European Conference on Environment and Health of the World Health Organization in Frankfurt-am-Main, Germany, on 8 December 1989,

Affirming the need to protect, preserve and improve the state of the environment and to ensure sustainable and environmentally sound development,

Recognizing that adequate protection of the environment is essential to human well-being and the enjoyment of basic human rights, including the right to life itself,

Recognizing also that every person has the right to live in an environment adequate to his or her health and well-being, and the duty, both individually and in association with others, to protect and improve the environment for the benefit of present and future generations,

Considering that, to be able to assert this right and observe this duty, citizens must have access to information, be entitled to participate in decision-making and have access to justice in environmental matters, and acknowledging in this regard that citizens may need assistance in order to exercise their rights,

Recognizing that, in the field of the environment, improved access to information and public participation in decision-making enhance the quality and the implementation of decisions, contribute to public awareness of environmental issues, give the public the opportunity to express its concerns and enable public authorities to take due account of such concerns,

Aiming thereby to further the accountability of and transparency in decision-making and to strengthen public support for decisions on the environment,

Recognizing the desirability of transparency in all branches of government and inviting legislative bodies to implement the principles of this Convention in their proceedings,

Recognizing also that the public needs to be aware of the procedures for participation in environmental decision-making, have free access to them and know how to use them,

Recognizing further the importance of the respective roles that individual citizens, non-governmental organizations and the private sector can play in environmental protection,

Desiring to promote environmental education to further the understanding of the environment and sustainable development and to encourage widespread public awareness of, and participation in, decisions affecting the environment and sustainable development,

Noting, in this context, the importance of making use of the media and of electronic or other, future forms of communication,

Recognizing the importance of fully integrating environmental considerations in governmental decision-making and the consequent need for public authorities to be in possession of accurate, comprehensive and up-todate environmental information,

Acknowledging that public authorities hold environmental information in the public interest,

Concerned that effective judicial mechanisms should be accessible to the public, including organizations, so that its legitimate interests are protected and the law is enforced,

Noting the importance of adequate product information being provided to consumers to enable them to make informed environmental choices,

Recognizing the concern of the public about the deliberate release of genetically modified organisms into the environment and the need for increased transparency and greater public participation in decision-making in this field,

Convinced that the implementation of this Convention will contribute to strengthening democracy in the region of the United Nations Economic Commission for Europe (ECE),

Conscious of the role played in this respect by ECE and recalling, *inter alia*, the ECE Guidelines on Access to Environmental Information and Public Participation in Environmental Decision-making endorsed in the Ministerial Declaration adopted at the Third Ministerial Conference 'Environment for Europe' in Sofia, Bulgaria, on 25 October 1995,

Bearing in mind the relevant provisions in the Convention on Environmental Impact Assessment in a Transboundary Context, done at Espoo, Finland, on 25 February 1991, and the Convention on the Transboundary Effects of Industrial Accidents and the Convention on the Protection and Use of Transboundary Watercourses and International Lakes, both done at Helsinki on 17 March 1992, and other regional conventions,

Conscious that the adoption of this Convention will have contributed to the further strengthening of the 'Environment for Europe' process and to the results of the Fourth Ministerial Conference in Aarhus, Denmark, in June 1998,

Have agreed as follows:

Article 1
Objective

In order to contribute to the protection of the right of every person of present and future generations to live in an environment adequate to his or her health and well-being, each Party shall guarantee the rights of access to information, public participation in decision-making, and access to justice in environmental matters in accordance with the provisions of this Convention.

Article 2
Definitions

For the purposes of this Convention,

1. 'Party' means, unless the text otherwise indicates, a Contracting Party to this Convention;
2. 'Public authority' means:
   (a) Government at national, regional and other level;
   (b) Natural or legal persons performing public administrative functions under national law, including specific duties, activities or services in relation to the environment;
   (c) Any other natural or legal persons having public responsibilities or functions, or providing

public services, in relation to the environment, under the control of a body or person falling within subparagraphs (a) or (b) above;

    (d) The institutions of any regional economic integration organization referred to in article 17 which is a Party to this Convention.

This definition does not include bodies or institutions acting in a judicial or legislative capacity;

3. 'Environmental information' means any information in written, visual, aural, electronic or any other material form on:

    (a) The state of elements of the environment, such as air and atmosphere, water, soil, land, landscape and natural sites, biological diversity and its components, including genetically modified organisms, and the interaction among these elements;

    (b) Factors, such as substances, energy, noise and radiation, and activities or measures, including administrative measures, environmental agreements, policies, legislation, plans and programmes, affecting or likely to affect the elements of the environment within the scope of subparagraph (a) above, and cost-benefit and other economic analyses and assumptions used in environmental decision-making;

    (c) The state of human health and safety, conditions of human life, cultural sites and built structures, inasmuch as they are or may be affected by the state of the elements of the environment or, through these elements, by the factors, activities or measures referred to in subparagraph (b) above;

4. 'The public' means one or more natural or legal persons, and, in accordance with national legislation or practice, their associations, organizations or groups;

5. 'The public concerned' means the public affected or likely to be affected by, or having an interest in, the environmental decision-making; for the purposes of this definition, non-governmental organizations promoting environmental protection and meeting any requirements under national law shall be deemed to have an interest.

Article 3
General provisions

1. Each Party shall take the necessary legislative, regulatory and other measures, including measures to achieve compatibility between the provisions implementing the information, public participation and access-to-justice provisions in this Convention, as well as proper enforcement measures, to establish and maintain a clear, transparent and consistent framework to implement the provisions of this Convention.

2. Each Party shall endeavour to ensure that officials and authorities assist and provide guidance to the public in seeking access to information, in facilitating participation in decision-making and in seeking access to justice in environmental matters.

3. Each Party shall promote environmental education and environmental awareness among the public, especially on how to obtain access to information, to participate in decision-making and to obtain access to justice in environmental matters.

4. Each Party shall provide for appropriate recognition of and support to associations, organizations or groups promoting environmental protection and ensure that its national legal system is consistent with this obligation.

5. The provisions of this Convention shall not affect the right of a Party to maintain or introduce measures providing for broader access to information, more extensive public participation in decision-making and wider access to justice in environmental matters than required by this Convention.

6. This Convention shall not require any derogation from existing rights of access to information, public participation in decision-making and access to justice in environmental matters.

7. Each Party shall promote the application of the principles of this Convention in international

environmental decision-making processes and within the framework of international organizations in matters relating to the environment.

8. Each Party shall ensure that persons exercising their rights in conformity with the provisions of this Convention shall not be penalized, persecuted or harassed in any way for their involvement. This provision shall not affect the powers of national courts to award reasonable costs in judicial proceedings.

9. Within the scope of the relevant provisions of this Convention, the public shall have access to information, have the possibility to participate in decision-making and have access to justice in environmental matters without discrimination as to citizenship, nationality or domicile and, in the case of a legal person, without discrimination as to where it has its registered seat or an effective centre of its activities.

Article 4
Access to environmental information

1. Each Party shall ensure that, subject to the following paragraphs of this article, public authorities, in response to a request for environmental information, make such information available to the public, within the framework of national legislation, including, where requested and subject to subparagraph (b) below, copies of the actual documentation containing or comprising such information:
   (a) Without an interest having to be stated;
   (b) In the form requested unless:
      (i) It is reasonable for the public authority to make it available in another form, in which case reasons shall be given for making it available in that form;
      or
      (ii) The information is already publicly available in another form.

2. The environmental information referred to in paragraph 1 above shall be made available as soon as possible and at the latest within one month after the request has been submitted, unless the volume and the complexity of the information justify an extension of this period up to two months after the request. The applicant shall be informed of any extension and of the reasons justifying it.

3. A request for environmental information may be refused if:
   (a) The public authority to which the request is addressed does not hold the environmental information requested;
   (b) The request is manifestly unreasonable or formulated in too general a manner; or
   (c) The request concerns material in the course of completion or concerns internal communications of public authorities where such an exemption is provided for in national law or customary practice, taking into account the public interest served by disclosure.

4. A request for environmental information may be refused if the disclosure would adversely affect:
   (a) The confidentiality of the proceedings of public authorities, where such confidentiality is provided for under national law;
   (b) International relations, national defence or public security;
   (c) The course of justice, the ability of a person to receive a fair trial or the ability of a public authority to conduct an enquiry of a criminal or disciplinary nature;
   (d) The confidentiality of commercial and industrial information, where such confidentiality is protected by law in order to protect a legitimate economic interest. Within this framework, information on emissions which is relevant for the protection of the environment shall be disclosed;
   (e) Intellectual property rights;
   (f) The confidentiality of personal data and/or files relating to a natural person where that person has not consented to the disclosure of the information to the public, where such confidentiality is provided for in national law;

(g) The interests of a third party which has supplied the information requested without that party being under or capable of being put under a legal obligation to do so, and where that party does not consent to the release of the material; or

(h) The environment to which the information relates, such as the breeding sites of rare species.

The aforementioned grounds for refusal shall be interpreted in a restrictive way, taking into account the public interest served by disclosure and taking into account whether the information requested relates to emissions into the environment.

5. Where a public authority does not hold the environmental information requested, this public authority shall, as promptly as possible, inform the applicant of the public authority to which it believes it is possible to apply for the information requested or transfer the request to that authority and inform the applicant accordingly.

6. Each Party shall ensure that, if information exempted from disclosure under paragraphs 3 (c) and 4 above can be separated out without prejudice to the confidentiality of the information exempted, public authorities make available the remainder of the environmental information that has been requested.

7. A refusal of a request shall be in writing if the request was in writing or the applicant so requests. A refusal shall state the reasons for the refusal and give information on access to the review procedure provided for in accordance with article 9. The refusal shall be made as soon as possible and at the latest within one month, unless the complexity of the information justifies an extension of this period up to two months after the request. The applicant shall be informed of any extension and of the reasons justifying it.

8. Each Party may allow its public authorities to make a charge for supplying information, but such charge shall not exceed a reasonable amount. Public authorities intending to make such a charge for supplying information shall make available to applicants a schedule of charges which may be levied, indicating the circumstances in which they may be levied or waived and when the supply of information is conditional on the advance payment of such a charge.

Article 5
Collection and dissemination of environmental information

1. Each Party shall ensure that:

(a) Public authorities possess and update environmental information which is relevant to their functions;

(b) Mandatory systems are established so that there is an adequate flow of information to public authorities about proposed and existing activities which may significantly affect the environment;

(c) In the event of any imminent threat to human health or the environment, whether caused by human activities or due to natural causes, all information which could enable the public to take measures to prevent or mitigate harm arising from the threat and is held by a public authority is disseminated immediately and without delay to members of the public who may be affected.

2. Each Party shall ensure that, within the framework of national legislation, the way in which public authorities make environmental information available to the public is transparent and that environmental information is effectively accessible, *inter alia*, by:

(a) Providing sufficient information to the public about the type and scope of environmental information held by the relevant public authorities, the basic terms and conditions under which such information is made available and accessible, and the process by which it can be obtained;

(b) Establishing and maintaining practical arrangements, such as:

(i) Publicly accessible lists, registers or files;

    (ii) Requiring officials to support the public in seeking access to information under this Convention; and

    (iii) The identification of points of contact; and

  (c) Providing access to the environmental information contained in lists, registers or files as referred to in subparagraph (b) (i) above free of charge.

3. Each Party shall ensure that environmental information progressively becomes available in electronic databases which are easily accessible to the public through public telecommunications networks. Information accessible in this form should include:

  (a) Reports on the state of the environment, as referred to in paragraph 4 below;

  (b) Texts of legislation on or relating to the environment;

  (c) As appropriate, policies, plans and programmes on or relating to the environment, and environmental agreements; and

  (d) Other information, to the extent that the availability of such information in this form would facilitate the application of national law implementing this Convention,

provided that such information is already available in electronic form.

4. Each Party shall, at regular intervals not exceeding three or four years, publish and disseminate a national report on the state of the environment, including information on the quality of the environment and information on pressures on the environment.

5. Each Party shall take measures within the framework of its legislation for the purpose of disseminating, *inter alia*:

  (a) Legislation and policy documents such as documents on strategies, policies, programmes and action plans relating to the environment, and progress reports on their implementation, prepared at various levels of government;

  (b) International treaties, conventions and agreements on environmental issues; and

  (c) Other significant international documents on environmental issues, as appropriate.

6. Each Party shall encourage operators whose activities have a significant impact on the environment to inform the public regularly of the environmental impact of their activities and products, where appropriate within the framework of voluntary eco-labelling or eco-auditing schemes or by other means.

7. Each Party shall:

  (a) Publish the facts and analyses of facts which it considers relevant and important in framing major environmental policy proposals;

  (b) Publish, or otherwise make accessible, available explanatory material on its dealings with the public in matters falling within the scope of this Convention; and

  (c) Provide in an appropriate form information on the performance of public functions or the provision of public services relating to the environment by government at all levels.

8. Each Party shall develop mechanisms with a view to ensuring that sufficient product information is made available to the public in a manner which enables consumers to make informed environmental choices.

9. Each Party shall take steps to establish progressively, taking into account international processes where appropriate, a coherent, nationwide system of pollution inventories or registers on a structured, computerized and publicly accessible database compiled through standardized reporting. Such a system may include inputs, releases and transfers of a specified range of substances and products, including water, energy and resource use, from a specified range of activities to environmental media and to on-site and offsite treatment and disposal sites.

10. Nothing in this article may prejudice the right of Parties to refuse to disclose certain environmental information in accordance with article 4, paragraphs 3 and 4.

Article 6
Public participation in decisions on specific activities

1. Each Party:
   (a) Shall apply the provisions of this article with respect to decisions on whether to permit proposed activities listed in annex I;
   (b) Shall, in accordance with its national law, also apply the provisions of this article to decisions on proposed activities not listed in annex I which may have a significant effect on the environment. To this end, Parties shall determine whether such a proposed activity is subject to these provisions; and
   (c) May decide, on a case-by-case basis if so provided under national law, not to apply the provisions of this article to proposed activities serving national defence purposes, if that Party deems that such application would have an adverse effect on these purposes.

2. The public concerned shall be informed, either by public notice or individually as appropriate, early in an environmental decision-making procedure, and in an adequate, timely and effective manner, *inter alia*, of:
   (a) The proposed activity and the application on which a decision will be taken;
   (b) The nature of possible decisions or the draft decision;
   (c) The public authority responsible for making the decision;
   (d) The envisaged procedure, including, as and when this information can be provided:
      (i)   The commencement of the procedure;
      (ii) The opportunities for the public to participate;
      (iii) The time and venue of any envisaged public hearing;
      (iv) An indication of the public authority from which relevant information can be obtained and where the relevant information has been deposited for examination by the public;
      (v)   An indication of the relevant public authority or any other official body to which comments or questions can be submitted and of the time schedule for transmittal of comments or questions; and
      (vi) An indication of what environmental information relevant to the proposed activity is available; and
   (e) The fact that the activity is subject to a national or transboundary environmental impact assessment procedure.

3. The public participation procedures shall include reasonable time-frames for the different phases, allowing sufficient time for informing the public in accordance with paragraph 2 above and for the public to prepare and participate effectively during the environmental decision-making.

4. Each Party shall provide for early public participation, when all options are open and effective public participation can take place.

5. Each Party should, where appropriate, encourage prospective applicants to identify the public concerned, to enter into discussions, and to provide information regarding the objectives of their application before applying for a permit.

6. Each Party shall require the competent public authorities to give the public concerned access for examination, upon request where so required under national law, free of charge and as soon as it becomes available, to all information relevant to the decision-making referred to in this article that is available at the time of the public participation procedure, without prejudice to the right of Parties to refuse to disclose certain information in accordance with article 4, paragraphs 3 and 4. The relevant information shall include at least, and without prejudice to the provisions of article 4:
   (a) A description of the site and the physical and technical characteristics of the proposed activity, including an estimate of the expected residues and emissions;

(b) A description of the significant effects of the proposed activity on the environment;

(c) A description of the measures envisaged to prevent and/or reduce the effects, including emissions;

(d) A non-technical summary of the above;

(e) An outline of the main alternatives studied by the applicant; and

(f) In accordance with national legislation, the main reports and advice issued to the public authority at the time when the public concerned shall be informed in accordance with paragraph 2 above.

7. Procedures for public participation shall allow the public to submit, in writing or, as appropriate, at a public hearing or inquiry with the applicant, any comments, information, analyses or opinions that it considers relevant to the proposed activity.

8. Each Party shall ensure that in the decision due account is taken of the outcome of the public participation.

9. Each Party shall ensure that, when the decision has been taken by the public authority, the public is promptly informed of the decision in accordance with the appropriate procedures. Each Party shall make accessible to the public the text of the decision along with the reasons and considerations on which the decision is based.

10. Each Party shall ensure that, when a public authority reconsiders or updates the operating conditions for an activity referred to in paragraph 1, the provisions of paragraphs 2 to 9 of this article are applied *mutatis mutandis*, and where appropriate.

11. Each Party shall, within the framework of its national law, apply, to the extent feasible and appropriate, provisions of this article to decisions on whether to permit the deliberate release of genetically modified organisms into the environment.

Article 7
Public participation concerning plans, programmes and policies relating to the environment

Each Party shall make appropriate practical and/or other provisions for the public to participate during the preparation of plans and programmes relating to the environment, within a transparent and fair framework, having provided the necessary information to the public. Within this framework, article 6, paragraphs 3, 4 and 8, shall be applied. The public which may participate shall be identified by the relevant public authority, taking into account the objectives of this Convention. To the extent appropriate, each Party shall endeavour to provide opportunities for public participation in the preparation of policies relating to the environment.

Article 8
Public participation during the preparation of executive regulations and/or generally applicable legally binding normative instruments

Each Party shall strive to promote effective public participation at an appropriate stage, and while options are still open, during the preparation by public authorities of executive regulations and other generally applicable legally binding rules that may have a significant effect on the environment. To this end, the following steps should be taken:

(a) Time-frames sufficient for effective participation should be fixed;

(b) Draft rules should be published or otherwise made publicly available; and

(c) The public should be given the opportunity to comment, directly or through representative consultative bodies.

The result of the public participation shall be taken into account as far as possible.

Article 9
Access to justice

1. Each Party shall, within the framework of its national legislation, ensure that any person who considers that his or her request for information under article 4 has been ignored, wrongfully refused, whether in part or in full, inadequately answered, or otherwise not dealt with in accordance with the provisions of that article, has access to a review procedure before a court of law or another independent and impartial body established by law.

   In the circumstances where a Party provides for such a review by a court of law, it shall ensure that such a person also has access to an expeditious procedure established by law that is free of charge or inexpensive for reconsideration by a public authority or review by an independent and impartial body other than a court of law.

   Final decisions under this paragraph 1 shall be binding on the public authority holding the information. Reasons shall be stated in writing, at least where access to information is refused under this paragraph.

2. Each Party shall, within the framework of its national legislation, ensure that members of the public concerned
   (a) Having a sufficient interest
   or, alternatively,
   (b) Maintaining impairment of a right, where the administrative procedural law of a Party requires this as a precondition,
   have access to a review procedure before a court of law and/or another independent and impartial body established by law, to challenge the substantive and procedural legality of any decision, act or omission subject to the provisions of article 6 and, where so provided for under national law and without prejudice to paragraph 3 below, of other relevant provisions of this Convention.

   What constitutes a sufficient interest and impairment of a right shall be determined in accordance with the requirements of national law and consistently with the objective of giving the public concerned wide access to justice within the scope of this Convention. To this end, the interest of any non-governmental organization meeting the requirements referred to in article 2, paragraph 5, shall be deemed sufficient for the purpose of subparagraph (a) above. Such organizations shall also be deemed to have rights capable of being impaired for the purpose of subparagraph (b) above.

   The provisions of this paragraph 2 shall not exclude the possibility of a preliminary review procedure before an administrative authority and shall not affect the requirement of exhaustion of administrative review procedures prior to recourse to judicial review procedures, where such a requirement exists under national law.

3. In addition and without prejudice to the review procedures referred to in paragraphs 1 and 2 above, each Party shall ensure that, where they meet the criteria, if any, laid down in its national law, members of the public have access to administrative or judicial procedures to challenge acts and omissions by private persons and public authorities which contravene provisions of its national law relating to the environment.

4. In addition and without prejudice to paragraph 1 above, the procedures referred to in paragraphs 1, 2 and 3 above shall provide adequate and effective remedies, including injunctive relief as appropriate, and be fair, equitable, timely and not prohibitively expensive. Decisions under this article shall be given or recorded in writing. Decisions of courts, and whenever possible of other bodies, shall be publicly accessible.

5. In order to further the effectiveness of the provisions of this article, each Party shall ensure that information is provided to the public on access to administrative and judicial review procedures and shall consider the establishment of appropriate assistance mechanisms to remove or reduce financial and other barriers to access to justice.

Appendix 1

Article 10
Meeting of the parties

1. The first meeting of the Parties shall be convened no later than one year after the date of the entry into force of this Convention. Thereafter, an ordinary meeting of the Parties shall be held at least once every two years, unless otherwise decided by the Parties, or at the written request of any Party, provided that, within six months of the request being communicated to all Parties by the Executive Secretary of the Economic Commission for Europe, the said request is supported by at least one third of the Parties.

2. At their meetings, the Parties shall keep under continuous review the implementation of this Convention on the basis of regular reporting by the Parties, and, with this purpose in mind, shall:

    (a) Review the policies for and legal and methodological approaches to access to information, public participation in decision-making and access to justice in environmental matters, with a view to further improving them;

    (b) Exchange information regarding experience gained in concluding and implementing bilateral and multilateral agreements or other arrangements having relevance to the purposes of this Convention and to which one or more of the Parties are a party;

    (c) Seek, where appropriate, the services of relevant ECE bodies and other competent international bodies and specific committees in all aspects pertinent to the achievement of the purposes of this Convention;

    (d) Establish any subsidiary bodies as they deem necessary;

    (e) Prepare, where appropriate, protocols to this Convention;

    (f) Consider and adopt proposals for amendments to this Convention in accordance with the provisions of article 14;

    (g) Consider and undertake any additional action that may be required for the achievement of the purposes of this Convention;

    (h) At their first meeting, consider and by consensus adopt rules of procedure for their meetings and the meetings of subsidiary bodies;

    (i) At their first meeting, review their experience in implementing the provisions of article 5, paragraph 9, and consider what steps are necessary to develop further the system referred to in that paragraph, taking into account international processes and developments, including the elaboration of an appropriate instrument concerning pollution release and transfer registers or inventories which could be annexed to this Convention.

3. The Meeting of the Parties may, as necessary, consider establishing financial arrangements on a consensus basis.

4. The United Nations, its specialized agencies and the International Atomic Energy Agency, as well as any State or regional economic integration organization entitled under article 17 to sign this Convention but which is not a Party to this Convention, and any intergovernmental organization qualified in the fields to which this Convention relates, shall be entitled to participate as observers in the meetings of the Parties.

5. Any non-governmental organization, qualified in the fields to which this Convention relates, which has informed the Executive Secretary of the Economic Commission for Europe of its wish to be represented at a meeting of the Parties shall be entitled to participate as an observer unless at least one third of the Parties present in the meeting raise objections.

6. For the purposes of paragraphs 4 and 5 above, the rules of procedure referred to in paragraph 2 (h) above shall provide for practical arrangements for the admittance procedure and other relevant terms.

Article 11
Right to vote

1. Except as provided for in paragraph 2 below, each Party to this Convention shall have one vote.

2. Regional economic integration organizations, in matters within their competence, shall exercise their right to vote with a number of votes equal to the number of their member States which are Parties to this Convention. Such organizations shall not exercise their right to vote if their member States exercise theirs, and vice versa.

Article 12
Secretariat

The Executive Secretary of the Economic Commission for Europe shall carry out the following secretariat functions:

(a) The convening and preparing of meetings of the Parties;

(b) The transmission to the Parties of reports and other information received in accordance with the provisions of this Convention; and

(c) Such other functions as may be determined by the Parties.

Article 13
Annexes

The annexes to this Convention shall constitute an integral part thereof.

Article 14
Amendments to the convention

1. Any Party may propose amendments to this Convention.

2. The text of any proposed amendment to this Convention shall be submitted in writing to the Executive Secretary of the Economic Commission for Europe, who shall communicate it to all Parties at least ninety days before the meeting of the Parties at which it is proposed for adoption.

3. The Parties shall make every effort to reach agreement on any proposed amendment to this Convention by consensus. If all efforts at consensus have been exhausted, and no agreement reached, the amendment shall as a last resort be adopted by a three-fourths majority vote of the Parties present and voting at the meeting.

4. Amendments to this Convention adopted in accordance with paragraph 3 above shall be communicated by the Depositary to all Parties for ratification, approval or acceptance. Amendments to this Convention other than those to an annex shall enter into force for Parties having ratified, approved or accepted them on the ninetieth day after the receipt by the Depositary of notification of their ratification, approval or acceptance by at least three fourths of these Parties. Thereafter they shall enter into force for any other Party on the ninetieth day after that Party deposits its instrument of ratification, approval or acceptance of the amendments.

5. Any Party that is unable to approve an amendment to an annex to this Convention shall so notify the Depositary in writing within twelve months from the date of the communication of the adoption. The Depositary shall without delay notify all Parties of any such notification received. A Party may at any time substitute an acceptance for its previous notification and, upon deposit of an instrument of acceptance with the Depositary, the amendments to such an annex shall become effective for that Party.

6. On the expiry of twelve months from the date of its communication by the Depositary as provided for in paragraph 4 above an amendment to an annex shall become effective for those Parties which have not submitted a notification to the Depositary in accordance with the provisions of paragraph 5 above, provided that not more than one third of the Parties have submitted such a notification.

7. For the purposes of this article, 'Parties present and voting' means Parties present and casting an affirmative or negative vote.

Article 15
Review of compliance

The Meeting of the Parties shall establish, on a consensus basis, optional arrangements of a non-confrontational, non-judicial and consultative nature for reviewing compliance with the provisions of this Convention. These arrangements shall allow for appropriate public involvement and may include the option of considering communications from members of the public on matters related to this Convention.

Article 16
Settlement of disputes

1. If a dispute arises between two or more Parties about the interpretation or application of this Convention, they shall seek a solution by negotiation or by any other means of dispute settlement acceptable to the parties to the dispute.

2. When signing, ratifying, accepting, approving or acceding to this Convention, or at any time thereafter, a Party may declare in writing to the Depositary that, for a dispute not resolved in accordance with paragraph 1 above, it accepts one or both of the following means of dispute settlement as compulsory in relation to any Party accepting the same obligation:
   (a) Submission of the dispute to the International Court of Justice;
   (b) Arbitration in accordance with the procedure set out in annex II.

3. If the parties to the dispute have accepted both means of dispute settlement referred to in paragraph 2 above, the dispute may be submitted only to the International Court of Justice, unless the parties agree otherwise.

Article 17
Signature

This Convention shall be open for signature at Aarhus (Denmark) on 25 June 1998, and thereafter at United Nations Headquarters in New York until 21 December 1998, by States members of the Economic Commission for Europe as well as States having consultative status with the Economic Commission for Europe pursuant to paragraphs 8 and 11 of Economic and Social Council resolution 36 (IV) of 28 March 1947, and by regional economic integration organizations constituted by sovereign States members of the Economic Commission for Europe to which their member States have transferred competence over matters governed by this Convention, including the competence to enter into treaties in respect of these matters.

Article 18
Depositary

The Secretary-General of the United Nations shall act as the Depositary of this Convention.

Article 19
Ratification, acceptance, approval and accession

1. This Convention shall be subject to ratification, acceptance or approval by signatory States and regional economic integration organizations.

2. This Convention shall be open for accession as from 22 December 1998 by the States and regional economic integration organizations referred to in article 17.

3. Any other State, not referred to in paragraph 2 above, that is a Member of the United Nations may accede to the Convention upon approval by the Meeting of the Parties.

4. Any organization referred to in article 17 which becomes a Party to this Convention without any of its member States being a Party shall be bound by all the obligations under this Convention. If one or more of such an organization's member States is a Party to this Convention, the organization and its member States shall decide on their respective responsibilities for the performance of their obligations under this Convention. In such cases, the organization and the member States shall not be entitled to exercise rights under this Convention concurrently.

5. In their instruments of ratification, acceptance, approval or accession, the regional economic integration organizations referred to in article 17 shall declare the extent of their competence with respect to the matters governed by this Convention. These organizations shall also inform the Depositary of any substantial modification to the extent of their competence.

Article 20
Entry into force

1. This Convention shall enter into force on the ninetieth day after the date of deposit of the sixteenth instrument of ratification, acceptance, approval or accession.
2. For the purposes of paragraph 1 above, any instrument deposited by a regional economic integration organization shall not be counted as additional to those deposited by States members of such an organization.
3. For each State or organization referred to in article 17 which ratifies, accepts or approves this Convention or accedes thereto after the deposit of the sixteenth instrument of ratification, acceptance, approval or accession, the Convention shall enter into force on the ninetieth day after the date of deposit by such State or organization of its instrument of ratification, acceptance, approval or accession.

Article 21
Withdrawal

At any time after three years from the date on which this Convention has come into force with respect to a Party, that Party may withdraw from the Convention by giving written notification to the Depositary. Any such withdrawal shall take effect on the ninetieth day after the date of its receipt by the Depositary.

Article 22
Authentic texts

The original of this Convention, of which the English, French and Russian texts are equally authentic, shall be deposited with the Secretary-General of the United Nations.

IN WITNESS WHEREOF the undersigned, being duly authorized thereto, have signed this Convention.

DONE at Aarhus (Denmark), this twenty-fifth day of June, one thousand nine hundred and ninety-eight.

Annex I
List of activities referred to in article 6, paragraph 1 (a)

1. Energy sector:
   — Mineral oil and gas refineries;
   — Installations for gasification and liquefaction;
   — Thermal power stations and other combustion installations with a heat input of 50 megawatts (MW) or more;
   — Coke ovens;
   — Nuclear power stations and other nuclear reactors including the dismantling or decommissioning of such power stations or reactors 1/ (except research installations for the production and conversion of fissionable and fertile materials whose maximum power does not exceed 1 kW continuous thermal load);
   — Installations for the reprocessing of irradiated nuclear fuel;
   — Installations designed:
     — For the production or enrichment of nuclear fuel;
     — For the processing of irradiated nuclear fuel or high-level radioactive waste;
     — For the final disposal of irradiated nuclear fuel;

— Solely for the final disposal of radioactive waste;

— Solely for the storage (planned for more than 10 years) of irradiated nuclear fuels or radioactive waste in a different site than the production site.

2. Production and processing of metals:

— Metal ore (including sulphide ore) roasting or sintering installations;

— Installations for the production of pig-iron or steel (primary or secondary fusion) including continuous casting, with a capacity exceeding 2.5 tons per hour;

— Installations for the processing of ferrous metals:

   (i)   Hot-rolling mills with a capacity exceeding 20 tons of crude steel per hour;

   (ii) Smitheries with hammers the energy of which exceeds 50 kilojoules per hammer, where the calorific power used exceeds 20 MW;

   (iii) Application of protective fused metal coats with an input exceeding 2 tons of crude steel per hour;

— Ferrous metal foundries with a production capacity exceeding 20 tons per day;

— Installations:

   (i)   For the production of non-ferrous crude metals from ore, concentrates or secondary raw materials by metallurgical, chemical or electrolytic processes;

   (ii) For the smelting, including the alloying, of non-ferrous metals, including recovered products (refining, foundry casting, etc.), with a melting capacity exceeding 4 tons per day for lead and cadmium or 20 tons per day for all other metals;

— Installations for surface treatment of metals and plastic materials using an electrolytic or chemical process where the volume of the treatment vats exceeds 30 m^3.

3. Mineral industry:

— Installations for the production of cement clinker in rotary kilns with a production capacity exceeding 500 tons per day or lime in rotary kilns with a production capacity exceeding 50 tons per day or in other furnaces with a production capacity exceeding 50 tons per day;

— Installations for the production of asbestos and the manufacture of asbestos-based products;

— Installations for the manufacture of glass including glass fibre with a melting capacity exceeding 20 tons per day;

— Installations for melting mineral substances including the production of mineral fibres with a melting capacity exceeding 20 tons per day;

— Installations for the manufacture of ceramic products by firing, in particular roofing tiles, bricks, refractory bricks, tiles, stoneware or porcelain, with a production capacity exceeding 75 tons per day, and/or with a kiln capacity exceeding 4 m^3 and with a setting density per kiln exceeding 300 kg/m^3.

4. Chemical industry: Production within the meaning of the categories of activities contained in this paragraph means the production on an industrial scale by chemical processing of substances or groups of substances listed in subparagraphs (a) to (g):

(a) Chemical installations for the production of basic organic chemicals, such as:

   (i)   Simple hydrocarbons (linear or cyclic, saturated or unsaturated, aliphatic or aromatic);

   (ii) Oxygen-containing hydrocarbons such as alcohols, aldehydes, ketones, carboxylic acids, esters, acetates, ethers, peroxides, epoxy resins;

   (iii) Sulphurous hydrocarbons;

   (iv) Nitrogenous hydrocarbons such as amines, amides, nitrous compounds, nitro compounds or nitrate compounds, nitriles, cyanates, isocyanates;

   (v)   Phosphorus-containing hydrocarbons;

   (vi) Halogenic hydrocarbons;

   (vii) Organometallic compounds;

   (viii) Basic plastic materials (polymers, synthetic fibres and cellulose-based fibres);

   (ix) Synthetic rubbers;

      (x) Dyes and pigments;

      (xi) Surface-active agents and surfactants;

  (b) Chemical installations for the production of basic inorganic chemicals, such as:

      (i)   Gases, such as ammonia, chlorine or hydrogen chloride, fluorine or hydrogen fluoride, carbon oxides, sulphur compounds, nitrogen oxides, hydrogen, sulphur dioxide, carbonyl chloride;

      (ii)   Acids, such as chromic acid, hydrofluoric acid, phosphoric acid, nitric acid, hydrochloric acid, sulphuric acid, oleum, sulphurous acids;

      (iii) Bases, such as ammonium hydroxide, potassium hydroxide, sodium hydroxide;

      (iv) Salts, such as ammonium chloride, potassium chlorate, potassium carbonate, sodium carbonate, perborate, silver nitrate;

      (v)   Non-metals, metal oxides or other inorganic compounds such as calcium carbide, silicon, silicon carbide;

  (c) Chemical installations for the production of phosphorous-, nitrogen- or potassium-based fertilizers (simple or compound fertilizers);

  (d) Chemical installations for the production of basic plant health products and of biocides;

  (e) Installations using a chemical or biological process for the production of basic pharmaceutical products;

  (f) Chemical installations for the production of explosives;

  (g) Chemical installations in which chemical or biological processing is used for the production of protein feed additives, ferments and other protein substances.

5. Waste management:

  — Installations for the incineration, recovery, chemical treatment or landfill of hazardous waste;

  — Installations for the incineration of municipal waste with a capacity exceeding 3 tons per hour;

  — Installations for the disposal of non-hazardous waste with a capacity exceeding 50 tons per day;

  — Landfills receiving more than 10 tons per day or with a total capacity exceeding 25,000 tons, excluding landfills of inert waste.

6. Waste-water treatment plants with a capacity exceeding 150,000 population equivalent.

7. Industrial plants for the:

  (a) Production of pulp from timber or similar fibrous materials;

  (b) Production of paper and board with a production capacity exceeding 20 tons per day.

8. (a) Construction of lines for long-distance railway traffic and of airports 2/ with a basic runway length of 2,100 m or more;

  (b) Construction of motorways and express roads; 3/

  (c) Construction of a new road of four or more lanes, or realignment and/or widening of an existing road of two lanes or less so as to provide four or more lanes, where such new road, or realigned and/or widened section of road, would be 10 km or more in a continuous length.

9. (a) Inland waterways and ports for inland-waterway traffic which permit the passage of vessels of over 1,350 tons;

  (b) Trading ports, piers for loading and unloading connected to land and outside ports (excluding ferry piers) which can take vessels of over 1,350 tons.

10. Groundwater abstraction or artificial groundwater recharge schemes where the annual volume of water abstracted or recharged is equivalent to or exceeds 10 million cubic metres.

11. (a) Works for the transfer of water resources between river basins where this transfer aims at preventing possible shortages of water and where the amount of water transferred exceeds 100 million cubic metres/year;

(b) In all other cases, works for the transfer of water resources between river basins where the multiannual average flow of the basin of abstraction exceeds 2 000 million cubic metres/year and where the amount of water transferred exceeds 5% of this flow.

In both cases transfers of piped drinking water are excluded.

12. Extraction of petroleum and natural gas for commercial purposes where the amount extracted exceeds 500 tons/day in the case of petroleum and 500,000 cubic metres/day in the case of gas.

13. Dams and other installations designed for the holding back or permanent storage of water, where a new or additional amount of water held back or stored exceeds 10 million cubic metres.

14. Pipelines for the transport of gas, oil or chemicals with a diameter of more than 800 mm and a length of more than 40 km.

15. Installations for the intensive rearing of poultry or pigs with more than:
    (a) 40,000 places for poultry;
    (b) 2,000 places for production pigs (over 30 kg); or
    (c) 750 places for sows.

16. Quarries and opencast mining where the surface of the site exceeds 25 hectares, or peat extraction, where the surface of the site exceeds 150 hectares.

17. Construction of overhead electrical power lines with a voltage of 220 kV or more and a length of more than 15 km.

18. Installations for the storage of petroleum, petrochemical, or chemical products with a capacity of 200,000 tons or more.

19. Other activities:
    — Plants for the pretreatment (operations such as washing, bleaching, mercerization) or dyeing of fibres or textiles where the treatment capacity exceeds 10 tons per day;
    — Plants for the tanning of hides and skins where the treatment capacity exceeds 12 tons of finished products per day;
    (a) Slaughterhouses with a carcass production capacity greater than 50 tons per day;
    (b) Treatment and processing intended for the production of food products from:
        (i) Animal raw materials (other than milk) with a finished product production capacity greater than 75 tons per day;
        (ii) Vegetable raw materials with a finished product production capacity greater than 300 tons per day (average value on a quarterly basis);
    (c) Treatment and processing of milk, the quantity of milk received being greater than 200 tons per day (average value on an annual basis);
    — Installations for the disposal or recycling of animal carcasses and animal waste with a treatment capacity exceeding 10 tons per day;
    — Installations for the surface treatment of substances, objects or products using organic solvents, in particular for dressing, printing, coating, degreasing, waterproofing, sizing, painting, cleaning or impregnating, with a consumption capacity of more than 150 kg per hour or more than 200 tons per year;
    — Installations for the production of carbon (hard-burnt coal) or electrographite by means of incineration or graphitization.

20. Any activity not covered by paragraphs 1–19 above where public participation is provided for under an environmental impact assessment procedure in accordance with national legislation.

21. The provision of article 6, paragraph 1 (a) of this Convention, does not apply to any of the above projects undertaken exclusively or mainly for research, development and testing of new methods or products for less than two years unless they would be likely to cause a significant adverse effect on environment or health.

22. Any change to or extension of activities, where such a change or extension in itself meets the criteria/thresholds set out in this annex, shall be subject to article 6, paragraph 1 (a) of this

Convention. Any other change or extension of activities shall be subject to article 6, paragraph 1 (b) of this Convention.

Notes

1   Nuclear power stations and other nuclear reactors cease to be such an installation when all nuclear fuel and other radioactively contaminated elements have been removed permanently from the installation site.
2   For the purposes of this Convention, 'airport' means an airport which complies with the definition in the 1944 Chicago Convention setting up the International Civil Aviation Organization (Annex 14).
3   For the purposes of this Convention, 'express road' means a road which complies with the definition in the European Agreement on Main International Traffic Arteries of 15 November 1975.

Annex II
Arbitration

1. In the event of a dispute being submitted for arbitration pursuant to article 16, paragraph 2, of this Convention, a party or parties shall notify the secretariat of the subject matter of arbitration and indicate, in particular, the articles of this Convention whose interpretation or application is at issue. The secretariat shall forward the information received to all Parties to this Convention.
2. The arbitral tribunal shall consist of three members. Both the claimant party or parties and the other party or parties to the dispute shall appoint an arbitrator, and the two arbitrators so appointed shall designate by common agreement the third arbitrator, who shall be the president of the arbitral tribunal. The latter shall not be a national of one of the parties to the dispute, nor have his or her usual place of residence in the territory of one of these parties, nor be employed by any of them, nor have dealt with the case in any other capacity.
3. If the president of the arbitral tribunal has not been designated within two months of the appointment of the second arbitrator, the Executive Secretary of the Economic Commission for Europe shall, at the request of either party to the dispute, designate the president within a further two-month period.
4. If one of the parties to the dispute does not appoint an arbitrator within two months of the receipt of the request, the other party may so inform the Executive Secretary of the Economic Commission for Europe, who shall designate the president of the arbitral tribunal within a further two-month period. Upon designation, the president of the arbitral tribunal shall request the party which has not appointed an arbitrator to do so within two months. If it fails to do so within that period, the president shall so inform the Executive Secretary of the Economic Commission for Europe, who shall make this appointment within a further two-month period.
5. The arbitral tribunal shall render its decision in accordance with international law and the provisions of this Convention.
6. Any arbitral tribunal constituted under the provisions set out in this annex shall draw up its own rules of procedure.
7. The decisions of the arbitral tribunal, both on procedure and on substance, shall be taken by majority vote of its members.
8. The tribunal may take all appropriate measures to establish the facts.
9. The parties to the dispute shall facilitate the work of the arbitral tribunal and, in particular, using all means at their disposal, shall:
    (a) Provide it with all relevant documents, facilities and information;
    (b) Enable it, where necessary, to call witnesses or experts and receive their evidence.
10. The parties and the arbitrators shall protect the confidentiality of any information that they receive in confidence during the proceedings of the arbitral tribunal.

11. The arbitral tribunal may, at the request of one of the parties, recommend interim measures of protection.

12. If one of the parties to the dispute does not appear before the arbitral tribunal or fails to defend its case, the other party may request the tribunal to continue the proceedings and to render its final decision. Absence of a party or failure of a party to defend its case shall not constitute a bar to the proceedings.

13. The arbitral tribunal may hear and determine counter-claims arising directly out of the subject matter of the dispute.

14. Unless the arbitral tribunal determines otherwise because of the particular circumstances of the case, the expenses of the tribunal, including the remuneration of its members, shall be borne by the parties to the dispute in equal shares. The tribunal shall keep a record of all its expenses, and shall furnish a final statement thereof to the parties.

15. Any Party to this Convention which has an interest of a legal nature in the subject matter of the dispute, and which may be affected by a decision in the case, may intervene in the proceedings with the consent of the tribunal.

16. The arbitral tribunal shall render its award within five months of the date on which it is established, unless it finds it necessary to extend the time limit for a period which should not exceed five months.

17. The award of the arbitral tribunal shall be accompanied by a statement of reasons. It shall be final and binding upon all parties to the dispute. The award will be transmitted by the arbitral tribunal to the parties to the dispute and to the secretariat. The secretariat will forward the information received to all Parties to this Convention.

18. Any dispute which may arise between the parties concerning the interpretation or execution of the award may be submitted by either party to the arbitral tribunal which made the award or, if the latter cannot be seized thereof, to another tribunal constituted for this purpose in the same manner as the first.

APPENDIX 2

Wildlife and Countryside Act 1981

SCHEDULE 1
BIRDS PROTECTED BY SPECIAL PENALTIES

Part I
At all times

Common name	Scientific name
Avocet	*Recurvirostra avosetta*
Barn Owl	*Tyto alba*
Bearded Tit	*Panurus biarmicus*
Bewick's Swan	*Cygnus columbianus*
Black Redstart	*Phoenicurus ochruros*
Black Tern	*Chlidonias niger*
Black-necked Grebe	*Podiceps nigricollis*
Black-tailed Godwit	*Limosa limosa*
Black-throated Diver	*Gavia arctica*
Black-winged Stilt	*Himantopus himantopus*
Bluethroat	*Luscinia svecica*
Brambling	*Fringilla montifringilla*
Cetti's Warbler	*Cettia cetti*
Chough	*Pyrrhocorax pyrrhocorax*
Cirl Bunting	*Emberiza cirlus*
Common Scoter	*Melanitta nigra*
Corncrake	*Crex crex*
Crested Tit	*Parus cristatus*
Crossbill	*Loxia curvirostra*
Dartford Warbler	*Sylvia undata*
Dotterel	*Charadrius morinellus*
Eurasian Spoonbill	*Platalea leucorodia*
European Bee-eater	*Merops apiaster*
Fieldfare	*Turdus pilaris*
Firecrest	*Regulus ignicapillus*
Garganey	*Anas querquedula*
Golden Eagle	*Aquila chrysaetos*
Golden Oriole	*Oriolus oriolus*
Goshawk	*Accipiter gentilis*
Great Bittern	*Botaurus stellaris*
Great Northern Diver	*Gavia immer*
Green Sandpiper	*Tringa ochropus*
Greenshank	*Tringa nebularia*
Gyrfalcon	*Falco rusticolus*
Hen Harrier	*Circus cyaneus*

Hobby	*Falco subbuteo*
Honey Buzzard	*Pernis apivorus*
Hoopoe	*Upupa epops*
Kentish Plover	*Charadrius alexandrinus*
Kingfisher	*Alcedo atthis*
Lapland Bunting	*Calcarius lapponicus*
Leach's Petrel	*Oceanodroma leucorhoa*
Little Bittern	*Ixobrychus minutus*
Little Gull	*Larus minutus*
Little Ringed Plover	*Charadrius dubius*
Little Tern	*Sterna albifrons*
Long-tailed Duck	*Clangula hyemalis*
Marsh Harrier	*Circus aeruginosus*
Marsh Warbler	*Acrocephalus palustris*
Mediterranean Gull	*Larus melanocephalus*
Merlin	*Falco columbarius*
Montagu's Harrier	*Circus pygargus*
Osprey	*Pandion haliaetus*
Pallid Harrier	*Circus macrourus*
Parrot Crossbill	*Loxia pytyopsittacus*
Peregrine	*Falco peregrinus*
Purple Heron	*Ardea purpurea*
Purple Sandpiper	*Calidris maritima*
Quail	*Coturnix coturnix*
Red Kite	*Milvus milvus*
Red-backed Shrike	*Lanius collurio*
Red-necked Phalarope	*Phalaropus lobatus*
Red-throated Diver	*Gavia stellata*
Redwing	*Turdus iliacus*
Roseate Tern	*Sterna dougallii*
Ruff	*Philomachus pugnax*
Savi's Warbler	*Locustella luscinioides*
Scarlet Grosbeak	*Carpodacus erythrinus*
Scaup	*Aythya marila*
Scottish Crossbill	*Loxia scotica*
Serin	*Serinus serinus*
Shore Lark	*Eremophila alpestris*
Short-toed Treecreeper	*Certhia brachydactyla*
Slavonian Grebe	*Podiceps auritus*
Snow Bunting	*Plectrophenax nivalis*
Snowy Owl	*Nyctea scandiaca*
Spotted Crake	*Porzana porzana*
Stone-curlew	*Burhinus oedicnemus*
Temminck's Stint	*Calidris temminckii*
Two-barred Crossbill	*Loxia leucoptera*
Velvet Scoter	*Melanitta fusca*
Whimbrel	*Numenius phaeopus*
White-billed Diver	*Gavia adamsii*
White-tailed Eagle	*Haliaeetus albicilla*
Whooper Swan	*Cygnus cygnus*

Wood Sandpiper	*Tringa glareola*
Woodlark	*Lullula arborea*
Wryneck	*Jynx torquilla*

Part II
During the close season

Goldeneye	*Bucephala clangula*
Greylag Goose	*Anser anser*
Northern Pintail	*Anas acuta*

Note: The common name or names given in the first column of the Schedule are included by way of guidance only; in the event of any dispute or proceedings, the common name or names shall not be taken into account.

SCHEDULE 2
BIRDS WHICH MAY BE KILLED OR TAKEN

Part I
Outside the close season

Common name	*Scientific name*
Canada Goose	*Branta canadensis*
Capercaillie	*Tetrao urogallus*
Common Pochard	*Aythya ferina*
Coot	*Fulica atra*
Crakes and Rails	*Rallidae*
Eurasian Wigeon	*Anas penelope*
Gadwall	*Anas strepera*
Golden Plover	*Pluvialis apricaria*
Goldeneye	*Bucephala clangula*
Greylag Goose	*Anser anser*
Grouse	*Tetraonidae*
Mallard	*Anas platyrhynchos*
Moorhen	*Gallinula chloropus*
Northern Pintail	*Anas acuta*
Northern Shoveler	*Anas clypeata*
Pink-footed Goose	*Anser brachyrhynchus*
Plovers	*Charadriidae*
Snipe	*Gallinago gallinago*
Teal	*Anas crecca*
Tufted Duck	*Aythya fuligula*
Waders	*Scolopacidae*
White-fronted Goose	*Anser albifrons*
Woodcock	*Scolopax rusticola*

Part II

[Repealed]

SCHEDULE 3
BIRDS WHICH MAY BE SOLD

Part I
Alive at all times if ringed and bred in captivity

Common name	*Scientific name*
Barn Owl	*Tyto alba*
Dunnock	*Prunella modularis*
Blackbird	*Turdus merula*
Song Thrush	*Turdus philomelos*
Jackdaw	*Corvus monedula*
Jay	*Garrulus glandarius*
Magpie	*Pica pica*
Starling	*Sturnus vulgaris*
Brambling	*Fringilla montifringilla*
Bullfinch	*Pyrrhula pyrrhula*
Chaffinch	*Fringilla coelebs*
Goldfinch	*Carduelis carduelis*
Greenfinch	*Carduelis chloris*
Linnet	*Carduelis cannabina*
Redpoll	*Carduelis flammea*
Reed Bunting	*Emberiza schoeniclus*
Siskin	*Carduelis spinus*
Twite	*Carduelis flavirostris*
Yellowhammer	*Emberiza citrinella*

Part II
Dead at all times

Rock Dove	*Columba livia*
Woodpigeon	*Columba palumbus*

Part III
Dead from 1 September to 28 February

Capercaillie	*Tetrao urogallus*
Common Pochard	*Aythya ferina*
Coot	*Fulica atra*
Eurasian Wigeon	*Anas penelope*
Golden Plover	*Pluvialis apricaria*
Mallard	*Anas platyrhynchos*
Northern Pintail	*Anas acuta*
Northern Shoveler	*Anas clypeata*
Snipe	*Gallinago gallinago*
Teal	*Anas crecca*
Tufted Duck	*Aythya fuligula*
Woodcock	*Scolopax rusticola*

SCHEDULE 4
BIRDS WHICH MUST BE REGISTERED AND RINGED IF KEPT IN CAPTIVITY

Common name	Scientific name
Andaman Serpent Eagle	*Spilornis elgini*
Barbary Falcon	*Falco pelegrinoides*
Bearded Tit	*Panurus biarmicus*
Black Honey Buzzard	*Henicopernis infuscata*
Black Redstart	*Phoenicurus ochruros*
Cetti's Warbler	*Cettia cetti*
Chough	*Pyrrhocorax pyrrhocorax*
Cirl Bunting	*Emberiza cirlus*
Crakes and Rails	*Rallidae*
Crested Tit	*Parus cristatus*
Crossbill	*Loxia curvirostra*
Dartford Warbler	*Sylvia undata*
Dwarf Sparrow Hawk	*Accipiter nanus*
Falcons	*Falconidae*
Fieldfare	*Turdus pilaris*
Firecrest	*Regulus ignicapillus*
Galapagos Hawk	*Buteo galapagoensis*
Golden Eagle	*Aquila chrysaetos*
Golden Oriole	*Oriolus oriolus*
Goshawk	*Accipiter gentilis*
Grey-backed Hawk	*Leucopternis occidentalis*
Gundlach's Hawk	*Accipiter gundlachii*
Gyrfalcon	*Falco rusticolus*
Hawaiian Hawk	*Buteo solitarius*
Hen Harrier	*Circus cyaneus*
Hobby	*Falco subbuteo*
Honey Buzzard	*Pernis apivorus*
Ibises and Spoonbills	*Threskiornithidae*
Imitator Sparrow Hawk	*Accipiter imitator*
Imperial Eagle	*Haliaeetus heliaca*
Kinabalu Serpent Eagle	*Spilornis kinabaluensis*
Lapland Bunting	*Calcarius lapponicus*
Lesser Kestrel	*Falco naumanni*
Madagascar Fish Eagle	*Haliaeetus vociferoides*
Madagascar Serpent Eagle	*Eutriorchis astur*
Marsh Harrier	*Circus aeruginosus*
Marsh Warbler	*Acrocephalus palustris*
Mauritius Kestrel	*Falco punctatus*
Merlin	*Falco columbarius*
Montagu's Harrier	*Circus pygargus*
New Britain Collared Sparrow Hawk	*Accipiter brachyurus*
New Guinea Harpy Eagle	*Harpyopsis novaeguineae*
Osprey	*Pandion haliaetus*
Pallas's Fish Eagle	*Haliaeetus leucoryphus*
Parrot Crossbill	*Loxia pytyopsittacus*
Peregrine	*Falco peregrinus*

Phillipine Eagle	*Pithecophaga jefferyi*
Plumbeous Forest Falcon	*Micrastur plumbeous*
Red Kite	*Milvus milvus*
Red-backed Shrike	*Lanius collurio*
Redwing	*Turdus iliacus*
Ridgway's Hawk	*Buteo ridgwayi*
Savi's Warbler	*Locustella luscinioides*
Scottish Crossbill	*Loxia scotica*
Serin	*Serinus serinus*
Shore Lark	*Eremophila alpestris*
Snow Bunting	*Plectrophenax nivalis*
Spanish Imperial Eagle	*Aquila adalberti*
Steller's Sea Eagle	*Haliaeetus pelagicus*
Two-barred Crossbill	*Loxia leucoptera*
Wallace's Hawk Eagle	*Spizaetus nanus*
White-necked Hawk	*Leucopternis lacernulata*
White-tailed Eagle	*Haliaeetus albicilla*
Woodlark	*Lullula arborea*
Wryneck	*Jynx torquilla*

Any bird one of whose parents or other lineal ancestor was a bird of a kind specified in the foregoing provision of this Schedule.

SCHEDULE 5
ANIMALS WHICH ARE PROTECTED

Common name	*Scientific name*
Adder	*Vipera berus*
Adonis blue	*Lysandra bellargus*
All bats	*Vespertilionidae and Rhinolophidae*
All dolphins, porpoises, whales	Cetacea
All turtles	*Cheloniidae and Dermochelyidae*
Allis shad	*Alosa alosa*
Apus	*Triops cancriformis*
Atlantic stream (white-clawed) crayfish	*Austropotamobius pallipes*
Barberry carpet	*Pareulype berberata*
Basking shark	*Cetorhinus maximus*
Beetle	*Hypebaeus flavipes*
Black hairstreak	*Strymonidia pruni*
Black-veined	*Siona lineata*
Brown hairstreak	*Thecla betulae*
Burbot	*Lota lota*
Carthusian snail	*Monacha cartusiana*
Chalkhill blue	*Lysandra coridon*
Checkered skipper	*Carterocephalus palaemon*
Common frog	*Rana temporaria*
Common toad	*Bufo bufo*
Couch's goby	*Gobius couchii*
De Folin's lagoon snail	*Caecum armoricum*
Dormouse	*Muscardinus avellanarius*

Duke of Burgundy	*Hamearis lucina*
Essex emerald	*Thetidia smaragdaria*
Fairy shrimp	*Chirocephalus diaphanus*
Fan mussel	*Atrina fragilis*
Fen raft spider	*Dolomedes plantarius*
Field cricket	*Gryllus campestris*
Fiery clearwing	*Bembecia chrysidiformis*
Fisher's estuarine moth	*Gortyna borelii*
Giant goby	*Gobius cobitis*
Glanville fritillary	*Melitaea cinxia*
Glutinous snail	*Myxas glutinosa*
Grass snake	*Natrix natrix*
Heath fritillary	*Mellicta athalia (Melitaea athalia)*
High brown fritillary butterfly	*Argynnis adippe*
Ivell's sea anemone	*Edwardsia ivelli*
Ladybird spider	*Eresus niger (cinaberinus)*
Lagoon sand shrimp	*Gammarus insensibilis*
Lagoon sandworm	*Armandia cirrhosa*
Lagoon sea slug	*Tenellia adspersa*
Lagoon snail	*Paludinella littorina*
Large blue	*Maculinea arion*
Large copper	*Lycaena dispar*
Large heath butterfly	*Coenonympha tullia*
Large tortoiseshell	*Nymphalis polychloros*
Lesser silver water beetle	*Hydrochara caraboides*
Lulworth skipper	*Thymelicus acteon*
Marine hydroid	*Clavopsella navis*
Marsh fritillary	*Eurodryas aurinia*
Medicinal leech	*Hirudo medicinalis*
Mire pill beetle	*Curimopsis nigrita*
Mole cricket	*Gryllotalpa gryllotalpa*
Mountain ringlet	*Erebia epiphron*
Natterjack toad	*Bufo calamita*
New Forest burnet	*Zygaena viciae*
New Forest cicada	*Cicadetta montana*
Norfolk aeshna	*Aeshna isosceles*
Northern brown argus	*Aricia artaxerxes*
Northern hatchet-shell	*Thyasira gouldi*
Otter	*Lutra lutra*
Palmate newt	*Triturus helveticus*
Pearl mussel	*Margaritifera margaritifera*
Pearl-bordered fritillary	*Boloria euphrosyne*
Pine marten	*Martes martes*
Pink sea-fan	*Eunicella verrucosa*
Purple emperor	*Apatura iris*
Rainbow leaf beetle	*Chrysolina cerealis*
Red squirrel	*Sciurus vulgaris*
Reddish buff	*Acosmetia caliginosa*
Sand lizard	*Lacerta agilis*
Sandbowl snail	*Catinella arenaria*

Silver-spotted	*Hesperia comma*
Silver-studded blue	*Plebejus argus*
Slow worm	*Anguis fragilis*
Small blue	*Cupido minimus*
Smooth newt	*Triturus vulgaris*
Smooth snake	*Coronella austriaca*
Southern damselfly	*Coenagrion mercuriale*
Stag beetle	*Lucanus cervus*
Starlet sea anemone	*Nematostella vectensis*
Sturgeon	*Acipenser sturio*
Sussex emerald	*Thalera fimbrialis*
Swallowtail	*Papilio machaon*
Tentacled lagoon-worm	*Alkmaria romijni*
Trembling sea-mat	*Victorella pavida*
Twaite shad	*Alosa fallax*
Vendace	*Coregonus albula*
Violet click beetle	*Limoniscus violaceus*
Viper's bugloss	*Hadena irregularis*
Viviparous lizard	*Lacerta vivipara*
Walrus	*Odobenus rosmarus*
Wart-biter	*Decticus verrucivorus*
Warty (great crested) newt	*Triturus cristatus*
Water beetle	*Graphoderus zonatus*
Water beetle	*Paracymus aeneus*
Water vole	*Arvicola terrestris*
Whitefish	*Coregonus lavaretus*
White-letter hairstreak	*Strymonidia w-album*
Wildcat	*Felis silvestris*
Wood white	*Leptidea sinapis*

SCHEDULE 6
ANIMALS WHICH MAY NOT BE KILLED OR TAKEN BY CERTAIN METHODS

Common name   *Scientific name*

Badger
Bats, Horseshoe (all species)
Bats, typical (all species)
Cat, Wild
Dolphin, bottle-nosed
Dolphin, common
Dormice (All species)
Hedgehog
Pine Parten
Common Otter
Polecat
Porpoise, Harbour or Common
Shrews (all species
Red squirrel

SCHEDULE 8
PLANTS WHICH ARE PROTECTED

Common name	Scientific name
Least Adder's Tongue	*Ophioglossum lusitanicum*
Small Alison	*Alyssum alyssoides*
Blackwort	*Southbya nigrella*
Bluebell	*Hyacinthoides non-scripta*
Bedstraw Broomrape	*Orobanche caryophyllacea*
Oxtongue Broomrape	*Orobanche loricata*
Thistle Broomrape	*Orobanche reticulata*
Lundy Cabbage	*Rhynchosinapis wrightii*
Wood Calamint	*Calamintha sylvatica*
Snow Caloplaca	*Caloplaca nivalis*
Tree Catapyrenium	*Catapyrenium psoromoides*
Alpine Catchfly	*Lychnis alpina*
Laurer's Catillaria	*Catellaria laureri*
Slender Centaury	*Centaurium tenuiflorum*
Rock Cinquefoil	*Potentilla rupestris*
Meadow Clary	*Salvia pratensis*
Triangular Club-rush	*Scirpus triquetrus*
Purple Colt's-foot	*Homogyne alpina*
Wild Cotoneaster	*Cotoneaster integerrimus*
Slender Cottongrass	*Eriophorum gracile*
Field Cow-wheat	*Melampyrum arvense*
Sand Crocus	*Romulea columnae*
Lizard Crystalwort	*Riccia bifurca*
Broad-leaved Cudweed	*Filago pyramidata*
Jersey Cudweed	*Gnaphalium luteoalbum*
Red-tipped Cudweed	*Filago lutescens*
Cut-grass	*Leersia oryzoides*
Diapensia	*Diapensia lapponica*
Shore Dock	*Rumex rupestris*
Marsh Earwort	*Jamesoniella undulifolia*
Field Eryngo	*Eryngium campestre*
Dickie's Bladder Fern	*Cystopteris dickieana*
Killarney Fern	*Trichomanes speciosum*
Norfolk Flapwort	*Leiocolea rutheana*
Alpine Fleabane	*Erigeron borealis*
Small Fleabane	*Pulicaria vulgaris*
South Stack Fleawort	*Tephroseris integrifolia (ssp maritima)*
Pointed Frostwort	*Gymnomitrion apiculatum*
Hedgehog Fungus Fungi	*Hericium erinaceum*
Oak Polypore Fungi	*Buglossoporus pulvinus*
Royal Bolete Fungi	*Boletus regius*
Sandy Stilt Puffball Fungi	*Battarraea phalloides*
Brown Galingale	*Cyperus fuscus*
Alpine Gentian	*Gentiana nivalis*
Dune Gentian	*Gentianella uliginosa*
Early Gentian	*Gentianella anglica*

Fringed Gentian	*Gentianella ciliata*
Spring Gentian	*Gentiana verna*
Cut-leaved Germander	*Teucrium botrys*
Water Germander	*Teucrium scordium*
Wild Gladiolus	*Gladiolus illyricus*
Stinking Goosefoot	*Chenopodium vulvaria*
Grass-poly	*Lythrum hyssopifolia*
Blunt-leaved Grimmia	*Grimmia unicolor*
Elm Gyalecta	*Gyalecta ulmi*
Sickle-leaved Hare's-ear	*Bupleurum falcatum*
Small Hare's-ear	*Bupleurum baldense*
Stinking Hawk's-beard	*Crepis foetida*
Northroe Hawkweed	*Hieracium northroense*
Shetland Hawkweed	*Hieracium zetlandicum*
Weak-leaved Hawkweed	*Hieracium attenuatifolium*
Blue Heath	*Phyllodoce caerulea*
Red Helleborine	*Cephalanthera rubra*
Young's Helleborine	*Epipactis youngiana*
Branched Horsetail	*Equisetum ramosissimum*
Green Hound's-tongue	*Cynoglossum germanicum*
Perennial Knawel	*Scleranthus perennis*
Sea Knotgrass	*Polygonum maritimum*
Lady's-slipper	*Cypripedium calceolus*
Churchyard Lecanactis	*Lecanactis hemisphaerica*
Tarn Lecanora	*Lecanora archariana*
Copper Lecidea	*Lecidea inops*
Round-headed Leek	*Allium sphaerocephalon*
Least Lettuce	*Lactuca saligna*
Alpine Sulphur-tresses Lichen	*Alectoria ochroleuca*
Arctic Kidney Lichen	*Nephroma arcticum*
Ciliate Strap Lichen	*Heterodermia leucomelos*
Convoluted Cladonia Lichen	*Cladonia convoluta*
Upright Mountain Cladonia Lichen	*Cladonia stricta*
Coralloid Rosette Lichen	*Heterodermia propagulifera*
Ear-loped Dog Lichen	*Peltigera lepidophora*
Forked Hair Lichen	*Bryoria furcellata*
Goblin Lights Lichen	*Catolechia wahlenbergii*
Golden Hair Lichen	*Teloschistes flavicans*
New Forest Beech-lichen	*Enterographa elaborata*
Orange Fruited Elm Lichen	*Caloplaca luteoalba*
River Jelly Lichen	*Collema dichotomum*
Scaly Breck Lichen	*Squamarina lentigera*
Stary Breck Lichen	*Buellia asterella*
Snowdon Lily	*Lloydia serotina*
Lindenberg's Liverwort	*Adelanthus lindenbergianus*
Leafy Liverwort	*Petallophyllum ralfsi*
Rough Marsh-mallow	*Althaea hirsuta*
Creeping Marshwort	*Apium repens*
Cambridge Milk-parsley	*Selinum carvifolia*
Moss	*Drepanocladius vernicosus*

Alpine Copper Moss	*Mielichoferia mielichoferi*
Anomodon, Long-leaved Moss	*Anomodon longifolius*
Baltic Bog Moss	*Sphagnum balticum*
Blue Dew Moss	*Saelania glaucescens*
Blunt-leaved Bristle Moss	*Orthotrichum obtusifolium*
Bright Green Cave Moss	*Cyclodictyon laetevirens*
Cordate Beard Moss	*Barbula cordata*
Cornish Path Moss	*Ditrichum cornubicum*
Derbyshire Feather Moss	*Thamnobryum angustifolium*
Dune Thread Moss	*Bryum mamillatum*
Flamingo Moss	*Desmatodon cernuus*
Glaucous Beard Moss	*Barbula glauca*
Green Shield Moss	*Buxbaumia viridis*
Hair Silk Moss	*Plagiothecium piliferum*
Knothole Moss	*Zygodon forsteri*
Large Yellow Feather Moss	*Scorpidium turgescens*
Millimetre Moss	*Micromitrium tenerum*
Multifruited River Moss	*Cryphaea lamyana*
Nowell's Limestone Moss	*Zygodon gracilis*
Polar Feather-moss Moss	*Hygrohypnum polare*
Rigid Apple Moss	*Bartramia stricta*
Round-leaved Feather Moss	*Rhyncostegium rotundifolium*
Scleicher's Thread Moss	*Bryum schleicheri*
Threadmoss, Long-leaved Moss	*Bryum neodamense*
Triangular Pygmy Moss	*Acaulon triquetum*
Vaucher's Feather Moss	*Hypnum vaucheri*
Welsh Mudwort	*Limosella australis*
Holly-leaved Naiad	*Najas marina*
Slender Naiad	*Najas flexilis*
Stalked Orache	*Halimione pedunculata*
Early Spider Orchid	*Ophrys sphegodes*
Fen Orchid	*Liparis loeselii*
Ghost Orchid	*Epipogium aphyllum*
Lapland Marsh Orchid	*Dactylorhiza lapponica*
Late Spider Orchid	*Ophrys fuciflora*
Lizard Orchid	*Himantoglossum hircinum*
Military Orchid	*Orchis militaris*
Monkey Orchid	*Orchis simia*
Caledonia Panneria	*Panneria ignobilis*
New Forest Parmelia	*Parmelia minarum*
Oil Stain Parmentaria	*Parmentaria chilensis*
Plymouth Pear	*Pyrus cordata*
Perfoliate Penny-cress	*Thlapsi perfoliatum*
Pennyroyal	*Mentha pulegium*
Alpine Moss Pertusaria	*Pertusaria bryontha*
Southern Grey Physcia	*Physcia tribacioide*
Pigmyweed	*Crassula aquatica*
Ground Pine	*Ajuga chamaepitys*
Cheddar Pink	*Dianthus gratianopolitanus*
Childing Pink	*Petroraghia nanteuilii*

Deptford Pink	*Dianthus armeria*
Floating-leaved Water Plantain	*Luronium natans*
Ragged Pseudo Cyphellaria	*Pseudocyphellaria lacerata*
Rusty Alpine Psora	*Psora rubiformis*
Fen Ragwort	*Senecio paludosus*
Martin's Ramping fumitory	*Fumaria martinii*
Spiked Rampion	*Phyteuma spicatum*
Small Restharrow	*Ononis reclinata*
Alpine Rock-cress	*Arabis alpina*
Bristol Rock-cress	*Arabis stricta*
Western Rustwort	*Marsupella profunda*
Norwegian Sandwort	*Arenaria norvegica*
Teesdale Sandwort	*Minuartia stricta*
Drooping Saxifrage	*Saxifraga cernua*
Yellow Marsh Saxifrage	*Saxifraga hirculus*
Tufted Saxifrage	*Saxifraga cespitosa*
Serpentine Solenopsora	*Solenopsora liparina*
Whorled Soloman's-seal	*Polygonatum verticillatum*
Alpine Sow-thistle	*Cicerbita alpina*
Adder's-tongue Spearwort	*Ranunculus ophioglossifolius*
Fingered Speedwell	*Veronica triphyllos*
Spiked Speedwell	*Veronica spicata*
Dwarf Spike Rush	*Eleocharis parvula*
Early Star-of-Bethlehem	*Gagea bohemica*
Starfruit	*Damasonium alisma*
Foxtail Stonewort	*Lamprothamnium papulosum*
Bearded Stonewort	*Chara canescens*
Strapwort	*Corrigiola litoralis*
Turpswort	*Geocalyx graveolens*
Fen Violet	*Viola persicifolia*
Viper's-grass	*Scorzonera humilis*
Ribbon-leaved Water-plantain	*Alisma gramineum*
Starved Wood-sedge	*Carex depauperata*
Alpine Woodsia	*Woodsia alpina*
Oblong Woodsia	*Woodsia ilvenis*
Field Wormwood	*Artemisia campestris*
Downy Woundwort	*Stachys germanica*
Limestone Woundwort	*Stachys alpina*
Greater Yellow-rattle	*Rhinanthus serotinus*

SCHEDULE 9

Part I
Animals which are established in the wild

Common name	*Scientific name*
Bass, large mouthed black	
Bass, rock	
Bitterling	
Budgerigar	

Capercaillie
Coypu
Dormouse, Fat
Duck, Carolina wood
Duck, mandarin
Duck, ruddy
Eagle, white-tailed
Frog, edible
Frog, European Tree or Common Frog
Frog, marsh
Gerbil, Mongolian
Goose, Canada
Goose, Egyptian
Heron, night
Lizard, common wall
Marmot (prairie dog)
Mink, American
Newt, Alpine
Barn Owl
Parakeet, Ring-necked
Partridge, chakar
Partridge, rock
Pheasant, golden
Pheasant, Lady Amhurst's
Pheasant, Reeves
Pheasant, silver
Porcupine, Crested
Porcupine, Himalayan
Pumpkinseed (Sun Fish or Pond Perch)
Quail, bobwhite
Rat, black
Squirrel, grey
Terrapin, European pond
Toad, African clawed
Toad, midwife
Toad, yellowbellied
Wallaby, red-necked
Wels, European Catfish
Zander

SCHEDULE 9

Part II
Plants

Common name	*Scientific name*
Hogweed, Giant	
Seaweed, Japanese	
Kelp, Giant	
Knotweed, Japanese	

Environmental Protection Act 1990 (c 43)

PART III

STATUTORY NUISANCES AND CLEAN AIR

Statutory nuisances: England and Wales

79. Statutory nuisances and inspections therefor

[(1) Subject to subsections (2) to (6A) below], the following matters constitute 'statutory nuisances' for the purposes of this Part, that is to say—

(a) any premises in such a state as to be prejudicial to health or a nuisance;

(b) smoke emitted from premises so as to be prejudicial to health or a nuisance;

(c) fumes or gases emitted from premises so as to be prejudicial to health or a nuisance;

(d) any dust, steam, smell or other effluvia arising on industrial, trade or business premises and being prejudicial to health or a nuisance;

(e) any accumulation or deposit which is prejudicial to health or a nuisance;

(f) any animal kept in such a place or manner as to be prejudicial to health or a nuisance;

(fa) any insects emanating from relevant industrial, trade or business premises and being prejudicial to health or a nuisance;

(fb) artificial light emitted from premises so as to be prejudicial to health or a nuisance;

(g) noise emitted from premises so as to be prejudicial to health or a nuisance;

[(ga) noise that is prejudicial to health or a nuisance and is emitted from or caused by a vehicle, machinery or equipment in a street [or in Scotland, road];]

(h) any other matter declared by any enactment to be a statutory nuisance;

and it shall be the duty of every local authority to cause its area to be inspected from time to time to detect any statutory nuisances which ought to be dealt with under section 80 below and, where a complaint of a statutory nuisance is made to it by a person living within its area, to take such steps as are reasonably practicable to investigate the complaint.

[(1A) No matter shall constitute a statutory nuisance to the extent that it consists of, or is caused by, any land in a contaminated state.

[(1B) Land is in a 'contaminated state' for the purposes of subsection (1A) above if, and only if, it is in such a condition, by reason of substances in, on or under the land, that—

(a) harm is being caused or there is a possibility of harm being caused; or

(b) pollution of controlled wastes is being, or is likely to be, caused;

and in this subsection 'harm' or 'pollution of controlled waters' and 'substance' have the same meaning as in Part IIA of this Act.]

(2) Subsection (1)(b), (fb) and (g) above do not apply in relation to premises—

(a) occupied on behalf of the Crown for naval, military or air force purposes or for the purposes of the department of the Secretary of State having responsibility for defence, or

(b) occupied by or for the purposes of a visiting force;

and 'visiting force' means any such body, contingent or detachment of the forces of any country as is a visiting force for the purposes of any of the provisions of the Visiting Forces Act 1952.

(3) Subsection (1)(b) above does not apply to—

      (i)   smoke emitted from a chimney of a private dwelling within a smoke control area,

      (ii) dark smoke emitted from a chimney of a building or a chimney serving the furnace of a boiler or industrial plant attached to a building or for the time being fixed to or installed on any land,

      (iii) smoke emitted from a railway locomotive steam engine, or

      (iv) dark smoke emitted otherwise than as mentioned above from industrial or trade premises.

(4)   Subsection (1)(c) above does not apply in relation to premises other than private dwellings.

(5)   Subsection (1)(d) above does not apply to steam emitted from a railway locomotive engine.

(5A) Subsection (1)(fa) does not apply to insects that are wild animals included in Schedule 5 to the Wildlife and Countryside Act 1981 (animals which are protected), unless they are included in respect of section 9(5) of that Act only.

(5B) Subsection (1)(fb) does not apply to artificial light emitted from—

      (a) an airport;

      (b) harbour premises;

      (c) railway premises, not being relevant separate railway premises;

      (d) tramway premises;

      (e) a bus station and any associated facilities

      (f) a public service vehicle operating centre;

      (g) a goods vehicle operating centre;

      (h) a lighthouse;

      (i) a prison.

(6)   Subsection (1)(g) above does not apply to noise caused by aircraft other than model aircraft.

[(6A) Subsection (1)(g) above does not apply to noise made—

      (a) by traffic;

      (b) by any naval, military or air force of the Crown or by a visiting force (as defined in subsection (2) above), or

      (c) by a political demonstration or a demonstration supporting or opposing a cause or campaign.]

(7)   In this Part—

      'airport' has the meaning given by section 95 of the Transport Act 2000;

      'appropriate person' means—

        (a) in relation to England, the Secretary of State;

        (b) in relation to Wales, the National Assembly for Wales.

      'associated facilities', in relation to a bus station, has the meaning given by section 83 of the Transport Act 1985;

      'bus station' has the meaning given by section 83 of the Transport Act 1985;

      'chimney' includes structures and openings of any kind from or through which smoke may be emitted;

      'dust' does not include dust emitted from a chimney as an ingredient of smoke;

      ['equipment' includes a musical instrument;]

      'fumes' means any airborne solid matter smaller than dust;

      'gas' includes vapour and moisture precipitated from vapour;

      'industrial, trade or business premises' means premises used for any industrial, trade or business purposes or premises not so used on which matter is burnt in connection with any industrial, trade or business process, and premises are used for industrial purposes where they are used for the purposes of any treatment or process as well as where they are used for the purposes of manufacturing;

      'goods vehicle operating centre', in relation to vehicles used under an operator's licence, means a place which is specified in the licence as an operating centre for those vehicles, and for the purposes of this definition 'operating centre' and 'operator's licence' have the same meaning as in the Goods Vehicles (Licensing of Operators) Act 1995;

'harbour premises' means premises which form part of a harbour area and which are occupied wholly or mainly for the purposes of harbour operations, and for the purposes of this definition 'harbour area' and 'harbour operations' have the same meaning as in Part 3 of the Aviation and Maritime Security Act 1990;

'local authority' means, subject to subsection (8) below,—

    (a) in Greater London, a London borough council, the Common Council of the City of London and, as respects the Temples, the Sub-Treasurer of the Inner Temple and the Under-Treasurer of the Middle Temple respectively;

    (b) outside Greater London, a district council; and

    [(bb) in Wales, a county council or county borough council;]

    (c) the Council of the Isles of Scilly; and

    (d) in Scotland, a district or islands council or a council constituted under section 2 of the Local Government etc. (Scotland) Act 1994;

'lighthouse' has the same meaning as in Part 8 of the Merchant Shipping Act 1995;

'noise' includes vibration;

['person responsible'—

    (a) in relation to a statutory nuisance, means the person to whose act, default or sufferance the nuisance is attributable;

    (b) in relation to a vehicle, includes the person in whose name the vehicle is for the time being registered under [the Vehicle Excise and Registration Act 1994] and any other person who is for the time being the driver of the vehicle;

    (c) in relation to machinery or equipment, includes any person who is for the time being the operator of the machinery or equipment;]

'prejudicial to health' means injurious, or likely to cause injury, to health;

'premises' includes land and, subject to subsection (12) below, any vessel;

'prison' includes a young offender institution;

'private dwelling' means any building, or part of a building, used or intended to be used, as a dwelling;

'public service vehicle operating centre', in relation to public service vehicles used under a PSV operator's licence, means a place which is an operating centre of those vehicles, and for the purposes of this definition 'operating centre', 'PSV operator's licence' and 'public service vehicle' have the same meaning as in the Public Passenger Vehicles Act 1981;

'railway premises' means any premises which fall within the definition of 'light maintenance depot', 'network', 'station' or 'track' in section 83 of the Railways Act 1993;

'relevant separate railway premises' has the meaning given by subsection (7A);

['road' has the same meaning as in Part IV of the New Roads and Street Works Act 1991;]

'smoke' includes soot, ash, grit, and gritty particles emitted in smoke;

['street' means a highway and any other road, footway, square or court that is for the time being open to the public;]

'tramway premises' means any premises which, in relation to a tramway, are the equivalent of the premises which, in relation to a railway, fall within the definition of 'light maintenance depot', 'network', 'station' or 'track' in section 83 of the Railways Act 1993.

and any expressions used in this section and in the [1956 c. 52.] Clean Air Act 1956 or the [1968 c. 62.] Clean Air Act 1968 have the same meaning in this section as in that Act and section 34(2) of the Clean Air Act 1956 shall apply for the interpretation of the expression 'dark smoke' and the operation of this Part in relation to it.

(7A) Railway premises are relevant separate railway premises if—

    (a) they are situated within—

        (i) premises used as a museum or other place of cultural, scientific or historical interest, or

        (ii) premises used for the purposes of a funfair or other entertainment, recreation or amusement, and

(b) they are not associated with any other railway premises.

(7B) For the purposes of subsection (7A)—

(a) a network situated as described in subsection (7A)(a) is associated with other railway premises if it is connected to another network (not being a network situated as described in subsection (7A)(a));

(b) track that is situated as described in subsection (7A)(a) but is not part of a network is associated with other railway premises if it is connected to track that forms part of a network (not being a network situated as described in subsection (7A)(a));

(c) a station or light maintenance depot situated as described in subsection (7A)(a) is associated with other railway premises if it is used in connection with the provision of railway services other than services provided wholly within the premises where it is situated.

In this subsection 'light maintenance depot', 'network', 'railway services', 'station' and 'track' have the same meaning as in Part 1 of the Railways Act 1993.

(7C) In this Part 'relevant industrial, trade or business premises' means premises that are industrial, trade or business premises as defined in subsection (7), but excluding—

(a) land used as arable, grazing, meadow or pasture land,

(b) land used as osier land, reed beds or woodland,

(c) land used for market gardens, nursery grounds or orchards,

(d) land forming part of an agricultural unit, not being land falling within any of paragraphs (a) to (c), where the land is of a description prescribed by regulations made by the appropriate person, and

(e) land included in a site of special scientific interest (as defined in section 52(1) of the Wildlife and Countryside Act 1981),

and excluding land covered by, and the waters of, any river or watercourse, that is neither a sewer nor a drain, or any lake or pond.

(7D) For the purpose of subsection (7C)—

'agricultural' has the same meaning as in section 109 of the Agriculture Act 1947;

'agricultural unit' means land which is occupied as a unit for agricultural purposes;

'drain' has the same meaning as in the Water Resources Act 1991;

'lake or pond' has the same meaning as in section 104 of that Act;

'sewer' has the same meaning as in that Act.

(8) Where, by an order under section 2 of the [1984 c. 22.] Public Health (Control of Disease) Act 1984, a port health authority has been constituted for any port health district, the port health authority shall have by virtue of this subsection, as respects its district, the functions conferred or imposed by this Part in relation to statutory nuisances other than a nuisance falling within paragraph (fb), (g) of subsection (1) above and no such order shall be made assigning those functions; and 'local authority' and 'area' shall be construed accordingly.

(9) In this Part 'best practicable means' is to be interpreted by reference to the following provisions—

(a) 'practicable' means reasonably practicable having regard among other things to local conditions and circumstances, to the current state of technical knowledge and to the financial implications;

(b) the means to be employed include the design, installation, maintenance and manner and periods of operation of plant and machinery, and the design, construction and maintenance of buildings and structures;

(c) the test is to apply only so far as compatible with any duty imposed by law;

(d) the test is to apply only so far as compatible with safety and safe working conditions, and with the exigencies of any emergency or unforeseeable circumstances;

and, in circumstances where a code of practice under section 71 of the [1974 c. 40.] Control of Pollution Act 1974 (noise minimisation) is applicable, regard shall also be had to guidance given in it.

(10) A local authority shall not without the consent of the Secretary of State institute summary proceedings under this Part in respect of a nuisance falling within paragraph (b), (d)[, or (e), (fb) [and, in relation to Scotland, paragraph (g) or (ga),] of subsection (1) above if proceedings in respect thereof might be instituted under Part I [or under regulations under section 2] of the Pollution Prevention and Control Act 1999.

(11) The area of a local authority which includes part of the seashore shall also include for the purposes of this Part the territorial sea lying seawards from that part of the shore; and subject to subsection (12) below, this Part shall have effect, in relation to any area included in the area of a local authority by virtue of this subsection—

(a) as if references to premises and the occupier of premises included respectively a vessel and the master of a vessel; and

(b) with such other modifications, if any, as are prescribed in regulations made by the Secretary of State.

(12) A vessel powered by steam reciprocating machinery is not a vessel to which this Part of this Act applies.

80. Summary proceedings for statutory nuisances

(1) Where a local authority is satisfied that a statutory nuisance exists, or is likely to occur or recur, in the area of the authority, the local authority shall serve a notice ('an abatement notice') imposing all or any of the following requirements—

(a) requiring the abatement of the nuisance or prohibiting or restricting its occurrence or recurrence;

(b) requiring the execution of such works, and the taking of such other steps, as may be necessary for any of those purposes,

and the notice shall specify the time or times within which the requirements of the notice are to be complied with.

(2) The abatement notice shall be served—

(a) except in a case falling within paragraph (b) or (c) below, on the person responsible for the nuisance;

(b) where the nuisance arises from any defect of a structural character, on the owner of the premises;

(c) where the person responsible for the nuisance cannot be found or the nuisance has not yet occurred, on the owner or occupier of the premises.

(3) The person served with the notice may appeal against the notice to a magistrates' court within the period of twenty-one days beginning with the date on which he was served with the notice.

(4) If a person on whom an abatement notice is served, without reasonable excuse, contravenes or fails to comply with any requirement or prohibition imposed by the notice, he shall be guilty of an offence.

(5) Except in a case falling within subsection (6) below, a person who commits an offence under subsection (4) above shall be liable on summary conviction to a fine not exceeding level 5 on the standard scale together with a further fine of an amount equal to one-tenth of that level for each day on which the offence continues after the conviction.

(6) A person who commits an offence under subsection (4) above on industrial, trade or business premises shall be liable on summary conviction to a fine not exceeding £20,000.

(7) Subject to subsection (8) below, in any proceedings for an offence under subsection (4) above in respect of a statutory nuisance it shall be a defence to prove that the best practicable means were used to prevent, or to counteract the effects of, the nuisance.

(8) The defence under subsection (7) above is not available—

(a) in the case of a nuisance falling within paragraph (a), (d), (e), (fa), (f) or (g) of section 79(1) above except where the nuisance arises on industrial, trade or business premises;

(aza) in the case of a nuisance falling within paragraph (fb) of section 79(1) above except where—

    (i)   the artificial light is emitted from industrial, trade or business premises, or

    (ii) the artificial light (not being light to which sub-paragraph (i) applies) is emitted by lights used for the purpose only of illuminating an outdoor relevant sports facility;

  (b) in the case of a nuisance falling within paragraph (b) of section 79(1) above except where the smoke is emitted from a chimney; and

  (c) in the case of a nuisance falling within paragraph (c) or (h) of section 79(1) above.

(8A) For the purposes of subsection (8)(aza) a relevant sports facility is an area, with or without structures, that is used when participating in a relevant sport, but does not include such an area comprised in domestic premises.

(8B) For the purposes of subsection (8A) 'relevant sport' means a sport that is designated for those purposes by order made by the Secretary of State, in relation to England, or the National Assembly for Wales, in relation to Wales.

A sport may be so designated by reference to its appearing in a list maintained by a body specified in the order.

(8C) In subsection (8A) 'domestic premises' means—

  (a) premises used wholly or mainly as a private dwelling or

  (b) land or other premises belonging to, or enjoyed with, premises so used.

(9) In proceedings for an offence under subsection (4) above in respect of a statutory nuisance falling within paragraph (g) of section 79(1) above where the offence consists in contravening requirements imposed by virtue of subsection (1)(a) above it shall be a defence to prove—

  (a) that the alleged offence was covered by a notice served under section 60 or a consent given under section 61 or 65 of the [1974 c. 40.] Control of Pollution Act 1974 (construction sites, etc); or

  (b) where the alleged offence was committed at a time when the premises were subject to a notice under section 66 of that Act (noise reduction notice), that the level of noise emitted from the premises at that time was not such as to a constitute a contravention of the notice under that section; or

  (c) where the alleged offence was committed at a time when the premises were not subject to a notice under section 66 of that Act, and when a level fixed under section 67 of that Act (new buildings liable to abatement order) applied to the premises, that the level of noise emitted from the premises at that time did not exceed that level.

(10) Paragraphs (b) and (c) of subsection (9) above apply whether or not the relevant notice was subject to appeal at the time when the offence was alleged to have been committed.

[80A. Abatement notice in respect of noise in the street

[(1) In the case of a statutory nuisance within section 79(1)(ga) above that—

  (a) has not yet occurred, or

  (b) arises from noise emitted from or caused by an unattended vehicle or unattended machinery or equipment,

the abatement notice shall be service in accordance with subsection (2) below.

(2) The notice shall be served—

  (a) where the person responsible for the vehicle, machinery or equipment can be found, on that person;

  (b) where that person cannot be found or where the local authority determines that this paragraph should apply, by fixing the notice to the vehicle, machinery or equipment.

(3) Where—

  (a) an abatement notice is served in accordance with subsection (2)(b) above by virtue of a determination of the local authority, and

    (b) the person responsible for the vehicle, machinery or equipment can be found and served with a copy of the notice within an hour of the notice being fixed to the vehicle, machinery or equipment,

a copy of the notice shall be served on that person accordingly.

(4) Where an abatement notice is served in accordance with subsection (2)(b) above by virtue of a determination of the local authority, the notice shall state that, if a copy of the notice is subsequently served under subsection (3) above, the time specified in the notice as the time within which its requirements are to be complied with is extended by such further period as is specified in the notice.

(5) Where an abatement notice is served in accordance with subsection (2)(b) above, the person responsible for the vehicle, machinery or equipment may appeal against the notice under section 80(3) above as if he had been served with the notice on the date on which it was fixed to the vehicle, machinery or equipment.

(6) Section 80(4) above shall apply in relation to a person on whom a copy of an abatement notice is served under subsection (3) above as if the copy were the notice itself.

(7) A person who removes or interferes with a notice fixed to a vehicle, machinery or equipment in accordance with subsection (2)9b) above shall be guilty of an offence, unless he is the person responsible for the vehicle, machinery or equipment or he does so with the authority of that person.

(8) A person who commits an offence under subsection (7) above shall be liable on summary conviction to a fine not exceeding level 3 on the standard scale.]

81. Supplementary provisions

(1) Where more than one person is responsible for a statutory nuisance section 80 above shall apply to each of those persons whether or not what any one of them is responsible for would by itself amount to a nuisance.

(2) Where a statutory nuisance which exists or has occurred within the area of a local authority, or which has affected any part of that area, appears to the local authority to be wholly or partly caused by some act or default committed or taking place outside the area, the local authority may act under section 80 above as if the act or default were wholly within that area, except that any appeal shall be heard by a magistrates' court having jurisdiction where the act or default is alleged to have taken place.

(3) Where an abatement notice has not been complied with the local authority may, whether or not they take proceedings for an offence under section 80(4) above, abate the nuisance and do whatever may be necessary in execution of the notice.

(4) Any expenses reasonably incurred by a local authority in abating, or preventing the recurrence of, a statutory nuisance under subsection (3) above may be recovered by them from the person by whose act or default the nuisance was caused and, if that person is the owner of the premises, from any person who is for the time being the owner thereof; and the court may apportion the expenses between persons by whose acts or defaults the nuisance is caused in such manner as the court consider fair and reasonable.

(5) If a local authority is of the opinion that proceedings for an offence under section 80(4) above would afford an inadequate remedy in the case of any statutory nuisance, they may, subject to subsection (6) below, take proceedings in the High Court for the purpose of securing the abatement, prohibition or restriction of the nuisance, and the proceedings shall be maintainable notwithstanding the local authority have suffered no damage from the nuisance.

(6) In any proceedings under subsection (5) above in respect of a nuisance falling within paragraph (g) of section 79(1) above, it shall be a defence to prove that the noise was authorised by a notice under section 60 or a consent under section 61 (construction sites) of the [1974 c. 40.] Control of Pollution Act 1974.

(7) The further supplementary provisions in Schedule 3 to this Act shall have effect.

[81A. Expenses recoverable from owner to be a charge on premises

(1)   Where any expenses are recoverable under section 81(4) above from a person who is the owner of the premises there mentioned and the local authority serves a notice on him under this section—

    (a)   the expenses shall carry interest, at such reasonable rate as the local authority may determine, from the date of service of the notice until the whole amount is paid, and

    (b)   subject to the following provisions of this section, the expenses and accrued interest shall be a charge on the premises.

(2)   A notice served under this section shall—

    (a)   specify the amount of the expenses that the local authority claims is recoverable,

    (b)   state the effect of subsection (1) above and the rate of interest determined by the local authority under that subsection, and

    (c)   state the effect of subsections (4) to (6) below.

(3)   On the date on which a local authority serves a notice on a person under this section the authority shall also serve a copy of the notice on every other person who, to the knowledge of the authority, has an interest in the premises capable of being affected by the charge.

(4)   Subject to any order under subsection (7)(b) or (c) below, the amount of any expenses specified in a notice under this section and the accrued interest shall be a charge on the premises—

    (a)   as from the end of the period of twenty-one days beginning with the date of service of the notice, or

    (b)   where an appeal is brought under subsection (6) below, as from the final determination of the appeal,

until the expenses and interest are recovered.

(5)   For the purposes of subsection (4) above, the withdrawal of an appeal has the same effect as a final determination of the appeal.

(6)   A person served with a notice or copy of a notice under this section may appeal against the notice to the county court within the period of twenty-one days beginning with the date of service.

(7)   On such an appeal the court may—

    (a)   confirm the notice without modification,

    (b)   order that the notice is to have effect with the substitution of a different amount for the amount originally specified in it, or

    (c)   order that the notice is to be of no effect.

(8)   A local authority shall, for the purpose of enforcing a charge under this section, have all the same powers and remedies under Law of Property Act 1925, and otherwise, as if it were a mortgagee by deed having powers of sale and lease, of accepting surrenders of leases and of appointing a receiver.

(9)   In this section—

'owner', in relation to any premises, means a person (other than a mortgagee not in possession) who, whether in his own right or as trustee for any other person, is entitled to receive the rack rent of the premises or, where the premises are not let at a rack rent, would be so entitled if they were so let, and

'premises' does not include a vessel.]

[(10) This sub-section applies to Scotland only.]

[81B. Payment of expenses by instalments

(1)   Where any expenses are a charge on premises under section 81A above, the local authority may by order declare the expenses to be payable with interest by instalments within the specified period, until the whole amount is paid.

(2)   In subsection (1) above—

'interest' means interest at the rate determined by the authority under section 81A(1) above, and 'the specified period' means such period of thirty years or less from the date of service of the notice under section 81A above as is specified in the order.

(3) Subject to subsection (5) below, the instalments and interest, or any part of them, may be recovered from the owner or occupier for the time being of the premises.

(4) Any sums recovered from an occupier may be deducted by him from the rent of the premises.

(5) An occupier shall not be required to pay at any one time any sum greater than the aggregate of—

   (a) the amount that was due from him on account of rent at the date on which he was served with a demand from the local authority together with a notice requiring him not to pay rent to his landlord without deducting the sum demanded, and

   (b) the amount that has become due from him on account of rent since that date.]

[(6) This sub-section applies to Scotland only.]

82. Summary proceedings by persons aggrieved by statutory nuisances

(1) A magistrates' court may act under this section on a complaint [or, in Scotland, the sheriff may act under this section on a summary application,] made by any person on the ground that he is aggrieved by the existence of a statutory nuisance.

(2) If the magistrates' court [or, in Scotland, the sheriff] is satisfied that the alleged nuisance exists, or that although abated it is likely to recur on the same premises, the court shall make an order for either or both of the following purposes—

   (a) requiring the defendant [or, in Scotland, defender] to abate the nuisance, within a time specified in the order, and to execute any works necessary for that purpose;

   (b) prohibiting a recurrence of the nuisance, and requiring the defendant [or defender], within a time specified in the order, to execute any works necessary to prevent the recurrence;

   and [in England and Wales,] may also impose on the defendant a fine not exceeding level 5 on the standard scale.

(3) If the magistrates' court [or the sheriff] is satisfied that the alleged nuisance exists and is such as, in the opinion of the court [or the sheriff], to render premises unfit for human habitation, an order under subsection (2) above may prohibit the use of the premises for human habitation until the premises are, to the satisfaction of the court [or the sheriff], rendered fit for that purpose.

(4) Proceedings for an order under subsection (2) above shall be brought—

   (a) except in a case falling within paragraph (b) or (c) below, against the person responsible for the nuisance;

   (b) where the nuisance arises from any defect of a structural character, against the owner of the premises;

   (c) where the person responsible for the nuisance cannot be found, against the owner or occupier of the premises.

(5) [Subject to subsection (5A) below, where] more than one person is responsible for a statutory nuisance, subsections (1) to (4) above shall apply to each of those persons whether or not what any one of them is responsible for would by itself amount to a nuisance.

[(5A) In relation to a statutory nuisance within section 79(1)(ga) for which more than one person is responsible (whether or not what any one of those persons is responsible for would by itself amount to such a nuisance), subsection (4)(a) above shall apply with the substitution of 'each person responsible for the nuisance who can be found' for 'the person responsible for the nuisance'.

(5B) In relation to a statutory nuisance within section 79(1)(ga) above caused by noise emitted from or caused by an unattended vehicle or unattended machinery or equipment for which more than one person is responsible, subsection (4)(d) above shall apply with the substitution of 'any person' for 'the person'.]

(6) Before instituting proceedings for an order under subsection (2) above against any person, the person aggrieved by the nuisance shall give to that person such notice in writing of his intention

to bring the proceedings as is applicable to proceedings in respect of a nuisance of that description and the notice shall specify the matter complained of.

(7) The notice of the bringing of proceedings in respect of a statutory nuisance required by subsection (6) above which is applicable is—

(a) in the case of a nuisance falling within paragraph (g) of section 79(1) above, not less than three days' notice; and

(b) in the case of a nuisance of any other description, not less than twenty-one days' notice;

but the Secretary of State may, by order, provide that this subsection shall have effect as if such period as is specified in the order were the minimum period of notice applicable to any description of statutory nuisance specified in the order.

(8) A person who, without reasonable excuse, contravenes any requirement or prohibition imposed by an order under subsection (2) above shall be guilty of an offence and liable on summary conviction to a fine not exceeding level 5 on the standard scale together with a further fine of an amount equal to one-tenth of that level for each day on which the offence continues after the conviction.

(9) Subject to subsection (10) below, in any proceedings for an offence under subsection (8) above in respect of a statutory nuisance it shall be a defence to prove that the best practicable means were used to prevent, or to counteract the effects of, the nuisance.

(10) The defence under subsection (9) above is not available—

(a) in the case of a nuisance falling within paragraph (a), (d), (e), (f), (fa) or (g) of section 79(1) above except where the nuisance arises on industrial, trade or business premises;

(aza) in the case of a nuisance falling within paragraph (fb) of section 79(1) above except where—

(i) the artificial light is emitted from industrial, trade or business premises, or

(ii) the artificial light (not being light to which sub-paragraph (i) applies) is emitted by lights used for the purpose only of illuminating an outdoor relevant sports facility;

[(aa) in the case of a nuisance falling within paragraph (ga) of section 79(1) above except where the noise is emitted from or caused by a vehicle, machinery or equipment being used for industrial, trade or business purposes;]

(b) in the case of a nuisance falling within paragraph (b) of section 79(1) above except where the smoke is emitted from a chimney;

(c) in the case of a nuisance falling within paragraph (c) or (h) of section 79(1) above; and

(d) in the case of a nuisance which is such as to render the premises unfit for human habitation.

(10A) For the purposes of subsection (10)(aza) 'relevant sports facility' has the same meaning as it has for the purposes of section 80(8)(aza).

(11) If a person is convicted of an offence under subsection (8) above, a magistrates' court may, after giving the local authority in whose area the nuisance has occurred an opportunity of being heard, direct the authority to do anything which the person convicted was required to do by the order to which the conviction relates.

(12) Where on the hearing of proceedings for an order under subsection (2) above it is proved that the alleged nuisance existed at the date of the making of the complaint, then, whether or not at the date of the hearing it still exists or is likely to recur, the court shall order the defendant (or defendants in such proportions as appears fair and reasonable) to pay to the person bringing the proceedings such amount as the court considers reasonably sufficient to compensate him for any expenses properly incurred by him in the proceedings.

(13) If it appears to the magistrates' court that neither the person responsible for the nuisance nor the owner or occupier of the premises can be found the court may, after giving the local authority in whose area the nuisance has occurred an opportunity of being heard, direct the authority to do anything which the court would have ordered that person to do.

Termination of existing controls over offensive trades and businesses

84. Termination of Public Health Act controls over offensive trades etc.

(1) Where a person carries on, in the area or part of the area of any local authority—

    (a) in England or Wales, a trade which—

        (i) is an offensive trade within the meaning of section 107 of the [1936 c. 49.] Public Health Act 1936 in that area or part of that area, and

        (ii) constitutes a prescribed process designated for local control for the carrying on of which an authorisation is required under section 6 of this Act; or

    (b) in Scotland, a business which—

        (i) is mentioned in section 32(1) of the Public Health (Scotland) Act 1897 (or is an offensive business by virtue of that section) in that area or part of that area; and

        (ii) constitutes a prescribed process designated for local control for the carrying on of which an authorisation is required under the said section 6, subsection (2) below shall have effect in relation to that trade or business as from the date on which an authorisation is granted under section 6 of this Act or, if that person has not applied for such an authorisation within the period allowed under section 2(1) above for making applications under that section, as from the end of that period.

(2) Where this subsection applies in relation to the trade or business carried on by any person—

    (a) nothing in section 107 of the Public Health Act 1936 or in section 32 of the Public Health (Scotland) Act 1897 shall apply in relation to it, and

    (b) no bye-laws or further bye-laws made under section 108(2) of the said Act of 1936, or under subsection (2) of the said section 32, with respect to a trade or business of that description shall apply in relation to it;

but without prejudice to the continuance of, and imposition of any penalty in, any proceedings under the said section 107 or the said section 32 which were instituted before the date as from which this subsection has effect in relation to the trade or business.

(3) Subsection (2)(b) above shall apply in relation to the trade of fish frying as it applies in relation to an offensive trade.

(4) When the Secretary of State considers it expedient to do so, having regard to the operation of Part I and the preceding provisions of this Part of this Act in relation to offensive trades or businesses, he may by order repeal—

    (a) sections 107 and 108 of the [1936 c. 49.] Public Health Act 1936; and

    (b) section 32 of the [1897 c. 38.] Public Health (Scotland) Act 1897;

and different days may be so appointed in relation to trades or businesses which constitute prescribed processes and those which do not.

(5) In this section—

'prescribed process' has the same meaning as in Part I of this Act; and

'offensive trade' or 'trade' has the same meaning as in section 107 of the Public Health Act 1936.

APPENDIX 4

Magistrates' Association: Fining of Companies for Environmental and Health and Safety Offences

In recent years the public has become increasingly concerned about dangers to the environment and the protection of employees' health and safety at work. There have been a number of high profile incidents sometimes involving death and major pollution problems. These concerns have been reflected in the greatly increased maximum fines for related offences. For example, under the provisions of the Environmental Protection Act 1990 the maximum fines for some offences dealt with summarily are £20,000 — far in excess of the financial penalties normally imposed by magistrates — while fines in the Crown Court are unlimited.

Defendants in such cases are frequently companies and sometimes multi-national companies with huge annual turnovers. We need to be reminded of the *Magistrates' Court Sentencing Guidelines* advice that our aim should be for any fine to have equal impact on rich or poor. This is true of companies as well as individuals.

Environmental and health and safety offences to be encountered in the magistrates' court include air or water pollution, the illegal deposit, recovery or disposal of waste, fly-tipping, the illegal extraction of water, failure to meet packaging, recycling and recovery obligations as well as a range of matters relating to the protection of the employee in the work place. A list of the main offences is set out on page 78 of the *Magistrates' Court Sentencing Guidelines*.

It is essential that the public feels confident that convicted companies receive proper and meaningful penalties. The financial penalties must relate to the companies' means and we should accustom ourselves, in appropriate cases to imposing far greater financial penalties than have generally been imposed in the past.

The Lord Chancellor in 1998 spoke to the Magistrates' Association about the disquiet being expressed about the level of sentences for these offences. He particularly suggested the maximum penalties were there to be used in appropriate cases. He said, 'You should not flinch from using them if you believe that they are deserved.'

New guidance

Some important guidance regarding the sentencing of companies for both categories of offence has now been given in the judgment in *R v F Howe and Son (Engineers) Ltd, R v Friskies Petcare UK Ltd* and in the Sentencing Advisory Panel's recent advice to the Court of Appeal on environment offences.

R v Howe relates to health and safety matters but the judgments can equally apply to environmental offences. Its main points are:

- Fines on companies need to be large enough to make an impact on shareholders — past fining levels were far too low
- A company is presumed to be able to pay any fine the court is minded to impose unless financial information to the contrary is available to the court before the hearing
- A deliberate breach of the legislation by a company or an individual with a view to profit seriously aggravates the offence

The judgment provides important guidance on the question of seriousness, in the factors we should take into account in deciding the sentence and in the reasons we give.

R v Friskies Petcare UK Ltd sets out important guidelines for prosecutors, defendants and the sentencing court in the event of a plea of guilty. It strongly recommends that the salient facts of the case, together with aggravating and mitigating features, should be presented to the sentencing court in the form of schedules, which should if possible be agreed in advance. There will therefore be no doubt about the basis on which sentence is passed, and any Higher Court dealing with an appeal against sentence will have the relevant facts at its fingertips. The procedure could easily be adapted to assist magistrates' courts which have to decide whether to commit for sentence following an indication of a guilty plea on plea before venue, or in cases involving a straightforward committal for sentence. The principles apply equally to environmental offences.

Procedures

When considering any of these cases one of the first questions to be asked if dealing with an either way offence is whether the seriousness of the offence is such that the sentencing powers of magistrates are inadequate. If so then the court should not deal with the case and commit to the Crown Court.

If the court is prepared to hear the case then the general procedure adopted in the *Magistrates' Court Sentencing Guidelines* should be followed. After an initial consideration of the seriousness of the offence, an appropriate type of penalty should be considered.

The penalty in these cases is usually a fine. The offences are 'non-violent' — but can cause or risk death, serious injury or ill health — and usually have no continuing threat to persons because the regulator will have used enforcement powers to prevent any such threat. They are often committed in situations where the defendant company has failed to devote proper resources to prevent a breach of the law — hence a financial penalty would usually be the appropriate response.

Seriousness — aggravating and mitigating

As in the sentencing guidelines, having heard the evidence and considered the seriousness of the offence and an appropriate form of penalty, the court considers those factors which could aggravate or mitigate the offence. The Howe case and the Sentencing Advisory Panel advice do suggest what some of the factors could be.

These factors are deemed to aggravate the seriousness of the offence:

- a deliberate or reckless breach of the law rather than carelessness
- action or lack of action prompted by financial motives — profit or cost saving
- disregarding warnings from a regulatory authority or the workforce
- an awareness of the specific risks likely to arise from action taken
- lack of co-operation with a regulatory authority
- serious extent of damage resulting from offence (but lack of actual damage does not render the offence merely technical; it is still serious if there is risk)
- previous offences of a similar nature
- death or serious injury or ill health of humans has been a consequence of the offence
- animal health or flora affected
- expensive clean up operation required
- defendant carrying out operations without an appropriate licence
- other lawful activities interfered with

Other factors may provide some mitigation:

- the offender's minor role with little personal responsibility
- genuine lack of awareness or understanding of specific regulations
- an isolated lapse

There may be some offender mitigation:

- prompt reporting
- ready co-operation with regulatory authority
- good previous record
- timely plea of guilt

Sometimes in a case much more damage has occurred than could have been reasonably anticipated. Any sentence should give weight to the environmental impact but should primarily reflect the culpability of the offender.

The level of fines — general approach

A fine is considered by the Sentencing Advisory Panel to be the appropriate form of penalty for both companies and individuals for these offences. The normal principles of the Criminal Justice Act 1991 should apply and the seriousness of the offence and the financial circumstances of the defendant should be taken into account. The level of fine should reflect the extent to which the defendant's behaviour has fallen below the required standard. High culpability should be matched by a high fine even though actual damage turned out to be less than might reasonably have been anticipated.

In line with *R v Howe*, the level of the fine should reflect any economic gain from the offence by failure to take precautions. It has been said that a deliberate failure to take the necessary precautions can be a form of stealing commercial advantage from law-abiding competitors.

In all cases with corporate offenders the company's financial circumstances must be carefully considered. No single measure of ability to pay can apply in all cases. Turnover, profitability and liquidity should all be considered. It is not usual for an expert accountant to be available in summary cases.

If a company does not produce its accounts the court can assume that the company can pay whatever fine the court imposes. In most cases it is hard to imagine a company failing to provide such information, although with large known companies of national or international standing this may not be a necessary requirement. Where necessary the payment of fines can be spread over a longer period than the usual twelve months, if payment in full would be unduly burdensome on say, a smaller company.

Fining too little?

A fine suited to the circumstances of a small local company would make no impact at all on a multi-national corporation with a huge turnover. The fine to any company should be substantial enough to have a real economic impact, which together with attendant bad publicity would pressure both management and shareholders to tighten their regulatory compliance. Such fines on large companies might often be beyond the summary fines limit and in such circumstances the case should be transferred to the Crown Court for trial or sentence. Where the court does not transfer the case of a larger company to the higher court magistrates should look to a starting point near the maximum fine level then consider aggravating and mitigating factors.

Fining too much?

Care should be taken to ensure that fines imposed on smaller companies are not beyond their capability to pay. The court might not wish the payment of the fine to result in the company not being able to pay for improved procedures or cause the company to go into liquidation or make its employees redundant.

Other sentencing options

Whilst fines will be the usual outcome in proceedings of this sort, other sentencing options are available.

- A discharge will rarely be appropriate.
- Compensation should be considered if there is a specific victim who has suffered injury, loss or damage. You should give reasons if you decide not to make a compensation order. The current limit is £5,000 per offence, although substantial civil claims are often pending in such cases.
- The legislation provides for the possibility of directors and senior managers appearing before the courts, and custodial sentences are available in specific instances. The courts have power to disqualify directors under the Company Directors Disqualification Act 1986. This is important particularly in health and safety enforcement, and breach of an order is itself a criminal offence carrying a term of imprisonment for up to two years.

Costs

The prosecution will normally claim the costs of investigation and presentation. These may be substantial, and can incorporate time and activity expended on containing and making the area safe. Remediation costs for pollution offences may also be significant. For water pollution offences enforcing authorities are able to recover them through the criminal courts (Water Resources Act 1991, as amended). In other cases there are powers for the courts to order offenders to remedy the cause of the offence, or for the Environment Agency to require them to undertake clean-up at their own expense, or for the agency to carry out remedial costs and seek to recover them through the civil courts.

The enforcing authorities' costs should be fully recouped form the offender.

The order for costs should not be disproportionate to the level of the fine imposed. The court should fix the level of the fine first, then consider awarding compensation, and then determine the costs. If the total sum exceeds the defendant's means, the order for costs should be reduced rather than the fine. Compensation should take priority over both the fine and costs.

Whilst the article has focused on companies as defendants, the reader will appreciate that individuals may also be prosecuted under these provisions. Wider sentencing options are then available.

As always, magistrates should seek the advice of the court clerk on sentencing options and guidelines in all cases.

APPENDIX 5

Part 54 — Judicial Review and Statutory Review

I Judicial Review

Scope and interpretation

54.1—(1) This Section of this Part contains rules about judicial review.

(2) In this Section—

(a) a 'claim for judicial review' means a claim to review the lawfulness of—

(i) an enactment; or

(ii) a decision, action or failure to act in relation to the exercise of a public function.

(b) revoked

(c) revoked

(d) revoked

(e) 'the judicial review procedure' means the Part 8 procedure as modified by this Section;

(f) 'interested party' means any person (other than the claimant and defendant) who is directly affected by the claim; and

(g) 'court' means the High Court, unless otherwise stated.

(Rule 8.1(6)(b) provides that a rule or practice direction may, in relation to a specified type of proceedings, disapply or modify any of the rules set out in Part 8 as they apply to those proceedings)

When this Section must be used

54.2—The judicial review procedure must be used in a claim for judicial review where the claimant is seeking—

(a) a mandatory order;

(b) a prohibiting order;

(c) a quashing order; or

(d) an injunction under section 30 of the Supreme Court Act 1981[1] (restraining a person from acting in any office in which he is not entitled to act).

When this Section may be used

54.3—(1) The judicial review procedure may be used in a claim for judicial review where the claimant is seeking—

(a) a declaration; or

(b) an injunction[(GL)].

(Section 31(2) of the Supreme Court Act 1981 sets out the circumstances in which the court may grant a declaration or injunction in a claim for judicial review)

(Where the claimant is seeking a declaration or injunction in addition to one of the remedies listed in rule 54.2, the judicial review procedure must be used)

(2) A claim for judicial review may include a claim for damages, restitution or the recovery of a sum due but may not seek such a remedy alone.

---

[1] 1981 c.54.

(Section 31(4) of the Supreme Court Act sets out the circumstances in which the court may award damages, restitution or the recovery of a sum due on a claim for judicial review)

Permission required

54.4—The court's permission to proceed is required in a claim for judicial review whether started under this Section or transferred to the Administrative Court.

Time limit for filing claim form

54.5—(1) The claim form must be filed—

    (a) promptly; and

    (b) in any event not later than 3 months after the grounds to make the claim first arose.

  (2) The time limit in this rule may not be extended by agreement between the parties.

  (3) This rule does not apply when any other enactment specifies a shorter time limit for making the claim for judicial review.

Claim form

54.6—(1) In addition to the matters set out in rule 8.2 (contents of the claim form) the claimant must also state—

    (a) the name and address of any person he considers to be an interested party;

    (b) that he is requesting permission to proceed with a claim for judicial review; and

    (c) any remedy (including any interim remedy) he is claiming.

    (Part 25 sets out how to apply for an interim remedy)

  (2) The claim form must be accompanied by the documents required by the relevant practice direction.

Service of claim form

54.7—The claim form must be served on—

    (a) the defendant; and

    (b) unless the court otherwise directs, any person the claimant considers to be an interested party, within 7 days after the date of issue.

Acknowledgment of service

54.8—(1) Any person served with the claim form who wishes to take part in the judicial review must file an acknowledgment of service in the relevant practice form in accordance with the following provisions of this rule.

  (2) Any acknowledgment of service must be—

    (a) filed not more than 21 days after service of the claim form; and

    (b) served on—

        (i) the claimant; and

        (ii) subject to any direction under rule 54.7(b), any other person named in the claim form,

    as soon as practicable and, in any event, not later than 7 days after it is filed.

  (3) The time limits under this rule may not be extended by agreement between the parties.

  (4) The acknowledgment of service—

    (a) must—

        (i) where the person filing it intends to contest the claim, set out a summary of his grounds for doing so; and

        (ii) state the name and address of any person the person filing it considers to be an interested party; and

    (b) may include or be accompanied by an application for directions.

  (5) Rule 10.3(2) does not apply.

Failure to file acknowledgment of service

54.9—(1) Where a person served with the claim form has failed to file an acknowledgment of service in accordance with rule 54.8, he—

    (a) may not take part in a hearing to decide whether permission should be given unless the court allows him to do so; but

    (b) provided he complies with rule 54.14 or any other direction of the court regarding the filing and service of—

        (i) detailed grounds for contesting the claim or supporting it on additional grounds; and

        (ii) any written evidence,

    may take part in the hearing of the judicial review.

  (2) Where that person takes part in the hearing of the judicial review, the court may take his failure to file an acknowledgment of service into account when deciding what order to make about costs.

  (3) Rule 8.4 does not apply.

Permission given

54.10—(1) Where permission to proceed is given the court may also give directions.

  (2) Directions under paragraph (1) may include a stay[^GL] of proceedings to which the claim relates.

    (Rule 3.7 provides a sanction for the non-payment of the fee payable when permission to proceed has been given)

Service of order giving or refusing permission

54.11—The court will serve—

    (a) the order giving or refusing permission; and

    (b) any directions,

    on—

        (i) the claimant;

        (ii) the defendant; and

        (iii) any other person who filed an acknowledgment of service.

Permission decision without a hearing

54.12—(1) This rule applies where the court, without a hearing—

    (a) refuses permission to proceed; or

    (b) gives permission to proceed—

        (i) subject to conditions; or

        (ii) on certain grounds only.

  (2) The court will serve its reasons for making the decision when it serves the order giving or refusing permission in accordance with rule 54.11.

  (3) The claimant may not appeal but may request the decision to be reconsidered at a hearing.

  (4) A request under paragraph (3) must be filed within 7 days after service of the reasons under paragraph (2).

  (5) The claimant, defendant and any other person who has filed an acknowledgment of service will be given at least 2 days' notice of the hearing date.

Defendant etc. may not apply to set aside[^GL]

54.13—Neither the defendant nor any other person served with the claim form may apply to set aside[^GL] an order giving permission to proceed.

Response

54.14—(1) A defendant and any other person served with the claim form who wishes to contest the claim or support it on additional grounds must file and serve—
  (a) detailed grounds for contesting the claim or supporting it on additional grounds; and
  (b) any written evidence,
  within 35 days after service of the order giving permission.
  (2) The following rules do not apply—
  (a) rule 8.5 (3) and 8.5 (4) (defendant to file and serve written evidence at the same time as acknowledgment of service); and
  (b) rule 8.5 (5) and 8.5 (6) (claimant to file and serve any reply within 14 days).

Where claimant seeks to rely on additional grounds

54.15—The court's permission is required if a claimant seeks to rely on grounds other than those for which he has been given permission to proceed.

Evidence

54.16—(1) Rule 8.6 (1) does not apply.
  (2) No written evidence may be relied on unless—
  (a) it has been served in accordance with any—
   (i) rule under this Section; or
   (ii) direction of the court; or
  (b) the court gives permission.

Court's powers to hear any person

54.17—(1) Any person may apply for permission—
  (a) to file evidence; or
  (b) make representations at the hearing of the judicial review.
  (2) An application under paragraph (1) should be made promptly.

Judicial review may be decided without a hearing

54.18—The court may decide the claim for judicial review without a hearing where all the parties agree.

Court's powers in respect of quashing orders

54.19—(1) This rule applies where the court makes a quashing order in respect of the decision to which the claim relates.
  (2) The court may—
  (a) remit the matter to the decision-maker; and
  (b) direct it to reconsider the matter and reach a decision in accordance with the judgment of the court.
  (3) Where the court considers that there is no purpose to be served in remitting the matter to the decision-maker it may, subject to any statutory provision, take the decision itself.
  (Where a statutory power is given to a tribunal, person or other body it may be the case that the court cannot take the decision itself)

Transfer

54.20—The court may
  (a) order a claim to continue as if it had not been started under this Section; and
  (b) where it does so, give directions about the future management of the claim.
  (Part 30 (transfer) applies to transfers to and from the Administrative Court)

II Statutory Review Under the Nationality, Immigration and Asylum Act 2002

Scope and interpretation

54.21—(1) This Section of this Part contains rules about applications to the High Court under section 101(2) of the Nationality, Immigration and Asylum Act 2002[2] for a review of a decision of the Immigration Appeal Tribunal on an application for permission to appeal from an adjudicator.

(2) In this Section—

(a) 'the Act' means the Nationality, Immigration and Asylum Act 2002;

(b) 'adjudicator' means an adjudicator appointed for the purposes of Part 5 of the Act;

(c) 'applicant' means a person applying to the High Court under section 101(2) of the Act;

(d) 'other party' means the other party to the proceedings before the Tribunal; and

(e) 'Tribunal' means the Immigration Appeal Tribunal.

Application for review

54.22—(1) An application under section 101(2) of the Act must be made to the Administrative Court.

(2) The application must be made by filing an application notice.

(3) The applicant must file with the application notice—

(a) the immigration or asylum decision to which the proceedings relate, and any document giving reasons for that decision;

(b) the grounds of appeal to the adjudicator;

(c) the adjudicator's determination;

(d) the grounds of appeal to the Tribunal together with any documents sent with them;

(e) the Tribunal's determination on the application for permission to appeal; and

(f) any other documents material to the application which were before the adjudicator.

(4) The applicant must also file with the application notice written submissions setting out—

(a) the grounds upon which it is contended that the Tribunal made an error of law; and

(b) reasons in support of those grounds.

Time limit for application

54.23—(1) The application notice must be filed not later than 14 days after the applicant is deemed to have received notice of the Tribunal's decision in accordance with rules made under section 106 of the Act.

(2) The court may extend the time limit in paragraph (1) in exceptional circumstances.

(3) An application to extend the time limit must be made in the application notice and supported by written evidence verified by a statement of truth.

Service of application

54.24—(1) The applicant must serve on the Asylum and Immigration Tribunal copies of the application notice and written submissions.

(2) Where an application is for review of a decision by the Tribunal to grant permission to appeal, the applicant must serve on the other party copies of—

(a) the application notice;

(b) the written submissions; and

(c) all the documents filed in support of the application, except for documents which come from or have already been served on that party.

(3) Where documents are required to be served under paragraphs (1) and (2), they must be served as soon as practicable after they are filed.

---

[2] 2002 c.41.

Determining the application

54.25—(1) The application will be determined by a single judge without a hearing, and by reference only to the written submissions and the documents filed with them.

(2) If the applicant relies on evidence which was not submitted to the adjudicator or the Tribunal, the court will not consider that evidence unless it is satisfied that there were good reasons why it was not submitted to the adjudicator or the Tribunal.

(3) The court may—

(a) affirm the Tribunal's decision to refuse permission to appeal;

(b) reverse the Tribunal's decision to grant permission to appeal; or

(c) order the Asylum and Immigration Tribunal to reconsider the adjudicator's decision on the appeal.

(4) Where the Tribunal refused permission to appeal, the court will order the Asylum and Immigration Tribunal to reconsider the adjudicator's decision on the appeal only if it is satisfied that—

(a) the Tribunal may have made an error of law; and

(b) there is a real possibility that the Asylum and Immigration Tribunal would make a different decision from the adjudicator on reconsidering the appeal (which may include making a different direction under section 87 of the 2002 Act).

(5) Where the Tribunal granted permission to appeal, the court will reverse the Tribunal's decision only if it is satisfied that there is no real possibility that the Asylum and Immigration Tribunal, on reconsidering the adjudicator's decision on the appeal, would make a different decision from the adjudicator.

(6) The court's decision shall be final and there shall be no appeal from that decision or renewal of the application.

Service of order

54.26—(1) The court will send copies of its order to—

(a) the applicant, except where paragraph (2) applies;

(b) the other party; and

(c) the Asylum and Immigration Tribunal.

(2) Where—

(a) the application relates, in whole or in part, to a claim for asylum;

(b) the Tribunal refused permission to appeal; and

(c) the court affirms the Tribunal's decision,

the court will send a copy of its order to the Secretary of State, who must serve the order on the applicant.

(3) Where the Secretary of State has served an order in accordance with paragraph (2), he must notify the court on what date and by what method the order was served.

(4) If the court issues a certificate under section 101(3)(d) of the Act, it will send a copy of the certificate together with the order to—

(a) the persons to whom it sends the order under paragraphs (1) and (2); and

(b) if the applicant is in receipt of public funding, the Legal Services Commission.

Costs

54.27—The court may reserve the costs of the application to be determined by the Asylum and Immigration Tribunal.

III Applications for Statutory Review Under Section 103A of the Nationality, Immigration and Asylum Act 2002

Scope and interpretation

54.28—(1) This Section of this Part contains rules about applications to the High Court under section 103A of the Nationality, Immigration and Asylum Act 2002[3] for an order requiring the Asylum and Immigration Tribunal to reconsider its decision on an appeal.

(2) In this Section—

(a) 'the 2002 Act' means the Nationality, Immigration and Asylum Act 2002;

(b) 'the 2004 Act' means the Asylum and Immigration (Treatment of Claimants, etc.) Act 2004[4];

(c) 'appellant' means the appellant in the proceedings before the Tribunal;

(d) 'applicant' means a person applying to the High Court under section 103A;

(e) 'asylum claim' has the meaning given in section 113(1) of the 2002 Act;

(f) 'filter provision' means paragraph 30 of Schedule 2 to the 2004 Act;

(g) 'order for reconsideration' means an order under section 103A(1) requiring the Tribunal to reconsider its decision on an appeal;

(h) 'section 103A' means section 103A of the 2002 Act;

(i) 'Tribunal' means the Asylum and Immigration Tribunal.

(3) Any reference in this Section to a period of time specified in—

(a) section 103A(3) for making an application for an order under section 103A(1); or

(b) paragraph 30(5)(b) of Schedule 2 to the 2004 Act for giving notice under that paragraph,

includes a reference to that period as varied by any order under section 26(8) of the 2004 Act.

(4) Rule 2.8 applies to the calculation of the periods of time specified in—

(a) section 103A(3); and

(b) paragraph 30(5)(b) of Schedule 2 to the 2004 Act.

(5) Save as provided otherwise, the provisions of this Section apply to an application under section 103A regardless of whether the filter provision has effect in relation to that application.

Application for review

54.29—(1) Subject to paragraph (4), an application for an order for reconsideration must be made by filing an application notice—

(a) during a period in which the filter provision has effect, with the Tribunal at the address specified in the relevant practice direction; and

(b) at any other time, at the Administrative Court Office.

(2) The applicant must file with the application notice—

(a) the notice of the immigration, asylum or nationality decision to which the appeal related;

(b) any other document which was served on the appellant giving reasons for that decision;

(c) the grounds of appeal to the Tribunal;

(d) the Tribunal's determination on the appeal; and

(e) any other documents material to the application which were before the Tribunal.

(3) The applicant must also file with the application notice written submissions setting out—

(a) the grounds upon which it is contended that the Tribunal made an error of law which may have affected its decision; and

---

[3] 2002 c.41   [4] 2004 c.19

(b)   reasons in support of those grounds.
(4)   Where the applicant—
    (a)   was the respondent to the appeal; and
    (b)   was required to serve the Tribunal's determination on the appellant,
    the application notice must contain a statement of the date on which, and the means by which, the determination was served.
(5)   Where the applicant is in detention under the Immigration Acts, the application may be made either—
    (a)   in accordance with paragraphs (1) to (3); or
    (b)   by serving the documents specified in paragraphs (1) to (3) on the person having custody of him.
(6)   Where an application is made in accordance with paragraph (5)(b), the person on whom the application notice is served must—
    (a)   endorse on the notice the date that it is served on him;
    (b)   give the applicant an acknowledgment in writing of receipt of the notice; and
    (c)   forward the notice and documents within 2 days
        (i)   during a period in which the filter provision has effect, to the Tribunal; and
        (ii)   at any other time, to the Administrative Court Office.

Application to extend time limit

54.30—An application to extend the time limit for making an application under section 103A(1) must—
(a)   be made in the application notice;
(b)   set out the grounds on which it is contended that the application notice could not reasonably practicably have been filed within the time limit; and
(c)   be supported by written evidence verified by a statement of truth.

Procedure while filter provision has effect

54.31—(1)   This rule applies during any period in which the filter provision has effect.
(2)   Where the applicant receives notice from the Tribunal that it—
    (a)   does not propose to make an order for reconsideration; or
    (b)   does not propose to grant permission for the application to be made outside the relevant time limit,
    and the applicant wishes the court to consider the application, the applicant must file a notice in writing at the Administrative Court Office in accordance with paragraph 30(5)(b) of Schedule 2 to the 2004 Act.
(3)   Where the applicant—
    (a)   was the respondent to the appeal; and
    (b)   was required to serve the notice from the Tribunal mentioned in paragraph (2) on the appellant,
    the notice filed in accordance with paragraph 30(5)(b) of Schedule 2 to the 2004 Act must contain a statement of the date on which, and the means by which, the notice from the Tribunal was served.
(4)   A notice which is filed outside the period specified in paragraph 30(5)(b) must—
    (a)   set out the grounds on which it is contended that the notice could not reasonably practicably have been filed within that period; and
    (b)   be supported by written evidence verified by a statement of truth.
(5)   If the applicant wishes to respond to the reasons given by the Tribunal for its decision that it—
    (a)   does not propose to make an order for reconsideration; or

(b) does not propose to grant permission for the application to be made outside the relevant time limit,

the notice filed in accordance with paragraph 30(5)(b) of Schedule 2 to the 2004 Act must be accompanied by written submissions setting out the grounds upon which the applicant disputes any of the reasons given by the Tribunal and giving reasons in support of those grounds.

Procedure in fast track cases while filter provision does not have effect

54.32—(1) This rule applies only during a period in which the filter provision does not have effect.

(2) Where a fast track order applies to an application under section 103A—

(a) the court will serve copies of the application notice and written submissions on the other party to the appeal; and

(b) the other party to the appeal may file submissions in response to the application not later than 2 days after being served with the application.

(3) In this Rule, a 'fast track order' means an order made under section 26(8) of the 2004 Act which replaces a period of time specified in section 103A(3) of the 2002 Act with a period shorter than 5 days.

Determination of the application by the Administrative Court

54.33—(1) This rule, and rules 54.34 and 54.35, apply to applications under section 103A which are determined by the Administrative Court.

(2) The application will be considered by a single judge without a hearing.

(3) Unless it orders otherwise, the court will not receive evidence which was not submitted to the Tribunal.

(4) Subject to paragraph (5), where the court determines an application for an order for reconsideration, it may—

(a) dismiss the application;

(b) make an order requiring the Tribunal to reconsider its decision on the appeal under section 103A(1) of the 2002 Act; or

(c) refer the appeal to the Court of Appeal under section 103C of the 2002 Act.

(5) The court will only make an order requiring the Tribunal to reconsider its decision on an appeal if it thinks that—

(a) the Tribunal may have made an error of law; and

(b) there is a real possibility that the Tribunal would make a different decision on reconsidering the appeal (which may include making a different direction under section 87 of the 2002 Act).

(6) Where the Court of Appeal has restored the application to the court under section 103C(2)(g) of the 2002 Act, the court may not refer the appeal to the Court of Appeal.

(7) The court's decision shall be final and there shall be no appeal from that decision or renewal of the application.

Service of order

54.34—(1) The court will send copies of its order to—

(a) the applicant and the other party to the appeal, except where paragraph (2) applies; and

(b) the Tribunal.

(2) Where the application relates, in whole or in part, to an asylum claim, the court will send a copy of its order to the Secretary of State.

(3) Where the court sends an order to the Secretary of State under paragraph (2), the Secretary of State must—

(a) serve the order on the appellant; and

(b) immediately after serving the order, notify the court on what date and by what method the order was served.

(4) The Secretary of State must provide the notification required by paragraph (3)(b) no later than 28 days after the date on which the court sends him a copy of its order.

(5) If, 28 days after the date on which the court sends a copy of its order to the Secretary of State in accordance with paragraph (2), the Secretary of State has not provided the notification required by paragraph (3)(b), the court may serve the order on the appellant.

(6) If the court makes an order under section 103D(1) of the 2002 Act, it will send copies of that order to—

(a) the appellant's legal representative; and

(b) the Legal Services Commission.

(7) Where paragraph (2) applies, the court will not serve copies of an order under section 103D(1) of the 2002 Act until either—

(a) the Secretary of State has provided the notification required by paragraph (3)(b); or

(b) 28 days after the date on which the court sent a copy of its order to the Secretary of State,

whichever is the earlier.

Costs

54.35—The court shall make no order as to the costs of an application under this Section except, where appropriate, an order under section 103D(1) of the 2002 Act.

Practice Direction — Judicial Review

THIS PRACTICE DIRECTION SUPPLEMENTS PART 54

1.1 In addition to Part 54 and this practice direction attention is drawn to:

- section 31 of the Supreme Court Act 1981; and
- the Human Rights Act 1998

The Court

2.1 Part 54 claims for judicial review are dealt with in the Administrative Court.

2.2 Where the claim is proceeding in the Administrative Court in London, documents must be filed at the Administrative Court Office, the Royal Courts of Justice, Strand, London, WC2A 2LL.

2.3 Where the claim is proceeding in the Administrative Court in Wales (see paragraph 3.1), documents must be filed at the Civil Justice Centre, 2 Park Street, Cardiff, CF10 1ET.

Urgent applications

2.4 Where urgency makes it necessary for the claim for judicial review to be made outside London or Cardiff, the Administrative Court Office in London should be consulted (if necessary, by telephone) prior to filing the claim form.

Judicial Review Claims in Wales

3.1 A claim for judicial review may be brought in the Administrative Court in Wales where the claim or any remedy sought involves:

(1) a devolution issue arising out of the Government of Wales Act 1998; or

(2) an issue concerning the National Assembly for Wales, the Welsh executive, or any Welsh public body (including a Welsh local authority) (whether or not it involves a devolution issue).

3.2 Such claims may also be brought in the Administrative Court at the Royal Courts of Justice.

Rule 54.5 — Time limit for filing claim form

4.1 Where the claim is for a quashing order in respect of a judgment, order or conviction, the date when the grounds to make the claim first arose, for the purposes of rule 54.5(1)(b), is the date of that judgment, order or conviction.

Rule 54.6 — Claim Form

Interested parties

5.1 Where the claim for judicial review relates to proceedings in a court or tribunal, any other parties to those proceedings must be named in the claim form as interested parties under rule 54.6(1)(a) (and therefore served with the claim form under rule 54.7(b)).

5.2 For example, in a claim by a defendant in a criminal case in the magistrates or Crown Court for judicial review of a decision in that case, the prosecution must always be named as an interested party.

Human rights

5.3 Where the claimant is seeking to raise any issue under the Human Rights Act 1998, or seeks a remedy available under that Act, the claim form must include the information required by paragraph 15 of the practice direction supplementing Part 16.

Devolution issues

5.4 Where the claimant intends to raise a devolution issue, the claim form must:

(1) specify that the applicant wishes to raise a devolution issue and identify the relevant provisions of the Government of Wales Act 1998, the Northern Ireland Act 1998 or the Scotland Act 1998; and

(2) contain a summary of the facts, circumstances and points of law on the basis of which it is alleged that a devolution issue arises.

5.5 In this practice direction 'devolution issue' has the same meaning as in paragraph 1, schedule 8 to the Government of Wales Act 1998; paragraph 1, schedule 10 to the Northern Ireland Act 1998; and paragraph 1, schedule 6 of the Scotland Act 1998.

Claim form

5.6 The claim form must include or be accompanied by –

(1) a detailed statement of the claimant's grounds for bringing the claim for judicial review;

(2) a statement of the facts relied on;

(3) any application to extend the time limit for filing the claim form;

(4) any application for directions.

5.7 In addition, the claim form must be accompanied by

(1) any written evidence in support of the claim or application to extend time;

(2) a copy of any order that the claimant seeks to have quashed;

(3) where the claim for judicial review relates to a decision of a court or tribunal, an approved copy of the reasons for reaching that decision;

(4) copies of any documents on which the claimant proposes to rely;

(5) copies of any relevant statutory material; and

(6) a list of essential documents for advance reading by the court (with page references to the passages relied on).

5.8 Where it is not possible to file all the above documents, the claimant must indicate which documents have not been filed and the reasons why they are not currently available.

Bundle of documents

5.9 The claimant must file two copies of a paginated and indexed bundle containing all the documents referred to in paragraphs 5.6 and 5.7.

5.10   Attention is drawn to rules 8.5(1) and 8.5(7).

Rule 54.7 — Service of Claim Form

6.1   Except as required by rules 54.11 or 54.12(2), the Administrative Court will not serve documents and service must be effected by the parties.

Rule 54.8 — Acknowledgment of Service

7.1   Attention is drawn to rule 8.3(2) and the relevant practice direction and to rule 10.5.

Rule 54.10 — Permission Given

Directions

8.1   Case management directions under rule 54.10(1) may include directions about serving the claim form and any evidence on other persons.

8.2   Where a claim is made under the Human Rights Act 1998, a direction may be made for giving notice to the Crown or joining the Crown as a party. Attention is drawn to rule 19.4A and paragraph 6 of the Practice Direction supplementing Section I of Part 19.

8.3   A direction may be made for the hearing of the claim for judicial review to be held outside London or Cardiff. Before making any such direction the judge will consult the judge in charge of the Administrative Court as to its feasibility.

Permission without a hearing

8.4   The court will generally, in the first instance, consider the question of permission without a hearing.

Permission hearing

8.5   Neither the defendant nor any other interested party need attend a hearing on the question of permission unless the court directs otherwise.

8.6   Where the defendant or any party does attend a hearing, the court will not generally make an order for costs against the claimant.

Rule 54.11 — Service of Order Giving or Refusing Permission

9.1   An order refusing permission or giving it subject to conditions or on certain grounds only must set out or be accompanied by the court's reasons for coming to that decision.

Rule 54.14 — Response

10.1   Where the party filing the detailed grounds intends to rely on documents not already filed, he must file a paginated bundle of those documents when he files the detailed grounds.

Rule 54.15 — Where Claimant Seeks to Rely on Additional Grounds

11.1   Where the claimant intends to apply to rely on additional grounds at the hearing of the claim for judicial review, he must give notice to the court and to any other person served with the claim form no later than 7 clear days before the hearing (or the warned date where appropriate).

Rule 54.16 — Evidence

12.1   Disclosure is not required unless the court orders otherwise.

Rule 54.17 — Court's Powers to Hear Any Person

13.1   Where all the parties consent, the court may deal with an application under rule 54.17 without a hearing.

13.2   Where the court gives permission for a person to file evidence or make representations at the hearing of the claim for judicial review, it may do so on conditions and may give case management directions.

13.3 An application for permission should be made by letter to the Administrative Court office, identifying the claim, explaining who the applicant is and indicating why and in what form the applicant wants to participate in the hearing.

13.4 If the applicant is seeking a prospective order as to costs, the letter should say what kind of order and on what grounds.

13.5 Applications to intervene must be made at the earliest reasonable opportunity, since it will usually be essential not to delay the hearing.

Rule 54.20 — Transfer

14.1 Attention is drawn to rule 30.5.

14.2 In deciding whether a claim is suitable for transfer to the Administrative Court, the court will consider whether it raises issues of public law to which Part 54 should apply.

Skeleton arguments

15.1 The claimant must file and serve a skeleton argument not less than 21 working days before the date of the hearing of the judicial review (or the warned date).

15.2 The defendant and any other party wishing to make representations at the hearing of the judicial review must file and serve a skeleton argument not less than 14 working days before the date of the hearing of the judicial review (or the warned date).

15.3 Skeleton arguments must contain:

(1) a time estimate for the complete hearing, including delivery of judgment;

(2) a list of issues;

(3) a list of the legal points to be taken (together with any relevant authorities with page references to the passages relied on);

(4) a chronology of events (with page references to the bundle of documents (see paragraph 16.1);

(5) a list of essential documents for the advance reading of the court (with page references to the passages relied on) (if different from that filed with the claim form) and a time estimate for that reading; and

(6) a list of persons referred to.

Bundle of documents to be filed

16.1 The claimant must file a paginated and indexed bundle of all relevant documents required for the hearing of the judicial review when he files his skeleton argument.

16.2 The bundle must also include those documents required by the defendant and any other party who is to make representations at the hearing.

Agreed final order

17.1 If the parties agree about the final order to be made in a claim for judicial review, the claimant must file at the court a document (with 2 copies) signed by all the parties setting out the terms of the proposed agreed order together with a short statement of the matters relied on as justifying the proposed agreed order and copies of any authorities or statutory provisions relied on.

17.2 The court will consider the documents referred to in paragraph 17.1 and will make the order if satisfied that the order should be made.

17.3 If the court is not satisfied that the order should be made, a hearing date will be set.

17.4 Where the agreement relates to an order for costs only, the parties need only file a document signed by all the parties setting out the terms of the proposed order.

INDEX